CHRIST AND OTHER MASTERS

CHRIST AND OTHER MASTERS:
AN HISTORICAL INQUIRY

INTO SOME OF

THE CHIEF PARALLELISMS AND CONTRASTS BETWEEN CHRISTIANITY

AND THE

RELIGIOUS SYSTEMS OF THE ANCIENT WORLD.

With special reference to prebailing Difficulties and Objections.

BY

CHARLES HARDWICK, M.A.

EDITED BY

FRANCIS PROCTER

GYAN

Published by

GYAN

Gyan Publishing House
5, Ansari Road
Daryaganj, New Delhi-110002
Phone: 011-47034999, 9811692060
E-mail: books@gyanbooks.com

Distribution Network
gyanbooks.com
India, USA, Canada, UK, Australia, France

ISBN: 978-81-212-7322-0 (PB)
First Published, 1882

2nd Impression 2023

Printed at: Gyan Press, Delhi.

CHRIST AND OTHER MASTERS
Author: CHARLES HARDWICK, Editor: FRANCIS PROCTER

CHRIST AND OTHER MASTERS

CHRIST AND OTHER MASTERS:

AN HISTORICAL INQUIRY

INTO SOME OF

THE CHIEF PARALLELISMS AND CONTRASTS BETWEEN CHRISTIANITY

AND THE

RELIGIOUS SYSTEMS OF THE ANCIENT WORLD.

With special reference to prevailing Difficulties and Objections.

BY

CHARLES HARDWICK, M.A.

LATE ARCHDEACON OF ELY, AND CHRISTIAN ADVOCATE IN THE UNIVERSITY OF CAMBRIDGE.

FOURTH EDITION. EDITED BY

FRANCIS PROCTER;

VICAR OF WITTON, NORFOLK; FORMERLY FELLOW OF ST CATHARINE'S COLLEGE, CAMBRIDGE.

"Are not Abana and Pharpar, rivers of Damascus, better than all the waters of Israel? May I not wash in them and be clean? So he turned, and went away in a rage."—2 KINGS v. 12.

London:

MACMILLAN AND CO.

1882.

'I have laid it down as an invariable maxim constantly to follow historical tradition, and to hold fast by that clue, even when many things, in the testimony and declarations of tradition, appear strange and almost inexplicable, or at least enigmatical; for so soon as in the investigation of ancient history we let slip that thread of Ariadne, we can find no outlet from the labyrinth of fanciful theories, and the chaos of clashing opinions.'—F. von Schlegel, *Phil. of Hist.* p. 81, Lond. 1847.

CAMBRIDGE: PRINTED BY C. J. CLAY, M.A. AT THE UNIVERSITY PRESS.

PREFATORY MEMOIR TO SECOND EDITION.

The present work contains the four Essays published by the late Archdeacon Hardwick in the years in which he held the office of 'Christian Advocate' in the University of Cambridge. It is simply a reprint of the first edition, with the introduction of a few notes from the author's manuscript.

The central point, around which his whole argument is constructed, is the exhibition of the real position and relation of Christianity in the presence of the other religions, which have had, and still have, the allegiance of so great a part of mankind. It was his intention, in a concluding volume, to discuss these religions as one great whole, and to determine the place of the present argument among our Christian defences and evidences; and to analyse more minutely the causes which rendered heathen systems so ineffective, and which led in so many instances to their rapid deterioration. He felt, however, that this was too much to undertake in one year. His publication therefore for the fifth and concluding year of his office as the last 'Christian Advocate' was intended to be a discussion of the genuineness of the Second Epistle of St. Peter, which had formed the subject of a Latin Thesis composed for his B.D. degree; and a few pages of this treatise were in type, when it, and the conclusion of the present elaborate work, and whatever else was occupying his ever-active mind, was cut short by a death regretted not only by a circle of private friends, but by all admirers of a sound and reasonable churchmanship.

To those who were acquainted with the Author in the University, his character of patient labour must be well known. To reckon simply the years, from 1845, when he was elected to a Fellowship, to the year of his death, 1859, and to compare this period with the number of books written and edited in the interval, will satisfy any one that there could have been but few idle days. But a more intimate acquaintance with his early life causes the greater wonder at the learning which produced these works. A slip of paper written during his undergraduateship, gives the particulars of his previous educational course, which would be hardly credited, if the story rested upon accounts picked up from hearsay evidence.

CHARLES HARDWICK was born September 22, 1821, at Slingsby, in the North Riding of Yorkshire. He received the first rudiments of English, writing and arithmetic, under Mr. Chapman, the schoolmaster in his native village, who survived his pupil by a few weeks. He was taught also the Latin Grammar by the Rev. Wm. Walker, at that time the Curate, and who afterwards held the Rectory of Slingsby. At the age of twelve, in 1833, he was sent to a school at Malton, kept by Mr. P. Corcoran, a Socinian minister, who is described as being a clever man. Here he began Greek: he did not, however, remain long under his teaching, but was sent to the Grammar School at Sheffield, where some relatives resided. Here again he only remained for one year: weak health compelled his removal home, and kept him there for six or eight months —*studying:* entering upon a course of self-education: preparing to obtain learning in the only way that seemed open to him, by assisting in teaching others. At the age of fifteen he was taken by Mr. Irving, on the recommendation of his friend Mr. Walker, as pupil and assistant in the Thornton Grammar School near Pickering; and he was there for eighteen months.

In the summer of 1838, while not yet seventeen, he removed to the academy at Malton, where he was assistant classical Tutor under Mr. Marshall. Here he remained for eighteen months. While in this situation, he delivered two lectures at the

Mechanics' Institute; and some of his youthful essays in Poetry were published in the Poet's Corner of the *York Courant.* A longer specimen of his talents in this department, in the shape of a sacred drama, was sent to Lord Carlisle through Mr. Walker, his lordship's chaplain; and this brought the youth a sovereign, and a word of encouragement. He continued to write poetry—sonnets and longer pieces—in his next situation; when he was engaged as assistant by the Rev. H. Barlow, who took pupils at Shirland Rectory, in Derbyshire. Here he enjoyed a salary of £40 a-year. But it does not appear that he was there for a full year—at all events not more than a year. He brought home a half-year's stipend, which enabled him to pay his Caution money.

In July 1840, he was entered for a sizarship at St. John's, but was unsuccessful at the examination in October. He then entered as a pensioner at Catharine Hall, and obtained a small scholarship after the College examination in the Easter Term in 1841.

The remainder of his undergraduate course is soon told. The hardworking youth was chiefly maintained by his scholarship, with helps that are obtainable in the University, and for which so steady a student could be safely recommended by Professor Corrie, the tutor of the College. He had also an exhibition (Lady Lumley's) of £15 for three years, from the Thornton Grammar School. This fact intimates that he was at that school as a scholar; or if he united the positions of teacher and scholar, he was sufficiently recognised in the latter capacity to be considered a member of the school.

In the examination at the end of his second year (1842) he was Prizeman in Divinity, 1st in classics, and 2nd in Mathematics. At the B.A. examination, in January 1844, he stood first Senior Optime.

Self-maintenance and self-improvement were still the rules of his working life. By the assistance of Professor Corrie, he soon became tutor in the family of Sir Joseph Radcliffe, then residing at Brussels. Here he used the opportunities open to him, and made himself master of French and German. He was unsuccessful in an examination for a Yorkshire Fellowship in the October Term of 1844: but nothing daunted, he continued his work with his pupils, and improved himself so far that he was elected in 1845.

He was now free to choose his own line of reading. His Fellowship giving him a title for orders, he was ordained Deacon in 1846, and Priest in 1847, in which year he proceeded to his M.A. degree.

In September, 1846, he received the thanks of the parishioners of All Saints, Cambridge, for duty done during the absence of the Vicar, the Rev. George Maddison. During this year, 1846, he was engaged, for the University Press, upon the new edition of Sir Roger Twysden's *Historical Vindication of the Church of England in point of Schism, as it stands separated from the Roman, and was reformed* 1° *Elizabeth;* and found the additional matter introduced into this edition, in Twysden's autograph, in an interleaved copy in the Library of the British Museum. As a Supplement to this work, he was induced to edit Archdeacon Fullwood's *Roma Ruit, or the Pillars of Rome broken:* Cambridge, 1847. He also completed, for the University Press, the edition of the Saxon and Northumbrian versions of St. Matthew's Gospel (1848), commenced by the late Mr. John M. Kemble.

His next work was an edition, for the Percy Society, of *A Poem on the Times of Edward II.* (1849), followed by an Anglo-Saxon *Passion of St. George* (1850): undertaken while engaged on the Catalogue of MSS. in the Cambridge University Library, of which Mr. Hardwick was appointed to be editor in chief, and to which he contributed the descriptions of the volumes of Anglo-Saxon, Anglo-Norman, and Early English literature. In 1849, also, he read before the Cambridge Antiquarian Society, *An Historical Enquiry touching St. Catharine of Alexandria;* which was printed with the addition of a *Semi-Saxon Legend,* and Glossary. (Cambridge, 1849.)

In 1850, he assisted in preparing an edition of the Book

of Homilies for the University Press, under the supervision of Professor Corrie, who fairly 'thanks his friend and former pupil for verifying a large proportion of the quotations from Scripture and ecclesiastical writers, and for his valuable aid in correcting the press and supplying an index.'

In December of this year he preached a course of sermons at Great St. Mary's, on the Connection of the Old and New Testaments.

In March of the year 1851, he was appointed by the Bishop of London (C. J. Blomfield) to be the Cambridge preacher at the Chapel Royal, Whitehall. He had at this time just completed his *History of the Articles of Religion.* An American edition of this work, of course without the author's sanction, was printed at Philadelphia in 1852.

In March 1853, at the conclusion of his Preachership at Whitehall, he became Professor of Divinity in Queen's College, Birmingham, an office, however, which he held only for a few months. Church History was occupying his attention. He printed a selection from his Whitehall sermons, under the title of *Twenty Sermons for Town Congregations;* and also the *History of the Christian Church during the Middle Ages.*

In 1855 he was appointed Lecturer in Divinity in King's College, Cambridge; and Christian Advocate, which office caused the composition of the Ist part of the present work. In 1856 he was elected a member of the Council of the Senate, and re-elected in 1858. Early in 1856 he published the 2nd volume of his *History of the Christian Church,* embracing the *Reformation Period;* and before the end of the year Part II. of this work. The IIIrd Part was written in 1857: and the IVth Part in 1858; in which year he also edited Thomas of Elmham's *Historia Monasterii S. Augustini Cantuariensis* in the Series, commenced in 1857, of "The Chronicles and Memorials of Great Britain and Ireland during the Middle Ages." In 1859, he carried through the press a second edition of the *History of the Articles,* much of the work being rewritten.

Mr. Hardwick had just been appointed by the Bishop (T.

Turton) to the Archdeaconry of Ely, when his work on earth was cut short. He died by a fall in the Pyrenees, August 19, 1859, and was buried in the Protestant Cemetery at Luchon.

No notice is taken in this survey of articles contributed to Reviews, or smaller papers read before the Antiquarian Society. Apart also from the works edited by Mr. Hardwick, which involved an amount of labour which a conscientious editor only can appreciate, the original works—the *History of the Articles*—the two volumes of *Church History*—and the four Parts of *Christ and other Masters*—have made him a name among the writers of the English Church, which will not soon be forgotten.

FRANCIS PROCTER.

AUTHOR'S PREFACE.

Many of the subjects I am here attempting to discuss have, in one shape or other, occupied the thoughts of previous writers, both at home and on the continent. To some of their productions, as the references annexed will testify, the present work has been indebted for valuable suggestions: and even where I am not conscious of appropriating the materials, or adopting the results of others, it can hardly be expected that my observations are always original, or my researches independent. The only recent treatise which professes to grapple with exactly the same class of difficulties, is a volume published in 1848 by Mr F. D. Maurice, with the title *The Religions of the World, and their relations to Christianity.* Like other writings of that gifted author, it has naturally attracted a large circle of admirers, offering as it does some very choice reflections on the spirit that pervaded the religious systems of antiquity, Muhammedanism included. Still it seems to me, at least, that Mr. Maurice's treatment of the subject would have proved far more successful, had his method been more rigorously historical. He rather helps us to philosophize on what may possibly have been the attributes of those religions, as viewed by the more elevated minds of heathendom, than to determine the precise complexion of the popular belief, and its true relation to the doctrines of the Gospel. I feel, moreover, that the growth and permanence of such systems are always traceable quite as much to their accordance with the lower and depraved tastes of humanity, as to supernatural influences exerted on their constitution by the ever-present Logos, or to fragments of primeval truth they are supposed to have retained.

The work itself will shew the animus with which objections have been met and answered. I hope that no assailant of Revealed Religion, with whom it is my duty to contend, will ever find his arguments misrepresented: and if in any case I manifest what seems to him a needless warmth of feeling, my apology must be the strong conviction which I entertain as to the sacredness of Christianity, and the exceeding blindness of those persons, who, having once embraced it, turn away from all its central doctrines with irreverence, coldness, or contempt. 'A politic man,' observes Lord Bacon[1], 'may write from his brain, without touch and sense of his heart, as in a speculation that appertaineth not unto him; but a feeling Christian will express in his words a character of zeal or love. The latter of which, as I could wish rather embraced, being more proper for these times, yet is the former warranted also by great examples.'

One word of comment on the startling verdict of the Royal Commissioners[2] with reference to the office which it is my privilege to fill. 'Objections,' they remark, 'have justly been made both to the name and to the office of Christian Advocate: for if the Christian religion requires defence, such defence should be a spontaneous act, not a hired service.'

This criticism, I would submit, is no less adverse

1 *Of Church Controversies*, Works, III. 135, Lond. 1765.
2 *Report of the Commissioners for the University of Cambridge*, p. 69.

to all kinds of religious endowments. Every one who enters into holy orders does so with the understanding that he has been called to preach, expound, and advocate, a definite system of belief; and every one who afterwards accepts ecclesiastical preferment, is converted by that step into a 'hired' defender of his principles. In what respect foundations like those of Hulse, Boyle, and Bampton, are peculiarly obnoxious to the charge of fostering a sordid spirit in the persons who have been entrusted with the functions they prescribe, it is not easy to determine. But while urging this, I would by no means be understood to argue, that such endowments have been uniformly applied in the best manner possible.

CONTENTS.

PART I.

INTRODUCTION.

CHAPTER I.

CHAPTER II.

CHAPTER III.

PART II.

RELIGIONS OF INDIA.

CHAPTER I.

CHAPTER II.

CHAPTER III.

CHAPTER IV.

PART III.

RELIGIONS OF CHINA, AMERICA, AND OCEANICA.

PART IV.

RELIGIONS OF EGYPT AND MEDO-PERSIA.

CHAPTER III.

CHAPTER IV.

PART I.

INTRODUCTION.

INTRODUCTION.

CHAPTER I.

On the Religious Tendencies of the Present Age.

'Αναπέμπει ἡμᾶς ἐπὶ ἐνθέως (ὡς λέγει) ποιητὰς καὶ σοφοὺς καὶ φιλοσόφους.—Origen, *contra Celsum*, Lib. VII. p. 359 (ed. Spencer).

Periodic agitations in the moral world. Examples of these agitations: (1) Sixth century before Christ. (2) Fifteenth and sixteenth centuries after Christ. The present aspect of political affairs. The mental activity of the age. In what respects peculiar. Different effects of this activity on religious inquiries. First variety of modern thought. Second variety of modern thought. Its parallel in the Primitive Church. Third variety of modern thought. Examination of its principles. How modified by the Idealistic philosophy. Universality of its sympathies. How affected towards Christianity. The tendency retrogressive: leading men to Pantheism. Main features of Pantheism. Antiquity of this class of objections. The Clementines. The first race of spiritualists. Celsus and his cavils. Neo-Platonism. Manichæism. Persistency of like objections. The spiritualists of the Reformation period. Lord Herbert. English and French Deists. Different modes of resisting these attacks. Plan and purpose of the present work.

THERE is no more striking aspect in the history of religion than the correspondencies which it from time to time exhibits in remote and disconnected quarters of the world. The scholar who investigates the laws of thought in almost any period, not confining his inquiries to a single people or one group of cognate tribes, is sure to be impressed with a belief that mighty and mysterious agencies do verily exist in the recesses of our spiritual nature, and that HE who regulates their action so as to produce phenomena which men are equally unable to create or to interpret, is not human but Divine.

Conjunctures of this kind will often furnish the historian with his resting-points, or epochs. After traversing, it may

1—2

be, centuries of stagnant uniformity, where all things promised to continue as they were, his thoughts are suddenly aroused by indications of a tempest, and the growth of some gigantic revolution. A new spirit, whence it came he cannot tell, begins to work at many different points below the surface of society, projecting a new order of ideas, stimulating sluggish faculties, and calling into active exercise another cycle of emotions. Many a problem which the former age abandoned as insipid, or intractable, begins to be discussed with fresh alacrity. The nature of God himself, His attributes, and His relation to the visible world; the origin, and future destiny of man,—are all regarded as it seems through other media: and these changes, propagated simultaneously, in countries where no outward currents of communication are detected, and in countries linked together by the ties of blood, of language, and of commerce, constitute a different phase of civilisation, if they do not actually commence an era in the fortunes of the human race.

Some faint analogy may be perceived in the occasional convulsions of the physical world; for instance, in great earthquakes, such as that of 1755. The shock that buried Lisbon never ceased to vibrate till it reached the wilds of Scotland, and the vineyards of Madeira. It was felt among the islands of the Grecian Archipelago; it changed the level of the solitary lakes that sleep beneath the shadows of the Noric Alps.

On turning to the annals of mankind we ascertain that few, if any, centuries have been more pregnant with events of universal moment than the sixth before the Christian era. While the members of the Hebrew commonwealth, honoured with the special custody of Holy Writ, were drooping in the grasp of Babylonic despotism, their sanctuary profaned, their liturgy suspended, and Jerusalem a heap of stones;—while they, alone in that desert of the nations, were conversing face to face with God, and learning more and more the perfect unity and spirituality of His essence, what a change was wrought meanwhile in other regions of the earth! In Greece, for instance, we behold a young and ardent people rising day by day to eminence in arts, in letters, and in arms. The founders of Hellenic speculation had but recently commenced their struggles for the disenthralment of the human spirit. Colonies like that which had been planted at Marseilles were widening the horizon of men's thoughts, and drawing Western Europe into union with the East; while swarms of Orphic brotherhoods, the fresh creations either of Thrace, of Egypt, or of Phrygia, were diffusing in all quarters the keen thirst they felt for reconciliation with the God of heaven, and an objective revelation of His will. In China a successful movement issued in the rehabilitating of the ancient state-religion. Almost every village of Persia was the theatre of changes more decisive and profound. A consciousness of some incurable antagonism among the elements of our moral being had there prompted Zoroaster to construct his theory of two rival principles. And, last of all, the birth of Gótama Buddha in 'the world of men' was made a pretext for dethroning the religious system of his forefathers,—replacing the mythology of the Bráhman by the cold and blank negations, which, in spite of all their dreariness, are still exerting a disastrous witchery on the teeming millions of the East.

Or glance we at a later stage of universal history, the fifteenth and sixteenth centuries after Christ; and we shall find a second cluster of these wonderful analogies. The day-star of religious liberty was rising in the north of Europe. As the multitude woke up from the protracted slumber of the Middle Ages, dreams that once bewildered them were fading from the mind. The old traditions, social, civil, and ecclesiastical, were shaken to their roots, and lost their hold in every quarter. God was meanwhile felt to be peculiarly near to us, the living God, the moral Ruler of the Universe, the righteous Lord not only of the Church collective, and of Christian commonwealths, but also of the human family at large, and every human conscience. It was mainly by the force of this conviction that the Saxon friar was impelled to lift his voice with such tremendous emphasis against the schoolmen and the Roman pontiffs, and enabled to attract so vast an audience from all parts of western Christendom. Yet, strange to say, the mighty movement which he headed found some parallels in still more distant regions. A new incarnation of the Lama of Thibet effected permanent changes in one branch of Buddhism; while Bába Nánuk of Lahore, the Luther of the Panjáb, felt himself constrained to reassert the absolute unity of God, and on the basis of that doctrine laboured to promote the fusion of the Bráhman and the Muslim in one religious confraternity.

Now persons are not wanting who affirm that agitations of our day betoken the approach, if not the actual presence, of some corresponding crisis in the history of man. I do not here allude to the momentous war, in which our statesmen have embarked,—a war, that after slaying thousands of our fellow-Christians, and disorganizing the political machinery of

Europe, threatens to extend itself indefinitely among the Asiatic nations, and involve them also in the struggle. Subjects of this kind might fairly, it is true, engage the notice of a Christian advocate, who, conscious that the world is God's, and that His arm is ever visible in guiding or confounding human projects, had been urged to combat what is termed the 'positive' philosophy of Comte and other sociologists: for nothing could have more discredited their baseless theories, than the combinations we have recently been called to witness and the perils that beset the future course of western civilisation. But such is not my purpose now. I rather wish to ask what are the *spiritual* characteristics of the age in which we live, and whether any of the fermentations in the moral and intellectual world have given birth to tendencies peculiarly detrimental to the interests of Christian truth.

That our own lot has been really cast within a period of extraordinary mental vigour and activity it is impossible to deny. The closer study of the human constitution, physical and psychological; the victories achieved by modern sciences inspiring an idea that every difficulty in nature may ere long be mastered by the progress of invention; the astonishing facilities of intercourse among ourselves and other members of the family of nations; the establishment of truer canons both in verbal and historic criticism; profound researches into the structure and affinities of language; the more copious inductions of ethnology, elucidating the condition of the ancient world, and helping us to track the pre-historic wanderings of influential tribes; a broader, and, in many cases, juster view of heathendom, the character of its divinities and its relation to the Church of God; a quick perception of the vastness of the rational creation, and the higher value we have learned to place on individual souls,—these all have, in a greater or less degree, assisted in the modification of established theories, in opening new veins of thought, and in exciting yearnings that were scarcely ever felt by earlier ages of the world. And, as we might have easily foreseen, the great enlargement of our sphere of knowledge, and our deeper sympathies with everything that bears the impress of humanity, have been combined in certain quarters with a feverish love of speculation, and an irrepressible desire of change. First principles are now more freely called in question, sifted with a bold and microscopic criticism, and not unfrequently rejected with an utter disregard of ancient prepossessions, maxims and authorities. Here also it appears that the portentous agitation is not limited to Christian countries, nor to those of them who as distinguished for their intellectual prowess have been commonly esteemed the champions of the right of free inquiry. It has even roused the Jew himself from his supineness[1]: it has taught him to interpret and defend his sacred books as he had never done before.

Of course, the epoch is not absolutely singular: there have been many like it, where the human mind was similarly quickened, and gave similar indications of the fevers that possessed it. Still the present generation has peculiar characteristics, and is often penetrated by a spirit of its own. I do not say that gifted individuals now reflect more deeply on particular questions, or have grown more clearly conscious of the difficulties by which those questions are encompassed. Who, for instance, ever looked the hardest problems of humanity more fully in the face than Origen or St. Augustine, Anselm or Aquinas? Who, so long as we continue in the present stage of our existence, will approximate more closely to the right solution of them than such men as Bacon, Butler, Pascal, and Leibnitz? But granting this, it must be also granted, first, that there has been of late a marvellous increase in the area of the field of speculation; and, secondly, that the number of speculative minds is multiplied almost indefinitely. What hosts of questions that had once been canvassed only in the narrow circle of divines and schoolmen and philosophers, are now dispersed among the mass of the community, and agitated far and near! The ever-teeming press exposes them to universal criticism; and thus attempts are making to resolve—to handle, weigh, and measure, one might say—the mysteries of God and man, of life, of death, and of eternity, alike in the saloons of opulence, the crowded halls of science, and the workshop of the rudest artisan. On every side we recognise the same determination to know more about the real ground of men's convictions, an impatience of restraint, a fearless self-assertion, and a fixed resolve to push whatever principle they may embrace to its remotest consequence, with small regard to other inferences no less legitimate, by which the former should in reason have been traversed and controlled.

§ 1. If our thoughts are concentrated on the single province

[1] 'Judaism, roused from her lethargy by the mighty upheavings of the age, has at length arisen and steps forth out of her long obscurity into the broad sunlight of general consciousness.' Philippsohn, *Development of the Religious Idea*, p. 3, Lond. 1855. This able work, written by a Jew, who speaks of the Old Testament almost in the style of Maurer and De Wette, is itself a sign of the times.

of religion, we shall see, as might have been anticipated, that the spirit of the age has there left very deep impressions of its power. One class, indeed, of educated Englishmen have never drifted far from the positions of the previous generation. They continue to look down unmoved on all the tossings of their neighbours. Nor can theirs be termed the silence of misgiving or the self-possession of indifference; it is rather the tranquillity of deep and living faith. For in their ranks are many of the brightest luminaries both of scholarship and science[1],—minds of a gigantic stature; minds, moreover, that are gifted with the finest critical acumen, and that never hesitate to exercise it in determining religious questions, such as in their judgment man may fairly hope to master. Subject to this limitation they are advocates of progress; and accordingly we hear them welcome every species of research that may contribute to the stores of sacred knowledge. They are foremost in acquiring and comparing languages, in tracing the descent of nations, and in disinterring such materials as are calculated to supply the blanks that we deplore in Jewish or in Christian history. On men like these, however, the effect of modern progress and discovery is to strengthen their belief in the announcements of the Bible. Whichever way they turn, its truthfulness is more completely vindicated, and their hold upon its mysteries proportionally confirmed[2]. They are most conscious, it is true, that in the kingdoms both of grace and nature, in the volume of God's works and in the volume of His word, a thousand difficulties remain which they are utterly unable to decipher; depths of thought they never hope to fathom, discords which they cannot harmonize, and elevations which they cannot climb. Such problems as the origin and growth of evil, that profound enigma into which so many others are eventually resolved;

[1] One of the highest types of this school was the late Regius Professor of Hebrew at Cambridge,—the lamented Dr. Mill, who, in the vastness of his erudition, in the grasp and clearness of his reasoning faculties, in his scientific attainments, and his unswerving orthodoxy, was more than a match for the apostles of modern scepticism and unbelief. See his *Christian Advocate's Publications*, passim. Few scholars ever knew so much, and fewer still when they have reached the utmost verge of human knowledge are animated by his reverential spirit.

'Nescire velle, quæ Magister Optimus
Docere non vult, erudita inscitia est.'

[2] 'Magis magisque mihi confirmabatur omnes versutarum calumniarum nodos, quos illi deceptores nostri adversus divinos Libros innectebant, posse dissolvi.' S. August. *Confess.*, lib. VI. c. 3. 'Titubabit autem fides, si divinarum Scripturarum vacillat auctoritas.' *De Doctr. Christ.*, lib. I. c. xxxvii.

such principles of the Divine œconomy as that of sacrifice or mediation, though they recognise its perfect fitness, and embrace it on their knees,—are felt to be immeasurably above their present comprehension; yet so numerous and convergent are the testimonies which commend the doctrines of the Gospel to their inmost heart[1], that all the arrows of the Tempter fall innocuous, blunted by the shield of faith. A man of this kind knows in what he has believed; and though he still sees darkly, communing with adumbrations of the truth, and not with truth itself, he waits in patience till that veil which separates the present from the future has been finally withdrawn, till Christianity has been divested of the earthly symbols under which it is presented to his faith, and he beholds it as it is. What happens in the physical world as the reward of patient observation, will, he is persuaded, happen also in the moral world. The seeming incongruities will form at last a *concordissima dissonantia*, and the riddles that now test and try us, will be then converted into proofs of harmony and vehicles of love.

2. But there is a powerful class of minds in England as in other parts of Europe, who are differently affected in their estimate of sacred topics by the fluctuations of the present day. The widening of their field of vision and the light that has been thrown on many of their favourite studies, so far from adding vigour to the principle of faith, has rather tended to disturb their intellectual balance, and induced a state of feeling which approaches, here and there at least, to very serious misbelief. The causes more immediately at work in the production of the change will doubtless vary with the tone and texture of the individual mind; but all whom I include in this division are alike dissatisfied with what they style 'the popular religion,' or the views of Christianity now current in different branches of the Church. Devoted in some cases to the study of the mechanism of nature, these persons form the habit of regarding the Almighty rather as a God of law and order, 'a great Mechanician,' who has, once for all, impressed upon his works the tendencies which they are bound to follow, than as ever

[1] After dwelling on the importance of criteria by which to separate the true religion from the false, Leibnitz (Théodicée, *Œuvres*, II. 42, Paris, 1842) does not fear to add: 'Cependant la foi divine elle-même, quand elle est allumée dans l'âme, est quelque chose de plus qu'une opinion, et ne dépend pas des occasions ou des motifs qui l'ont fait naître: elle va au delà de l'entendement, et s'empare de la volonté et du cœur, pour nous faire agir avec chaleur et avec plaisir, comme la loi de Dieu le commande, sans qu'on ait plus besoin de penser aux raisons, ni de s'arrêter aux difficultés de raisonnement que l'esprit peut envisager.'

present with the sacred family and as ever active in the government of all things. Hence a disposition to reduce the supernatural elements of Christianity within the smallest possible compass, and in many cases to escape from the consideration of barely physical miracles, without, however, any conscious wish to call in question the abstract possibility of a miraculous intervention. The nature, method, limits, and effects of prophecy, and generally of that mysterious influence exercised upon the mind and spirit of the sacred writers which is termed their inspiration, have on similar grounds provoked the criticism of this school of theologians. In their eyes *the* evidence of Christianity, the single ground on which it ever must depend, is the inherent fitness of its central doctrines to appease their moral and emotional wants. But this position, where exclusively asserted, has involved them in the maintenance of others less consistent with the 'popular theology.' They contend for the importance, not to say necessity, of discriminating between the form of a religion and its essence; or, in other words, require us to abstract the kernel of the truth from what is merely husk and shell, and so determine what portions of the Holy Scriptures are divine, and really entitled to the designation 'Word of God.' Their chief criterion in conducting such a process they derive from what are called 'the pure instincts' of our spiritual nature, which it is affirmed enable us to call in question and correct some representations of the sacred writers, more especially of the Old Testament; the letter of which is held to be deficient in moral dignity, and even said to violate in some respects the perfect law of conscience. 'How inscrutable also,' it is whispered, 'are the views there furnished of the character of God Himself! How stern the aspects under which He is presented in His dealings with the world at large! How awful and repulsive the idea that beings gifted with such scanty opportunities of knowledge should have power to make themselves incorrigible in the present life, and so consign themselves to hopeless misery in the next! How terribly mysterious the arrangement in virtue of which an inconsiderable fraction of the human family has ever been elected from the guilty mass; while others are abandoned to their own devices, or have only faint and flickering lights to guide them in their searchings after God.' Allusions to these topics have exposed their authors to the charge of striving to disparage the supremacy of Christianity, by placing it in the same line with philosophical systems of the heathen world, and recognising also in such systems a prophetic office and a genuine revelation. It is not my purpose to determine how far the charge has been substantiated. I notice it in order to bring out more clearly the supposed connexion of these modes of thought with others that will be discussed hereafter. But candour, in the meantime, urges me to add that wild as may have been the intellectual aberrations of the former class, they are not consciously opposed to Christianity itself. Their reverence for the Person of our blessed Lord is warm and constant; their devotion to His service is indisputable.

We understand them, in so far at least as their opinions are connected with the present subject, by reverting to the mental struggles of the early Church at Alexandria. As soon as ever Christian truth had come in contact with the speculative yearnings that prevailed in heathendom, its own adherents were divided into schools of thought considerably diverging from each other. One of these predominated in the West, the second in the East, especially in what was then a kind of philosophical exchange for all the various theorizers of the age,—the schools of Alexandria. Origen and others whom he represented, after weighing and contrasting the claims of Christianity with those of the prevailing heathen systems, occupied a somewhat new position[1]. They had listened to the pleas of Gnosticism; they saw it ramifying in all quarters and assuming everywhere the most grotesque expression; yet instead of treating it as an utter falsification of Christianity, they sympathised with it so far as to allow that real mental wants had given birth to many of its theories. They strove accordingly to satisfy the cravings of the pseudo-Gnosis by the substitution of a Gnosis properly so-called. They granted that the faith of ordinary Christians (πίστις) was in many points a popular adaptation rather than a sci-

[1] Mr. R. W. Mackay (*Rise and Progress of Christianity*, p. 193) will not, however, concede the name of philosophy to the Alexandrian speculations, because 'a philosophy tied to dogmatic authority is a manifest self-contradiction.' His meaning probably is that philosophy in his peculiar acceptation of the term cannot coexist with an objective revelation; and yet the phenomena of nature which are the subject of all natural philosophy are as truly such a revelation as the Holy Scriptures profess to be. 'The chief distinction,' he continues (p. 194), 'of the so-called philosophy seems to have been an enlarged and more liberal comprehension of former systems; the admission, against dogged ignorance, of the general claims of heathen wisdom as well as Jewish, as part of a universal revelation; and on the other hand the assertion, against the onesidedness of heretical Gnosis, of the plain doctrines of Christianity.' A more exact account of the principles and tendencies of this school is furnished by Guerike, *De Schola quæ Alexandriæ floruit, etc.*

entific expression of the truth; and that beneath the terminology of the Church there lay a richer vein of doctrines which philosophers, and they alone, could thoroughly appreciate. Such thoughts would necessarily colour all the stream of Alexandrine theology, and especially the views of Clement, Origen, and their disciples, with regard to the position of the heathen world. No absolute boundary was drawn between the Christian Church and it; philosophy standing in the same relation to the one as did the law of Moses to the other, and serving as a kind of pedagogue to bring men unto Christ[1]. They raised the Gospel, it is true, indefinitely above all previous systems, and regarded it as superseding and completing them; but a profound anxiety to place it on a broader basis and in more intelligible connexion with ancient history as well as with the literary and artistic culture of mankind at large, impelled them to approximate as closely as the nature of the case allowed to the position of the pseudo-Gnostics. On the other hand, the Latin fathers, and especially their sternest type, Tertullian[2], as uniformly laboured to repel those foreign elements which Gnosticism would fain have mingled and incorporated with the primitive belief. The barrier which they raised between the old and new convictions was impassable. The pagan world to them was anti-Christian in its very core;

[1] See, for instance, the remarkable passage in Clemens Alexand. *Stromata*, lib. I. c. 5 (p. 331, ed. Potter), and others in Mr Trench's *Hulsean Lectures* (1846), p. 157, note. It should, however, be remembered that the eulogies of the Greek Fathers were generally limited to Platonism, a system which had doubtless acted here and there as a positive preparation for the Gospel. Many Platonists were numbered among the early converts, and some appear to have retained their scholastic mantle, esteeming what they had embraced the true philosophy: see Justin's *Dialog.* c. 3, c. 8, and Eusebius IV. 26, § 4. Their main positions were (1) that the Logos (ἄσαρκος or σπερματικός) had constantly communicated to men the seeds of Divine truth, so that the doctrines of Plato were in many cases not essentially different from those of Christ: (2) that portions of the truth as taught by Plato were derived directly from the Hebrew scriptures: Gieseler, *Eccl. Hist.* I. 163, n. 5, Edinb. 1846.

[2] In his *De Anima*, c. 23, he calls Plato 'omnium hæreticorum condimentarius;' but a more complete specimen of his modes of thought is furnished in the *De Præscriptione Hæreticorum*, c. 7 and c. 8: 'Quid ergo Athenis et Hierosolymis? Quid academiæ et ecclesiæ? Quid hæreticis et Christianis? Nostra institutio de porticu Salomonis est: qui et ipse tradiderat, Dominum in simplicitate cordis esse quærendum. Viderint qui Stoicum et Platonicum et dialecticum Christianismum protulerunt. Nobis curiositate opus non est post Christum Jesum, nec inquisitione post Evangelium. Cum credimus, nihil desideramus ultra credere:' cf. *Adv. Hermogenem*, c. VIII. and Hippolytus, *Philosoph.* v. 6, Oxon. 1851.

and even if it could be proved that correspondencies to any rites or dogmas of the Church were manifest in heathen systems, Tertullian and his school evaded the objections drawn from such phenomena, by urging that the whole of Gentilism was only a distorted copy of primordial truth, or else was actually derived from a perusal of the Old Testament Scriptures[1]. The traces left by both these parties on the current literature of the Church it is superfluous to point out.

3. But then, as now, there was a third variety of sentiment with reference to the claims of Christianity and its relation to the heathen world. I cannot tell how far the members of this third school draw their tenets from the writings of the Alexandrines, or have been affected by the speculations of their modern representatives. The path was very short and slippery from the standing-ground of orthodox Gnosticism to that of Marcion or Carpocrates. Nor can it be disputed that a like transition has been simplified in recent times by treatises of Christian philosophers, who themselves are checked in their descent to scepticism and disbelief. If men like Coleridge have indulged in vehement and indiscriminate charges of 'bibliolatry,' intending by that phrase all deference to the letter of our sacred books as absolutely true; if they have openly repudiated what they term the popular theology as destitute of Christian life and spirit, and have even represented some of its foremost doctrines as no better than a species of 'devil-worship,'—one need hardly marvel if a second generation of reformers claim the right of drawing bolder inferences from such ideas, and resolve to free themselves entirely from the

[1] Thus he asks in his *Apolog.* c. XLVII: 'Unde hæc, oro vos, philosophis aut poetis tam consimilia? nonnisi de nostris sacramentis: si de nostris sacramentis, ut de prioribus, ergo fideliora sunt nostra magisque credenda, quorum *imagines* quoque fidem inveniunt.' The Latin Fathers in the age of St. Augustine had considerably modified their tone in treating of these subjects. Thus in the *De Civitate Dei*, lib. VIII. c. 11, we read: 'Mirantur autem quidam nobis in Christi gratia sociati, cum audiunt vel legunt Platonem de Deo ista sensisse, quæ multum congruere veritati nostræ religionis agnoscunt.' He explains the affinity by urging that Plato borrowed from the Hebrews. In his *Confessiones*, lib. VII. c. 20, he also alludes to the preparatory effect produced on his own mind by the writings of the Platonists, but is careful to point out the insufficiency of everything short of the Holy Scriptures to teach the way to heaven. His cautious language is explained when we remember that he had to deal with Christian Platonists, 'Qui dicere ausi sunt omnes Domini nostri Jesu Christi sententias, quas mirari et prædicare coguntur, *de Platonis libris* eum didicisse:' cf. *De Doctrina Christiana*, lib. II. c. 28.

irksome fetters of tradition. If it be again contended, that all branches of the human family possess the same kind of inspirations, owing to the universal presence of the Word of God within them; if the Holy Ghost be rather sent to waken up a slumbering consciousness of Christianity already planted in the soul than to infuse the elements of supernatural life, and bring the fallen spirit back to fellowship with Christ, a door is opened for the broad and specious theory, that the Gospel is at best a higher stage of natural religion, or, it may be, one of numerous forms, in which the spiritual instincts of humanity have found an utterance for themselves.

With this remark on what appears to be at least a possible affinity between the second and third varieties of modern thought, I pass to an examination of the principles enunciated in the latter school. And first, it is observable that when a similar class of questions were discussed some years ago, the dress which they assumed was very different. What is known as the 'sensational' philosophy was then in the ascendant, or was not so commonly abandoned as it now is; and the fashion, therefore, was to ransack all the chambers and the tombs of history in quest of some objective bases for explaining the resemblances between the heathen systems and that founded by our blessed Lord. It was usual to suppose that certain general truths had been communicated in the infancy of the human race, by means of 'a primeval preternatural revelation[1],' and that Christianity may therefore have preserved at least some fragments of such revelation, like the other extant creeds. They all, it was contended, were ultimately reducible to the same level; yet as none of them was altogether earthly in its origin, or merely a projection from the spiritual consciousness of man, the hope was entertained that in proportion to the growth of criticism, the aboriginal form of true religion might be rescued from accretions under which it lay concealed.

During the last twenty years, however, there has been a mighty change in the character of the established philosophy, and that change has gradually influenced the complexion of

[1] Such, for example, was the solution adopted by the Unitarian author, Mr. Belsham; but Mr. W. J. Fox, originally of the same sect (*Religious Ideas*, p. 66, Lond. 1849), corrects his predecessor. 'That early revelation,' he urges, 'is better looked for in the source of all revelations, in that with which all revelations must be identified to be genuine,—the moral constitution of human nature, the human mind and heart.'

assaults on Christianity itself. A species of idealism is now the favourite system. The invisible world is recognised as one province of creation; a belief in what is spiritual and supersensuous has returned. Men's thoughts have been directed inward, so that speculators are impelled to search amid the silent depths of their own being, for the oracle that is to satisfy their cravings and to disentangle their perplexities. The primitive idea of God, it is maintained, by a spontaneous process of self-evolution leads directly upward to the purest and noblest conceptions of His nature, prompts the various 'races' of mankind to fashion their theologies in harmony with the instincts of the human spirit, and thus determines the religious character of every age and people. While the former generation struggled by the aid of criticism to weaken and destroy the credibility of Holy Scripture, or evacuated and etherialised the special doctrines of Christianity where these could not be utterly expunged, the new school commonly admit that some such doctrines were announced by Christ or His immediate successors, but profess to treat them as so many natural products of the ordinary human mind, as self-devised expedients for appeasing a peculiar class of human wants and aspirations, or as forms assumed by the ideas of God in one peculiar stage of their development. Religions generally, and the Gospel as one member of the class, are therefore mere expressions of the fundamental beliefs inherent in our spiritual nature. These writers commonly refuse to be indebted for their guidance to a sacred book or any kind of outward revelation[1]. We no longer hear of Christ importing into Palestine the precious lore which had been gathered from the lips or volumes of the Eastern sages. We have not to answer the objection that His doctrines and precepts may be traced to this or that enlightened Hebrew, or were simply modern adaptations of maxims and traditions which had long been current in some Jewish sect. Objections of this kind have broken down, or balanced and destroyed each other. Of course the

[1] In this respect the system of the Mormons, which in other features is not unlike the Absolute Religion, occupies a very different place. It allows that revelations of God's will have been made to all the world, so that there is no people who have not some portions of the truth among them. It even shews extreme indulgence to idolaters. Yet in sifting all other creeds, which it professes to have done (Gunnison, *The Mormons*, pp. 60, 61, Philadelphia, 1852), it makes use of what is held to be the genuine book-revelation, and does not appeal to mere instincts of humanity.

general resemblance of Christ's teaching to the teaching of His predecessors is affirmed, but such resemblance is attributed by spiritualists to the unaided operation of the religious sentiment in man, awakened and directed by peculiar circumstances.

Nor can these be termed the speculations of a band of ignorant or dreamy mystics. They are entertained by men of learning; who profess moreover a peculiar interest in the progress of civilisation, and who labour to advance what they believe to be the disenthralment of the human spirit. They affirm that something higher, deeper, heavenlier, is reserved for us; that growth must be expected and promoted not only in our apprehension of religious truth, but in the orb of truth itself; that their peculiar mission is to hasten this result by shewing man his real dignity and destiny, by sounding all the depths of human consciousness, and calling to their aid the newest facts of history and the last discoveries of science. They do not, indeed, contemn the worthies of antiquity. The statues of Confucius, Moses, and Pythagoras; of Socrates, and Zoroaster; of Buddha, Christ, and Apollonius; of Máni and Muhammad, are all elevated side by side in the Walhalla of spiritualism. These all in different measures are applauded as the saints, the prophets, the apostles of their age; yet, notwithstanding the enormous latitude of his belief, the spiritualist is not content with any of the forms in which religion has hitherto appeared on earth. However well adapted to peculiar countries or to transitory phases of the human mind, they are unequal to the wants and capacities of the present century. He would not himself have worshipped either with his 'swarthy Indian who bowed down to wood and stone,' or with his 'grim-faced Calmuck,' or his 'Grecian peasant,' or his 'savage,' whose hands were 'smeared all over with human sacrifice;' but rather aims, by analysing the principles of heathenism and cultivating a deeper sympathy with what is termed the 'great pagan world,' to organise a new system which he calls the Absolute Religion, the Religion of humanity, the Religion of the Future. From it all special dogmas are to be eliminated; sentiments which every one may clothe according to his fancy, are to occupy the place of facts; the light of a spontaneous Gospel is to supersede the clumsy artifice of teaching by the aid of a historical revelation. Thus, while the promoters of this scheme affect the greatest reverence for the wisdom and the so-called 'inspiration' of the past, they aim to soar indefinitely above it. Nearly all the doctrines of ancient systems are abandoned or explained away[1], as things which really have no stronger claim upon us than the cycle of luxuriant mythes that captivated Greek imaginations in the pre-historic period. The Christ and Christianity of the Bible are thus virtually denied: 'superior intellects' are bidden to advance still higher, to cast off as worthless or ill-fitting the old garments of the Church, to join the standard of the Absolute Religion, and so march forward to 'the promised land.' Mr. Theodore Parker, one of their chief oracles, shall tell us what it is that we are summoned to believe; or rather (for his system cannot boast of its constructiveness) what points they are that we are urged to throw away. After dwelling on *the* article of his faith—belief in what is called an 'Infinite God'—he thus proceeds, with painful flippancy of manner far too common in the schools of 'spiritualism:'

'Of course I do not believe in a devil, eternal torment, nor in a particle of absolute evil in God's world or in God. I do not believe that there ever was a miracle, or ever will be; everywhere I find law,—the constant mode of operation of the Infinite God. I do not believe in the miraculous inspiration of the Old Testament or the New Testament. I do not believe that the Old Testament was God's first word, nor the New Testament his last. The Scriptures are no finality to me. Inspiration is a perpetual fact. Prophets and Apostles did not monopolize the Father: He inspires men to-day as much as heretofore. In nature, also, God speaks for ever....I do not believe in the miraculous origin of the Hebrew Church, or the Buddhist Church, or the Christian Church; nor the miraculous character of Jesus. I take not the Bible for my master, nor yet the Church; nor even Jesus of Nazareth for my master.....I try all things by the human faculties.....But at the same time, I reverence the Christian Church for the great good it has done to mankind; I reverence the Mahometan Church for the good it has done,—a far less good[2].'

Such is one example of the creed commended as a substitute for Christianity. We are to hold the doctrine of one Infinite God, and then are left at liberty to disbelieve whatever else we please. Nor is the process of negations even here exhausted. The principles of spiritualism have carried many of their owners, by a course of fearless logic, into a denial of the Personal God Himself; and more who join the movement, who inscribe the name of freedom on their banners and talk loudly of the progress and perfectibility of man, are drifting in the very same direction,—to that vortex in which faith and morals

[1] 'Religion,' says Mr. F. W. Newman, 'was created by the inward instincts of the soul: it had afterwards to be pruned and chastened by the sceptical understanding.' *Phases of Faith*, p. 232.

[2] *Theism, Atheism, and the Popular Theology*, pp. 263, 264. Other extracts, serving to elucidate the principles of this School, are added in Appendix I.

also will be finally engulfed. For all the tendencies of this belief, whatever its apostles may affirm, are absolutely *retrogressive;* it is carrying men afresh to paganism[1]. In spite of all its claims to a superior illumination, it leaves its votary with no intelligible object of worship but himself: it does not solve one mystery of his being; nay, it cannot even guarantee the immortality of his soul.

Mr. Parker, it is true, with small regard to the coherence of his principles, contends for the idea of God, which he has borrowed from the Bible, as 'different in kind from what is called the Universe, as self-subsisting and unchangeable[2].' He also, it must be acknowledged, is impressed with the reality and universality of the 'religious sentiment,' which he deems 'the strongest and deepest element in human nature;' and some other writers of his school are doubtless under the influence of like convictions. Still it is indisputable that for the last twenty years or more the monstrous form of Pantheism has threatened to devour a host of minor infidelities. The young Hegelians of Germany[3] are pantheists to a man; and even the eclectic philosophy of M. Cousin[4] is not easily vindicated from the charge of fostering the same delusion.

1 Philippsohn, the Jewish writer above cited, has some striking observations on this tendency of modern thought, tracing it into its inevitable effects on morals as well as theology. One section of the anti-Talmudic Jews appears to be influenced by it. 'The Human Idea,' he concludes, p. 253, 'ever produces its own resolution into its various successive phases; each of these phases abrogates that which it followed, till it reaches its ultimate stage, the virtual disavowal of its own system. Such was its course in the religions of antiquity; in the philosophemes of the Greeks; in the later philosophemes of Des Cartes and Spinosa as in that of Hegelism. *It is a circle that ever terminates in itself, the serpent that holds its own tail in its mouth.*' The Pantheism of many Jewish speculators in the Middle Ages has been noticed by Van Mildert, *Boyle Lectures*, I. 258 sq.

2 *Theism, Atheism, and the Popular Theology*, pp. 105 sq.

3 One of Neander's latest warnings referred to the gigantic progress of this evil: 'Die eigentliche und alles verschlingende Gefahr wahrhaft liegt in dem sich nähernden entscheidenden Kampfe *für das wahre Dasein des Christenthums selbst, des Sittengesetzes, des Glaubens an einen persönlichen Gott;* ein Kampf, gegen welchen ganz unbedeutend erscheinen müssen alle Streitigkeiten zwischen verschiedenen christlichen Gemeinschaften, und wogegen zurücktreten müssen die untergeordneten Gegensätze zwischen Katholicismus und Protestantismus.' *Deutsche Zeitschrift*, for May, 1850, p. 163.

4 See Morell's *Hist. of Phil.* II. 512, 513, Maret's *Essai sur le Panthéisme dans les Sociétés Modernes*, 3me ed., Paris, 1845,—a work of great ability, but now and then one-sided, especially when it tries to shew that orthodox 'Protestantism' may be convicted of Pantheistic tendencies. The learned author ought to have reflected

I shall not here dwell upon the ravings of 'material' pantheists, a minor class of speculators who rejoice to think with Comte that the religious sentiment in man is always necessarily weakened in proportion to his intellectual development, and who accordingly have joined the clamour for some 'Nouveau Grand-Être;' that is, for no God at all. But disregarding such, we find that even the more 'spiritual' section of the pantheists adopt the same ideas respecting Christianity as those already censured. The universe is in their system deified, or transubstantiated into God, its laws and processes are all identified with Him; humanity at large becomes a *necessary manifestation* of the Absolute. He is the ocean, we the waves. The various forms of human thought are all therefore equally inevitable and equally legitimate; evil is itself phenomenal, and nothing more,—the point of departure to a second moral state, which men distinguish by the name of good; while error is no more than uncompleted truth, or truth at some inferior stage of its development. Religions, in like manner, being based on what is termed 'the spontaneity of the human reason,' or the natural inspirations flowing from the breasts of seers and sages who resign themselves entirely to the guidance of the light within them, are equally fatuitous, and vary with the age and people in the midst of which they flourish. They can never hope to rise above the spiritual level of their authors; yet they all are to be viewed as true, because the genuine products of humanity, and adapted to the ends they are intended to subserve[1].

that Romanism is far more open to the charge of denying 'une vérité absolue et immuable' and of advocating 'la notion d'une vérité progressive et mobile' (p. 24). Thus a Romanist writer in the *Revue des Deux Mondes*, 1854, Tome VIII. p. 1097, contends: 'Le catholique prenant le dogme *tel que le temps l'a fait* est, en un sens, bien plus près de la grande philosophie que le protestant, qui cherche à revenir sans cesse à une prétendue formule primitive du Christianisme.'

[1] This plea for universal 'toleration' has, doubtless, commended the philosophical Pantheism of the day to one class of English minds: yet even Mr. F. W. Newman (*Hebrew Monarchy*, p. 26, 2nd ed.) is compelled to admit that in early times 'the pure monotheistic faiths' could not have been preserved except by what he calls 'intolerance,' *i.e.* want of sympathy with error. Heathenism in our own age is still most lenient in its estimate of 'collateral polytheistic systems.' M. Huc's *Travels* furnish several instances of this, and the following extract shews that the Bráhmans are actuated by the same spirit: 'Although stedfast in his faith, the Hindoo is not fanatical: he never seeks to make proselytes. If the Creator of the world, he says, had given the preference to a certain religion, this alone would have

It will be shewn hereafter how the same denial of the Personality of God pervaded nearly all the heathen systems of the ancient world, and everywhere produced the same results in ethics and theology. At present I shall only draw attention to the periodical recurrence of a similar spirit in the times posterior to the promulgation of Christianity. This course will serve a twofold purpose: it will render us familiar with the parentage of the objections which are levelled at the Gospel by our modern adversaries; it will indicate how deep is the vitality of truth, how constant its resistance, and how sure its final triumph.

For if adversaries, starting up on every side, and armed with every species of objection, sought in vain to strangle Christianity at its birth; if they were baffled when the fashion was to scoff it down as the religion 'of weavers, shoemakers, and slaves;' if they retired before it till the symbol of the cross surmounting the conquered dragon was impressed on the imperial coinage, and till heathenism itself became 'the faith of peasants' (paganismus); if they won no credit even as supported by the zeal, the learning, and the power of Julian; if they furbish the old weapons only to be once again repulsed, when Julian's taunting prophecy has been for centuries confuted by experience, when those very nations which he deemed impervious to the Gospel rank among its foremost champions, and send forth the missionary in whose hands it is transplanted fresh at the antipodes, we may assuredly discover in this growth the evidence of supernatural life, the auguries of better things to come.

When Christianity was first announced in the great theatres of Oriental speculation it was forced at once into collision with those very systems out of which its modern enemies would fain extract it; and the struggle that ensued elicited in every case an opposition similar to that which it encounters now from persons who are studying to malign it or betray it with a kiss. Among the first assailants of the Pentateuch[1], we find a writer who disparaged the idea of all objective reve-

prevailed upon the earth; but as there are many religions, this proves the approbation of them by the Most High. Men of an enlightened understanding, says the Bráhman, well know that the Supreme has imparted to each nation the doctrine most suitable for it, and He therefore beholds with satisfaction the various ways in which He is worshipped.' Björnstjerna, *Theogony of the Hindoos*, p. 67, Lond. 1844.

[1] Cf. Neander, *Ch. Hist.*, I. 490, and Schliemann, *Die Clementinen*, pp. 193—199, Hamburg, 1844.

lation[1], such as Christians entertained from the beginning. In the room of this it was proposed to substitute the inward revelation of the heart. An early race of Gnostics in like manner drew their inspirations altogether from within. Their composite system, borrowed partly from the Gospel, partly from the ancient creeds of Asia, was designed for the 'superior intellects' of the day, whom intuition (so they urged) exalted far above the sphere of faith, and liberated from the bondage of original Christianity. Hence they gloried in the name of 'spiritualists[2],' and called 'the man of the Church' by a contemptuous title, intimating that he was still in subjection to the grosser elements of his nature. For a time the flattering speculations of this school obtained extensive currency; it put out branches in all quarters; it attracted multitudes of proselytes; and yet we search in vain for any of those noble fruits brought forth by Christianity. The system of the early Gnostic would not work; and therefore it has been extinct for centuries, unless perchance some trace of it is still discernible among the Druses of Mount Lebanon, whose doctrines here and there remind one of the creed of Basilides[3].

Again, it was by weapons such as those which had been wielded in the school of 'spiritualism,' though weapons of a coarser edge, that Celsus undertook to stem the progress of the early Church. 'He,' says Neander[4], 'is the original representative of a class of intellects which, in the various attacks on Christianity, has over and over again presented itself to our notice: wit and acumen, without earnestness of purpose or depth of research; a worldly understanding that looks at things merely on the surface, and delights in hunting up difficulties and contradictions.' Celsus was, moreover, an avowed spiritualist. He taunts the Christian as belonging to an abject and

[1] See the *Clementine Homilies*, ed. Dressel, XVIII. 6: *'Αποκάλυψίς ἐστι τὸ ἐν πάσαις καρδίαις ἀνθρώπων ἀπορρήτως κείμενον κεκαλυμμένον, ἄνευ φωνῆς τῇ αὐτοῦ* [sc. *υἱοῦ*] *βουλῇ ἀποκαλυπτόμενον.*

[2] See Irenæus *Contra Hæres.* Lib. III. c. XV. § 2. The following passage is significant: 'Plurimi autem et contemtores facti, quasi jam perfecti, sine reverentia et in contemtu viventes, semetipsos *spiritales* vocant, et se nosse jam dicunt eum, qui sit intra Pleroma ipsorum, refrigerii locum.' The Montanists in like manner boasted that they were *πνευματικοί* as being in possession of the last developments of truth; while ordinary Christians were only *ψυχικοί*: Gieseler, I. 148, and cf. Stieren's note on Irenæus, Lib. III. c. XI. § 9.

[3] Other remnants of the early Gnostics may possibly be discoverable among the 'Yezidis,' or 'Devil-worshippers' of Armenia: see Von Haxthausen's *Transcaucasia*, p. 263, Lond. 1854.

[4] *Ch. Hist.* I. 227.

a sense-bound race[1], insists upon the duty of turning from all outward things to gain a deeper intuition of God through the perceptions of the mind, and more especially denounces the idea of all particular revelations to a single people, on the ground that they induce contracted and unworthy notions of the Supreme Being. Yet this champion of a purer creed than Christianity, this propagator of more lofty thoughts, which he affected to support by what he terms the 'inspirations' of the heathen writers, does not scruple to decry 'the jealous monotheism of the Christians[2],' apologising even for the worship of the 'dæmons,' or divine agencies in nature. He treats the history of Christ Himself in a profane spirit, sneers at Christian humility as a debased and stupid misconception of the Platonic sentiment, has no idea of sin except that it is either necessary or unreal, and is therefore at a loss to understand the meaning of redemption[3].

But the supernatural character of the Christian faith was meanwhile threatened by a more insidious adversary. On the confines of the Church appeared a number of inquiring spirits who were anxious to escape from the prevailing nature-worship, and sustain, if possible, the tottering cause of heathenism by giving to it a more spiritual constitution; and from them originated the idea of fusing Christianity with their eclectic system. Affecting to guide mankind into a knowledge of the Absolute, it took the name of Neo-Platonism; and as the founder of it was acquainted with the Gospel, which he once indeed professed[4], some precious elements of Christian truth were blended with the empty legends and philosophisings out of which it was compounded. Christ, however, was admitted there as only one of many creatures who had taken rank with the immortals. Pythagoras was to stand on nearly the same level, being honoured by the

[1] Δειλὸν καὶ φιλοσώματον γένος. Origen, *cont. Celsum*, Lib. VII. p. 357, ed. Spencer.

[2] See the confession of one of his more recent admirers, Mr. Mackay, *Rise and Progress of Christianity*, p. 159.

[3] Cf. Neander, as above, pp. 231 sq.

[4] It is curious to notice how Porphyry himself, a Neo-Platonist opponent of the Gospel, speaks of Ammonius Saccas becoming 'a thinker:' Ἀμμώνιος μὲν γὰρ Χριστιανὸς ἐν Χριστιανοῖς ἀνατραφεὶς τοῖς γονεῦσιν, ὅτε τοῦ φρονεῖν καὶ τῆς φιλοσοφίας ἥψατο, εὐθὺς πρὸς τὴν κατὰ νόμους πολιτείαν μετεβάλετο: in Eusebius, *Hist. Eccl.* VI. 19. Here, however, as in most other cases where a search after the Absolute was undertaken independently of revelation, it issued in Pantheism; since the Absolute and the Personal, the Finite and the Infinite, are only reconciled in Christ: cf. Maret, as before, pp. 145 sq.

Neo-Platonist professors as an incarnation of the Deity, who was 'sent to bring down the light of happiness and philosophy for the salvation of the human race[1].' Some of them asserted also that the genuine teaching of our Lord Himself had harmonised with theirs, but was corrupted by His followers[2]. Yet they all evinced the heathen bias of their system by repudiating the monotheism of Christianity, by consenting to adapt their doctrines to the grossest forms of popular superstition, and by teaching that all nations had their own peculiar 'dæmons,' whom it was the duty of the masses to propitiate and adore. So plausible were many of the arguments alleged in aid of this religious syncretism that emperors for a while embraced it; and had Christianity assented to the compromise, the rage of persecution might have ceased. We read that in the private oratory of Severus, Abraham was now associated with Orpheus, and Apollonius of Tyana with our blessed Lord Himself[3]; and Hadrian, captivated by a similar class of speculations, was anxious at one period to enthrone the Founder of Christianity among the gods of the metropolis, desisting only after he had calculated the profound and sweeping changes which this measure would have certainly produced[4].

And now the Christian, whose uncompromising temper had survived the calumnies and scoffs, the torture and the flame, of Western heathenism, was called to meet another class of adversaries,—one that brought to the encounter not only the familiar

[1] Such was the language of Iamblichus, one of his biographers: Mackay, p. 161.

[2] 'Ita enim volunt et ipsum credi, nescio quid aliud scripsisse, quod diligunt, *nihilque sensisse contra deos suos*, sed eos potius magico ritu coluisse; et discipulos ejus non solum de illo fuisse mentitos, dicendo illum Deum, per quem facta sint omnia, *cum aliud nihil quam homo fuerit*, quamvis excellentissimæ sapientiæ; verum etiam de diis eorum non hoc docuisse, quod ab illo didicissent.' S. Augustin. *de Consensu Evangelistarum*, Lib. I. § 52, ed. Bened.

[3] 'Matutinis horis in larario suo in quo et divos principes, sed optimos, electos, et animas sanctiores, in queis et Apollonium, et, quantum scriptor suorum temporum dicit, Christum, Abraham et Orpheum, et hujusmodi cæteros habebat, ac majorum effigies, rem divinam faciebat.' Lampridius, in *Vit. Sever. Alex.* c. 29.

[4] *Ibid.* c. 43. Speaking of the early Christian centuries Mr. Max Müller remarks (Bunsen's *Univ. Hist.* I. 119): 'It was a period of religious and metaphysical delirium, when everything became everything, when Mâyâ and Sophia, Mitra and Christ, Virâf and Isaiah, Belus, Zarvan, and Kronos were mixed up in one jumbled system of inane speculation, from which at last the East was delivered by the positive doctrines of Mohammed, the West by the pure Christianity of the Teutonic nations.'

mythes of pagan Greece and Rome, but tortuous subtleties and huge abstractions, which had long engaged the pensive and ascetic spirits of the East. The pure and lofty Theism of the Church already, it is true, had vanquished many forms of Eastern speculation, when the earliest race of Gnostics had been driven from the field of controversy. Still another and more formidable series of attacks, all aiming to confound the Gospel with the old religions of Asia, date their rise from the appearance of the Persian Máni, who flourished at the opening of the fourth century. His main position[1] is, that on comparing the systems of Zoroaster and Buddha with that of Jesus Christ, the same divine ingredients are observable in all, though under various shades and modifications. Hence it was proposed to bring about a reconciliation of the three systems, or rather to incorporate the older creeds with what had been more recently revealed in Christianity. Máni was himself to be the organ of God (the 'Paraclete') for carrying on this fresh development, and one of his chief duties was to purify the intellects of men in order that they might be rescued from all servile bondage to the past, and more particularly from what was held to be a special artifice of the evil principle, the Old Testament œconomy. To promote this separation he affirmed that inspirations granted to himself enabled him to point out what was merely human, transitory, or accommodated to the prejudices of the Jewish people, in the records of the New Testament; his dictum being pressed on all as absolutely infallible, because it was affirmed that he in his own person represented the last progress in the knowledge of religious truth. But Máni, though he struggled hard and was supported by a train of energetic followers, could not shake the constancy of the more earnest Christians. They perceived that his religion was erected on a fundamental misconception, and was utterly antagonistic to their own. He started with ideas of God and His relation to the world, which if not absolutely pantheistic bordered very closely upon pantheism, and must result in it eventually. His Ahriman they felt was not the Satan of the Bible. But they saw still more distinctly that if his principles were true, they would produce an utter severance of the Old and New Testaments. These they had been taught to recognise as equally divine, as so indissolubly bound together and so mutually interpenetrating that to rob them of the first would be to tear the second into shreds and tatters.

[1] Cf. Neander, *Ch. Hist.* II. 157 sq.

We occasionally encounter the descendants of such misbelievers even during the inertness of the Mediæval period. As many tenets of the Neo-Platonist were re-adopted in the ninth century by John Scotus Erigena[1], so the errors of the Manichæan[2] found a simultaneous echo in the pulpits of Paulicians, Cathari, and Albigenses. Other instances might be collected from the annals of the following period; but as soon as the study of the pagan poets and philosophers revived, the general tendency of thought was somewhat different. Oriental speculations were less known, and writers like Boccaccio[3] prove their heathenish turn of mind, by using heathen phraseology to designate the highest mysteries of Holy Writ, and otherwise promoting the amalgamation of the two religions. Prayers are offered in the most offensive spirit to Jupiter, to Juno, and to Venus. The incarnation of 'the son of Jupiter' is mentioned; he is said to have visited the earth, that he might forward its redemption. Other scholars[4] of this stamp proceed yet further; they place our blessed Lord in juxtaposition with Socrates and Plato, identify the Persons of the Holy Trinity with heathen deities, and under the patronage of the Medici at Florence threaten to obliterate the characteristic doctrines of the Gospel, or confound them with the theories of Greek philosophy[5].

With the Reformation of the sixteenth century, levelling as it did so many of the ancient boundaries of human thought, and breaking off so many time-worn fetters, came a signal for the reappearance of free-thinkers still more cognate with misguided zealots of the present day. Servetus and the rest of

[1] See a recent article in the *North British Review*, No. XLV. pp. 121, sq. The writer shews, however, that Scotus 'never lost his faith entirely either in the personality of God or in the supernatural teaching of the Bible.'

[2] The following extract from a *Formula Receptionis Manichæorum* belonging to the period, shews that Buddha, Máni, Zoroaster, Christ and the Sun, were then treated as different manifestations of the same power: *Ἀναθεματίζω τοὺς τὸν Ζαράδαν καὶ Βουδᾶν καὶ τὸν Χριστὸν καὶ τὸν Μανιχαῖον, καὶ τὸν ἥλιον, ἕνα καὶ τὸν αὐτὸν εἶναι λέγοντας.* Tollius, *Itiner. Italic.* p. 134. Traject. 1696.

[3] This may be seen especially in the *Filocolo* (al. *Filocopo*), where, as Sismondi (*Liter. of Southern Europe*, I. 300) has remarked, Boccaccio 'seems determined to confound the two religions, and to prove that they are in fact the same worship, under different names.'

[4] Roscoe's *Life of Leo X.*, II. 87, 88. Hence the frightful growth of infidelity at Rome itself immediately before the Reformation: see, for instance, Erasmus, *Epist.* lib. XXVI. ep. 34, ed. Le Clerc.

[5] Cf. the determinations of the Council of Lateran, Labbe, XIV. 188.

the 'Illuminati' were, in fact, precursors of the English spiritualists[1]. They all opposed themselves to the idea of an objective revelation, often substituting for the Holy Scriptures the distempered products of their own imaginations, and claiming the infallible guidance of the Holy Spirit, whom, in cases where the plea was more convenient, they represented as superior in authority even to the Lord Himself. Their utter subjectivity involved them also in the absolute denial of the cardinal doctrines promulgated by the Church, impelled them to devise eccentric institutions, and assert that 'every man shall be saved by the law or sect which he professeth[2].' It was not, however, till the following century that men of learning and intelligence were seriously possessed by the desire of founding what is called an Absolute Religion. Lord Herbert of Cherbury was the first in England who approximated closely to the ground of Mr. Parker. Grievously perplexed by the phenomena of heathenism, he entered on the task of sifting the peculiarities of all religions. Out of the residuum he attempted to compile a creed[3], consisting of five simple articles, which all the world, he ventured to predict, would recognise as true, and deem sufficient as a term of communion and a warrant of salvation.

Many of his followers in that century and the next proceeded to far greater lengths[4]. In Tindal, Collins, Blount,

[1] See the evidence collected in Mr. Riddle's *Bampton Lectures* (1852), pp. 394 sq. The error there noted of Castellio, who 'separated Scripture from the Spirit,' has been very common both before and since the Reformation. Thus Milton hinted (*Prose Works*, IV. 449, Bohn's ed.) that 'the Spirit which is given us is a more certain guide than Scripture, whom, therefore, it is our duty to follow.'

[2] Art. XVIII. of the XXXIX. The Scottish Confession of 1560 speaks in like manner, 'of those that affirm, that men quhilk live according to equitie and justice, shall be saved, what religioun soever they have professed,' in Knox's *Works*, II. 108, ed. Laing.

[3] After announcing his own five articles, he adds: 'quos non nostri tantum sed universi Orbis cœtus pro veris indubitatisque habere debent.' *De Religione Gentilium*, p. 2, Amstel. 1663. This treatise, together with its companion *De Veritate* published as early as 1624, has been examined at length by Leland, in his useful *View of the Principal Deistical Writers* (XVIIth and XVIIIth cent.), 5th ed. 1798. See also on the general question of modern Deism, the sketch given by Van Mildert in his *Boyle Lectures* (1802—1805), Lect. IX.—Lect. XII.

[4] In speaking of Tindal, whose *Christianity as old as the Creation* first appeared in 1730, Leland remarks (I. 127): 'Others have attacked particular parts of the Christian scheme, or of its proofs. But this writer has endeavoured to subvert the very foundations of it, by shewing that there neither is

Chubb, Woolston, and Bolingbroke at home; and in Dupuis, Voltaire, and D'Alembert on the continent, we find a class of writers who resolved at every hazard, and with confidence[1] proportioned to their daring, to destroy the credibility of Holy Writ, to pour contempt on all external revelations, and conduct us back if possible to heathenism, or 'the religion of nature[2].' But in vain; the truth of God was still victorious. Notwithstanding the depressed condition of theology, and notwithstanding the corrupted spirit and materialistic temper of the age, the flood of intellectual licence was again rolled back. The ark still rode in conscious majesty upon the bosom of the surging

nor can be any external revelation at all, distinct from what he calls *the internal revelation of the law of nature in the hearts of all mankind,'* &c. Tindal was a veritable forerunner of the spiritualists. 'He sometimes speaks as if he thought the deists were infallibly guided, in making use of the reason God hath given, to *distinguish religion from superstition*, so that they are sure not to run into any errors of moment' (p. 128). Other persons who were in favour of an external revelation he called 'Demonists.'

[1] Thus, when Dupuis published his *Origine de tous les Cultes*, the volume on Christianity started with the boast, 'qui doit faire une révolution dans le monde religieux et dans le culte de plusieurs grandes nations' (ed. Auguis, v. 1). He tells us immediately after, 'Christ sera pour nous ce qu'ont été Hercule, Osiris, Adonis, Bacchus. Il partagera en commun avec eux le culte que tous les peuples de tous les pays et de tous les siècles ont rendu à la Nature universelle et à ses agens principaux.'

[2] 'The present unbelievers,' writes Waterland ('Wisdom of the Ancients,' *Works*, v. 4), 'are setting up what they call natural religion to rival supernatural: human reason in the heart of man, in opposition to Divine reason laid down in the Word of God; or to say all in short, *Pagan darkness* in opposition to Scripture light.' The kind of worship which these heralds of the Absolute Religion would fain establish in the room of what they found among the Christians of their times, may be gathered from *An Apology for professing the Religion of Nature in the Eighteenth Century of the Christian Æra* (Twelve Letters addressed to Bishop Watson), 1789. The author then adds *A Liturgy on the Principles of Theism* 'in which philosophers might join without insulting their understandings or corrupting their hearts.'

The 'First Service' commences thus:

'Powerful Ruler of the Universe! whatever Thou art—whether Nature necessarily existing; or the animating spirit of mortals,—we adore Thee, who by impenetrable methods conductest all things to Thy purposes.'. . . .

The 'First Service' ends:—

'Despotic government has not produced a tyrant; human nature has not generated a monster, so cruel, so revengeful, so wicked as the odious phantom to which superstition is devoted!'

In the 'Second Service' (p. 195), the pantheism is avowed.

'How shall we speak of Nature, or of Nature's God! Everything tends to convince us, we should not, for we cannot seek the Deity out of Nature. Everything to us is impossible which is not produced by its laws.'

waters; while many rival systems, fabricated in compliance with 'the instincts of humanity,' and directed by 'the light of nature,' perished in the storm they had provoked. It is remarkable that not a few of the objections ventilated at this period by the English 'Deists' found their way across the channel, and in Germany communicated a fresh impulse to the Rationalistic movement[1]. They are now returning home, etherialised indeed, and moulded into more fantastic shapes, although substantially the same objections as before. England once the master has become the ardent, apt, and credulous disciple; and when numbers of our brethren on the continent are just emerging from the fogs of scepticism and welcoming the earliest dawn of better days, it seems as though the English were resolved to venture out again into the same dreary regions,—only to be taught again the utter fruitlessness of all endeavours to resolve the arduous problems of humanity without the aid of Holy Writ.

Impelled by the necessity of coping with these wild and retrogressive tendencies, the Christian advocate has never shrunk from the encounter, and has seldom found his labours altogether unsuccessful. He may not indeed be always guided by a sound discretion; he may fail to understand the nature of the malady in certain cases, and in others may suggest an antidote that does not work its cure; but still his consciousness of the profound importance of the issue has been ever visible. He feels that to reduce our blessed Lord into the category of human seers is practically to dethrone Him. Christianity will tolerate no rival. They who wish to raise a tabernacle for some other master, be it even for the greatest worthies of the old œconomy,—a Moses or Elias,—must be warned that Christ, and Christ alone, is to be worshipped: they must hear *Him*.

The Eastern Church, as we have seen, appeared at first to use less emphasis in their assertion of this truth than the contemporary Latin writers; or rather by evincing a disposition to multiply the points of contact between Christianity and other systems, and so recognising a prophetic element in Gentilism, they gave a handle to the laxer party who had little or no reverence even for the character of Christ. But all such tenderness for the religions of the heathen world was everywhere forgotten in the Middle Ages[2]. They who issued

[1] Tholuck has drawn attention to this fact in his *Glaubwürdigkeit der evangel. Gesch.*: cf. also Mr. Riddle's *Bampton Lectures*, p. 397.

[2] When Bede was pressed with the objection that many heathen philosophers had evinced a large amount of moral sensibility, he

forth to plant the cross among the northern and eastern nations, had to deal with men who were not absolutely hostile to the Saviour, but who recognised in Him no more than a pre-eminently gracious Being to be added to the number of their dark divinities[1], or else esteemed the Gospel only one manifestation of the Absolute akin to their own religions[2]: and hence the ardent missionary, full of zeal, though sometimes wanting in intelligence, was tempted to commence his exhortations by decrying all their gods as evil spirits, and exaggerating the guilt of their departed ancestors. A milder tone, however, grew more common at the period of the Reformation. Many rose to advocate the salvability of the nobler class of heathen, gloried to have found sublimer thoughts in their philosophers, or more tender precepts in their poets, and even went so far as to maintain, that some of them had access to the highest truths, and were instructed by the Word of God unwritten. A most zealous Swiss reformer[3] on the one side and a learned bibliothecarius[4] of the Roman pontiff on the other, represented this new

answered that none who were ignorant of Christ, the virtue of God and the wisdom of God, could have either *true* virtue or *true* wisdom. Yet he adds: 'In quantum vero vel gustum aliquem sapientiæ cujuslibet vel virtutis imaginem habebant, *totum hoc desuper acceperunt;* non solum munere primæ conditionis, verum etiam quotidiana ejus gratia, qui creaturam suam nec se deserentem deserens, dona sua, prout ipse judicaverit hominibus et magna magnis et parva largitur parvis.' *Expositio in Cant. Canticorum;* Opp. IX. 197, ed. Giles.

[1] See an example in Neander, V. 397.

[2] See the striking testimony of a Franciscan missionary in Raynald. *Annal. Eccl.* ad an. 1326, § 31.

[3] Walter (Gualther) was under the necessity of defending Zwingli on account of the freedom with which he had praised the heathen poets and philosophers, which exposed him to the charge of ranking idolaters and Epicureans with the Christian saints. The apologist then proceeds: 'Cum vero illud [*i.e.* Verbum Dei] non vacuum redire, nec fructu suo carere dicat Dominus, nemo opinor negabit plures ex gentibus quoque ad salutem pervenisse, si nimirum eos Dei verbo vel *externo* vel *interno* aliquo modo instructos fuisse demonstraverimus,' &c. Pref. to Zwingli's *Works*, ed. 1545, sign. ε, 4. Cf. Browne, *On the Articles*, II. 75. Erasmus and others used similar language: Hey, *Lectures*, II. 360.

[4] The *De Perenni Philosophia* of Augustinus Steuchus Eugubinus, titular bishop of Kisamos, was published at Basle in 1542. His principles may be gathered from Lib. X. c. 23: 'Claret igitur post multa secula missam diuinitus Theologiam, nihil aliud fuisse quam priscorum seculorum caligantis iam et obscuræ, quam animis hominum impresserat Deus, et uoce sua in creatione, post in secuto tempore per nuncios tradiderat, scientiæ reuelationem. Neque enim fieri potest, quod postea cœlitus est apertum, quodque perfecte declaraturus uenit e cœlo in terras Deus, ante aduentum eius alia ratione

phase of thought. The latter even did not hesitate to urge that the philosophy of the ancients was a kind of 'tacit Christianity,' and that the promulgation of the Gospel only took away the inmost veil and brought us into full communication with the source of supernatural truth. Since then the records of the ancient world have been repeatedly examined in order to obtain fresh light for the determination of these questions. Theophilus Gale endeavoured to establish[1], 'that the proud sophists of Greece, esteemed the eye of the world for wisdom,' were 'fain to come and light their candles at the sacred fire, which was lodged in the Jewish Church.' While Cudworth, 'anxious to satisfy those amongst us who boggle so much at the Trinity, and look upon it as the choke-pear of Christianity[2],' employed his deep and ponderous erudition in maintaining that a similar doctrine was known among the Platonists; this being, in fact, one only out of many consequences that resulted from the co-existence of a true philosophy external to the sphere of revelation. But with Cudworth, it should be remembered, such a view in no wise tended to discredit the Old Testament, or to excite the faintest prejudice against it. In the present day the same investigation is actively proceeding; and now that every corner of the heathen world has been explored, a somewhat different explanation of

celebre fuisse quam eadem ipsa quod diuinitus esset traditum.' In 1548 appeared the *Historia de diis gentilibus* of Greg. Sylv. Gyraldus; in allusion to which Eckermann, *Religionsgeschichte und Mythologie*, I. 12 (Halle, 1848), remarks: 'Schon seit dem Anfange des sechszehnten Jahrhunderts hatte man *besonders in Italien* angefangen, die Theologie und die Mythologie des heidnischen Alterthums in mannigfaltige nähere Beziehung zu setzen. Man fing an zwischen den Mythen des Heidenthums und den Sagen des Alten Testaments Vergleichungen anzustellen, und gründete namentlich die Ansicht, dass sämmtliche polytheistische Religionem nur als Abartungen aus, oder Abfälle von dem Hebräischen Monotheismus anzusehen seien, und war emsig bemüht, dieselbe auf gelehrte Weise zu begründen.'

[1] *Court of the Gentiles*, 'Advertisements to the Reader.'

[2] *Intellectual System*, Pref. p. xliii., cf. II. 428 sq. But in making out as good a case as possible for the heathen, whose polytheism he appears to have considered as little more than a monotheism in disguise, this great writer confounded the religion of ancient nations with the theological opinions of the leading poets and philosophers: see Mosheim's note, in Vol. II. p. 251. Coleridge was nearer to the truth, when he wrote as follows: 'Across the night of Paganism, philosophy flitted on, like the lantern-fly of the Tropics, a light to itself, and an ornament, but alas! no more than an ornament of the surrounding darkness. Christianity reversed the order.' *Aids to Reflection*, I. 146, Pickering's ed.

the correspondencies between the Gentile and Christian systems has been generally adopted, at least by all those writers who preserve the ancient reverence for the Bible. There is now no general wish among the orthodox to trace such parallelisms *exclusively* to the diffusion of the Hebrew Scriptures[1]. There is even less occasion to suspect that any critical pressure will be used for bringing the philosophy of heathenism into more perfect unison with the distinctive doctrines of the Church. Yet on the other hand the features of resemblance, few and dim and fragmentary though they be, are welcomed as so many testimonies to the truth of revelation—as 'unconscious prophecies of heathendom,' or else as portions of that spiritual heritage which men and tribes bore with them from the cradle of the human race. A living writer[2] has observed, that 'the noblest and most effectual way of defending Christianity is not to condemn everything which preceded it,—to turn all the virtues of distinguished heathens into splendid vices,—but rather to make them testify in its favour.'

Such is also my conviction; and with kindred feelings I now purpose to reopen the investigation of those leading facts and the analysis of those ideas of heathenism which the opponents of Christianity have been accustomed to adduce as parallel to what is found in the sacred volume, and as, therefore, placing Gentile systems on a level with the Church of God. Such points of correspondency, where they in truth exist, I hold to be explainable without in any way diminishing the lustre of the Gospel or detracting in the least degree from

[1] The evidence that can be urged in favour of this view has been recently collected in Mr. Tomkins's *Hulsean Prize Essay* (1849).

[2] Schaff, *Ch. Hist.* I. 168. It is gratifying to remark that Creuzer in his elaborate *Symbolik*, though he manifests no very decided prepossessions in favour of Christianity, is not influenced by any fanatical dislike of it, and that the French scholar (M. Guigniaut) who translated and enlarged the work of Creuzer is of the same mind. For example, he echoes the following sentiment: 'Pour moi,' dit M. Creuzer, 'la meilleure religion est celle qui conserve avec la plus grande pureté le caractère moral et prescrit aux peuples la règle des mœurs la plus sévère. Je suis loin de penser, toutefois, que dans la morale réside toute l'essence de la religion; je sais au contraire que les plus nobles âmes, et les peuples les plus mémorables des temps anciens et modernes, ont demandé à cette dernière des lumières plus hautes sur le mystère de notre existence et sur nos futures destinées. Entre toutes les religions connues, le christianisme me paraît avoir le mieux satisfait à ce double besoin de l'homme: mais, soit dans sa doctrine, soit dans les formes de son culte, il avait été et avait dû être préparé par les religions antérieures.' *Religions de l'Antiquité*, 'Avertissement,' p. 7.

the supremacy which it enjoys in the affections of the Christian world.

The order I propose to follow in discussing the religious systems where minute comparison has been thought desirable[1], is this:—

The Religions that arose and still prevail in Hindústán and some adjoining countries.

The Religions of Mexico, of China, and the Southern Seas.

Both these groups appear to have always been entirely external to the sphere of Hebrew influence.

The Religions of Ancient Egypt and Persia.

These, it is alleged, have both at different periods actually modified the development of thought among the Hebrews; the first, during their long residence in Egypt; the second, during the Babylonish captivity.

The Religions of Ancient Greece and Rome.

With these the planters of Christianity were brought into immediate contact at the very opening of their work, and over these they won a triumph in the first five centuries of the present era.

The Religions of the Saxon, Scandinavian, and Slavonic tribes.

Among these tribes the principles of heathenism appear to have been strongest; and some of them in fact were not converted to Christianity for a thousand years after its promulgation.

But before proceeding to determine the characteristics of these several groups[2], on each of which I purpose to bestow a

[1] If it be asked why Muhammadanism is not included in the series, my reply is, that I consider it a debased form of revealed religion,—a Christian, or more properly, a Jewish heresy. Paret, in the *Studien und Kritiken*, 1855, 2tes Heft, p. 295, calls it 'eine niedere Abart oder, wenn man will, Abklatsch der Offensbarungs-religion.'

[2] Objections have been urged against this arrangement on the ground that it does not recognise 'the great watersheds of thought and language which divide the principal families of the human race' (*Col. Ch. Chr.* March, 1858, p. 105). The plan proposed by one reviewer is to take the threefold division of the human race, the Semitic, the Aryan, and the Turánian, and assuming that the spheres of language and religion are generally conterminous to arrange all the religions of which we have any authentic information under these three different heads. 'There is the Semitic family with its spiritual monotheism, the Aryan family with its worship of nature, and the Chinese and Turánian races with their vague belief in a Divine Being, neither spiritual nor natural, but hovering in its ghostly unreality between heaven and earth, filling

separate investigation, it is necessary to my argument that certain other points should be established. These will be comprised in two preliminary chapters.

One of them has refereuce to the question touching *the unity of the human race*—a question intimately bound up with my present subject. For if it be in any measure probable that all varieties of men originated in a single pair, I shall be *pro tanto* justified in urging this important fact, as one medium of accounting for traditions which were afterwards diffused through all the human family.

The second point concerns what may be called the *characteristic features of the Old Testament religion*, and its vital coherence with the system founded in and by our blessed Lord. For if this close connexion be established, I am able to point out the ancient germ and nucleus of which Christianity became the *true* development; and if the principles pervading both the stages of Revealed Religion be fundamentally the same, a standard will have been erected in the ancient world whereby to estimate the real character and tendencies of those contemporary religions, which, as we shall see hereafter, sprang up wild in different soils of paganism.

the human heart with fear and superstition, but unable to inspire its votaries with the joy and confidence of the Aryan suppliant, or the awe and reverence of the Semitic worshipper.'

But this criticism, even if the counter-theory could be established, seems to emanate from a misconception of the work on which I am now occupied. I am not writing a history of all religions, but am comparing the chief religions of heathendom with Christianity or Revealed Religion. *That* is my centre.

CHAPTER II.

On the Unity of the Human Race.

'Quanquam in hoc ipso non mediocriter peccent quod non *hominis* causa dicunt, sed *hominum*. Unius enim singularis appellatio totum comprehendit humanum genus. Sed hoc ideo, quia ignorant unum hominem a Deo esse formatum, putantque homines in omnibus terris et agris, tanquam fungos, esse generatos.' LACTANTIUS, *Divin. Instit.* lib. VII. c. 4.

Impugners of the unity of the human race. Mitigation of these assaults. Reasons of the change. Objections. Answers. Mental and moral properties common to man. Universal response to the appeals of Christianity. Objections answered. Explanation of physiological varieties. Objection I. *Answer. Objection* II. *Answer. Classification of human languages. Are these three groups reducible to one? Philology has not answered the question. Its bearing on the truthfulness of the Bible. Gradual formation of heathen theologies. Their infinite variety. Truth and unity in the Church.*

THE object of this chapter is to indicate, as briefly as may be, the general nature of the evidence producible in favour of the oneness of the human species, or the derivation of the various tribes of man from one common stock[1]. I cannot hope to enter far into the details of so vast a question; nor indeed will it be necessary. For the main conditions of the argument are satisfied, if I can prove that modern sciences, so far from damaging in this respect the credibility of the sacred record, are all tending to establish and confirm it. In other words, I shall be content with shewing that researches of the present

[1] Any comparative view of the religions of the world would be valueless, indeed philosophically impossible, unless we may regard them as all concerned with one subject-matter; contemplate them as phenomena of the spiritual relations of the same class of rational creatures with the same Divine Being who is over all. Hence the questions of the unity of the human race and the unity of God, as vindicated in the Old Testament, are preliminary to our main investigation.

age conspire to warrant a belief in the original unity of men, and therefore serve to justify the expectation, that traditions current in the various tribes and peoples of antiquity had very much in common, having emanated from the same primordial source.

During the last century, when scepticism of every kind was rampant, and when France was in particular embarking on her infidel crusade against all noble theories of man, of God, and of the universe, the fashion was to scoff at this idea of consanguinity among the different nations of the globe. Language was regarded as a mere conventional apparatus gradually devised by the untutored savage: 'positive religions' were decried as engines of a crafty priesthood, or as 'heresies' of what was called 'the religion of nature:' while man himself had been reduced to little more than one of the varieties of animal life.

The same degrading notions led the French Encyclopédists to deny not only the objectivity of human nature, but the common origin of men. It will be found that all intelligent belief in the unity of the human race is naturally associated with belief in God's own unity and paternity, with real consciousness of sin, with ardent longings for redemption, and particularly with a recognition of the fact, that Christ and the apostles planted a religious system which provides for men of every age and climate, and is capable of indefinite expansion. These truths the unbelievers of the last century assailed with blasphemous vituperation: and, therefore, we are not surprised to hear them advocating the hypothesis of independent human species. According to Voltaire, none but a blind man can doubt, that the whites, negroes, Albinos, Hottentots, Laplanders, Chinese and Americans, are entirely distinct races. Since that time, however, there has been a vast reaction in the mind of European scholars. It is true, assailants are not wanting who repeat among ourselves the oft-exploded cavils of the French Encyclopédists. The most cultivated nations are still said to have been formed in the very lowest grade of savage life, and to have struggled year by year into their present stage of moral, social, and religious elevation; passing from the grossest Fetishism to a refined and flexible Polytheism, and so upwards, till they were at last enabled, by some means or other, to evolve the true idea of God[1]. But even where these principles of

[1] So think M. Comte, Mr. F. W. Newman, and many others, regardless of the fact, conceded even by Mr. W. J. Fox (*Religious Ideas*, p. 65), that in the very oldest records, 'we often find symptoms of a more distinct conception of Divine grandeur and infinity than

development are entertained, their authors do not speak so positively as the sceptics of the former age, against the oneness of the human family[1]; while others who refuse on different grounds to acquiesce in the scriptural account of man's origin, have, notwithstanding, been constrained by philosophical reasons to postpone their judgment on the subject[2]. Modern science has in fact materially contributed, in this case also, to revive the lustre and to vindicate the truth of revelation. She has wrested from the grasp of unbelief a number of its choicest weapons, and has wielded them against itself with irresistible effect.

In the first place, Cuvier[3], by a series of historical and geological researches, proved that man has not been very long an occupant of the earth; that none of the existing varieties can trace their origin beyond the point at which the Bible seems to place the introduction of the human species; and, therefore, that the modern theory of 'creative laws,' acting by 'myriads of ages,' is adverse to the facts of history and the

prevailed in later ages.' Alex. von Humboldt (*Cosmos*, II. 113) seems to shrink from expressing any positive opinion either way; and yet instances of tribes *relapsing* into a savage and almost brutal state are not unfrequent; *e.g.* the Bushmen of Southern Africa.

[1] Thus Mr. Theodore Parker (*Discourse*, &c., p. 75) acknowledges 'the identity of the human race,' which refers, however, to ideas and sentiments common to mankind, without implying, in his opinion, the doctrine of a common origin. He also admits that the view in favour of *several* originating pairs is equally without any direct historical proof. It is afterwards added: 'No one can determine what was the primitive state of the human race, or when, or where, or how mankind, at the command of God, came into existence. Here our conclusions can be only negative,' (p. 76): *i.e.* after we have rejected the evidence of the Bible and extinguished the traditions of the ancient world, we find ourselves in utter darkness.

[2] Niebuhr, for example (*Lect. on Ancient History*, I. 6, Lond. 1852), evades the consideration of the main problem in the following passage: 'Whether all nations were originally of different origin and belonged to different races, or whether their original identity were changed in form and language by a series of miracles, these are questions which do not belong to ancient history; and we must leave to others to discuss them. Without a direct and minute revelation from God, we *cannot arrive at any certain results on these points*, and in reference to them the Book of Genesis cannot be considered as a revelation.' William von Humboldt seems to have hesitated in like manner to the very close of his life (see Chev. Bunsen's *Outlines of the Philosophy of Universal History*, I. 59, 60, Lond. 1854); but his illustrious brother, the author of *Cosmos*, obviously inclines to the hypothesis of unity: see I. 351, Sabine's edition.

[3] *Essay on the Theory of the Earth*, ed. Jameson, §§ 30 sq.

phenomena of science. Mr Lyell[1] rendered similar service to the cause of Christian truth, when he demolished the analogous theory of Lamarck, which represented man as one of the numerous links in a graduated chain of beings, successively developed into higher stages; his bodily organism being a modification of the ape, and his mental prerogatives no more than the expanded form of faculties which he enjoys in common with the brute creation. But what has tended most of all perhaps to silence the objections of the antichristian 'philosophers,' are the strange affinities which have been brought to light by the investigations of comparative philology. When India fell into the hands of Britain, and a class of enterprising scholars, headed by Sir William Jones, began to work the precious mines of history which that conquest opened to the western world, it was established that the 'Aryan' race beyond the Indus spoke a language fundamentally akin to that of Germany and England. Other languages, in which affinity had hitherto been unsuspected, were also found to range themselves within the same group; an Aryan, or Indo-European, family was constituted; and as the new principles of classification were extended into wider regions, it grew obvious that all known varieties of human language, once a dreary chaos, were reducible into a small number of harmonious groups; while in these groups themselves, some evidence was thought to be detected of a radical connexion, such as leads to the belief that all are only modifications of an older and more general type.

Meanwhile a different process had been leading to the same result. Comparative physiology was moving hand in hand with comparative philology. The skill and industry of Blumenbach[2] in that department, served to shew that in respect of their physical structure and the laws of their animal œconomy, the varieties of the human race are in like manner all reducible to a very few groups; and Prichard[3], by a happy combination of these sciences, was able to push forward the great problem, and, as some imagined, went so far as to establish the original oneness of the human family.

[1] *Principles of Geology*, III. 4 sq. 6th ed.: cf. Prof. Sedgwick's *Discourse on the Studies of the University of Cambridge*, Pref. pp. xviii. sq. 5th ed.

[2] His great work is entitled *De Generis Humani varietate nativa*, Gotting. 1775: but his examination and comparison of skulls proceeded until 1828.

[3] See his *Researches into the Physical History of Mankind*, 3rd ed.

Several lines of proof must, therefore, be regarded as converging to the point in question:—(1) the Scriptural, (2) the Psychological, (3) the Physiological, (4) the Philological.

1. *Scriptural Proof.*

I should have judged it quite superfluous to insist upon this head in dealing with avowed assailants of dogmatic Christianity; but there is reason to believe that several persons who revere the Bible as in some degree a supernatural record, strenuously deny the derivation of the human family from one single pair. Thus, when Professor Agassiz[1] is reminded of St. Paul's assertion, that 'God hath made of one blood[2] all nations of men, for to dwell on all the face of the earth' (Acts xvii. 26), his answer is, that this 'figurative expression applies to the higher unity of mankind, and not to their supposed genital connexion by natural descent.' He also argues that the Book of Genesis, to which allusion is here made by the apostle, 'must be considered as relating chiefly to the history of the *white* race, with special reference to the history of the Jews.'

Now both these statements seem to me most arbitrary and evasive. (1) Until it has been shewn that such expressions as 'made of blood' are used to signify any species of relation or descent, save that of natural generation[3], we are scarcely justified in seeking for a figurative import. St. Paul there told the men of Athens, among whom polytheism had grown into a sort of passion, that God was really one, the single Lord, the absolute Creator of the universe. He next proceeded to announce the great correlative truth, that God has left an image of His own oneness in the oneness of humanity; and that this fact was certified by the production of the human species from one common stock[4]. All nations were declared to be His offspring;

[1] See his contribution to the *Christian Examiner* (American), July, 1850, pp. 135—137. This periodical is an organ of the Boston Unitarians.

[2] A second reading, adopted by Lachmann, omits αἵματος altogether.

[3] The only 'higher unity' connecting men together, is the spiritual nature they derive in common by regeneration from Christ, the New Head of humanity: but this birth is most expressly said to be 'not of blood' (αἱμάτων), John i. 13. Neither, as St. Paul instructs us elsewhere, could it be predicated of all men indiscriminately; for according to him the unconverted Gentiles (Eph. iv. 17, 18) are still 'alienated from the life of God through the ignorance that is in them.'

[4] See Neander's excellent paraphrase (*Planting*, I. 192, Lond. 1851). 'In the polytheistic standing-point,' he adds (*note*), 'a knowledge of the unity of human nature is wanting, because it is closely connected with a knowledge of the

since they all were sons of Adam, 'which was the son of God' (Luke iii. 38).

(2) The second argument is equally unfounded, inconsistent with the general tenour of the sacred narrative, the statements of particular texts, and all the varied prophecies of redemption. Who in reading the Book of Genesis, without a theory in his eye, is likely to suspect that he is tracing out the origin and early fortunes of one section of the human race? Our first mother was herself called Eve, because (the sacred penman has been careful to inform us) 'she was the mother of all living' (Gen. iii. 20): and whenever it was subsequently foretold how the disasters that had overwhelmed her progeny should terminate on the appearance of some Great Deliverer, every nation from the rising of the sun to the going down thereof, all tribes, wherever scattered and however brutalised, are said to be the objects whom He comes to bless and rescue, to exalt and re-unite. And with this view the writings of the New Testament entirely correspond. Adam is there represented as a 'caput gentis,' whose descendants constitute the self-same race that has been reconstructed in the second Adam[1]. 'As by the disobedience of the one (τοῦ ἑνὸς), the many (οἱ πολλοὶ) were made sinners, so by the obedience of the one shall the many be made righteous' (Rom. v. 19). 'As in Adam all die, even so in Christ shall all be made alive' (1 Cor. xv. 22). In Him

unity of God:' and when it is remembered how the Athenians boasted that they were αὐτόχθονες, the drift of St. Paul's observation is still more obvious. Cf. on the whole of this wonderful speech Baumgarten, *Acts of the Apostles*, II. 157 sq. Edinb. 1854.

[1] When Mr. F. W. Newman calls in question the oneness of the human family, and asks what in that case 'becomes of St. Paul's parallel between the first and second Adam, and the doctrine of headship and atonement founded on it;' a writer in the *Quarterly Review* (No. cxc. p. 474, note) attempts to meet the difficulty by replying that, 'even if mankind had not descended from a single pair, the truths laid down by St. Paul in the passage referred to would be untouched; for when he speaks of all men as *dead in Adam*, he is speaking of Adam as the representative of human nature in its natural and fallen state.' But such interpretation of St. Paul's language seems to me unjustifiable. Adam is affirmed to be the origin of death to all men, just as strictly as our blessed Lord is the origin of life (1 Cor xv. 21, 22); and unless it be contended that in St. Paul's teaching Christ is only the *representative* of redeemed humanity, and not the actual bringer-in of the redemption, Adam must be also far more than a representative; see Rom. v. 19, where the parallelism is most remarkable. I ought to add, however, that the *Quarterly Reviewer* does not admit the truth of Mr. Newman's hypothesis. He holds that scientific research *has* established 'the extreme probability' of a single origin for all the human family.

the course of degradation that commenced with Adam, and was tending to dissever man from man, and one community from another, is arrested and reversed. Humanity has found a second Head, a nobler Representative: it is generically born again in Christ; and, therefore, all the individual members of the species, Jew or Greek, barbarian, Scythian, bond or free, are made susceptible of Christian influences. 'Go ye,' was the charge of Him, who is the 'Second Man,' 'the Lord from Heaven,' (Mark xvi. 15,) 'Go ye into all the world, and preach the Gospel to every creature (πάσῃ τῇ κτίσει);' 'for we know,' writes the Apostle (Rom. viii. 22), 'that the whole creation (πᾶσα ἡ κτίσις) groaneth and travaileth in pain together until now.'

2. *Psychological Proof.*

This argument depends entirely on the fact that, notwithstanding every minor variation in feeling or capacity, in taste or temperament, by which we are enabled to distinguish one people from another, there are certain moral, spiritual, and mental elements, inherent in humanity itself, and underlying all the national types and local characteristics. At first indeed, when our attention is directed to the subject, a picture meets us not of unity but of diversity. We everywhere encounter groups of human beings, each betraying some peculiar tendencies, with manners as dissimilar as their physical conformation; with intellectual habits, indicating all degrees of power and culture; with sentiments, in one case, harsh and barbarous, in a second, gentle, tender, and refined:—a class of variations warranting, as we might judge, the supposition that each separate group is radically independent, and has always formed an independent species. But more thoughtful observation leads us to abandon this hypothesis as crude and superficial. It enables us to see that very many of these wide diversities exist at present, and have long existed in the same country, being multiplied in homogeneous populations, or at least in populations where the race of men has been comparatively unaffected by foreign admixtures. Some diversity, therefore, is not utterly incompatible with unity of origin; and thus we are admonished to carry our analysis still deeper, in the hope of separating what is merely special in the mind of man or accidental in the phases of society, from broader and more fundamental characteristics. To the latter class we shall most reasonably assign whatever has been held in common by the various families of nations, be their state of culture what it may; those great specific properties of mankind, the aspirations, faculties, and sentiments, which have in every period been distinguishing the human from the brute creation.

Men are like each other, and unlike the rest of animated nature, not only as endowed with similar feelings and affections, or impelled by similar appetencies and aversions, but as speaking, reasoning, and reflecting creatures. Wheresoever man is, there we find these marks of his superior dignity. No depths of barbarism have yet been able to obliterate them, however much their brilliance may at times be clouded, or their sphere of action circumscribed. Or look at man as a *progressive* being, when he differs *toto cœlo* from the lower animals. The progress has indeed been slow in certain cases where the soil was uncongenial, or the civilising agents inefficient; but experience teaches us that some advance is uniformly possible; that in the breasts of all men there are latent and mysterious faculties; that all are capable of passing gradually into the higher stages of existence, and readily adapting themselves to novel circumstances and conditions. If we grant that in so far as our domestic instincts are concerned, a parallel is found among the other orders of creation, it is no less obvious, that wherever such exist in man, their character is uniform, their operation is identical: while in that loftier province of his being, where he is immediately connected with the 'God of the spirits of all flesh,' the traces of a common nature are peculiarly discernible. It is a fact that all varieties of men exhibit the same kind of spiritual perceptions, much as these may vary both in sensibility and clearness: all are actuated by sentiments of awe and deference to superior genii, blunted though these be, alike in savage and in civilised communities: all are able to appreciate high and noble deeds, and are susceptible of generous impulses: while all are gifted with the faculty of rising out of their subjection to the influence of the senses, and believe in some hereafter. Even where the human type is lowest, where it reaches the extreme of degradation, bordering almost on brutality, as, for example, in the natives of Australia, the philanthropist is, notwithstanding, cheered by frequent glimpses of the same distinctive nature, and enabled to detect at least the groundwork of a desecrated temple.

And if this general correspondency of mind and heart is tending to establish that all members of the human species constitute but one great family, much more is such connexion vindicated by presentiments which all of them alike evince in favour of the Christian faith. Wherever it has penetrated, the

Good Shepherd's voice is heard, and wakes an echo in the consciences of men; and what in every case attracts them to His fold, is also that which makes them truly conscious of the universal brotherhood subsisting in all nations. With the sole exception of Muhammadanism,—a heresy that drew its dogmas and its very life-blood from Revealed Religion,—we shall find that all the systems of the ancient world were limited in their design and local in their range. They were the images of separate nationalities; they issued from within; they represented special modes of thought and harmonised with states of feeling and imagination that prevailed in certain districts: but with Christianity the case was altogether different. It came fresh from God: it rested on a series of objective revelations: it was active and diffusive as the light, and all-embracing as the firmament of heaven: it dealt with man as man, and never faltered in its claim to be regarded as a veritable 'world-religion.'

Obstacles it doubtless met with in appealing to the various tribes and nations whom it struggled to convert; yet few if any of these obstacles can fairly be ascribed to idiosyncrasies arising from diversity of race. The Hebrews, among whom the Gospel was indigenous, became ere long its most implacable opponents; and at present, when it is accepted by the bulk of the Germanic nations, other members of the Indo-European family have manifested no peculiar warmth in their appreciation of its offer. It knows, in truth, of no distinctions in the pedigree of human souls, because it is the one religion, *the* religion of mankind. Accordingly it reaps in every soil a harvest of conversions. Heralds of the doctrine of the cross had scarcely issued from their lowly birthplace in Judæa, when they found a welcome in the neighbouring states, and even in the capitals of pagan Greece and Rome. They taught both intellectual and imperial masters of the age to bow before the simple majesty of evangelic truth. They civilised the rude but manly nations of the north. They penetrated far into the plains of Central Asia. They discoursed as freely and effectively in tents of wandering tribes, as in the schools and temples of the land of Egypt. And though century after century expired, the Gospel shewed no symptom of decay or imbecility; it was adapted, as at first, to the necessities of every climate, to the temperament of every 'race,' and all the varied phases of society.

Nor at the present day are we without examples of this universal fitness. The families of Western Africa, including that which some have deemed a separate and originally lower type of man, are daily proved to be convertible, are folded in the Christian Church, and are invested with the Christian character. The warlike tribe of the Zulus in Southern Africa, the crouching Dyaks on the coasts of Borneo, multitudes of South-sea islanders, who form together an assemblage of the greatest physical variations, are all yielding to the same appeals; while in New Zealand, where but thirty years ago the natives were ferocious cannibals, the scourge of neighbouring islands, and the terror of the British seaman who was driven to their shores, we now behold a population almost as generally Christian as our own. The chiefs and people vie together in their zeal for the advancement of religion, and exhibit all that catalogue of virtues which distinguish the regenerate nature, 'love, joy, peace, long-suffering, gentleness, goodness, faith, meekness, temperance.'

But in urging facts like these to prove the radiation of the human family from one common point, we meet with some objections:

(1) It is said, for instance, that identity of disposition may exist without implying an identity of origin[1]. Thus in the large group of cats, including the leopard, tiger, lion, and other species, the same general temperament and habits are everywhere observable, and yet it is alleged such animals were originally made to constitute distinct varieties. To this it is sufficient to reply, that man, as we may gather from the faculties of speech and reason, from his moral susceptibilities, his spiritual nature, and his vast capacity of progress, must be treated as a being *sui generis;* or, at least, that where differences like these exist we are not justified in reasoning so completely to his case from that of the inferior animals. It is not of course denied that with regard to what are called the animal appetencies and aversions of his nature, and even to one class of sensuous habits, such analogy may be adduced with justice, and pursued into its consequences. But in doing this, we must not overlook the fact that all varieties of men are far more intimately related than the class of animals in question. The various *species* of the feline genus either intermingle very seldom, or evince a strong repugnance to such union. If hybrids be occasionally produced, and if they threaten by their propagation to commence an intermediate or degenerate race of animals, the wayward tendency is soon arrested by their absolute

[1] This argument is also urged by Professor Agassiz, as above, p. 118.

sterility; and thus the species do not lose their original characteristics. On the other hand, such intermixtures are both possible and permanent among the different families of man. The 'races' which are thought to be peculiarly distinct from each other (the 'Caucasian' and the negro), are most ordinary examples of this law; alliances between them issuing in a fruitful progeny, and, what is specially worthy of remark, the nobler type ere long predominating and absorbing the degraded[1].

(2) It has also been contended that even were we at liberty to assume that the genus *homo* has only one species, *i.e.* to assume that no specific variety exists among the different tribes of man, this fact would never justify us in determining the derivation of all mankind from one single pair; for 'similar causes,' it is urged, 'operating on two or more points of the globe under similar circumstances would necessarily produce similar results[2].' But surely it is far more philosophical to prefer the simpler of two hypotheses, where it will adequately explain the various phenomena of any given question; in other words, it is unworthy of a thoughtful mind to advocate the notion of 'similar causes' and 'similar circumstances,' when the facts before us do not call for such plurality. The spread of population and the present variations in the human species can be perfectly interpreted without this multiplying of productive centres. 'Nothing short of necessity,' to quote a modern writer[3], whom we shall not readily convict of superstitious deference to the letter of the Old Testament, 'should induce us to seek for an autochthony in different parts of the globe, which would break the ties of blood-relationship that bind all men together; and so far are we from being able to point out any necessity in this case, that all the attainable evidence clearly points in the opposite direction.'

3. *The Physiological Proof.*

The axiom I have just advanced respecting the preference always due to simple hypotheses, will equally apply to this

[1] Chev. Bunsen, *Phil. of Universal History*, II. 108, where the writer adds: 'Nature always tends towards perfection, and the image of God, hidden under deviations from the perfect type, returns, *jure postliminii*, as soon as outward impediments are removed.'

[2] This argument, which has become very current, is so stated in Mr. Blackwell's edition of Mallet's *Northern Antiquities*, p. 25.

[3] Dr. Donaldson, *New Cratylus*, 2nd ed. p. 100.

division of the argument The chief authorities for conducting it are Blumenbach and Prichard, whose laborious researches into tho physical history of man will ever be esteemed[1] among the richest contributions to the study of our present subject. They have shewn that animals acknowledged to form one species will, under the adventitious influences of domestication, climate, and the like, divide into a number of subordinate varieties; and thus establish a presumption that at least in respect of all the functions of his animal œconomy, man will undergo a similar modification. They have shewn that distinctions in the families of men are not so strongly marked, so uniform or permanent as exist in any given tribe of animals. They have shewn that all diversities insensibly pass into each other by graduated shades of difference, and, what is still more remarkable, that hardly any specimen can be adduced in which the actual transition is not capable of historical proof. Examples have been multiplied to shew that with regard to human skeletons and crania in particular, the conformation is substantially the same in all types of man; while deviations from the nobler types all range themselves within comparatively narrow limits, and present so many intermediate forms as to render the transition very gradual from one case to another. Similar results have flowed from investigations into the varieties of human colour and the texture of the human hair, which had been formerly regarded as the most abiding characteristics of a race, and are at present vaunted by the friends of slavery and the adversaries of Revealed Religion. Colour is now proved to vary in a great degree with the peculiarities of climate; while 'woolly' hair is only one extreme gradation in a large scale of varieties, and is no longer to be treated as the necessary concomitant of a black skin and negro features[2].

These statements, however, have not been suffered to pass on without a challenge. Prichard's work is far from popular in some districts of America; and two zealous writers[3], bent as

[1] See, for instance, Dr. Wiseman's *Lectures on the Connexion between Science and Revealed Religion*, Lect. III, IV. Lond. 1836, and Carpenter's *Principles of Human Physiology*, pp. 55 sq. Lond. 1846. 'Up to the present moment,' adds the Chevalier Bunsen, in speaking also of Prichard's great work, 'there exists no book which treats that question with equal depth and candour:' as above, I. 48. Some additional facts have been more recently collected in Smyth's *Unity of the Human Races*, New York, 1850.

[2] *Cosmos*, I. 352.

[3] Both these gentlemen have long distinguished themselves by the emphasis with which they speak and write on this subject (see Smyth, p. 110), but their chief

it would seem on proving at all hazards that the negro type of man is radically distinct from others, have been labouring hard for years to undermine the truth of man's original unity by various artifices. While the great majority of thoughtful Germans are at length persuaded that 'the unity of the human species is a fact established as firmly as the unity of any other animal species[1],' that conclusion is repudiated in the strongest terms by Messrs. Nott and Gliddon.

(1) One of their objections which they urge in common with Agassiz is, that the analogy between the human and other animated species, requires us to assign to the varieties of men as well as to the different animals an origin according with their present geographical distribution.

But to this it may be answered, that even if we should allow that different species of animals were all created each within some zoological district of its own—a point which those who make the statement cannot *prove*,—it would by no means follow of necessity that men were also first of all located in the regions which they now inhabit. This argument again is guilty of neglecting all the higher properties of man: it deals with him as nothing more than a variety of animal life. Besides, the facts of history are themselves irreconcilable with the supposed analogy. The tribes of men *are* found to emigrate, and, after some few generations, flourish equally in very different climates. For example, the aborigines of the American continent itself, comprising tribes of very different grades of civilisation, from the Esquimaux of the polar regions to the Aztecs of Mexico, are now acknowledged, even by the opponents of our theory, to be strictly homogeneous, *i.e.* scions of one parent stock. Of course, it is conceivable that adaptations do exist and have existed always in the human organisation, fitting this or that variety of man for some peculiar province. It is

work has not been long before the public. Its title is: '*Ethnological Researches*, based upon the Ancient Monuments, Painting, Sculptures, and Crania of Races, and upon their Natural, Geographical, Philosophical, and Biblical History, &c....by J. C. Nott, M.D., and George R. Gliddon, &c. Philadelphia, 1854.' A large portion of it is devoted to attacks on what is called the Mosaic chronology. The authors also dwell upon some recent 'facts' supplied as they maintain by geology and palæontology, especially the discovery of human fossils in the peninsula of Florida. These they urge are fatal to received ideas respecting the date of man's creation. But neither of the latter topics falls within the scope of the present chapter. See an examination of the authors' statements in the *British Quarterly*, No. XLIII. pp. 1 sq.

[1] In Bunsen, as above, I. 352.

also possible that like beneficent arrangements were already in process of formation and development anterior to the date of the earliest emigrations. Such marks of fitness every true philosopher is always ready to examine and appreciate; but he nevertheless demurs to the assumption that the human species had no power of self-accommodation to diversities of climate, and no buoyancy enabling men to rise almost indefinitely beyond the limits of their primitive condition.

(2) It is alleged against one of Prichard's main positions, that the principal types of the human species have *not* been variable, but that, on the contrary, as far as records will enable us to go, the broader characteristics of man's physical organisation have been absolutely fixed and inelastic.

A favourite illustration of this argument is borrowed from Egyptian excavations, where monuments are said to prove that in the very earliest dawn of history the great distinctions that exist between the negro and the white man are quite as strongly marked as at the present day[1]. Unfortunately, so long as the enigmas of Egyptian chronology remain unsolved, we have no hope of ascertaining the precise dates of the inscriptions here referred to. Some are placed as early as the older Pharaohs, and one is cited as belonging to a most remote antiquity[2]. If we are justified in drawing any inference from these remains[3],

[1] See Morton's *Crania Egyptiaca*, p. 66; Smyth, *Unity of the Human Races*, p. 40.

[2] The authority for this statement is a communication made to Mr. Gliddon by Lepsius, in whose opinion negroes are mentioned at Ṣakkara by the name of KESH, on monuments of the sixth dynasty, B.C. 3000: see Hamilton, *The Pentateuch and its Assailants*, p. 277, and 'postscript,' p. 338: Edinb. 1852.

[3] Hamilton, as above, p. 315, note; cf. Prichard, II. 346 sq.; Wiseman, I. 153 sq. See Prichard, III. 227 sq.: from the evidence cited it must be concluded that 'the subjects of the Pharaohs had something in their physical character approximating to that of the negro' (p. 230). Still considerable diversity existed, as to figure and complexion, among the old Egyptians. One was μελανχρώς, another μελίχρως. In Smith's *Dict. of Gr. and Rom. Geogr.*, art. ÆGYPTUS (p. 38), it is contended that, notwithstanding the dark hue of the Egyptians, they 'were not a negro race,—a supposition contradicted alike by osteology, and by monumental paintings, where negroes often appear, but always either as tributaries or captives..... The Egyptians may be said to be intermediate between the Syro-Arabian and Ethiopic type; and as at this day the Copt is at once recognised in Syria by his dark hue, the duskier complexion—brown, with a tinge of red—of the ancient Egyptians may be ascribed solely to their climate, and to those modifying causes which, in the course of generations, affect both the osteology and the physiology of long-settled races.' 'Im Grossen und

it is in favour of the clear distinctness of the negro and the old Egyptian families at a very early period. Yet no evidence whatever is furnished by this fact against the doctrine of their common origin. *How soon* the various types of man had been developed, whether variations did not actually exist to some degree among the sons of Noah[1], is a question wrapt, and likely to continue wrapt, in utter mystery. Science freely grants that she has no ability to solve it[2]; and the Christian therefore may repose in his belief that men are really one species, till the scriptural narrative has been discredited by arguments more cogent and conclusive than the advocates of slavery have as yet extracted from Egyptian hieroglyphics.

4. *The Philological Proof.*

By following out his principles of classification, Blumenbach concluded that the human species is divisible into three primary and two secondary varieties (Caucasian, Mongolian, American, Ethiopian, and Malay). Prichard distributed them afresh into seven classes (Iránian, Turánian, American, Hottentots, Negroes, Papuas, and Alfourous); while others have since raised the number as high as eleven, conceiving that there is no middle ground between this classification and the reduction of them all to one. But as the question was more fully canvassed, thoughtful writers found it quite impossible, even from a physiological point of view, 'to recognise in the groups thus formed any true typical distinction, any general and consistent

Ganzen,' says Knobel (pp. 277, 278), 'gehörten die Aegypter zur dunkelfarbigen Abtheilung der Erdbevölkerung.' Yet he continues, 'Diese Angaben machen jedoch die Aegypter noch nicht zu rabenschwarzen und wollhaarigen Negern.'

[1] This supposition may perhaps receive encouragement from the fact that two at least of the sons of Noah bear names expressing a distinctive colour. Thus *Ham*, of which the root is found alike in the Semitic (חמם) and the Coptic (chame), signifies 'hot,' 'sunburnt,' 'black,' *Japhet* (יֶפֶת from יָפָה) in like manner signifies 'beauty,' referring more especially to fairness of complexion: cf. Knobel, *Die Völkertafel der Genesis*, Giessen, 1850, pp. 239, 22, 13. It is further probable that any original difference of type in the family of Noah would be very rapidly developed: for, as Dr. Carpenter observes (*Principles of Human Physiology*, p. 53, Lond. 1846), 'there would be a greater tendency to the perpetuation of these varieties, in other words, to the origination of distinct races, during the earlier ages of the history of the race, than at the present time, when in fact, by the increasing admixture of races which have long been isolated, there is a tendency to the *fusion* of all these varieties, and to a return to a common type.'

[2] See the language of the great anatomist, Johannes Müller, in Humboldt's *Cosmos*, I. 352, 353; and cf. Mr. Parker's admission, above, p. 36, n. 1.

natural principle[1].' They all were felt to be conventional, vague, and artificial; tending thus in no small measure to enforce the supposition that all human forms were only modifications of a single species. And the same results are flowing from the generalisations of philology. The two inquiries should indeed be kept as independent as possible, because we are not warranted in affirming that the classification of language will ever strictly coincide with the classification of physiology. The variations in the structure of the human frame may *not* have taken place concurrently with the confusion and disruption of human language; and, therefore, we are unable to predict that all who carried with them kindred elements of speech would be distinguished by the same varieties of physical organisation. Still the labours of philology, by disentangling the perplexities in which the subject is involved, all point us to a few grand sources, out of which the various languages of man may have originally welled.

According to Bopp's arrangement[2], which he based on purely philological considerations, the division ought to be tripartite: (1) Languages with monosyllabic roots, but incapable of composition, and therefore without grammar or organisation; (2) Languages with monosyllabic roots which are susceptible of composition, and in which the grammar and organisation depend entirely on this; (3) Languages which consist of dissyllabic verbal roots, and require three consonants in the vehicles of their fundamental signification. The second and third of these classes are known to scholars as the Aryan, or Indo-European, and the Aramaic, or Semitic. From the circumstance that persons speaking these languages have always occupied a high position in the history of mankind, our knowledge of them is considerable, and nearly all their properties are fully analysed in works of modern scholars.

Such, however, cannot be affirmed of members of the group which Bopp arranges first in his classification. That group is meant to comprehend all other languages of man,—those, namely, in Europe, Asia, and Africa, which are not included in the second and third groups, together with the various aboriginal dialects of America. As a first approximation to more systematic treatment, Mr. Max Müller[3] has proposed to form a

[1] *Cosmos*, I. 353.

[2] See *Comparative Grammar*, I. 102, 103; Lond. 1856.

[3] See his able report on the 'Last results of the Researches respecting the Non-Iránian and Non-Semitic Languages of Asia or Europe,' in Bunsen, as above, I. 263—486.

separate class, which he entitles the Turánian, making it to comprehend all European, Asiatic, and Polynesian languages, that do not harmonise either with the Aryan or Semitic type. Of this Turánian group the principal branches are Tungusic, Mongolic, Turkic, and Finnic in the north, Taïc, Malaïc, Bhotîya, and Tamilic in the south; it being confessed, however, that they cannot offer such distinctive traits of family-likeness, as we find among the members of the other groups. They are rather like so many 'radii diverging from a common centre,' than 'children of a common parent[1].'

But supposing such affinities to be established, supposing that we are not under the necessity of admitting different independent beginnings in structure and lexicography for the elements of the Turánian, as we certainly are not for those of the Semitic and Aryan branches, what is to be said of the sporadic languages in Africa and America, which have not hitherto been definitely placed in any of these groups? Are they spontaneous products of the several regions where they flourish? or are they really connected with the languages of Europe and Asia, though the links of union be now lost? The latter supposition is not only more probable on ethnological and traditional grounds, but has received distinct corroboration from researches of the present day[2]. The native languages of North-America, it is stated, are not only uniform in their grammatical type, as had been long acknowledged, but exhibit many clear analogies to the Turánian forms of Northern Asia; thus according with a supposition, which is rendered probable on other grounds, that the elements of American population were all transported from that quarter. Many interesting results have also been obtained from recent investigations into the languages of Africa[3], the general tendency of which suggests

[1] Mr. Max Müller's 'Last Results of the Researches, &c.,' as before, I. 478.

[2] The Government of the United States are now printing, under the editorship of Mr. Schoolcraft, a series of volumes containing *Historical and Statistical Information respecting the History, Condition, and Prospects of the Indian Tribes.* According to the report of the Chevalier Bunsen 'the linguistic data before us, combined with the traditions and customs, and particularly with the system of pictorial or mnemonic writing (first revealed in this work), enable me to say, that the Asiatic origin of all these tribes is as fully proved as the unity of family among themselves:' as before, II. 112.

[3] Bunsen, II. 115 sq. The same writer draws attention (p. 114) to the fact established by William von Humboldt that most of the Polynesian languages are connected with the Malay, *i.e.* are capable of being classed with the Turánian group. But whether the remark can be extended to the Papua languages spoken in Australia, New Guinea, &c., is not yet ascertained.

the grouping of them with Semitic and Turánian idioms, and connects the spread of population over that continent, partly with the northern states that border on Abyssinia, and partly with the southern tribes in which the Káfir dialects prevail.

The arduous question now remaining for philologers is this: to ascertain if, when the individual languages have been arranged in groups, the groups themselves be also capable of reduction under one primordial group; or rather to establish, if not the absolute confluence of all languages to one common source, at least the *possibility* of their original divergence from one common center. Those of which we are best able to affirm the nature and affinities all indicate the table-land of Upper Asia[1] as the birthplace of the civilisation they were instrumental in communicating to other districts. Starting therefore from this point we may perhaps divine the general course of man's migrations into Europe and Asia, and the nature of the process by which tribes were gradually separated from each other in the various provinces of the earth. The earliest emigrants may have proceeded eastward into China, since the language of that country is least of all organic in its structure and the least developed of Turánian tongues. But as like impulses were constantly at work, new colonies would be continually projected till a layer of population had been actually expanded over many parts of Europe and Asia[2]. It is also

[1] I would here draw attention to the confidence with which Sir William Jones pronounces on this subject. After expressing his belief in the more than human origin of the Mosaic narrative, he adds: 'It is no longer probable only, but it is absolutely certain, that the whole race of man proceeded from Irán, as from a centre, whence they migrated at first in three great colonies; and that those three branches grew from a common stock which had been miraculously preserved in a general convulsion and inundation of this globe:' *Works*, I. 137, Lond. 1799. Cf. A. Fr. Gfrörer, *Urgeschichte des menschlichen Geschlechts*, Schaffhausen, 1855, who also recognises the truthfulness of the Hebrew narrative respecting the dispersion of the human family. The same may be affirmed of Knobel's learned work *Die Völkertafel der Genesis*, cited above, for although he favours what is called the document-hypothesis, professing to ascribe the 10th chapter of Genesis to the older (or 'Elohistic') hand, he is no less persuaded of its vast importance in all questions of ethnography. 'Die Stammväter' (he writes, p. 9) 'sind mythische Personen, während die von ihnen abgeleiteten Völker geschichtlich sind.'

[2] Rawlinson. *Early Hist. of Babylonia* (Journal of the Royal As. Soc. xv. 232), has recently made the following suggestions with respect to the course of the Scythic (Hamitic or Turánian) races:—'Leaving it, therefore, still a matter of speculation whether the prehistoric period may be more correctly estimated at two thousand or four thousand years; I will only

easy to conjecture how the isolation of each tribe, and other disuniting agencies, promoted the rapid growth of different dialects, and how the progress of confusion would be expedited by the introduction of secondary formations, tending to obscure the old affinities and hide the verbal roots which all may have imported from the mother-country. But many of the early settlers appear to have been subsequently overflowed, pushed forward, or exterminated by fresh waves of population, issuing from the districts where the Aryan and Semitic idioms had been planted; since the former of these grew predominant in the north of India, and in nearly all the European continent, while the latter flourished far and wide in western Asia, and diffused itself, as some conjecture, under certain modifications, into Egypt and the north of Africa. Such, I say, was probably the course and order of these primitive migrations; yet, even had we evidence to justify us in pronouncing definitely on the subject, it would never by itself explain the vast varieties of human speech. Three families of man, or rather three original groups, in which the several members of each group possessed the means of intercommunication in the same mother-tongue, may have been either simultaneously, or in succession, parted from each other, and propelled across the continents and islands of the globe; but how these groups themselves originated is a more recondite question. In truth, as physiology, though it establish the identity of the human species, can of itself determine nothing as to the precise condition and the actual birthplace of the aborigines, so are the oracles of philology all silent touching what occurred before the founding of the primitive types of human speech. The question, therefore, in so far as these two sciences extend, is left enveloped in uncertainty.

remark, that it must have been during this interval that nationalities were first established; and that the aboriginal Scyths or Hamites appear to have been the principal movers in the great work of social organisation. They would seem, indeed, simultaneously or progressively to have passed in one direction by southern Persia into India; in another, through southern Arabia to Æthiopia, Egypt, and Numidia. They must have spread themselves at the same time over Syria and Asia Minor, sending out colonies from one country to Mauritania, Sicily, and Iberia; from the other, to the southern coasts of Greece and Italy. They further, probably, occupied the whole area of modern Persia, and thence proceeding to the north by Chalcis and the Caucasus, they penetrated to the extreme northern point of the European and Asiatic continents.' He adds that 'independently of all reference to the Scriptural record, we should still be able to fix on the plains of Shinar, as the focus from which the various lines had radiated.'

Among our English scholars, for example, there are many, who although persuaded that the principles which led to the formation of Indo-European and Semitic families are incontrovertible, despair of bridging over the great gulf that lies between them, so as to establish their correspondence either in organisation, in grammatical structure, or in vocabulary; and when it is further urged that both these families may be scientifically connected with the more sporadic forms of language which we call 'Turánian,' such philologers declaim against the gross injustice of the torture, and deny that the generic unity of man is demonstrable by this process. Others, on the contrary, are no less confident that the identification will be ultimately established. As the science of philology advances, they predict that more and more traces of family-likeness will be generally recognised; that radicals, which, under various changes and disguises, have survived in all these different groups of language ever since the first migrations, will be more and more readily detected; and that, while it is most unphilosophical to derive any one of these groups from the other, they will all at last be proved to have been emanations from some great primordial tongue, the leading elements of which were either broken in the lapse of time, or buried in some vast catastrophe.

Now, whatever be the issue of those learned labours, and whatever be the fate of these dissuasives on the one hand, or these confident predictions on the other, they give rise to a reflection of the utmost value to all Christians. The veracity of Holy Scripture, far from being weakened by them, is considerably enhanced. The book of Genesis afforded by anticipation the best medium for explaining such linguistic phenomena. It tells us that there was in early times a great divulsion in the elements of human language, that whereas the whole earth was formerly 'of one lip' (Gen. xi. 1), the unity of speech was broken on the plain of Shinar, and the human family dispersed from thence 'upon the face of all the earth.' And as the sacred narrative does not specify the nature nor degree of this 'confusion,' it is equally reconcileable with either of the current theories of philology: it will hold its ground unshaken, whether we are led eventually to the hypothesis that the primitive language is entirely lost, or whether portions of the tangled threads survive in various languages, thus serving to connect us with the earliest fathers of mankind.

What then is the general inference to be gathered from this chapter in elucidation of our main inquiry? We may sum it up as follows :—Man is a religious being. The ideas of God, of sacrifice, of prayer, have been inwoven with his spiritual constitution, and have, therefore, always struggled for expression in his personal and social life. Approach him where you will, in England, in the tropics, or at the antipodes, and he exhibits this unfailing proof of his humanity, especially in all the sober moments, when he communes most profoundly with himself, in trouble, sorrow and perplexity, in solitude, in sickness, or when verging close upon the grave. Exactly, therefore, in proportion as we have established the unity of his origin, we have established also a presumption that the various families of man inherited from age to age a stock of sacred knowledge, and conveyed it with them in their wanderings from the cradle of the human race.

But it is obvious that in beings ever liable to fall, and ever prone to substitute their speculations for the holy will of God, this great substratum of religion might in course of time be overgrown and buried; just as primitive forms of speech would disappear beneath a crop of secondary formations. The effect of individual character, of isolation, of climate, the phenomena of nature, and a host of adventitious agencies, would soon be visible in the altered aspects of traditions; while a corresponding modification of the forms of social life would gradually affect the tone and sensibility of the human spirit. Where the tribe, or people, sank in moral culture, the idea of God would also be enfeebled and debased[1]. The worshipper whose heart was shrinking from the presence of the High and Holy One, would speedily betake himself to more congenial objects. He would look no higher than the earth, and finding, as he grew more selfish and irreverent, that some powers of nature with which he stood connected were antagonistic to him, and opposed the gratification of his wishes, he would chiefly strive to overcome them, or would struggle to disarm their vengeance, by re-

[1] The following confession of A. W. von Schlegel is the more remarkable, because its author was entirely influenced by the force of historical truth, and not by theological prepossessions. Here at length he was of one accord with his distinguished brother. 'Je mehr ich in der alten Weltgeschichte forsche, um so mehr überzeuge ich mich, dass die gesitteten Völker von einer reinern Verehrung des höchsten Wesens *ausgegangen sind;* dass die magische Gewalt der Natur über die Einbildungskraft des damaligen Menschengeschlechts erst später die Vielgötterei hervorrief, und endlich in dem Volksglauben die geistigen Religionsbegriffe ganz verdunkelte, während die Weisen allein im Heiligthume das uralte Geheimniss bewahrten.' *Vorrede* to the German translation of Prichard's *Egyptian Mythology*, p. xvi.

sorting to a multitude of exorcisms and other like devices. All his worship would eventually be nature-worship; all his prayers would take the abject form of deprecation. Or in different regions, where external nature was more joyous and propitious, and where man himself, by the development of his reflective and imaginative faculties, had gained a higher measure of intelligence; the creed of paganism would also be considerably idealised, it would become more sentimental and poetic. Its mythes would be far loftier in conception, and would all be cast in gentler moulds. The pagan worshipper might still, indeed, address his homage to the good or evil energies of nature, but no longer to a formless power or an impersonal divineness: he would fashion for himself a group of new divinities, to whom he could attribute human shapes and human properties; and thus the highest effort of this class of heathen was to bring about the deification of humanity.

But as in every case the drapery of imagination with which they clothed their gods was the spontaneous product of their own locality, the cycle of religious mythes would be indefinitely enlarged. Each town and village would give birth to fresh divinities, until at length it grew almost impossible in any part of heathendom to recognise the purer doctrine of the earliest ages, to distinguish even broken echoes of the first traditions, or to disentangle the few elements of primitive truth from an interminable mass of aftergrowths, which had corrupted and concealed it. So hopeless seemed the task of restoration, so remote from men's perceptions the idea of one all-ruling, all-embracing God, that, in the fourth century of the present era, when Julian and his pagan followers laboured to disparage Christianity, on the ground that it was far too modern and exclusive, they were driven to avow that a plurality of religions is inevitable, nay, is actually demanded by the diverse forms of human thought, and by the multiplicity of 'human races[1].' And the same convictions still prevail, as we have seen, in England and elsewhere among the heralds of the Absolute Religion.

Yet, in spite of every wayward tendency of human nature,

[1] Cf. Neander, *Ch. Hist.* III. 135 sq. After some general remarks on the question of man's origin, Julian himself proceeds as follows: Ἐνταῦθα δὲ ἀρκέσει τοσοῦτον εἰπεῖν, ὡς ἐξ ἑνὸς μὲν καὶ μιᾶς οὖσιν, οὔτε τοὺς νόμους εἰκὸς ἐπὶ τοσοῦτον παραλλάξαι· οὔτε ἄλλως τὴν γῆν ὑφ' ἑνὸς ἐμπλησθῆναι πᾶσαν.... Πανταχοῦ δὲ ἀθρόως, νευσάντων θεῶν, ὅνπερ τρόπον ὁ εἷς, οὕτω δὲ καὶ οἱ πλείους προῆλθον ἄνθρωποι, τοῖς γενεάρχαις θεοῖς ἀποκληρωθέντες. *Opp.* ed. Spanheim, I. 292.

disuniting men from God, and substituting for the steadier light of old traditions, the capricious glimmerings of their own imagination; there was ever on the earth one ark of refuge, and one beacon planted on a hill. The Church of God, the keeper and the witness of the true religion, rested on a sure and stable basis, so that while the heathen were abandoned to themselves to test the systems of their own devising, and were 'given over to a reprobate mind;' its inmates had continual access to the oracles of God,—the children of Israel had light in their dwellings. There, in what is verily the moral center of the world, midway between the principal seats of ancient civilisation, God exemplified upon a single people[1] the restoring and exalting process, under which humanity at large, when ready for the great experiment, should be cured of all its guilty wanderings and infatuations, and made one again in Christ.

[1] Cf. Theodoret, *De Providentia*, Orat. x.: *Opp.* IV. 454, Paris, 1642: Οὕτω δι' ἑνὸς ἔθνους τοῦ Ἰσραὴλ πάντα τὰ ἔθνη, τὰ τὴν αὐτὴν ἔχοντα φύσιν, εἰς τὴν τῆς εὐσεβείας κοινωνίαν ἐκάλει.

CHAPTER III.

On the Characteristics of Religion under the Old Testament.

Οὐδὲ γὰρ διὰ Ἰουδαίους μόνους ὁ νόμος ἦν, οὐδὲ δι' αὐτοὺς μόνους οἱ προφῆται ἐπέμποντο, ἀλλὰ πρὸς Ἰουδαίους μὲν ἐπέμποντο, καὶ παρὰ Ἰουδαίων ἐδιώκοντο· πάσης δὲ τῆς οἰκουμένης ἦσαν διδασκάλιον ἱερὸν τῆς περὶ Θεοῦ γνώσεως, καὶ τῆς κατὰ ψυχὴν πολιτείας. S. Athanasius, *contra Gentes*, cap. xii. (p. 57, ed. Benedict.).

The non-finality of Hebraism. Progressive character of the old œconomy. Importance of just ideas respecting God. The Hebrew doctrine of God: its peculiar sublimity. How illustrated by the Exodus: and in the Book of Psalms. This doctrine essentially moral. Example drawn from Solomon's prayer. Contrast between the Hebrew and the Phœnician theology. Phœnician divinities. Hebrew doctrine of man. Character of sin. The malignity of sin especially asserted. Effects of this training. Objections to the ritual branches of the Law. Peculiar temperament and position of the Hebrews. Symbolic mode of teaching. Distinction between types and symbols. General principles inculcated by the sacrificial system. Example. Different classes of transgressions. Operation and effects of the Levitical offerings. Suggestive features of the sanctuary. Relation of the Law to the Gospel. The Protevangelium. The call of Abraham. Indefinite form of the early Promise. Objections to the received views of prophecy. Germinant accomplishments of prophecy. State of feeling on these subjects among the Jews. Admissions of modern sceptics. The scriptural account of prophecy: its reality and objectivity. Assailants of this view. Hebrew prophecy as based on history, and intertwined with it. Particular instances. Prophecy in the age of David. The Messiah was to be a King: of superhuman dignity; and also a Priest. Doctrine of a suffering *Messiah. Prophecy in the age of the Captivity. The new Kingdom. The new Covenant.*

HAVING now in some measure cleared a way to our investigation, first, by pointing out the special tendencies of modern disbelief, and secondly, by undermining one of the more plausible positions which its advocates have sought to occupy, I shall proceed to ascertain the leading traits by which Revealed Religion was distinguishable in all the earlier stages of its progress. For since Christianity professes to reach backward into periods long anterior to the human lifetime of its Founder; since it claims to be most vitally connected with the Old-Testament œconomy, and since the roots from which it sprang are there; we see not only the importance, but necessity, of analysing the ideas embodied in the Hebrew institutions, of reverting to the solemn ordinances of the Law, and studying the oracular voices of the Prophets.

We shall thus be able to compare the aspects of religious thought and feeling as displayed in members of the sacred commonwealth with contemporary systems of the heathen world. If Hebraism resemble these in such a manner as to justify the inference that it was derived from any or from all of them, then Christianity, in turn, professing to have grown directly out of it, is ultimately resolvable into heathen elements. Or, if again the principles alike of Heathenism and Hebraism be nothing more than natural projections of religious instincts, mere expedients of the human understanding to escape from what is felt to be a burden and a paradox, then Christianity may also be subjective in its origin,—a fresh development of that which, having issued from the human breast in ruder times, was afterwards remodelled in accordance with the riper judgments of humanity in the Augustan period.

Now the two great principles of Hebraism, the poles, one might affirm, on which the system absolutely turned, were (1) the LAW, and (2) the PROMISE; that designed to keep alive the elementary idea of God, and superintend the education of the human spirit during the comparative infancy of the race; while this was occupied in opening out a brighter and more blissful future, where the limits of the Church of God would be indefinitely widened, and the happiness of all its members inexpressibly enhanced.

For that Hebraism was never meant to be an ultimate stage in the unfolding of the true religion, is apparent from confessions and arrangements of its own sacred books. They frequently proclaim its non-finality[1]. The prophets, keeping

[1] If no other text existed, Jerem. xxxi. 31 sq. as compared with Heb. viii. would be sufficient to establish this position. On the attempts of Jewish writers to evade the force of it, see Schöttgen's *Horæ Hebraicæ*, I. 969, Dresdæ, 1733. Yet one at least of the later Rabbis (Albo) distinctly recognises the temporary character of the Mosaic institute: 'When God, who is highly to be extolled, gave the Law, He knew that this form of education was sufficient for a certain period, which His wisdom had fixed, that it was sufficient to prepare those who received it, and incline their minds to receive the second form, although God has revealed this to no man; but when the time shall

pace with the spiritual development of the nation, carry on men's thoughts beyond a merely ritual service, and lay greater stress on the obedience of the heart; and in the age of the Captivity, when the observance of the Law was made to some degree impossible, 'a new covenant' is placed in actual *contrast* with the old, and dignity assigned to it which is denied to the preceding. Yet the kernel of that ancient system,—the profound relations it exhibited between Jehovah and His people, the principles that underlay its sacrifices and that breathed through all its symbols,—was imperishable. The Law was not to sink without the prospect of some glorious sublimation; it did not expire without transfusing its own life into the heart of a successor. Christianity is the legitimate offspring of the elder dispensation, because, according even to De Wette, the Old Testament 'is a great prophecy, a great type of Him who was to come and has come[1];' because the Law in all its breadth and depth is tributary to the Gospel, and because the Saviour came not to destroy, but to transfigure and complete.

This thought, however, of substantial identity between the old and new œconomies, has frequently been misconceived, or overstated, in the popular teaching of divines. Persuaded that the Church of God was not without her 'Acts and Monuments before Christ incarnate[2],' zealous above all things to maintain the unity and fixity of truth, and to announce those glorious principles that give coherence to the history of redemption, they have seemed to speak of the Old Testament as though it were an absolute and perfect revelation, and have therefore laboured to evolve from it the special doctrines of the Gospel[3].

come, God will reveal that second form to men:' quoted in Tholuck, *On the Ep. to the Hebrews*, I. 294.

[1] See Bähr, *Symbolik des Mosaischen Cultus*, I. 16, note, Heidelberg, 1837. 'Das Christenthum,' writes Wuttke (*Gesch. des Heidenthums*, I. 18, Breslau, 1852), 'im weltgeschichtlichen Sinne *beginnt nicht* erst mit dem Auftreten Jesu Christi, sondern Christus ist der *Mittelpunkt* des Christenthums, und mit ihm bricht die schon lange vorhandene Knospe zur vollen Blüthe auf.'

[2] The title of Bp. Montague's work, published in 1642.

[3] The true distinction was, however, clearly seen even during the period when there was a strong tendency to Judaize, and reduce the Gospel into a kind of 'New Law.' Thus we find a writer of the 12th century expressing himself as follows: 'Primus gradus est cognitionis fidei quo nihil minus unquam fides habere potuit: credere videlicet Deum esse et eum Salvatorem et Remuneratorem expectare. Hæc cognitio fidei simplicibus ante incarnationem Verbi ad salutem sufficere potuit, videlicet ut et Deum crederent et Salvatorem expectarent: quamvis ejusdem salvationis suæ modum et tempus non cognoscerent. Duo enim in homine tantum sunt, natura et culpa: et Creator ad naturam refertur, Sal-

They consult it with the eyes of Christians rather than of Hebrews, and neglecting to shade off the full illumination which our Lord and the apostles turned upon it, feel themselves at liberty to urge that what is now made clear to us, must have been also luminous from the beginning. And a like forgetfulness to vary the point of view from which we contemplate the records of the Elder Church, has often issued in a disregard of those great laws of sequence and progression that characterise its general history. God, who in the Son spake once and absolutely, had communicated only parcels of the truth (πολυμερῶς), and these at various seasons, by the ministry of the prophets (Heb. i. 1). His communications then, as ever, were adapted to the exigencies of the age, and were proportioned to the receptivity of the people. For in the training of the sacred corporation, as in that of individuals under discipline, there was a gradual exercise and evolution of the spiritual powers of man,—a growth from the half-consciousness of childhood to the larger views, the deeper reasonings, the accumulated wisdom of maturity; and, therefore, it is easy to observe how, corresponding with this growth in the capacity of the subject, the illumination granted from on high had also passed through different stages in a measurable progress. Clearer insight into some of the great mysteries of the Cross was only the reward of patient waiting, or the fruit of

vator ad culpam. Sub lege autem scripta crevit cognitio, quando jam de persona Redemptoris manifeste agi cœpit, et Salvator per legem promitti, et post promissionem expectari. Sub gratia autem adhuc amplius excrevit cognitio, cum ipse jam Salvator, non ut prius a multis putabatur solum homo, sed et Deus verus manifestatus est. Et ipse redemptionis modus non in terrenæ culmine potestatis, sed in morte probatus est constare Salvatoris.' H. de S. Victore, *Erudit. Theolog. ex Miscellan.* Lib. I. Tit. XVIII. *Opp.* III. 73. Mogunt. 1617.

The same writer (*De Sacramentis*, Lib. I. pars x. c. vi.) discusses the question, 'an secundum mutationes temporum mutata sit fides' (*Opp.* III. 412 sq.), and concludes in the following passage:—'Crevit itaque per tempora fides in omnibus, ut major esset, sed mutata non est, ut alia esset. Ante legem, Deus creator credebatur, et ab eo salus et redemptio expectabatur; per quem vero et quomodo eadem salus implenda et perficienda foret, exceptis paucis quibus hoc scire singulariter in munere datum erat, a cæteris etiam fidelibus non cognoscebatur. Sub lege autem persona Redemptoris mittenda prædicebatur, et ventura expectabatur. Quæ autem ipsa persona hæc foret homo an angelus, an Deus, nondum manifestabatur. Soli hoc cognoverunt, qui per Spiritum singulariter ad hoc illuminati fuerunt. Sub gratia autem manifeste omnibus, jam et prædicatur et creditur, et modus redemptionis et qualitas personæ Redemptoris.' And similar principles were inculcated on the English nuns at the beginning of the next century: 'Nimeð god ʒeme, mine leoue sustren, uor hwi me ouh Him to luuien. Erest, ase a mon þet woweð — ase a King

tedious and (as many deem) circuitous probation[1]; while of other truths that constitute the household words of Christianity, the prophet and the saint alike were ignorant; they were left to 'inquire and search diligently' (1 Pet. i. 10), until the Pedagogue was superseded by the heavenly Teacher[2], and 'the fulness of the times' had come.

With this conviction clearly present to the mind, I now purpose to examine the character of the Law, and some of the peculiar functions it was destined to perform in the continuous training of the Hebrews; not of course excluding from our survey what is termed the patriarchal dispensation, since in all its leading characteristics (those of prayer and sacrifice, for instance) it is one with the Mosaic system.

þet luuede one lefdi of feorrene londe, and sende hire His sondesmen biforen, þet weren þe patriarkes and þe prophetes of þe Olde Testament, *mid lettres isealed.* A last He com Him suluen, and brouhte þet gospel *ase lettres iopened,* and wrot mid His owune blode saluz to His leofmon.' *Ancren Riwle* (ed. Camden Soc. 1853), p. 388.

[1] The objection based upon the length of interval that elapsed between the fall of man and his redemption, is as old as Celsus and Porphyry. Leo the Great repels it in the following passage, radiant with the light of true philosophy: 'Cessent igitur illorum querelæ, qui impio murmure divinis dispensationibus obloquentes, de Dominicæ nativitatis tarditate causantur, tanquam præteritis temporibus non sit impensum, quod in ultima mundi ætate est gestum. Verbi incarnatio hæc contulit facienda (?), quæ facta (?) et sacramentum salutis humanæ in nulla unquam antiquitate cessavit. Quod prædicaverunt apostoli, hoc annunciaverunt prophetæ; nec sero est impletum, quod semper est creditum. *Sapientia vero et benignitas Dei hac salutiferi operis mora capaciores nos suæ vocationis effecit;* ut quod multis signis, multis vocibus, multisque mysteriis per tot fuerat secula prænunciatum, in his diebus Evangelii non esset ambiguum; et nativitas, quæ omnia miracula, omnemque intelligentiæ erat excessura mensuram, tanto constantiorem in nobis gigneret fidem, quanto prædicatio ejus et antiquior præcessisset et crebrior. Non itaque novo consilio Deus rebus humanis, nec sera miseratione consuluit; sed a constitutione unam eandemque omnibus causam salutis instituit. Gratia autem Dei, qua semper est universitas justificata sanctorum, *aucta est* Christò nascente *non cœpta.*' Sermo III. de Nativitate: *Opp.* p. 16, col. I, B, Paris, 1639.

[2] Gal. iii. 24. This metaphor of St. Paul is most expressive, pointing out the true relation of the Law to the Gospel, and vindicating its claim to be regarded as an agent (though but elementary and subordinate) in the moral education of the Church. St. Chrysostom (*in loc.*) expands the same idea with great clearness:—Ὁ δὲ παιδαγωγὸς οὐκ ἐναντιοῦται τῷ διδασκάλῳ, ἀλλὰ καὶ συμπράττει, πάσης κακίας ἀπαλλάττων τὸν νέον, καὶ μετὰ πάσης σχολῆς τὰ μαθήματα παρὰ τοῦ διδασκάλου δέχεσθαι παρασκευάζων· ἀλλ' ὅταν ἐν ἕξει γένηται, ἀφίσταται λοιπὸν ὁ παιδαγωγός.

§ 1. *The Law.*

The moral force and grandeur of religions are in every case to be determined by the worthiness of their ideas of God, His nature and His attributes. It has been frequently remarked, that, 'as man is, so is the divinity he worships;' but the converse is more rigorously correct: what God is, such His worshipper becomes. If the sacred institutes of any people manifest a disposition to obscure the unity of God, to tamper with His holiness, to waver in their statements touching His essential independence of the properties of matter or of man, that system has been incapacitated in the same proportion for directing and exalting the religious life of the community. If God be represented as no more than the stupendous aggregate of all created spirits; if divinity be ascribed to nature as a whole, to this or that energy of nature, and to this or that ideal representative of men, no standing-ground is left for urging the intrinsic excellence of virtue: faith, love, justice, purity, and liberty itself, have no intelligible basis; they become the mere subjective forms of human sentiment and the conventionalities of human law. Or if again, while the Creator is not actually confounded with the laws and operations of the universe, His power be notwithstanding liable to any species of constraint or limitation; if He be thwarted by some other substance, fate, or time, or matter, or chaos, or evil, it must also follow that the moral consciousness of the worshipper is wounded and distracted; he abandons the resistance he was offering to the downward tendencies of his nature; he drifts away to the conclusion, either that sin is absolutely inevitable, or that righteousness is for the present banished from the earth.

1. Now all the teaching of the Hebrew Scriptures on these points is far above suspicion. They announce at every turn, and under every kind of illustration, the cardinal doctrine of *One, Living, Personal God, the Maker and the moral Governor of all things.* They draw the broadest possible line of demarcation between humanity and Divinity. They make the consciousness of the Creator essentially distinct from that of each and all created beings. They demand for Him the worship of the human spirit, because He is a God of unapproachable perfection, self-existent, absolutely free, and altogether righteous. Such, indeed, appears to be the foremost object of the old œconomy. Destined as it was for the instruction of an age that was peculiarly exposed to fascinations of polytheism

on one side and of dualism on the other, it pointed with especial frequency to what alone was able to supply a refuge from these desolating errors,—to the doctrine of the monarchy of God[1]. While subjects which might possibly have interfered with it in minds incapable of deep reflection are passed over, or left standing in the background, *it* is ever prominent in place and definite in expression. Instances there doubtless are in which both ancient and modern spiritualists have been offended by expressions that ascribe to God the organs, faculties, and passions of mankind. Those thinkers do not recognise the clear necessity of such expressions for communicating any definite ideas of God and His relations to the creature; but treat them as mere relics of primeval barbarism, exhorting us to soar at length above all human images, and gain a true conception of the Infinite and All-pervading. Yet, in spite of numerous cavils rising out of these anthropomorphisms, it is generally acknowledged that the Hebrew creed, for some cause or other, was pre-eminently pure and monotheistic,—a concession which, one might have fancied, also proves at least the possibility of worthy thoughts of God existing with and under figurative representations[2]. 'This must be confessed,' writes Mr. Parker[3], 'that under the guidance of divine Providence, the great and beautiful doctrine of one God seems quite early embraced by the great Jewish lawgiver, incorporated with his national legislation, defended with rigorous enactments, and slowly communicated to the world.' How deeply, for example, is this truth inscribed on the Mosaic record of creation! While the heathen systems, we shall see at large hereafter, had so abandoned the true idea of God as to acknowledge the co-eternity of matter and to represent the highest object of man's worship fettered more or less by the conditions of the transitory and the limits of the mundane[4], it was very different with the Hebrews.

[1] 'To understand the nature of the Jewish œconomy, we must begin with this truth, to which every page of the five books of Moses is ready to bear witness, That the separation of the Israelites was in order to preserve the doctrine of the Unity, amidst an idolatrous and polytheistic world.' Warburton, *Divine Legation*, II. 419, Lond. 1846.

[2] 'The humanity of God,' says Hengstenberg, 'had its corrective in the doctrine of His true Divinity, by which it was indefinitely exalted above all heathenism.' *Dissertations on the Genuineness of the Pentateuch*, II. 369, Edinb. 1847.

[3] *Discourse*, &c. pp. 65, 66.

[4] It is here granted that isolated declarations do exist in heathen writers, affirming the essential independence of the Divine Being (cf. Archbp. Sumner's *Records of Creation*, &c. I. 123 sq., 185 sq. Lond. 1816, and Mosheim's *Dissert.* in Cudworth, III. 140 sq. Lond. 1845); yet, as Baumgarten justly adds (*Acts of the Apostles*, II. 193),

God was there confessed not merely as the animating principle of all things, but the sole and absolute Creator[1]. He spake and it was done. His fiat quickened all the pulses of the universe, —and as material laws that govern it are only indications of His presence and expressions of His legislative will, so in the world at large He ever acts as on a theatre objective to Him, regulating the destinies alike of the community and of the individual spirit. And the subsequent disclosures of the Bible are in perfect harmony with what is thus recorded in the earliest pages of it. They are one continuous attestation of the unity, the personality, the righteousness of God, revealed in mandates or in prohibitions, and reiterated by the 'fiery law,' or a succession of stupendous acts. To look no further than the earliest crisis in the national history of the Hebrew race, the Exodus itself was nothing but a grand religious triumph; where the majesty of God was vindicated in the presence of a people foremost in the rank of civilisation, yet peculiarly be-

these declarations are no more than 'abstract ideas which do indeed convey an inkling of the truth, but possess no vital energy. The general popular notion of the gods and of their nature was stamped on their mythes, their hymns and religious ceremonies; and this view [the limitation of the Divine Being] held its way undisturbed by all the philosophical thoughts and well-meaning words that went on alongside of it.' The same remark is even more applicable to the doctrine of the *Unity* of God, which, as Mr. Mackay urges (*Progress of the Intellect*, I. 133, Lond. 1850), was never entirely lost sight of, even by those who were in act polytheists. The truth is, it was so far in the background as to exercise very little practical influence: cf. Weisse, *Philosoph. Dogmatik*, I. 670 sq. Leipzig, 1855.

[1] Many writers (*e.g.* Milton, *Prose Works*, IV. 176) have stoutly denied that God, even according to the Scriptural cosmogony, created the world *out of nothing:* and whether the fact of such creation be deducible from the language of Gen. i. 1, may very fairly be disputed (see Bp. Pearson, *On the Creed*, pp. 76—84, Lond. 1842, Witsius, *Exercitationes Sacræ*, 'De Creatione,' Amst. 1697; and Hävernick, *Introd. to the Pentateuch*, p. 94, note, Edinb. 1850). Other texts, however, insist with great emphasis on the absolute sovereignty of God in the world of matter, and some of these appear totally inconsistent with the laxer theory of creation, *e.g.* Heb. xi. 3, *Πίστει νοοῦμεν κατηρτίσθαι τοὺς αἰῶνας ῥήματι Θεοῦ, εἰς τὸ μὴ ἐκ φαινομένων τὸ βλεπόμενον γεγονέναι*, where Bengel aptly remarks: 'Ut creatio fundamentum et specimen est omnis œconomiæ divinæ, sic fides creationis est fundamentum et specimen omnis fidei.' The tradition of the Jews to the same effect is preserved in 2 Maccab. vii. 28: *Ἀξιῶ σε, τέκνον, ἀναβλέψαντα εἰς τὸν οὐρανὸν καὶ τὴν γῆν, καὶ τὰ ἐν αὐτοῖς πάντα ἰδόντα, γνῶναι ὅτι ἐξ οὐκ ὄντων ἐποίησεν αὐτὰ ὁ Θεὸς, καὶ τὸ τῶν ἀνθρώπων γένος οὕτως γεγένηται.* 'Diese aegyptische Kosmogonie hat viele Aehnlichkeit mit der mosaischen, die ohne Zweifel aus ihr hervorgegangen; es findet sich in derselben Nichts von einem

sotted by their worship of the various energies of nature. There it was that Israel also had defiled themselves with the idols of Egypt (Ezek. xx. 7); they were on the point of losing the traditions that connected them with Abraham and with the Evangelic promise; they were melting fast away into the mass of heathenism by which they were encircled, when the Lord Himself came forward to their rescue. He asserted the unrivalled greatness of His sovereignty. 'Against all the gods of Egypt[1] I will execute judgment: I am the Lord' (Ex. xii. 12). The influences of nature He employed as agents of His mighty purpose, now restraining them with a miraculous discrimination, and now wielding them with a terrific aim for the confusion of the adversary, till ere long the ransomed multitude could chant in concert with their noble captain, 'I will sing unto the Lord, for He hath triumphed gloriously . . . Who is like unto Thee, O Lord, among the gods? Who is like thee, glorious in holiness, fearful in praises, doing wonders?...Thou in Thy mercy leadest forth Thy people which Thou hast redeemed; Thou guidest them in Thy strength unto Thy holy habitation' (Ex. xv. 1, 11, 13).

And the same magnificent spectacle recurs at every stage of Hebrew history. Who has not remarked amid the grandeur of the choral hymns and other lyrics of the Israelites, how the idea of God as the one Lord of all things is ever present to the writer's mind, and how the varied forms of nature are but living testimonies to the personality of their Creator! Had there been a single germ of pantheism lurking in the Hebrew

ungeordneten Chaos, wie bei Griechen und Römern; auch bei den Aegyptern ist die Welt aus Nichts geschaffen, Alles Vorhandene aus der allmächtigen Hand der schaffenden Gottheit Osiris hervorgegangen.' Uhlemann, *Thoth.* pp. 27, 28, Göttingen, 1855.

[1] Cf. Ex. xviii. 11, xx. 23, Numb. xxxiii. 4, Ezek. xx. 7, 8, which justify the authorized version of וּבְכָל־אֱלֹהֵי מִצְרַיִם (= LXX. *καὶ ἐν πᾶσι τοῖς θεοῖς τῶν Αἰγυπτίων*). When Mr. Newman infers from texts like these (*Hebrew Monarchy*, p. 26, 2nd ed.), that 'the Hebrew creed was not monotheistic in the sense of denying the *existence* of other gods,' his language is in one respect admissible, *viz.* if it be taken to mean that the Hebrews looked upon idolatry as the work of evil spirits, and so ascribed a personality to the false object of worship. But that this idea of superhuman intelligences was never suffered to trench upon the doctrine of the Divine Unity and Omnipotence, is clear from numerous texts like Deut. iv. 39: 'the Lord he is God in heaven above and upon the earth beneath: there is none else.' In other passages where the thoughts of the writer are exclusively confined to the visible idol, he speaks of heathen gods as actually non-existent. See Is. xxxvii. 19.

system it would doubtless have shewn itself in this class of writings, as we may infer especially from the complexion of the Védas and the hymns of ancient Greece. Yet, on the contrary, the sacred writer, notwithstanding the peculiar sensibility which he displays in picturing the rich and glowing beauties of the universe, is never tempted to invest it with the attributes of God. His poetry is 'a reflex of monotheism:' and nature comes before us 'not as self-subsisting, or glorious in her own beauty, but ever in relation to a higher, an overruling, a spiritual Power[1].'

But the God of the Old Testament is not only the most powerful Being in the universe; He is not only the Absolute, the Undefined, the Infinite, who having called the creatures out of nothing, rules them as the grand Proprietor, and doeth whatsoever pleaseth Him. This thought of God is there associated with a second. He is indeed the ELOHIM and EL SHADDAI, but He is JEHOVAH also[2]. His attributes are moral, and not merely physical. He is raised as to His essence indefinitely above the sphere of things created, yet He mingles with them as their Governor, as the Rewarder of the upright, the Avenger of the wronged, 'long-suffering, abundant in goodness and truth, keeping mercy for thousands, but not always pardoning the guilty[3].' Thus the monarchy of God is ever based on righteousness; and after the selection of the Hebrew family to constitute the visible kingdom of Jehovah, and to act as conservators of the true religion in the midst of Gentilism, it is continually proclaimed that they are Israelites indeed who labour to be God-like; that such alone are properly the subjects

[1] Humboldt's *Cosmos*, II. 44. This author instances the civth Psalm. 'Nature is conceived as having the ground of its existence in another,—as something posited, created; and this idea, that God is the Lord and Creator of Nature, leads men to regard God as the Exalted One, while the whole of Nature is only His robe of glory, and is expended in His service.' Hegel, *Phil. of Hist.* p. 204, Lond. 1857.

[2] I am here following Dr. Hengstenberg, who in his *Dissertations on the Pentateuch*, II. 213—393, has investigated the Names of God, as they occur in the Books of Moses, with singular felicity. The plural form of אֱלֹהִים, he suggests, may intimate that the true God possesses in Himself what men were disposed to divide among a plurality.

[3] See Ex. xxxiv. 6, 7, a passage which develops the great truths implied in the name JEHOVAH. The clause וְנַקֵּה לֹא יְנַקֶּה is variously interpreted, but the rendering here adopted seems most in harmony with the remainder of ver. 7: cf. Nah. i. 3.

of the Lord of hosts, and are entitled to approach the seat of His peculiar presence[1].

It is not easy to recal a passage of the Bible where these statements are more fully verified than in the prayer and benedictions uttered by king Solomon at the dedication of the temple just completed on Mount Zion (1 Kings viii.). Where, it might be urged, are we more likely to encounter gross conceptions of the nature of God's presence, or those narrow and unspiritual views of worship, which opponents of the Old Testament are in the habit of ascribing to all branches of the legal institute? And yet there is no lack of testimony that the Hebrews were most truly conscious of the spirituality and universal empire of Jehovah, as well as of their own exalted mission in respect of other nations. Solomon, it is true, was penetrated by the thought that God was very near to Israel; that they were His inheritance; that He had separated them from all the people of the earth (ver. 53); that He had borne them up on eagles' wings, and brought them to Himself (Ex. xix. 4). He was no less certain that the Lord of Israel would be present with His choicest gifts and blessings to the worshippers who bent their knees and made their offerings in the precincts of the sanctuary. Yet he felt that such a national limitation was compatible with universal sovereignty: that God as to His essence was infinite and incomprehensible; that 'the heaven and heaven of heavens could not contain Him' (ver. 27); that if we ascribe to Him a special dwelling-place it is exalted far above the limits of the seen and transitory (ver. 30); that the earthly temple was symbolical of something higher, of a truer and more blissful presence; and that even the election of the Israelites itself had reference to a glorious future in the progress of the sacred family, when all the people of the earth should know, as Israel knew already, that 'the Lord is God, and that there is none else' (vers. 43, 60).

From such conceptions of the God of Israel, apprehended

[1] See especially Psalm xxiv, where the transition from one view of the God of Israel to the other is very remarkable. The thought of Him as the great Proprietor of the world and all that dwell therein, is made the basis of an argument for purity and reverence in the Hebrew worshipper, to whom He was pleased to reveal Himself in a peculiarly near relation. 'With other gods there may be an animal love and a favouritism for their own worshippers, without regard to their hearts and lives; but the God of Israel, who is God in the true sense of the word, cannot without absurdity be spoken of as having connexion with any except such as are of a pure heart.' Hengstenberg, *On the Psalms*, I. 417. Edinb. 1846.

not in later periods of the Hebrew commonwealth, but as early as the first consolidation of their empire, let us turn aside and glance at the theology of a neighbouring state, whose ruler was on terms of special amity with Solomon. The Phœnicians had been long the merchants and the leading colonisers of the district. Commerce tended to evolve their intellectual powers, and gave them such preponderance among the nations of the East, as had enabled them in numerous instances to propagate their civilisation and religious system[1], and even it would seem to captivate the mind of Solomon himself[2]. Nor was the intercourse then subsisting between the courts of Sidon and Jerusalem the oldest bond of union which connected the two peoples. They were, in fact, descended from the same ancestors; the languages they spoke were dialects of the same mother-tongue; and as early as the residence in Egypt the Israelites had been acquainted with Phœnician modes of thought, the Hyksos[3], who were then the masters of the throne of Egypt and their patrons, being also of Phœnician origin. Everything is therefore tending to beget the expectation, that if the general form of men's religious principles depend upon locality, or race, or on the

[1] Movers, *Die Religion und die Gottheiten der Phönizier*, pp. 12 sq. Bonn, 1841. The aggressive spirit of their system is illustrated in the history of Jezebel, herself a princess of the court of Sidon.

[2] See 1 Kings xi. 5. The worship of Ashtoreth (Astarte) thus tolerated at Jerusalem was not altogether abolished till the reign of Josiah: 2 Kings xxiii. 13. An adventurous school of modern critics have indeed laboured to convince us that what they call the 'Reformation of Jehovism' in the reign of Josiah was the substitution of the worship of a Supreme God for that of the Phœnician divinities, which had till then been 'the established religion' even in the kingdom of Judah: see Mr. Mackay's *Progress of the Intellect*, II. 442. In other words, they are pleased to represent what holy Scripture tells them of the frequent lapses of the Hebrews into the idolatrous worship of their neighbours, as a proof that such apostasy was not occasional or partial, but the normal state of the nation. The unfairness of this mode of procedure is most flagrant. The Bible gives a perfectly candid and consistent, not to say a highly probable account, when it confesses that the Israelites notwithstanding the emphatic warnings of their Lawgiver (Lev. xviii. 21) did forget that Jehovah was the true God and relapsed into forbidden worship (*e.g.* Judges ii. 11; iii. 7; x. 6; 1 Kings xvi. 31). That account ought therefore to be either accepted or rejected as a whole. If we reject it, Hebrew history is so far a blank, and there is no material left for theorising: if we accept it, the conclusion is inevitable that the Hebrews from the very earliest period were in possession of religious principles incapable of all amalgamation with those of the adjacent countries.

[3] Cf. Kurtz's chapter 'Die Hyksos und die Israeliten,' in his *Gesch. des alten Bundes*, II. 173 sq. Berlin, 1855.

influence of a dominant and proselytising neighbour, the theology and worship of the Hebrew church will bear considerable resemblance to those of which Phœnicia has supplied the clearest and the boldest type. We ask accordingly what were the views there current with respect to that which is the fundamental characteristic of religious systems,—the doctrine of God? 'The religion of the Phœnicians,' to quote from Movers,[1] one of the most critical and impartial writers on the subject, 'was like that of the kindred Semitic tribes of the ancient Asiatics in general,—essentially a nature-religion, *i. e.* a deification of the energies and laws of nature, an adoration of the objects in which those energies were thought to be present, and by which they became active and efficient. In this cycle of Religions the Godhead is not a Power distinct from nature and ruling it without restraint, *as in the religion of the Hebrews;* but it is the secret energy in nature herself, as she is manifested according to fixed laws, now shaping, animating, sustaining, now again destroying her own works, whom man is therefore wont to supplicate with different kinds of homage, according to her various operations.' This writer acknowledges indeed that in the earliest period of Phœnician history, the object of their worship was identical with that of Israel[2]: and the notice of Melchisedec may also lead us to conjecture that the true idea of God still lingered here and there among the circumjacent tribes; yet long before the age of Solomon it is certain that some mighty changes had been wrought in their religious system, and that both in creed and morals the Phœnicians had grown frightfully corrupt. Belief in God, the Holy One, the personal Creator, was supplanted by luxuriant forms of nature-worship, in which carnage alternated with licentiousness, and groans of abject

[1] Movers, *die Religion und die Gottheiten der Phönizier*, p. 148.

[2] 'Wenn sie [the Phœnician religion] von Alters her uns als Vergötterung der Natur, ihrer Kräfte und Gesetze erscheint, so sind wir doch weit entfernt, sie, und damit alle Religionen des Semitismus, für Naturreligion von Haus aus zu erklären. *Dies war die phönizische ebensowenig ursprünglich wie die hebräische.* Wir werden an seinem Orte den Spuren nachgehen, die sich namentlich in dem Entwicklungsgange der Ideen vom Baal oder El bedeutsam hervordrängen, und es wird sich zeigen, dass der Gott des monotheistischen Hebraismus der höchste Gott auch aller übrigen Stämme der Semiten war und blieb, dass jedoch der Naturdienst die reinere Gottesidee einer ältern Religionsstufe *allmählich verdunkelt*, aber nie auch in der phönizischen Religion völlig vertilgt hat:' p. 168. In pp. 312 sq. it is contended that the El of the Phœnicians was identical with the God of the Hebrew patriarchs, but was afterwards confounded with Moloch, the old fire-god of the Chaldaic-Assyrian mythology.

terror with the frantic songs of revelry. In strict accordance with human analogies the Godhead was now apprehended by them as male and female, and those special energies of nature were attributed to each that seemed to correspond most aptly to the functions of the different sexes[1]. Baal was the male-divinity,—a personification of the active or generative power in nature, the giver and withholder of that life which circulates through all the animal and vegetable kingdoms, and the ruler of their destinies. Ashtoreth was the female-divinity,—a personification of the passive or maternal principle in nature, the Aphrodite of Semitic tribes, enkindling the desire of sensual gratification, and enlisting all the grosser passions of her votaries. The fundamental unity of both these powers was also represented in Phœnicia by transferring to the masculine divinity the attributes of the feminine, so as to produce another God, in whom the forms and properties of male and female are exhibited in mystic combination[2].

I leave the reader to determine if a system such as this, whose gods were nothing more than the personifications of external nature, and reflections of corrupt humanity, had ought in common with the lofty and severely moral theism of the Hebrews. I ask him also to consider if the mere existence of their pure and elevating creed upon the borders of a dominant form of nature-worship be not calculated to supply additional proofs that they were guardians of a supernatural revelation, and that God was dealing with no other people as He dealt with them.

2. But the doctrine of one, personal, holy God, was not the only truth on which the Law insisted, and to which its institutions were designed to draw the thoughts of every Hebrew. It unfolded also the true *doctrine of man:* his *dignity* and *wretchedness.* It urged not one of these great verities, but both: for only where the origin and grandeur of the human species are fully apprehended, can we hope to understand the

[1] Movers, pp. 149 sq. It is also plain, however, that this tendency of thought was commonly associated by the Phœnicians with a disposition to find peculiar *symbols* of their gods among the heavenly bodies. Thus Baal, as Gesenius shews, was often identified not only with the sun, but with the planet Jupiter, *stella Jovis,* as the guardian or giver of good fortune; and Astarte (עַשְׁתֹּרֶת = ستارة = star) in like manner sometimes represented the moon, but more especially the planet Venus: cf. Movers, pp. 601 sq. On the dualism of China, see Wuttke, II. 12.

[2] The story of Hermaphroditus was carried by the Phœnicians to Cyprus and other regions: Movers, p. 149.

turpitude of moral evil and the real nature of the fall of man. The Bible tells us that there is in him a high and God-like element, that instead of being fashioned on the lower model of the brute creation, he came forth into the world erect in stature and impressed with the Divine similitude; that in virtue of this kinship human life is sacred (Gen. ix. 6), and that human spirits, on the dissolution of the body, will return to God who gave them[1] (Eccles. xii. 7).

The leading property in which the high original of man has ever been distinctly traceable is the freedom of his will, his power of self-determination. Here lay his greatest dignity and here his greatest peril. He is never represented by the sacred writer as the victim of some stern necessity, or some irrevocable fate[2], like that which the Muhammadans imported into their religion from the heathen creeds of western Asia. He is made in the image of God; and the pre-eminence thus awarded to him is that which helps us to conceive the possibility of the first deflection from the path of rectitude, and to define the character of sin in general.

Sin is the effect of self-complacency. It springs entirely from

[1] I shall not enter far into the question why the doctrine of prolonged existence after death was rather hinted than explicitly affirmed in all the earlier writings of the Old Testament. It may be that the prevalence of a false doctrine of immortality, especially in Egypt, tended to unfit the ancient Hebrews for receiving more specific communications on this subject (Hengstenberg, *Dissert. on the Pentateuch*, II. 473). It may be that the thought of individual immortality was often suffered to merge itself in that of the indestructibility of the Hebrew nation (cf. Jerem. xxxi. 16, 17; Ezek. xxxvii. 11—14). Hegel, *Phil. of Hist.* p. 205: 'The individual never comes to the consciousness of independence, on that account we do not find among the Jews any belief in the immortality of the soul.' But the principal reason for the silence, or at least reserve, of the Old Testament is traceable to the fact that so long as the future world was merely an indefinite expanse, untrodden by human footsteps and devoid of human imagery, an appeal to it for motives in aid of the legal institute must have proved inoperative. The character of the whole dispensation was visible and earthly, and with these peculiarities the faint allusions to the world of the invisible entirely responded. See a very thoughtful article on this subject in the *Christian Remembrancer*, 1849, I. 164 sq. Meanwhile the pious Jew, as it is there observed, would find his ground of confidence in the doctrine of one supreme God. 'Fixed upon that spiritual basis of life, as upon a rock, he felt himself secure, come what might. Amid all the changes and decay of nature, constant and enduring, he placed his future in Almighty love, and reposed with a serene content upon an indefinite eternity...prepared in God to go he knew not and he asked not whither.'

[2] Philippsohn, *Religious Idea*, pp. 40, 41.

beneath[1]. It is a voluntary surrender to external tempters, or a self-induced disturbance in the equilibrium of man's will. It is a perverted quality of the creature, by which he is impelled into antagonism with the Creator, refuses to continue in the attitude of worship and dependence, and claims to be his own divinity. When the narration of the Fall is once regarded as a veritable history, and as originally designed for the instruction alike of peasant and philosopher in every age, it furnishes the most intelligible guide within our reach for the elucidation both of ancient records and of moral paradoxes in our own experience. Man knows that he is ever drawn in opposite directions, that when he would do good, evil is present with him. He is no longer what he was designed to be, nor what he feels he might become. Apart from revelation he is sadly conscious of his malady; the Bible, therefore, tells him of its

[1] This, of course, is not the same as if I wrote, 'entirely from *within*.' Such language would exclude the doctrine of a personal Tempter, and therefore would impugn both intimations of the Old Testament, and direct assertions of the New. Attempts, however, have been made of late, and that by members of the Church of England, to resolve the Fall into an outbreak of sexual concupiscence, or inharmonious action of the lower elements in man's own nature. The violence of these attempts may be estimated from the specimens contained in *A Vindication of Protestant Principles*, by Phileleutherus Anglicanus, Lond. 1847, and in Dr. Donaldson's recent speculations on the *Book of Jashar*, pp. 65 sq. In both works, the existence of any order of intelligences higher than the human is positively denied; and with regard to the language of our blessed Lord and the Apostles on the subject of a personal Tempter, these authors either contend that they felt themselves obliged 'to carry on what had become, and in the opinion of some persons still is, a necessary illusion' (*Vindication*, p. 77); or else maintain that passages alleged in proof of such external solicitations to evil ought really to be construed in a different sense, so as to make Satan only a personification of moral evil inherent in humanity. Now the former statement is entirely at variance with the general character of our Saviour's teaching. Did He not shew Himself the fearless adversary of all lax interpretations and 'traditions' which the superstitious Jews had grafted on the genuine revelation? And is it likely therefore that such a Teacher would have winked at serious 'errors'—errors which, in the opinion of our modern critic, are so vital as to trench upon the unity and absolute supremacy of God? To answer the second argument, I would ask the reader to examine for himself the principal texts in question, and try if the idea of an internal struggle will fairly satisfy the language of the sacred penman. This is Dr. C. J. Vaughan's suggestion (*Personality of the Tempter*, &c. p. 20. Lond. 1851), who repudiates the proposed explanation of such passages as utterly untenable, and then adds: 'from which consequently we must infer, by the strictest rules of reasoning, either the personality of the Tempter, or (I speak as a man) the error, and therefore the imposture, of Christ.'

origin, its depth and its malignity; and to impress and foster this belief the legal institute was more especially directed. It dealt with man as with a wretched and degraded, yet recoverable, creature. It exhibited at every turn the perfect majesty and holiness of God, and through that exhibition deepened man's conviction of his littleness, depravity, and ruin. By the Law was the knowledge of sin. This function it especially came forward to discharge. The clouds of wrath indeed are ever fringed with hope: a prospect of some glorious restoration is unfolded in the distant background: intimations of God's love and placability accompany the most terrific manifestations of His anger; or, in other words, the sternest tokens of the truth that sin and holiness are incompatible, nay, absolutely antagonistic, are allied with frequent hints that God and man have found a place of meeting and of reconciliation. Still the ordinary and habitual operation of the Law was to excite the conscience of the Hebrew worshipper, to make him clear and sensitive as to the grand distinctions of morality, to waken longings which it could not satisfy, to preach divisions in the heart of man which it could neither remedy nor relieve. Its author knew that to improve the quality of human actions it is necessary to command the will, and regulate the wishes, nay, that such a course is an essential precondition to the fuller understanding of the truth. He knew, moreover, that until these elementary principles of religion are worked, or drilled, as I might say, into the human heart, there is no basis for ulterior training, no foundation for that superstructure, which it was the purpose of Jehovah to erect at some future period.

Accordingly, the office of the old œconomy regarded merely on the legal side is that of a schoolmaster; its tone is stern, severe, and peremptory. God is, for the most part, represented rather as the King, the Judge, and the Avenger of iniquity, than as the Pardoner and Redeemer. A whirling, wasting flame, the symbol of His purity, the proof that evil cannot 'dwell with Him,' is visible upon the confines of that spot, which had originally formed an earnest to the human family of their Maker's love and nearness[1]; and like images of awe and

[1] Yet the very banishment from Eden, and the planting of the sword-like flame upon its confines, were not altogether unrelieved by intimations of God's mercy. I have shewn elsewhere (*Sermons*, p. 49) that the cherubim were emblems, or rather one compounded emblem, of the highest forms of creature-life, especially the human; and that their appearance was a pledge to man of his continued interest in the seat from which he was expelled: cf. Bähr, *Symbolik des*

terror are associated in all future periods with His more immediate presence. Man is driven to confess at every step, that sin is a profound reality; and that by sinning he becomes an alien and an exile, at enmity with God, creation, and his proper self.

It would be easy to adduce examples where the Hebrew shewed a strong conviction of the force and fitness of these verities: but such examples are not wanted in the present stage of our inquiry. The moral sensibility of the whole Hebrew nation, as compared with that of the adjoining states, is commonly admitted, even by a section of those writers who deny that it was due in any measure to a supernatural revelation. While Greece is recognised as their instructress in the principles of beauty and of science; while Rome is the great fountain of their knowledge with respect to jurisprudence and municipal rights, they are content to be indebted to the Jew for clear conceptions of 'the holiness of God, and of His sympathy with His servants[1].'

3. But another portion of the legal institute awakens very different feelings in this class of speculators. 'What,' they ask triumphantly, 'can you allege in vindication of the ritualism and sacrificial cultus of the Hebrews? Is *it* worthy of a place in the religious system, which you argue sprang from heaven, and which we too acknowledge inculcates the purest and most spiritual views of God? Must *it* not rather be an artifice of Satan, or, as Satan is a mere nonentity, of Jewish priests,—a spurious after-growth that rooted itself in the dark ages, or possibly amid the last convulsions of the Hebrew monarchy?'

Indeed, the ceremonial law, as it is called, has proved itself a stumbling-block to every form of spiritualism. The school of Philo made it tolerable only by concealing it beneath a multitude of allegorical interpretations. The Alexandrines, in like manner, were perplexed by not a few of its provisions, and in reference to the main principles on which it was constructed, viewed it chiefly as a condescension to the weakness of the carnal mind[2]; while many Deists of the last century, and some of their descendants in the present, have not hesitated to de-

Mosaischen Cultus, I. 311 sq.; Fairbairn, *Typology of Scripture*, I. 221 sq. 2nd ed.

[1] Newman's *Hebr. Monarchy*, p. 332, 2nd ed.: cf. *Phases of Faith*, pp. 188, 231.

[2] It is remarkable that Spinosa in like manner (*Tractatus Theologico-Politici*, cap. ii. p. 27, Hamburgi, 1670) places Solomon higher than the Law by reason of his intellectual eminence: 'nam ea *iis tantum* tradita est, qui ratione et naturalis intellectus documentis carent.'

nounce the ceremonial law in terms of obloquy, abhorrence, or contempt[1]. Their opposition is, I think, attributable partly to mistaken views respecting the nature and effects of ritualism in general, but still more to want of insight into the condition of the ancient world and the capacity of its inhabitants. Till we have placed ourselves, as far as possible, upon the standing-ground of those for whom the Law of Moses was designed; till we have tried to look upon it with their eyes, and think afresh the thoughts which burnt and struggled in their bosoms, we shall fail to understand the drift of very many of its ordinances, we shall be incompetent judges of the way in which a system such as that was calculated to excite, instruct, and edify the members of the Elder Church.

The Hebrew was in race and temperament a western Asiatic. The very genius of his native language, corresponding there as always to the bent and constitution of the human mind, bore witness to his general inaptitude for deep and abstract thought or metaphysical inquiries[2]. He was, accordingly, far more dependent than the cultivated nations of the present day on the ideas derived from outward action. He lived far more than they in the impressions made upon the senses[3]; and on passing into the province of religion manifested an especial quickness in appreciating representations of the truth that had been cast into a concrete shape and carried their appeal directly

[1] Von Bohlen's language on this subject (*Einleitung*, p. 175) is merely a reiteration of De Wette's earlier views: but the author neglects to tell us that De Wette afterwards modified them very considerably in his *Biblische Dogmatik*, § 54. See Hengstenberg, *Dissert. on the Pentateuch*, II. 504. According to another class of writers (*e. g.* Bunsen, *Kirche der Zukunft*, p. 77) the whole of the Levitical system was 'introduced in God's anger,' and therefore only interposed new obstacles between Him and His creatures. This was also the view of Spinosa: see Hegel, *Phil. of Hist.* p. 205, Lond. 1857. The single text that furnishes a plea in favour of this theory is Ezek. xx. 25, 26, where God declares that after the defection of the Israelites He gave them 'statutes that were not good, and judgments whereby they should not live.' But it is obvious from the order in which this punishment occurs, that the prophet did not mean the laws and institutions of the Mosaic covenant, all of which were in fact promulgated soon after the exodus from Egypt. He was, on the contrary, referring to cruel and licentious customs of the neighbouring heathen, to which the Lord declares that He abandoned the Israelites for their unfaithfulness to Him and to the Law: cf. 2 Thess. ii. 11, and Fairbairn's *Ezekiel*, pp. 176, 177, Edinb. 1851.

[2] See Wiseman's *Lectures on the Connexion between Science and Revealed Religion*, I. 139.

[3] Cf. O. Müller, as quoted in Hengstenberg, *Dissert.* II. 513.

to the ear and eyesight. Hence for men like him the language of symbolic action might be aptly substituted, here and there at least, for that of speech and writing, on the ground that it would be more urgent, scenic, and expressive. It accorded with the mental habits of the period; it fell in completely with the prevalent modes of thought. An emblem borrowed from the outer world, an institution clad in picturesque and vivid imagery was to him the most efficient sign and best interpreter of things invisible; for although the popular mind of antiquity when labouring to give utterance to a supersensuous truth, might be impelled by some internal necessity to use symbolic language, there is no reason to infer that it must always have apprehended such truths exactly in the form assumed in their expression[1], or could never have been able to detach the thing communicated from its vehicle and outer covering.

The Hebrew was, moreover, as to the degree of his religious knowledge and his capability of reflection in the childhood of his being. As such his character was marked by childlike simplicity. A stranger to all deep and long-sustained abstraction, he was most accessible to teaching that approached him through the channel of the senses, that spoke to him in ritual acts, in the arrangements of a solemn and imposing liturgy, that fetched its motives from external and immediate objects, from rewards that followed close upon obedience, or from penalties that touched his body, and were ever 'lying at the door.' Jehovah 'led him by the hand' in matters of religion[2], rescued him from the seductions of heathen worship, by providing forms adapted to his temperament and his capacity, yet making all such forms the vehicles of pure ideas and noble aspirations, and thus gradually prepared him for the time when his religion would be less outsided and more spiritual, when 'the true worshippers' would 'worship the Father in spirit and in truth' (John iv. 23).

For these and other reasons it was most expedient to clothe some revelations of the Old Testament in figurative drapery, to

[1] Bähr, *Symbolik*, I. 24, 25. Tholuck (*Ep. to the Hebrews*, I. 107) quotes a remarkable testimony on the subject from the Persian philosopher Mahmúd.

[2] Cf. Bp. Law's *Considerations on the Theory of Religion*, p. 152, 7th ed., and Chandler's *Bampton Lectures*, pp. 49, 50. Irenæus had already expressed himself to the same effect: Ὡς οὖν ἡ μὲν μήτηρ δύναται τέλειον παρασχεῖν τῷ βρέφει τὸ ἔμβρωμα, τὸ δὲ ἔτι ἀδυνατεῖ τὴν αὐτοῦ πρεσβυτέραν δέξασθαι τροφήν· οὕτως καὶ ὁ Θεὸς αὐτὸς μὲν οἷός τε ἦν παρασχεῖν ἀπ' ἀρχῆς τῷ ἀνθρώπῳ τὸ τέλειον, ὁ δὲ ἄνθρωπος ἀδύνατος λαβεῖν αὐτό· νήπιος γὰρ ἦν. Lib. IV. c. 37, § I.

employ symbolic and prophetic action[1] as an ordinary means of teaching spiritual truths and leading men to an approximate acquaintance with transcendant mysteries, which some ulterior revelation would more perfectly unveil. The forms of Hebrew worship in particular were meant to be a sort of acted parable, precluding, it may be, the fullest measure of religious knowledge, and, as when the Saviour spoke in parables, implying man's unworthiness and his imperfect receptivity[2]; yet, meanwhile, bringing to the eyes of docile and inquiring spirits many a truth which they might otherwise have failed to apprehend. We should, moreover, bear in mind that symbolic actions were not the only media then employed in the communication of sacred knowledge. The emblems of the legal institute were something more than hieroglyphics, which the future ages of the world might possibly decipher. In many cases where they did not speak emphatically to the warm imagination of the oriental, they would doubtless be explained by Moses, or the line of prophets who succeeded in his room, and thus would borrow fresh significance from naked and explicit forms of teaching by which they were accompanied. The initiatory rite of circumcision will supply us with an instance of the truth of this remark. Its own suggestive character is assumed in admonitions of the Hebrew legislator, as though it were intelligible to all classes of his subjects; yet the moral duty which it indicates is, notwithstanding, forcibly repeated both by him and by the prophet Jeremiah[3].

I am here expressing no opinion as to the degree of insight which the Israelite enjoyed into the correspondency between the ritual service of the Law and the events of Christianity, *i.e.* respecting the didactic office of the legal institute regarded as a series of prophetic types. Such correspondency[4], I doubt not,

[1] Witsius, *de Prophetia et Prophetis*, devotes a chapter (Lib. I. c. xii.) to this mode of instruction. Ezekiel himself (xxiv. 24) told the Jews distinctly that he was on one occasion 'a sign' (εἰς τέρας) to them: 'according to all that he hath done shall ye do; and when this cometh, ye shall know that I am the Lord God.'

[2] Some interesting reflections on this analogy will be found in Mr. Isaac Williams's *Study of the Gospels*, Part II. § 3.

[3] Deut. x. 16; xxx. 6; Jerem. iv. 4. That many of the later Jews were still in the habit of assigning spiritual meanings to the symbols of the temple service is shewn by Tholuck, *Ep. to the Hebrews*, II. 18, 19.

[4] The great points of correspondency, as noticed in the writings of the New Testament, are investigated with much learning and sobriety by Mr. Fairbairn, *Typology of Scripture*, 2nd ed. The author is fully conscious of the distinction

was intended, and is now distinctly traceable: but whether it was seen by worthies of the old œconomy is a very different question. They who pondered the suggestive emblems of the sanctuary, who prayed for fresh illumination to 'behold wondrous things out of the Law' (Ps. cxix. 18), may doubtless have obtained in it some passing glimpses of the evangelic Promise[1]: yet others, when they worshipped either in the wilderness or on the sacred hill of Sion, may have gathered from the multiplicity of public sacrifices no acquaintance with the holy Victim of the Cross. Their own condition intellectually may have

I am here endeavouring to establish between the typical and symbolical aspects of the Law: cf. Bähr, *Symbolik des Mosaischen Cultus*, I. 15 sq.

[1] Archbp. Magee appears to overstate the measure of this insight, when he gathers that 'the ancient sacrifices, those prescribed to the patriarchs, and those enjoined by the law, were types and figures, and *known to be such*, of that one great sacrifice, which was, at a future day, to be offered upon the cross for the sins of the whole human race.' *On the Atonement*, I. 381, 3rd ed. The authority adduced to justify this inference is the following passage of Eusebius, *Demonst. Evangel.* lib. I. c. x. (p. 36, Paris, 1628): Ἕως μὲν οὖν οὐδέπω, τὸ κρεῖττον, οὐδὲ τὸ μέγα καὶ τίμιον, καὶ θεοπρεπὲς σφάγιον παρῆν ἀνθρώποις, ταῖς διὰ ζώων θυσίαις λύτρα τῆς ἑαυτῶν ζωῆς, καὶ ἀντίψυχα τῆς οἰκείας φύσεως προσηκόντως ἀποδιδόναι χρῆν τῷ Θεῷ; ὡς δὲ ἔπραττον οἱ πάλαι θεοφιλεῖς, σεμνόν τι καὶ θεοφιλὲς καὶ μέγα ἱερεῖον ἥξειν ποτὲ εἰς ἀνθρώπους τῷ θείῳ πνεύματι προειληφότες, τὸ τοῦ παντὸς καθάρσιον κόσμου, οὗ καὶ τὰ σύμβολα τέως ἐπιτελεῖν αὐτοὺς προφήτας ὄντας, καὶ τὸ μέλλον ἔσεσθαι προτυπουμένους. But if this passage really warranted the inference that the Hebrews, as a nation, were so conversant with all the mysteries of redemption, it would be impossible to explain such texts as I Pet. i. 11, 12, or indeed to understand the utter dulness of the first apostles in not perceiving that He whom they revered as the Messiah must go to Jerusalem and be killed, and must rise again the third day (Matt. xvi. 22; Luke xviii. 34). Archbp. Magee himself acknowledges the force of a similar difficulty arising out of what is called 'the mystical sacrifice of the Phœnicians' (Euseb. *Præpar. Evangel.* lib. I. c. x; I. 90, ed. Gaisford): for he there perceives (p. 389), that if such offering had contained the typical references assigned to it by Bryant (*Observations on Ancient History*, pp. 286 sq. Camb. 1767), the idolatrous inhabitants of Canaan would have possessed 'a more exact delineation of the great future sacrifice' than was accorded to the Hebrews at the same early period. The truth is, that the 'typical' character of the sacrifice in question cannot be established. The phrase κατεσφάττοντο δὲ οἱ διδόμενοι μυστικῶς signifies that human victims were immolated on these occasions 'with mystic or secret rites,' without implying a prophetic reference to some higher Victim. This consideration also furnishes an answer to Mr. W. J. Fox (*Religious Ideas*, p. 110), when he dwells upon the theory of Bryant, and endeavours to elicit an argument in favour of his 'religion of humanity,' from such fancied parallels between the Christian and Phœnician views of expiation.

resembled that of the woman in St. Matthew's Gospel, whose devotion was accepted and rewarded by the Saviour, but who knew not that in pouring the ointment on His body, she had done it for His burial (Matt. xxvi. 12).

Apart, however, from its typical design, the Hebrew system had been calculated to exert a present influence on the life and spirit of the worshipper. It was not only a collection of prophetic types that should hereafter grow more luminous, explicit and convincing when the Antitype Himself arose; it was *symbolical* of truths already current in the Elder Church; it was suggestive of ideas that operated then and there upon the springs of moral action. The sacrificial cultus, for example, which is properly esteemed the root and centre of the legal system, was no empty pageant for exciting a fantastic or appeasing a blood-thirsty populace: it was no mere state-machinery for keeping Israelites together, or retaining them in their allegiance to some earthly potentate. It symbolised a number of profound realities, affecting man's position in the sight of God, and illustrated on what terms the spirit of the human suppliant could approach the glorious Object of his worship. It set forth, especially, in vivid characters and certified in blood of sacrificial victims the great truth, which every nation more or less admitted and deplored, the truth that sin and holiness are utterly incompatible, and that only by surrendering life can the relations which iniquity subverts be re-established and renewed.

To render this more plain and forcible, I shall select an instance from the ordinary worshippers of the time of David, when the ark had come in triumph to the new metropolis, and when the cycle of the Hebrew liturgy was celebrated in its fulness. Such a man would find that he was planted in the midst of a minute and solemn ritual, its centre in the holy tabernacle, or rather in the ark of the covenant, where God, who 'rideth upon the heaven of heavens' (Ps. lxviii. 33), had condescended to approach His fallen creatures, and dispense His gifts of grace.

The tabernacle itself was curtained from the outer world, and subdivided into three compartments, each with its appropriate office in the worship of Jehovah. The forecourt was a gathering-point for all the congregation of the Israelites: the holy place was destined for a special order[1], for the mem-

[1] The distinction does not, however, prove the existence of a sacerdotal *caste* among the Hebrews. The idea of caste is inseparably connect-

bers of the sacerdotal family, whom God, in carrying out His purpose, had brought nigh unto Himself: while only one of these, and he upon a single day of the year, was authorized to pass beyond a veil suspended at the extremity of the holy place, that he might offer incense near the mercy-seat, or covering of the ark of witness, and so minister in the holiest of all. But other circumstances urged the Hebrew layman in the same direction, and constrained him to reflect on the provisions of the Law. He was most deeply interested in the multifarious acts of worship ever celebrated in the mother-city of Judæa. Like his countrymen in general he was circumcised: he stood in a peculiar nearness, or in covenant-relations to the God of Abraham; and in virtue of this connexion prayed to God as to his own God, and was able to participate in what is found to be an all-pervading element of Hebrew worship, the rite of sacrifice.

He felt, moreover, that the system under which he lived was such as to accuse, convict, and punish him when he deflected from the course of action it prescribed. Of these delinquencies one section were the open violations of the Moral Law which contravened the letter of the Decalogue; the rest were all transgressions of inferior branches of the legal system, partly moral, partly positive or ceremonial. Now the former class embracing all varieties of heinous sin the worshipper knew would subject him to excommunication or else to death itself. The Law was able to prescribe no remedy for them: it claimed 'the blood not of a vicarious victim, but of the transgressor[1].' He was, therefore, either separated, where the sin was public and notorious, from all intercourse with other Hebrews, and was driven to confess with shame and bitter self-reproaches, 'Thou desirest not sacrifice, else would I give it;' or was sentenced to die 'without mercy,' an example of the just severity of God, a warning to his neighbours. Hope there might be

ed with that of different origins (*e.g.* the Bráhmans, and they alone, are said to have issued from the *head* of Bráhma). Besides, it was announced in early times to all the Israelites without exception, (Ex. xix. 5, 6) that if they were true to God's covenant, they would be a special people and a 'kingdom of priests' (cf. 1 Pet. ii. 9, where Christians are also entitled γένος ἐκλεκτὸν, βασίλειον ἱεράτευμα): in other words, that as contrasted with Gentile nations, every Hebrew would know God in His revealed character and stand to Him in a relationship peculiarly near. And that the Israelites felt themselves thus 'consecrated as a whole people,' so as to become 'priests and prophets for all mankind,' is stated by Philo, *De Abrahamo*, Opp. II. 15. ed. Mangey; *De Mose*, Ibid. II. 104.

[1] Davison, *On Sacrifice*, p. 80.

for such culprits, even at this dark extremity, but the source from which it sprang was not distinctly indicated by the ordinances of the Law.

It was, however, different with a second class[1] of crimes, where the offence was either purely ceremonial, or, if moral, one in which the turpitude was not so glaring nor so utterly devoid of palliating circumstances. For all these the Law of Moses had provided means of expiation. An Israelite, for instance, has been sworn as witness, but is guilty of concealing portions of the truth (Levit. v. 4—6). He can preserve his standing in the sacred commonwealth only by the aid of 'trespass-offerings[2]'—a lamb or kid of the goats which must be offered in his name in strict compliance with the regulations of the Law. He therefore travels to mount Zion, to the holy tabernacle of God. He brings his offering to the altar: his hand is pressed upon the head of the devoted animal, which he is taught will be accepted as the means of rescuing the

[1] Offences for which an atonement was provided may be classed as follows: 1. Bodily impurity. 2. Ceremonial omissions and transgressions. 3. Sins of ignorance and inadvertency, or offences unwittingly committed (ἀγνοήματα). 4. Certain specified cases of moral transgression, knowingly committed, in favour of which exceptions from the general severity of the Law appear to have been recognised. Davison, *Ibid.* p. 78. Still it is quite possible that the pardon of grosser acts of immorality and even of most deadly sins may have been symbolised, and in so far as related to men's outward position in the theocracy, may have been really effected, on the great day of atonement: for the confession of the high priest then extended to 'all the iniquities of the children of Israel, and all their transgressions in all their sins,' *i. e.* to sins of every kind. Maimonides (as quoted by Magee, I. 351), declares that 'the scapegoat made atonement for all the transgressions of the Law, both the lighter and the more heavy transgressions,' provided the sinner was himself truly penitent: but this theory of the Jewish schoolman rests upon a total misconception of the Levitical sacrifices. None of these 'could make him that did the service perfect, as *pertaining to the conscience*,' (Heb. ix. 9, 10; x. 1, 11): they were in respect of it impotent and insufficient: they were symbols only of the genuine purification that was to be effected by other agencies, and therefore did not reach beyond 'the time of reformation.'

[2] The words אָשָׁם (= πλημμέλεια, sacrificium pro delictis), and חַטָּאת (= ἁμαρτία, περὶ τῆς ἁμαρτίας, sacrificium pro peccatis) are so interchanged in this passage (Lev. v. 1—13), that it is well-nigh impossible to say whether allusion is really made to the 'trespass-offering,' or 'the sin-offering:' see Winer, *Realwörterbuch*, II. 431 sq. 3rd ed. I have adopted that view which seems more probable on the whole, making the trespass-offerings refer to an offence in which the individual only is concerned, and the transgression known exclusively to himself.

offender from the outward penalty of his misdeed. The blood, or vehicle of life, is taken by the priest who sprinkles part of it upon the altar, and pours the rest upon the ground. The flesh is then abandoned to the ministers of the sanctuary, and in cases such as that we are considering, is consumed by them within the precincts of the tabernacle: while the offerer is at liberty to turn his footsteps homeward, reinstated in his old position as a member of the sacred family, and so far at peace with God whose laws he had infringed.

Now this was only one of multitudinous rites that exercised the faith and tested the obedience of the Hebrew, that constrained him to reflect on the surpassing majesty and purity of God, that deepened in his heart the sentiments of fear and reverence, and that kept alive the consciousness of moral evil. The operation of his sacrifice was plainly two-fold[1]. It produced a real change in him with reference to the outward laws and privileges of the theocracy under which he lived: it symbolised and represented, though it did not actually impart, those better gifts of grace, affecting his relations to the Searcher of the human spirit, and promoting the purification of the conscience. I will here revert a moment to the case before adduced, and indicate the probable emotions and reflections which the rite of sacrifice was calculated to excite in ordinary Hebrews of the age of David, when they worshipped in a pious spirit, such as that which animates the Book of Psalms. The one locality at which their offering must be made in order to secure acceptance would itself contribute to impress the doctrine of God's unity[2]. How sacred also and how awful was that place! How radiant to the eye of such a worshipper with glorious and profound associations! 'It is here that Thou, O God, the Unapproachable, hast condescended to draw nigh and bless the waiting multitude. Dreadful art Thou, O Lord, out of Thy sanctuaries, the God of Israel; He gives might and strength unto His

[1] Cf. above, p. 81, n. 1, and Mr. Thomson's *Bampton Lectures* (1853), p. 65. Grotius already insisted strongly on the same distinction: 'Lex vetus dupliciter spectatur; aut carnaliter, aut spiritualiter. Carnaliter, qua instrumentum fuit πολιτείας, *reipublicæ* Judaicæ. Spiritualiter, qua σκίαν εἶχε τῶν μελλόντων, *umbram habebat futurorum*...Ex his quæ diximus perspicuum jam est, quomodo victimæ pro peccato in Veteri Fœdere peccata expiarint; nimirum Deum movendo, ut pœnam carnalem remitteret, idque per satisfactionem quandam *etc.*' *Defensio Fidei Cathol. de Satisfactione Christi*, c. x. *Opp. Theolog.* III. 331, 333.

[2] Εἷς ναὸς ἑνὸς Θεοῦ· φίλον γὰρ ἀεὶ παντὶ τὸ ὅμοιον. κοινὸς ἁπάντων, κοινοῦ Θεοῦ ἁπάντων. Joseph. *contra Apion.* lib. II. § 23: *Opp.* II. 485, ed. Havercamp.

people. Blessed be God' (cf. Ps. lxviii. 35). So mused he as he wound his way along the sacred slopes of Zion; or perchance he asked himself with trembling earnestness, 'Who shall ascend into the hill of the Lord, or who shall stand in His holy place?' and heard the answer of the Psalmist, 'He that hath clean hands and a pure heart; who hath not lifted up his soul unto vanity, nor sworn deceitfully. He shall receive the blessing from the Lord, and righteousness from the God of his salvation' (Ps. xxiv. 3—5). Where he enters the tabernacle in this spirit, the feelings that subdue him as he stoops beneath the sacred curtain will continue to direct his thoughts in all his subsequent devotions, and will save him from presenting 'the sacrifice of fools.' He leads his offering to the altar, and as he is there again reminded that the victim must be perfect of its kind, without spot or blemish, in full possession of that life which constitutes the noblest gift of God, how calculated is it to suggest and strengthen the conviction that purity, internal purity, will also be demanded of the worshipper, that while he brings an offering to the altar and expresses there his sense of imperfection and dependence, he must also learn the arduous task of self-surrender, he must give his soul a living sacrifice to God[1]. His hand is placed upon the victim, in whose struggles he beholds the image and the representative of punishment

[1] Bähr, who has been followed by some English writers of distinction, is not satisfied with considering this as *one aspect* of the rite of sacrifice, but argues that the surrender of the human life and will to God was at the very root of the idea. He draws attention, it is true, to the blood sprinkled on the altar, but only to blood as the *vehicle of life*, not as giving an especial prominence to the death of the victim. 'Der symbolische Charakter des Opfers besteht aber nun darin dass das Dar- oder Nahebringen (הקריב) des Nephesch in Opferblute auf den Altar, als den Ort der Gegenwart und Offenbarung Gottes, Symbol von dem Dar- oder Nahebringen des Nephesch des Opfernden an Jehova, den Heiligen ist. Wie jenes Darbringen des Thierblutes (Seele) ein Hin- und Aufgeben des Thierlebens in den Tod ist, so soll auch das seelische, d. i. selbstische im Gegensatz zu Gott befindliche Leben des Opfernden hin- und aufgegeben werden, d. h. sterben; weil aber dies Hingeben ein Hingeben an Jehova, den Heiligen ist, so ist es kein Aufhören schlechthin, nicht etwas blos Negatives, sondern ein Sterben, welches eo ipso zum Leben wird' u. s. w. II. 210. According to this theory there is nothing strictly substitutionary or vicarious in any sacrifice, and therefore not in the sacrificial death of Christ, who merely surrendered His life to God as an example of perfect self-renunciation to be imitated spiritually by all His people. See a full examination of Bähr's positions in Kurtz, *Das Mosaische Opfer*, Mitau, 1842, and cf. Fairbairn's *Typology*, Vol. II. Append. B.

which he provoked[1], and he is smitten with a deeper consciousness of his pollution and demerit; he feels that if Jehovah were to deal with him according to his works, the penalty would fall directly, and would overwhelm himself instead of the vicarious offering. 'Lo! now,' his plea is, 'I repent, and am truly sorry for my misdeeds; let this victim be my expiation[2].' Its death is speedily accomplished, and he finds in that event another symbol both of the displeasure and the placability of God. He learns from what is represented to his eyesight that 'without shedding of blood there is no remission;' yet he reasons that as natural life is cherished by the agency of food derived from the inferior animals, the love of God is also manifested in arrangements which provide that their life shall be taken as a substitute for his. And therefore when he gazes on the flame of the completed sacrifice, new hopes are simultaneously awakened in his bosom. He feels that God, who has not turned away from the oblation thus presented in accordance with His will, who visibly delivers the offender from the temporal consequence of his transgression, may also be induced to hear his cry of penitential grief, to purge the soul with hyssop, and to heal the broken and the contrite heart (Ps. li. 7, 17).

The internal arrangements of the sanctuary itself would in like manner serve to generate these deeper principles of faith, of reverence, of humility. The earnest worshippers, for instance, uniformly revered the ark of the covenant as the proper shrine of God, the Self-Existent One, and therefore as a pledge that notwithstanding their demerit He was still the ever-present Guardian of the Israelites, and that His tabernacle was with man. The same was vividly suggested by the mercy-seat, or mystic covering of the Law, where God was pledged to commune with His people (Ex. xxv. 22), and extended to them foretastes of His reconciling love. Yet different thoughts were also prompted by this indication of His saving presence. So long as the most sacerdotal Hebrews were excluded from the holiest portion of the tabernacle, the truth could scarcely fail to print itself upon the least reflecting mind among them, that an age of

[1] That the Mosaic sacrifices were in this sense *vicarious*, and really instrumental in releasing the offender from the temporal punishment due to his transgression, is distinctly affirmed in Levit. i. 4: 'And he shall put his hand upon the head of the burnt-offering; and it shall be accepted for him, to make atonement for him' (וְנִרְצָה לוֹ לְכַפֵּר עָלָיו): cf. the arguments and authorities in Magee, Vol. I. No. XXXVIII. No. XXXIX.

[2] See this and other traditional forms in Outram, *De Sacrificiis*, Lib. I. c. XV. § 10, 11. Lond. 1677.

full and absolute communion with the Holy One was still to be expected, that the way into the inner glories of the sanctuary 'was not yet made manifest' (Heb. ix. 8), that veils were interposed between the human soul and God, and would continue to be there suspended till a mystery 'kept secret since the world began' was finally unveiled at the inauguration of some new œconomy, and discovered 'to all nations for the obedience of faith' (Rom. xvi. 25, 26).

Nor does this version of the Law, regarded under its *symbolic* aspect, differ in essential points from the deductions which the Christian is enabled to derive from *typical* arrangements of the old œconomy. On the contrary, it will be found that the two lines of thought are strictly parallel. They both exhibit the same general elements of supernatural truth; they both are tending to produce the same kind of principles and feelings in their subjects, though the last has reference to far higher platforms, and to modes of action far more spiritual, heavenly, and profound[1]. In different words, there is exactly the same kind of disproportion between the Hebrew and Christian versions of the Law as that which, from the nature and necessities of the case, exists between the office of the pedagogue and the professor. There is a disproportion, but no dissimilitude: the first is elementary; it hints, suggests, and shadows forth what is distinctly inculcated and effected by the second. In the first, as Moses emblematically veiled his countenance, we have a system veiled, in order that the plenary light of truth

[1] Mr. Fairbairn (*Typology of Scripture*, I. 58, 59) has embodied nearly the same idea in the following passage: 'In the immediate ends to be accomplished, and the apparatus provided for accomplishing them, the two dispensations are as far asunder as heaven is from the earth: but in both alike, we see a pure and holy God, enshrined in the recesses of a glorious sanctuary, unapproachable by guilty and polluted flesh, but through a medium of powerful intercession and cleansing efficacy, —yet to those who so approach, most merciful and gracious, full of loving-kindness, and plenteous in redemption: while in every act of sincere approach on their part, there is necessarily brought into exercise the same feelings of contrition and abasement, self-renunciation, realising faith, childlike dependence and adoring gratitude. So that the preparatory and the ultimate dispensations, considered in their general character and design, disclosed substantially the same views of God, and in doing so awoke the same feelings in the hearts of His worshippers: but the former only as the shadow of the latter, a resemblance but not the substance, a representation in outward, earthly, and perishable materials, and with respect to the concerns of flesh and time, of the spiritual ideas and principles which the dispensation of the Gospel embodies in things not made with hands and with respect to objects truly heavenly and divine.'

might not be prematurely manifested, and so dazzle the imperfect vision of the subject (2 Cor. iii. 13); in the second, when the fulness of the time had come, the light of the knowledge of the glory of God is ready to shine forth into the heart of every child of Adam from the face of Jesus Christ (2 Cor. iv. 6). And thus the Law is found to have been neither silenced, abrogated, nor subverted by the coming of the Son of God. Its real character is vindicated; it is shewn to be a lower form of one and the same religion. It has passed into the Gospel. Its dim and shadowy outlines are filled up by the effusion of the Holy Spirit; its graphic and mnemonic symbols are converted into quickening and sustaining sacraments; its bloody sacrifices pointing ever to the spotless Lamb of God, who taketh away the sins of the world, have been exchanged[1] for prayers and hymns, and eucharistic offerings, where the worshipper presents himself, his soul and body, a living sacrifice, holy, acceptable to God, which is our reasonable service (Rom. xii. 1). Faint and transitory 'preludes' of the Incarnation, granted in the time of Hebraism, were just enough to indicate that God was placable, and might hereafter bring Himself into more intimate relations with the human family. But in the Gospel heaven and earth are reconciled and re-united. God has been 'manifest in the flesh,' assuming all our nature, body, soul and spirit, into perfect and indissoluble union with divinity. The fulness of time arrived, and 'God sent forth His Son, made of a woman, made under the Law, to redeem them that were under the Law, that we might receive the adoption of sons' (Gal. iv. 4, 5). The Christian, therefore, is not left to raise himself by means of a symbolic ritual to the full perception of these blessed facts, and a belief in these transcendent mysteries: before our eyes Jesus Christ hath been evidently set forth crucified amongst us (Gal. iii. 1). In his character of the burnt-offering, He was immolated to replace mankind in their original subjection to the Godhead: as the peace-offering, He completed our imperfect vows and our defective praises: as the sin-offering, He bore in His sinless body to the tree the concentrated weight of penal suffering that was due to man's iniquities. He blotted out the handwriting that was against us, nailing it

[1] *Οὐκοῦν καὶ θύομεν καὶ θυμιῶμεν· τοτὲ μὲν τὴν μνήμην τοῦ μεγάλου θύματος, κατὰ τὰ πρὸς αὐτοῦ παραδοθέντα μυστήρια ἐπιτελοῦντες, καὶ τὴν ὑπὲρ σωτηρίας ἡμῶν εὐχαριστίαν δι' εὐσεβῶν ὕμνων τε καὶ εὐχῶν τῷ Θεῷ προσκομίζοντες· τοτὲ δὲ σφᾶς αὐτοὺς ὅλῳ καθιεροῦντες αὐτῷ, καὶ τῷ γε Ἀρχιερεῖ αὐτοῦ Λόγῳ, αὐτῷ σώματι καὶ ψυχῇ ἀνακείμενοι.* Eusebius, *Demonst. Evangel.* Lib. I. c. x. (p. 40, Paris, 1628).

to the cross. He died the just for the unjust that He might bring us back to God. He passed in triumph from the earth, or outer-court of the eternal sanctuary, and entered not 'into the holy places made with hands, which are the figures of the true; but into heaven itself, there to appear in the presence of God for us' (Heb. ix. 24).

§ 2. *The Promise.*

The possibility of this reconcilement between God and His offending creatures was already hinted, as we saw, in shadowy and symbolic ordinances of the legal system. But there was another and a more explicit way in which the future exaltation of mankind was intimated to the members of the Hebrew Church. As early as the time of Abraham, the evangelic 'Promise' had obtained a definite expression; the Gospel had been 'preached before' (Gal. iii. 8).

I shall not reopen old discussions touching the amount of hope derivable from the sentence passed on him who tempted our first parents. Many Christians have discovered there a kind of 'Protevangelium,' or 'grand charter of God's mercy after the fall[1];' others, the incipient germ which every future promise only served to ripen and develope[2]; and St. Paul appears himself to countenance these expositions when the victory of Christ is represented as the bruising of Satan's power beneath the feet of Christians (Rom. xvi. 20). It may nevertheless be granted that the language used in Genesis might originally produce in man no very definite ideas either of the Person, or the nature of his future Champion. All that our first parents gathered from it may have been the vast but vague assurance that their forfeited possession, with its peace and harmony and innocence, was not lost for ever, but would be restored on the

[1] Bp. Sherlock, *On Prophecy*, Disc. III. p. 78.

[2] Fairbairn, *Typol. of Scripture*, I. 193. This is not the place to take in hand a critical refutation of the views propounded in the recent work of Dr. Donaldson with reference to the correct interpretation of Gen. iii. 15. As one of the assailants of those views most truly urges, the translation of 'what is usually considered as the first Messianic promise' is 'so gross that it will not bear rendering into English.' *Remarks on Dr. Donaldson's Book, entitled* 'Jashar,' by Mr. J. J. S. Perowne, 2nd ed. p. 24. It is however satisfactory to add, that all Hebrew scholars with whom I have had an opportunity of conversing on the subject, strongly reprobate the exposition there advanced. They hold that it is philologically desperate, and could never have possessed itself of such a mind as Dr. Donaldson's, had he not found it useful in the vindication of his favourite theory, touching the non-existence of all moral agents other than the human: cf. above, p. 72, note.

discomfiture of him whose instigations led to their expulsion. In that case the *how* and *when* would be reserved for some ulterior promise.

It is however certain that a root and starting-point of such explicit revelations has been found in Abraham, the friend of God, the father of the faithful; and after his progeny was elected as the special vehicle of true religion, and its guardian in a world fast lapsing from the worship and the fear of God, or growing vain in their imaginations (Rom. i. 21), fuller beams of light were thrown continually upon the future history of his race, and on the hopes and prospects of mankind in general. 'From this time began that line of the divine oracles, which, first being preserved in his family, and afterwards secured in record, has never been broken nor lost, but having successively embraced the Law, the Prophets, and the Gospel, is now completed, to remain the lasting and imperishable monument of Revealed Truth in the world[1].' Accordingly we ascertain that while the better and more thoughtful class of heathen were compelled to seek relief in their embarrassments by dreaming of some golden age that might eventually come round afresh, and reinstate them in some lost inheritance; the Hebrew always proved himself a man of the future. The genius of his religion was pre-eminently hopeful. He was ever in the attitude of expectation[2], ever reaching forward to an age of glory, of enlargement, of deliverance, when his race would be superlatively blessed, and prove itself the bearer of unuttered blessings to all tribes and families of man.

I grant that in its earlier form the prophecy to which these hopes were clinging with so much of ardour and tenacity was comparatively dim, indefinite and enigmatical; nor could it, under Hebraism, assume the spiritual aspect which the promises of God possess when contemplated by ourselves from Christian points of view. Yet on the other hand we should remember that such characteristics harmonise with the prevailing methods, tone and spirit of the old œconomy. The symbolical and typical versions of the legal system have their parallel in what may be esteemed the Hebrew and the Christian versions of the

[1] Davison, *Discourses on Prophecy*, p. 97, 4th ed.

[2] '*Expectation* then,' says the lamented Archer Butler, 'is the inward spirit of the Old Testament, as Fulfilment of the New. Wonderful itself, its function clearly is to testify wonders more august to come. From Moses to Malachi, these Hebrew Scriptures are, as it were, one long-drawn sigh of sorrowful hope.' *Sermons*, 1st series, p. 212, 3rd ed.

Promise. Thus, the very first conceptions of man's rescue from the consequences of the fall may have been only rude approximations to the great reality. They may have reached no further than the thought of some divine interposition which should mitigate the ills of life, and make the earth a more congenial habitation. Again, although the wording of the curse[1] denounced on men's seducer (Gen. iii. 15), would have doubtless made it evident that God was on *their* side, and not on his; the question whether a destructive blow then threatened was to be inflicted by the human species generally, by some peculiar race of Eve's descendants, or a single champion of that race, was for the present left unanswered.

Nor am I contending that when Abraham received the promise, 'In thee (*or*, in thy seed) shall all the nations of the earth be blessed,' the language was entirely free from corresponding ambiguity[2]. The patriarch himself would pro-

[1] The word זֶרַע (properly 'the act of sowing,' hence 'seed' and 'progeny' in general) would not of itself convey the idea of an individual, but rather of a plurality of descendants: cf. Rom. xvi. 20, and below, note 2. Accordingly Kurtz (*Gesch. des Alten Bundes*, I. 62, 63), although recognising the prophetic character of the verse, takes the expression 'seed of the woman,' as equivalent to all the human race. 'Das ganze Menschengeschlecht (der Weibessame) soll den Kampf mit dem Urheber der Sünde kämpfen, und soll ihn kraft des göttlichen Willens *siegreich* kämpfen.'

[2] Gen. xii. 2, 3; Gal. iii. 8. On a future occasion (Gen. xxii. 18) the phrase 'in thee' is explained 'in thy seed' (בְּזַרְעֲךָ), and in this expanded form the promise was republished, (1) in the case of Isaac (Gen. xxvi. 4), and (2) in that of Jacob (Gen. xxviii. 14). But the difficulty of applying the expression זֶרַע to an individual is apparent even at this last stage of the promise: for in the earlier member of the same verse (v. 14) it is prophesied that the seed of Jacob (זַרְעֲךָ) shall be as numerous 'as the dust of the earth:' cf. xxii. 17, 18. On the other hand it has been argued from St. Paul's distinction between 'seed' and 'seeds' (Gal. iii. 16), and his exposition of the 'one seed' as prophetic of the Messiah, that the patriarchs may have been taught by such expressions as occur in Gen. xxii. 18, to expect an individual Saviour. I do not think it unlikely that they had by some course or other arrived at this conclusion: the language of our Lord Himself implies as much, when He says, 'Your father Abraham rejoiced to see my day; and he saw it, and was glad' (John viii. 56). Still it is next to certain that St. Paul, in the passage above quoted, did not mean to rest this inference on the Hebrew equivalent of 'seed.' His meaning rather is, that the promise was not given to all the σπέρματα (posterities, or descendants) of Abraham, but only to the single line of Isaac, that, *viz.* of which 'Christ' (the κεφαλή and πλήρωμα of all the Christian body) was the representative and consummation: see ver. 29. The form σπέρματα is used in this way by Joseph. *Antiq.* VIII. 7, 6 (παῖς ἐκ βασιλικῶν σπερμάτων): and St. Paul elsewhere (1 Cor. xii. 12) con-

bably discover there allusion to an individual Benefactor of the Abrahamic race. He may have also been enabled more and more, by his own want of territory, and his fuller insight into the mysterious ways of God, to separate the spiritual from the temporal branches of the Promise[1], to see through the earthly blessing more and more distinctly in proportion as it was deferred, and so recognise in the Messiah, not only an illustrious Chieftain who should stretch His sceptre over all the land of Canaan, but a glorious Agent for disseminating true religion, and restoring peace and righteousness to man. Yet even thus the image of the future Christ was little more than outline. Subsequent disclosures were required to fill the outline up, to introduce fresh features, to supply more special characteristics, to combine ideas of death and suffering with ideas of conquest and of glorification, till the Personage who stands before us in the visions of Isaiah[2] might hereafter be at once identified with the exalted Son of Mary, and apostles be enabled to establish from the ancient Scriptures that Jesus is the Christ[3].

But the peculiar forms and aspects thus assumed from time to time by Messianic intimations of the Old Testament have proved a fruitful source of modern scepticism. The evidence of prophecy to which all fathers and apologists of the Early Church assigned the very greatest prominence[4], and

siders ὁ Χριστὸς as involving mystically the whole spiritual organism, the Church united with Him: cf. Tholuck's Appendix to Dissert. I. *Epist. to the Hebrews*, ii. 230 sq.

[1] See the reasoning on this subject in Hebr. xi. 9, 10.

[2] 'What less have we in the single book of Isaiah than the *scheme* of the Gospel, and the *establishment* of it, unfolded? The mission of Christ into the world, his original Divine Nature, his supernatural birth in his incarnation, his work of mercy and his kingdom of righteousness; his humiliation, sufferings, and death; the sacrifice of atonement for sin made by his death; the effusion of the gifts and grace of the Holy Spirit; the enlarged propagation of his religion; the persecutions of it; the moral characters of it; the blindness and incredulity of the Jewish people in the rejection of it; the adoption of the Gentile world into the Church and people of God; the peace of the righteous in death, and the triumph and victory of God's mercy, in behalf of man, over death?' Davison, *On Prophecy*, pp. 272, 273. Even Mr. F. W. Newman was so affected by some of these passages that, to use his own expressions, 'they were the very last link of my chain that snapt.' *Phases of Faith*, pp. 195, 196.

[3] See, for instance, Acts iii. 24 sq.; xviii. 28; xxiv. 14; xxvi. 22 sq.; xxviii. 23. This method they had learned from Him, who, 'beginning at Moses and all the prophets, expounded unto them *in all the Scriptures* the things concerning Himself:' see Luke xxiv. 24—27.

[4] Thus, Justin Martyr, speaking of the evidence of prophecy, says,

which in fact secured for Christianity a number of its ablest champions and its brightest luminaries[1], is decried as shallow, impotent, and inconclusive. A living writer who described the several steps by which the old 'religion of the letter' is gradually 'renounced,' informs us that the Christian Church has been crippled ever since the first century by its acquiescence in the following proposition, *viz.* that 'the Jewish teacher Jesus fulfilled the conditions requisite to constitute him the Messiah of the ancient Hebrew prophets[2].' Others, who decline to say expressly whether they have also lost their faith in the Messiahship of Jesus, manifest the same antipathy to all external evidences, and more especially to that by which His claims to such an office have been hitherto supported. The prophets, it is urged, *may* have in every case had reference primarily to events and persons of their own day, or at least so nearly contemporaneous that the spiritual gift they exercised was rather one of predication than prediction; and therefore that the Christian acts unfairly to the Holy Scriptures when he construes language spoken primarily of Hebrew kings, or of the sacred family at large, as a direct and literal prophecy of Christ. Such language, say our critics, can be honestly adduced in no other way than as the language of allegory or of general illustration.

Now without pausing to remind objectors of this second class that all their animadversions will extend far higher even than the saints and worthies of the ancient Church, it may suffice to answer that the strength of such an argument is

ἥπερ μεγίστη καὶ ἀληθεστάτη ἀπόδειξις καὶ ὑμῖν, ὡς νομίζομεν, φανήσεται: *Apol.* I. c. 30. St. Augustine has numerous passages to the same effect: *e. g.* 'Nam de prophetia convincimus contradicentes paganos. Quid est Christus? dicit paganus: cui respondemus, Quem prænunciaverunt prophetæ.' *Tractat.* xxxv. *in Johan.* § 7, ed. Benedict.

[1] Justin Martyr, Clemens Alexandrinus, Tertullian, Lactantius, and Arnobius were all originally heathen, and all attribute their conversion to the intimate correspondence between the facts of the New Testament and the predictions of the Old: Lyall's *Propædia Prophetica*, p. 88.

[2] Newman's *Phases of Faith*, p. 202. He adds (p. 225) that the heavy yoke imposed on Christians of the present day arises from our claiming 'Messiahship for Jesus.' 'This,' it is alleged, 'gave a premium to crooked logic, in order to prove that the prophecies meant what they did not mean, and could not mean. This put the Christian church into an essentially false position, by excluding from it in the first century all the men of most powerful and cultivated understanding among the Greeks and Romans:' cf. the language of an ancient scoffer in Origen, *contra Celsum*, Lib. I. p. 39, ed. Spencer.

drawn from considerations neither probable in themselves, nor warranted by the phenomena of Holy Scripture. For even were we to admit that *all* the prophecies are capable of being referred to circumstances actually or proximately contemporaneous,—an assumption[1] than which nothing is more arbitrary and unjustifiable,—does it necessarily follow that a second Person, standing in the same relations, or a second series of analogous events, may not have been embraced within the scope of the original prediction[2]? May not one fulfilment of a prophecy be leading up men's thoughts and aspirations to another less immediate but more literal? May not an imperfect realisation of the prophet's language be the pledge and prelude of a second still more glorious and exhaustive? Is the Bible such a plain and superficial document that the discovery of these fresh and deeper meanings should in any wise offend us? The truth is, that a mind impressed with reverence for the Holy Scriptures, searching them with the conviction that Christ is to be found in every quarter, in the

[1] Take, for instance, one of the first passages in which both Jews and Christians of all times have recognised the promise of a personal Messiah (Gen. xlix. 8—10). Whether the true reading (in ver. 10) be שִׁילֹה (retained in the Samaritan), or שִׁלֹה (=LXX. τὰ ἀποκείμενα αὐτῷ and ᾧ ἀπόκειται), between which critics are divided: and whether, secondly, we interpret שִׁילֹה as the *subject* of the verb, 'Man of Rest,' 'the Rest-bringer,' corresponding to 'the Prince of Peace,' in Is. ix. 5; or with those moderns who virtually reject the Messianic interpretation, make שִׁילֹה the *object* of the verb, and translate (1) 'until he (Judah) comes to Shiloh' (the well-known locality in Ephraim); or else (2) 'until he (Judah) comes to rest,' *i.e.* rest in the land of Canaan,—the fulfilment of Jacob's language is in every case removed into a distant future. The same is equally true of the next important prophecy mentioned in the Pentateuch (Numb. xxiv. 17): for whether the 'Star out of Jacob' be an image of the Israelitish royalty in general, or of an actual king like David, or of Christ Himself, *the* king of Israel, a mighty interval exists between the date of the prediction and the earliest fulfilment of it. Other instances are the 2nd and 72nd Psalms, the latter of which Mr. Newman himself urges 'was never fulfilled by any historical king:' *Phases*, p. 194.

[2] Bacon suggests that all interpreters should allow 'that latitude which is agreeable and familiar unto divine prophecies, being of the nature of their Author, with whom a thousand years are but as one day, and therefore are not fulfilled punctually at once, but have springing and germinant accomplishment throughout many ages; though the height or fulness of them may refer to some one age.' *Advancement of Learning*, Bk. II. Works, I. 49. Lond. 1765: cf. Nares, *View of the Prophecies*, pp. 92 sq., Lond. 1805, and Davison, pp. 195 sq.

Law of Moses, in the prophets, and in the Psalms, will be prepared for such phenomena. Whatever they may be to others, they will constitute for him a portion of that marvellous fulness and fertility which characterise the works of the Omnipotent. He sees, for instance, that when prophets of the age of the Captivity foretell the grandeur of the Messianic period, very many of their figures are derived from the anterior age of David. The name[1] of him who governed Israel as the righteous representative of God becomes the name of the Messiah; the seat of empire is the Holy Land; the growth and ultimate glorification of the theocracy is shadowed out as a reunion of Judah and Israel on their return from the dispersion: and why? Because the elder system was in all its parts prophetic; because it typified, and was designed to pass into the later; because the Christ of prophecy was the all-righteous King of Judah, and has verily succeeded to the throne of His father David; because the restoration from captivity was itself an earnest and a prelude of the Messianic deliverance; and because all nations, when they met as brethren in the bosom of the Church of Christ, have recognised in Jerusalem the birth-place and metropolis of the new œconomy, and are ready to exclaim with Jews and proselytes of old, 'All my fresh springs shall be in thee' (Ps. lxxxvii. 7). Or if the sacred writer contemplate the fortunes of the Hebrew commonwealth as in many ways repeated in the life of the Messiah[2]: if he shew, for instance, that our blessed Lord in early childhood was compelled by hard necessity to sojourn in the land of Egypt, finding an asylum in that very region which supplied a cradle to the Hebrew race, such incidents are placed together as related, harmonising and analogous, because the Christ is

[1] See, for example, Ezek. xxxvii. 24, 25, which is peculiarly perplexing to Mr. Newman (*Phases*, p. 193). He fails to perceive that the whole of the prophet's description is *ideal*, though the re-appearance of 'David' on the earth is sufficient to intimate this, and that a barely 'literal' fulfilment is not to be expected. 'The prophecy,' as Mr. Fairbairn remarks, (*Ezekiel*, p. 363) 'is a detailed picture of coming good, drawn, as such a picture must have been, under the form of the old covenant-relations.... The whole earth is as much Christ's rightful heritage as the territory and people of Canaan were David's; and only when it becomes His actual possession can the prophecy respecting Him, as the New Testament David, reach its destined accomplishment.'

[2] Cf. Dr. Mill's *Christ. Adv. Publ.* (1844), pp. 411 sq., who justly observes in treating of a similar case (p. 408): 'There are other matters necessary to the right understanding of sacred prophecies beside the bare rules (which no sane man despises) of grammatical interpretation.'

verily *the* promised Seed; because He is the Head and Antitype of God's collective First-born; and because He only realised in all their fulness the exalted characteristics which Israel as a nation was commissioned to exhibit and diffuse.

And that Hebrews were themselves alive to such ulterior and more perfect realisations of the elder covenant, and frequently discerned the fitness of this ὑπόνοια in the language and general structure of the prophecies, we are enabled to establish fully from their extant literature[1]. They welcomed every voice that issued from the desert with the faintest whispers of Messiah. His birth, His life, His kingdom, widely as they often erred in estimating the nature, colouring and effect of these, were constantly suggested to their thoughts; and therefore when St. Matthew, writing for the special benefit of Jews, alluded to examples where predictions were fulfilled in that higher sense, or when St. Paul, endeavouring to reclaim the Judaizers of Galatia, declared that the arrangements of the Abrahamic family with reference to the child of promise were so ordered as to intimate that such a child must be extraordinary and begotten from above, they neither of them ran the risk of serious misconception, nor were open to the charge of sheltering their arguments beneath a fanciful exegesis.

I grant that earnest minds have varied in their power of tracing and appreciating the great ideas that connect these deeper meanings of the Bible with the naked and more primary sense. I grant that in the present day the general tendency of thought is adverse to such methods of interpretation[2], and that writers who pride themselves on the superiority of their critical acumen are never more successful, in the judgment of the undiscriminating and the superficial, than in their attempts to underrate the mysteries of Holy Scripture. But the course of my argument is not affected by this circumstance. I am

[1] See Schöttgen, *Horæ Hebraicæ*, passim: and Mill, as above, p. 418.

[2] It should, however, be stated that the age is not without examples of a healthier tendency. Thus the reaction in De Wette's mind impelled him to make the following acknowledgment in addition to what has been already cited (p. 59): 'Kein durchaus leeres Spiel war die typologische Vergleichung des A. T. mit dem N. T. Auch ist es schwerlich blosser Zufall, dass *die evangelische Geschichte in den bedeutendsten Momenten der mosaischen parallel geht.* Im Judenthum lag, wie im Keime Blätter und Früchte, das Christenthum. Freilich bedurfte es der göttlichen Sonne um hervorzubrechen.' And Umbreit has very recently (*Studien und Kritiken*, 1855, 3tes Heft, pp. 573 sq.) abandoned the un-Messianic interpretation of Is. vii. 14, which he had formerly endeavoured to establish.

endeavouring to ascertain what were the leading features of the Old-Testament religion as interpreted by persons occupying the position of the Hebrews; and with reference to the topic now before us, it remains indisputable that either owing to the character of their sacred books, or to some other agency, they were emphatically men of hope. In spite of every storm that darkened the immediate future of the Church, they looked with yearning confidence to what they called 'the times of restitution and refreshing,' of peace, forgiveness, and redemption. They took refuge in this 'world to come[1],'—an age when temporal evils would be all corrected or exhausted, when mercy and truth would meet together, and righteousness and peace would kiss each other, when Zion under the benignant rule of Christ would shew herself the mother-city of a world-embracing system, and 'all nations flow' to her for solace and for light.

And it is most observable that, however modern sceptics may account for the origin and intensity of this conviction, its existence at the birth of Christ is now commonly admitted. The recognition of His claims by many of His fellow-countrymen in Palestine and other regions, is attributed to the fact that He was generally expected. And this fact indeed is absolutely necessary to the establishment of the Straussian hypothesis on the composition of the sacred Gospels. The national mind, it is discovered, must have been occupied completely with expectations of some great Deliverer, or ideal portraits such as those ascribed to Jesus of Nazareth by His followers, could not possibly have been conceived. And with this view accords the language of Mr. Mackay, a main pillar of the Absolute Religion. 'The fund of Hebrew hope,' he writes[2], 'was as

[1] Schöttgen, II. 23 sq.: cf. *Ep. to Hebrews*, II. 5, VI. 5. Winer, who is certainly not inclined to overestimate the Divine element in Holy Writ, makes the following statement on this subject: 'Nur in einer Beziehung treten sie [die Propheten] aus ihrem durch die Zeitverhältnisse bedingten Gesichtskreise heraus und richten den Blick des Volks auf eine fern liegende ideale Zukunft, dann nämlich, wenn sie, durch die Betrachtung der nächsten Zukunft nicht befriedigt, von dem grossen Nationalretter (Messias) und dem hochbeglückten Zeitalter reden,' u. s. w. *Realwörterbuch*, s. v. *Propheten*, II. 279, 3rd ed.

[2] *Progress of the Intellect*, II. 209. He refers to the same phenomenon in his later work (*Rise and Progress of Christianity*, p. 15, Lond. 1854): 'Through a long series of misfortunes the Jews had been constantly supported by the expectation of a great deliverer, called emphatically the anointed king, or Messiah, who would restore the ancient glory of their theocracy, or Divine Kingdom, as it existed under David and Solomon, inaugurating at the same time a new reign of righteousness.'

immeasurable as the power of the invisible Sovereign; and it was even anticipated that the prospective kingdom would embrace universal dominion, a dominion coextensive with the theoretical (?) empire of the Deity over the whole earth.' According to Mr. Mackay, the origin of these profound convictions was entirely human and subjective. The Messiah-doctrine, he conjectures[1], was 'a joint product of the misfortunes of the times and of the theocratic constitution,' the experience of a want in this and other instances exciting 'the imagination to fill up the blank out of its own resources.'

But there is one other class of writers whom we ought in fairness to examine before this startling verdict is accepted. We shall always, it is true, be grateful to the advocate of the 'religion of humanity' who confesses the existence of Messianic predictions, or at least discovers new presentiments in favour of the Gospel; yet he must excuse us if, when he proposes such inadequate explanation of the origin of these presentiments, we seek elsewhere for less fantastic guides and more intelligible reasons. Mr. Mackay and his friends may treat the Hebrew prophets as the μαντεῖς, or the preachers, as the rhetoricians, or the improvisatori of the times in which they flourished; he may find in all their loftiest utterances no more than natural guesses of a thoughtful mind, or the creations of an eastern fancy: but we who look at them with different eyes, who have been taught to 'worship the God of our fathers, believing all things which are written in the Law and in the prophets,' shall rather form our estimate of the phenomena in question after hearing what the sacred writers tell us of themselves and of their own experiences.

Now prophecy, in their meaning of the term, is a peculiar characteristic of Revealed Religion. There is doubtless no lack of oracles and divination, of augurs and of fortune-tellers in the various records of the heathen world[2]; but we shall look in vain to them for what is everywhere discovered in the Bible[3].

[1] *Progress of the Intellect*, II. 210.

[2] On the fundamental distinction between prophecy and all forms of heathen divination, see Hävernick, *Einleitung*, II. ii. 29 sq., and J. Smith's chapter on the 'Difference of the true prophetical spirit from all enthusiastical imposture:' *Select Discourses*, pp. 190 sq. Lond. 1660.

[3] Cf. Mr. Morgan's *Christianity and Modern Infidelity*, pp. 120 sq. Lond. 1854. 'The Hebrew Scriptures, then,' writes Archer Butler, 'themselves, and the people and polity which form their singular subject, intimate a wonderful *future*, and point altogether to it, and are wholly inexplicable unless on the supposition of it. This at once distinguishes it [? them] from every other ancient writing of the same

We shall look in vain for series of explicit prophecies, arising not from a mastery which the seer possesses over hidden powers of nature, nor from the effects of some delirious intoxication, where his reasoning faculties are all suspended, but from holy, calm, and conscious intercourse with God Himself, the personal Revealer, who in due time vindicates the character of the prophecy by bringing it to pass. 'Produce your cause, saith the Lord: bring forth your strong reasons, saith the King of Jacob. Let them bring them forth, and shew us what shall happen: let them shew the former things what they be, that we may consider them, and know the latter end of them; or declare us things for to come. Shew the things that are to come hereafter, that we may know that ye are gods[1].' And as Jehovah challenges the idols of the heathen, bidding them establish their title to divinity by putting forth prophetic gifts, so all His messengers were ever conscious of the special nature of their calling, and have drawn the clearest possible distinctions between the true and false in prophecy. 'Woe,' their cry was, 'unto the foolish prophets, that *follow their own spirit, and have seen nothing*' (Ezek. xiii. 3). They were persuaded that the office of the genuine seer had brought him into close communion with the fountain of all knowledge; and prophecy was therefore, in his case, a real opening of things secret, an objective revelation of the plans and purposes of God[2] (Amos iii. 7; Is. xliii. 12). He *saw* what he describes: he was assured of it by some immediate intuition[3]. Exalted to a higher sphere of thought,

kind; *among all national literatures this makes the Jewish unique.*' Sermons, 1st ser. pp. 209, 210, 3rd ed.

[1] Is. xli. 21—23. Bp. Lowth (*Isaiah*, p. 106, Lond. 1778) translates the second member of v. 21: 'Produce these your mighty powers,' making the challenge apply directly to the false divinities. St. Jerome (*in loc.*) sees in the passage an allusion to the fact that heathen oracles were all silenced at the coming of Christ. 'Si ergo suum interitum non potuere prædicere, quomodo aliena, vel mala, vel bona, potuerint nunciare?' He then adds: 'Quod si aliquis dixerit, multa ab idolis esse prædicta, hoc sciendum quod semper mendacium junxerint veritati; et sic sententias temperarint, ut seu boni seu mali quid accidisset, utrumque posset intelligi.'

[2] Witsius in one of his able *Miscellanea* ('De Prophetis et Prophetia') establishes the following definition of prophecy: 'Cognitio et patefactio rerum arcanarum, quas quis non ex propria solertia neque ex aliorum relatu, sed ex cœlesti atque extraordinaria Dei revelatione novit:' Lib. I. c. 2, § 1.

[3] See the recent discussion of this subject in Mr. Lee's *Inspiration of Holy Scripture*, pp. 167 sq. Lond. 1854;—a treatise well deserving the attention of all biblical scholars who rejoice to see exactness of thought combined with fulness of knowledge and a reverential spirit.

admitted to a deeper survey of the world invisible, the prophets for the time were made recipients of supernatural communications. These the Lord Himself presented to them, and these they apprehended by an organ of the soul which corresponded to their outer vision, and which equally convinced them of the truth and objectivity of what they saw. While, on the contrary, all forms of pseudo-prophecy were utterly subjective. There was no external fact according with its utterances, nor with the impulse of the human spirit. The diviner may in many casés have been perfectly sincere, and many of the heathen oracles when consulted on religious questions may have given answers highly calculated to protect the interests of morality: but all their best vaticinations, if not due exclusively to human shrewdness and reflection, were so many vague forebodings and presentiments: they spoke 'out of their own hearts' (Ezek. xiii. 2).

Such then is the grand distinction which the sacred writers uniformly draw between the nature of prophetic visions and all merely human efforts to obtain a knowledge of the will of God, and penetrate the mysteries of the invisible. Yet strange to say, the testimony of the prophets on this subject is rejected by the speculators of the present day, in order to make room for novel theories, wild and arbitrary in their form[1], if not completely pantheistic in their tendency. Where prophecies of redemption are not construed as the mere projections of the human consciousness, or yearnings prompted by the want of some Redeemer, they are all resolved into peculiarities of natural temperament, in such a way as to discard the operation of the Holy Spirit, and repudiate every trace of an objective element. The founder of this school was Benedict de Spinosa. Starting as he did with a belief that God was only a generalised expression for all natural causes, he laboured to obliterate the distinction between a personal Revealer and

[1] Thus, Mr. Edward Strachey, writing on *Hebrew Politics in the times of Sargon and Sennacherib*, (Lond. 1853), does not scruple to make the following unqualified assertion (p. 5): 'The prophets were the preachers, not the predicters, the forth-speakers of God's eternal plan and methods of governing man, not foretellers of particular events of and to their nation. *This was what our Lord and his apostles understood by the name, and so has it always been understood in modern times of earnestness and zeal.*' In a postscript (p. 352) the author adds: 'I have not now first to acknowledge how greatly I owe to Mr. Maurice my principles and method of considering Hebrew prophecy; but their application is my own.'

the subject of the revelation. He held that the real source[1] of all predictions lay in the imaginative faculty; that when the prophets are said to have been full of the Holy Ghost, the meaning is[2] that they were men of singular virtue and exalted piety; and that as their admirers were ignorant of the true causes of prophetic knowledge, they were in the habit of ascribing it, like other portents, to an act of God Himself. As one corollary from his main positions he contended that 'prophetic' gifts were not peculiar[3] to the Hebrew nation, but diffused in every part of heathendom. These principles when first advanced by Spinosa were generally execrated as 'atheistic;' but after passing through the crucible of certain German theologians[4], they are not unfrequently espoused in England by the friends of progress, and the adherents of the Absolute Religion. In spite of all the protests which their authors have inserted to the contrary, the prophecies in general, not excluding those which are entitled Messianic, are stripped of their divine authority, and treated as the outbreak of an ardent patriotism, a feverish zeal, or an exuberant imagination.

I grant indeed that some few sparks of truth may be detected here and there amid the theorisings of this modern school. The prophet, for example, never lost his individuality[5].

[1] *Tractatus Theologico-Politici*, c. II. p. 15, Hamburg, 1670. 'Qui igitur,' it is added, 'sapientiam, et veram naturalium et spiritualium cognitionem ex Prophetarum libris investigare student, tota errant via: quod, quoniam tempus, philosophia et denique res ipsa postulat, hic fuse ostendere decrevi, parum curans quid superstitio oggานniat, quæ nullos magis odit quam qui veram scientiam, veramque vitam colunt.'

[2] *Ibid.* c. I. p. 13.

[3] He infers this chiefly from the case of Balaam, who although a true prophet is called by Joshua (xiii. 22) הַקּוֹסֵם, the 'diviner.' But see Kurtz, *Gesch. des Alten Bundes*, II. 457 sq., where it is shewn (after Hengstenberg) that Balaam was really verging to the confines of heathen magic, though he had not altogether lost his early faith in the One true God.

[4] The name of Schleiermacher must be added to this number. His views respecting the Old Testament in general were most derogatory. For instance, he maintains the following position in his treatise *Der Christliche Glaube* (I. 77 sq. 3rd ed. Berlin, 1835): 'Das Christenthum steht zwar in einem besonderen geschichtlichen Zusammenhange mit dem Judenthum; was aber sein geschichtliches Dasein und seine Abzweckung betrifft, so verhält es sich zu Judenthum und Heidenthum gleich.' With regard to the Messianic predictions of the Old Testament, he observes (*Ibid.* p. 96) that their chief value to us arises from the evidence they furnish of a 'striving of human nature towards Christianity,' and of the preparatory aim of earlier institutions: cf. p. 80.

[5] Cf. Lee, as above, p. 179; Fairbairn, *Ezekiel*, Pref. p. vii.

His natural faculties were not suspended nor coerced by the incoming of a higher agency. The style, the language, the poetic colouring, the restricted knowledge of all subjects not designed to be included in the scope of the prediction, were his own. He was an inspired *man*, the human and Divine factors coalescing, harmonising, and co-operating in the exhibition of the thing revealed. But after these concessions have been made, it seems to me unquestionable, that no theory will explain the statements of the sacred prophets, nor account for the sublime phenomena of revelation, which neglects to recognise in prophecy the workings of a supernatural Agent, opening, elevating and directing the spirit of the seers, presenting to their inner vision images of things to come, and thus supplying an objective and historic basis for the faith and aspirations of the Israelite. And such is certainly the view adopted by the writers of the New Testament. Respecting that salvation which has been accomplished in Christianity, the prophets are said to have 'inquired and searched diligently, who prophesied of the grace that should come unto us; searching what, or what manner of time the Spirit of Christ which was in them did signify, when it testified beforehand the sufferings of Christ, and the glory that should follow' (1 Pet. i. 10, 11): 'for prophecy came not in old time by the will of man; but holy men of God spake as they were moved by the Holy Ghost' (2 Pet. i. 21).

Nor are those the only criteria by which genuine prophecy is separable from all human substitutes, and from the auguries and divinations of the heathen world. It stood from first to last in vital union with monotheism: it kept pace with the expansion of man's faculties, and aided in the gradual training of the sacred commonwealth. As one agent in the mighty course of operations that has issued in the planting of a catholic Church, its form and structure were peculiarly adapted to the exigencies of the period[1] out of which it grew. Pro-

[1] This peculiarity was noticed long ago by St. Augustine (*Epist.* CII. § 15: *Opp.* II. 211, ed. Bened.); 'Et tamen ab initio generis humani, alias occultius, alias evidentius, *sicut congruere temporibus* divinitus visum est, nec prophetari destitit, nec qui in eum crederent defuerunt, ab Adam usque ad Moysen, et in ipso populo Israel, quæ speciali quodam mysterio gens prophetica fuit, et in aliis gentibus antequam venisset in carne.' Mr. Trench, *Hulsean Lectures* (1845) p. 86, suggests the same thought: 'And thus (did time allow) we might trace in much more detail how not only in the idea of type and prophecy there is obedience to that law of advance and progress, which we have everywhere been finding, but in the very order and sequence of the prophecies themselves.'

phecy, in other words, was so completely interwoven with the fortunes of the Abrahamic race as to supply continual answers in the moment of perplexity, and even to convert the darkest epochs of their lifetime into fresh occasions for directing them to the Messiah, and that period when they should 'receive of the Lord's hand double for all their sins.' While the presentiments that rose in other countries were but dim and floating visions of the night, with nothing in the past or present where they could attach themselves, and therefore destitute of moral power and practical results; the Messianic doctrine of the Hebrews was real, living, and coherent. In their nation where it is confessed[1] no period seems to have existed when the 'historical sense' was not developed, prophecy obtained immense advantages by calling to its aid the associative faculty[2], by clothing future incidents in imagery consecrated by the memories of the past, and finding in the altered aspects of society a stock of fresh material[3] for increasing the vividness of its descriptions and the area of its field of vision.

Prophecy was thus the living voice of God that went along continually with the development of the Hebrew nation. When it spoke the parched and joyless desert seemed to blossom like the rose, and minister fresh streams of comfort and of blessing: men 'drank of the spiritual Rock which followed them, and that Rock was Christ.' It smoothed the pillow of the dying patriarch, convincing him that there was still some better and enduring substance in reserve: it taught his children to

[1] Grote's *Hist. of Greece*, I. 492, Lond. 1849. This writer thinks that the 'historical sense' did not arise in the superior intellects of Greece till B.C. 700.

[2] Cf. Mr. Lee's remarks on this subject (*Inspiration of Holy Scripture*, pp. 149 sq.) which he introduces in the following passage: 'In considering the single predictions of Scripture apart from the complete structure of Prophecy, we may observe, that a certain method has been almost uniformly pursued, which constitutes, as it were, the *Law* according to which the different portions of God's Revelation have been communicated;—namely, that each prediction, with scarcely an exception, proceeds from and attaches itself to some definite fact in the historical present.'

[3] 'Mir ist die Weissagung eine objective Mittheilung göttlichen Wissens an den Menschen, aber eine solche, die den Zuständen der jedesmaligen Gegenwart sich lebendig anschliesst, ihren Bedürfnissen entgegenkommt, den Factoren der Entwicklung sich organisch einfügt. Die Abhängigkeit der Weissagung von der Geschichte ist für mich keine andre als die, dass Gott die Samenkörner der Weissagung nicht eher ausstreut, als bis durch die von Ihm gelenkte Geschichte der Boden bereitet ist, dessen das Samenkorn bedarf, um Wurzel zu schlagen und Frucht zu bringen.' Kurtz, *Gesch. des Alten Bundes*, II. 550.

exclaim, as Jacob did before them: 'I have waited for Thy salvation, O Lord' (Gen. xlix. 18). It inspired the Israelites, when they went forth a youthful people with the Lord Jehovah at their head, to occupy the soil which He had promised to their fathers. It consoled them in the midst of sterner scenes at Horeb; it allayed the apprehensions there awakened by the awful promulgation of the Decalogue; and as 'the light that shineth in a dark place,' it pointed to the possibility of milder institutions and the coming of a second Legislator[1]. It grew more definite and explicit in proclaiming the Messiah, when an actual kingdom had been founded in Judæa, when the conquests of the son of Jesse had well-nigh exhausted the more secular branches of the Abrahamic promise, and the faithful had before their eyes a noble champion of the true religion. During all that gloomy series of disasters which ensued on the degeneracy of Solomon, and the divulsion of the sacred tribes, the deep-toned voice of prophecy was heard with greater frequency alike in Israel and in Judah. It guided and sustained a remnant of both countries by unfolding to their view the picture of reunion and enlargement, when after some thorough sifting of the Hebrew race, the fallen tabernacle of David[2] would be re-established in the midst of them; when exiles would return to 'seek the Lord their God, and David their king[3];' when enemies of truth and righteousness would disappear like some majestic forest; while the Branch[4] emerging

[1] See Deut. xviii. 15—19, Acts iii. 22, vii. 37, Hebr. xii. 18, 19: and cf. Sherlock, Disc. VI. pp. 127 sq. That the Jews and also the Samaritans of our Lord's age adopted the Messianic interpretation is rendered highly probable by John vi. 14, v. 45—47, iv. 25. Some writers in modern times have argued that a general reference to the 'prophetic order' of the Old Testament is included in the word נָבִיא; while they maintain, however, that the one Prophet in whom the idea of such an order was fully realised, is the Messiah. See the arguments in favour of both views in Hengstenberg, *Christology of the Old Testament*, I. 95 sq. Edinb. 1854, and Kurtz, *Gesch. des Alten Bundes*, II. 513 sq. The latter expresses himself 'unconditionally for the exclusive reference to a single definite Person, *i.e.* to the Messiah' (p. 514).

[2] Amos ix. 11, 12: cf. Acts xv. 16, 17, and Hengstenberg, *Ibid.* I. 314 sq.

[3] Hosea iii. 4, 5. Hengstenberg (*Ibid.* I. 282) observes that 'by the *king David* the whole Davidic house is to be understood, which is here to be considered as an unity, in the same manner as is done in 2 Sam. vii. and in a whole series of Psalms which celebrate the mercies shewn, and to be shewn, to David and his house. These mercies are most fully concentrated in Christ.'

[4] Cf. Is. x. 33, 34 (where the proud armies of Assyria are mentioned under the figure of a mighty

from the roots of Jesse would embrace the world beneath His shadow, would inaugurate a brighter era, would be called the Wonderful Counsellor, the Mighty God, the Everlasting Father, the Prince of Peace. When heavier ills descended, when the temple was itself defiled, and when the latest caravan of captives brought the tragic news of this calamity to Babylon, the land of the oppressor, it was still the Messianic promise of a righteous King and an eternal kingdom, that came forward to sustain the drooping spirit of the solitary mourner. And when at length the voice of prophecy was going to be hushed entirely, when the Church was to be left in solemn stillness, waiting for the manifestation of the glory of the Lord, the latest breath of Malachi, though stern and terrible for Israelites[1] who would not rise to any true conception of the Messianic character, was full of hope and solace for the rest: it intimated the approach of times when every Gentile nation would unite in prayer and offerings with the holier section of the Hebrews, and the Sun of Righteousness arise with healing in His wings (Mal. i. 11; iv. 2).

Abundant illustrations of this view of prophecy, elucidating the fitness of the various seasons when it spoke, and its peculiar adaptation to the wants, the faculties, and prospects of the Hebrews, are furnished in all parts of the sacred volume: but my present purpose will be answered if I draw attention to the age of David and the Babylonic exile.

(1) In order to retain the Hebrews in the attitude of expectation, the time at which the Messianic promise would be realised was always indeterminate; and therefore when the sceptre came at length into the hands of David, many an eye would turn to him with ardent longing, and behold in him that son of Abraham, on whom their faith had long been centered. 'Is this not he that should come?' may well have been the general question. 'Peace is everywhere established from Dan to Beersheba; Moab, Ammon, Edom, and Philistia, who have hitherto curtailed our borders and wasted the flower of our armies, are content to rank among the vassals of the sacred

forest) with the opening verses of Is. xi. That the mysterious 'Child' of Is. ix. 6 is identical with the 'Immanuel' of Is. vii. 14, and both of them with the eternal 'Ruler' pointed out by a contemporary (Micah v. 2 sq.), can scarcely admit of any question.

[1] See, for example, Zech. xi. where many of the Israelites are shewn symbolically to be filling up the measure of their fathers by rejecting the Good Shepherd; and in Malachi iii. 1—3, the Messenger of the Covenant whom they professed to delight in enters on His work by sifting not the heathen but the sacred family itself.

family; the last fortress of the Canaanite has been reduced; and he who was the guiding spirit of those mighty operations is the head and life of our religious system. His hymns are on every tongue, and he has vowed that he will never rest until the worship of the Lord is firmly planted in his new metropolis, and also in the heart and conscience of his people.'

Now this juncture was the time selected for relieving men's disquietude, and pouring a fresh flood of light upon the Promise. The well-known intimations then conveyed to David form the basis of all future prophecies. Israel was instructed that his kingdom would supply the origin and groundwork of a greater, that when David had been gathered to his fathers, a posterity[1] descended from his loins would rear a temple to Jehovah; and that the throne of this posterity would be established for ever, yea, that God would be to it a Father, and it would be to Him a son (2 Sam. vii. 11—14). When Solomon was born this prophecy indeed *began* to be accomplished, and was more entirely brought to pass when he completed the erection of the temple, and the glory of the Lord was visible within its courts: yet he might learn from David to extend his views into the distant future[2], and appears himself to have been conscious that his own achievements were utterly unable to exhaust the fulness of its meaning (1 Kings viii. 26, 27). From this time, however, the Messiah was expected as *the* King, the King of Israel, exalted on the throne of David, and, in virtue of His close communion with the Lord Jehovah, an object of universal reverence,

[1] The word is still זֶרַע (cf. above, p. 89, n. 1), and may therefore be understood collectively, *i.e.* of descendants in general, but as constituting an ideal unity. That the reference is not exclusively to Christ we must infer from vv. 14, 15: while, on the other hand, none but a superhuman Personage could realise the absolute perpetuity of the race, and fully satisfy the remaining conditions of the prophecy: cf. Acts ii. 30. On its intimate connexion with Ps. ii. and the light which is thereby thrown upon it, see Ebrard, *On the Epistle to the Hebrews*, pp. 39, 40, Edinb. 1853.

[2] In 2 Sam. vii. 19, David says, in his address to the Almighty, 'Thou hast spoken also to Thy servant's house of things far distant' (לְמֵרָחוֹק); adding the remarkable words וְזֹאת תּוֹרַת הָאָדָם אֲדֹנָי יֱהוִֹה, which, as compared with 1 Chron. xvii. 17, are thought by some to indicate the superhuman rank of the Messiah. See the different renderings in Mr. Barrett's *Synopsis of Criticisms*, II. 545 sq. Immediately before his death we find David occupied with the same magnificent thoughts respecting the destiny of his house (2 Sam. xxiii. 5): 'For is not my house so with God? For He hath made with me an everlasting covenant, ordered in all things and sure; for all my salvation and all my pleasure, should He not make it grow?'

exercising justice and dispensing mercy to the various families of men.

The Hebrews thus obtained one definite image of the Christ; an image which enabled every thoughtful mind among them to approximate more closely to a true conception of the great Deliverer. But the humanity of Christ was not the only characteristic which the prophet of that period was commissioned to unveil. A hymn[1] composed by David on a subsequent occasion represents his future Son returning as a warrior from conflicts where His enemies were miserably put to flight, and traces at the same time His majestic course to more than human impulses. The Son of David as there pictured occupies a most exalted station. He is David's Lord as well: He sits on no earthly throne, but at the side of God, the Unapproachable, a sharer of His glory, and a joint-administrator of His Kingdom.

And in order to prepare the Hebrew mind for still more wondrous revelations, and in order to exalt the thoughts and spiritualise the feelings with respect to their Messiah, and the elevation of His throne from earth to heaven, this passage also represents the Son and Lord of David in a different aspect, and a totally distinct capacity. The Law of Moses furnished no idea of any priesthood in connexion with the tribe of Judah (Heb. vii. 14): the union of royal and sacerdotal offices was made impossible by the arrangements of the old œconomy; and yet the Christ is there seen by David invested with the dignities of both[2]. He is the Priest-king of the Hebrews, in order that some work of expiation may be accomplished before a people are prepared to offer themselves willingly to God, and so be worthy of enlistment in the cause of the Messiah, and of sharing in His universal conquests.

But this image of the Priest, suggesting as it does the thought of sacrifice, reminds us of new lessons which the Psalms of David would impress on every one who waited for redemption in Israel. It might indeed have been anticipated from the first that He who undertook the office of our Champion would encounter the resistance of the evil power which com-

[1] Ps. cx. which is continually cited in the New Testament as David's and as also Messianic; *e.g.* by our Lord Himself, Matth. xxii. 43 sq.: cf. Hengstenberg, *On the Psalms*, III. 326 sq.

[2] See the remarkable parallel in Zech. vi. 12, 13, where the Man, whose name is the Branch, sits and rules as a Priest upon the throne, and the royal and sacerdotal offices are united in His person ('the counsel of peace shall be between them both').

passed our defeat and ruin; yet never till the age of David was the Church invited to reflect distinctly on the picture of a Christ involved in danger, suffering and humiliation. The persecutions and distresses of the Israelitish monarch, and the obloquy which he endured in his attempts to vindicate the true religion, and promote the welfare of his country (Ps. lxix.), had prepared men for the thought that even righteous princes may not claim to be exempted[1] from the evils incident to our condition while on earth; and therefore had prepared them in some measure for the wondrous revelations of the 22nd Psalm. The servant of the Lord is there assailed by every species of malicious mockery. His enemies have pierced his hands and feet, and parted his garments among them; and, unsated by this foul barbarity, they feast their eyes upon the spectacle, and heighten his distress by shouts of savage exultation. Now in reading such a psalm as this, a thoughtful Israelite may well ask his neighbour, 'Of whom speaketh the prophet? of himself, or of some other man?' and when no adequate fulfilment of that language can be traced in circumstances of the period, he will naturally regard it as predictive of some future sufferer; while the closing portions[2] of the Psalm compel him to identify that Sufferer with the glorious King he is expecting. For notwithstanding the extreme violence of persecution, the holy speaker is not overwhelmed by it. He is conscious that Jehovah interposes for his rescue, and he therefore registers a vow that he will dedicate to God a special service of thanksgiving; that high and low, of Israel and of every nation under heaven, shall be invited to a sacrificial feast, and join in celebrating his deliverance to all future ages. The truth appears

[1] The same lesson was forcibly inculcated in the whole Book of Job. 'By the side of a long line of prophecy, as a whole outwardly gorgeous and flattering, and promising in the Messiah a successful potentate and opener of a glorious temporal future for the Jewish nation, there rose one sad but faithful memento, and all that appearance of approaching splendour was seen in qualifying connexion with other truths.' *Christian Remembrancer* (1849), p. 208.

[2] The transition takes place at v. 22, and the magnificent picture of the whole world, as one result of the deliverance of God's servant, consecrating themselves to Jehovah, can only be realised in Gospel times. Τούτων γὰρ οὐδὲν ἐπὶ τοῦ Δαβὶδ ὁρῶμεν γεγενημένον, οὐδὲ ἐπί τινος τῶν ἐκ Δαβίδ. Μόνος δὲ ὁ Δεσπότης Χριστὸς, ὁ ἐκ Δαβὶδ κατὰ σάρκα, ὁ ἐνανθρωπήσας Θεὸς λόγος, ὁ ἐκ Δαβὶδ λαβὼν τὴν τοῦ δούλου μορφήν. Πᾶσαν γὰρ γῆν καὶ θάλασσαν τῆς θεογνωσίας ἐπλήρωσε, καὶ πέπεικε τοὺς πάλαι πλανωμένους, καὶ τοῖς εἰδώλοις προσφέροντας τὴν προσκύνησιν, ἀντὶ τῶν οὐκ ὄντων, τὸν ὄντα προσκυνῆσαι Θεόν. Theodoret, *in Psalm.* xxi: *Opp.* Tom. I. 481, Paris, 1642.

to be that David on this and other like occasions spoke not merely for himself, but in the name of his posterity; nor is it difficult to trace a reason why the Psalms should bring to light the bitter sufferings of the king Messiah, and why earlier ages should be left comparatively ignorant of such truths. The Hebrew Church was, under David, passing from a state of meanness and depression, into one of ease, prosperity and triumph. As a nation they began to feel their outward and material strength, and therefore ran the risk of sinking down into voluptuous self-security. If the idea of their Messiah had not been lost entirely, they might still have learned with many of their children in the days of Christ to picture Him as nothing but a temporal prince, combining the military strength of David with the peaceful pomp of Solomon. Checks were, therefore, given to these earthly tendencies by stating prominently how David suffered, and associating with this fact another truth, that sorrow and humiliation were reserved for his descendant. The unworldly visage of the Crucified was now uplifted for the study of the Hebrew Church[1]: the sufferings of Messiah were revealed as necessary preconditions of His universal empire and of the glory that should follow.

(2) We shall see, if I mistake not, further illustrations of these characteristics, or rather of this law of prophecy, if we turn to the disastrous age of the Captivity. How heavy a blow was then inflicted on the house of David and the hopes of all the Israelites! The kingdom of the ten tribes had been already 'broken from being a people:' they had fallen to the heathen level of impurity and licence, and were swallowed up in the Assyrian empire. In the meanwhile partial reformations of the neighbouring state of Judah had in vain put off the evil day; corruption seemed incarnate in the person of Jehoiachin; the Hebrew Church was ripe for chastisement, and ready to pass under an eclipse: the promises of God were on the point of abrogation: the visibility of the theocracy was going to be lost;

[1] 'Et encore que le règne de ce grand Messie soit souvent prédit dans les Écritures sous des idées magnifiques, Dieu n'a point caché à David les ignominies de ce bénit fruit de ses entrailles. Cette instruction était nécessaire au peuple de Dieu. Si ce peuple encore infirme avait besoin d'être attiré par des promesses temporelles, il ne fallait pas pourtant lui laisser regarder les grandeurs humaines comme sa souveraine félicité et comme son unique récompense: c'est pourquoi Dieu montre de loin ce Messie tant promis et tant désiré, le modèle de la perfection et l'objet de ses complaisances, abîmé dans la douleur. La croix paraît à David comme le trône véritable de ce nouveau roi.' Bossuet, *Discours sur l'Hist. Universelle*, Partie II. § 4.

and all the members of the sacred commonwealth abandoned to the grasp of an imperious and blaspheming power. Yet the very moment when the prophet Jeremiah was commissioned to foretel this dread calamity, when he published what must have appeared to many the death-warrant of his nation, was also chosen as the time for granting to the Church a further glimpse of blessings to be afterwards her own. The picture of recovery from the power of Babylon appears to break entirely through the background of more gloomy visions, and the menace of the stern reformer ultimately softens down into an evangelic benediction[1]. Although the royalty of such a ruler as Jehoiachin must perish, and although his house shall never prosper, 'behold the days come, saith the Lord, that I will raise unto David a righteous Branch, and a King *shall* reign and prosper;' like his prototype the ancient David (2 Sam. viii. 15), 'he shall execute judgment and justice in the earth.' The tribes who constituted the ideal Church of God shall be hereafter reinstated in their lost possessions; the sacred family shall inherit every blessing that was then associated with residence in Canaan, and proximity to God Himself; and so great will be this restoration that the old deliverance from the land of Egypt will cease to be the turning-point of Hebrew history. Its memories will be all absorbed by those of the Messiah, and the consciousness of true redemption. After a second passage through the wilderness, a moral isolation in the desert of the nations (Ezek. xx. 35, 36), there will be a glorious coming back to Zion, and a fresh incorporation in the family of God.

But in addition to this general fitness of the shape assumed by the Messianic promise, its republication at the time of the Captivity had one peculiar feature. In the leading prophets of the age (in Jeremiah and Ezekiel), there are plain allusions to a new œconomy[2], different and distinct from that originally confirmed with Israel on their exodus from Egypt. In this new covenant God no longer writes His law externally, so as to render it a cold series of mandates and requirements, but imparting first of all the remission of sins, imparts therewith

[1] Cf. Jerem. xxii. 30 with xxiii. 5 sq. In Ezek. xxi. 25—27 we have the same kind of contrast; the period of suffering and desolation was to continue only till the age of the Messiah, 'until he comes to whom the judgment, or the right, belongs,' and then would follow a time of restoration when the mitre and the crown are transferred to Him in all their glory: cf. above, p. 105, n. 2.

[2] Jerem. xxxi. 31—34, Ezek. xxxvi. 22—33, on the latter of which passages see Fairbairn's *Ezekiel*, pp. 342 sq.

fresh impulses in aid of man's obedience, and exalts the character of his worship by making it spontaneous, the outpouring of a warm and renovated heart. Nay, such a change was shewn to be essential in all Israelites who wished for reinstatement in the favour of Jehovah, and the visible tokens of His goodness.

Now what period in the history of the Jews was more propitious for the inculcation of these truths? So long as they remained in Palestine, so long as the continuity of their national existence was unbroken, and so long as all the ordinances of the Law were celebrated with their former regularity, the worshipper might seldom realise the possibility of fundamental changes in the system under which he lived. But when the sanctuary itself was levelled with the ground, when sacrifices were no longer offered, when the priest and people had been left to mourn the desolation of their country, some while clinging to its wretched ruins, others in their lonely musings by the streams of Babylon, how much was there in an emergency like this to lift their thoughts above the legal institutions, and constrain them to reflect on better things to come! How local and how limited those institutions would appear to men, whom change of place prevented from complying with them! How full of deep suggestions on the differences between the real and symbolical, the moral and the ceremonial, the perfect and the partial, the future and the past! And if we glance at the predictions of Daniel, and still more at those of Zechariah, we discover how entirely both these prophets were enabled to detach themselves from old associations, how the earthly and material temple is replaced by one not made with hands; and, in a word, how Christian subjects stand completely out, and fill the vision of the seer.

Thus in spite of all the sternness of the legal institute; in spite of all the trials, troubles, and reverses which befel the race on whom that yoke had been 'imposed until the time of reformation,' no feeling of despondence was ever generated in the bosom of the Israelites. On the contrary, the elder system died in hope; or rather its development was closed by giving birth to Christianity. Those innumerable threads of golden light, that run through all the annals of the Hebrew nation, went on increasing both in number and variety, until they met harmoniously in Him, from whose abundance they had issued, by whose Spirit they were scattered in the ancient world, at sundry times, in divers manners. The grand Subject of prediction came at last. He took our human nature, died that we might live, and reigns that we may triumph. He is 'the Root and the Offspring of David, and the bright and morning Star.' The Christian, therefore, can appropriate every word of the exalted song which gushed originally from the heart of one that stood upon the very confines of the new œconomy, and that spoke in sight of him whose ministry was destined to become the living link connecting Law and Prophets with the Gospel: 'Blessed be the Lord God of Israel, for He hath visited and redeemed His people, and hath raised up an horn of salvation for us in the house of His servant David; as He spake by the mouth of His holy prophets, which have been since the world began.'

If it be found hereafter on a strict examination of their sacred books and other ancient documents that nearly all the heathen systems were defective in those very points which form the leading characteristics of Revealed Religion; if the general tendency of pagan thought was in philosophers to pantheism, or the worship of nature as a whole, and in the many to polytheism, or the deification of particular energies of nature; if sin was there regarded as eternal and as necessary, or in other cases as unreal, notwithstanding those frequent reclamations of the moral consciousness that drove men to devise new rites of worship, and to rear new altars in honour of the 'unknown' divinity: if being thus 'without God in the world,' the heathen were also 'without hope,' the victims in their thoughtful moments of distracting doubts, of abject terror, and of withering desperation, we may thence derive not only a fresh stock of motives for disseminating truths that we possess, but special reasons for abstaining from all heathenish speculations, and for listening with more docile spirit to 'the oracles of God.'

APPENDIX I.

The Absolute Religion.

THE following extracts will give the reader a complete view of the 'reforms' demanded by the advocates of what they term 'the absolute religion,' or, 'the religion of humanity.' Mr. Parker has the credit of being, if not their most cultivated, certainly their most intelligible exponent, and we therefore draw our first quotations from his works. In his *Discourse of Matters pertaining to Religion* (cheap reprint, London, 1850, pp. 180, 181), he tells us:

'Christianity agrees generally with all other forms in this, that it is a religion. Its peculiarity is not in its doctrine of one Infinite God, of the immortality of man, nor of future retribution. It is not in particular rules of morality; for precepts as true and beautiful may be found in heathen writers, who give us the same view of man's nature, duty and destination. The great doctrines of Christianity were known long before Christ; for God did not leave man four thousand years unable to find out his plainest duty......Every imperfect form of Religion was, more or less, an anticipation of Christianity. So far as a man has real Religion, so far he has Christianity. This is as old as the human race. By its light Zoroaster, Confucius, Socrates, with many millions of holy souls, walked in the early times of the world.'

In an earlier chapter of the same work (pp. 71, 72), Mr. Parker gives us further insight into the 'paradise' of his religion:

'In passing judgment on these different religious states [*viz.* Fetichism, Polytheism, and Monotheism], we are never to forget that there is no monopoly of Religion by any nation or any age. Religion itself is one and the same. He that worships truly, by whatever form, worships the Only God. He hears the prayer, whether called Brahma, Jehovah, Pan, or Lord; or called by no name at all. Each people has its prophets and its saints; and many a swarthy Indian, who bowed down to wood and stone—many a grim-faced Calmuck, who worshipped the great God of storms—many a Grecian peasant, who did homage to Phœbus-Apollo when the Sun rose, or went down—yes, many a savage, his hands smeared all over with human sacrifice, shall come forth from the east and west, and sit down in the Kingdom of God, with Moses and Zoroaster, with Socrates and Jesus,' &c.

A later work by the same author, entitled *Theism, Atheism, and the Popular Theology*, Lond. 1853, Introd. p. xxvi, contains a fuller development of his eclectic principles:

'Luther,' he says, 'endeavoured to make new ecclesiastical raiment for mankind, tired of attempting to mend and wear the old and ill-fitting clothes of the church, which became only the worse for botching. In the present time there is the same problem: to gather from the past, from the Bible, from the Catholic and Protestant Churches, from Jew and Gentile, Buddhist, Brahman, and Mahometan, every old truth which they have got embalmed in their precious treasures; and then to reach out and upwards towards God and get every new truth that we can, and join all these together into a whole of theological truth—then to deepen the consciousness of God in our own soul, and make the Absolute Religion the daily life of men.'

Again (pp. 132, 133):

'As "Christian Theology" professes to be derived from a verbal revelation of God,—represented, by the Church, as the Catholics say; by the Scripture, as the Protestants teach,—so the Absolute Religion is derived from the real revelation of God, which is contained in the Universe; this outward universe of matter, this inward universe of man; and I take it we do not require the learned and conscientious labours of a Lardner, a Paley, or a Newton, to convince us that the Universe is genuine and authentic, and is the work of God, without interpolation. We all know that. I call this the Absolute Religion, because it is drawn from the absolute and ultimate source; because it gives us the Absolute Idea of God,—God as Infinite; and because it guarantees to man his natural rights, and demands the performance of the absolute duties of human nature:' cf. pp. 263, 264, where Mr. Parker throws additional light upon his theory by telling us what he does *not* believe. The residuum, it appears from that passage, is slight indeed (quoted above, p. 17).

Mr. W. J. Fox (*The Religious Ideas*, Lond. 1849) evinces that he too has departed from the older 'Unitarian' views, and set up what he calls a 'religion of humanity.' It is substantially the same as Mr. Parker's. He informs us that the source of all revelation is the 'moral constitution of human nature, the human mind and heart' (p. 66); that religions are not revealers by virtue of what is peculiar to them, but 'in what is common to them with other religions' (p. 49); adding that 'what they have as a peculiarity is something which will ill bear the test of time, as compared with what is essential.' We are afterwards told that his religion of humanity is not subordinated to the influences of climate, but is always the same, is found wherever man is found, 'common in sense, and reason, thought and feeling, mind and heart:' that 'it is free from the collisions which ever attend specific theologies,' &c. (pp. 166, 167).

The same general principles pervade the different writings of Mr. R. W. Mackay, being enunciated in the most startling form at the commencement of his *Sketch of the Rise and Progress of Christianity*, Lond. 1854. He tells us, for example, that 'to the truths already uttered in the Athenian prison, Christianity added little or nothing, except a few symbols, which though perhaps well calculated for popular acceptance, are more likely to perplex than to instruct, and offer the best opportunity for priestly mystification' (pp. 19, 20).

Again (p. 21):

'If Christianity so much resembles its antecedents, containing positively nothing which may not be satisfactorily accounted for as a spontaneous development of thought or natural requirement of the mind and heart, why unfairly divorce it from historical analogies; why need we be astonished, or allow our astonishment to represent as marvellous or miraculous a modification rendered inevitable, and which indeed was already pre-established in the mind before Christianity supplied a symbol for expressing it.'

But the very ablest organ by which the principles of the Absolute Religion are advocated in this country is the *Westminster Review*. A favourable specimen is subjoined:

'It is not the *presence* of God in antiquity, but his presence *only* there,—not his inspiration in Palestine, but his withdrawal from every spot besides,—not his supreme and unique expression in Jesus of Nazareth, but his absence from every other human medium,—against which these writers protest. They feel that the usual Christian advocate has adopted a narrow and even irreligious ground; that he has not found a satisfactory place in the Divine scheme of human affairs for the great Pagan world; that he has presumptuously branded all history but one as "profane;" that he has not only read it without sympathy and reverence, but has used it chiefly as a foil to shew off the beauty of evangelic truth and holiness, and so has dwelt only on the inadequacy of its philosophy, the deformity of its morals, the degenerate features of its social life; that he has forgotten the Divine infinitude when he assumes that Christ's plenitude of the Spirit implies the emptiness of Socrates. In their view, he has rashly undertaken to prove, not *one positive* fact,—a revelation of Divine truth in Galilee;—but an *infinite negative;*—no inspiration anywhere else. To this *negation* and to this alone is their remonstrance addressed. They do not deny a *theophany* in the gift of Christianity; but they deny two very different things, viz. 1, That this is the *only* theophany; and 2, That this is theophany *alone;* that is, they look for *some* divine elements elsewhere, and they look for *some* human here. It is not therefore a smaller, but a larger, religious obligation to history, which they are anxious to establish; and they remain in company with the Christian advocate so long as his devout and gentle mood continues; and only quit him when he enters on his sceptical antipathies.' (July, 1852, pp. 203, 204.)

It is instructive to place in contrast with these views of Christianity the main positions of one of its more learned assailants before the birth of Spiritualism and the discovery of the Absolute Religion.

Dupuis, *Origine de tous les Cultes* (new ed. Paris, 1822, pp. 181, 182), after citing examples of correspondency between the doctrines and ceremonies of Hebraism and those of the Persian religion, as represented by Hyde, proceeds as follows: 'Il nous suffit des traits que nous avons rassemblés pour faire voir qu'il n'y a rien de nouveau dans la secte des Chrétiens, rien qui soit à elle, et qu'elle a absolument le caractère de toutes les religions orientales et en particulier de celle des Perses, à laquelle nous la rapportons comme à sa source. Nous nous sommes attachés à saisir le caractère ou le génie original des religions des grands peuples de l'Asie et de l'Afrique, des Égyptiens, Phéniciens, Arabes, Phrygiens et Perses, parceque c'est du sein de ces peuples qu'est sortie la religion de Christ, dont le berceau est en Orient et presque au centre des nations ci-dessus nommées.'

'Nous avons vu que la grande divinité de ces pays était le soleil adoré sous différens noms, Osiris en Égypte, Bacchus en Arabie, Adonis en Phénicie, Atys en Phrygie, Mithra en Perse, etc. Nous avons observé que, dans toutes ces religions, le Dieu-soleil était personnifié,' &c.

He afterwards undertakes to establish the agreement between the

Christian and other 'mythologies' in point of doctrine, not ascribing it to any other necessary evolution of human thought, but rather to external derivation:

'Nous ferons voir également que la théologie des Chrétiens est fondée sur les mêmes principes que celles des païens, Égyptiens, Grecs, Chaldéens, Indiens, et qu'elle renferme les mêmes idées que celles qui faisaient partie de la métaphysique universellement reçue quand le christianisme a paru. On reconnaîtra que leurs docteurs parlent le même langage qu'on parlait dans les écoles les plus fameuses de ce siècle-là, en sorte que la religion des Chrétiens, dans sa partie théologique comme dans sa partie cosmologique, n'a rien que n'appartienne aux autres religions, et qui ne s'y retrouve bien des siècles avant l'établissement du christianisme, et cela de l'aveu des auteurs chrétiens, de leurs pères qui nous fournissent presque toutes les autorités sur lesquelles est appuyée notre démonstration. Ainsi, nous pouvons dire à juste titre: Nil sub sole novum.' (p. 192.)

PART II.

RELIGIONS OF INDIA.

RELIGIONS OF INDIA.

CHAPTER I.

Varieties of Religious Thought among the Hindús.

'Εν τῇ σοφίᾳ τοῦ Θεοῦ οὐκ ἔγνω ὁ κόσμος διὰ τῆς σοφίας τὸν Θεόν.

Alexander's expedition to India. Unhistorical character of the Hindú mind. Date of Hindú civilisation. § I. Védaism. The chief gods of the Védas. How far the idea of unity was retained. Growth of polytheism. How far pantheistic. Moral tone. Imperfect consciousness of sin. Early date of the Védas. Argument from the language: from the picture of society: from the theology. § II. Bráhmanism. Character of the new theology. Occasional marks of progress. Organization of the system. The twice-born. New phase of pantheism. Máyá. The Hindú triad. Hindú theory of man; and of the world. Transmigration. Popular religion. Philosophical religion. Probable age of Bráhmanism. § III. Schools of philosophy—(a) The Sánkhya school. Its materialism. Practical aim of Kapila and his followers.—(b) Buddhism. Early biography of Gautama. Foundation and propagation of Buddhism. Points of contact with Bráhmanism. Doctrine of sin: of Caste-system: of causation. Nirvána. Buddhist ethics. —(c) The Eclectic school. Asceticism. The Bhagavad-Gítá. Theological and ethical system. Re-assertion of the law of caste. New theory of genuine devotion.

THE European who first fought his way across the passes leading to the north of India was Alexander the Great. As early as the summer of 327 B.C. his veterans rested one whole month upon the banks of the Hydaspes. But although an opportunity was thus afforded to the band of scientific Greeks, who joined his expedition, for investigating the religions of the Panjáb and for studying the peculiar genius of the vanquished, the reports which they have left us on these questions are extremely meagre and uncritical. The honour of unlocking, that mysterious treasure-house in which the literary wealth of India had been hoarded up from prehistoric ages was reserved for other conquerors.

Nor, if Aristotle had himself attended his heroic pupil, is it likely that our knowledge of the primitive history of Hindústán would be materially augmented. Doubtless an experienced eye, like the Stageirite's, would have noted with especial interest and intelligence the aspects of the physical world thus opened to the eager gaze of the Hellenes. The grandeur of the mountain-scenery, culminating in the snow-crowned summits of the Hindú-Kúsh, the richness of the foliage, the fertility of the soil, the mighty forests, the luxuriant rivers, the prodigious size and the grotesque proportions of the animals and plants, would all in turn have furnished topics for reflection and comparison to the mind of such a traveller. He would have probably assisted also in determining the physiological characteristics of the native population, and while remarking, as did others, the dyed beard, the tunic of white linen, the ornaments of gold and ivory, the timid air and almost feminine softness of the men, their passionate love of music, juggling, and gymnastics, have enabled us to speak more definitely in reference to their moral elevation and the nature of their intellectual training. He might further have investigated more at length the contrasts which already marked the different orders of Hindú society,—such, for instance, as the distribution into castes, or the specific points of difference then observable between the courtly and accomplished 'Bráchman,' and the anchoret who mortified the flesh amid the silence and discomforts of the jungle. Nay, it is conceivable that a mind which mastered the whole compass of Hellenic wisdom might have been able to anticipate some triumphs of the modern ethnologist; he might have traced those common elements of thought and feeling, language and mythology, which, binding Greek and Persian and Hindú together, pointed backwards to the early dawn of civilisation and the cradle of the human family.

Yet, high as were the expectations not unnaturally raised by Alexander's expedition, one peculiarity in the mental constitution of Hindús prevented both the ancients and ourselves from gaining any accurate knowledge of their aboriginal condition. Rich as their literature is found to be in other products, it has never given birth to formal histories[1]; and

[1] The only exception is *Rája Taringini*, a quasi-historical account of Kashmir; and even this, according to Prof. Wilson (*Asiatic Researches*, xv. 1 sq.), dates no higher than the XIIth century after

what is even more remarkable, the Hindú scholar is deficient in those very qualities which indicate the presence of historic consciousness. He gazes with a cold, if not contemptuous, spirit on the vanities of sense and time, and therefore is disposed to treat all questions of chronology with arrogant indifference. He lives, or rather dreams away his lifetime, in the midst of intellectual problems, labouring hard to measure the immeasurable, to circumscribe the absolute. Compared with such recondite speculations, every incident of life is a mere ripple on the boundless ocean, as fleeting, as phenomenal. What now is, may, for ought he cares, have been a thousand times already, and may frequently come round afresh. The object of his interest is reunion with Divinity, a reabsorption of the finite soul into the primal source of being; and that destiny, according to the various creeds of Hindústán, implies obliviousness in reference to all earthly knowledge, and entire abstraction from all shadows and illusions of the past.

Now, whether it is exclusively owing to the operation of such feelings that the literary monuments of Hindústán are seldom found to be available for historical purposes, I do not venture to determine. But this may be affirmed with certainty, that if the annals of India were less blank and barren, modern Europe would have been far less bewildered than it is by theories and counter-theories. Here, as in like cases, where the evidence is dim and fragmentary at the best, imagination is too often suffered to take wing, and even to usurp the throne of history.

On one side we have seen a race of orientalists so dazzled by the brilliance of their own discoveries, so intoxicated by the novelty and beauty of the region into which they were the first to penetrate, that India is for them the fountain of all wisdom and the mother of all civilisation. Glowing with this fancy, they are anxious to persuade us that in ages long before the birth of Moses or Sesostris, a religious system, which has since remained well-nigh immutable, was fabricated by the genius of some Hindú rishi on the banks of the Yamuná, or in

Christ. We are elsewhere told by the same authority, that the ancient (Bráhmanical) records of India have scarcely enabled us to determine more than one important historical fact, viz. the identity of Chandragupta, one of the kings of Magadha, with the Sandracottus, or Sandracoptus, of the Greek writers. The reign of the latter monarch began about 312 B.C.; whereas if any credit were conceded to the list of dynasties preserved in the Puráńas, this event would have to be placed 1200 years earlier (Lassen, *Indische Alterthumskunde*, I. 501, Bonn, 1847).

the plain of the Ganges; and that thither we must go if we desire to find the master-key which can alone explain the mysteries of later systems, which alone can solve the problems of our spiritual nature, and give back to western states the uncorrupted form of Christianity[1].

On the other side it has been vigorously contended, for example in the school of Niebuhr[2], that the civilisation of India is both modern and derived—a thing of yesterday, if we compare it with the mental history of some other nations. The Hindús, when vanquished by the troops of Alexander, and described by Megasthenes, had (so these writers argue) recently emerged from utter barbarism; they were kinsmen of the 'black and savage Indians,' whom we meet with in the pages of Herodotus; while Sanskrit literature, for which the opposite school asserted an unfathomable antiquity, had borrowed all its choicer portions from Greek treatises imported by the Arabs in the middle ages.

But truth, we now are justified in stating, was equidistant from these two extreme positions. When the first intoxication of the orientalist was over; when the monuments of ancient India were decyphered by a race of scholars more sagacious

[1] See, for instance, Holwell's *Original Principles of the ancient Bramins*, &c. (Lond. 1779). This writer glories in the name of 'orthodox Christian Deist' (p. 91), and claims direct affinity with the Hindús, who 'from the earliest times have been an ornament to the creation,' on the ground that both he and they are strict monotheists. He deems the Bráhmanical religion the first and purest product of a supernatural revelation. The Hindú scriptures, he supposes, contain, 'to a moral certainty, the original doctrines and terms of restoration, delivered from God himself, by the mouth of his first-created Birmah, to mankind, at his first creation in the form of man' (p. 71). According to Holwell's theory, our blessed Lord was a reappearance of 'Birmah,' but the exact substance of His teaching can be no longer ascertained, owing to grievous corruptions and disfigurements which it was made to undergo at the hands of the apostles and their followers.

[2] 'This opinion concerning the antiquity of Indian civilisation, which has sprung up especially within the last forty years [Niebuhr wrote as far back as 1830], is, indeed, spreading farther and gaining stability. I cannot decide upon it, and cannot say what it is founded upon; but from the assurance of a very competent Englishman, I believe that people will soon come to the conviction, as some highly competent persons have already done, that all the alleged knowledge of the Indians does not by any means belong to the centuries of Moses and Sesostris, to which it has been assigned, but that the greater part of their literature belongs to the middle ages; that for the most part it is borrowed from the Greek, through the medium of Arabic translations,' &c.: *Lectures on Ancient History*, I. 138.

than a Holwell and less credulous than a Voltaire; when fresh materials had been disinterred in various quarters, and a flood of light had broken unexpectedly into this field of literature from China and Nepál on one side, and Ceylon upon the other; random guesses were exchanged for logical deductions, and philosophizing tamed or baffled by the stubborn strength of facts. It was now obvious, that if Hindús were not historians their religion had a history; that this religion, far from being uniform and stationary in its character, had undergone a series of important changes, not to say of revolutions; that instead of being a spontaneous product of the soil of Hindústán, and therefore unconnected in its growth with other ancient systems, the original Hindúism bore in every feature the most legible indications of a northern parentage, and indications which connect the elements of its mythology, as well as of its speech, with other sections of the 'Indo-European' family.

The phases of religious thought which the immediate object of the present work has made it necessary for me to examine, are reducible under three descriptions:

1. Védaism, or the Vaidic religion.
2. Bráhmanism.
3. Schools of Hindú philosophy, including Buddhism.

§ 1. *Védaism.*

It is now almost universally admitted that to ascertain the basis of Hindú civilisation, or, rather, to become acquainted with the earliest utterances of the Hindú religion, we must have recourse directly to the class of sacred books entitled Védas[1].

[1] See Colebrooke's Essay *On the Védas, or Sacred Writings of the Hindús*, first published in the *Asiatic Researches*, VIII. 377—497. They are four in number, and are denominated the Rig-Véda, the Yajur-Véda, the Sáma-Véda, and the Atharva-Véda. The Rig-Véda (Véda of Praise) is the one genuine collection. The Sáma-Véda is only a short extract from the Rig-Véda, containing such hymns as had to be chanted during the sacrifice. The Yajur-Véda is a similar manual intended for another class of priests, who had to mutter certain hymns of the Rig-Véda, together with invocations and other sacrificial formulas. The Sanskrit text of the Rig-Véda is being edited by Prof. Max Müller: it has also been translated in part by Prof. Wilson, and entirely by M. Langlois. The White Yajur-Véda is edited with a translation, by Prof. Weber of Berlin. The Sáma-Véda is edited, with a translation, first by Mr. Stevenson, and secondly by Prof. Benfey of Göttingen. The fourth Véda, though some of its materials are more recent, is regarded by the Hindús themselves as of co-ordinate authority. It has just been edited by Prof. Roth and Mr.

Here I take my stand, and without entering very far into particulars either as to the theology which they contain, or the precise date of their composition, I shall try to give the reader such a general view of both as for the present purpose will be found sufficiently approximate.

Two remarks are necessary at the outset.

First, I shall exclude from this inquiry all reference to the aboriginal (*i. e.* non-Áryan) tribes of India. The Védas have been ever the possession of one dominant race[1],—a race which, having crossed the Indian Alps at some remote period, was gradually diffused into the Panjáb, and ultimately over a large portion of the whole Peninsula. Who and what was the 'barbarian' (mléchchha) they drove out before them; who and what the abject serf, or Śúdra, they had forcibly converted to their own religion, are extraneous questions, interesting in themselves, but not admissible within the limits of the present survey[2].

Secondly, I ought to mention that in forming an estimate of the Védas, my materials have been gathered from the oldest portion of those treatises, the Védas proper, and not from Bráhmañas and Upanishads, in which the Vaidic doctrines are idealised and systematically developed by later hands[3]. For

Whitney. Supplementary works in illustration of the texts of the Védas have also been published. Especially valuable is the *Nirukta*, an original glossary and commentary, which has been also edited by Prof. Roth: Göttingen, 1852.

[1] On the origin of the Hindús and their gradual occupation of India, see Lassen, *Ind. Alterth.* I. 511 sq. They distinguished themselves from other ancient tribes by the name Árya = 'noble,' 'well-born,' a designation originally belonging also to the Medes (Ἄριοι, Herod. VII. 62), and afterwards preserved in the district *Ariana*, and in the modern *Ari* and *Arikh*, applied by the Armenians to the natives of Media. Is árya derived from arya 'a householder,' originally used as the name of the third caste or the Vaiśyas, who formed the great bulk of the immigrants or new settlers. [Cf. Max Müller, *The Science of Language*, pp. 240 sq. Lond. 1862.] See further illustrations in Lassen, I. 6 sq., and Dr. Donaldson's *New Cratylus*, pp. 118, 119, 2nd ed. The former of these authorities asserts (p. 511) that we find no traces of their foreign extraction in the ancient literature of the Hindús themselves; but he is here not quite accurate, as Weber pointed out in his *Indische Studien*, 2tes Heft, 1850, p. 165.

[2] See *Appendix* I. at the end of this Part.

[3] These treatises are (1) the Bráhmañas, commentaries partly liturgical and partly theological in their character, containing, it would seem, a much fuller development of the Bráhmanical system, and (2) the Upanishads, a kind of supplement to other sacred books. Speaking generally, each Véda may be said to consist of two parts, the Mantras, or prayers, and the

although many of these productions are said to breathe the spirit of the Védas, and although some of them may fairly claim, on philological and other grounds, a very high antiquity, it is impossible with our present knowledge to determine their exact position in reference to the sacred texts which they interpret.

Of the documents which Hindús have always held in special veneration, the Rig-Véda is the first and foremost. It contains as many as 1017 'mantras,' *i.e.* canticles and prayers. These, with slight exceptions, are *religious* in their character. About one half of them are found to be addressed either to Indra, the god of light[1], or Agni, the god of fire[2]; who therefore occupy the foremost place in the mythology of the Védas. The next divinity to which a certain prominence appears to be awarded is Varuńa, the god of water; but none of these can be distinguished absolutely from a multitude of other gods, which

Bráhmańas, or treatises: Colebrooke, as above, pp. 387, 388 (cf. also *Des Védas*, par M. J. B. Saint-Hilaire, pp. 10, 11, Paris, 1854). All the Bráhmańas are believed in point of time to lie between the Védas on the one side, and the heroic poems on the other; and Professor Wilson, arguing from internal evidence, seems to have made it not improbable that one of the number, the Aitaréya Bráhmańa (which, however, is not, he maintains, an integral part of the Rig-Véda) was written as far back as the sixth century before the Christian era: see *Journal of the Asiatic Society*, XIII. 105. The Véda alone is called *śruti*, or revelation; everything else, however sacred, can only claim the title of *smriti*, or tradition. The revelation was supposed to be handed down by inspired rishis, till at last it reached the minds of common believers, and was accepted by them as absolute truth. Few Bráhmans at the present day can read and understand the Véda. They know little more of it than a few hymns and prayers. Instead of the Véda, they read the Laws of Manu, the six systems of philosophy, the Puránas and the Tantras.

[1] Indra, the Hindú Jupiter, is not unfrequently styled 'lord of heaven,' (divaspati = diespiter). The name 'Indra' is itself of doubtful origin, meaning either (1) 'blue' (an epithet of the firmament), or (2) 'the illuminator,' or (3) 'the giver of rain:' Wuttke, *Gesch. des Heidenthums*, II. 242, Breslau, 1853. His attributes, though for the most part terrible in their manifestation, are essentially *creative* or *productive*, and sometimes absolutely *beneficent;* as when he is said to chase away evil spirits from the clouds, or send refreshing showers upon the earth, in spite of the malevolence of Vritra or Ahi, the demon who withholds them.

[2] The Agni (= Ignis) of the Védas is not so much the god presiding over the element of fire, as the element of fire itself, considered partly as the vivifying principle of vegetation, and partly as a *destructive agent*, 'Agni ist die dem Indra gegenüberstehende Naturmacht; Indra erzeugt das Leben, Agni verzehrt es.' Wuttke, *Ibid.* p. 241: cf. however, Prof. Wilson, *Rig-Véda*, Vol. I. 'Introd.' p. xxvii.

either act as representatives of the chief divinities, and so are Indra, Agni, and Varuńa with different names, or else appear as deifications of some single aspect in the powers and processes of nature. Trinity or triad there is none[1]. Much less can we observe among the ancient hymns of India a complete and systematic theogony. The Vaidic gods are for the most part isolated beings, shadowy and impersonal energies, as multiform in character and manifestation as the elements with which they are connected, not to say identified. The earliest grouping of them into a system must be dated from the subsequent period[2], when the image of one, holy, personal Creator being broken more and more, and fading more and more completely from the Hindú mind, it was attempted to regain the thought of unity, which man was sadly conscious he had lost, by calling to his aid the light of metaphysics and the generalisations of natural philosophy.

The doctrine of one great First-Cause was not indeed, as we shall see hereafter, absolutely banished from the heart of bards and rishis; yet their extant hymns should satisfy the most incredulous that the idea of God as one, supreme, and spiritual, never formed a prominent article in the early creeds of India. It retired far-off into the background. It seldom operated as a principle of life. It was the feeble and expiring echo of an older and a purer revelation; and even where it shewed its power at all, where Indra for the moment was absorbed completely by some brighter and more spiritual being, the God of whom such visions preached was not a thinking, willing, loving Spirit, personal and self-conscious, ruling over nature as His work and as the Father of the spirits of all flesh, but rather a great That[3], a neuter abstract, separable from the world of

[1] Those writers who labour to establish that the Hindús have worshipped a triad of divinities from the very earliest period, give the second or third place in it to Varuńa (Οὐρανός): Wuttke, *Ibid.* p. 243. He is, in their view, the *preserving* and *directing* agent of the Vaidic system, the sphere of his operation lying between those of Indra and Agni. It deserves to be further noted, that as far back as the Védas, sexual distinctions were attributed to the gods. Each of the three leading divinities is attended by a wife, who reflects his own special energy: Indráńí, Varuńáńí, Agnáyí.

[2] 'In der Védischen Götterlehre findet sich kein System, obwohl *Indra* schon der mächtigste der Götter ist:' Lassen, I. 768. He then sketches the oldest systematic representations as we find them in the *Nirukta.*

[3] The Sanskrit word (Tad) is literally *That.* And the same idea was in all probability expressed by the mystic monosyllable Óm (aum), by which the hymns of the Védas were uniformly prefaced. Some writers, referring the three letters

matter in idea, but not in essence; spiritualised indeed, but spiritualised, ennobled, deified by the poetic faculty of the worshipper. He was a nature-god, and not the God of nature.

1. Accordingly if we proceed to analyse the psychological peculiarities which tended to protect that early creed of the Hindú, the point which strikes us most is the profound devotion he had always paid to natural phenomena. This tendency he manifested in common with all nations of remote antiquity; for though we cannot trace the Áryan backward to his haunts in central Asia, nor speak positively of the effect produced upon him by the savage scenery of those regions he had traversed in the course of his migrations, it is certain that on crossing the Hindú Alps he bowed at once in adoration of the new and beauteous world to which he was transplanted. The earthly bias of the spirit had received fresh impulses; the witchery exercised upon the senses was entire and irresistible. How potent were such impulses, how absolute such fascination in the other tribes of Western Asia, may be gathered from the noble protest of the patriarch: 'If I beheld the sun when it shined, or the moon walking in brightness, and my heart hath been secretly enticed, or my mouth hath kissed my hand; this also were an iniquity to be punished by the judge; for I should have denied the God that is above' (Job xxxi. 26—28). And like the patriarch in sensibility, though not in fear and reverence, were the authors of the sacred books of Hindústán. The 'golden-handed' sun, dispensing as the lord of heaven his gifts of radiance and fertility; the starry firmament, inspiring awe and deepening wonder; the freshness of the morning and the calm of evening twilight, whispering in man's heart of supernatural genii; season following season, and one element commingling with another; the scorching wind, the lightnings flashing forth in majesty and armed with speedy vengeance, rain and dew and drought,—these all excited in their turn the sentiments of pain or pleasure, joy or sadness, confidence or apprehension. All were felt to indicate the presence of invisible powers, at peace or else at enmity with man, and therefore recognised as objects worthy of his prayers[1]. Such veneration of the elements may

to a triad of the elements, explain *a* of Agni (fire), *u* of Varuńa (water), and *m* of Marut (wind): but the true etymology of the word appears to be suggested by the old Persian 'avam' (=aum), meaning 'That': see Lassen, I. 775, n. 3.

[1] 'It is the peculiar character of the Indian mythology to combine a gigantic wildness of phantasy, and a boundless enthusiasm for nature, with a deep mystical import, and a profound philosophic sense.' F. von Schlegel, *Phil. of Hist.* p. 154, Lond. 1847.

not indeed have consciously involved the worshipper at first in a denial of God's sovereignty. He may have read in them the tokens, symbols, agents of a spiritual Intelligence. The harmony of natural laws, the wondrous and majestic revolution of the stars and planets, most of all the glorious element of light from which the Áryan borrowed the generic name[1] of his divinities, may have, at least to elevated minds, suggested other and far higher spheres, of which the present world is only a distorted copy and a feeble adumbration. Yet ere long a change came over men's ideas; the golden thread was broken which connected 'the invisible things of God,' His power, His righteousness, His personality, His fatherhood, with objects that solicit and bewitch the senses. Popular imagination ultimately believed its own allegories, and not only so, but construed them according to the letter. The mythe became an object not of fancy but of faith; and the relations of natural and supernatural being thus inverted and obscured, the law was substituted for the Legislator, and the Giver hidden from men's eyes by the effulgence and the multiplicity of His gifts.

In other words, the Védas, taken as a whole, reveal to us an aspect of religious feeling, always bordering upon pantheism, often passing quite across the border. Wheresoever in the world around him the Hindú observed extraordinary manifestations of the brilliant or the beautiful, the barren or prolific, the sombre or the terrible; wherever the action of the elements was such as to produce extraordinary effects upon himself, his

[1] Déva, *nom.* dévas (=*deus*, *θεός*, Goth. *tius*, A. S. *tiw*), is derived from the Sansk. *deva*, 'luminous,' 'resplendent' (cf. *sub divo*);—an etymology which of itself suggests the leading feature of Hindú polytheism. Light, accordingly, became the aptest symbol of the Divine Being. Thus the *Gáyatrí*, or holiest verse of the Védas, is addressed to the sun-god, and contains the following passage among others: 'Let us meditate on the adorable light of the divine sun (Savitri): may it guide our intellects. Desirous of food, we solicit the gift of the splendid sun (Savitri), who should be studiously worshipped. Venerable men, guided by the understanding, salute the divine sun (Savitri) with oblations and praise.' *Asiat. Researches*, VIII. 400: cf. Wuttke, II. 260—262, where other evidence is adduced to shew that the sun was at first regarded as an image in the visible world of what the supreme Essence is in the world invisible. 'Perhaps,' says Ritter (*Hist. of Ancient Philosophy*, I. 92, Oxf. 1838), 'there is nothing more instructive in Indian archæology than (so to express ourselves) the *transparency* of their mythology, which permits us to perceive how, with a general sense of the divine, the coexistence of a special recognition thereof in the separate phenomena of nature was possible, and how out of the conception of the one God a belief in a plurality of gods could arise.'

children, or his property, he betrayed the consciousness of his dependence by some special act of homage. He acknowledged in such powers the presence of divinity; he called the influence which affected him or his a *dêva* ('deus'); it was pregnant for the time with a divine or diabolic efficacy, and therefore it became a fitting object of desire or dread, of adoration or of deprecation, according to the aspects it assumed in reference to the worshipper. Hence, also, every province of creation was soon peopled by spiritual energies, all varying in their character with human hopes and fears, with human interests and passions. Nay, so far was the Hindú impelled in this direction that he deified the sacrifice itself[1], from which he hoped to profit; he worshipped his own offering, he worshipped the solemn form of words by which his offering was accompanied.

But although these objects had been each invested by imagination with a kind of personality, the *dêvas* of the Hindú populace, throughout the Vaidic period, were little more than formless powers and colourless abstractions. Human properties, it is true, were frequently ascribed to them: it was believed that even gods are ultimately mortal, and can only purchase an exemption from the common lot by drinking of the potent *amrita*[2], the draught of immortality; yet how vague was the impression made by this or that particular god we gather from the fact that the same element is connected at different times with different divinities; the names are interchanged, the powers confounded with each other; and thus, owing to the want of individuality, the veneration of the ancient gods grew obsolete; their memory vanished with the phases of society from which they had emerged, or with the momentary gushings of religious sentiment in some peculiar locality. Even Indra, occupying as he did the foremost place among the group of Vaidic gods, and wielding powers, as it would seem, identical with those of the Supreme Being, is, nevertheless, presented in

[1] For example, the hymns comprising one whole section of the Rig-Véda are addressed to Soma, the milky juice of the moon-plant (asclepias acida), which the worshipper had learnt to deify. Thus, in Langlois's translation (Tome I. p. 174) the following is the last petition of such a prayer: 'Dieu fort, ô Soma, que ta divine prudence nous accorde la part de richesses (que nous désirons)! Combats pour nous; personne ne peut lutter contre toi. Tu es le maître de la force, et règnes sur les deux partis: donne-nous la supériorité dans la bataille.' This deification of the Soma is still more prominent in the Sáma-Véda.

[2] As early as the Rig-Véda, the Soma sacrifice is called *amrita* (='immortal'); and in a secondary sense the liquor which communicates immortality (*Ibid.* p. 173).

the Rig-Véda as the offspring of Aditi[1], the mother of the universe; the dignities with which he is invested are equally ascribed to Agni, Rudra, and the rest; while, in the next period of Hindú mythology, the same Indra is depressed into a deity of the second order; his heaven (or 'swarga') is only fourth in rank among the bright localities, entitled superhuman, and even his throne itself is rendered insecure. He has to tremble at the prospect of still further humiliation, if, peradventure, some daring mortal shall complete the horse-sacrifice, or qualify himself for ruling in the place of Indra by extraordinary acts of penance. Such are the indefinite forms and such the varying aspects of Hindú polytheism at the early stage of its development.

2. But if the Védas thus abound with indications that the worshipper in ancient times was gifted only with a superficial consciousness of one Almighty God, and if the texture of his hymns and prayers were such as to obscure that consciousness still further by interposing an innumerable crowd of fresh divinities, we are prepared to find a corresponding deterioration in his moral and religious sentiments. And such is really the case. The physical attributes of God and of superior genii are confessed and venerated; but the traces of belief in His moral government are only few and indistinct[2]. The worshipper, for instance, moved by some good fortune has prepared his eucharistic offering, the oiled butter or the juices of a sacred plant; he bends in supplication; he invites his favourite god to come and taste of his abundance. Winds and fire and sunlight, these are all profusely welcomed to the banquet; but the God of nature, He who framed the world and reigns supreme above the elements, appears to have been utterly overlooked; He has no part in the oblation, except, perhaps, allusion to Him be intended in that solemn muttering (Óm), by which the ceremony is preceded. Or, again, the worshipper is overwhelmed by sorrow and perplexity; his hopes are blasted or his fortune wrecked, and with the spirit of a famished menial he determines to apply for aid and compensation to some fresh divinity. His voice, which quivers with emotion, has at length found utterance in a passionate prayer; yet what that prayer in almost every case solicits is exemption from the physical ills of life, a fuller and more sparkling cup of temporal prosperity. Large and healthy families, cows and horses, fertile pastures,

[1] Langlois, II. 238; cf. III. 42, 492.

[2] See Saint-Hilaire, *Des Védas*, pp. 172, 173, who corroborates this inference.

bounteous harvests, victory over public and domestic foes, are found to be the leading, not to say the solitary topics in the supplications of the Védas. We shall look in vain for penitential psalms, or hymns commemorating the descent of spiritual benefits.

This want of moral sensibility, this slowness to admit the presence and malignity of moral evil, and the holiness of Him with whom we have to do, is not by any means peculiar to the creed of Hindústán. If prayers suggested in the Védas differed in some points from those of the adjacent countries, all such differences were only matters of degree. If Persia, for example, soon discovered that the greatest struggles which affect humanity are not the struggles of the sun and clouds, the waters and the winds, but struggles raging in the breast of living men between the elements of light and darkness, and the powers of good and evil, it is notwithstanding an indisputable fact that even in the brighter spots of ancient heathendom the supplications offered to the gods are nearly always prompted by the wish for temporal prosperity[1]. Exceptions there would doubtless be, since the conviction of man's moral bondage is inseparable from himself, and cannot be obliterated in the lowest depths of sensuality. Accordingly we may discover here and there examples bearing witness to the glimmerings of such consciousness as far back as the earliest prayers of the Védas. 'O Varuńa, by our invocations, by our sacrifices, by our holocausts, we desire to turn away thine anger. Come, thou giver of life; relieve us, prudent king, from our offences[2].' 'Soma

[1] 'They are supplicated to confer temporal blessings upon the worshipper, riches, life, posterity; the short-sighted vanities of human desire, which constituted the sum of heathen prayer in all heathen countries.' Prof. Wilson, *Lectures*, pp. 9, 10, Oxf. 1840. Stuhr, *Die Religions-Systeme der heidnischen Völker des Orients*, Berlin, 1836, 'Einleitung,' p. xii, has pointed out the strong contrast in this particular between the worship of the heathen and the Christian; and indeed of all the extant heathen prayers a very small fraction only are offered in the hope of calling down moral or spiritual benefits. An example of the latter may be seen in Creuzer's *Symbolik*, IV. 629, Leipzig, 1842.

[2] *Rig-Véda*, ed. Langlois, I. 41. In a subsequent hymn (*Ibid.* I. 79) there are also allusions to moral turpitude; but the last verse is differently rendered by Saint-Hilaire (*Des Védas*, p. 56). I am very glad to find myself again supported in the view here taken of the Védas by the high authority of Prof. Wilson, who, after mentioning some other peculiarities, remarks: 'There is little demand for moral benefactions, although, in some few instances, hatred of untruth and abhorrence of sin are expressed; a hope is uttered that the latter may be repented of or expiated; and the

[the personified libation] has declared to me that in the waters are all medicines [*or*, medicinal plants]. Agni works the happiness of all: the waters cure all evils. Salutary waters, guard my body from disease [*or*, perfect all medicines for the good of my body], that I may long behold the sun. Purifying waters, cleanse away from me whatever is impure or criminal, every evil I have done by violence, by imprecations, by injustice[1].' It should also be remembered that the same conviction of impurity might not unfrequently suggest the offering of material sacrifice, to which allusion has been made above. Of human[2] victims no example is preserved in any of the Védas; nor in that early age did man so frequently evince his consciousness of imperfection by inordinate displays of animal sacrifices[3]. What the Hindú mainly offered was clarified butter poured upon the fire, or else the fermenting juice of the soma-plant[4], which he presented in ladles to the deity whom he invoked. In this, which may at first have been commended to him by its potent and exhilarating properties, he afterwards beheld an emblem of the vital sap whereby the universe itself is made productive; but in bringing such oblation he was actuated chiefly by the hope of gratifying the animal wants of his divinity, not by the idea of deepening his own sense of guilt, or compensating for his own demerit. Still, as we have seen, he was at times oppressed by a misgiving that the gods were hostile to him; that the Rákshasas (or evil spirits) interfered to vitiate his offerings, and that Yama, the sovereign of the dead, was planning his destruction. He grew anxious therefore to disarm their vengeance, and to replace himself if possible upon the moral elevation which he felt that he had forfeited. Iniquity had left its deadly poison in the spirit of the sinner; yet through lack of some unerring guidance he could only dream about the cause of his disorder, and could only guess at the appropriate remedy.

gods are in one hymn solicited to extricate the worshipper from sin of every kind.' 'Introd.' to his translation of the *Rig-Véda*, I. p. xxvi.

[1] *Rig-Véda*, ed. Langlois, I. 38, and, as repeated, IV. 143.

[2] They can, however, be plainly traced as far back as the Aitaréya Bráhmana: see Prof. Wilson's paper in the *Jour. of the Asiat. Soc.* XIII. 105.

[3] There is allusion, however, in the Rig-Véda, as well as in the Yajur-Véda, to the sacrifice of a horse ('aśwamédha'), which afterwards obtained a new importance in the Hindú worship. Still as offered in the Rig-Véda, its object is simply to acquire additional wealth and prosperity, not, as in the Puránas and in Southey's *Curse of Kehama*, to assist in dethroning Indra and exalting the sacrificer to his place: see Wilson's *Rig-Véda*, Vol. II. 'Introd.' pp. xii. sq.

[4] Wuttke, II. 344 sq.

3. If we now pass forward from this sketch of early Hindú worship to the questions touching the antiquity of the Védas, it must be conceded that one class of arguments adduced by Indian scholars will hardly stand the test of rigorous criticism. Sir William Jones[1] endeavoured, for example, to fix the precise date of the Yajur-Véda by calculating backwards through the lives of two-and-forty sages by whom the document is said to have been handed down to us. But the point of departure in this calculation is the age of Parásara, which in its turn depends upon the accuracy of astronomical observations. By the aid of such a process, Jones had placed the composition of the Yajur-Véda as far back as 1580 B.C. Colebrooke, in like manner, having satisfied himself that a Vaidic calendar which he examined ought to be referred to the 14th century B.C., obtained a very similar conclusion. But it seems that this great scholar subsequently staggered under the enormous difficulties of the problem, and was finally disposed to treat his chronological statements as precarious and conjectural[2]. The same opinion must be formed of other calculations resting on the astronomical works of India; nor can vague disclosures of the Cashmir chronicle be entitled to a higher place[3]. Converging as they do, however, these various testimonies must be held to have created a presumption in favour of the early dating of the Védas, and such presumption is again supported if we estimate the worth of the internal evidence.

(1) The language of the Védas, when compared with later writings of the Indo-Áryan race, is characterised by a profusion of archaisms. The grammatical forms are less developed, the diction far more rustic, and the style more rugged, primitive and elliptical. To use the illustration of Sir William Jones, the Sanskrit of the Védas differed from the Sanskrit of the classic age, as did the Latin of the age of Numa from the Latin of the age of Cicero. Or, in other words, if we might reason from one member of the family of nations to a second, the

[1] See the *Preface* to his translation of the *Laws of Manu.*

[2] Cf. Saint-Hilaire, *Des Védas*, p. 140. Prof. Wilson, in like manner, *Rig-Véda*, 'Introd.' Vol. I. p. xlviii., observes that in proposing dates on this subject, nothing more than conjecture is intended.

[3] Prichard, who appears to be satisfied with Davis's treatise on the astronomy of the Hindús (*Researches into the Physical History of Mankind*, IV. 102), attaches great importance to the agreement of the results obtained by these different modes of computation. He is, accordingly, prepared to place the Great War, which separates the historic from the pre-historic period of Indian antiquities, in the 14th century before the Christian era. *Ibid.* p. 104.

peculiarities of the Véda-dialect imply an interval as wide as that which parts the English of the venerable Cædmon from the English of the Caroline divines. Those scholars who devote particular attention to the study of the Védas, have moreover noticed great diversities in the language of the several volumes[1], implying that as the hymns which they contain were gradually indited, the language of the Áryan tribes had passed through several stages of development; while on comparing the 'Mantras,' or Védas proper, with the Bráhmañas, which were intended for their illustration, the existence of fresh intervals between the composition of the text and commentaries is thoroughly ascertained.

(2) But other proofs, more generally appreciable, and to certain minds more cogent and conclusive, are derived from the peculiar pictures there presented of Hindú society. As the Vaidic hymns were, notwithstanding the extravagant claims advanced in their behalf, composed at various times by different poets, and only strung together in the time of the half-mythical Vyása ('the Arranger'), they reflect the life and feelings of the Áryan under very different circumstances. At first we see a man of patriarchal simplicity, a hunter or a cowherd. His ideas are circumscribed within the narrow limits of his clan, the chief of which, surrounded by a multitude of cattle, is the father and perhaps the priest[2] of all his followers. In some points these primitive chieftains are not much unlike the petty kings of the Homeric age[3]; but apter parallels are found in Hebrew patriarchs, or in modern Arabs of the desert. According to this version of his life, the Áryan colonist was originally nomadic in his habits: he was led from plain to plain, or from one lofty plateau to another, in quest of milder skies and richer pasturage. At length, indeed, a mighty change comes over his ideas: the shepherd is transformed into a warrior, and we see him on the other side of the great alpine frontier, permanently settled in the north of Hindústán. Yet even there no manifest traces are discerned of a political or religious organization; we look in vain for cities, temples, images and the like. One section of the colonists appears to be engaged in agriculture: groups of them have been collected and arranged in villages: they are planting, sowing, building; on the one side anxious to propitiate the ungenial powers of nature, on the other actively engaged in warring

[1] Saint-Hilaire, p. 152, who appeals to the authority of Roth, Benfey and Weber.

[2] In the later hymns of the Rig-Véda the power of the priestly order (Purohiti) is established.

[3] Cf. Langlois, *Rig-Véda*, 'Introduction,' p. x.

with the dark-complexioned 'Dasyus,' or, in different words, expelling the old tenants of the soil[1].

But rude and simple though he be, the Áryan of the Véda is no savage. He begins to manifest his aptitude for intellectual culture[2]: he is earnest, thoughtful, enterprising: he learns to speak of ships and commerce: he is not entirely ignorant of astronomical science. A worker in the precious metals, and a manufacturer of musical instruments, he has already given proofs of his perception both of the conveniences and the amenities of social life. He has moreover learned in some degree the power, the richness and the flexibility of his native language, and from time to time there rises up a bard, or rishi, whose poetic genius gives expression to the varied feelings that are working in the breast of the community. This rishi is the oracle of his village: in the songs and prayers which he composes lie the elements of common worship, and the germs of that far mightier system, which on its development is destined to unite all Indo-Áryan tribes together, and diffuse its humanizing influence to the southernmost point of Hindústán. Such grand ideas, however, were not present to the fancy of the ancient bards: and he who is desirous of realizing in some measure the important changes afterwards wrought in Hindu life, has only to transfer his thoughts from the original aspects of society, as pictured in the Védas, to that stage when the ambassador of Seleucus found a welcome at the Court of Chandragupta, or when Kálidása, in the century before the Christian era, charmed his audience by the elegant drama of the *Fatal Ring*.

(3) There is one more criterion which enables us to judge of the remote antiquity of the Védas. It may be entitled theological. We find it, partly, in the fact that some divinities

[1] We catch occasional glimpses of this contest in the hymns of the Védas: *e. g. Rig-Véda Sanhitá*, I. 137, 138, ed. Wilson,—a passage which also proves that the invaders thought themselves the champions of true religion: 'Discriminate,' is the prayer to Indra, 'between the Áryas and they [? them] that are Dasyus [enemies]: restraining those who perform no religious rites, compel them to submit to the performer of sacrifices:' and III. 34, 9: 'Destroying the Dasyus, Indra protected the Áryan colour' (varna = caste).

[2] Prof. Wilson has drawn attention to some of the points here specified: but he seems to overstate his case when he adds (*Rig-Véda*, Vol. II. p. xvii.): 'These particulars, although they are only briefly and incidentally thrown out, chiefly by way of comparison, or illustration, render it indisputable, that the Hindús of the Vaidik era even had attained to an advanced stage of civilisation, little if at all differing from that in which they were found by the Greeks at Alexander's invasion.'

who stand conspicuous in these books have either undergone most serious transformations, or else have vanished altogether from the literature of the next period[1]: partly, in the absence from the Védas of some doctrines which had afterwards become the cardinal points of the Hindú system. Such, for instance, are the doctrines of caste[2], of transmigration and of incarnation[3]; none of which have hitherto been discovered in the oldest records of Hindúism.

[1] The following extract from Prof. Wilson's 'Introd.,' as above, pp. xxvi, xxvii, is valuable on more accounts than one, and especially as shewing how very inexact some modern writers are in their philosophisings on these subjects: 'The divinities worshipped [in the *Rig-Véda*] are not unknown to later systems, but they there perform very subordinate parts, whilst those deities, who are the great gods—the *Dii majores*—of the subsequent period, are either wholly unnamed in the *Véda*, or are noticed in an inferior and different capacity. The names of Śiva, of Mahádéva, of Durgá, of Kálí, of Ráma, of Krishńa, never occur, as far as we are yet aware: we have a Rudra, who, in after-times, is identified with Śiva, but who, even in the *Puráńas*, is of very doubtful origin and identification; whilst in the Véda he is described as the father of the winds, and is evidently a form of either Agni or Indra. The epithet Kapardin, which is applied to him, appears, indeed, to have some relation to a characteristic attribute of Śiva,—the wearing of his hair in a peculiar braid; but the term has probably in the *Véda* a different signification...at any rate, no other epithet applicable to Śiva occurs, and there is not the slightest allusion to the form in which, for the last ten centuries at least, he seems to have been almost exclusively worshipped in India,—that of the *Linga* or *Phallus*. Neither is there the slightest hint of another important feature of later Hindúism, the Trimúrtti, or Tri-une combination of Brahmá, Vishńu and Śiva, as typified by the mystical syllable *Óm*, although, according to high authority on the religions of antiquity [*viz.* Creuzer's], the Trimúrtti was the first element in the faith of the Hindús, and the second was the Lingam.'

[2] 'The existence of but one caste in the age of purity, however incompatible with the legend which ascribes the origin of the four tribes to Brahmá, is everywhere admitted.' Wilson, *Vishńu Puráńa*, p. 406, n. 8. Lond. 1840. This admission is strengthened by the fact that other races kindred to the Áryans were unacquainted with the distinction of caste. It should, however, be remarked that one single hymn in the *Rig-Véda* favours a contrary hypothesis: 'Le Brahman a été sa bouche; le prince (Râjanya) ses bras; le Vêsya, ses cuisses: le Soudra est né de ses pieds' (Langlois, IV. 341). But this hymn is allowed on all hands to be of later date (*Ibid.* pp. 498, 499; Lassen, I. 794). There is also in the *Rig-Véda* (see Langlois, IV. 489, n. 62) an instance of the early use of *dwijas* (*i. e.* 'twiceborn'), which is afterwards applied to members of the three superior castes, who as such underwent a special form of initiation; but in that remote period the expression seems to have been used merely for the priests ('les premiers-nés de Rita').

[3] 'Dieses Dogma ist den Vêda fremd, und die wenigen Anspielungen, die in ihnen auf Mythen vor-

What length of interval was necessary for producing all these changes, social, mental, and linguistic, it is now impossible to state with anything like confidence or precision. The development of cognate languages, the culture and expansion of the human intellect, as well as the formation of the framework of society, may all have varied much in different climates and in different periods of man's history. But, what is most essential to our purpose, no eminent critic of the present day will venture to maintain that Hindú civilisation, as represented by its literature, is capable of being carried backwards to a period more remote than that of Joshua and the Exodus,—the age when Hebrew literature began to flourish, and, in contrast to the Áryan, manifest a thoroughly historic character,—the age, moreover, when the literature, if such it can be called, of other ancient nations can present to the inquirer little more than monstrous legends, or fantastic mythes, or barren lists of dynasties.

§ 2. *Bráhmanism.*

It seems that when the Áryans had secured their conquests in the country of the Five Rivers, and, as some conjecture, offshoots following the course of the Indus had been planted as far south as Cutch and Guzerat, the chief attention of the invaders was directed to the spread of civilisation in the other parts of the Peninsula. The centre of their earliest operations was a narrow strip of territory, watered on one side by the Saraswati, from whence new colonies were propagated year by year, until the plain of the Ganges was entirely rescued from the grasp of the 'barbarian.'

On proceeding to inspect the institutions now completed, we approach another epoch in the history of Hindústán. The twilight of intelligence is passed. The age when elements and processes of nature had by man's poetic faculty been converted, first, into the symbols of religious feeling, and then into the objects of religious worship, is succeeded[1] by an age entitled 'the

kommen, die später in die Avatâra des Vischnu aufgenommen worden sind, zeigen, dass in der ältesten Zeit die Lehre von der periodischen Menschwerdung des erhaltenden Gottes zur Vertilgung des Uebels noch nicht gebildet worden war:' Lassen, I. 488.

[1] The divinities of the Vaidic period, who most resemble the heroes of the next age, are the two demigods Aswins, *Aświnau* (dual), children of the sun, endowed with youth and beauty, travelling in a three-wheeled and triangular car, physicians of the gods and

heroic age of India,' when the gods are more completely *humanized*, assume a definite shape in the imagination of the worshipper, and exhibit all the ordinary signs of individuality.

Philosophers are not unfrequently disposed to welcome this new species of polytheism, on the ground that it contains a germ of something more exalted and more ethical. They think that the idea of God as one, as personal, as righteous, an idea which in the former period was extruded from the popular belief, was far more likely to be rescued and restored to its supremacy when the inquirer started from the notion of man-like gods, than when he bowed in adoration to a host of shadowy genii or impersonal abstractions. On the other hand, it should be recollected that the Hindú populace would also be more prone to acquiesce in a polytheism of its own creation, and lose sight of spiritual facts which had their symbols in the primitive mythology. In the worship of the elements, the veil between the seen and unseen had remained comparatively slender; in the worship of anthropomorphic gods in whom all human excellencies found their utmost limit, the new object was more satisfying because it was more human, but on that account was far less calculated to suggest a higher class of truths.

We must allow, indeed, that intellectually the Áryans gained a more exalted point of civilisation in the second period of their history. The field of knowledge had been everywhere enlarged: the power of abstract thinking and the tendency to metaphysical speculation, scarcely traceable in the Védas, were now rapidly developed in all quarters: the refinement of men's taste had shewn itself, if not in graceful and voluptuous works of art, at least in the unrivalled majesty and music of their language as employed in the heroic poems. It is also true that in proportion as they grew familiar with antagonisms in nature, they betrayed a somewhat deeper consciousness of discord in themselves; and that with keener sense of moral turpitude, there came the habit of self-loathing and the aspiration after some deliverance from the fetters of the flesh. Such yearnings might be often silenced by the thought that purity, attractive though it be, is for the present unattainable, that the character

benefactors of the human race. Their name is derived from *aśwa* (equus), since they are said to have been begotten by the sun during his metamorphosis as a horse; but as their mother is once called the sea (Sindhu), many writers identify them simply with the sun and moon, which appear to rise out of the ocean: cf. Prof. Wilson, 'Introd. to *Rig-Véda*, Vol. I. p. xxxvi. and Vol. II. p. 179.

of gods themselves is full of grievous stains and blemishes, that the obligation to a holy life is seldom if ever urged in the most sacred institutions of their forefathers; yet notwithstanding every drawback and abatement, the existence of a higher tone of moral sensibility appears unquestionable; and therefore we may gladly acquiesce in Ritter's verdict[1], that 'the retrogression in the second period of Indian religion was not unattended with an element of progress.'

Special features of this new system will be more fully noticed when we come to trace the parallelisms which they exhibit to the facts and verities of Christianity. At present suffice it to enumerate a few of the more prominent characteristics. The Divine has been distinctly apprehended under the form of the human; and thus the pantheon is inhabited by beings of godlike grace or power or dignity, conspicuous alike in counsel and in action, and especially enlisted in diffusing the Áryan faith among the old possessors of the soil. The system also of which these are the most popular divinities is made to undergo extensive modifications. It has now a far more definite creed, a cumbrous and elaborate ritual, a code of laws, a dominant order of religious teachers. The Védas, we have noticed, bear no marks of a distinction such as that which forms the basis of the Hindú castes; indeed the royal and the sacerdotal offices are there at times united in one eminent person; but in all the commentaries on the Védas, and still more throughout the Laws of Manu[2], the social system of the Indo-Áryans is completely organized. The whole population, as we there see them, are distributed into four hereditary classes. One of these embraces, it would seem, the conquered natives[3], whose position is accordingly most abject. The

[1] *Hist. of Ancient Philosophy*, I. 94.

[2] These were edited and translated under the title *Mánava Dharma-Śástra* by Sir G. C. Haughton, who based his labours on the older version of Sir W. Jones. Scholars are, however, still divided as to the antiquity of this compilation: cf. Ritter, I. 72 sq. with Elphinstone, *Hist. of India*, pp. 226 sq. 3rd ed. Of course many of the materials were far more ancient: but the most probable date of the appearance of the code in its present form is about the fifth century B.C. (later than the rise of Buddhism, and earlier than the great epic poems).

[3] Lassen, I. 799. So impure and abject were the members of this fourth class, that Bráhmans might not read the Védas, even to themselves, in the presence of a śúdra; while to teach him the law, or instruct him in the mode of expiating sin, was sure to sink a Bráhman into the hell called Asamvrita (Elphinstone, pp. 16, 17). Yet the chańdála, or offspring of intercourse which violated the law of caste, was held to be even more contemptible. He was classed with 'dogs and crows.'

remainder, who form the Áryan part of the community, are (1) Bráhmans, or religious teachers, (2) Kshatriyas, or knights, and (3) Vaiśyas, or tradesmen. But in social rank the Bráhman always rises very high above his fellows. He is the depository of Divine wisdom and authority. A belief in his exalted origin[1] secures him the profoundest reverence even of the royal family. His duties are indeed so rigorously defined, his life is so divided between study, labour, and austerities, that he is precluded from intermeddling in affairs of state or from otherwise exceeding the bounds of his position; yet in all that appertains to knowledge, secular or sacred, he is absolute and unimpeachable.

The steps by which the Bráhman gained this vast ascendency are matters only of conjecture. Traces may be found of some mighty conflict between him and the Kshatriya, between the champion of intelligence and the champion of physical prowess; and even after the Bráhman was victorious, the distinction he had won was far less absolute than that which separated all the three superior classes from the wretched śúdras they had crushed. Each individual of those three classes was *dwija*, 'twice-born:' on arriving at maturity, they all received a special tonsure, and were all invested with a thread that symbolised their elevation far above the multitude, that gave them access to the Védas, and, it may be, intimated a belief that souls of a superior order had in recompense of previous merits been permitted to spend another life in tenements so honourable[2].

But the Hindú doctrine of caste is intimately connected with other central verities of their religion. The Bráhman occupied the highest place in the gradations of society, because he was believed to stand in the most intimate relation to the Supreme Being, because the Spirit of the Universe had been most clearly imaged forth in him. For during all this second period of Hindúism we shall find the various species of existence ultimately traced to unity, on the ground that each is a constituent part of God, and that its special character depends upon its distance, or the measure of its aberration, from the primal source of being. In the creed of Bráhmanism, as methodised by 'orthodox' philosophy, God alone is truly said to be: all other forms of life are, as to their material properties, but empty and illusive; while, as to their spiritual properties,

[1] See above, p. 134, n. 2.

[2] Cf. Fred. von Schlegel, *Phil. of Hist.* pp. 156, 157; Wuttke, II. 318.

they are but transient scintillations of His glory. Alone, supreme, and unapproachable, a feeling of dissatisfaction with Himself had crossed the mind of the Great Solitary. He longed for offspring, and at length determined to resolve the primitive simplicity of His essence, and transform Himself into a world which might contrast with His eternal quietude. From this desire of God has sprung whatever is, or is to be: the earth, the sky, the rock, the flower, the forest, the innumerable tribes of gods and men, of beasts and demons,—these, so far as they possess a true existence, are all consubstantial with divinity. The basis underlying all the forms which they assume is the Ineffable, the Uncreated. God may be regarded as the undeveloped world, the world as the development of God. He is both the fountain and the stream, the cause and the effect, the one Creator and the one creation. 'As the spider spins and gathers back [its thread]; as plants sprout on the earth; as hairs grow on a living person; so is this universe, here, produced from the imperishable nature. By contemplation the vast one germinates; from him food [*or*, body] is produced; and thence, successively, breath, mind, real [elements], worlds and immortality arising from [good] deeds[1].' Expressions of this kind had not unnaturally suggested to some minds the inference that the pantheism of ancient India was simple and materialistic: but a further insight into the philosophy, at least so far as it appears in monuments of the Bráhmanic age[2], will prove such inferences to be erroneous. We may not indeed, be able to decide with confidence respecting the complexion of the earliest Hindú metaphysics, since the Védas, notwithstanding the ingenuity of their commentators[3], will be found to have contained a very slender metaphysical element: but as soon as ever an attempt was made to bring the ruder superstitions of their forefathers into harmony with more refined conceptions of the Godhead, the whole tone of Hindú pantheism is subtilized,

[1] An extract given by Colebrooke (*Asiat. Researches*, VIII. 475) from a upanishad of the fourth Véda.

[2] A specimen is subjoined from the first chapter of the *Laws of Manu* (Jones' *Works*, III. 66, 4to. ed.): 'He, whom the mind alone can perceive, whose essence eludes the external organs, who has no visible parts, who exists from eternity, even *He*, the soul of all beings, whom no being can comprehend, shone forth in person. He, having willed to produce various beings *from His own divine substance*, first with a thought created the waters, and placed in them a productive seed,' &c.

[3] For instance, they have tried to evolve the principal dogmas of the Védánta philosophy, on the unity and universality of spirit, from a long hymn of the *Rig-Véda*, II. 125 sq., ed. Wilson.

to the extent of questioning the reality of the material world itself. All forms assumed by matter are then held to be not only transient but illusive. The semblance of reality which they possess is due to Máyá[1],—the personification of God's fruitless longing for some being other than His own,—the power, by which, in different words, the Absolute had been Himself beguiled from His original quietude. But while matter is thus held to be essentially non-existent, that which underlies and animates the whole of the phenomenal universe is one with the Divinity, who, by a species of self-analysis, has brought Himself under the conditions of the finite and the temporal, and must in future so continue till the visible is ultimately reabsorbed by the invisible, and multiplicity reduced afresh to simple unity.

It must not, however, be supposed that this idea of one original and all-pervading spirit (Mahán-Átmá) was irreconcileable with the old polytheism. On the contrary, the pantheon of the Indo-Áryans was enlarged instead of narrowed in the progress of this second period, till, as seen in the Puráńas, it has reached a most appalling magnitude. I shall hereafter have occasion to refer specifically to the sacred triad of the Bráhmans, and shall therefore only touch upon it here, as one example of a law by which the mind of the Hindú was constantly disposed to view all forms of being under triune aspects[2].

[1] On this peculiar feature of Bráhmanism, see Wuttke, II. 282 sq., who shews that in the Vaidic period, *máyá* meant no more than the desire of evolution. However, the idea of *máyá*, as fully developed, always implies 'illusion,' 'unreality:' it means that God, who in himself had no attributes, was beguiled into a belief that He possessed them by his union with *máyá*, or his own longing; and so appeared to create, preserve, and destroy. The following illustration from the *Probodha-Chandrodaya*, as translated by Goldstücker (Ibid. p. 284), will throw further light upon this subject: 'Maja [*i. e.* Máyá] ist unbegreiflich. Gleich einer unzüchtigen Dirne lässt sie den höchsten Geist Dinge sehen, die gar nicht existiren, und täuscht ihn so. Der Göttliche, dessen Glanz dem Krystalle gleicht, der niemals sich verändert, ward durch sie, die Unehrbare, in heftige Unruhe versetzt. Er, der Wissende, hing unklaren Phantasien nach, und da er in den von der Maja bereiteten Schlummer fiel, erblickte er betäubt vielgestaltige Träume: ich bin, diess ist mein Vater, diess meine Mutter, diess mein Feld, mein Reichthum *u. s. w.* ...Wie ein See in den Truggebilden der Mittagssonne erscheint, so entfaltete sich das fleckenlose Licht aus unrichtiger Erkenntniss als Äther, Luft, Feuer, Wasser, Erde.'

[2] Wuttke, with a truly Germanic passion for symmetrical arrangement, and well-rounded theories, has represented this tendency in a genealogical form:

Addicted from the first to the examination of natural phenomena, he could not fail to witness year by year the rise, the growth, the death (in order to the reproduction) of vegetable matter. The concentration of his thoughts on such a process had induced the habit of generalizing his conceptions, and finally of picturing all the changes of the universe as an effect of generating, preserving, and dissolving forces. It was by this process also that the properties of creation, of preservation, of destruction (as the medium of regeneration) were personified and worshipped as Brahmá, Vishńu, and Śiva. The absolute and self-existent, the impersonal That, by which the universe was first projected into being, whose creative energies still operate in never-ending cycles, had been thus presented to the Hindú mind as 'three only[1]:' while some elevated spirits, searching after the one supreme God, 'if haply they might find Him,' laboured to identify the object of their search with the first member of the sacred triad. As he was called Brahmá (masculine), they named it Brahma (neuter). But results which we have noticed in the Vaidic age were no less visible in this. The lofty product of man's generalizing faculty was too ethereal and transcendent for the cognizance of ordinary spirits. So remote was Brahma from the sphere of sinful finite beings, so unloving and impersonal his character, that no temple was erected and no victim offered in his honour: and even his more concrete image, the personified Brahmá, has never, in historic times, conciliated to himself a share of popular veneration[2].

Das sich entfaltende Brahma

	Entstehen	Bestehen	Vergehen
	Geburt	Leben	Tod
	Satva	Radschas	Tamas
	Licht	Luft	Feuer
	Himmel	Oberwelt	Unterwelt
	Indra	Varuna	Agni
	Brahmá	Vischnu	Çiva
	Götter	Menschen	Thiere
	Geist	Seele	Körper
(Seele:)	Selbstheit	Gemüth	Verstand
(Körper:)	Kopf	Brust	Bauch
	Brahmanen	Xatrija	Vaiçja.

[1] See *Asiatic Researches*, VIII. 395—397, where Colebrooke quotes a remarkable passage from the *Nirukta*, affirming that the gods are 'only three' in number. It will be noticed more at length in Chap. II.

[2] See Stuhr, *Religions-systeme des Orients*, I. 97, 98. He is still

No apter illustration can be furnished of the shifting and capricious genius of Hindú mythology, than the fact that of those three divinities who rank foremost in the system of the Bráhmans, Śiva had been previously unhonoured and unknown. The other two had, in like manner, held subordinate positions, Vishńu figuring in the Védas as an elemental god like Varuńa, and Brahmá, if there identical with Brahman[1], being merely an equivalent for Agni. And in strict accordance with these facts, the highest tenants of the Hindú pantheon are still viewed as finite beings, liable, when certain revolutions are completed, to dethronement and extinction. They partake of the phenomenal character of the universe; and therefore the eventual winding up of all things will necessitate their reabsorption.

It is thus apparent that the fundamental dogma of the Bráhmans is the dogma of *emanation*. The Divinity is believed to be resolved, diffused, discerpted, and so weakened. All things are imperfect, because all are in a state of flux and reflux; their intrinsic character depending on their ever-varying distance from the centre of unity, or on the number of the intermediate links by which they are removed from the original essence.

And the same idea will help us more than any other to elucidate the Hindú theory of man. The 'orthodox' philosopher uniformly started, in his speculations on this subject, from the Divine side of things, because with him spirit is all-important, and the human spirit consubstantial with the Spirit of the universe. But owing to a happy inconsistency, which reappears in many later speculations, Hindú pantheism could not altogether blast those instincts of the soul which lead man to assert his individuality and the inherent freedom of his choice. A few who called themselves philosophers yielded, it is true, to logical pressure, and adopted the degrading error of the fatalist; they argued that the foulest crimes of man are ultimately wrought by Brahma, and therefore that the guilt is not attributable to the human instrument[2]: but even his own distorted

worshipped by one class, the Bráhmans, at sunrise every morning: but (as Mr Elphinstone remarks) he 'was never much worshipped, and has now but one temple in India' (p. 89, 3rd ed.).

[1] See Langlois, *Rig-Veda*, IV. 386: where we find a hymn on the marriage of Brahman and Júhú. In many other passages of the *Rig-Véda* Brahmanaspati = Agni, where Brahman appears to mean 'priest.'

[2] The Christian missionary of the present day is not unfrequently repulsed, when speaking of righteousness and judgment to come, by such assertions as the following: 'I have neither sin nor guilt, for every thing is wrought in me by Brahma:' cf. Wuttke, II. 332. 'Adhuc enim mihi

version of the Fall will testify that the Hindú was dimly conscious all the while of his original freedom and nobility. According to that tradition[1] God, when he determined to project the universe, gave birth at once to all particular souls. At first, they were both free and happy, but, impelled by envy and ambition, they eventually broke away still further from the primal essence, and so forfeited their eminent place among celestial intelligences. A world, or rather purgatory, was then constructed for their habitation: it came forth already blighted and disorganized; and out of it was made the human body of the same debased material, in order to supply more deadly instruments of torture, and more dismal cells for the incarceration of the damned[2]. The Here and visible had thus become in Bráhmanism the dark antithesis of the Hereafter and invisible; and we learn, accordingly, how from the doctrine of *emanation* had sprung up a second characteristic principle of this creed,—the doctrine of *dualism*. So lost, however, is the human spirit, so oppressed by the ungenial atmosphere around it, and so weakened by the sinful burdens of the flesh, that though in every case believed to be recoverable, many a life of pain and penance will be ordinarily needed for promoting its exaltation and securing its return. It may at first, for instance, be united with the lowest species of organic life; and, under favourable circumstances, may ascend in its successive births 'into the bodies of spiders, of snakes, of chameleons' and the like, until deemed worthy of inhabiting a human tenement. The trial then begins which will determine all its future destiny. An opportunity has been given it of achieving its own liberation; and according to the present quality of its actions it will mount directly upwards through the ranks of demi-gods and gods, or plunge again into the lower region of existence, and commence a fresh series of births. It may be that this vast idea of transmigration was suggested partly by man's growing consciousness of his demerit, partly by his inability to account for the existing distribution of rewards and punishments, partly by observing points of contact and resemblance between faculties and instincts of the lower animals and those of human beings. But, however prompted, the idea of transmigration became at length so deeply rooted in the creed of Hindústán, that even the most rampant forms of infidelity were unable to dislodge it. The first aim of

videbatur, non esse nos qui peccamus, sed nescio quam aliam in nobis peccare naturam.' S. August. *Confess.* v. 10.

[1] See more on this subject in Chap. III.

[2] See the picture of a human body in *Manu*, chap. VI. §§ 77, 78.

the Bráhmanical system, as interpreted alike by peasant and philosopher, was to shorten the duration of such wanderings, or diminish the amount of purgatorial suffering: and the highest glory of that system, in the eyes of all its votaries, was to furnish rules or grant indulgences, by which they might attain immediate and complete exemption from such terrible necessity[1].

What, then, are the methods which the Bráhman has prescribed for the attainment of supreme felicity, or reabsorption into God? These methods are reducible to two. The first, adapted to the character and capacities of the many, consisted chiefly, not to say exclusively, of outward and mechanical acts of worship. Moral merit[2] was by them confounded with ritual punctuality. The repetition of the sacred texts which they had gathered from the teaching of the Bráhmans, though the súdra-class was rigorously denied this scanty privilege; the invocation of a host of deities; the deprecation of evil spirits; dutiful obedience to the priestly order, and merciful regard for every class of sentient creatures[3],—these were deemed the fittest passport, not indeed to absolute repose, but to a loftier and more hopeful stage of being on the dissolution of the present body.

It was very different with the second and far smaller class, the early mystics and philosophers of Hindústán. By these the doctrine of God's abstract unity was more completely realized, and therefore when they countenanced the worship of the *dévas*, it was only as the old Socinian worshipped Christ, or as the Roman Catholic of the present age professes to adore the saints[4].

1 'This belief [in a metempsychosis] is not to be looked upon as a mere popular superstition: it is the main principle of all Hindú metaphysics; it is the foundation of all Hindú philosophy. The great object of their philosophical research in every system, Bráhmanical or Buddhist, is the discovery of the means of putting a stop to further transmigration; the discontinuance of corporeal being; the liberation of soul from body.' Wilson, 'Pref.' to the *Sánkhya Káriká*, p. x. Oxf. 1837.

2 For instance, it is declared in the *Laws of Manu* (ch. II. § 79: Jones' *Works*, III. 94): 'A twice-born man [*i. e.* a member of any of the three superior castes], who shall a thousand times repeat those three (or Óm, the vyáhritis, and the gáyatrí) apart [from the multitude] shall be released in a month even from a great offence, as a snake from his slough.' Again (§ 82): 'Whosoever shall repeat day by day, for three days, without negligence, that sacred text, shall [hereafter] approach the Divine essence, move freely as air, and assume an ethereal form.' Cf. also the consentient testimony of the late Col. Sleeman, a very acute observer of the peculiarities of the Hindú mind, in his *Rambles and Recollections*, II. 18, 19.

3 See *Manu*, ch. XII. § 83.

4 See the language of a Portuguese missionary in Von Bohlen, *Das alte Indien*, I. 153.

They even shrank from the idea of giving attributes to God, and so reducing Him within the sphere of human sympathies, but laboured, on the other hand, to raise humanity at once into complete equality with the Divine. Their favourite motto was, 'He who knows the Supreme God becomes God.' On the wings of knowledge, therefore, these philosophers hoped to rise indefinitely until they lost themselves in that which is alone true being,—the abysses of the Absolute and Universal. They did not, it may be, reject the ceremonial worship of their forefathers; they did not feel exonerated from the duty of restraining their sensual appetites, but rather would insist upon the need of violent austerities in order to escape more easily from every fascination of the natural life: yet, on the other hand, the pinnacles on which they stood were so exalted and so inaccessible to the many, that a total separation was now forming between them and other classes of their fellow-countrymen, between the follower of the Hindú Gnosis and the herd of vulgar and unlettered souls: and, as the tradesman could never gain the social eminence of the soldier, nor the soldier of the Bráhman, none but members of the learned class were they to whom immediate liberation was made possible. The rest had, speaking generally, been doomed to wander on for ages, and to undergo an almost endless series of new births.

The object of these pages does not make it necessary for me to adjudicate respecting the antiquity of the religious system, which had manifestly reached its prime on the appearance of the Institutes of Manu. Nearly all competent scholars are inclined to place it far higher than the date of Alexander's expedition[1], arguing partly from allusions interspersed in Greek writers of the period, and still more from evidence surviving in the two great epic poems of Hindústán, the Rámáyana and Mahábhárata, which not only testify to the continuous struggle of that system,

[1] Almost the only writer of intelligence who now advocates the contrary is Col. Sykes: see *Asiat. Journal*, Vol. VI. He there affirms, 'After a careful collation of facts, I unhesitatingly declare, that I have not met with evidence to satisfy my mind that Bráhmanism *was ever in the ascendant*, until after the fall of Buddhism' (p. 448). He believes that Buddhism was the old religion of the Áryans, and that Bráhmanism first became the popular creed, when Sankhara Áchárya established the exclusive worship of Síva in the 9th century after Christ. In like manner Col. Sykes is of opinion that the Pali is an older language than the Sanskrit, and especially presses the point that, although we have many old inscriptions and coins of Buddhist kings (in Pali), we have none whatever of Bráhmanical kings until the fourth, nay probably until the seventh century after Christ.

in the south of India, with the older form of heathenism, with 'monsters, giants and barbarous men,' but also indicate the vast predominance obtained by the Bráhmanical order. Yet, however this question may be finally decided, little doubt exists that long before the inroads of the Macedonian hero, adversaries of the 'orthodox' belief were silently arising and acquiring strength beneath its very shadow. As the primitive religion of the Védas was transformed from year to year, until, in spite of their ingenious commentators, we are able to detect few traces of its earlier characteristics, so the creed of Bráhmanism itself was finally assaulted by the learned artifices of the sceptic, and transmuted in the crucible of the philosopher.

§ 3. *Schools of Philosophy*[1].

While the influence of the sacerdotal order was rapidly increasing, while the Vaidic doctrines were recast in more ideal moulds, and while the popular mind of India, vigorous and creative as before, was on the one side adding to the number of its mythes, and on the other forming new religious confraternities exclusively devoted to the worship either of Śiva or Vishńu, the thinking class of the community was more and more estranged from the religion of their fathers. They began to pry into such questions as the following: 'What is the original element, or power of nature, lying at the base of all phenomena? What is man, and whence? Whither is he tending? Which of all things is the most important? What is truth? And what must be my aim in order that I may have done what is fitting to be done?' These questions might be

[1] The two schools entitled to the name of 'orthodox,' are (1) the *Púrva* (earlier) *Mimánsá*, founded by Jaimini, with the design of facilitating the interpretation of the Védas, and (2) the *Uttara* (later) *Mimánsá*, or *Védánta*, attributed to the half-mythical sage Vyása, or by others more correctly to Vyása, named Krishńa Dwaipáyana. The name Védánta (anta='end') sufficiently denotes the spirit which pervaded the latter system: although the basis of that system must be sought not so much in the Védas proper, as in the Upanishads. See Colebrooke's *Essays on the Philosophy of the Hindús*, as edited, with additions, by Pauthier, Paris, 1833; and the very useful edition of the *Aphorisms* of various schools, printed for the Benares Government College, under the care of Dr. Ballantyne. For a copy of the latter series I am indebted to the courtesy of John Muir, Esq., a true friend of India, who has himself published *An Examination of Religions*, in Sanskrit and English, Part I., Mirzapore, 1852, and Part II., Calcutta, 1854; and a collection, with an English translation, of *Original Sanskrit Texts on the Origin and Progress of the Religion and Institutions of India*, Lond. 1858.

turned aside or deemed unanswerable by many to whom they were presented; but others, reeling under the burden they imposed, would not unfrequently retire for comfort to the neighbouring forest, and as followers gathered round them, each might finally become the centre of a literary circle, if not the founder of a school. At first, however, the contemplative philosopher might be unconscious, or but slightly conscious, of his opposition to the 'sacred' writings. He might even, like the earliest race of Christian schoolmen, be desirous of employing philosophic methods only to establish popular belief on a more rational and lasting basis. To his efforts, therefore, we may be indebted for the systematic moulding of Hindúism, which appears in the post-Vaidic writings; since every school of 'orthodox' philosophy manifests the deepest veneration both for lyric and dogmatic portions of the Védas. These are deemed the utterances of God himself; and, as partaking of His essence, they are absolute, infallible, eternal[1].

Yet other thoughtful spirits, who have frequent representatives in later times and distant countries[2], grew more daring in their philosophical speculations. They were more disposed to start afresh in their pursuit of knowledge, to devise a theory of religion for themselves, and gather the materials mainly, if not solely, from their observation of the world around them. It was rather in the open book of nature than in the traditionary hymns and legends that they hoped to find a satisfactory solution of their multiplying doubts.

This bolder race of Hindú speculators we shall most conveniently study in three classes, (*a*) the 'atheistic' Sánkhya, (*b*) Buddhism, (*c*) the eclectic, or intermediate school, as represented in the Bhagavad-Gítá.

a. Sánkhya Philosophy.

The author of the Sánkhya philosophy was Kapila, who, like the great majority of educated Hindús, was probably a

[1] For example, it is stoutly contended by the school of Mímánsá (*Aphorisms*, Part I. pp. 32 sq. ed. Ballantyne) that the Védas are retrospectively eternal, notwithstanding the occurrence in them of names of men, &c.

[2] Cousin, while engaged in lecturing on the philosophy of the last century, found himself carried back to India as the birthplace of systems which are often thought to be of modern extraction: 'En effet,' he writes, 'la philosophie indienne est tellement vaste, que tous les systèmes de philosophie s'y rencontrent, qu'elle forme tout un monde philosophique, et qu'on peut dire à la lettre que l'histoire de la philosophie de l'Inde est un abrégé de l'histoire entière de la philosophie.' *Cours de l'Hist. de Philosophie*, I. 180, Paris, 1829.

Bráhman; though his later followers hold that he obtained his knowledge of the twenty-five categories, which formed the basis of his teaching, 'merely by birth;' in other words, that he was himself an incarnation of the Deity[1]. The system which he founded was entitled Sánkhya[2], apparently because the author deemed it a result of pure reason, or deliberate judgment. It professed to remedy the various ills of life, external and internal, by resolving intellectual difficulties, and by revealing to its votary 'the real nature of all that is.' It does not, like some other systems, spend its strength in trying to discriminate between existence and non-existence; it puts the further question, What *made* things as they are? and thus, excepting soul, which is a mute, inert, and passionless spectator of the process, every thing is by the Sánkhya represented under the two aspects of 'producer' and 'production[3].'

In this creed, the plastic origin of all material things, the primary productive essence[4] (*prakriti*), whose properties come before us in sensation, is the 'undiscrete,' the indestructible, the all-embracing, or, in modern phraseology, the Absolute. 'Creation' is the individualising of this universal principle: yet the motive power is due in no case to a conscious and designing Agent, but rather to blind impulses, evolving first intelligence, or *buddhi*, one of the inherent properties of the material essence, and then self-consciousness, the third in order of the Sánkhya principles[5]. The consciousness of individual existence (*ahan-kára*) is thus, according to the present system, an attribute of matter[6]: its organ is material: it can only be connected with the soul by self-illusion: it is no proper and original element of man; and in the school of Kapila, the aim is so to educate the young philosopher, that he is prepared to lay aside the pronoun *I* entirely, to affirm that souls have individually no interest either in human passions or possessions,

[1] See Dr. Ballantyne's *Lecture on the Sánkhya Philosophy*, embracing the text of the *Tattwa-Samása*, Mirzapore, 1850.

[2] Sánkhya from sankhyá = 'number,' and also 'reason.' Hence the 'rational system.' Others find in the name a reference to something like the Pythagorean theory of numbers. It is worth observing that the modern Buddhists of Ceylon frequently call their teachers 'the clergy of reason:' Tennent, *Christianity in Ceylon*, p. 192.

[3] *Lecture*, as above, p. 53.

[4] On its affinity with the ὕλη of Plato and Aristotle, see M. Pauthier's note on Colebrooke, *Essais*, p. 17.

[5] *Lecture*, as above, pp. 26, 54.

[6] See *Sánkhya Káriká*, ed. Wilson, pp. 175, 176, where it is distinctly affirmed that the soul or spirit can have no attributes, and is entirely passive.

and in this sense to declare, as the grand climax of his teaching, 'Neither I am, nor is ought mine, nor is there any I[1].'

Another feature of the system is that, without impugning the reality of spirit, or refusing to it some directive agency, the active principle in man is always held to be a property of body, and action itself regarded as material. Kapila did not wish, as it would seem, to enter on elaborate discussions touching the origin and destination of man's spiritual nature. Philosophy, he concluded, ought to deal chiefly with phenomena, not with final causes, and excepting hints to the effect that *buddhi*, or intelligence, though itself material, is the link between the soul and matter, we shall look in vain for any definite theory as to the connexion and disconnexion of the visible and the invisible. The Sánkhya speculator had before him two distinct classes of effects, a world produced by nature, and a multitude of souls proceeding from a spiritual essence. The first attracted his chief interest. He did not, however, fail to recognise the fact that souls are in the ordinary state of man possessed, or, he would say, deluded by the consciousness of individuality, and that this consciousness will haunt them till, so far as they are interested, all the processes of nature have completed their development. He also held that such activity of nature has no other object than the liberation of the soul: it is an instance of unselfishness: the process will go on with reference to that liberation, till it is no longer needed,—'as a man boiling rice for a meal desists when it is dressed[2].' 'Generous nature, endued with qualities, does by manifold means accomplish without benefit [to herself] the wish of ungrateful soul, devoid of qualities[3]:' expressions, which, if I mistake not, were among the earliest evidences that philosophic minds were rising to the great conception of self-sacrifice, or rather of spontaneous action in behalf of others.

How far the Sánkhya system is obnoxious to the charge of atheism, has been frequently disputed[4]. Kapila himself affected to discern, in his peculiar theory of nature, the solution of all human problems, and consequently was disposed to treat assertions of a primal and intelligent Cause, distinct from matter and surpassing nature, as extremely doubtful, or, at least, as

[1] Colebrooke, p. 44. The original is remarkable: Násmi na mé náham.

[2] *Sánkhya Káriká*, ed. Wilson, p. 168.

[3] *Ibid.* p. 171.

[4] Cousin, who treats the Sánkhya philosophy as the sensualism [sensationalism] of India, declares that it must always issue in 'materialism, fatalism, atheism' (*Cours* &c. I. 200).

philosophically superfluous. Hence opponents[1], in whose eyes religion and philosophy were convertible terms, assailed him chiefly on this ground, asseverated that his teaching was 'unscriptural' and absurd, repudiated his attempts to shelter himself beneath a figurative interpretation of the Védas, and branded all his speculations with the title 'atheistic' (*niríśwara, i. e.* 'without an *íśwara,*' or 'lord'). But his disciples might have urged in mitigation of this charge that Kapila does not entirely overlook the presence of spirit in the midst of the material universe,—inert, indeed, and passionless, 'a bystander, a spectator[2],' but still a real entity,—and further, that he is not unwilling to assign the origin of individual souls to some great central essence[3], gifted with volition, and as such, analogous to the abstract God of the Védántins. The truth appears to be that Kapila, in recoiling from their system, rushed at once into the opposite extreme. They laboured to get rid of contradictions between visible and invisible by questioning, and finally denying, the reality of the former. He, perplexed as much as they by the anomalies and apparent dualism of the world, allotted the first place to matter, or at least invested it with all active properties. What was Máyá, or illusion, in the 'orthodox' creed, became reality in his: it was the true foundation of the visible universe.

The Sánkhya was, however, thoroughly Indian in the practical bent of his philosophy. He was striving, like the rest, to purchase an exemption from the fatal liability to repetition of birth; he hoped to further the emancipation of the spirit from the bonds of individuality. And knowledge was the single recipe which he would deign to offer in promoting these desir-

[1] See the *Aphorisms of the Vedánta Philosophy*, Bk. I. ch. I. sect. II. (ed. Ballantyne), containing a 'confutation of the Atheistic doctrines of the Sánkhyas.' One argument is well put, *viz.* that man, who by the philosopher is called upon to identify himself with the course of the world, cannot without absurdity be called upon to identify himself with what is unintelligent.

[2] Colebrooke, ed. Pauthier, pp. 40, 180. In reply to the question, What is soul? it is answered (*Lecture*, as above, p. 17): 'Soul is without beginning, subtile, omnipresent, intelligent, without [the three] qualities, eternal, spectator, enjoyer, not an agent, the knower of body, pure, not producing aught.'

[3] This is disputed by a writer in the *Colonial Church Chronicle*, XI. 108; quoting Colebrooke's Essay, where it is maintained that the soul is, according to the Sánkhyas, 'neither produced nor productive: it is multitudinous' [*i. e.* there is a multitude of souls, and not one only universal soul], 'individual, sensitive, eternal, unalterable, immaterial.' The view taken in the text is supplied by J. C. Thompson, Introd. to the *Bhagavad Gítá*, p. lxvii. and elsewhere.

able results. He laid no stress whatever on the influences of moral goodness; while sacrifice and every form of ritual observance, though the merit of them was in general terms conceded, could possess no charm for him, because they only served to place the worshipper upon a level with the perishable *dêvas*, and secured no more than temporary liberation[1]. Such grovelling aims can never satisfy the aspirations of the true philosopher. He, therefore, hastens to strike out a new and independent pathway, free, as he maintains, from every shadow of 'impurity, excess, or deficiency[2].'

If we ask, What is the special character of the remedy to which these wondrous powers may be attributed?—the answer is that it consists of a profound acquaintance with the Sánkhya philosophy, as digested in twenty-five categories; or, in other words, implies a perfect knowledge of the way in which mankind are constituted, and the means by which they can escape from the entanglements of self. No sooner have these principles been mastered than the Sánkhya is elevated, potentially at least, to the ultimate stages of existence. Pain and pleasure, vice and virtue cease to operate for him. He is no more susceptible of qualities so accidental and so earthly. It is true that, owing to the force of impulses already given, he must continue for a while to occupy a human body, and must act like other mortals, 'as the potter having set his wheel whirling puts on it a lump of clay, fabricates a vessel and takes it off, and leaves the wheel continuing to turn round[3];' yet all the *consequences* of action are prevented when the soul is once illuminated by true knowledge. Or if it be asked again, By what peculiar channels man obtains this salutary illumination?—the answer is, By inference, by perception, and, last in order, by tradition or 'right affirmation[4].' For Kapila was driven to confess not only that some truths may far exceed the range of human vision and the powers of human logic, but that, on their revelation, such high verities are capable of being handed down to future ages. He himself

[1] *Aphorisms of the Sánkhya Philosophy*, Bk. I. Aph. 83: *Sánkhya Káriká*, ed. Wilson, p. 15. In the aphorism, it is maintained, that all liberation, supposed to be wrought out by ritual observances, will be found imperfect and temporary, just because it was the result of *act*, or was accomplished by *means*.

[2] *Sánkhya Káriká*, p. 14. It is curious to observe that the 'impurity' of the Vaidic method arose partly from the countenance there given to *animal* sacrifices.

[3] *Sánkhya Káriká*, pp. 184, 185.

[4] *Lecture*, as above, p. 49. Some of the matters not proveable by perception or by inference are said to be, the existence of Indra, the northern Kurus, the golden mountain Méru, the nymphs in Paradise.

had, for example, been indebted to the ancients for more than one ingredient of the system he had founded.

With regard to the capacities of the human subject, Kapila pursued a very independent line. He went so far as to suggest ideas fatal to the vast prerogatives of the Bráhmans. Human souls, he argued, though personally distinct[1], are all of equal worth and elevation. Present inequalities in their condition he referred to the specific structure of men's bodies, or rather to the distribution of the primary elements from which their bodies are compounded. These elements[2] together form a triad. They are purity or goodness (*sattwa*); imperfection, pain or foulness (*rajas*); blind indifference, stupidity or darkness (*tamas*). In proportion to the dominance obtained by one or other of the primary elements, man approaches, first, to the divine or noble; secondly, to the selfish, or the barely human; thirdly, to the bestial, the inert, or the besotted. He alone who by obeying the dictates of true philosophy rises high above the ordinary level is exempted from the risk, or rather the necessity, of emigrating step by step through various forms of bodily organisation. Here, as we have hinted, Kapila was always true to the received opinions; nay, so deeply rooted in his mind was the idea of transmigration, that he started an elaborate theory for its defence. When some began to ask, How souls which he believed to be inactive have the power of passing from one body to another? or secondly, How it happens that emancipation is not universally effected in the act of disembodiment?—his answer was, that every soul upon its first emission and association with matter, is invested also with a subtile and elastic framework (*linga-śaríra*)[3], the reflection of the more

[1] The rival doctrine of the Védántins is presented in the following extract: 'This soul of all worlds is but one: by *whom* is it made more? Some speak of soul as several—seeing that knowledge and other mental states are observable [simultaneously—some being happy whilst others are sad]; but in the Bráhman, the worm and the insect; in the outcaste, the dog and the elephant; in goats, cows, gadflies and gnats, the wise behold the same' [single soul]: *Lecture*, as above, p. 24.

[2] *Ibid.* p. 27. Such a distribution, with other objects, was perhaps much older than Kapila (Lassen, *Ind. Alt.* I. 832): yet the *guna* of the Sánkhyas is no mere attribute, but a substance discernible by soul through the medium of the faculties. In Prakriti, or nature absolute and unmodified, we have the three qualities in perfect equipoise: Wilson, on *Sánk. Kár.* p. 52.

[3] Colebrooke, pp. 24, 25, with Pauthier's notes. The latter points out the close affinity of this notion to certain speculations of the Greek philosophers and early Fathers of the Church, respecting the corporeity of the soul.

substantial body. This it cannot afterwards abandon till the hour of ultimate emancipation; and a vehicle is consequently found in which the passive soul may be transferred from one material tenement to another.

Acute, however, as the author of the Sánkhya system was, he failed eventually to satisfy the anxious questions of Hindús respecting the Supreme Intelligence. When they demanded by *whom* the human spirit had been made to emanate, or *why* the great primordial element was individualised in human bodies, Kapila could only urge that such had been the necessary order of development, one step of some inscrutable and eternal process. The uniform vagueness of his language on these questions led to the formation of another school, entitled the 'theistic' Sánkhya[1]. It ascribed no will to *prakriti*, or the material essence; it recognised an *íśwara*, or lord, and therefore did not hesitate to preach that God exists, that God is the intelligent Source of being, that God allots those varying passions, powers and faculties which men continually exhibit, and that God is the great Judge who punishes or rewards according to their conduct. Modified by the accession of these new and better influences, the Sánkhya system grew, and flourished in some districts; though at present hardly any traces of it are discernible in the literary circles of Hindústán[2].

b. Buddhism.

From the school of Kapila to that of Buddha[3] the transition is most obvious and direct. The close affinity between them did not escape the eye of Colebrooke, and, in spite of Ritter's disbelief, the truth of his remark has been continually verified[4].

[1] *Ibid.* pp. 34 sq. Wuttke (II. 424) is of opinion that this modification is due to Christian influences: nor is there anything in the chronology adverse to his view; for when Lassen (I. 833) places Patanjali, with whom it is associated, in the 2nd century before Christ, he allows that the evidence for so doing is extremely slight.

[2] In the present day, if it survive at all, we have to search for it among the labyrinths of German metaphysics. Prof. Wilson says: 'During the whole of my intercourse with learned natives, I met with but one Brahman who professed to be acquainted with the writings of this school.' Pref. to the *Sánkhya Káriká*, p. viii.

[3] See a new work by C. F. Kœppen, *Die Religion des Buddha und ihre Entstehung*. Berlin, 1857.

[4] See, for instance, Lassen, I. 830, 831: Saint-Hilaire, *Des Védas*, p. 147. The latter observes with justice, that all the indianists 'n'hésitent pas à reconnaître dans le bouddhisme, devenu plus tard une religion, un développement et une copie du sânkhya de Kapila. La ressemblance ne peut faire le moindre doute pour qui se donnera la peine d'étudier les deux doctrines: les bases de l'une et de l'autre sont identiques.'

One system is indeed no more than the extension and practical embodiment of the other. I am not desirous of maintaining absolutely that principles allied in some degree to those of Buddhism were unknown to other Asiatics in still earlier times[1]. What I intend by Buddhism, is the system of metaphysical and social philosophy, organised by Śákya-muni, or Gautama Buddha. Neither am I speaking here of Buddhism in its modern development, as modified by intermixtures either with the popular forms of Bráhmanism, or with the older superstitions of the countries where it afterwards gained a footing: for that view of it will come more properly before us, when we pass from Hindústán to China, and the other regions where it still possesses a complete ascendancy. In different words, we shall be dealing now with a philosophy rather than with a religion.

Although in passing to a survey of the principles of Buddhism, we entirely quit the region of the mythe and enter that of the historic legend, and although the ground we have to traverse is in general less encumbered by chronological difficulties, the point of starting has not hitherto been absolutely determined. The narratives that wear the greatest semblance of probability are the Chinese on one side, and the Sing'halese on the other; while of these conflicting authorities, the latter is preferred by nearly all competent writers of the present day[2].

1 'It may be,' says Mr. Hardy, (*Manual of Buddhism*, p. 88, Lond. 1853) 'that Gótama presented himself to the world as the successor of men, whose claims to supreme authority were thus acknowledged; but I have not yet met with any well-authenticated data of their doctrines or deeds.' Yet even this has been positively denied by W. von Humboldt in his great work, *Ueber die Kawi-Sprache*, I. 290: 'Sowohl die Annahme eines Vor-Brahmanischen, als eines ursprünglich Ausser-Indischen Buddhismus, bedarf keiner Widerlegung mehr.' Cf. on the other side, Col. Sykes, as above, p. 145, n. 1. I may here also add, that the religion of the Jains, which still survives in Guzerat and other parts of India, is connected in its origin, if not absolutely one with Buddhism: see Colebrooke, *Asiat. Res.* IX. 279 sq. Stuhr, *Die Religions-systeme*, &c. I. 61 sq.

2 E. Burnouf, *Introduction à l'histoire du Bouddhisme indien*, Pref. p. iii. p. 587, Paris, 1844; Lassen, II. 51 sq.; Elphinstone, pp. 111, 112, 3rd ed.; Hardy, *Manual of Buddhism*, p. 353. Mr. Elphinstone makes the following observations, in the justice of which almost every one is now disposed to acquiesce: 'These discrepancies are too numerous to be removed by the supposition that they refer to an earlier and a later Budha; and that expedient is also precluded by the identity of the name Sakya, and of every circumstance in the lives of the persons to whom such different dates are assigned. We must, therefore, either pronounce the Indian Báudhas to be ignorant of the date of a religion which arose among themselves, and at the same time

The death of Gautama is thus ascribable to the year 543 B.C., *i. e.* two centuries before the date of Alexander's expedition.

When the primitive story is divested of the countless fables[1] in which it has been decked by later superstition, Gautama is there presented not as one of many incarnations of the Deity[2],

must derange the best established part of the Hindú chronology; or admit that an error must have occurred in Cashmír or Tibet, through which places it crept into the more eastern countries, when they received the religion of Budha, many centuries after the death of its founder. As the latter seems by much the most probable explanation, we may safely fix the death of Budha about 550 B.C.' There are persons who identify Buddha with the prophet Daniel, and ascribe the appearance of Buddhism in India to the captivity and dispersion of the Jews!! See Wilson's paper in *Journal of As. Soc.* (1856), XVI. 233.

[1] See the very copious legends of Gótama (or, more properly, Gautama = a descendant of Gotama) in Mr. Hardy's *Manual of Buddhism*, pp. 139—353. These are drawn exclusively from Sing'halese sources, but are identical with accounts now circulated in Birmah and Siam, and have also very much in common with the Tibetan traditions, as previously reported by Csoma Körösi, and still more fully in the *Rgya Tch' er Rol Pa* (a Tibetan history of Buddha, *circ.* 150 B.C. ed. Foucaux, Paris, 1847); with the Nepálese traditions, as reported by Mr. B. H. Hodgson; with the Mongolian. (Tataric) traditions, as reported by M. Schmidt, and with the Chinese as preserved in the *Foe Koue Ki*, and translated by Abel Rémusat. Professor Wilson (as above, pp. 247, 248) has suggested various considerations, which in his judgment throw suspicion on these narratives, and 'render it very problematical whether any such person as Śákya Sinha, or Śákya-muni, or Śramaña Gautama, ever actually existed.' The reader is also referred to an admirable sketch of Śákya-muni in M. Saint-Hilaire's recent work *Du Bouddhisme*, pp. 28—123, Paris, 1855, where the historical and legendary elements are separated with great care and acumen.

[2] On the story which had reached St. Jerome, and was repeated by Ratramnus, respecting the birth of Gautama from the side of a *Virgin*, see Lassen, III. 370. In the *Lalita Vistara* (included in M. Foucaux's Tibetan history of Buddha, and assigned by him, and Wilson after him, to about 150 B.C.) Gautama is said to have previously attained the rank of Bódhisatwa (which is inferior only to that of Buddha) in the Tushita heaven, where he taught the doctrine to innumerable millions of Bódhisatwas, &c. To rise to the elevation of a perfect Buddha one existence more on earth was necessary, and he therefore becomes incarnate as the son of the Śákya prince Suddhódana, king of Kapilavastu, and Máyá his wife: he is born miraculously from his mother's side, who died seven days after his birth. Wilson, in *Journal of As. Soc.* (1856), XVI. 243. The feeling which prompted this peculiar theory of incarnation was subsequently shared by the Valentinians, and in the 16th century by our Joan of Kent: see Hardwick's *Hist. of Reformation*, pp. 278, 279, and n. 6. In the fabulous legend of Lao-tse, composed as late as A.D. 350, he also is said to have issued from the left side of his mother, who carried him in her womb for 72 years: see the 'Introd.' to S. Julien's edition of the *Tao-te-King*, p. xxiii.

nor as the sole receptacle of the divine Intelligence, but simply as a man,—a man of gentle, ardent, pensive, philanthropic nature. Descended from a royal house in one of the most polished provinces of central India, he was nurtured in the midst of luxury, and with the prospect of unbroken happiness. But ere he reached the flower of manhood Gautama grew weary of the pomp and pleasures of his father's court. Presentiments by which he seems to have been haunted almost from his cradle, and the ever-darkening pictures which he drew of human wretchedness and mutability, had filled his heart with sadness bordering on despair. At last, abandoning his favourite wife, he stole away entirely from the palace; and at the age of nine-and-twenty sought relief in the society of Bráhmans, with whom he lived six years a life of study and asceticism. It was while occupied in these pursuits, resisting the temptations to sensual pleasure, and mourning over the prostration of the universe at large, that he awoke to the idea of standing forth among his fellow-men in the capacity of liberator and informer[1]. Hitherto he was but Śákya-muni, the 'solitary' of the race of Śákya; now he fancied himself entitled to the appellation *Buddha*, 'the awakened,' 'the enlightened.' He collected, in the midst of spiritual ecstasies, that during the present cycle of the universe he was exalted to the very highest point of being, and that by renunciation of the world he had been freed from all the limitations of natural existence. For the sake, however, of promoting the emancipation of others, he did not pass away immediately into his ultimate condition. He resolved to be the founder of a school; but instead of acting like the Bráhmans, he exhibited at once the deep and comprehensive basis on which he thought a worthier fabric should be reared. He preached in public at Benares (Varanásí), and afterwards in other parts of northern and central India, fascinating a large crowd of followers, by the beauty of his person, the feminine suavity of his manners, his ardour, his austerities, the touching eloquence of his address,

[1] He finally thought himself capable of becoming the deliverer of the whole universe. See the narrative in Saint-Hilaire, pp. 55 sq. 'Il avait enfin trouvé la voie forte du grande homme, la voie du sacrifice des sens, la voie infaillible et sans abattement, la voie de la bénédiction et de la vertu, la voie sans tache, sans envie, sans ignorance, et sans passion...la voie qui mène à la possession de la science universelle, la voie du souvenir et du jugement, la voie qui adoucit la vieillesse et la mort, la voie calme et sans trouble, exempte des craintes du démon, qui conduit à la cité du Nirvána:' *Ibid.* p. 57.

the mildness and philanthropy of his doctrines[1], the use of the vernacular language, and, according to the legends, a profuse display of wonder-working powers.

When Gautama breathed his last, at the advanced age of eighty, Buddhism had been firmly rooted in some parts of Hindústán. The sayings of the founder were gradually collected into Sútras[2], which, on being augmented by the Vinaya and Abhidharma (disciplinary and metaphysical treatises), became the rivals of the Vaidic literature. These all were duly authorised in synods[3]; and ere long the doctrines which they

[1] 'The two most successful religious impostures, which the world has yet seen, are Buddhism and Muhammádanism. Each creed owed its origin to the enthusiasm of a single individual, and each was rapidly propagated by numbers of zealous followers. But here the parallel ends: for the *Kurán* of Muhammad was addressed wholly to the "passions" of mankind, by the promised gratification of human desires both in this world and in the next; while the *Dharma* of Sákya Muni was addressed wholly to the "intellect," and sought to wean mankind from the pleasures and vanities of this life by pointing to the transitoriness of all human enjoyment. . . The former propagated his religion by the merciless edge of the sword; the latter by the persuasive voice of the missionary. The sanguinary career of the Islamite was lighted by the lurid flames of burning cities; the peaceful progress of the Buddhist was illuminated by the cheerful faces of the sick in monastic hospitals [for the crippled, the deformed, the destitute], and by the happy smiles of travellers reposing in Dharmasálás by the road-side. The one was the personification of bodily activity and material enjoyment; the other was the genius of corporeal abstinence and intellectual contemplation.' Cunningham, *Bhilsa Topes*, pp. 53, 54. Buddhism has been defined as a 'puritan-quietist' offshoot from Hindúism.

[2] 'Sútra' is properly a philosophical aphorism; but, like other Sanskrit words, it acquired a technical meaning from its adoption by the Buddhists. The oldest of their *Sútras* are written, for the most part, in simple prose, the text, as now preserved, belonging to the first century after Christ. The genuine *Sútras*, whether in Sanskrit or in Pali, all begin with the expression, 'This has been heard by me,' implying that they are the *ipsissima verba* of Sákya. 'We may consider it established upon the most probable evidence that the chief *Sanskrit* authorities of the Buddhists still in our possession were written, at the latest, from a century and a half before, to as much after, the era of Christianity.' Wilson, *Buddha and Buddhism* (*Journ. of As. Soc.* XVI. 240). The *Páli* works of southern India date from the fifth century after Christ. The later compositions indicate the influence of foreign admixtures, and in one the parable of the Prodigal Son is said to have been distinctly reproduced: Wuttke, II. 522: see also Saint-Hilaire, *Du Bouddhisme*, p. 126. One of the most interesting relics of 'orthodox' Buddhism is the *Lotus de la bonne Loi*, translated from the Sanskrit by Burnouf, Paris, 1852.

[3] See a full account of these extraordinary assemblies in Cunningham, pp. 55 sq.

recommended had so far prevailed that they were threatening to eradicate the ancient system. Of Hindú kings who manifested an especial interest in the spread of Buddhism, none was more conspicuous than Aśoka[1], who, on abandoning the hereditary faith, endeavoured at the middle of the third century before Christ to give the new religion a predominance in districts far beyond the boundaries of Magadha. The Bráhmans had in early times diffused their influence, either by the agency of the sword, or of religious solitaries, who, bent on self-renunciation, settled in the territory of the unbeliever, and bore silent witness to the creed and worship of their forefathers. Bráhmanism, however, could not propagate itself except by making śúdras of all people whom it vanquished; for to spread the higher elements of religious knowledge among those who were not genuine Áryans, was believed to be peculiarly profane. Buddhism, on the other hand, made no distinction in the quality of the persons it addressed; and. in a synod held 246 B.C. a regular plan was organised for propagating the new faith by means analogous to those employed hereafter in conducting Christian *missions*,—by pacific and persuasive teaching, and translating Buddhist writings into foreign languages.

The first-fruits of their mighty harvest were gathered in Kashmír: and under Ming-Te the flexible creed of Buddhist emissaries won for them admission to the court of the 'celestial empire,' A.D. 61,—exactly at the time when Christianity was marching forth in all its pristine vigour to subdue the kingdoms of the western world. The Buddhists, it is true, could not eventually retain their hold on India. After thriving for a thousand years, and writing a triumphant history in monasteries[2], and enormous temples excavated from the living rock, there came a vast and terrible revulsion in the feelings of the populace. The younger sister was violently extruded by the elder from all parts of Hindústán[3], if we except one scanty

[1] See the narrative in Lassen, II. 213 sq. Buddhism thus became *the* religion, the state-religion of India, in the third century, B.C. The dynasties, which reigned in the chief cities of India, were Śúdras. Buddhism was losing ground rapidly in the seventh century of our era; and was extirpated under Sankara-Áchárya.

[2] Viháras = monasteries: Sthúpas ('topes') = monuments erected over Buddhist reliquiæ (between the third and seventh centuries of our era).

[3] In the eleventh century Buddhism was limited to a few localities; and in the 16th, Abulfazl, the minister of Akbar, being anxious to explore the characteristics of all religions, could find no one to assist him in his enquiries respecting Buddhism.

remnant at the foot of the Himálaya. Yet meanwhile Buddhism had evinced a property unknown to every other heathen system. It was far more capable of transplantation. It flourished with peculiar freshness and luxuriance in Tibet, and ultimately in the Tartar tribes of central Asia. Above all, it kept possession of its ancient fortress in the island of Ceylon; and thither in the early centuries of our era flocked a multitude of foreign pilgrims, anxious by such visit to abridge their term of penitential suffering, to venerate the relics of Gautama Buddha, or to kiss the print of his gigantic foot.

What then were the characteristics of this marvellous system as originally constituted? Its founder, we discern at once, had common ground with Bráhmanism, which, notwithstanding, he endeavoured to demolish. He took for granted the hereditary doctrine of transmigration; he argued, like his predecessors, for eternal cycles of the universe, and infinite successions of births and new births. It was a fundamental article of the Buddhist creed that 'he who is now the most degraded of the demons may one day rule the highest of the heavens; he who is at present seated upon the most honourable of the celestial thrones may one day writhe amidst the agonies of a place of torment; and the worm that we crush under our feet may, in the course of ages, become a supreme Buddha[1].' It was also held that liberation from this terrible necessity of repeated births was the grand aim of all religions. Buddhism, in like manner, recognised the wretchedness of individual being, and fell in with the prevailing tendency to quietude, to mortification of the flesh, to abstract and ecstatic contemplation.

[1] Hardy, *Manual of Budhism*, p. 36. Saint-Hilaire, *Du Bouddhisme*, p. 183, seems of opinion that in the possible extent to which transmigration may be carried, Buddhism is even more exacting than Bráhmanism. According to the Buddhist no increase is possible in the number of personal spirits, so that there is a constant tendency to the depopulation of the world of appearance (Sansára); and in the long run every such spirit will pass into the Buddha-world, will become a Bódhisatwa, and finally reach *nirvána*. 'Alles, was da lebt und athmet, soll und muss Buddha werden:' Schott, p. 3; cf. p. 10. Before the final step is taken by which the Bódhisatwa becomes a perfect Buddha, he may undergo repeated births either into the world of dévas or of men. In this case he is represented as a saviour, whose mission is to rouse men from their slumbers, and incite them by his own example to a course of self-renunciation and philosophy. A thousand of these Bódhisatwas appear in the world of men during each great Kalpa (Mahákalpa); all are born in the north of India. That period of the world in which we live has already beheld four of these Bódhisatwas. The last was Śákya-muni, whose successor is expected at the end of 5000 years. *Ibid.* p. 13.

In many other points, where it diverged entirely from the old religion, it was following, consciously or unconsciously, the path marked out by Kapila, and trodden by his disciples. The founder of the Sánkhya philosophy had taught that Brahmá himself was only at the head of the elemental creation, and, as such, was finite, mortal, subject to contingencies like pain and ignominy. The supreme authority of the Védas might accordingly be questioned; their tenets might be all subordinated to other forms of knowledge. Gautama intensified this feeling, and completed the Sánkhya innovation by rejecting the Védas altogether. As the 'enlightened' one, and as believing in the infinite capacity of his own intellect, he placed his tripod far above[1] the throne of beings like Brahmá, or Mahéswara; he was himself the 'lord and teacher,' not of one section of the universe, but of all 'the three worlds.'

Another blow inflicted by him on the old religion, and especially on the power of the Bráhmanical order, was the absolute rejection of animal sacrifice. Some indication of a like repugnance is traceable to early times[2], and in the creed of Kapila, the shedding of blood was openly denounced as one example of 'impurity[3].' But in Buddhism the rejection rests on deeper and more subtle grounds. The Buddhist has no consciousness of guilt, because he utterly denies the freedom of the creature. Sin is in his view a necessary thing: it is a cosmical and not a personal evil: its vitiation is inherent in the world of matter, and inseparable from all forms of transient being. If the Buddhist sins, the punishment which nature has attached to his demerit will inevitably take effect: the law *must* have its course. He therefore manifests no wish for reconcilement: he has no idea of mediation, of satisfaction, of propitiation[4]. On the other hand, a keener insight into all

[1] This affinity between Kapila and Gautama is pointed out in Lassen, I. 831. In the Sing'halese Buddhism of the present day, which is largely intermixed with Bráhmanical elements, the Mahá-Brahmá is notwithstanding only the ruler of a 'bráhma-lóka': Hardy, p. 41. This idea of the gods being made subject to the will of a mortal by his performance of superhuman austerities was not entirely new in Hindústán.

[2] See Roth, *Nirukta*, 'Einl.' p. xxxiii.

[3] See above, p. 151, n. 2.

[4] Cf. Mr. Thomson's *Bampton Lectures*, pp. 44, 45. In speaking of Sing'halese Buddhism at the present day, Sir E. Tennent observes that 'neither in heaven nor on earth can man (according to the Buddhist doctors) escape from the consequences of his acts; that morals are in their essence productive causes, without the aid or intervention of any higher authority; and hence forgiveness and atonement are ideas utterly unknown.'

the possible consequences of the Hindú doctrine of transmigration would naturally serve to deepen his repugnance to traditionary usages involving the destruction of animal life[1]: from both which causes it results that Buddhism stands conspicuous in the midst of heathendom as a religion without sacrificial cultus. The very name of sacrifice (*yajna*) has been discarded, and the simple worship of the Buddhists almost universally restricted to the offering up of prayers and flowers and perfumes, in memory of their founder. It is true that orders of religious teachers[2], corresponding to the Christian clergy, were instituted as early as the reign of Aśoka; but excepting in the Lama-hierarchy of Tibet, which may hereafter call[3] for more particular notice, Buddhist priests perform no functions that are strictly sacerdotal; they are rather confraternities of mendicants, who act as patterns of the sternest form of self-renunciation, or as mere teachers of the populace.

It was contended in the class-rooms of the Sánkhya philosophy that human spirits, in whatever bodies they may dwell, are all intrinsically equal[4]. Gautama was also a believer in this doctrine, and went so far as to reduce it into practice. He could not shut his eyes, indeed, to the existence of the caste-system; and, accepting it as an established fact, attributed distinctions in the various orders of society to differences of conduct in a former life: but notwithstanding such admission, men of every caste were equally invited to his lectures, and arranged according to their age and worth; and, as he taught that all, whatever be their natural gifts or opportunities or condition, are entitled to the same spiritual advantages, and have access to the means of liberation, he prepared his hearers for the ultimate dissolution of the caste-system[5], and the overthrow of Bráhmanism. Indeed the universe itself, and not the

[1] 'The Báudha religionists carry their respect for animal life much further than the Bramins: their priests do not eat after noon, nor drink after dark, for fear of swallowing minute insects; and they carry a brush on all occasions, with which they carefully sweep every place before they sit down, lest they should inadvertently crush any living creature.' Elphinstone, p. 107. Still, at the present day, as the same writer adds in a note, 'the laity eat animal food without restraint; even the priests may eat it, if no animal is killed on their account.'

[2] Burnouf, *Hist. du Bouddhisme*, pp. 293 sq.; Wuttke, II. 557.

[3] See *Appendix* II.

[4] 'The Bráhman is born of a woman, so is the chańdála' (outcaśte). 'My law is a law of grace for all.' 'My doctrine is like the sky. There is room for all without exception—men, women, boys, girls, poor and rich.'

[5] It is retained, however, in Ceylon: Hardy, pp. 71, 78.

narrow confines of the Áryan tribes, was chosen as the theatre on which the new religion sought to operate: the Buddha, though he taught in northern Hindústán, was anxious to deliver and enlighten all things.

(1) But besides these general principles, there were, in Buddhism, other characteristics which deserve particular consideration. Some of them may be regarded as speculative, or metaphysical; the rest as practical, or moral. In Kapila's system, we already noticed, the idea of God was never prominent: it was in danger of evaporating altogether in the midst of philosophical refinements. But Gautama went further still: the system which he founded is more openly atheistic. It not only disregarded, but denied the one eternal God, the Maker and the Ruler of all other forms of being. Whatever symptoms of intelligence and design, whatever powers of organisation it might recognise, they all were held to be inherent properties of matter. The world and all things in it rise into existence, are transformed, and ultimately vanish in obedience to some natural order, some inscrutable necessity: they are like regular undulations of the ocean flowing one into another; they are links in some eternal chain of causes and effects. To Bráhmans God is everything; to Buddhists God is nothing. Bráhmanism, when fully and minutely analysed, is found to be all centre; Buddhism all circumference. The first contended, that because the abstract Brahma is one only and immutable, all things subject to mutation are unreal; they merely seem to be. The second argued, that because all things are now multiform and mutable, they cannot have a single and immutable basis. In the one, the spirit underlying every form of matter is an efflux of the Godhead; in the other, while the world appears to be undeified, the only God is not confessed. The Buddhist breaks entirely loose from the ideal pantheism of the Bráhman, but he finds no refuge in the sanctuary of truth; his creed is purely negative and nihilistic[1].

[1] The following statement of Professor Wilson entirely corroborates the inferences I had drawn respecting the atheistic character of primitive Buddhism: 'Belief in a supreme God, the Creator and Ruler of the universe, is unquestionably a modern graft upon the unqualified atheism of Śákya Muni: it is still of very limited recognition. In none of the standard authorities translated by M. Burnouf, or Mr. Gogerly, is there the slightest allusion to such a First Cause, the existence of whom is incompatible with the fundamental Buddhist dogma of the eternity of all existence. The doctrine of an Ádi-Buddha, a first Buddha, in the character of a supreme Creator, which has found its way into Nepál, and perhaps into western Tibet, is entirely local, as is that of the Dhyání Buddhas, and the Bódhi-

Exception[1] may perhaps be made in favour of one school or sect, the Buddhists of Nepál and western Tibet, who, owing to their close proximity to Bráhmanism, or other causes, seem to have inherited a loftier and more spiritual faith, transferring their idea of God to one supreme Intelligence, whom they designate Ádi-Buddha[2]: but of Buddhism, as it stands depicted in the oldest class of monuments, we need not hesitate to affirm, that no single trace survives[3] in it of a Supreme

satwas, their sons and agents in creation, as described by Mr. Hodgson. They are not recognised in the Buddhist mythology of any other people, and have no doubt been borrowed from the Hindús. There can be *no First* Buddha, for it is of the essence of the system that Buddhas are of progressive development: any one may become a Buddha by passing through a series of existences in the practice of virtue and benevolence, and there have been accordingly an infinitude of Buddhas in all ages and in all regions.' *Journal of Asiat Soc.* (1856), XVI. 255, 256. Weber (*Indische Skizzen*, Berlin, 1857, p. 67, *note*) takes substantially the same view.

[1] See Elphinstone, pp. 104, 105. Wuttke, following Burnouf, is, however, of opinion that the sect is comparatively modern (II. 529), especially as no trace of it is found in China, and as the nearest approximation to such theism in the speculative philosophy of the Buddhists (see Hodgson, in *Asiat. Researches*, XVI. 435 sq.) does not go beyond the Sánkhya doctrine of a spiritual essence.

[2] Cunningham (*Bhilsa Topes*, p. 39) seems to be of opinion that the earliest race of Buddhists differed most materially from the Sánkhyas, and instead of holding the eternity of matter, contended that everything was the creation of the self-existent Ádi-Buddha, who willed it, and it was.

[3] 'In den Sutra und den wichtigsten andern Religionsschriften ist keine Spur eines höchsten weltbildenden Wesens:' Wuttke, II. 527. In this verdict concur Burnouf, Schmidt (as there cited, p. 529); Tennent (*Christianity in Ceylon*, p. 208, *note*); Hardy, *Manual of Budhism*, p. 399; Saint-Hilaire, *Du Bouddhisme*, p. 245. It should, however, be stated on the other side, that Col. Sykes (*Journal of Asiat. Soc.* VI. 377) endeavours to screen the Buddhists from the charge of atheism. His chief appeal is to a curious hymn, composed, as many think, by Gautama himself, at the moment when he became Buddha. It is printed, with three versions somewhat differing, in Mr. Hardy's *Manual*, pp. 180, 181: but there is nothing in it to militate against the view here adopted. It merely states that Gautama had found the 'artificer' (*Gehakáraka* = 'the House-builder') of the human frame, *i.e.* the key explaining the true doctrine of existence, and had thus secured exemption from all future wanderings. Major Cunningham (*Bhilsa Topes*, p. 36, and elsewhere) maintains that the *primitive* Buddhism was 'theistic,' in the sense that Gautama admitted the bare existence of a Supreme Being, but denied His providence. On the contrary, Schott, a very great authority, in his treatise *Über den Buddhaismus in Hochasien und in China* (Berlin, 1846) declares: 'Die ursprüngliche, ungefälschte Buddha-Lehre weiss von keiner ewigen Individualität, und somit verdankt auch das Weltgebäude keiner solchen sein Dasein' (p. 2). Speaking of the present

Being, either like the Óm of the Vaidic period, or the Brahma of the Laws of Manu. Buddhism even went so far as to reject the Sánkhya theory of an active material essence, on the ground that all such arguments are contradicted by the mutable phenomena of the universe. 'Beings are not created,' says a writing of high authority among the Buddhists, 'by one God, or lord (*íśwara*), neither by one spirit (*purusha*), neither by matter (*pradháná*). If there were indeed a single cause of all things, as God, or spirit, or matter, then, by the simple fact of the existence of this cause, must the world at once have been created in its entirety, since a cause cannot exist without producing its due effect. But all things may be seen to come into the world, according to a law of succession, some issuing from the parent-womb, others from the germ. It must accordingly be concluded that there is a series of causes, and that God is not the single cause[1].'

To elucidate this doctrine of causation was indeed one principal object in the teaching of 'the sons of Sákya.' They believed that theoretically the first approach to liberation involves a knowledge of the way in which all life has been produced. Starting, therefore, with the old hypothesis, that the cycles of the universe had no beginning, individual life, with all its ills and accidents, its faculties of mind and body, is traceable backwards through twelve stages[2] to the first term in the circle of generation, which is 'ignorance' (*avidyá*), and consists in mistaking for durable that which is but evanescent and precarious; or, in other words, assigning to the universe a

state of Buddhism in China, Gutzlaff declares: 'It is heresy to talk of a causation, or a primary Author, for all things have existed since numberless Kalpas, and by their natural tendency return to annihilation.' *Journ. of As. Soc.* XVI. 80. 'It is a grand machinery, without an intellectual propelling power:' *Ibid.* p. 81. The most ancient and genuine school of Buddhism is that of the Swabhávikas, whose doctrine is thus summarily indicated in a Buddhist Páli book: 'Whencè come existing things? from their own nature,—*swabhávát.* Where do they go to after life? into other forms, through the same inherent tendency. How do they escape from that tendency? Where do they finally go? into vacuity,—*sunyatá.*' Wilson, in *Journ. of As. Soc.* XVI. 256.

[1] Quoted from the *Yasomitra*, in Burnouf, p. 572.

[2] See Saint-Hilaire, pp. 188—190. This 'ignorance' is an abstract quality producing another abstract quality, merit and demerit, *karma;* which *karma* gives birth to a third abstraction, consciousness; and this being endowed with physical power, produces body and mind, and so on: Hardy, p. 392. Yet the Buddhist does not profess to enlighten us either respecting the origin of *avidyá*, or the manner in which *karma* operates.

reality which it does not actually possess. For Buddhism, in this matter, went beyond the elder system; it regarded all 'the three worlds' as 'empty[1],' as no better than a shadowy and illusive phantom. Having lost all faith in God the Author of the universe, the Buddhist was propelled to the conclusion, that the sensible forms around him ought not to exist: they had no right to be, and therefore since they are, they must be evil; and the object was accordingly to liberate all sentient creatures from their bondage to the non-existent. So entirely was the mind of Gautama possessed by this idea, that of the elementary lessons which he taught men in conjunction with his doctrine of the twelve-fold chain of causes, nearly all had reference to the rise and remedy of human suffering. The universality of that suffering, its birth from passion and desire, the possibility of escaping from it, and the method of escape, these constitute the 'four grand verities[2]' impressed in early youth upon the memory of Buddhists.

And if the special character of this deliverance be investigated, we find it summed up in the word *nirvána*, 'extinction,' 'blowing out.' Such was the supreme felicity of the Buddha: such the goal to which he ever pointed the aspirations of his followers. It was formerly disputed whether more is meant by the expression *nirvána* than 'eternal quietude,' 'unbroken sleep,' 'impenetrable apathy:' but the oldest literature of Buddhism will scarcely suffer us to doubt that Gautama intended by it nothing short of absolute 'annihilation[3],' the destruction of all elements which constitute existence[4].

[1] Schmidt has pointed out (*Mémoires de l'Académie de Saint Pétersbourg*, I. 98 sq.) that the two main principles of Buddhism are (1) that the three worlds are empty, and (2) that there is no difference between being and non-being.

[2] Saint-Hilaire, p. 127.

[3] *Ibid.* pp. 195 sq.; Burnouf, *Hist. du Bouddhisme*, p. 589: Wuttke, II. 570. The last writer (p. 571) cites the following passage from a Mongolian catechism: 'Der Sansára [*i.e.* the world of appearance] ist seiner Wesenheit nach *leer*, seiner Form nach trügerisch, seinen Wirkungen nach verderblich: Nirvána ist auch seiner Wesenheit nach *leer*, aber er vernichtet jede Täuschung und befreit von allem Uebel.' Prof. Wilson (*Journ. of As. Soc.* XVI. 256, 257) adopts the same view as that which I have stated in the text. Life is the cause of evil, from which there is no escape but by ceasing to be. In Buddhism there is no recipient for the liberated soul.

[4] *Nirvána* is sometimes used to signify the *Buddha-world*, the world inhabited by Bódhisatwas (candidates for Buddhaship); but the more abstract meaning is the true one. 'In Nirwána aber fliesst alles befreite Geistige zu einer absoluten Monas zusammen; aus den unzähligen Buddha's wird unpersönliches Buddha:' Schott, p. 10. *Nirvána* is aptly defined as 'ein von allem Etwas ewig befreites Nichts:' p. 11.

Neither Bráhmanism nor Buddhism could feel happy in the present world: to both it was a prison-house, a place of torture and of ignominy. But the gulf between the two rival systems was in this respect immeasurable. Bráhmanism contended that true being does exist beyond the world of phenomena (Sansára); Buddhism, that being is the same in all the 'three worlds,' but nowhere is possessed of more than the appearance of reality. The Bráhman, writhing under the calamities of life, was anxious to emancipate himself as soon as possible from the world of phantoms, that he might revert to his original oneness with divinity: the Buddhist, driven to desperation by witnessing the same calamities, was no less anxious to escape, but was content if he could ultimately pass beyond the verge of that enchanted circle which was fatal to his peace, and so attain to non-existence. Both alike gave utterance to the grief which preyed upon their inmost being; but the Buddhist sorrowed as the man who has no hope, and his philosophy is therefore the philosophy of despair.

(2) But while we charge the creed of Gautama with atheism and nihilism, we must acknowledge that it rose in one respect superior to all other heathen systems,—in the loftier tone of its morality. It was a *practical*, and not a speculative philosophy, concerning itself not with God and the invisible, but with the charities and duties of the present life. Here indeed we find the secret of its mightiness, the key to its majestic progress in the whole of eastern Asia. The grand picture of a royal youth, abandoning his home and honours to become the gentle, apt, and sympathetic teacher of the people, was alone sufficient to evoke a class of sentiments forgotten by the old religions. And in course of time fresh arguments were found to strengthen the devotion which this picture of philanthropy excited. 'A great part of the respect paid to Gótama Budha arises from the supposition that he voluntarily endured, throughout myriads of ages, and in numberless births, the most severe deprivations and afflictions, that he might thereby gain the power to free sentient beings from the misery to which they are exposed under every possible form of existence. It is thought that

'Existence is a tree: the merit or demerit of the actions of men is the fruit of that tree and the seed of future trees; death is the withering away of the old tree from which the others have sprung; wisdom and virtue take away the germinating faculty, so that when the tree dies there is no reproduction. This is Nirvána.' From the *Brahma-jála*, a *Páli Sútra*, where Śákya-muni is made to confute sixty-two Bráhmanical heresies: Wilson, as above, p. 257.

myriads of ages previous to his reception of the Budhaship, he might have become a *rahat* [one who is entirely rescued from all evil desire], and therefore ceased to exist; but that of his own free-will he forewent the privilege, and threw himself into the stream of successive existence, for the benefit of the three worlds[1].' Nor was the founder of Buddhism merely anxious to exhibit his commiseration for the calamities of other men. He laid unwonted stress on social and domestic duties, while the Bráhmans, in their teaching, rather aimed at the production of ceremonial punctuality[2].

Believing that, in spite of some paramount necessity, the individual has the power of punishing himself by an illicit course of action, every Buddhist, whether lay or cleric, was enjoined[3] to kill no living thing, to be honest in his dealings, to indulge no sensual appetites, to abstain from lying, and intoxicating liquors; while a further series of more rigorous injunctions was provided for the guidance of the monks, the celibates, the devotees[4]. In carrying out these regulations it is easy to perceive that the most exemplary Buddhists had no true idea of the distinctive properties of soul and body, and of their reciprocal relations. On the one side, they identified intelligence with sensibility[5]: on the other, they regarded the external organs as the only seat of evil and the single enemy of mankind. The body was even treated by them as consubstantial with brute matter; and to curb its wayward passions, to seal up the various inlets of temptation, to mortify and extirpate the sensual appetites, and by *dhyána*, 'contemplation,' rivet the desires exclusively upon the ultimate destination of the

[1] Hardy, *Manual of Budhism*, p. 98: cf. Prof. Max Müller, in Mr. Thomson's *Bampton Lectures*, p. 36. One of the reflections ascribed to the youthful Gautama in a Tibetan biography is to the same effect (in Saint-Hilaire, p. 39): 'En faisant voir la clarté de la loi aux créatures obscurcies par les ténèbres d'une ignorance profonde, je leur donnerai l'œil qui voit clairement les choses; je leur donnerai le beau rayon de la pure sagesse, l'œil de la loi, sans tache et sans corruption.'

[2] See the drama called *Mrichchhakati*, which is said to represent Buddhist institutions with singular fidelity.

[3] The list of commandments varies somewhat in different writings: see Stuhr, I. 180, Prichard, IV. 124. Upham (*Historical and sacred Books of Ceylon*, III. 12, 158; cf. pp. 162, 163) gives a list, ten in number, more closely resembling the second table of the Decalogue.

[4] The Bhikshus and Bhikshunís are all separated from the world, and engage to lead a life of self-denial, celibacy and mendicancy, and to estrange themselves from all domestic and social obligations. Prof. Wilson (*Journ. of As. Soc.* XVI. 255) animadverts on the rigour and inhumanity of these regulations.

[5] See Saint-Hilaire, p. 226.

human subject, was the highest aim of ethical philosophy. The conviction of present wretchedness, which throws a shade of melancholy over the whole life of the Buddhist devotee and furnishes a clue to most of his speculations, is thus deepened by a course of self-inflicted torture. So far indeed was he bent on carrying his renunciation of the sensible world and its enjoyments, that he stigmatised his Bráhman rival as a man who lived in bondage to the present and the visible[1].

Nor was passive self-control the only point to which importance was attached in Buddhist ethics. Man was there exhorted to promote his extrication from the bonds of individuality by sharing the calamities of others: he was to facilitate his own escape by making others rise superior to the fatal law of transmigration. It is probable that here and there a Buddhist might be influenced by the same generous self-devotion which had characterised the framer of his creed: but generally his eye was fastened on the prospect of remuneration; he believed that by assisting others he should be smoothing his own pathway to *nirváṇa.* Merit, with demerit the correlative, is the power by which, according to Buddhism, the destiny of all sentient beings is controlled[2]; and when this principle was fully apprehended the acquisition of a stock of merits became the great concern of life: religion was converted into a regular system of profits and losses[3].

Still we must not overlook the emphasis which Buddhism uniformly placed upon a class of gentle and retiring virtues, which were well-nigh banished from the rest of heathendom,—meekness, resignation, equanimity under suffering, forgiveness of injuries. Much as these are found to differ from the corresponding virtues of the Christian, and symptomatic as they often are of womanly, instead of manly and heroic qualities,

[1] Stuhr, I. 187. 'Chose étrange,' says M. Pavie, referring to some moral maxims of the Buddhists, 'ceux qui méditent sur ces belles pages, au lieu de conclure qu'il y a une autre vie où l'âme humaine doit trouver la satisfaction de ses immenses désirs, se retirent dans une négation désespérée. Ils dédaignent tous les biens de la vie comme une illusion, comme un leurre qui séduit l'esprit et l'entraîne dans le tourbillon des naissances à venir. Mieux vaut pour eux cesser d'être, s'abîmer dans un incompréhensible néant: c'est donc l'art de mourir une fois pour toutes, que le novice vient étudier dans le monastère:' *Revue des Deux Mondes*, 1854, Tome v. p. 133.

[2] Hardy, p. 445. *Karma* is properly 'that which is to be done.'

[3] *Ibid.* p. 507, where reference is made to the Chinese practice of keeping a debtor and creditor account of the acts of each day, and transferring the balance from one year to another: see also Saint-Hilaire, pp. 215 sq.

they could scarcely fail to benefit a multitude of savage tribes to which they were propounded. For example, when the Buddhist finds himself assailed by calumny or open violence, he restrains his animosity by reflecting that the blow has been necessitated by misdemeanors committed in some previous existence. He is thankful that no heavier penance has fallen to his lot; and even at the last extremity, when death itself must be confronted, he can welcome it as the appointed means of liberation from 'this unclean body[1].'

Truth, however, calls for the addition, that fair and lovely as might be the outward forms of Buddhism, its inherent principles were such as made it well-nigh powerless in the training of society, and therefore it has left the countries which it overran the prey of superstition and of demon-worship, of political misrule and spiritual lethargy. Confessing no supreme God, who is at once the Legislator and the Judge, its moral code was ultimately void of all authority. Denying also the true dignity and freedom of the human agent, it invested moral sentiments and relations with a kind of physical outsidedness; they were all parts of a great system with which the fortunes of the Buddhist, why he knew not, were mechanically connected. He spoke indeed of 'laws,' but these were only common rules of action, according to which all things are found to happen[2]: vice had no intrinsic hideousness, and virtue was another name for calculating prudence; while love itself was in the creed of Buddhism little more than animal sympathy, or the condolence of one sufferer with his fellow. Buddhism also could discourse of 'duty;' but such duty, as it had no object and no standard, was devoid of moral motive: it shrank into a lifeless acquiescence in some stern necessity, a blind submission to some iron law. The Buddhist's principle of action was 'I must;' he could not say 'I ought.'

c. The Eclectic School of India.

To understand the origin of this eclectic school we must remember that, in addition to the systems of philosophy already noticed, there had been from early times a strong and passionate bias in favour of asceticism[3]. Partly owing to the climate,

[1] Wuttke, II. 579.

[2] See Mr. R. A. Thompson's *Christian Theism*, I. 187 sq. on the ethics of Spinosa.

[3] See Wuttke, II. 362 sq. The old Bráhmanical ascetic was first known as *Sramaṅa* (cf. the Σαρμᾶναι of Megasthenes); but after the time of Aśoka, the word seems to have been exclusively assigned to the

which induced inertness and disposed to contemplation, man had at the close of the Vaidic age begun to muse profoundly on the paradoxes of the world around him. He sighed for peace and unity, and everything that thwarted this desire and made him conscious of his isolation and estrangement from the primal source of being, he was anxious to repudiate and uproot. He also mused upon the conflicts which he felt among the moral elements of his nature, and ere long arrived at the conclusion that the seat of all disorder is the region of the senses. By indulging these he was persuaded that the soul is lured from the pursuit of spiritual and heavenly things, and therefore drew up special rules of discipline by which the downward tendency might be corrected and reversed. By 'exercise and dispassion,' by 'asceticism and mortification,' the mind was thought to be capable of reaching a state of absolute calm in which one single object may be contemplated to the exclusion of all others. This object was at first to be the Lord (*íśwara*): 'but as the practised swimmer parts with his last cork or bladder, so the soul of the ascetic must in due course part with every object, and at length meditate without an object at all[1].' His principles, as wrought into a system, constitute the *Yoga school* of Hindú philosophy, in which the *yogin*, or devotee, aspires to perfect union ('yoking') with the Divine Being.

At last, perhaps when many centuries[2] had been allowed for the development of these tendencies, there rose in northern Hindústán a poet and philosopher, who, while faithful to the main positions of the ancient Bráhman, sought to reconcile his metaphysical tenets with the speculations of the Sánkhya school;

Buddhist devotees (Lassen, II. 449, 700, n. 3). Cf., however, Wilson, in *Journ. of As. Soc.* XVI. 230. It still exists in the Páli form *Samana*, and is sometimes used by the Chinese Buddhists as equivalent to 'priest,' but must not in that connexion be confounded with the *shaman* of demon-worship. See Schott, p. 18, n. 1, who points out that the word *saman* = shaman is Tungusic. Weber on the contrary (*Indische Skizzen*, p. 66, Berlin, 1857) thinks that the *shaman* of the devil-worshippers was a corruption of *śramańa;* and so Caldwell, *Grammar of the Drávidian Languages*, p. 519, *note*, Lond. 1856.

[1] See *Aphorisms of the Yoga*, Bk. I. §§ 17, 18, ed. Ballantyne.

[2] It is now generally conceded that the date of the Bhagavad-Gítá is post-Christian. Even Lassen, who contends for the antiquity of Krishńa-worship, places this poem in a later period of Hindú history, 'in welcher die Vischnuiten in Secten zerfielen und ihre Religionslehre mit philosophischen Lehren in Einklang zu bringen versuchten:' II. 494. Mr. J. C. Thomson, its recent editor and translator (Hertford, 1855), is disposed to place it between 100 B.C. and 300 A.D.

and while confessing the advantages to be derived from the contemplative mode of life, contended that principles of self-renunciation were reconcileable with devotion to all active duties. This writer was himself a Bráhman and a Vaishńava, *i. e.* a member of the sect which had invested Vishńu[1] with the attributes of the Supreme Being, and which worshipped him in preference to the rival Śiva. The work which he composed, the Bhagavad-Gítá[2], was dexterously inlaid by him in one of the great literary monuments of his forefathers, where 'it reads like a noble fragment of Empedocles or Lucretius introduced into the midst of an Homeric epic[3].' The later portions of it are chiefly occupied with philosophical theories which were already glanced at in our survey of the Sánkhya system; and indeed the only novel feature of speculative value is the effort made to harmonise the varying elements of that system by supposing the material and spiritual essences to be alike eternal, 'by uniting them in one Supreme Being, and thus making nature, or the material essence, a portion of the great eternal Deity[4].' Here indeed the teaching of the Bhagavad-Gítá seems to have approximated to the theism of revealed religion[5]; but

[1] See, for instance, ch. XVIII. (p. 121 of Mr. Thomson's translation), where Arjuna is charged by his divine instructor not to reveal his knowledge to misbelievers or revilers of Krishńa, the incarnate form of Vishńu.

[2] This poem is, for the most part, a colloquy between Arjuna and Krishńa. Arjuna is one of the sons of Páńdu, and after being in banishment for years, is making a grand effort to dethrone his uncle and cousin by whom he had been iniquitously expelled. His sufferings moved the pity of Vishńu (Krishńa), who had become his bosom-friend, his councillor and charioteer. When the dialogue opens, the two hostile armies are drawn up in battle-array, but Arjuna recoils from the encounter on reflecting that it must lead to the slaughter of his near relations. The object of Krishńa is to overrule this feeling.

[3] *Quarterly Review*, Vol. XLV. pp. 6, 7.

[4] See Mr. Thomson's 'Introd.' pp. xcv. xcvi.

[5] The following extract from a rapturous prayer of Arjuna, on discovering the real greatness and supreme divinity of his companion, should be cited here, because it has few parallels in the whole area of Hindú literature: 'The universe, O Krishńa! is justly delighted with thy glory, and devoted to thee. The Rákshasas [evil spirits] flee, affrighted, to the divers quarters of heaven, and all the multitudes of the Siddhas [demi-gods] salute thee. And, indeed, why should they not adore thee, O great one! thee, the first creator, more important even than Brahmá himself? O infinite king of gods! habitation of the universe! thou art the one indivisible, the existing and not existing [spirit and matter], that which is supreme. Thou art the first of the gods, the most ancient person. Thou art the supreme receptacle of this universe. Thou knowest all, and mayest be known, and art the supreme man-

a closer survey will convince us that the two ideas are really incompatible. For since matter in the Hindú system remains an independent substance, coessential with divinity, or since God is there supposed to fashion all things by changing Himself into the material universe, His own supremacy is so far questioned and invaded; while by attributing to every individual a portion of the Supreme Being, which, according to that later system, exists in him together with his own individual soul, each form of animated nature is said to have within it particles of divinity; and on this ground polytheism, hero-worship, and even animal-worship, are reasserted and defended[1].

It is, however, to the ethical portions[2] of the poem that I draw attention more particularly, as enabling us to trace the highest flight of philosophical Hindúism, in its efforts to determine the right course of human conduct.

(1) A primary object of the writer was to vindicate the institution of caste, which had been sorely shaken by the Buddhist revolutions, and perhaps we may infer impugned by members of the Kshatriya-class, who were beginning to exceed their own province. So absolute and so inviolable, it is taught, are duties which the law of caste imposes, that these transcend and overpower all earthly considerations. For example, it was the intention of the poet to establish that love of kindred, though a virtue in itself, must be sacrificed whenever it is generating in the warrior's breast a feeling of compassion for his enemies. His province is to fight, and fight he must on all occasions, and at any cost whatever. 'It is better to do one's own duty, even though it be devoid of excellence, than to perform another's duty well[3].'

sion. By thee is this universe caused to emanate, O thou of endless forms....Thou All! Of infinite power and immense might, thou comprehendest all; therefore thou art All. As I took thee merely for a friend, I beseech thee without measure to pardon whatever I may, in ignorance of this thy greatness, have said from negligence or affection, such as, O Krishna! O son of Yadu! O friend! and everything in which I may have treated thee in a joking manner, in recreation, repose, sitting, or meals, whether in private, or in the presence of these, eternal One! Thou art the father of the animate and inanimate world.' ch. XI. (transl. pp. 79, 80). Krishńa had already (ch. VII. pp. 51 sq.) prepared his companion for this outburst of adoration, by declaring, 'I am the cause of the production and dissolution of the whole universe. There exists no other thing superior to me...On me is all the universe suspended, as numbers of pearls on a string;' adding also, that he was the mystic syllable *Óm* in all the Védas.

[1] Cf. 'Introd.' as before, p. cii.

[2] Ch. I.—ch. VI., ch. XII., ch. XVIII.

[3] See p. 26, and, more fully, pp. 118 sq. In pp. 66, 67, there is a

(2) The second object is to modify the Yoga-doctrines in such a manner that devout persons may feel under no pressing obligation to consume their lives in violent austerities and maceration of the body. The author does not, it is true, deny the efficacy and numerous excellences of that older system; but he argues[1] that when transformed into the *Karma-Yoga*, by adapting principles of renunciation (*sannyása*) to all the duties of common-life, it is still worthier of acceptance, and of greater efficacy in forwarding the process of emancipation. In the earlier system men's surrender of the world was outward, local, physical; in the later it was to become more inward, spiritual, and complete. The one, persuaded that evil always enters through the inlet of the senses, laboured to impair and so destroy the sinful medium; the other, acquiescing in this doctrine as to the peculiar province of temptation, urged the duty of subjugating the heart in such a manner that sensual impressions were disarmed and made inoperative. In other words, the way to overcome the world, was not to leave it, and seek out asylums in the jungle, but to extirpate all wishes and affections that produced attachment to it. Action was the proper element in which the devotee should undergo his training; yet action was at last to be entirely free from passion or emotion, and entirely irrespective of all consequences. 'Let the motive for action be always in the action itself, never in its reward[2].' 'He into whom all desires enter in the same manner as rivers enter the ocean, which is [always] full, yet does not move its bed, can obtain tranquillity; but not he who loves desires[3].' The author did not, it is true, deny that adequate reward is always given to acts of ritual worship. On the contrary, he maintained that whenever actions are performed with interested motives they involve[4] the agent in a series of necessary bonds or consequences (*karma-bandha*); sometimes purchasing admission for him to the heaven of Indra; sometimes, where he is the victim of base fear, and sacrifices to the demons, entailing on him an abode in less exalted spheres of being. Yet the one reward, and that which to the Hindú is alone desirable, was

passage which intimates that members of the vaiśya-class had now fallen, rather than risen in the scale of religious privileges, for they are ranked with 'women and Śúdras.'

[1] 'Introd.' as before, p. cviii.

[2] Ch. II. (p. 16). In the previous page there is a remarkable passage reflecting on those who were misled by 'flowery' sentences to assign the chief importance to the letter of precepts quoted from the Védas.

[3] Ch. III. (p. 19).

[4] Ch. IV. (pp. 31 sq.).

allotted to a different class of devotees. Where true devotion, action without passion, filled the spirit of the worshipper, he soared directly upwards to his ultimate condition. Having learned to concentrate his thoughts entirely on the Supreme Being, he obtained a perfect mastery over his whole nature: he subdued not only the irregular appetites, but every movement of the natural affections; he was 'of the same mind to friends, acquaintances, and enemies, to the indifferent and the neutral, to aliens and relatives, to the good and bad[1].' As 'candles placed in shelter from the wind do not flicker,' so this perfect devotee has been translated far above the sphere of earthly perturbations: he is utterly unmanned.

Such may be regarded as the last development of Hindú philosophy; for the monuments of the succeeding, or Puranic period, notwithstanding all the rich profusion of mythological novelties, give few if any indications of mental progress. Here and there the surface of religious thought may have been rippled, for a while, by the attempts of earnest individuals[2] to remodel the ancestral creed and lead men back to primitive institutions. The Kurán also, borne along the bloody stream of Arab conquest, was for ages dominant in various parts of India, but infused no higher life into the native population. Excepting the religious movements headed by Nanuk in the fifteenth century, and by Akbar in the sixteenth, both advancing from eclectic principles in the direction of a purer form of deism, the historian of Hindú philosophy will have little to record of universal interest till the master-minds of the Peninsula shall start from their lethargic slumber, and shall learn to vibrate once again beneath the potent touch of Christianity.

[1] Ch. VI. (p. 44).

[2] One of the most remarkable was the learned Bráhman, Rammohun-Roy, who laboured in the first quarter of the present century to expound the Védánta philosophy among his fellow-countrymen, with the hope of establishing a more general belief in one only God. Since his death a society, calling itself *Tatwa-bodhini Sabhá* ('Truth-expounding Society'), and meditating the same object, has continued to exist at Calcutta: see *Journal of the As. Soc.* XIII. 210.

CHAPTER II.

Apparent Correspondencies between Hindúism and Revealed Religion.

......'So werden wir es unmöglich finden, in der indischen Religion eine Quelle oder eine Rivalin in Beziehung auf die Grundidee des Christenthums zu finden.' DORNER.

Relations of Hindúism to Christianity. Theory of primeval prophecies: of diabolic counterfeits: of natural coincidences. External communication. Probable allusion to Christianity in the Mahábhárata.

§ 1. *Hindú monotheism. Practical polytheism. God in relation to matter: no real object of trust and worship. Source of this debased theology.*

§ 2. *Hindú trinities, or triads. Real nature of the Bráhmanical triad. How it excluded the truth of the Divine unity; and substituted the worship of created beings. Christian doctrine of the Trinity in Unity. Sánkhya triad. Buddhist triad.*

§ 3. *Hindú avatáras, or incarnations, especially that of Krishńa. Their origin. Their general forms and characteristics. The Krishńa-legend. Resemblances to sacred history. Heathen parallels. Krishńaism, properly so called, subsequent to Christianity. Influence of the spurious Gospels. Fundamental differences between Krishńaism and Christianity.*

Two inferences are commonly drawn by the opponents of Christianity from the remarkable series of phenomena exhibited in the foregoing chapter. It has been alleged (1) that those exalted products of man's theorising faculty will prove how very much of truth may be discovered without invoking the assistance of particular revelations; and that consequently we are justified in treating the Gospel as one of many signs of spiritual activity, as a further egress and embodiment of 'the religion of nature,' as a novel way of working out ideas and instincts latent in the breast of all the human species. Or else it is objected (2) that both Hindúism and Christianity are for the most part vestiges of some primeval and barbaric superstition, from which it is reserved for true philosophy and the doctors of the Absolute Religion to emancipate alike the churches and the world.

As my present object is chiefly historical, I shall say nothing of the contradictions involved in these two different pleas of modern scepticism. Both of them I hope to answer most effectually by ascertaining how far alleged resemblances between the Christian and heathen systems really extend, and then suggesting in each case what seems the obvious medium of communication or the natural ground of correspondence.

Some general observations, bearing both on this and on the following chapter, will be necessary by way of preface.

1. It must be pleaded that the cogency of many arguments which unbelief has urged against the supernatural character of Christianity is due to indiscreet assertions of the Christian apologist. Exaggerating the amount of light possessed in primitive times by the adherents of revealed religion; exaggerating also the antiquity of many Gentile systems which were made almost coeval with the first dispersion of mankind, he frequently approached the study of such systems with a confident expectation of detecting in them fresh analogies to truths which have been only brought to light by the announcements of the Gospel. When, for instance, a new world of intellectual enterprise was opened through the cultivation of Sanskrit literature, it was presumed by numbers of our fellow-countrymen who led the way in those researches, that the harvest to be reaped in India would not only confirm the older portions of Mosaic history, but also rescue from oblivion many a clear and pointed prophecy of the Incarnation and the Cross. If man had always, from the infancy of time, been fully conscious of these central facts of our religion, why not search for remnants of such knowledge and expressions of such consciousness in all parts of heathendom? That dim traditions of the Fall of man, that distant echoes of some promise of redemption do in fact survive wherever human steps have wandered, will be shewn hereafter when we come to *real* parallelisms between the Christian and other systems: but the sanguine expectations of mythologists were doomed to disappointment, when, assuming that the old deposit of traditionary knowledge had been well-nigh coextensive with the field of revelation, they attempted to translate familiar mythes of Hindústán into the language of the Old and New Testament. Nor did the evil consequences of the theory cease with its explosion. Works, in which it was developed, are still found to operate injuriously upon the cause of true religion, by supplying scoffs and cavils to that class of misbelievers who would fain reduce the Gospels to a level with the sacred books of India. 'Zeal,' says a thoughtful

writer on the Hindú pantheon, 'sometimes has in its results the same effect as infidelity, and one cannot help lamenting that a superstructure requiring so little support should be encumbered by awkward buttresses, so ill applied, that they would, if it were possible, diminish the stability of the building that they were intended to uphold. Of this description were the zealous researches of some missionaries, who, in Brahmá and Saraswatí, easily found Abraham and Sarah; and the Christian Trinity is as readily discovered in the monstrous triad of the Hindús. Of this description also, I am disposed to think, are the attempts at bending so many of the events of Krishńa's life to tally with those, real or typical, of Jesus Christ[1].'

2. There is another mode of contemplating such phenomena which deserves a passing notice, chiefly from the fact that it was sanctioned by those venerable writers, who first struggled, hand to hand, with pagans in defence of Christianity. It rests, however, on a vague presumption rather than on tangible and valid evidence. Its authors argue that heathendom, in regions where the light of genuine prophecy was quenched, had been occasionally misled by 'diabolic mimicries' of Christianity, projected by malignant demons, who, in order to preoccupy the spirit of their votaries and indispose men to accept the Gospel, coined a number of those base equivalents which still pass current in the Gentile world. Accordingly it is believed that, in addition to the series of primeval facts, which, under somewhat different versions, were preserved in most heathen countries, certain rites and dogmas, which are commonly held to be of Christian origin, had been already counterfeited and caricatured in far older creeds: and hence

[1] Moor, *Hindú Pantheon*, p. 200, Lond. 1810. In Maurice's *Hist. of Hindústán*, II. 225, Lond. 1824, and in Mr. Haslam's more recent work, *The Cross and the Serpent*, pp. 149 sq. Lond. 1849, the legend of Krishńa is confidently regarded as a remnant of some primeval tradition concerning the future life of the Redeemer. The Jesuits were at first divided as to the wisdom of the ancient Chinese, but eventually agreed in attributing to them a knowledge of the True God, and connecting them with the patriarchs of the Holy Scripture. 'Der Orden erklärte sich von nun an für die sogennante alte Weisheit der Chinesen, die sie aus irgend einer antediluvianischen Verbindung mit den biblischen Erzvätern errettet hätten. Andere stiegen nun bis zur Sündfluth empor und meinten, Noa's Kinder seyen die ersten Weisen des Landes gewesen; noch Andere wollten zwischen Jao, Noa oder gar Jehova eine ganz besondere Aehnlichkeit finden. *So leicht findet* man, was man sucht und wünscht.' Prof. Neumann, in Illgen's *Zeitschrift* (1837), Band VII. pp. 13, 14.

a living writer has not scrupled to contend that 'no external resemblances to any part whatever of the catholic system form any kind of presumption against that system, seeing that such anticipations of *parts* of it are, upon this theory, to be expected[1].'

3. It was perhaps in the recoil from theories of this nature, overstrained and made incredible, that other writers have been since propelled into an opposite conclusion. In their eyes, the correspondencies between the heathen and Christian systems, where not purely casual and external, may be almost universally referred to some internal affinity, to principles inherent in the constitution of man, and stimulated by necessities of his moral nature; the grand merit of Christianity, so they think, consisting in the fact, that it has spoken with authority on the character and bearing of those fundamental principles, and taught men how to regulate the course of their development. But while granting, as I do, that such assumptions will account for several of the points in question, there are many other indications of affinity so minute and so specific, that we cannot fairly pass them over with this short and summary explanation. By so acting, the opponent of Christianity incurs the charge of sheltering his objections under words that may hereafter prove no more than empty generalities. In any case it were unreasonable to call for our assent to his hypothesis till further questions have been asked and answered. What is the amount of probability that *some outward channel of communication existed at, or prior to, the birth of Christ, between Hindú philosophers and the doctors of the western world?* And if so, is it further probable, from the character and circumstances of the age, that any interchange or fusion would take place between the various and conflicting doctrines then in course of circulation? These inquiries are, I think, deserving of more notice than they have commonly received from modern speculators: for exactly in proportion as the answer is affirmative will natural media be discovered for explaining some of the more close resemblances which I have undertaken to investigate.

Now with reference to the former question, it is certain

[1] See Mr. Morris's *Essay towards the conversion of learned and philosophical Hindús*, pp. 201 sq. Lond. 1843, where the opinions of the Fathers on this subject are recited at length. In declining to accept the view there taken of heathen worship, I have no desire to call in question the great truth that evil spirits were concerned in instigating and appropriating such worship, and that the Gentiles, therefore sacrificed δαιμονίοις, καὶ οὐ Θεῷ (1 Cor. x. 20).

that a lively intercourse subsisted in the earliest age of Christianity between the western marts of Hindústán, and those of Persia and Egypt. Thoughtful minds were also actively employed in tracing the divergencies and points of contact in the different systems of philosophy, and in searching for some common ground on which they all could meet together. This eclectic tendency is manifest on one side in the schools of Alexandria, which, after it absorbed the commerce both of Tyre and Carthage, was the centre and emporium of all forms of philosophic speculation; and on the other side in many schools of India where the publication of a treatise, like the *Bhagavad-Gítá*, bears witness to the ruling wish for peace, for union, for amalgamation. We might, therefore, be prepared to find that in the traffic carried on between the east and west, regard was sometimes had to higher interests than those of merchandise. But further it is argued to the satisfaction[1], not to say delight, of adversaries of the Gospel, that many rampant heresies, by which the primitive Church was torn and weakened, had been generated in attempts to blend the truths of Christianity with notions borrowed from the heathen creeds of Hindústán and Persia. The riddle which the founders of the Gnostic sects were all struggling to interpret had reference to the origin of physical and moral evil[2]; and the various guesses which these sects propounded have betrayed, in almost every case, their eastern origin. If it be doubtful whether Buddhist emissaries, panting for fresh fields of action, penetrated through the towns and villages of Parthia, and even reached the shores of the Mediterranean, there is no lack of evidence enabling us to specify some individual links by which the interchange of articles of faith might be most naturally effected. Bardesanes[3], for example, one of the more brilliant spirits of the latter half of the second century, had himself travelled from Edessa

[1] See Von Bohlen, *Das alte Indien*, I. 571 sq. He concurs in many of the views adopted by J. J. Schmidt, in his treatise, *Über die Verwandschaft der gnostisch-theosophischen Lehren mit den Religionen des Orients, vorzüglich dem Buddhaismus*, Leipzig, 1828; and afterwards, in the main, by Neander, *Ch. Hist.* II. 159 sq. Bohn's ed. See also Prof. Wilson's Preface to the *Vishńu Puráńa*, p. viii.; and the more recent investigation in Lassen, III. 379 sq.

[2] *e. g.* Euseb. *Hist. Eccl.* v. 27: τὰ Μαξίμου περὶ τοῦ πολυθρυλλήτου παρὰ τοῖς αἱρεσιώταις ζητήματος, τοῦ πόθεν ἡ κακία, καὶ περὶ τοῦ γενητὴν ὑπάρχειν τὴν ὕλην.

[3] Von Bohlen, as above, p. 572. According to Lassen (III. 404), Bardesanes did not actually travel to India, but derived his knowledge of Bráhmanism from intercourse with ambassadors sent from India to Antoninus Pius.

to some part of Hindústán, expressly with the purpose of there studying the religion of the Bráhmans: while Mani[1], who endeavoured to construct a composite religion, of which Christianity was made a leading element, had wandered far and near in quest of knowledge, and contracted in his wanderings an especial fondness for the creed of Gautama, which he studied under the roof of some Buddhist grotto in Turkistán.

If the above considerations make it probable that intercourse did actually exist between the early misbelievers and the speculative minds of Hindústán, I hold myself at liberty to argue, on the other side, that Christian influences might be as readily made to operate through corresponding channels, and assist, to some degree, in modifying the old principles of Hindúism. But the question is not one of plausibilities and bare presumptions. Many circumstances raise it higher in the scale of probability. I shall not insist upon the fact that copies of the Gospels, both in their genuine and corrupted form, obtained a very wide circulation in all regions of the east. I shall not exaggerate the value of the evidence which traces the extant community of 'Christians of St. Thomas'[2] to the apostolic age. Eusebius[3] has distinctly mentioned, that when a learned doctor of Alexandria, at the close of the second century, was impelled by missionary zeal as far east as India, he found the seeds of Christianity already scattered, and already bearing fruit. The same diffusion of the Gospel at this early period is attested by the Arian writer, Philostorgius. He informs[4] us of a missionary with the surname Indicus (ὁ Ἰνδός),

[1] Neander, II. 170. This writer guards himself, however, against the construction that he means to explain *all* the parallelisms between true and false religions on the theory of external influences. He accordingly adds (p. 164): 'Analogies of this sort, having a perfectly internal origin, often recur in the historical development of Christianity, wherever *corruptions of purely Christian truth* have sprung up.' Cf. Lassen, III. 407, 408. Major Cunningham (*Bhilsa Topes*, pp. 133 sq.) is of opinion that Porphyry, 'the learned Pagan, was in fact a European Buddhist.'

[2] See Hough, *Hist. of Christianity in India*, I. 32 sq. Wiltsch (*Kirchl. Geographie*, I. 18, n. 8) declares himself in favour of the old traditions on this subject: 'Die Annahme, dass der Apostel Thomas in *India Asiatica*, seu *Orientali* die christliche Kirche gegründet habe, ist fast allgemein, und wenn je eine Nachricht der Kirchen-Historiker verdient geglaubt zu werden, so ist es diese.'

[3] *Hist. Eccl.* V. 10, where in speaking of Pantænus, he writes: *ὡς καὶ κήρυκα τοῦ κατὰ Χριστὸν εὐαγγελίου τοῖς ἐπ' ἀνατολῆς ἔθνεσιν ἀναδειχθῆναι, μέχρι καὶ τῆς Ἰνδῶν στειλάμενον γῆς*: cf. Neander, I. 113.

[4] *Hist. Eccl.* III. 4. The native place of Theophilus (c. 5) was Dvípa Sukhatara, the modern Diu Sokotora: Lassen, II. 1101.

who, on visiting his native land and other parts of the Hindú Peninsula, was not surprised to meet with fellow-Christians, whose peculiar rites attested their antiquity, as well as their comparative isolation from Christendom at large. The date of this testimony is about the year 350, and two centuries later every doubt as to the permanent presence of Christianity is dissipated by accurate reports of an Egyptian writer[1], whose extensive travels gained for him the title 'Indicopleustes.' Among other places where Christian bodies had been organised he mentions Taprobane (Ceylon), Male or Mangalor on the coast of Malabar, and Calliana, a settlement near Bombay[2].

And if it be alleged that nearly all this evidence points to southern rather than to northern Hindústán, the answer is that we have frequent traces of Christianity in that quarter also. The prolific missions[3] of the old Chaldæan or 'Nestorian' Church, diffused with marvellous rapidity over regions far beyond the Tigris, had ere long their offshoots in the heart of Bactriana and the northern provinces of India. There a knowledge of the Gospel lingered through the Middle Ages; for as late as 1503[4] we find the Nestorian patriarch ordaining a metropolitan and three bishops for the regulation of the Church of India; while in 1666, owing partly to these influences and partly to the rival missions of the Latin Church, the Christian population in the north-western provinces was roughly estimated at 25,000 families[5].

It is not then so improbable that while India on the one hand stimulated the formation of the early Christian heresies, genuine Christianity may in turn have imported some of its distinctive elements into the speculations of Bráhmanical and Buddhist doctors. One of the most able Hindú scholars of the present day[6] has even found allusion to such modifications in

[1] See Neander's remarks on this account of Cosmas, *Ch. Hist.* III. 165, 166, and Lassen, II. 1101.

[2] Cf. Renan (in *Journal Asiatique* (1856, p. 251) for some account of a Buddhist monk who in the sixth century became a Christian.

[3] A 'Notitia' of the very numerous sees founded by Nestorian influence is given in Assemani, *Bibl. Orient.* III. pt. ii. pp. 705 sq.

[4] Wiltsch, II. 361.

[5] Sleeman, *Rambles and Recollections*, I. 15, quoting Thevenot, the traveller.

[6] Weber, *Ind. Studien*, I. 400, note. His deductions from the passage in the *Mahábhárata* are as follows: 'Dass Bráhmanen über das Meer nach Alexandrien oder gar Kleinasien gekommen seien zur Zeit der Blüthe des ersten Christenthums, und dass sie, heimgekehrt nach Indien, die monotheistische Lehre und einige Legenden desselben auf den einheimischen, durch seinen Namen an *Christus* den Sohn der *göttlichen* Jungfrau erinnernden, und vielleicht schon vorher göttlich verehrten Weisen oder

the ancient literature of India, and pointed out particular links of intercourse through which the Christian influence may have been conveyed. His chief authority is a passage of the *Mahábhárata*, allowed on all hands to be one of the last additions[1] made to that gigantic poem; and as such it may have been no earlier than the second century of the Christian era. According to it, three Bráhmans crossed the sea upon a visit to some neighbouring region (Śvétadvípa), whose peculiarities, if the story be divested of poetic adjuncts and embellishments, consisted mainly in the fact that the inhabitants were light complexioned, and also in religion were monotheists (*ékántinas*). During this visit of the Bráhmans they acquired a stock of knowledge which enabled them on their return to introduce improvements into the hereditary creed, and more especially to make the worship of Krishńa (Vásudéva) the most prominent feature of their system. The foreigners from whom they borrowed these ideas are said to have also worshipped the one God without the intervention of images, to have been gifted with superior faith (*bhakti*), to have assigned peculiar efficacy to prayer when offered up in spirit, and to have confidently hoped that their specific doctrines would ere long attract to them a larger circle of adherents. Without entering on the controversies touching the precise date or the locality of this interview, or claiming any knowledge of the more immediate effects which it produced on one party or the other, I am surely justified in drawing from it the conclusion that as intercourse may thus be shewn to have subsisted between the Christian and the Bráhman, it is not impossible that some ideas and traditions of the latter were subjected to the transforming influences of Christianity.

Heros *Krishńa Dévakíputra* [Sohn der Dévakí "*Göttlichen*"] übergetragen haben, im übrigen die christlichen Lehren durch Sánkhya- und Yoga-Philosophemata ersetzend, wie sie umgekehrt ihrerseits vielleicht auf die Bildung gnostischer Sekten hingewirkt hatten." Lassen, who controverts some portions of Weber's theory (*Ind. Alterthum.* II. 1096 sq.) believes, notwithstanding, that the people visited by the Bráhmans were really Christians (p. 1099), and conjectures that the interviews took place in Parthia.

[1] Lassen. II. 1096, n. 1. A writer in *Col. Ch. Chron.* (XI. 146 sq.) is of opinion that the Bráhmans were not likely to borrow *religious* ideas from foreign sources. He translates the whole passage from the *Mahábhárata* (Bk. XII. ss. 337—341), and is inclined to think that Lassen has expressed himself with too great certainty in regard to the origin of the legend. Weber (*Indische Skizzen*, Berlin, 1857) has one essay entitled, 'Die Verbindungen Indiens mit den Ländern im Westen.' He resumes the discussion of Krishńa-worship (pp. 92 sq.).

Placing, therefore, all these facts and inferences before the reader to guide him in his judgment of what follows, I shall now proceed to the investigation of particular points in which the two religions have been thought to touch, if not entirely coincide. These have reference to—

1. Hindú monotheism.
2. Hindú triads, or trinities.
3. Hindú *avatáras*, or incarnations, especially that of Krishńa.

§ I. *Hindú Monotheism.*

The observation is now current that whatever else the old inhabitants of India may have gradually forgotten or distorted, their idea of God has always been the same, and always far superior to conceptions that prevailed in other parts of heathendom. 'The Gospels themselves,' wrote Belsham, 'teach not a purer monotheism than do the sacred writings of the Hindoos[1].' Voltaire, in his endeavours to destroy the supernatural character of Christianity by pointing out its close resemblance to other systems, had paraded the same boast in many of his writings; but when he sought to justify his language by appealing to the *Ezour-Veidam*[2], which he took an active part in rescuing from oblivion, he betrayed at once the weakness of his cause and his own blind credulity. The production was in fact no genuine monument of ancient India; it was the fabrication of a Jesuit missionary, who had put it forth in order to facilitate the conversion of the more learned class of Hindús by shewing that some truths of Christianity were not unknown to their forefathers. This fact alone should have suggested to mythologists that belief in one Supreme Being was less prominently stated in the genuine Védas than the 'patriarch of infidelity' was willing to suppose. And if we turn from vague assertions or disjointed extracts, and examine the documents themselves, it is quite obvious (1) that current statements on the purity and sublimity of early Hindú worship are very much exaggerated, and (2) that where traces of monotheism exist at all, they indicate a tenet far inferior to the lofty theism of Christianity.

My own belief is that no absolutely true idea can be

[1] Quoted in W. J. Fox's *Religious Ideas*, p. 11.

[2] See the account in Saint-Hilaire, *Des Védas*, pp. 15 sq., and Adelung's *Sketch of Sanskrit Literature*, pp. 75, 76, Oxf. 1832. Voltaire imagined that the work was composed before the date of Alexander's expedition: but the real author, it is said, was Roberto de' Nobili, a nephew of Bellarmine, who went on a mission to India about 1640.

obtained with reference to these subjects till a deeper study of Hindú literature shall have enabled us to discriminate more accurately between the lyric and dogmatic portions of the Védas, *i.e.* between those portions which are manifestly ancient, but in which there is a general absence of the metaphysical element, and those of later growth in which that element is active, and preponderates. It is also most desirable to separate as far as may be the præ-Christian treatises from those which are allowedly post-Christian; since suspicions are fast gaining ground[1] that even the Bráhmanical ideas of God were somewhat modified and exalted by intercourse with Christianity.

If we lay aside expressions in the Vaidic hymns which have occasionally transferred the attributes of power and omnipresence to some one elemental deity, as Indra for example, and by so doing intimated that even in the depths of nature-worship intuitions pointing to one great and all-embracing Spirit could not be extinguished, there are scarcely a dozen 'mantras' in the whole collection where the unity of God is stated with an adequate amount of firmness and consistency. The great mass of those productions either invoke the aid, or deprecate the wrath, of multitudinous deities, who elsewhere are regarded as no more than finite emanations from the 'Lord of the creatures'[2] (*Prajápati*); and therefore in the sacred books themselves polytheism was the feature ever prominent, and, what is more remarkable, was never openly repudiated. In other words, where a belief in the supremacy of God is manifest at all, it looks as though it were unable to assert itself in practice, owing to the uncongenial atmosphere by which it was surrounded.

[1] See above, p. 153, n. 1. Weber also has pronounced distinctly in favour of this view: 'Wenn ich nun schon oben, p. 400, aus einer bestimmten Sage des MBh. speciell die Verehrung Krishńa's als Eingottes, als durch das Bekanntwerden der Bráhmańa mit dem Christenthum veranlasst gemuthmasst habe so kann ich nicht umhin hier es auch weiter als meine Vermuthung auszusprechen, dass überhaupt die spätere exclusiv monotheistische Richtung der indischen Sekten, welche *einen bestimmten persönlichen Gott* verehren, um seine Gnade flehen und an ihn glauben (*bhakti* und *çraddhá*) eben durch das Bekanntwerden der Inder mit den entsprechenden Lehren des Christenthums influenzirt worden ist:' *Ind. Stud.* I. 423, and, as reiterated, II. 169.

[2] Thus in the remarkable hymn entitled 'Au Dieu Créateur' (*Rig-Véda*, ed. Langlois, IV. 409, 410) the last clause runs as follows: 'O Pradgâpati, ce n'est point un autre que toi qui a donné naissance à tous ces êtres. Accorde-nous les biens pour lesquels nous t'offrons le sacrifice. Puissions-nous être les maîtres de la richesse!' And just before the supremacy of One God is distinctly recognised: 'Parmi les dieux il est le Dieu incomparable. A quel (autre) dieu offririons-nous l'holocauste?'

Still, we must allow, that of those hymns in which monotheism is predominant, some exhibit true conceptions of the power, the spirituality, and the unrivalled majesty of God. The following is a specimen; it is taken from the last division of the Rig-Véda, and entitled by a commentator, the Supreme Spirit[1] (*Paramátmá*):—

"Nothing then existed, neither being (*sat*), nor non-being (*asat*); no world, no air, no firmament. Where was then the covering of the universe? where the receptacle of the water? where the impenetrable depths of air? Death was not, nor immortality, nor anything that marked the boundaries of day and night. But THAT (*Tad*) breathed in solitude without afflation, absorbed in His own thought (*swadhá*). Besides THAT nought existed. The darkness was at first enveloped in darkness; the water was devoid of movement; and everything was gathered up and blended together in THAT. The Being reposed on the bosom of this void; and the universe was at last produced by the strength of His devotion (*tapas*). In the beginning desire (*káma*) was formed in His spirit (*manas*): and this was the first productive principle. It is thus that the wise men, pondering in their heart, have explained the union of being and non-being.

"But who can know such things exactly? Or who can declare them? These beings, whence come they? This creation, whence did it originate? The *dévas* were themselves created or produced. But THAT, who knows His nature and His origin? Who can tell how all this varied world has issued into being? Can it, or can it not, support itself? He who, from the heights of heaven, is gazing on the universe, He alone can tell whether it exists, or only seems to exist."

It is obvious from the character of this exalted hymn and the position which it occupies in the Rig-Véda, that it was the product of an age in which the speculations of India were assuming the peculiar forms presented to our view in the Bráhmanic period. And, we saw already, a belief in the common origin of the phenomenal universe was, in this second stage of the Hindú religion, lying at the root of all men's theorisings. Unity became the central, though it might be esoteric[2], doctrine of the 'orthodox' philosopher. Every thing that is,

[1] Langlois, IV. 421. I have followed his translation in the main, comparing it with Colebrooke's (*Asiat. Researches*, VIII. 404) and Saint-Hilaire's (*Des Védas*, p. 60).

[2] It is remarkable that this *doctrina arcani*, on which Cudworth and others have insisted as a fundamental characteristic of ancient systems of philosophy, was recognised as late as the sixteenth century. In one of Xavier's conversations with a Bráhman, he was told *confidentially* that the learned Hindús all believed in the unity of God; and further, that it was revealed in their ancient writings, 'que toutes les fausses religions cesseroient un jour, et qu'un temps viendroit où tout le monde garderoit une même loi:' Bouhours, *Vie de S. François Xavier*, pp. 95, 96, Louvain, 1822.

and every thing that seems to be, comes forth originally from God, who is the primal source of being, and eventually is gathered up afresh in Him, the all-pervading Soul or Spirit. The *dêvas*, worshipped by the undiscerning multitude, are held to be no more than scintillations of His majesty: they emanate from Him, who, when the worlds were brought into existence, had proceeded to create the 'guardians of the worlds.' Hence God is, ultimately, every thing, and every thing is God. He 'is Brahmá; he is Indra; he is Prajápati: these gods are he, and so are the five primary elements, earth, air, the etherial fluid, water, and light[1].'

The attributes and operations of this one great Spirit are nowhere brought before us with such fervour and sublimity, as in the *Ísa-Upanishad*, a kind of pendant to the second Véda: for not only is He there exhibited as the All-glorious and Supreme, but also as the proper object of man's worship, the restorer of the fallen spirit, and the author of eternal happiness. The following passage[2] will give the reader a just idea of the whole:

"One sovereign ruler pervades this world of worlds. Nurture thyself with that single thought, abandoning all others, and covet not the joys of any creature. He who in this life performs his religious duties may desire to live a hundred years; but even to the end thou shouldest have no other occupation. It is to regions, left a prey for evil spirits and covered with eternal darkness, that those men go after death, who have corrupted their own soul. This one single Spirit, which nothing can disturb, is swifter than the thought of man. This primal Mover the *dêvas* even cannot overtake. Unmoved itself, it infinitely transcends all others, however rapid be their course. It moves the universe at its pleasure: it is distant from us, and yet very near to all things: it pervades this entire universe, and yet is infinitely beyond it. The man who has learned to recognise all beings in this supreme Spirit and this supreme Spirit in all beings, can henceforth look upon no creature with contempt. The man who understands that all beings only exist in this single being; the man who is made conscious of such profound identity, what trouble or what pain can touch him? He then arrives at Brahma himself: he is luminous, apart from body, apart from evil, apart from matter, pure, and rescued from all taint: he knows, he foreknows, he rules every thing: he sees only by himself alone, and things appear to him such as they were from all eternity, always like themselves......Let the wind, the breath immortal, carry off this body of mine, which is mere ashes; but, O

[1] See Colebrooke's translation from the *Aitarêya Áranya*, in *Asiat. Res.* VIII. 421, 422.

[2] It is translated with the title *Ísávásyam*, in Sir W. Jones's *Works*, VI. 423 sq. 4to. ed., by Rammohun Roy, *Translation of several principal books, &c. of the Veds*, pp. 101 sq. Lond. 1832; and still more exactly from a somewhat different text, by Saint-Hilaire, *Des Védas*, pp. 86 sq.

Brahma, remember my intentions, remember my efforts, remember my deeds. O Agni (spirit of fire), conduct us by sure pathways to eternal happiness. O God, who knowest all beings, purify us from every sin, and we shall be enabled to consecrate to thee our holiest adorations. My mouth is seeking truth only in this golden cup. It is I, O Brahma! I who adore thee under the form of the resplendent sun. O Sun eternal, hearken to my prayer."

The striking similarity in tone and sentiment between this prayer and the more lofty passages[1] of the *Bhagavad-Gítá* has not unnaturally induced a modern writer to assign their composition to the same period of Hindú literature; and at the same time hinted that, as the date of the latter was subsequent to the diffusion of Christianity, the former may be possibly indebted for some of its more ethical properties to the superior light of revelation. But, however all such points may be eventually decided, it is certain that no higher specimen of heathen worship has been hitherto found in the surviving monuments of Bráhmanism. 'One is tempted to ask,' writes[2] a learned translator of it, 'whether the Himálaya or Mount Sinai was the first to listen to these sacred verses.' But he adds immediately afterwards: 'That grand idea of the unity of God was lost in India, instead of being developed: it was swallowed up in pantheism; and these precious germs have therefore perished under a mass of most deplorable superstitions.'

Here indeed is one of the peculiarities to which I would direct the special notice of the reader. The Hindús have been, from first to last, a tribe of creature-worshippers, a nation of polytheists. Belief in one supreme Intelligence, so far from elevating the character of their institutions and obtaining an exclusive utterance in their sacred poetry, has been an heirloom only of the favoured few. It was so, in the Vaidic period, when the young imagination of the Áryan, intoxicated by the beauties of external nature and led astray from God, sought refuge in the deification of the elements. It was so, when his descendants had been taught to clothe the genii of that earlier period with the attributes of human heroes and of god-like sages. It is so at present, when a Hindú writer has been heard deploring the incurable idolatry of his countrymen, and affirming that 'the allegorical adoration of the true Deity[3],' which anti-Christian scholars had professed to recog-

[1] See a specimen above, p. 171, n. 5.

[2] Saint-Hilaire, p. 89.

[3] In the 'Introduction' to his *Translation*, &c., Rammohun Roy declares that the Hindús of the present day 'have no such views of the subject, but firmly believe in the real existence of innumerable

nise in the existing forms of worship, is totally unknown among themselves.

But I shall go yet further. Passing by the question as to whether any changes were, in this particular, effected through the agency of the Gospel and Kurán, I feel justified in asserting that the best conceptions formed of the supreme Being, in the highest systems of Hindú philosophy, are all imperfect and one-sided: they fall short of those which have impressed themselves on almost every chapter in the records of the true religion.

1. The Jehovah of the Hebrews and the God of Christians is so purely spiritual and so entirely supramundane, that His worshippers could never run the risk of identifying their Divinity either with the forms of matter, or with powers and processes of the material universe. He is in essence totally distinct from each and all of these. The world of matter is objective to Him, and so far from thwarting His divine omnipotence, it is one single product of His legislative will, an instrument, a vassal. On the other hand, the Brahma of Hindústán is evermore confounded with the vital properties of nature, or is only made coordinate and coequal with them. Creation itself is there preceded by a something[1], that restrains and fetters the sovereignty of the Creator; or else, as in the Sánkhya system, where it was attempted to establish a peculiar principle of causality by extruding the revealed idea of God, creation is no more than the spontaneous evolution of a primary essence, irrespectively of any conscious and designing Agent. God, in other words, is not supreme according to the doctrine of Hindú philosophers. Some of them indeed allow us to regard Him as the everpresent basis and the sole substratum of the universe, the life and starting-point of all its varied operations: but in no case do the energies inherent in His being enable Him to rise superior to mysterious laws which regulate the course of nature. Even where the Sánkhyas had, in later times, so modified[2] their tenets that volition was ascribed to the Almighty and His moral attributes more fully recognised, this virtual limitation of His freedom, this entrenchment on His absolute supremacy, continues to be visible.

And since Hindús were rarely able to conceive of God as altogether separable from the world of phenomena without

gods and goddesses, who possess, in their own departments, full and independent power; and to propitiate them, and not the true God, are temples erected and ceremonies performed:' p. 5; cf. above, pp. 141, 142.

[1] See Prof. Wilson's *Lectures*, p. 53.

[2] Above, p. 153.

plunging into utter atheism, so their noblest thoughts of Him are in the same proportion leavened and debased by pantheistic elements, of which the logical issue is denial of His proper personality. 'This whole,' it had been taught in schools of 'orthodox' philosophy, 'this whole is Brahma, from Brahmá to a clod of earth. Brahma is both the efficient and the material cause of the world. He is the potter by whom the fictile vase is formed: He is the clay of which it is fabricated[1].' Nor, as other phases in the history of Bráhmanism present themselves for our investigation, are evils of this kind corrected and removed. The system in which the freedom of God appeared to be entirely compromised was followed by a subtler form of pantheism, which contended that whatever *is* resulted from the internal necessities of the Divine nature; so that the idea of God, as known to Christendom, instead of gaining clearness with the growth of metaphysical acumen, had remained as evanescent and impersonal as before. Men argued that all essences, which underlie the various grades of being and impart to the material world whatever of reality it may possess, originate in one great Spirit, who is subjected to periodic resolution and is periodically reabsorbed in simple unity. Creation, therefore, must be construed still more nakedly as another name for emanation. God Himself is one, because the universe is one mighty organism, and all the forms of animated nature, being consubstantial with divinity, or containing in themselves a particle of the all-pervading Spirit, are thereby shielded from the violence of man, or made the fitting objects of his worship. Such is even the theology of portions of the *Ísa-Upanishad*, from which an extract has been given above: and such is also one main tenet of the *Bhagavad-Gítá*, where, in the midst of efforts to establish the universality of God, the language put into the mouth of the divine interlocutor breathes the sternest kind of pantheism, and pursues the principle of absolute necessity to its furthest and most fearful consequences.

2. But granting that relations between God and matter are not always so far misinterpreted; granting that some higher

[1] Wilson, *Ibid.* p. 49; and above, p. 139; although, as Prof. Wilson justly remarks, the full extent of these materialistic illustrations may not have been intended. Rammohun Roy, as before, p. 12, explains the phrase 'All that exists is indeed God' as equivalent to 'Nothing bears true existence excepting God;' and the phrase 'Whatever we smell or taste is the Supreme Being' as equivalent to 'The existence of whatever thing appears to us relies on the existence of God.' But surely this refinement is excessive.

thoughts than such as we have just reviewed were struggling here and there for utterance through the pantheistic terminology of Bráhmanism; granting that the unity of which it speaks is something more than Nature[1], as traced backwards to its primary germ and basis by a generalising process of the intellect, or Nature, as idealised and deified by the poetic faculty of the worshipper; granting, also, that the current dogmas, with regard to the great Spirit of the universe, are sometimes capable of interpretations which do not of necessity exclude the thought of His self-consciousness and independent personality; how poor are, notwithstanding, the most elevated of Hindú conceptions as compared with that which has, in every age, been printed on the heart of Christians and of Hebrews! There the Author of the universe, as represented by philosophy, is so unknown, so abstract, so incapable of definition, so devoid of everything that constitutes a bond of sympathy with created beings, as to exercise no power on the direction of the human will or the formation of the human character. No man is able to hold converse with the Absolute; no *déva* can describe the being or mark out the path of the Ineffable. The thought of Him inspires not confidence and hope, but awe, distrust, and apprehension. He has no *paternal* character[2]. The world and the affairs of men may all indeed be subject to fixed laws which had their origin in Him, but no account is taken by this doctrine of the providence by which He regulates the course of individuals and the destinies of nations. Much less are men regarded as the objects of His love and pity, as the wanderers He would fain recover from their blind infatuation, as the prodigals whom He is ever yearning to reclaim and elevate, to pardon and renew. Belief in the Supreme God is therefore with such persons barely *speculative*: it does not warm the heart; it does not quicken the religious sentiment; it does not foster gratitude; it is not perfected by love. The Brahma of the Hindú schoolman still

[1] Yet Wuttke (II. 262) is indisposed to grant more than this: 'Das Brahma,' he writes, 'ist nichts als die auf ihre Einheit zurückgeführte Natur, das Natur-Eins, die einheitliche Grundlage aller natürlichen Dinge, ist nicht mehr und nicht weniger.' When Christianity, as he contends, was brought into communication with Hindúism, the resulting idea of God was a mixture of 'Christian monotheism' and 'Hindú naturalism.'

[2] See Creuzer's *Symbolik*, I. 171, 172, Leipzig, 1836, on the difference between the Christian and heathen use of the word 'Father' as applied to God. 'Wenn der Christ seinen Gott *Vater* nennt so ist es ungetheiltes Vertrauen, was ihm dieses Wort eingiebt. Der Christ *kennt* seinen Gott.'

continues a great *It*, a vast but cold abstraction, shewing little or no interest in the world and in the fortunes of his human progeny, or at the best receding far beyond the cognizance of ordinary spirits. Hence it has resulted that the great majority of Hindús have always, during the historic period, substituted for the one true God a host of demi-gods and other parasitical divinities, like those which crowd their pantheon at the present day. Each group they have invested with some one or other of the attributes of God, and made supreme in some one province of creation. These are held to exercise on man the personal government which seemed unworthy of the abstract Brahma, or entirely foreign to His nature. These, it is maintained, are still accessible to mortals; these can listen to the prayer and quaff the grateful sacrifice; these punish or reward according to the quality of actions; and whatever therefore of religious sentiment is now evoked in the great mass of Hindú worshippers, is not so much the issue of half-conscious gropings after the Unknown God, whose image is not utterly obliterated from the human spirit, as a tribute consciously and freely paid to those who are 'no gods.'

Before passing to another division of the subject, I cannot help remarking how completely the internal character of the doctrines here compared unites itself with different kinds of evidence in shewing that if Bráhmanism and Christianity have borrowed from each other, the obligation is upon the side of India, not of Palestine: for while many traits of the scriptural ideal of God can never be explained by reference to Bráhmanic speculations, nothing pure or noble is distinguishable in the latter, which might not have been derived from more explicit statements of the former. I incline, however, to the intermediate view already urged by St. Augustine in his controversy with the Manichæans of his day: 'Be it known,' he writes, 'to Faustus, or those rather who are charmed by his productions, that our doctrine of divine Monarchy is not borrowed from the heathen, but that, on the other hand, the heathen themselves had not so wholly lapsed into the worship of false gods as to relinquish all belief in the one True God, from whom is every order of created being[1].'

§ 2. *Hindú Trinities, or Triads.*

It is difficult to understand how any one, whose judgment was not clouded by some theory of his own respecting the

[1] *Contra Faustum*, lib. xx. c. 19: *Opp*. VIII. 345. ed. Bened.

extent of the primeval revelation, or who on the other hand was not desirous at all hazards to impair the sacred character of Christianity, could ever have adduced the Hindú triad as the parallel of that transcendant mystery which forms the basis of the Catholic faith. Sir William Jones, who commonly shewed himself as eager as the rest of his contemporaries to detect the slighest shadows of affinity between the Bible and the sacred books of India, was in this case strenuous in denying the reality of the alleged resemblances[1]. And fresh investigations have completely justified the verdict of that eminent critic. The *trimúrrti* of India, which eventually is represented under the symbol of a body with three heads, has no foundation in the Védas[2], nor have any traces of it been discovered in the Laws of Manu. It was clearly the production of a later age,—an age when thoughtful persons, anxious to regain their hold on the idea of unity, began to study all the various processes of physical life, and to reduce them into three kinds or phases, generation, preservation, and destruction[3]. Each of these was deemed the efflux of a special energy, and Brahmá, Vishńu, and Śiva were selected as the verbal representatives of natural causes contemplated in their three-fold character. So long as the idea of God as one, supreme, and personal was consciously preserved, those titles would not necessarily issue in impiety. Men felt that Brahmá, the Ineffable, whose proper dwelling is in gloom and silence, had notwithstanding made a revelation of Himself in nature, and that under three ideal forms expressing His distinctive operations in that province, men were able to conceive of Him and pay Him adoration.

But however this may be, it is quite certain that ere long the physical attributes of God, as the Creator, the Preserver,

[1] *Asiatic Researches*, I. 273. He complained that missionaries, in their zeal for the conversion of the natives, had been foolish enough to urge that 'the Hindús were even now almost Christians, because their Brahmá, Vishńu and Mahésa [Śiva] were no other than the Christian Trinity.' One of these missionaries was the Jesuit Bouchet, who in the words of Chateaubriand (*Génie du Christianisme*, V. 10) sent home a number of most curious details 'sur le rapport des fables indiennes avec les principales vérités de notre religion, et les traditions de l'écriture.' On the contrary, a learned Jewish writer, Philippsohn, *Development of the Religious Idea*, p. 156, has pointed out that the 'trinitarian Godhead of Christianity' differs from all other triads in being 'exclusively and wholly good; whereas in heathenism one of the three divine powers was conceived to be opposed to the other two, the principle of evil.'

[2] See above, p. 134, n. 1.

[3] Above, pp. 140, 141.

the Destroyer, were so rigorously personified, that they not only superseded the more elemental of the Vaidic deities, but practically excluded from men's thoughts the personality of God Himself. Brahmá, for instance, who in theory constituted the first link of some grand chain of emanations, was eventually saluted[1] as the 'great creator,' the 'father of the universe,' the 'founder and the governor of all things:' while other epithets, no less exalted and as plainly inconsistent with belief in unity, were gradually transferred by similar processes to Śiva and Vishńu. These three together represented everything that was divine; all other objects in the pantheon were reducible to these, and were held to be new phases of the three superior gods. 'The deities are only three,' says a high authority[2] of Bráhmanism, 'whose places are the earth, the intermediate region, and heaven; *viz.* fire, air, and the sun. They are pronounced to be [the deities] of the mysterious names severally; and *Prajápati*, the Lord of the creatures, is [the deity] of them collectively. The syllable *Óm* intends every deity. It belongs to *Paraméshthí*, him, who dwells in the supreme abode; it appertains to *Brahmá*, the vast one; to *Déva*, God; to *Adhyátmá*, the superintending soul. Other deities belonging to these several regions are portions of the [three] Gods; for they are variously named and described, on account of their different operations: but [in fact] there is only one Deity, the Great Soul (*Mahán-Átmá*).' This passage, interesting on other accounts, will more especially enable us to realise the thought which underlies all seeming inconsistencies in statements of different Hindú writers respecting the essential character of the members of their sacred triad. Brahmá, Vishńu, and Śiva are deemed worthy of the highest honour, and in act have been so worshipped, because they gather up and place before the worshipper everything that he can possibly know of God; yet all the while they are, as to their essence, creatures[3] separable from

[1] Wuttke, II. 269 sq.

[2] Quoted by Colebrooke in *Asiat. Res.* VIII. 395 sq.

[3] The following passage is very explicit: 'You are not to consider Vishńu, Brahmá, and Mahádéva (Śiva), and other incorporate beings as the Deity, although they have each of them the denomination of Déva, or divine. They are all created; while the Supreme Being is without beginning or end, unformed, and uncreated; worship and adore Him.' The writer then explains that worship is paid to inferior deities in order that men's 'minds may be composed, and conducted, by degrees, to the essential Unity.' Quoted in Lord Teignmouth's *Life of Sir Wm. Jones*, II. 284, 8vo. ed.

Brahma, differing in degree but not in nature from the members of the human species, and all destined to eventual reabsorption like other finite beings. Hence also, as the consequence of this conception, each of them is represented in the ancient books of India accompanied by a wife (*śakti*), who forms the counterpart of his own energies[1]; Saraswatí reflecting the peculiar powers of Brahmá, Lakshmí of Vishńu, and Parvatí of Śiva.

It were needless to point out in detail how this Hindú triad differs from the Catholic doctrine of the Holy Trinity,—that, I mean, for which the primitive Church had never ceased to struggle with the utmost jealousy[2] when assaulted by a host of pagan theories on the right hand and the left. The opposition between such doctrines is entire and fundamental. The germ of the Christian Trinity is not discoverable in any or in all the processes of physical nature. The actual development of the idea is neither tritheistic nor Sabellian. Christians have indeed been ever constant in maintaining the grand principle of the divine Monarchy. They believe in one only True God, one starting-point, one Head, one ἀρχή, one original, supreme and indivisible Essence. They believe, accordingly, that while the Godhead of the Father is entirely independent, and of none, the God ead of the Second Person in the blessed Trinity is derived, —derived from all eternity, by the communication to Him of the Godhead of the Father: and a similar remark is applicable to the mode in which the Third Person has eternally coexisted in that infinite Being. They believe, in other words, that the Divine essence, though incapable of multiplication, was not absolutely sterile, yea rather, that in virtue of its communicability, those three transcendent and profound relations have arisen which justify the titles Father, Son, and Holy Spirit.

On the other hand, all Catholic Christians have maintained with equal firmness that as each of the Three Personalities is properly Divine, so each must be regarded as the subject of attributes, as one distinct and personal Agent. The Word of God, for instance, is no simple quality, constituting one person with the Father; as a man together with his faculties is said to form one human subject. Neither is the Son of God a

[1] See Stuhr, I. 100, Wuttke, II. 270: and cf. above, p. 124, n. 1.

[2] Thus St. Athanasius, *Contra Arianos*, Oratio II. (Opp. I. 325, Colcn. 1686) protests with his wonted vehemence against the tendency of the pagan mind to represent the Persons of the Holy Trinity as created intelligences: 'Αλλ' οὐκ ἂν ἀνάσχοιτό τις Χριστιανῶν τῶν τοιούτων αἱρετικῶν· Ἑλλήνων γὰρ ἴδια ταῦτα, ὥστε γενητὴν εἰσάγειν Τριάδα, καὶ τοῖς γενητοῖς αὐτὴν συνεξισάζειν, κ. τ. λ.

deified intelligence, exalted far above the level of his fellows, and entrusted with the joint administration of the universe. However much these views of Christ and of His Person may be advocated here and there by the professing Christian, they differ *toto cœlo* from the principles inherited by early saints and martyrs; for otherwise the opposition offered to the Gospel by the pagan scoffer and half-pagan heretic would be utterly inexplicable.

No greater resemblance will again be found between the Christian Trinity and some ideal combinations which arise from time to time in systems of Hindú philosophy. One of these appears to have been prompted by a wish of later Sánkhyas to get rid of the Bráhmanical triad, and replace it by a something more in harmony with their own peculiar speculations. They accordingly affirmed[1] that *buddhi*, or intelligence, the second in order of their 'principles,' became distinctly known as three gods, by the agency of the three 'qualities;' and was thus to be esteemed 'one person' (*múrrti*) distributed in 'three *dévas*,' or, in other words, Brahmá, Vishńu, and Śiva.

Buddhism, in like manner, had in later times put forth its own peculiar triad. Intelligence, the first principle, was in the monasteries of Nepál associated with *Dharma*, the principle of matter; while a mediating power, or *Sangga*, was combined with the two others in order to secure their union and harmonious co-operation[2]. But this latter class of triads will more fitly come before us, on proceeding to examine[3] what is called

[1] Colebrooke, *Essais*, ed. Pauthier, pp. 17, 18.

[2] Cf. Cunningham (*Bhilsa Topes*, pp. 35, 36; p. 358: Lond. 1854), who traces back this triad as far as B.C. 247. Schott *Uber den Buddhaismus in Hochasien*, pp. 39, 40) has some interesting revelations on this subject. The three most precious things in the estimation of Buddhists are Śákya-muni, his religion (*Dharma*), and the community of religious men (*Sangga*). 'Unter *Dharma* und *Sangga* versteht man im ganzen buddhaistischen Hochasien und eben so in China *keine mit Buddha eins ausmachenden Personen* oder seinem Wesen emanirten Kräfte.' Still the Buddhists of those regions are sometimes in the habit of grouping three objects of worship together; *e.g.* Śákya-muni, his next predecessor, and his next successor (*Ibid.* p. 40). On Egyptian and other triads, see Wilkinson, 2nd series, I. 185 sq.; and Bunsen's protest 'in the name of philosophy' against the abuse of the word; *Egypt's place in Universal History*, I. 365.

[3] In the meantime I refer the reader to C. Morgan's able *Investigation of the Trinity of Plato, &c.*, who, in treating of the Catholic doctrine of the Holy Trinity, remarks (pp. 154, 155, Camb. 1853): 'But the cultivators of human wisdom appear to have been total strangers to it, till it was disclosed to them by a teacher of philosophy,

the 'Platonic trinity,' a doctrine which has often since the days of Plotinus been put forward as subversive of the loftier claims of Christianity.

§ 3. *Hindú* avatáras, *or incarnations, especially that of Krishńa.*

A remark which I have made already in allusion to the Hindú triads may as safely be extended to the Hindú theory of incarnations. That theory again has no existence either in the Védas[1], or the Laws of Manu[2]. It is, therefore, a development, or rather I should say, an aftergrowth, of which no trace appears until we reach a later stage in the religious history of Hindústán. There was, however, a clear tendency in the direction of this dogma, when philosophers had once begun to realize the principle of emanation; for if all created beings had within them particles of Divinity, it was easy to believe that heroes, whether physical or moral, had been gifted with so large a share of the divine, that God might, without impropriety, be said to dwell in them, to speak in them, to use them as material instruments whereby His purposes were carried out.

The name of *avatára*, or descent, has been, however, for the most part limited to certain manifestations of Vishńu, the second member of the mythological triad, who is made to vindicate his character as god and guardian of humanity, or as a middle-term between the powers of generation and destruction, by stepping down from his celestial dwelling-place for the deliverance of the earth at large, or for the special benefit of his worshippers. The *avatáras* of this class are ten in number. First of all Vishńu is represented as inhabiting the shape of an enormous fish, by which a remnant of the human family was rescued from a general deluge; secondly, as incarnate in a tortoise, by whose help the *dévas* were enabled to manufacture for themselves a new elixir, or ambrosia, which imparted immortality; thirdly, in a boar, which, when the earth was carried by a demon to the bottom of the sea, dived

[Plotinus], who had been educated in the bosom of Christianity. Then, and not till then, they used it as a key to unlock the abstract subtilties of Plato, and to throw a decent veil over the extravagant and licentious fables of Pagan mythology.'

[1] Above, p. 134, n. 3.

[2] Vishńu is only once noticed in this ancient code (Bk. XII. § 121), and then as a divinity of inferior rank.

down and rescued it; and then advancing, in the fourth place, to the highest order of animal life, and clothing himself with attributes more terrible and avenging, he appears as Narasingha, the 'Man-Lion.' The fifth incarnation, that of Vámana, the Dwarf, exhibits him rather in the light of a diplomatist, who had recovered for the *dévas* the possession of the 'three worlds' when they were conquered by the demon Bali.

We shall see hereafter that the earliest of these legends was not destitute of all historic basis, and others, as the second, third, and fourth, and possibly the fifth, are equally susceptible of such an explanation. The tenth, or Kalki *avatára*[1], is believed to be still future, pointing to some fearful crisis, when Vishńu, in human form, and seated on a 'white horse,' shall give the signal for extinguishing this visible universe. The four remaining *avatáras* (the sixth, seventh, eighth, and ninth) are all so far historical, that a real basis for them is discoverable in the annals of the Áryan conflicts, either with the savage aborigines of the Peninsula, or with other foes of the Bráhmanical religion[2]. Vishńu, in every case, is thought to be incarnate in the person of some sage or hero; he struggles with malignant spirits, whether men or demons, and having rescued his own followers from their grasp, recedes again into the sphere of absolute divinity.

But one of these remarkable incarnations, that of Krishna, or the eighth of the foregoing series, will demand a fuller investigation, not only as the leading member of a group, but also as peculiar in its characteristics[3], and presenting many obvious points of similarity to incidents recorded in our Gospels.

In the earlier *avatáras*, Vishńu is said to have emitted only

[1] Cf. Rev. vi. 8, which intimates the Christian origin of this legend. It will be considered again in Chap. III.

[2] For instance, the startling phenomena of Buddhism were finally explained by some of its Bráhmanical opponents on the supposition that Gautama Buddha was an illusory form emitted from the substance of Vishńu (the *ninth* in the series), and that his mission really was to deceive and so destroy the Daityas, or lower classes, who from their ascetic habits had grown too powerful: see *Vishńu Pur.* ed. Wilson, pp. 336 sq.

[3] Krishna-worship, according to M. Pavie, *Bhagavat Dasam Askand*, Pref. p. xi. (Paris 1852) is 'le plus moderne de tous les systèmes philosophiques et religieux qui ont partagé l'Inde en sectes rivales. Basé sur la théorie des incarnations successives que n'admettaient ni le Véda, ni les législateurs de la première époque brahmanique, le krichnaïsme *diffère sur tant de points* des croyances particulières à l'Inde, qu'on a été tenté de le considérer comme un emprunt fait aux philosophies et aux religions étrangères.'

a portion (*anśa*) of his godhead, and so to have established an imperfect relation with the forms of animal and human life; but Krishńa, on the contrary, reflected the most glorious image of the god of preservation. The god himself was actually incarnate; he descended as a real man upon the theatre of humanity, while claiming for himself the attributes of the Supreme Being, with whom he is identified. The first example of this great conception meets us in the pages of the *Bhagavad-Gítá*, in which the poet makes him speak as follows[1]: 'Even though I am unborn, of changeless essence, and the lord also of all which exist, yet, in presiding over nature (*prakriti*), which is mine, I am born by my own mystic power (*máyá*). For whenever there is a relaxation of duty, O son of Bharata! and an increase of impiety, I then reproduce myself for the protection of the good, and the destruction of evildoers. I am produced in every age for the purpose of establishing duty.' But although the name of Krishńa and the groundwork of his legend were thus fully apprehended at an early period, it was only in the course of ages that Krishńäism was able to embody itself into a sect[2], and only after further intervals that the legend was invested with the fulness and luxuriance which it manifests in the Puráńas,[3]—documents belonging to what is termed the 're-naissance of Bráhmanism,' *i. e.* a period not earlier than the eighth, nor later than the twelfth century of the Christian era.

I subjoin an extract of the legend[4] as derived from these

[1] Chap. IV. (p, 30, ed. Thomson). Elsewhere Krishńa is represented as the Lord of the world, the Creator, the 'Lord of Brahmá, Vishńu and Śiva:' Wuttke, II. 339.

[2] Elphinstone, *Hist. of India*, p. 102, 3rd ed., places the formation of all the sects, which are founded on the worship of particular incarnations, later than the beginning of the 8th century of the Christian era: and Colebrooke (*As. Res.* VIII. 495) believes that the 'worship of Rama and of Crishna by the Vaishnavas, and that of Mahadeva and Bhavani by the Saivas and Sactas, have been generally introduced since the persecution of the Bauddhas and Jainas.' Lassen, in like manner (*Ind. Alt.* II. 446), considers that prominence was given to Krishńa-worship in the hope of counterbalancing the influence of Buddhism at the time when it was threatening to become universal in the Peninsula.

[3] See the *Vishńu Puráńa* as edited by Prof. Wilson, and the *Bhágavat-Pouráńa*, as edited by M. Burnouf. As all this class of writings are thoroughly *sectarian* in their character, they must have originated after the growth of the rival sects into which Bráhmanism was at length divided; and the general opinion now is that no Purán, *as it now exists*, can claim the high antiquity which was formerly assigned to it (Lassen, I. 479 sq.).

[4] In Mr. Thomson's edition of the *Bhagavad-Gítá*, pp. 134 sq. A longer summary will be found in M. Pavie's edition of the *Bhagavat Dasam Askand*, Pref. pp. xxxiv. sq.

sources by a recent hand with no unfriendly or polemical object:

"The king of the Daityas or aborigines, Áhuka, had two sons, Devaka and Ugrasena. The former had a daughter named Devakí, the latter a son called Kansa. Devakí (*the divine*) was married to a nobleman of the Áryan race named Vasudeva (or Anakadundubhi), the son of Súra, a descendant of Yadu, and by him had eight sons. Vasudeva had also another wife named Rohiní. Kansa, the cousin of Devakí, was informed by the saint and prophet Nárada, that his cousin would bear a son, who would kill him and overthrow his kingdom. Kansa was king of Mathurá, and he captured Vasudeva and his wife Devakí, imprisoned them in his own palace, set guards over them, and slew the six children whom Devakí had already borne. She was now about to give birth to the seventh, who was Balaráma, the playfellow of Krishńa, and, like him, supposed to be an incarnation of Vishńu; but by divine agency, the child was transferred before birth to the womb of Vasudeva's other wife, Rohiní, who was still at liberty, and was thus saved. Her eighth child was Krishńa, who was born at midnight, with a very black skin[1], and a peculiar curl of the hair called the *Śrívatsa*, resembling a Saint Andrew's cross, on his breast. The gods now interposed to preserve the life of this favoured baby from Kansa's vigilance, and accordingly lulled the guards of the palace to sleep with the Yoga-nidrá, or mysterious slumber. Taking the infant, its father Vasudeva stole out undiscovered as far as the Yamuná, or Jumna, river, which seems to have been the boundary between the Áryans and the aborigines. This he crossed, and on the other side found the cart and team of a nomad Áryan cowherd, called Nanda, whose wife, Yashodá, had by strange coincidence just been delivered of a female child. Vasudeva, warned of this by divine admonition, stole to her bedside, and placing Krishna by her, re-crossed the river, and re-entered the palace, with the female baby of Yashodá in his arms, and thus substituted it for his own son. When Kansa discovered the cheat, he for a while gave up the affair, and set the prisoners at liberty, but ordered all male children to be put to death. Vasudeva then entrusted Krishńa to the care of Nanda, the cowherd, who took him to the village of Gokula, or Vraja, and there brought him up. Here Krishńa, and his elder brother Balaráma, who joined him, wandered about together as children, and evinced their divine character by many unruly pranks of surprising strength, such as kicking over the cart, which served as conveyance and domicile to Nanda and his family. The female Daitya Pútaná was sent to suckle him, but the refractory baby, discovering the trick, showed his gratitude by slaying her. Later in life he vanquished the serpent Kalíya in the middle of the Yamuná (Jumna) river. A demon, Arishta, assuming the form of a bull; another, Keshin, that of a horse; and a third, Kálanemi, all undertook to destroy the boy, but each fell victims to his superhuman strength. Krishńa now incited Nanda and the cowherds to abandon the worship of Indra, and to adopt that of the cows, which

[1] *Krishńa*, as an adjective, means simply *black*, which ought at once to dispose of the vulgar cavil that χριστός is Krishńa slightly disguised. Each word grows naturally out of the character of the personage with whom it is associated.

supported them, and the mountains, which afforded them pasturage. Indra, incensed at the loss of his offerings, opened the gates of heaven upon the whole race, and would have deluged them, had not our hero plucked up the mountain Govarddhana, and held it as a substantial umbrella above the land. He soon took to repose from his labours, and amused himself with the Gopís, or shepherdesses, of whom he married seven or eight, among whom Radhá was the favourite, and to whom he taught the round dance called *Rása-*, or *Mańdala-nrityam.* Meanwhile Kansa had not forgotten the prophecies of Nárada. He invited the two boys, Krishńa and Balaráma, to stay with him at Mathurá; they accepted, and went. At the gates, Kansa's washerman insulted Krishńa, who slew him, and dressed himself in his yellow clothes. He afterwards slew Kansa himself, and placed his father Ugrasena on the throne. A foreign king of the Kálayavana (Indo-Scythian) race soon invaded the Yadu, or Áryan, territory, whereupon Krishńa built and fortified the town of Dwáraka, in Guzerat, and thither transferred the inhabitants of Mathurá. He afterwards married Satyabhámá, daughter of Satrájit, and carried off Rukmińí, daughter of Bhíshmaka. His harem numbered sixty thousand wives, but his progeny was limited to eighteen thousand sons. When afterwards on a visit to Indra's heaven, he behaved, at the persuasion of his wife, Satyabhámá, in a manner very unbecoming a guest, by stealing the famous Párijáta tree, which had been produced at the churning of the ocean, and was then thriving in Indra's garden. A contest ensued, in which Krishńa defeated the gods, and carried off the sacred tree. At another time, a female Daitya, Ushá, daughter of Bána, carried off Krishńa's grandson, Aniruddha. His grandfather, accompanied by Ráma, went to the rescue, and though Bána was defended by Śiva and Skanda, proved victorious. Pauńdraka, one of Vasudeva's family, afterwards assumed his title and insignia, supported by the king of Benares. Krishńa hurled his flaming discus (*chakra*) at this city, and thus destroyed it. He afterwards exterminated his own tribe, the Yádavas. He himself was killed by a chance shot from a hunter. He is described as having curly black hair, as wearing a club or mace, a sword, a flaming discus, a jewel, a conch, and a garland. His charioteer is Sátyaki, his city, Dwáraka; his heaven, Goloka."

The reader will not fail to notice in this legend more than one exact coincidence with circumstances in the human history of our blessed Lord. Remote as are the main ideas which it embodies from the principles of Holy Writ, there is sufficient also of external correspondence to account for the alacrity with which the modern infidel has seized upon the tale of Krishńa, and has tortured it into an argument against the truth of Christianity. Nor has the abstract I have just been quoting brought before us every minor point[1] in which the incidents of the Gospel are supposed to be as clearly visible. Other versions of the Krishńa-legend tell us how, in addition to the marvellous birth at midnight, choirs of *dévatas*, resembling the angelic host

[1] See a pointed summary of these in Maurice's *Hist. of Hindústán*, II. 222, 223, Lond. 1820.

of Bethlehem, saluted the divine infant as soon as he was born. They give still greater prominence to the massacre of the innocents by Kansa, and his failing to secure possession of the child by whom he was at last to be supplanted. They narrate how, in the train of miracles that follow this deliverance, the young hero, to the great amazement of his parents and a troop of cowherds by whom he was attended, overcame the serpent Kálíya, and trampled on its head; while of particular acts ascribed to him in after-years by the compilers of the more expanded version of the story, the cleansing of lepers, the raising of the dead, his own descending to the world invisible and reascending to the proper paradise of Vishńu, are not the least conspicuous.

It is true indeed that not a few of these minute resemblances to sacred history, if taken one by one, have also parallels in other realms of heathendom, and therefore may be possibly explained as merely outward and fortuitous, or else as borrowing their chief force from arbitrary combinations and the specious and deceptive colouring under which we are accustomed to present them. Two or three examples from Greek writers will best illustrate my meaning. If Krishńa was violently persecuted in his infancy, it might be answered, so was Hercules exposed to the implacable rage of Juno. If Krishńa, in his triumphs, comes before us crowned with flowers and at the head of dancing milkmaids and intoxicated satyrs, the description will apply to Bacchus also. If Krishńa, veiling his divinity, is said to have been concealed beneath the roof of Nanda, the cowherd, Apollo, in like manner, acted like an ordinary mortal when he sought a shelter in the household of Admetus. Or again, if Krishńa is to be regarded as a purely human and historical hero, doomed to death in childhood from forebodings that his life would prove the ruin of another, we can find his parallel in the elder Cyrus, who had also been entrusted to the care of herdsmen, to preserve him from the vengeance of his royal grandfather, whose death it was foretold he should eventually accomplish.

Yet in placing these analogies before the reader, as suggesting to one class of minds a *possible* medium for explaining the resemblances which form the subject of our investigation, I am willing to admit that such a method does not give what seems to me a satisfactory account of all the parallels in question, more especially when we include the minor topics furnished by more ample versions of the Krishńa-legend. Many of these, I grant, might have been accidental; but *all* can scarcely be so treated, without violence to probability and ordinary experience. If then we adopt the theory of external intercourse as furnishing the simplest and most adequate explanation of the present phenomena, it must follow either that Christianity has borrowed from Hindúism or Hindúism from Christianity.

Now the former supposition is at once repudiated by the fact that our doctrine of the Incarnation and Messiahship of Christ is perfectly original in itself and perfectly consistent with the language of the Hebrew prophets. Even the astounding incidents of the Saviour's childhood, which are thought to be most nearly related to the Krishńa-legend, are proved, in our own Gospels, to have been foretold by men who flourished long before the Bráhman had begun to dream of *avatáras:* and with reference to the Promise generally, its form was thoroughly *Hebrew*, interwoven from first to last with the exalted destinies of Abraham and David, pointing ever with a firmer hand and larger measure of illumination to the wondrous facts of Nazareth and Bethlehem, foreshadowing the persecutions which befel the Man of Sorrows as the necessary precondition of the 'glory that should follow;' and in all the course of this mysterious evolution, blending with itself no heterogeneous or extrinsic element, much less an element originating on the far-off borders of the Yamuná, and in the cloister of some Bráhman devotee.

But if the character of our Messianic doctrine be thus singular and self-consistent, and if all attempts to draw it out of foreign sources are discovered to be futile, what are we to think of the other hypothesis, according to which the Krishńa-legend is indebted for at least a portion of its richness and embellishment to influences diffused by Christianity? Can we offer any adequate explanation of the Christian elements in Krishńäism, by supposing that there was an actual intercourse of some kind or other between the two religions?

To answer this question, we must distinguish, in the first place, between Krishńa considered as an ancient hero, and the Krishńa who is ultimately said to be identical with the Supreme Being, and the leading member in a system of religion and philosophy.

Now that Krishna, though unnoticed in the very oldest literature of India, may have already figured as a local hero in the period preceding the Great War, and subsequently, as the Hercules of the Panjáb, may have attracted to himself the reverence of his fellow-countrymen, are suppositions by no means improbable. The allusion of Megasthenes[1] to some such

[1] Megasthenis *Indica*, ed. Schwanbeck, p. 290: καθαρὰν ποιῆσαι τῶν θηρίων γῆν τε καὶ θάλατταν: cf. Lassen, I. 647, 648.

hero, far surpassing other men in strength of mind and body, and especially distinguished by his zeal in purifying land and water and destroying every form of noxious animal, will bear to be interpreted of Krishńa, as well as Balaráma and the rest, whom popular superstition had exalted far above the rank of ordinary mortals. Yet this reference of the language has not been suffered to pass on without a challenge[1]; and other arguments, alleged in favour of the high antiquity of Krishńa, have been weakened more and more by modern criticism. When, for instance, he was represented as the central object[2] of the *Mahábhárata*, the statement was devoid of all solid basis. The real heroes of that poem are the Páńdavas; and if it be remembered that of the 100,000 distichs in the poem only 24,000[3] can be shewn to have entered into the original composition; and further, that the tales relating to Krishńa's boyhood, his frolics at Vrindávan, and even his destruction of the Asuras, 'have all a modern complexion[4],' we may fairly doubt if the author of the poem, as it stood at first, knew anything of Krishńa beyond his character of hero, prince, or chieftain. This, at least, may be regarded as extremely probable, *viz.* that the splendid episode (the *Bhagavad-Gítá*) which made us first acquainted with his claims to superhuman power and dignity, which first identified his being with that of the Supreme, and first brought out distinctly the idea of sympathy with the human species and of periodic births in order to promote their welfare, was composed as late as the third century of the Christian era. It may be inferred accordingly, that all our certain knowledge respecting Krishńa, in the times preceding the diffusion of the

[1] Lassen, in replying to some of Weber's observations (cf. above, p. 181, n. 6) on the peculiarities of Krishńaïsm, investigates the origin of the Avatára-system (II. 1106 sq.), and concludes that the doctrine of Vishńu's incarnations was formed at least three centuries before the Christian era, although the number and order of such incarnations were first settled at a later period. To these arguments Weber has replied in detail (*Ind. Stud.* II. 409 sq.), questioning, among other things, the identity of Krishńa with the Indian Hercules of Greek writers. In any case, he argues, this hero or demi-god was no incarnation, in the proper sense of the language, and was very different from the Krishńa of later times. In the Avatára-system the grand peculiarity consisted not in the fact that some divinity assumed a human or animal form, and in it protected and purified the earth, but rather 'dass der Gott aus Mitleid mit der leidenden, aus Zorn gegen die sündige Menschheit *selbst* als Mensch geboren wird und ein menschliches Dasein führt.' (p. 411.)

[2] See, for instance, Elphinstone's *India*, p. 93, 3rd ed.; and a rectification of the statement in Lassen, I. 488.

[3] Lassen, I. 484, 489.

[4] Wilson, *Pref.* to *Vishńu Puráńa*, p. lxxi. and p. 492, note.

Gospel, is confined to very few particulars. He was, first of all, a man possessed of more than ordinary virtue and intelligence; and secondly, a hero acting as the leader of the shepherd-chieftains in his own immediate neighbourhood: and thirdly, a demigod or emanation, it may be, especially connected with Vishńu, and zealous for the purity and permanence of physical creation. As to the development of this idea and its amalgamation with the higher thoughts propounded in the *Bhagavad-Gítá*, I think them products of external agencies connected with the spread of Christianity. It has been shewn elsewhere how numerous, in the early ages of the Gospel, were the causes predisposing men to interchange religious speculations, and how numerous also were the channels by which intercourse might have been readily effected. I have also quoted[1] the opinion of a critic conspicuous in this field of ancient literature, who maintains that in one of the latest additions to the *Mahábhárata* allusion to such intercourse is clearly traceable, as well as hints of the effect produced by it, in modifying men's ideas of God, and also in imparting a fresh form and colour to the Hindú theory of incarnations. Nor is this opinion, in so far as Krishńa is concerned, of recent origin. Sir William Jones, whose interest was excited by minute resemblances between the legend of Krishńa in its newest form and certain narratives of Holy Writ, attempted to explain the 'motley story' on the supposition that 'spurious Gospels, which abounded in the first age of Christianity, had been brought to India, and the wildest part of them repeated to the Hindús, who engrafted them on the old fable of Césava, the Apollo of Greece[2].' The same view has, in substance, been adopted by many other scholars[3], who have also pointed out that one of the chief media by which Hindú mythographers obtained their knowledge of the early history of our Lord, and the peculiar source from which they borrowed hints for the embellishment of their story, was the *Evangelium Infantiæ*[4], an apocryphal writing known originally by the title of 'Gospel of St. Thomas,' and, perhaps from a supposed connexion with him, circulated at an early period on the coast of Malabar. It is significant also that this gospel was already current[5] among heretics, but reprobated by the Church herself, as early as the time of Irenæus, and was subsequently held in special honour

[1] Above, p. 184, n. 1.
[2] *Asiat. Reser.* I. 274.
[3] *e.g.* Maurice, *Hist. of Hindústán*, II. 218 sq. Lond. 1820.
[4] Printed in the *Codex Apocryphus*, ed. J. A. Fabricius, I. 127 sq.
[5] *Adversus Hæres*, lib. I. c. 20, ed. Stieren.

by the followers of Mani[1], and by other misbelievers like him; their object being, as we know, to blend the creed, the legends, and the institutes of paganism with some of the distinctive elements of supernatural religion.

But leaving all these questions, as we must do, in comparative obscurity, it is important to observe that Krishńäism, when purged from all the lewd and Bacchanalian adjuncts which disfigure and debase it, comes indefinitely short of Christianity. Regarded in its brighter aspect, it will prove that man is far from satisfied with the prevailing forms of nature-worship, and is struggling to become more conscious of the personality of God, and panting for complete communion with Him. It recognises the idea of God descending to the level of the fallen creature and becoming man[2]. It welcomes Krishńa as one realisation of this great idea, as the hero who was sent to lighten many a burden of pain and misery under which the universe was groaning, as the teacher who alone could save mankind by pointing out a method of escape from the necessity of repeated births. These yearnings after something higher, purer, and more heavenly, are discernible at intervals amid the very sternest forms of pantheism; they bear witness, notwithstanding all the flagrant contradictions in the system with which they are connected, to a consciousness of moral guilt, as well as to a sense of physical evil; they give rise to the anticipation, that mankind will ultimately burst the trammels of their adversary and be reconciled to God.

Yet, on the other hand, the dogma of Hindús, when measured by a Christian standard, is but shadowy and unsatisfying. The most perfect incarnation of Vishńu, as found in Krishńa, is *docetic* merely; it rather seems to be than is[3]. According to the theory of matter, which prevailed among his followers, the Divine and human could not truly come together, and could not permanently coexist. The one essentially excludes the other. Krishńa, therefore, on going back to his celestial home, or, in

[1] See the 'Testimonia' collected by Fabricius, pp. 133, 136, 138, 140. In the decree of Pope Gelasius, *De libris apocryphis*, it is called 'Evangelium nomine *Thomæ* apostoli, quo utuntur Manichæi.'

[2] See Wilson's *Vishńu Puráńa*, p. 492, n. 3, where it is explained that although Krishńa as to his human properties and condition was only 'a part of a part' (*anśánśávatára*) of the supreme Brahma, yet he was in reality 'the very supreme Brahma.' The commentator adds an observation acknowledging it to be 'a mystery how the supreme should assume the form of a man.'

[3] Dorner (*Lehre von der Person Christi*, I. 7 sq., Stuttgart, 1845) has some excellent remarks on this point.

the language of philosophy, on his reabsorption into the Great Spirit of the universe, entirely lays aside the perishable flesh, which he had once inhabited. He quits his human body; he abandons 'the condition of the three-fold qualities;' he unites himself with 'his own pure, spiritual, inexhaustible, inconceivable, unborn, undecaying, imperishable and universal spirit, which is one with Vásudeva[1].' In this respect he differs altogether from the God-man of the Christian Church,—the Mediator in whom Divine and human are completely reconciled, the Meeting-point where earth and heaven, the finite and the Infinite, the personal and Absolute, have coalesced for ever, and are wedded in the bonds of an indissoluble union. And as one result of such imperfect and confused idea, it followed that the blessings said to have been brought by Krishńa were not real and abiding: they could only last until the close of one particular age, or period, when the powers of evil, softened and repressed, but still, according to this view, incapable of subjugation, would break forth again with irresistible violence, and be everywhere triumphant. It is written in one of the *Puráńas*: 'The day that Krishna shall have departed from the earth will be the first of the Kali age[2].'

[1] *Vishńu Pur.* ed. Wilson, p. 612. The death of Krishńa is here ascribed to a random shot of the hunter Jará (*i. e.* infirmity, old age, decay).

[2] *Ibid.* p. 487. In like manner it is stated (p. 486), 'As long as the earth was touched by his sacred feet, the Kali age could not affect it.'

CHAPTER III.

Real Correspondencies between Hindúism and Revealed Religion.

'Nulla porro falsa doctrina est, quæ non aliqua vera intermisceat.'

ST. AUGUSTINE.

Unity of the human race. Transmission of religious knowledge. Hindú reverence for tradition. Points most likely to be transmitted.

§ 1. *The primitive state of Man. The original pair. Innocence of primeval men. Buddhist legend. Bráhmanical and Buddhist reminiscences of Paradise.*

§ 2. *The Fall of Man. General form of the Hindú doctrine. Chronological cycles. More precise traditions of the Bráhmans. Buddhist traditions. Bráhmanical doctrine of the Tempter. The serpent considered as an image of matter generally; as an image of the devil.*

§ 3. *The Hindú version of the Deluge. Modern form of the legend. Version of the Satapat'ha Bráhmana.*

§ 4. *Hindú rite of sacrifice. Moral insensibility of the Hindús. Bráhmanical sacrifices. Remote antiquity of sacrificial rites. Design of Hindú sacrifices. Propitiatory sacrifices. Hindú conviction of unworthiness. Sacrifice according to the philosophers.*

§ 5. *The Hindú hope of restoration. How far an historical Saviour was expected. The Kalki avatára; its probable origin.*

IT has been shewn[1] how various but converging arguments, for which we are indebted mainly to the light of modern science, have all tended to corroborate the scriptural narrative with reference to the common origin of men. Exactly therefore in proportion as this point has been established, it is likely that the different sections of the human family will preserve in their dispersion many an interesting fragment of primeval knowledge, and contribute to the reconstruction of primeval history. If all have radiated from one centre; if all inherit the same human faculties, and have been actuated by the same peculiar instincts,

[1] Part I. ch. II.

we shall be prepared to find, with local variations, and at different depths below the surface, many a link of that great chain which girdles the whole globe, and binds humanity together.

Proofs of common parentage may all indeed have been obscured and weakened by a multitude of disuniting agencies, as climate, isolation, force of character, and the like. Two stories of the ancient world may in the process of transmission have been blended into one. The names of persons may have been entirely lost or hopelessly corrupted. The scene of this or that catastrophe may have been altered for the gratification of individual caprice or national vanity. A race of simple shepherds, with none of the explicit guidance which is furnished by a written document, may have so magnified, embellished, and confused the stories and traditions of their ancestors, that all the ingenuity of modern criticism will prove unequal to the work of disentangling the historic from the mythic, and of weeding out the genuine from the false. Yet, notwithstanding these formidable obstructions, we are warranted, on the hypothesis of unity, in searching everywhere, as far as human steps have wandered, for remains of a substratum of primeval knowledge; confident that such remains had once extended on all sides with the extension of the human species, however much they are at present buried and corrupted, broken and displaced. And the tenacity with which the popular mind has ever clung to what is ancient and established, will further justify us in predicting that the many would retain their hold on the original traditions of the Indo-Áryan race, long after the philosopher had ceased to care about them, or provide a place for them in his new system of ethics and religion.

Let us, then, inquire, as far as may be, whether such hints can be derived from any of the extant documents of India, and more particularly from one class of writings, the Puráńic[1], which, as meant for the instruction of the people, may be naturally expected to embody and reflect the popular traditions. We are not a little strengthened in these expectations by the fact that nearly all the ancient writings of Hindús, so far from advocating the notion that truth is self-evolved, or a discovery of the human reason[2], recognise in God the only Source of

[1] It is true, as I have more than once observed, that the Puráńas in their present form are thoroughly sectarian, and therefore must have been all modernized; but whenever the remodelling of them took place there can be no doubt that very old materials were extensively employed. See Prof. Wilson's Pref. to the *Vishńu Puráńa*, p. lxiii.

[2] Thus, for example, it is expressly said by a philosopher, (*San-*

supernatural teaching; and so far from urging that the present age alone is in possession of such teaching, they proclaim their frequent obligation to the purer wisdom of antiquity, and to the guidance of the 'sages who have delivered it to us[1].' 'Truth,' they say, 'was originally deposited with men, but gradually slumbered and was forgotten: the knowledge of it returns like a recollection[2].'

Now the points that were most likely to be cherished in the memory of the ancient world were not so much the details of primeval history, as those marvellous and momentous facts, which, happening in the infancy of time, and prior to the date of the original dispersion, were supposed to bear directly on the hopes, and fears, and general fortunes of the human species, or were fitted by the startling or attractive shape which they assumed in primitive lays and legends to excite the cravings of the earnest heart, and fire the popular imagination.

Such points are:

1. The primitive state of man.
2. His fall.
3. His punishment in the deluge.
4. The rite of sacrifice.
5. The primitive hope of restoration.

§ 1. *The Primitive State of Man.*

Inconsistent as may be the various Hindú stories touching the creation of this visible universe, and the original innocence and dignity of men, 'it is not difficult,' writes a high authority[3], 'to detect through all their embellishments and corruptions, the tradition of the *descent of mankind from a single pair*[4], however much they have disguised it, by the misemployment of the figures of allegory and personification.'

cara, ed. Fr. Windischmann, p. 106), 'dass man nicht durch Vermittelung von Vernunftgründen, sondern durch Hülfe der von jeher überlieferten Lehren Brahma erreichen könne.'

[1] *Yajur-Véda*, xl. 10, 13, as quoted by Morris, *Essay*, p. 60.

[2] See Humboldt's *Cosmos*, II. 112, 113, Sabine's ed.

[3] Prof. Wilson, *Lectures*, p. 56. Buddhism, on the contrary, having lost all faith in a Creator, and contending that the rise and perishing of the world is 'by nature itself,' rejected the idea of an original pair. 'There was no such thing as that of the creation of the first man and woman.' Upham, *Sacred Books of Ceylon*, III. 1, 2, Lond. 1833. Yet this statement is somewhat modified, p. 17.

[4] 'There was formerly only one Véda, only one God, one fire, and one caste. From Purúravas came the triple Véda in the beginning of the Tréta age.' From the Bhágavata Puráńa.

According to one view, Brahmá, the god of creation, had converted himself into two persons, the first man, or the Manu Swáyambhuva, and the first woman, or Śatarúpá[1]: this division into halves expressing, it would seem, the general distinction of corporeal substance into two sexes, and Śatarúpá, as hinted by the etymology of the word itself, denoting the great universal mother, the one parent of a 'hundred forms.' A second representation is that, in the opening of the present *kalpa*, Brahmá created out of his own substance as many as a 'thousand pairs[2]' of each of the four classes, into which mankind has been distributed. But since these statements are both found at no great distance from each other in the same *Puráńa*, they are probably intended to be reconciled by supposing that in the former case we have a Hindú reminiscence of the history of creation, and in the second an ideal picture of the primitive race of human beings. Be this, however, as it may, the Hindú legends are agreed in representing man as one of the last products of creative wisdom, as the master-work of God, and also in extolling the first race of men as pure and upright, innocent and happy. 'The beings who were thus created by Brahmá are all said to have been endowed with righteousness and perfect faith; they abode wherever they pleased, unchecked by any impediment; their hearts were free from guile; they were pure, made free from soil by observance of sacred institutes. In their sanctified minds Hari dwelt; and they were filled with perfect wisdom by which they contemplated the glory of Vishńu[3].'

The first men were accordingly the best. The Krita age, 'the age of truth,' the reign of purity, in which mankind, as it came forth from the Creator, was not divided into numerous conflicting orders, and in which the different faculties of man all worked harmoniously together, was a thought that lay too near the human heart to be uprooted by the ills and inequalities of actual life. In this the Hindú sided altogether with the Hebrew, and as flatly contradicted the unworthy speculations of the modern philosopher, who would fain persuade us that human beings have not issued from one single pair, and also that the primitive type of men is scarcely separable from that

[1] *Vishńu Pur.* pp. 51, 52. In the *Laws of Manu* (I. 32) the same notion is expressed in a somewhat different form. After stating (§ 31) that for the multiplication of the human race, the Creator caused the four castes to proceed respectively from his mouth, his arm, his thigh and his foot, it is added: 'Having divided his own substance, the mighty power Brahmá became half male and half female.'

[2] *Vishńu Pur.* p. 45 and n. 4.

[3] *Ibid.*

of ordinary animals. In the former of these conclusions it is true he may appeal on his behalf to theorisings of the Buddhists; but with reference to the latter, they also were equally unable to cast off the tenets of their forefathers. It is held that a distinguished group of beings (*brahmas*) whose merit was insufficient to support them any longer in superior worlds[1], took refuge on the earth, and as the lustre of their ancient greatness lingered round about them, they retained one class of superhuman attributes; they were able to subsist without food, and gifted with the power of passing through the air at will. No change of seasons, and no alternation of night and day could be experienced in their neighbourhood; and free from all the present accidents of humanity, they lived for ages in unbroken peace and inexhaustible felicity. Whether this legend of the *brahmas* be regarded as an echo of some old tradition pointing to the first estate of men, or to the fall of angels, is comparatively immaterial: it evinces a belief that primitive inhabitants of the earth ranked higher than the beasts that perish, and were strangers to the guilt and darkness which have pressed so heavily on their descendants.

The Bráhman and the Buddhist, in like manner, have preserved some recollections of the nature of the spot in which those first inhabitants were planted. According to legends of the former[2], the abode of man in his primeval innocence was the fabled mount Méru the 'centre' of the globe. 'It is a high and beauteous mountain. From the glittering surface of its peaks the sun diffuses light into the far-off regions. Arrayed in gold it forms a worthy habitation for the *dévas* and *gandharvas*. Hideous dragons guard this mountain; they frighten back the sinner who ventures to approach it. The sides are covered over with plants of heavenly origin; and no finite thought can soar as high as the cloud-piercing summit. It is adorned with graceful trees and limpid waters; and on every side resounds the music of the birds.' To this description of the *Mahábhárata*, some other features may be added from different sources. The position of Méru is in the centre of a region called Ilávrita[3]; it is said to be enclosed by the river Ganges, 'which, issuing from

[1] Hardy, *Manual of Buddhism*, p. 64.

[2] See Lüken's *Traditionen des Menschengeschlechts*, pp. 65, 66, Münster, 1856; Faber's *Origin of Pagan Idolatry*, I. 314 sq. Lond. 1816, and Bähr's *Symbolik des Mosaischen Cultus*, I. 168. Heidelberg, 1837.

[3] Mr. Faber attempts, but unsuccessfully, to connect this name *Ilávrita*, which he also writes *Ida-Vratta*, with *Eden*. (I. 326.)

the foot of Vishńu, and washing the lunar orb, falls here from the skies, and, after encircling the city, divides into four mighty rivers, flowing in opposite directions[1].' On the summit of the mountain is the dwelling-place of Śiva, as well as the capital of Brahmá. There also is the home of blessed spirits; there is Nandana, the grove of Indra[2], and there the Jambu-tree[3], whose apples, large as elephants, feed the Jambu-river with their juices, and secure to all who drink of it unvarying health and happiness, and exemption from all physical decay. It is manifest that the scene of all this blessedness was placed by the Hindú mythographers among the lofty peaks of the Himálaya. In sight of them the Áryan had originally settled when he crossed the alpine frontier; and as time went over, and his children were still further severed from the primitive haunts of man, the glorious high-lands of the north were peopled by his ever active imagination with groups of mythic beings. There was the locality from which the founders of the Indo-Áryan race had issued: and there the theatre on which, according to his dreams, had been enacted all the mysteries of the ancient world. Those legends, therefore, notwithstanding a huge mass of wild exaggerations, will bear witness to primeval verities. They intimate how in the background of man's visions lay a Paradise of holy joy,—a Paradise secured from every kind of profanation, and made inaccessible to the guilty; a Paradise full of objects that were calculated to delight the senses and to elevate the mind; a Paradise that granted to its tenant rich and rare immunities, and that fed with its perennial streams the tree of life and immortality. The waters also of Ilávrita, divided as they were into four channels, and flowing towards the cardinal points, may not unnaturally suggest comparison with the primitive river that 'went out of Eden to water the garden; and from thence was parted, and became into four heads' (Gen. ii. 10): although in course of time, when mount Méru was commonly identified with the summits of the Hindú Alps, we might expect that those four streams would in like manner be discovered in the principal rivers that descend from the Himálaya[4].

[1] *Vishnu Pur.* ed. Wilson, pp. 169, 170.

[2] *Ibid.* p. 169.

[3] *Ibid.* p. 168.

[4] The names of the rivers in the *Vishńu Puráńa* are the Sítá (the river of China, or Hoangho), the Alakanandá (a main branch of the Ganges), the Chakshu (? the Oxus), and the Bhadrá (the Oby of Siberia): see Prof. Wilson's note, p. 171. The Buddhists also have their four holy rivers, and place the sacred garden at the foot of mount Méru, towards the south-west, and at the source of the Ganges: Faber, I. 325.

This legend of the Bráhmans in the hands of Buddhist rivals has been subjected to fresh embellishment. The latter in depicting Mahá-Méru, informs us[1] of 'square-faced inhabitants,' who are exempted from all kinds of sickness, and from other evils incident to humanity. 'They do not perform any kind of work, as they receive all they want, whether as to ornaments, clothes, or food, from a tree called *kalpa-wurksha*. This tree is 100 yojanas high, and when the people require anything, it is not necessary that they should go to it to receive it, as the tree extends its branches, and gives whatever is desired. When they wish to eat, food is at that instant presented; and when they wish to lie down, couches at once appear. There is no relationship, as to father, mother, or brother. The women are more beautiful than the *dévas*. There is no rain, and no houses are required. In the whole region there is no low place or valley. It is like a wilderness of pearls; and always free from all impurities, like the court of a temple or a wall of crystal. The inhabitants live to be a thousand years old; and all this time they enjoy themselves like the *dévas*, by means of their own merit and with the assistance of the kalpa-tree.'

§ 2. *The Fall of Man.*

But while so many legends of the ancient Áryan intimate with singular unanimity that man as he came forth from his Creator was both innocent and happy; while they point us to an age of truth, of light, of perfectness, and lead us backward to a spot, whose primal beauties were unsullied by the breath of physical and moral evil, they have spoken as distinctly of some fearful retrogression, of degeneracy without us and within us, of bodily decay, of mental obscuration, of estrangement from the Source of Life, and of expulsion from our first inheritance. 'The deep sense of this fact,' writes Coleridge[2], 'and the doctrines grounded on obscure traditions of the promised remedy, are seen struggling, and now gleaming, now flashing, through the mist of pantheism, and producing the incongruities and gross contradictions of the Bráhman mythology: while in the rival sect,—in that most strange phenomenon, the religious atheism of the Buddhists, with whom God is only universal matter considered abstractedly from all particular forms—the fact is placed among the delusions natural to man.'

[1] Hardy's *Manual of Buddhism*, pp. 14, 15.

[2] *Aids to Reflection*, I. 225, 226, Pickering's ed.

If we consider only the more popular doctrine of the Bráhmans, it is found to be in substance that which has impressed itself on all religions of antiquity, and forms the basis of all creeds whatever: *viz.* that sufferings were entailed upon the world at large by the disordered will or appetite of individuals, impelling them to seek for gratification by eating of some interdicted products of the soil. This vivid consciousness of retrogression, in its moral aspect, was obscured, indeed, from time to time by the Hindú philosopher, who, advancing from pantheistic premises, adopted the well-known hypothesis of chronological cycles. In his teaching every perfect revolution in the fortunes of the universe (*mahá-yuga*) is divided into four shorter periods[1], which are each in turn invested with specific qualities corresponding to assumed distinctions in the general history of man. Thus, after the Krita or Satya-age, when everything is true and perfect, comes the Tretá-yuga, or age of sacrifice, when virtue having 'lost one foot' and the divine ingredient in our spirit[2] waxing feeble, 'the innate perfectness of human nature is no more evolved.' After this appears the Dwápara-age, the age of doubt, of scepticism, of infidelity; and last of all the Kali-age, through which the world is said to be at present passing, when the powers of darkness and disorder have become predominant in the soul of man, and when external nature groans beneath the burden of iniquity.

Yet side by side with such elaborate theories on the origin of evil and the probable course of its development from generation to generation, there lingered in the memory of Hindús a far more definite knowledge of primeval history, and of the agencies through which the present lot of man was rendered so abnormal. They had learned that human misery is the fruit of

[1] *Vishńu Pur.* Book I. chap. iii. As Professor Wilson remarks, 'It does not seem necessary to refer the invention [of these cycles] to any astronomical computations, or to any attempt to represent actual chronology.'

[2] Vishńu on becoming subject to the conditions of time (Kála) is said to have himself 'infused into created beings sin, as yet feeble though formidable, or passion and the like.' (*Ibid.* p. 45.) This led directly to the loss of the eight kinds of perfection, which the human race had once enjoyed: (1) *Rasollásá*, the spontaneous or prompt evolution of the juices of the body, independently of nutriment from without: (2) *Tripti*, mental satisfaction, or freedom from sensual desire: (3) *Sámya*, sameness of degree: (4) *Tulyatá*, similarity of life, form and feature: (5) *Visoká*, exemption alike from infirmity or grief: (6) Consummation of penance and meditation, by attainment of true knowledge: (7) The power of going everywhere at will: (8) The faculty of reposing at any time and in any place.

disobedience; that the physical ills of life originate in moral delinquency, and that of parent sins, by which the world at large was ultimately overrun, the chief are pride and self-complacency, ambition, and self-worship. One legend out of many shall be cited in illustration of this topic. As the old traditions of their ancestors were gradually distorted, the Hindús appear to have identified the first man (Manu Swáyambhuva) with Brahmá himself, of whom, as of the primary cause, he was the brightest emanation; while Śatarúpá, the wife and counterpart of Manu, was similarly converted into the bride of the creative principle itself. Brahmá, in other words, was 'confounded with the male half of his individuality[1],' so that the narratives which in sacred history relate to Adam and Eve, were not unfrequently transferred to Brahmá and to his female counterpart,—Śatarúpá, or, according to a different form, Saraswatí. Brahmá thus humanized is said to have become the subject of temptation[2]. To try him, Śiva, who is, in the present story, identified with the Supreme Being, drops from heaven a blossom of the sacred *vata*, or Indian fig,—a tree which has been always venerated by the natives on account of its gigantic size and grateful shadow, and invested alike by Bráhman and by Buddhist with mysterious significations[3], as 'the tree of knowledge or intelligence' (*bódhidruma*). Captivated by the beauty of this blossom, the first man (Brahmá) is determined to possess it. He imagines that it will entitle him to occupy the place of the Immortal and hold converse with the Infinite: and on gathering up the blossom, he at once becomes intoxicated by this fancy, and believes himself immortal and divine. But ere the flush of exultation has subsided, God Himself appears to him in terrible majesty, and the astonished culprit, stricken by the curse of heaven, is banished far from Brahmapattana and consigned to an abyss of misery and degradation. From this, however, adds the story, an escape is rendered possible on the expiration of some weary term of suffering and of penance. And the parallelism which it presents to sacred history is well-nigh completed when the legend tells us further that woman, his own wife, whose being was derived from his, had instigated the ambitious hopes which led to their expulsion, and entailed so many ills on their posterity.

It is also worthy of remark, that Buddhism, in spite of deep

[1] *Ibid.* p. 53, note.

[2] The story is thus extracted in Lüken's *Traditionen des Menschengeschlechts*, pp. 83, 84.

[3] Lassen, I. 255—260.

and fundamental misconceptions[1], has retained at least a glimmering of primeval truth in reference to the fall of man as well as to his origin and loftier destinies. The Buddhists of Ceylon, for instance, have been taught that a class of spirits, who survived the wreck of previous worlds and systems, had, on their migration to the human sphere of being, lost another portion of their primal dignity. They were deprived of their perfections, we are told, by reason of 'their covetousness and by eating of all sorts of food, which lust effected in them. Thus they became man and woman, according to their fate, from whom we have all proceeded[2].'

But while some Hindú philosophers attributed the fall of man to a necessity inherent in the very nature of all finite emanations; while others saw in it the consequence of our association with time and matter; and while a third division, more alive to the realities of life and to the moral bearings of the fall, were willing to regard it as a penalty incurred by guilty spirits in a previous stage of their existence, the majority of the people clung more closely to traditions of their ancestors. The Buddhist, it is true, denied emphatically that the origin of evil is ascribable to any cause except 'the mischievous and corrupted temper of man[3]:' but in the creed of popular Bráhmanism, the sin of our first parents was traced up directly to the guile and malice of a tempter, not within us but without us. The tempter was, in form at least, a serpent. 'Almost all the nations of Asia,' is the forced confession of a modern rationalist[4], 'assume the serpent to be a wicked being, which has brought evil into the world.' 'How strangely,' writes a second[5], 'is the serpent everywhere mixed up with the development of the religious sentiment in man.' As such it had become, in almost every part of heathendom, an object of religious worship[6], or, to speak more properly, a symbol of those deadly and terrific powers, which, present (as men thought) in serpents, were the objects of continual dread, and therefore, of religious deprecation.

[1] See above, p. 160; and Hardy's *Manual*, pp. 65, 66.

[2] *Sacred Books of Ceylon*, ed. Upham, III. 17.

[3] *Ibid.* p. 157. When the further question is asked, 'Is the devil, or any other powerful spirit, the cause of sin?'—the Buddhist is taught to answer, 'by no means.'

[4] Von Bohlen, *Das alte Indien*, I. 248: cf. Hävernick, *Intr.* I. *to the Pentateuch*, p. 101 (Edinb. 1850), where the fact that local peculiarities are wanting in the Hebrew narrative is referred to as a proof of its originality.

[5] Priaulx, *Quæstiones Mosaicæ*, p. 85, Lond. 1842.

[6] See Deane's *Worship of the Serpent*, pp. 65 sq. Lond. 1830.

Serpents may indeed have been occasionally welcomed by the ancient Áryan as the bringers or restorers of good fortune, just as they are sometimes fed in our day with reluctant interest at the doors of Hindú cottages and temples; but the common attitude which they assume in all descriptions both of ancient and modern writers is one of absolute antagonism to man. The Hindú serpent is the type and emblem of the evil principle in nature; and as such, we see it wrestling with the goddess Parvatí, or writhing under the victorious foot of Krishńa when he saves from its corrupting breath the herds that pasture near the waters of the Yamuná. And as a further illustration of this view, it is contended, that many Hindús who feel themselves constrained to pay religious worship to the serpent, regard it, notwithstanding, as a hideous reptile, whose approach inspires them with a secret awe and insurmountable horror.

But it may be necessary to investigate these questions somewhat more particularly, for the purpose of discriminating, if possible, between the character of the serpent when it forms the subject of a Hindú mythe, and when the subject of a Hindú legend. According to the first view, it is believed to be a symbol of primitive matter generally; according to the second, it is an image of the evil spirit, the seducer and arch-enemy of man. We are reminded[1] that anterior to the human epoch, when Brahma is still sleeping on the waters and preparing to diffuse himself through all the various orders of creation, the *dévas* already brought into existence are anxious to ascertain what part has been reserved for them in the ensuing process. They petition the Great Father of beings (*Mahápitri*), and are made at his suggestion to precipitate themselves upon the earth in the shape of material elements, fire, air, water, and the like, with Indra as their head and leader. At this epoch also comes into the world the chief of the serpents (Kulikétu)[2], who has soon occasion to complain most bitterly to the Lord of the universe, that, for no fault of his, he was continually tormented by the Suras,—or inferior gods inhabiting *Swarga* and composing the great army led by Indra in his conflict with the Asuras. In answer to the prayer of Kulikétu, Brahma is said to have enjoined that he should henceforth receive adoration like the *dévas* from each human being, and that mortals who refused to pay such worship to him, should be cut off by some unnatural death

[1] See an interesting paper *Sur le Mythe du Serpent chez les Hindous*, in the *Journal Asiatique*, Mai-Juin, 1855, pp. 469—529.

[2] The same as Kulika, one of the chiefs of the Nágas, or serpents: *Ibid.* p. 481.

and made incapable of rising higher in the scale of created beings.

I think it not improbable that the right interpretation of this mythe is one which has already been suggested. It directs us to behold in Kulikétu an emblem of the earth before it had been subjected to human culture, when it felt itself tormented by the Suras, or, in other words, assaulted by the armies of the firmament,—the rain, the lightning, and the tempest. In the midst of this disorder, man, who had been hitherto regardless of the soil on which his lot is cast, and the material out of which his body is constructed, was bidden by the Lord of creation to render homage to the powers and processes of nature, to propitiate the ungenial elements, and welcome in all forms around him the immediate presence of Divinity.

According therefore to this mythe the serpent was not absolutely and directly charged with the origination of all evils; yet suspicions of such agency were nevertheless implied from first to last in the conception of the story. There was lurking under its fantastic imagery an idea that matter in the whole compass and duration of it was intrinsically evil; and might therefore be identified with that which was the recognised embodiment of the evil principle. And other tales of ancient India bring this truth before us in the greatest prominence. Side by side with representations of the serpent as a type of primitive matter was unfolded the analogous conception of him as *the* enemy of the human race[1]. For instance, at the opening of the *Mahábhárata* itself, we find a touching illustration of this subject. The young and beautiful Pramadvará had been affianced to the Bráhman Ruru, but just before the celebration of their nuptials she is bitten by a deadly serpent and expires in agony. As tidings of her death are carried round the neighbourhood, the Bráhmans and aged hermits flock together; and encircling the corpse of the departed mingle their tears with those of her disconsolate lover. Ruru is himself made eloquent by grief; he pleads the gentleness of his nature, and his dutiful observance of the laws of God: and finally, as the reward of his superior merits, Pramadvará is given back to him; yet only with the sad condition that he must surrender for her sake the half of his remaining lifetime. If this legend will not altogether justify the supposition[2] that a reference is intended by it to the

[1] *Ibid.* p. 488.

[2] 'N'y a-t-il point, dans cette donnée, comme un ressouvenir du couple primitif condamné à une vie courte et précaire à cause de la femme surprise par le serpent? ... Dans la légende indienne, comme dans la fable grecque [*i.e.* of O-

primitive pair of human beings, whose existence was cut short by a disaster inflicted on the woman by the serpent, it may serve at least to shew us how familiar was the Hindú mind with such a representation, and how visions of the fall of man had never ceased to flit with more or less confusion across the memory of the ancient bards.

§ 3. *The Hindú version of the Deluge.*

I shall not ask the reader to investigate a series of those minor points in which attempts are made to institute a clear connexion between the earliest Hindú legends and corresponding pages in the Scriptural history of man. But there is one catastrophe which, if the record of it in the Book of Genesis be accepted, could not fail to make a most profound impression in all quarters of the globe which had been visited by human footsteps. That catastrophe is the Deluge. The annals of the world begin afresh in Noah. The ark in which he rode securely to his destination is the second birth-place of the human family.

Now here again it is important to observe, that the Hindú traditions, notwithstanding the grotesque embellishments they underwent, from time to time, at the hands of the mythographers, were all in close accordance with the principal facts of revelation. They inform us how, amid an age of deep corruption, when the world was drowned by the avenging waters of a deluge, the Deity Himself came down to earth, in order to ensure the preservation of a righteous king, Manu, and to deposit with him in a ship the seeds of all created beings. Like other legends of antiquity, the present one has varied greatly with the lapse of ages, and been coloured by the varying conceptions of the people among whom it was diffused. I shall first extract[1] the popular, or Puráńic, version which, as might have been anticipated, is the most exuberant of the forms transmitted to us:

"Desiring the preservation of herds, and of Bráhmans, of genii and of virtuous men, of the Védas, of law, and of precious things, the Lord of the universe assumes many bodily shapes: but, though he pervades, like the air, a variety of beings, yet he is himself unvaried,

pheus and Eurydice], comme dans le récit biblique, c'est à la femme que le serpent s'adresse; il la choisit pour première victime, parce qu'elle est moins prudente, moins ferme en ses pensées que l'homme, son maître et son appui. Et dans quelles circonstances encore? Lorsque le bonheur sourit aux jeunes couples, et qu'aucun malheur ne semble les menacer de près ni de loin.' *Ibid.* pp. 490, 491.

[1] *Asiat. Researches*, I. 230 sq.

since he has no quality subject to change. At the close of the last Kalpa, there was a general destruction occasioned by the sleep of Brahmá; whence his creatures in different worlds were drowned in a vast ocean. Brahmá, being inclined to slumber, desiring repose after a lapse of ages, the strong demon Hayagríva came near him, and stole the Védas which had flowed from his lips. When Hari, the preserver of the universe, discovered this deed of the prince of Dánavas, he took the shape of a minute fish called Sap'harí. A holy king, named Satyavrata, then reigned; a servant of the spirit which moved on the waves, and so devout that water was his only sustenance. He was the child of the Sun; and, in the present Kalpa, is invested by Naráyańa in the office of Manu, by the name of Sráddhadéva, or the god of obsequies. One day, as he was making a libation in the river Kritamála, and held water in the palm of his hand, he perceived a small fish moving in it. The king of Dravira immediately dropped the fish into the river together with the water, which he had taken from it; when the Sap'harí thus pathetically addressed the benevolent monarch: 'How canst thou, O king, who shewest affection to the oppressed, leave me in this river-water, where I am too weak to resist the monsters of the stream, who fill me with dread?' He, not knowing who had assumed the form of a fish, applied his mind to the preservation of the Sap'harí, both from good nature, and from regard to his own soul; and, having heard its very suppliant address, he kindly placed it under his protection in a small vase full of water; but, in a single night, its bulk was so increased, that it could not be contained in the jar, and thus again addressed the illustrious prince: 'I am not pleased with living miserably in this little vase; make me a large mansion, where I may dwell in comfort.' The king, removing it thence, placed it in the water of a cistern; but it grew three cubits in less than fifty minutes, and said: 'O king, it pleases me not to stay vainly in this narrow cistern; since thou hast granted me an asylum, give me a spacious habitation.' He then removed it, and placed it in a pool; where, having ample space around its body, it became a fish of considerable size. 'This abode, O king, is not convenient for me, who must swim at large in the waters: exert thyself for my safety, and remove me to a deep lake.' Thus addressed, the pious monarch threw the suppliant into a lake; and, when it grew of equal bulk with that piece of water, he cast the vast fish into the sea. When the fish was thrown into the waves, he thus again spoke to Satyavrata: 'Here the horned sharks, and other monsters of great strength, will devour me; thou shouldest not, O valiant man, leave me in this ocean.' Thus repeatedly deluded by the fish who had addressed him with gentle words, the king said: 'Who art thou, that beguilest me in that assumed shape? Never before have I seen or heard of so prodigious an inhabitant of the waters, who like thee, hast filled up in a single day a lake of a hundred leagues in circumference. Surely thou art Bhagavat, who appearest before me; the great Hari, whose dwelling was on the waves, and who now, in compassion to thy servants, bearest the form of the natives of the deep. Salutation and praise to thee, O first male; the lord of creation, of preservation, of destruction! Thou art the highest object, O supreme ruler, of us thy adorers who piously seek thee. All thy delusive descents in this world give existence to various beings; yet I am anxious to know for what cause that shape has been assumed by thee. Let me not, O lotus-eyed, approach in vain the feet of a deity, whose perfect benevolence has been extended to all; when thou hast shewn, to our amazement, the appearance of other bodies, not in reality existing but successively exhibited.' The lord of the universe, loving the pious man who thus implored him, and intending to preserve him from the sea of destruction caused by the depravity of the age, thus told him how he was to act. 'In seven days from the present time, O thou tamer of enemies, the three worlds will be plunged in an ocean of death; but, in the midst of the destroying waters, a large vessel, sent by me for thy use, shall stand before thee. Then shalt thou take all medicinal herbs, all the variety of seeds; and, accompanied by seven saints, encircled by pairs of all brute animals, thou shalt enter the spacious ark, and continue in it, secure from the flood, on one immense ocean, without light, except the radiance of thy holy companions. When the ship shall be agitated by an impetuous wind, thou shalt fasten it with a large sea-serpent on my horn; for I will be near thee: drawing the vessel with thee and thy attendants, I will remain on the ocean, O chief of men, until a night of Brahmá shall be completely ended. Thou shalt then know my true greatness, rightly named the supreme godhead. By my favour all thy questions shall be answered, and thy mind abundantly instructed.' Hari, having thus directed the monarch, disappeared; and Satyavrata humbly waited for the time, which the ruler of our senses had appointed. The pious king, having scattered towards the east the pointed blades of the grass *darbha*, and turning his face towards the north, sat meditating on the feet of the god who had borne the form of a fish. The sea, overwhelming its shores, deluged the whole earth; and it was soon perceived to be augmented by showers from immense clouds. He, still meditating on the command of Bhagavat, saw the vessel advancing, and entered it with the chiefs of Bráhmans, having carried into it the medicinal creepers and conformed to the directions of Hari. The saints thus addressed him: 'O king, meditate on Kéśava; who will surely deliver us from this danger, and grant us prosperity.' The god, being invoked by the monarch, appeared again distinctly on the vast ocean in the form of a fish, blazing like gold, extending a million of leagues, with one stupendous horn: on which the king, as he had been before commanded by Hari, tied the ship with a cable made of a vast serpent, and, happy in his preservation, stood praising the destroyer of Madhu. When the monarch had finished his hymn, the primeval male, Bhagavat, who watched for his safety on the great expanse of water, spoke aloud to his own divine essence, pronouncing a sacred Puráňa, which contained the rules of the Sánkhya philosophy: but it was an infinite mystery to be concealed within the breast of Satyavrata; who, sitting in the vessel with the saints, heard the principle of the soul, the Eternal Being, proclaimed by the preserving power. Then Hari, rising together with Brahmá from the destructive deluge which was abated, slew the demon Hayagríva, and recovered the sacred books. Satyavrata, instructed in all divine and human knowledge, was appointed in the present Kalpa, by the favour of Vishňu, the seventh Manu, surnamed Vaivaswata: but the appearance of a horned fish to the religious monarch was Máyá or delusion; and he, who shall devoutly hear this important allegorical narrative, will be delivered from the bondage of sin."

This Puráňic version of the Deluge (for to that catastrophe alone has any of our modern scholars ventured to refer it) is, according to its own admission, coloured and disguised by allegorical imagery. It avows, for instance, that one prominent object in the picture, the phenomenon of the horned Fish, is *máyá*, or is based upon illusory ideas; while other features of it have an air of gloom and mysticism peculiar to productions of the Hindú mind in the ascetical, or Yoga, period of its history. There is, however, a different version[1] of the legend, shorter and far less ornate, in one of the great epic poems of India. That version contains no reference either to the sleep of Brahmá, the pilfering of the Védas, or the systems of Hindú chronology, which, as resting on the thought of a succession of similar worlds, may have themselves been primarily suggested by the story of the Deluge[2]. It is further silent with regard to the specific power by which Manu was able to collect together seeds of all existing things: nor was the author of it acquainted with those mighty serpents, who, in the Puráńic version, are said to have approached Manu and acted as the cords by which his ark was fastened to the horns of the enormous Fish. In one case also, it is Vishńu that becomes incarnate, mainly with the purpose of preserving the integrity of the Védas; in the other, it is Brahma, or the 'Lord of all things,' who is mercifully stooping to the level of the creatures for the rescue of his uncorrupted servant.

Still the outlines of the legend are precisely the same in both versions; and their close resemblance to each other, and also to the scriptural narrative of the Deluge, has induced a recent critic[3] to conclude that all the knowledge of this subject which Hindús have ever manifested was originally derived from a Semitic source. He has not, however, specified a channel, by which the transfer was likely to be effected; and if his meaning be that some account of the Deluge was first transmitted to the Panjáb in comparatively modern times, the conjecture is not only in itself improbable, but adverse to Hindú traditions. Another of these was happily brought to light a few years ago

[1] Edited by Bopp, Berlin, 1829, with the title, *Die Sündfluth, nebst drei anderen der wichtigsten Episoden des Mahá-Bhárata*. The writer of this version, as it now stands, is made to refer, as his authority, to the account of the Matsya avatára, which has been given above; but Prof. Wilson argues (Pref. to *Vishńu Puráńa*, p. li.) that the story in the *Mahábhárata* is really more ancient.

[2] Cf. Lüken, *Traditionen des Menschengeschlechts*, pp. 187, 188.

[3] Burnouf, *Bhágavata-Pourána*, Tome III. Pref. pp. xxiii. sq., where the points of divergence between the Puráńic and the Epic legends are fully pointed out. 'In the ancient historical fragments [preserved in Josephus] of the Assyrian or Babylonian history belonging to the Semitic race, the Hindú fable has a close parallel in the story of Xisuthrus and his flood, and the fish-god Oannes.' Prichard, III. 198.

by the publication of the Yajur-Véda. Appended to it is an ancient commentary, the *Satapat'ha-Bráhmańa*[1], in which the Hindú story of the Deluge is again presented to us in a still simpler dress, and, what is worthy of especial notice, accompanied by allusions which imply that Áryans had themselves referred the Deluge to a high antiquity, and also had retained a glimmering consciousness of some connexion between it and their migrations from the northern side of the Himálaya.

I am induced to give this legend also in its entirety, that ample means may be afforded for ascertaining what the Áryan of an early day had handed down to his posterity in reference to the marvels of the Flood, its nature and its consequences:

"One morning the servants of Manu brought him water for ablutions, as the custom is to bring it in our day when men's hands have to be washed. As he proceeded to wash himself he found a fish in the water, which spoke to him, saying, 'Protect me and I will be thy Saviour.' 'From what wilt thou save me?' 'A deluge will ere long destroy all living creatures, but I can save thee from it.' 'What protection, then, dost thou ask of me?' 'So long as we are little,' replied the Fish, 'a great danger threatens us, for one fish will not scruple to devour another. At first, then, thou canst protect me by keeping me in a vase. When I grow bigger, and the vase will no longer hold me, dig me a pond, and protect me by keeping me in it; and when I shall have become too large for the pond, then throw me into the sea; for henceforward I shall be strong enough to protect myself against all evils.' The Fish ere long became enormous (*jhasha*), for it grew very fast, and one day it said to Manu, 'In such a year will come the deluge; call to mind the counsel I have given thee; build a ship, and when the deluge comes, embark on the vessel thou hast built, and I will preserve thee.' Manu, after feeding and watching the Fish, at last threw it into the sea, and in the very year the Fish had indicated, he prepared a ship and had recourse [in spirit] to his benefactor. When the flood came, Manu went on board the ship. The Fish then reappeared and swam up to him, and Manu passed the cable of his vessel round its horn, by means of which he was transferred across yon Northern Mountain. 'I have saved thee,' said the Fish, 'now lash thy vessel to a tree, else the water may still carry thee away, though thy vessel be moored upon the mountain. When the water has receded, then also mayest thou disembark.' Manu implicitly obeyed the order, and hence that northern mountain still bears the name of Manu's descent[2]' (*Manor avasarpańam*). The deluge swept away all living creatures; Manu alone survived it. His life was then devoted to prayer

[1] Weber's *Ind. Stud.* I. 161 sq.

[2] In the *Mahábhárata* the name of the mountain is Naubandhana (='ship-bond'); and, what is very remarkable, Manu is there supposed to be resident in India when the deluge comes, and to be carried by it as far as Mount Himavat; whereas in this version of the story, it is implied that his original seat was on the *north* of the Himálaya range, and that he crossed over from thence into India (*atidudráva*): see Weber, p. 165.

and fasting in order to obtain posterity. He made the Páka-sacrifice[1]; he offered to the Waters the clarified butter, cream, whey, and curdled milk. His offerings were continued, and at the end of a year he thereby fashioned for himself a wife[2]: she came dripping out of the butter; it trickled on her footsteps. Mitra and Varuña approached her and asked 'Who art thou?' She answered, 'The daughter of Manu.' 'Wilt thou be our daughter?' 'No,' the answer was: 'My owner is the author of my being.' Their solicitations were all vain; for she moved directly onward till she came to Manu. On seeing her, he also asked her, 'Who art thou?' And she answered, 'Thine own daughter.' 'How so, beloved, art thou really my daughter?' 'Yes; the offerings thou hast made to the Waters, the clarified butter, the cream, the whey, and the curdled milk have brought me into being. I am the completion of thy vows. Approach me during the sacrifice. If so, thou shalt be rich in posterity and in flocks. The desire which thou art cherishing shall be entirely accomplished.' Thus was Manu wedded to her in the midst of the sacrifice, that is, between the ceremonies that denote the opening and the close of it. With her he lived in prayer and fasting, ever-anxious to obtain posterity: and she became the mother of the present race of men, which even now is called the race of Manu. The vows which he had breathed in concert with her were all perfectly accomplished."

Here again it would be quite superfluous to enlarge upon the shifting and capricious character of the Hindu legend, and still more to specify the points of contact which exist between it and the narrative preserved to us in Holy Scripture. Both these observations will immediately suggest themselves to every reader. But there is another point which, if it be less obvious, is certainly no less deserving of attention. The simplicity of the account in Genesis; the truthful and historic air of every part of it; its close coherence with all other facts of revelation, as well as with the scriptural theory of man and of the universe; the absence from it of those manifest depravations, which are only capable of being rectified and made intelligible when brought into the light which it diffuses, give additional weight to the authority on which it is received by Christians, and vindicate its claim to be regarded as a genuine copy of the old

[1] 'The *Pákayajna*, or sacrifice in which food is offered, implies either the worship of the Viśwadévas, the rites of hospitality, or occasional oblations, or building a house, the birth of a child, or any occasion of rejoicing.' Wilson, *Vish. Pur.* p. 292, n. 3.

[2] The following passage of the legend is, perhaps, an allegorical embellishment, the idea being that praise (Ídá), the daughter of Manu, is the medium and accomplice by which he was able to bring about the creation of new orders of being. In this manner the present legend is made to harmonize with that in the *Mahábhárata*, where the new creation is said to be achieved by the extraordinary penance of Manu. But the birth of Ídá from the Waters, and the overtures of Mitra and Varuña (? Day and Night), are still involved in mystery. Cf. Weber, I. 169.

tradition that descended, age by age, from Noah to all members of the sacred family.

§ 4. *Hindú Rite of Sacrifice.*

Attention has been drawn already[1] to some characteristics of the Védas, intimating how very low was the degree of moral sensibility once prevalent in the Áryan tribes of Hindústán. And this remark is further illustrated by the versions of the Deluge we have just been criticising. Although the human race, according to Hindú legends, was so utterly overwhelmed that Manu had become the second head and parent of our species, it is obvious, and especially obvious in the oldest form of the tradition, that the moral bearings of the Deluge were comparatively forgotten. It was rather treated as a dire catastrophe, originating in some physical necessities, than as the fruit and punishment of human sin. So far indeed the Buddhist[2] rose superior to the Bráhman. He was clearly conscious that although there *must* be periodic revolutions of the universe, their consequences may be all averted from the individual, who is open to the terrible warnings by which they are preceded. When a *déva* issues forth, according to the legends of Ceylon, arrayed in mourning and with trembling voice and streaming eyes announces, through the various regions doomed to desolation, that in a hundred thousand years the present *kalpa* will be finished, he is also commissioned to declare how every man is able to escape the dread calamity: 'Let him assist his parents, respect his superiors, avoid the five sins, and observe the five obligations.'

The Bráhman, however, notwithstanding the dulness of his moral intuitions, had always differed from the Buddhist in the care which he bestowed on the performance of sacrificial rites. There was no period in the lifetime of the Indo-Áryan people when altars were not reared and sacrifices offered[3]. For exam-

[1] Above, pp. 129, 130.

[2] See the whole passage in Hardy's *Manual*, pp. 29, 30. 'The beings in the world in great fear approach the *déva*, and ask him whether he has learnt this by his own wisdom, or has been taught it by another; when he replies, that he was sent by Mahá-Brahmá, the *déva* of many ages. On hearing this declaration the men and *dévas* of the earth regard each other with affection, from the fear that comes upon them; by which merit is produced, and they are born in a brahma-loka.'

[3] Lassen, I. 789. He urges among other points the existence of the three words *hu* (*dhu*), *θύω*, and Lat. *fio*, which shew that sacrificial rites, and even offerings made by fire, were older than the original dispersion of the Indo-European family.

ple, as early as the hymns of the Rig-Véda, men appealed to the abundant blessings which were granted to their forefathers in virtue of the soma-sacrifice. 'O Soma [thus personifying the libation], thy bounties have been all remembered. Thou conductest us along the best of pathways. Under thy protection, O thou whose surname is *Indu* [liquor], our holy and wise ancestors have won the favour of the *dêvas*[1].' And, in harmony with this tradition, we noticed how the Hindú legend of the Deluge not only testified to the existence of primeval sacrifices, but extolled their wondrous merit. As Noah, on issuing from the Ark, is said to have built an altar unto the Lord, the Self-existent, that he might propitiate His anger by 'burnt-offerings' (Gen. viii. 20—22); so the first anxiety of Manu was to people the earth afresh, by means of prayer and mortification, and still more by what was held to be the grand 'accomplisher of all desires,' by various forms of sacrifice. But though the early prevalence of this rite among the Indo-Áryans must in future be regarded as indisputable, there remains no small confusion in some quarters with regard to the precise direction and design of the oblations thus presented.

1. First, then, it should be remembered, that during the historic period, oblations were seldom or never made to God, the abstract Brahma, excepting where the worshipper had half-unconsciously identified Him with one or other of the elemental deities, with Indra, Agni, Soma, and the like, or else with some illustrious demi-god, the special organ of divinity. In other words, the Hindú offered his material sacrifices not to God, but to the gods[2]. As we behold him pictured in the sacred books of his religion, the objects of his worship differ only in degree, and not in nature, from the worshipper himself. They too are *creatures*, and as such are ultimately doomed to perish in the winding-up of all things. And the prevalent ideas of sacrifice entirely corresponded with this low conception of the nature of the beings to whom it was referred. 'By sacrifices the gods are nourished[3].' Rain and fire and sunlight were believed to gather strength and potency proportioned to the size of the oblation, and the fervour of the human spirit. It was, therefore, not so much the feeling of unworthiness, or the intention to deny one's self, that prompted a large class of the Hindú obla-

[1] *Rig-Véda*, Tome I. p. 171, ed. Langlois.

[2] Above, pp. 141, 190—191. Wuttke corroborates the view there taken: 'Nicht zu dem Ur-Brahma steigt das Gebet und der Opferrauch empor, sondern nur zu den dem Menschen ebenbürtigen creatürlichen Göttern:' II. 353.

[3] *Vishńu Pur.* p. 44.

tions. Man was thoroughly persuaded[1] that the gods were capable of receiving benefit from his services, that they were fed by the abundant products of his field or garden, were exhilarated by the juices of the holy soma-plant, were nerved by his impassioned prayers, were solaced by the music of his hymns, and that in recompence for all such acts of piety, the gods became propitious to him: his pastures grew more fertile; his flocks and herds were multiplied; a numerous family gathered round his table, and the foe that threatened to destroy or vex him was more readily circumvented and despatched.

2. But while such feelings were most prominent in many of the oblations of the ancient Áryan, he also proved that he was never destitute of those convictions which form the proper basis of the rite of sacrifice; he shewed a sense of personal unworthiness, and a desire of making good his imperfections by offering to God the choicest of his hopes, and sacrificing the best of his possessions. Hence the offerings which he brought were sometimes far more costly and more obviously piacular. As early as the composition of the third Véda, they were all reduced under five heads[2]: (1) *Agnihotra*, burnt offerings, or libations of clarified butter on sacred fire; (2) *Derśapaurńamása*, sacrifices at new and full moon; (3) *Cháturmásya*, sacrifices every four months: (4) *Paśuyajna* or *Áswamédha*, sacrifice of a horse or other animals; (5) *Soma-yajna*, offerings and libations of the juice of the acid asclepias, or moon-plant. A peculiar virtue was, however, generally ascribed to that one class of sacrifices which, as it involved the strangulation of the subject offered, would run counter to the prejudices of the later Áryan, who had mastered the ideas arising out of his belief in transmigration. While the other offerings were all mainly eucharistic, these were held to be propitiatory. While in other cases the god worshipped was invited to come down and share the offering with his suppliant, these were all religiously committed to the flames. While others had but little reference to the moral standing of the worshipper, these all derived their meaning from his felt antagonism to powers above him, and his dread of their impending vengeance. While the rest were, for the most

[1] See the passages collected from the Védas in Wuttke, II. 342, 349, and contrast with them Psalm L. 7—15. That worthier views were however subsequently far more common is evident from passages quoted in Bähr, as below, II. 273, 274.

[2] *Vishńu Pur.* p. 275, n. 1: cf. Bähr, *Symbolik des Mosaischen Cultus*, II. 222, 223, who points out, that, generally speaking, the unbloody sacrifices were naturally presented to Vishńu, and the bloody sacrifices to Śiva.

part, offered to some individual member of the Hindú pantheon, a sin-offering contemplated the whole group of *dévas*, and in them, it may be, recognised the majesty of the Supreme Intelligence. 'The worshipper,' it was taught, 'who offers up an animal duly consecrated by Agni and by Soma, is therewith able to buy off all deities at once[1].'

In this conception of the Hindú rite of sacrifice, ascending step by step through various orders of animals, and culminating in the grand oblation of the horse[2], the 'king of sacrifices,' we are able to detect the clearest parallelism to some of the provisions of the Mosaic economy[3]. Animal sacrifice was uniformly prompted by a deep conviction of personal unworthiness, and the necessity in every worshipper to compensate for his shortcomings and imperfect consecration of himself to God. His life was felt to have been placed in peril, or rather it was wholly forfeited to the Divine Proprietor, whose will he had resisted, and whose laws he had transgressed. He laboured, therefore, by renouncing some of his chief goods, to symbolise and make apparent both to the Divinity and to himself his consciousness of guilt and misery, and, if possible, to clear away the barriers that obstructed his approach to God. Hence also, by a terrible distortion of the rite of sacrifice, had grown the custom of devoting human life itself to the offended *dévas;* for although there is no public trace of such oblations[4] in the very earliest period of Hindú religion, the revolting spectacle was seen at last, and

[1] See the remarkable extract from the *Aitaréya Bráhmańa* in Roth's 'Einleitung' to his edition of the *Nirukta*, p. xxxiii. In the same passage the editor points out the close resemblances between the customs of the early Hindús in slaying their sin-offerings, and the corresponding customs of the Greeks and Romans.

[2] See above, p. 130, n. 3; *Manu*, ch. v. § 39, § 53, ch. XI. § 261; *Rámáyańa*, I. 13, ed. Schlegel.

[3] Above, pp. 83, 84.

[4] Above, p. 130, and n. 2. It may be mentioned, in addition to the paper of Prof. Wilson's there referred to, that Roth has also examined the remarkable legend of Sunahsépa (Weber's *Ind. Stud.* I. 457 sq., II. 112 sq.), and that he regards it as proving the existence of human sacrifices at an early period. 'Als Mittelpunkt der Sage in dieser Form erscheint offenbar die Rettung Çunahçepa's vom Opfertode, ihre nächste Beziehung ist also die religiös-sittliche, gerichtet gegen den Gräuel des Menschenopfers. So mag denn diese Legende, die einzige indische der Art, für das brahmanische Volk dieselbe Bedeutung gehabt haben, wie die Sage von Iphigenia oder von Phrixos für die Hellenen, die von Abraham und Isaak für das hebräische Alterthum. Die Aehnlichkeiten in einzelnen Zügen liessen sich manche namhaft machen: es möge genügen darauf hinzuweisen, dass die indische Erzählung für den dem Tode entzogenen Menschen keinen Ersatz auf dem Altare selbst eintreten lässt: die Bitte um Gnade

was repeated by some barbarous and fanatic spirits from that day to our own.

3. On the other hand, the teaching of the earnest and enlightened Áryans had been deflecting more and more from the revealed idea of substitutive suffering. They laboured to effect their own recovery without the intervention of a Mediator. Sacrifices might, indeed, be offered, and might possibly appease the wrath of some inferior *déva*, but the only offering which philosophy could stamp with its approval, was the conscious dedication of the individual spirit to the Spirit of the universe. According, therefore, to these doctors, the whole life of man must be a great oblation of himself, intended to promote his absolute deliverance from the fetters of the selfish and the natural. Exactly in proportion as he continues to possess an individual being[1], he is broken off from God, he is encompassed with infirmities, he is the victim of his appetites, the slave of his affections, and as such, abandoned to the powers of evil. Hence wherever this conception was fully realised, the form of man's devotion was most rigorous and ascetical. Though 'suitable acts of expiation had been enjoined by the great sages for every kind of crimes[2],' they all were far from satisfying the rules of penance which the ardent devotee was willing to impose upon himself. The proper sacrifice, he urged, is that which, springing from an utter abnegation of the individual, aims at nothing short of God and self-annihilation.

§ 5. *The Hindú hope of Restoration.*

The grand idea of an historic Saviour, entering once for all into the line of humanity, and once for all achieving its redemption by the offering of Himself to God, was utterly unknown to

genügt um das Gräuliche schlechthin aufzuheben.' In later times the offering of human victims was generally confined to the worshippers of Śiva, and his wife Kálí or Durgá.

[1] The following extract from the *Probodha-Chandrodaya* (ed. Goldstücker, p. 55) will serve to illustrate the whole subject: 'Wenn sie den Höchsten in Banden legten, den Einigen zur Vielheit theilten und den ewigen Herrscher in körperliches Dasein warfen und zu der Stufe der Sterblichkeit brachten, so werde ich eine Busse vollbringen, die dem Leben dieser Brahmatheiler ein Ende macht und ihn wieder zu seiner Einheit führt.'

[2] *Vishńu Pur.* p. 210. Yet in accordance with the laxer principles of the Puranic age, and of the Hindú sectaries, it was finally maintained that 'reliance upon Krishńa is far better than any such expiatory acts as religious austerity and the like.' Remembrance of Hari (Vishńu) is said to be the 'best of all expiations.' *Ib.*

every class of ancient Áryans. Sacrifices may have taught men the imperative need of some such intervention, and may further have suggested the conception of some Victim higher than the cows and horses which they strangled, and more holy than the holiest *yogin* who consumed his life in penance and austerities; but the actual course of Hindú thought was rather tending to diminish than increase the keenness of these cravings and the force of these suggestions. While the many had been more and more disposed to acquiesce in a routine of ceremonial observances, relying for the rest on some particular *déva,* whom they specially selected for their patron; the philosopher had grown more confident of his resources, and more daring in his efforts to mount upward on the wings of knowledge and asceticism, and consummate his fellowship with God. Yet notwithstanding all these wayward tendencies, diverging, each in opposite ways. from principles of true religion, there was always in the heart of man a yearning after some external Saviour; there was always a presentiment that such a Saviour would eventually stoop down from heaven, and by an act of grace and condescension master all our deadliest foes, and reinstate us in our lost inheritance.

This dim and elementary idea, pointing to a future *religatio* of the human and Divine, and so pervading all systems of religion, was especially manifest in the traditions of Hindús respecting the descent of God to earth in various forms of creaturely existence. I have already drawn attention to the legend of the Deluge, where, according to one version of it, Brahmá, and, according to another, Vishńu, is said to have appeared as an enormous Fish, in order to promote the welfare of his righteous follower, and preserve the continuity of the human species. Other legends bring before us different kinds of *avatáras,* where the rescue of mankind from the dominion of malignant spirits is no less conspicuous. Earth herself complains[1] how she is reeling under the vast load of guilt and wretchedness, yet her complaints are all eventually carried to Vishńu, who comforts her by the assurance that her wrongs shall be redressed and all her enemies brought to shame and silence. The hope of such emancipation is, we saw, most formally expressed in recent versions of the Krishńa-legend. There a series of periodic interventions in behalf of man is definitely asserted, while the object contemplated by them is no less distinctly said to be a *moral* object,—the suppression of impiety, the protection of the good, and the establishment of duty[2].

[1] *Asiatic Res.* x. 27.

[2] Above, p. 198.

But, as if to satisfy us that the faith of the Hindú in champions of his own devising was extremely feeble at the best, we see him ready to abandon them and willing to accept a novel incarnation of Vishńu, whose advent is still future. For example, in the close of the Kali-yuga, when the world, relapsing more and more into impiety, has reached the brink of annihilation, the Hindú expects a fresh deliverer, human both in form and aspect, seated on a white horse, and armed with a destructive scythe. To him will be awarded the eight faculties[1] which constituted man's original perfection: he will also be a genuine 'portion of Brahma,' 'the Beginning and the End[2].' 'By his irresistible might he will destroy all the *mléchchas* and thieves, and all whose minds are devoted to iniquity. He will then re-establish righteousness upon earth; and the minds of those who live at the end of the Kali-age shall be awakened, and shall be pellucid as crystal. The men who are thus changed by virtue of that peculiar time shall be as the seeds of human beings, and shall give birth to a race who shall follow the laws of the Krita-age, or age of purity[3].' Yet the modern origin of documents in which this legend is preserved, as well as its position in the series of Hindú *avatáras*, and the glaring contradiction which it offers to older representations of the sacred books in reference to the yuga-system, all require us to place it in an age far subsequent to the diffusion of the Gospel. On the other hand, the manifest resemblances which it exhibits to some visions of the Apocalypse will as clearly justify us in imputing its origin to Gnostic, if not Christian, influence[4]; an identification fatal to the cavils of a modern rationalist, who, after citing the Kalki-legend with an air of triumph, goes on to tell us that 'the Jews have the same belief,' but that 'with them it is an after-thought.' The truth is that, so far from being either secondary or derived, the expectation of a Christ, all-righteous and all-merciful, a Christ in whom all nations of the earth may find a blessing, was imprinted on the heart and memory of the Hebrew people from the time of Abraham: it was the pivot of their firmest hopes, it was the key to all their Scriptures.

[1] Above, p. 214, n. 2.

[2] *Vishńu Pur.* p. 484.

[3] *Ibid.* Cf. Lüken *Traditionen*, p. 320.

[4] 'Der Kalkin insbesondere mit seinem weissen Rosse ist schwerlich eine indische Erfindung, da er dem Yugasystem, welches am Ende *jedes* Kaliyuga eine *Zerstörung* der Welt verlangt oder wenigstens verlangen sollte, direkt widerspricht, erklärt sich dagegen vortrefflich aus den ähnlichen Vorstellungen der Gnostiker.' Weber, *Ind. Stud.* II. 411.

CHAPTER IV.

Contrasts in the general development of Hindúism and Revealed Religion.

'In the present impure age, the bud of wisdom being blighted by iniquity, men are unable to apprehend pure unity.'

HINDU PHILOSOPHER.

Ἡμῖν δὲ ἀπεκάλυψεν ὁ Θεὸς διὰ τοῦ Πνεύματος αὐτοῦ.—ST. PAUL.

Abraham contrasted with an ancient Áryan. His faith: his moral superiority: his hopeful spirit. Continuity of true religion. Bráhmanism, how far analogous to Hebraism. Hereditary priesthood. Narrowness of range. Buddhism, how far analogous to Christianity. Real coincidences between India and the West. Root of such resemblances: Essenism: early Christian heresies: Monasticism. Hindúism and Christianity in their ultimate consequences. Buddhism, as a popular religion. Hindú ideas of God and the universe; how opposed to Christianity. Degeneracy inherent in Bráhmanism. The remedy supplied in Christianity.

1. IF one were asked to single out the main criterion by which patriarchs, like Abraham, may be distinguished from the Áryan chief, whose portrait is preserved among the oldest hymns of the Rig-Véda, it would turn far less upon the difference in their mental organisation and their outward forms of worship, than on sentiments by which that organisation was directed and those forms of worship were upheld. The men to be contrasted are both primitive and simple-hearted. Both are nomades, far inferior, it may be, to their descendants in the strength and clearness of their intellectual powers, though more than equal in poetic sensibility; collecting wisdom as they move from spot to spot in search of regular modes of life and permanent habitations. The wealth of each is in his flocks and herds; his strength in the devotion of his clansmen and posterity. Both are also conscious of their moral wants, and their dependence on

superior genii; both are men of praise, of prayer, of sacrifice. And yet how very different are the aspects of their inner life, the real character of their religious worship, their relations to the world invisible.

The father of the Hebrew race, as we behold him in the Book of Genesis, abandoning his paternal roof, and then encamping, year by year, beneath a foreign sky, is ever influenced by the consciousness of supernatural guidance. The arm on which he leans is that of the Omnipotent. The Lord Himself is with him in the course of his migrations: his misgivings are all hushed when he reflects that God, the Self-Existent, is his shield, and his exceeding great reward (Gen. xv. 1). The patriarch, in other words, has such a faith in God as justifies his claim to be a Christian by anticipation, 'the father of the faithful.' That organ of the soul by which we realise as present what is actually beyond the range of human vision, was in him directed to the object where alone it can be satisfied. The God of Abraham was living, personal, ever-present, irresistible, no cold Abstraction of the logical faculty, no distant Something which could only be defined by negatives, but a willing Friend, a righteous Judge, a sympathetic Father. Abraham's road may lie along the trackless plain or the inhospitable mountain-side, and yet he fears no evil: his trust is in a living God and Guardian, who will never fail His own. He may be called to suffer, but he suffers at the hands of One who will convert the scourge itself into an instrument of blessing. He may have to sacrifice the fairest of his earthly prospects, yet he knows to whom the sacrifice is made. He wanders childless in the land of promise, yet as often as he gazes up to heaven, he welcomes in the stars that spangle the unclouded firmament, an image of his own posterity. Abraham 'believed in the Lord; and He counted it to him for righteousness' (Gen. xv. 6).

The Indo-Áryan, on the other hand, had no such faith in God, and no such trust in His protection. Indisposed to love God, he was equally unwilling to retain God in his knowledge. In proportion as he left his Father's house to wander forth in quest of this or that debasing pleasure, faith was dimmed and paralysed within him, till the thought of a supreme Intelligence, distinct from matter and transcending all material processes, had well-nigh vanished from his soul. Instead of finding peace in God, he vainly sought it in the adoration or deprecation of the elements; and having abandoned himself to this inferior kind of worship, he oscillated from one *dêva* to another, but had real faith in none.

It is indeed remarkable, that the efficacy of a principle analogous to Christian faith was never plainly recognised in India till after the propagation of the Gospel[1]. Then it was that the idea began to shew itself in one particular Hindú sect, where men adopted phraseology which might have been mistaken almost for the language of the early Church. They spoke of worshipping God in spirit: they ascribed a wonderful significance to faith (*bhakti*); yet even this new verity was in the end so much distorted, that the spurious 'faith' of India had become no better than a cloke for heartless apathy or gross licentiousness. Belief in one particular *dêva*, or a firm reliance on the merit of some special *avatára*, would, according to this system, obviate the need of virtue, and would sanctify all kinds of vice[2].

How different was the faith of Abraham! It did not terminate in *dêvas* like Vishńu or Śiva, Krishńa or Gańéśa: and the object being raised indefinitely higher, and invested with distinctly moral attributes, the principle of faith had also gained a corresponding elevation. 'I am the Almighty God: walk before me, and be thou perfect' (Gen. xvii. 1). Such was the original basis of the covenant which brought the patriarch into a new relationship with God. The Being whom he worshipped was not only righteous, but was righteousness itself. He was no local deity with limited jurisdiction or with human partialities. He was the Judge of all the earth (Gen. xviii. 25): and to impress this grand idea on Abraham and his posterity was the uniform design of all the elder revelation. The satisfying of men's intellectual cravings was but secondary and subordinate, compared with the enlivening of their conscience, the rectifying of their wishes, and the purification of their heart. The will of man, as one essential organ needed for the due appropriation of Divine knowledge, as one leading element in the spiritual constitution of our race, was made in Hebraism the

[1] See Lassen, II. 1096, 1099, and above, p. 182.

[2] Elphinstone, pp. 98, 121, and Wilson, *Lectures*, p. 31. The latter of these authorities, who has enlarged upon the question in his *History of the Hindú Sects*, remarks that by teaching the doctrine of 'faith alone,' the Hindú sectarian has rendered conduct 'wholly immaterial.' 'It matters not how atrocious a sinner may be, if he paints his face, his breast, his arms, with certain sectarial marks; or, which is better, if he brands his skin permanently with them with a hot iron stamp; if he is constantly chanting hymns in honour of Vishńu; or, what is equally efficacious, if he spends hours in the simple reiteration of his name or names; if he die with the word Hari, or Ráma, or Krishńa, on his lips, and the thought of him in his mind, he may have lived a monster of iniquity,—he is certain of heaven.'

subject of a special education: it was moulded step by step into conformity with the will of God. He asked the patriarch and his descendants whether, with the knowledge of Him which they had already, they would still believe in Him, and follow Him as their supreme Director, even though His path might sometimes be mysterious, and the truths He taught them might sound harsh and paradoxical. And the effect of this divine œconomy is clearly seen from day to day in Abraham himself. The patriarch can never be indifferent, for example, to his earthly prospects and position; for the present world to him is not a 'vast mirage' of unsubstantial phantoms, but is full of deep realities. He longs for offspring, he aspires to see his family in possession of the land of Canaan; yet whenever God appears to be rescinding the original promise, Abraham as often bows to the decision, and resigns his own will to the will of God: and when at last old age is creeping over him and he is still like one who sojourns in a strange country, and must buy himself a sepulchre, his walk with God continues to uphold and purify him; he can look more clearly through the temporal promise to the principles which underlie it; the postponement first, and then the partial realisation of it, teach him to reflect more deeply on some brighter and enduring heritage; and his spirit being thus exalted to a closer converse with the things invisible, he dies, as he has lived,—in faith.

On the other hand, it seems as though the Indo-Áryan were far less susceptible of moral culture, and that culture far more seriously retarded by the rank luxuriance of his other powers, the vividness of his imagination, and the acuteness of his speculative faculty. 'In the hymns of the Véda, we see man left to himself to solve the riddle of the world[1].' As soon as he relinquishes the primary faith in God, he dooms himself to wander without light or guidance in the midst of endless mazes, and to struggle with gigantic and insoluble enigmas. Nay, the obscuration has extended far and deep into the spiritual province of his nature. He is 'alienated from the life of God through the ignorance that is in him, because of the blindness of his heart.' The oracle of conscience may still speak indeed, but its decisions are continually disputed and rejected. The monitor within him, his own inmost self, may raise its frequent protest in behalf of righteousness, and drive him to invoke the help of Indra, or the mercy of the purifying Waters; yet he finds in them no real and abiding comfort; he is tempted to

[1] Prof. Max Müller, in Bunsen's *Phil. of Univ. Hist.* I. 134.

resign himself afresh to the dominion of the power of darkness, and to give up the battle of humanity for lost.

Abraham, 'believing Him faithful that promised,' was conspicuous also as a man of hope, of large ideas, of glowing aspirations. He shewed himself most conscious of his noble destiny; he realised, as few had done before, the glories which had been reserved for all adherents of the true religion. He saw the day of the Messiah; he saw it, and was glad. Directed by the light of the prophetic spirit, he beheld not only the detention of his children's children in a land that was not theirs, and their eventual recovery from bondage after a definite term of years (Gen. xv. 13, 14), but also their migration to the land of promise, the commencement of some Hebrew dynasty, and last of all the advent of *the* Son of Abraham, in whom all nations of the earth are blessed. We ought not, doubtless, to exaggerate the area of his field of vision, nor represent him as possessed of all those truths which, after the diffusion of a perfect light, we may discover in the oldest version of the Gospel-promise. The reality itself may be as different in degree from aught which Abraham anticipated, as the future glory of the Christian may transcend the imagery by means of which he now approximates to some idea of it. Still Abraham was in his day the champion of the ancient faith; and as he wandered far and near and saw the nations lapsing one by one into idolatry and creature-worship, he could hardly fail to understand that the election of his family, as the family of God, was for some high and holy purpose, that the basis of the covenant was a moral basis, and that He, in whom the stock of Abraham would finally put forth its choicest branch and reach its highest glory, was to spread the blessings of this covenant in all the scattered tribes of man.

But where in any of the Védas can we find a parallel to this patient trust in God, this glowing hope of an imperishable kingdom? There were echoes, it may be, confused, and often contradictory echoes of the primitive condemnation of man's tempter; and as evil seemed to propagate itself from age to age, and as the malice of the demons grew still more intolerable, earnest hearts would grope, despairing of all human saviours, for a God of truth, of holiness, of mercy: yet oft as heathendom put forth these dim presentiments, and fondly as it clung to these half-conscious prophecies of redemption, it was never able to decipher[1] them until the promise was in fact fulfilled, and

[1] 'The universal heart of mankind, from out of the depths, invoked the presence of the Restorer, though it would not read its own involuntary prophecy.' Archer Butler, *Sermons*, 1st series, p. 241.

meaning was imported into them by the announcements of the Gospel. The heart had always striven in the direction of Christianity, but never till the advent of the Saviour was that striving made intelligible even to itself.

Now the contrast here exhibited between the father of the faithful and the more elevated of those Áryan colonists who chanted in their first migrations the impassioned hymns of the Rig-Véda, is in general true of the religious systems under which the Hebrew and Hindú were being educated. In the one we have stability, in the other, fluctuation; in the one, development, in the other, discontinuity; in the one, progress, in the other, retrogression. In the first, the Object of belief entirely fills the spirit of the worshipper, He is the same yesterday, today, and for ever; in the second, the divinities all change, or vanish in the lapse of ages; they are 'old' and 'young[1],' are less and greater, this supplanting or eclipsing that, and all extinguishable by the very law of their existence. Moreover, out of Abraham there grew a family which proved itself the champion of monotheism, and which acted as the shelter of the purest forms of worship and the guardian of the oracles of God. That family in spite of all adverse influences was one and indestructible: it stood in reference to the world at large as stood the sacred ark of Noah in the midst of the avenging waters. It surmounted all the storms and fluctuations of all ages; it carried in its bosom the beginnings of a new creation, and the germs of supernatural life that should hereafter leaven all the mass of humanity.

As centuries revolved, the creed of that sacred family had doubtless grown more definite and luminous; the measure of man's light was greater, and his knowledge of his future destiny more certain and explicit; but the several steps by which these vast accessions were produced are all apparent in the marvellous annals of the Hebrew people. So far from standing in a line with heathenism, so far from borrowing its distinctive properties from any or from all the Gentile systems, the religion of the Old Testament, if we believe its own assertions and denunciations, was from first to last in diametric opposition to them. They were from beneath; it was from above. They all were issuing from the brain and heart of man; they varied with the variations of his temperament and with the growth of intellectual culture: it was the result of an objective revelation, which,

[1] The Védas themselves distinguish between the great gods and the less, between the young gods and the old. Wilson, *Rig-Véda*, I. 71.

coming down immediately from God, was radiant with the light of His perfection, and was based upon relations between God and man which neither time nor space can modify. As early as the patriarchal period it was taught how every ethnic system would be finally superseded; how the 'Shiloh' would inherit all the royalty of Judah, and how Gentiles would all flock to Him for light, for shelter, for nutrition. And when Christianity was actually established it was far from disappointing these anticipations of the ancient world. It grew out of that anterior system, as the ripening flower unfolds itself organically from the bud, or as the daylight is the natural sequence of the dawn. The Church of God has not been planted on the ruins of the old theocracy, but is its proper consummation. The Son of Abraham is now the Prince of Peace and King of Glory, and all 'who are Christ's are Abraham's seed and heirs according to the promise.'

2. Nor if special features of the Hebrew and Hindú systems be compared in chronological order, shall we often find that the alleged resemblances between them are more than superficial; provided only that our estimate of revealed religion is based entirely on original and authentic documents. This proviso is the more important, since analogies far deeper *do* exist, as we shall see hereafter, between the genuine creeds of Hindústán and certain depravations of revealed truth as it was first communicated. It might be urged, for instance, with considerable plausibility that Bráhmanism, in reference to the general course of its development, will stand to Buddhism in the same relation that Mosaism stands to Christianity; or, in other words, that if we place the principles enunciated in the Védas and the Laws of Manu side by side with those contained in the Old Testament, and if we place the principles of Gautama side by side with those of Christ and the Apostles, the comparison will lead us to infer some inward, if not outward and historical affinity, between the different systems of belief. These questions both demand a more particular examination.

(1) First, then, Bráhmanism was but a secondary stage in the formation of the Indo-Áryan institutions. It appears to have adapted to the wants of nations what before had been restricted to the family, the clan, the disconnected tribe. In this respect the office of Mosaism was not only analogous, but identical. Both, in order to effect such purpose, had engrafted new elements upon the worship of the previous period; both had multiplied the number of sacrificial rites, and, while reviving

many of the ordinances which had the sanction of the former generations[1], fresh importance seems to have been given to ritual uniformity, as though, in that peculiar phase of human progress, the language of symbolic action was peculiarly expressive and intelligible. But while I grant the perfect truth of all such representations, the objector needs to be reminded that the moral system of the Hebrews was meanwhile indefinitely superior to that of popular Hindúism. The institutes of Moses added, it may be, to what had formerly prevailed; they authorised a far more solemn and elaborate liturgy; but, unlike the institutes of Manu, they insisted at the same time more emphatically on the need of spirituality in the worshipper: the tone of every interdict and admonition grew more penetrating and severe. 'Will I eat the flesh of bulls, or drink the blood of goats? Offer unto God thanksgiving; and pay thy vows unto the Most High; and call upon Me in the day of trouble: I will deliver thee, and thou shalt glorify Me. But unto the wicked God saith, What hast thou to do, to declare My statutes, or that thou shouldest take My covenant in thy mouth?' (Ps. L. 13—16). The symbols of the Hebrew law were thus far more than barren and unmeaning ceremonies: they suggested to the worshipper a multitude of deep and spiritual relations. Man was taught to separate the visible imagery under which divine things were brought down more fully to his present understanding from ideas and principles enveloped in them, and especially to hear the doctrine of the unity, the placability, the holiness, and the supremacy of God, proclaimed in every chapter of their ritual institute.

Again, the system, re-enacted under Moses, like that which owed its birth to Manu, had a powerful and hereditary priesthood, whose prerogatives were guarded by a list of stringent prohibitions. None but they could minister in holy things. Yet here, in spite of all apparent similarities, the difference is essential and extreme. The Hebrew legislator had most plainly recognised the unity of the human race: he gave no sanction to the law of caste, by which the Bráhman had been lifted far above his fellows, not in office only but extraction and inherent worth. The son of Aaron was an ordinary Israelite; he was descended from an ordinary member of the patriarchal family, —no emanation from the head or reason of Brahmá, while others were the offspring of the feet. And, as the consequence of this original equality, the high-priest of the Hebrews, though

[1] Cf. Blunt's *Undesigned Coincidences*, pp. 8, 9. Lond. 1847.

invested with superior rank and ministering before God, not only for himself, but also in behalf of other men, had never shewn a disposition to invade the privileges of his brethren. His official dignity was felt to be compatible with the sacerdotal character of every Israelite, who, owing to his moral elevation and particularly to his knowledge of the one True God, had always been a member of a 'royal priesthood,' and a 'prophet for all mankind[1].' Accordingly the insight into heavenly mysteries, and access to 'the oracles of God,' had never been confined, among the Hebrews, to one narrow circle, or one favoured class. The many were not left to gather up such crumbs and fragments of religious truth as chanced to fall from the abundant table of some haughty doctor like the Bráhman. The provisions of the Law had rendered it possible for every one to know the will of God, and make it known to others; and each father, in pursuance of this principle, was urged to teach his children, 'to the intent that when they came up they might shew their children the same.'

The point, however, which is more especially insisted on by those who institute comparisons between the Hebrew and Bráhmanic systems is the partial and exclusive spirit manifest in both. That narrowness, indeed, may fairly be ascribed to every aspect of the latter system, no one has yet ventured to dispute. Its very constitution was harsh and inelastic. It knew of no expansion beyond the members of the three superior ('twice-born') classes; for the śúdra, though reduced by the victorious arm of the invader and associated with the rest in the capacity of a serf, was held to be excluded, by impurity of descent, from all acquaintance with the Védas[2] and from other like advantages. But can the same exclusiveness be fairly charged against the Hebrews and their system? Doubtless one great object of it was to fence them in from the contamination of the neighbouring heathen, and by educating them apart to render them a single and peculiar people; yet there never was a period in their history when they were treated as a higher and distinct 'race' of beings, or the proselyte rejected from communion with the genuine Hebrew. Men, for instance, like the Kenites or the Rechabites, retaining the ancestral faith in one True God without conforming to the ritual law of Moses, lived for centuries on terms of amity with Israel and were sheltered near the sanctuary of God. The psalmist and the prophet are both heard exulting in the thought that Zion was the home

[1] See above, p. 79, n. 1. [2] See above, p. 137, n. 3.

and mother-city not of Israel only, but of gentile nations also. At the dedication of the temple Solomon did not forget the 'strangers' coming out of far countries to worship in Jerusalem. They also were embraced within the circle of the prayer; 'That all people of the earth may know Thy name, to fear Thee, as do Thy people Israel' (1 Kings viii. 43). And as the number of such proselytes went on increasing, the energy of Hebraism itself would be recruited by admixtures from the heathen world. The single difference in point of expansibility between the Christian and Hebrew systems lay in this;—that under the more perfect institution converts are relieved from the necessity of compliance with the ancient ritual, on the ground that man, exalted by incorporation into Christ, is now attaining his majority,—is capable of higher and more spiritual forms of education. Still it should not be forgotten that nothing would at first conduce more largely to the spread of Christian influences than the existence of those Jewish proselytes in every district both of east and west. They served as starting-points for missions to the heathen; they were links, or rather living stones, made ready in the providence of God for binding all the world together, and for building up a Catholic Church.

(2) But, secondly, do other and more obvious points of similarity exist between the general aspects of Buddhism and those of Christianity? Was Buddhism, for example, in its main particulars the offspring of an older system? Christianity was also this, but with the grand distinction that it never for one moment ceased to venerate the holy writings and traditions of its predecessor; whereas Buddhism entered on the work of revolution by rejecting or contemning the authority of the Védas. Or, did Buddhism labour to emancipate the ancient world from the dominion of an irksome and elaborate ritual? Christianity has in turn effected this emancipation; not, however, by the violent uprooting of the older forms of service, but by placing in the very centre of its dogmatic system the reality which they foreshadowed, and thus elevating and refining the whole character of worship. Or, again, did Buddhism venture to repudiate every species of animal sacrifice? The Gospel did the same, but in obedience to a very different theory both of God and man. So far from questioning the truth of instincts which had found expression in the ancient sacrifices, it was ever pointing to 'the Lamb of God which taketh away the sin of the world:' it taught men how the offering of all other victims was eclipsed and superseded not by the development of human reason or the riper dictates of philosophy, but 'through the

offering of the body of Jesus Christ once for all.' Did Buddhism lay unwonted stress on ethics? Christianity did the same, but building on a true foundation, all the lessons which it inculcated were sustained by deep and heavenly motives; they grew directly out of its theology, deriving thence their highest virtue and most touching illustration. To be good is, in the moral system of the Christian, to be God-like: while in Buddhism, where the thought of the Creator and the Judge is virtually rejected, the moral code itself is stripped of its supreme authority. Or was Buddhism from the first distinguished by the feminine mildness of its tone, the gentleness of its demeanour, the diffusiveness of its philanthropy? These crowning excellencies of the heathen system were again transcended by the genial spirit of Christianity; for though it has distinctly recognised the freedom of the human agent, and so carried its appeal directly to the manlier province of our being, it has taught men with unequalled emphasis to put away 'all bitterness and wrath and anger and clamour and evil speaking, with all malice,' and has charged them to be 'kind one to another, tender-hearted, forgiving one another, even as God for Christ's sake hath forgiven them.' Or, lastly, did the followers of the Buddha rise at length to the conception of an ever-widening empire, and embark on the conversion of far-distant nations? Have their tenets been in fact accepted, not by Hindús only, but by countless multitudes in China and Tibet, and still more recently by Japanese and Burman, Mongol and Malay? The Gospel in like manner claims to be a 'world religion.' It has never faltered in that claim since He, whose errand was to rescue and restore humanity, commissioned the small band of Galilæan peasants to go forth into the world and 'preach the Gospel to every creature.' By the majesty and life inherent in the Gospel it has subjugated, step by step, the first, the mightiest, the most highly-gifted nations; and although, in some localities, the tide of conquest has receded and the vantage-ground been lost, the course of Christianity was on the whole triumphant and progressive. Every year is adding largely to the proofs already given of supernatural vigour, and indefinite expansibility: and thus the Gospel is, in fact, what Buddhism vainly strove to be,—*the* agent in the hands of God for working the regeneration of the human family[1].

[1] It is melancholy to hear a weak and half-infatuated writer of the present day, in discussing the great question, *What is Truth?* (Lond. 1856), complain of 'the partial littleness, the narrowness of conception, and circumscribed application of our Christian invention,

Yet, while I would contend that most of the alleged resemblances between the spirit which pervades the Bible on the one side, and the Hindú *sútras* on the other, are but slight and superficial, I am far from saying that no analogies whatever can be traced in the historical development of the religions we are now comparing. What, then, is the general nature of these points of contact? I answer: they are, for the most part, not discoverable in the genuine dogmas of revealed religion, but in later depravations of it,—not in Hebraism as founded on the ancient Scriptures, and embodied in the temple-service, not in Christianity as once for all delivered by the Lord and His Apostles to the keeping of the early Church, but in some schools and systems, drawing their original life from these, yet leavened and corrupted by other elements of foreign or extrinsic growth.

Nor will the bare existence of such resemblances be matter of surprise to him who soberly reflects upon the way in which they are produced. As soon as ever the mind of man is anxious to break loose from what is supernaturally revealed; as soon as ever the authority within him is suffered to resist and overrule the authority without him, he at once relapses, in the same proportion, to a state of nature: the religious system he constructs is so far standing on a level with heathenism; and whenever such internal affinity has been established[1] there is reason to expect, in cases even where no outward agents are at work, a general similarity between tenets of two independent doctors, and, it may be, in the structure of their sacred institutions.

I shall notice one or two examples. Of the three great sects who figured in Judæa at the close of the Old-Testament œconomy,

and the isolated instances of beneficence exhibited in the ministry of Christ,' as compared with the Buddhist's 'sublime picture of an exulting universe,' &c. p. 156.

[1] See above, p. 180, n. 1. Quinet (*Le Génie des Religions*, pp. 215, 216, Paris, 1851) appears to have been startled by the discovery of some of the resemblances between Buddhism and the Romanism of the Middle Ages:—'On reste d'ailleurs confondu en voyant comment, à travers toutes les différences de temps et de lieu, la même empreinte spirituelle a produit, dans le catholicisme du moyen âge et dans le bouddhisme de la haute Asie, des institutions, des mœurs, des singularités, si parfaitement semblables qu'on croirait l'Orient et l'Occident plagiaires l'un de l'autre. Dans les légendes des bouddhistes de Ceylan, comme dans les chroniques des monastères de Cîteaux et de Saint-Gall, ce ne sont que fondations de couvents d'hommes ou de femmes, missions chez les peuples étrangers, pèlerinages, bénédictions de reliques, indulgences, prédications, conciles œcuméniques pour combattre les schismes, extirper l'hérésie, maintenir l'orthodoxie.' On some of the points here cited, see Appendix II.

one of the most remarkable was the confraternity of the Essenes; which, though entirely Jewish in its main complexion, may remind us here and there not only of Pythagoras and the 'Polistæ,' but of Gautama Buddha and his school[1]. There is the same mystic glow upon the spiritual life of the Essene. Repelled and wearied by the frigid ritualism of the Pharisee, and disgusted by the selfishness and scepticism of the Sadducee, his feelings had impelled him to withdraw entirely from the town; he lost his reverence for the temple-service, he endeavoured to arrive at fuller knowledge of the things of God by analysing his own emotions. Meanwhile, however, he was not a mere recluse, inactive, meditative, and unpractical. He saw in every human being the image of the one Creator; he abhorred all forms of slavery; he was ardently desirous to promote the moral and material interests of his fallen countrymen. But here, as in the case of Buddhism, while attempting to remodel and regenerate, the Essene abandoned his belief not only in the errors and extravagances of other sects, but in some vital principles of true religion. He estranged himself from the divine society where God was more immediately present. The spirit which he more and more betrayed was, in the language of Neander, 'monkish and schismatic.' Like the Buddhist he believed in some arbitrary and irrevocable fate[2], necessitating human action. Like the Buddhist also he repudiated the ancient doctrine of mediation, propitiation, and redemption, by disparaging, if not abjuring, the rite of sacrifice, in which that doctrine was embodied; and thus, in spite of all the amiability and gentleness of his nature, we hear of no Essenes among the little company of Hebrews 'who first trusted in Christ.'

Or, take again the swarm of heresies that soon invaded

[1] A late writer (Mr. J. H. Gouldhawke), in his extravagant production, *The Solar Allegories*, Calcutta, 1855, attempts to prove that 'the greater number of personages mentioned in the Old and New Testaments are allegorical beings. He has also laboured to connect the philosophy of the Essenes with that of the Pythagoreans and Hindú philosophers (p. 20); and in particular traces back the growth of Christian monasticism to influences diffused by them and their associates in the schools of Alexandria. Neander, in considering a similar objection, has admitted (*Life of Christ*, p. 40, London, 1851) that the sect of the Essenes, though strictly Jewish in its origin, contained within it some infusion of Oriental theosophy, but is at the same time very careful to point out the fundamental contradiction between the special principles of Essenism and those of Christianity.

[2] *Τὸ δὲ τῶν Ἐσσηνῶν γένος, πάντων τὴν εἱμαρμένην κυρίαν ἀποφαίνεται, καὶ μηδὲν ὃ μὴ κατ' ἐκείνης ψῆφον ἀνθρώποις ἀπαντᾷ.* Joseph. *Antiq.* XIII. v. 9.

almost every province of the early Church. Abandoning, as they did, the more essential of the supernatural truths of revelation, they were virtually and in effect revivals of paganism; and family-likeness may accordingly be traced among the older speculations current in the schools of heathen philosophy. In discussing, for example, the nature of the Divine Sonship, Sabellius and his party taught a doctrine very similar to that already noticed in the *trimúrrti* of India; while Docetism, starting from a notion that the spiritual and material cannot permanently coexist, had merely reproduced the Hindú doctrine of *avatáras.* The inward correspondence in the texture of ideas had issued in a similar depravation of revealed truth.

Or if, penetrating below the surface, we investigate the elementary thoughts and feelings that hereafter found an utterance in monastic institutions of the Church, we find that on the one side those ideas are alien from the spirit of primitive Christianity, and on the other that they had been long familiar in the east before they were appropriated or unconsciously reproduced among one class of Christians in Syria and Egypt. India was the real birthplace of monasticism[1], its cradle being in the haunts of earnest *yogins* and self-torturing devotees, who were convinced that evil is inherent not in man only but in all the various forms of matter, and accordingly withdrew as far as possible from contact with the outer world[2]. At first indeed the Christian hermit like the earliest of his Hindú prototypes had dwelt alone upon the outskirts of his native town or village, supporting himself by manual labour and devoting all the surplus of his earnings to religious purposes. But during the fourth century of the present era many such hermits began to flock together in the forest or the wilderness, where regular confraternities were organised upon a model more or less derived from the Egyptian Therapeutæ and the old Essenes of Palestine; the members, in their dress and habits, most of all resembling[3] those of the religious orders who still swarm in Tibet and Ceylon. When Christianity was suffered to ally itself with the monastic tendencies so characteristic of the eastern mind, some justification would be doubtless found in the ungenial aspect of

[1] Prof. Wilson, in *Asiat. Res.* XVI. 38. See also Mr. Hardy's *Eastern Monachism*, and M. Pavie's critique on it in the *Revue des Deux Mondes*, 1854, Tome v. 'The type of those devotees,' writes Mr. H. T. Prinsep (*Tibet*, p. 150, Lond. 1852), 'who practised penances and sat on pillars, like Simeon Stylites,' are still found at Koon-boom and in Tibet.

[2] See above, pp. 169, 170.

[3] See Elphinstone's *India*, p. 107.

the age and in the feelings which might naturally impel an earnest spirit to recoil from the great centres of corruption, and erect itself a shelter from the inroads of barbarians and the storms of public life. It is indisputable also that, in spite of morbid symptoms[1] pointing to a different conclusion, a new character was at once imparted to this foreign mode of life by contact with the principles of the Gospel; and that, being thus ennobled, the monastic institute was frequently converted by the gracious providence of God into an apt and salutary agent for the training of the Christian scholar and the propagation of the Christian faith. Yet after all such benefits are estimated at their very highest worth, monasticism remains in its idea and essence inconsistent with the proper genius of revealed religion. It can draw no sanctions from the writings of the Old Testament[2]; it is repugnant to the spirit of the New. Though Christianity is found to be unsparing in its condemnation of all forms of worldliness, and though it teaches as was never taught before 'a total separation from all bonds considered as merely earthly,' it has nevertheless repudiated the heathenish idea[3] that any creature of God is evil in itself, or is, in other words, the product of ungodlike beings like the Gnostic demiurgus. Christianity so far from doing violence to any of our natural duties and relationships has consecrated all of them afresh; so far from labouring to pluck up the instincts and affections proper to humanity, it renders them more true and sensitive, because it renders them more Christ-like; purifying and refining and ennobling. Christianity, again, forbids the spiritual warrior to throw down his arms and quit the post of danger and of duty. His vocation is to benefit the world by his example,

[1] The histories and legends of the fourth and following century abound in illustrations of the lamentable errors and extravagances resulting from the prevalent passion in favour of monasticism. Some examples are collected by Neander, *Ch. Hist.* III. 337 sq. He particularly draws attention to the sect of Euchites, who, as he reminds us, constituted the first order of 'mendicant friars' (p. 342) within the pale of Christianity.

[2] It is worthy of notice that when Beda was requested by his friend, the bishop of Hexham, to compile an exposition of the first book of Samuel, he felt himself constrained to use the allegorical method of interpretation, because, as he remarked, the literal would no more apply to persons who alone were in a condition to profit by his labours; 'quibus ecclesiasticæ vitæ consuetudine longe fieri ab uxoris complexu et cœlibes manere propositum est.' *Works*, ed. Giles, VII. 369.

[3] Dr. Kay, Principal of Bishop's College, Calcutta, has recently discussed this subject, with special reference to Hindú theories, in his excellent essay on *The Promises of Christianity*, Oxf. 1855.

to be *in* it, but not *of* it, and, himself made luminous by fellowship with Christ, to 'let his light so shine before men, that they may see his good works, and glorify his Father who is in heaven.' And such was also the conviction of the early Christians. When the heathen were disposed to charge them with indifference to the practical business of society and the requirements of the state, the accusation was indignantly rejected by their ardent and severe apologist[1]: 'We are no Brachmans,' he could add, 'nor Indian Gymnosophists, dwellers in woods, estranged from the affairs of life. We know that our duty is to give thanks for every thing to God, the Lord and the Creator. We are far from wishing to repudiate any one of His works. We are temperate, it is true, and learn to use without abusing.'

(3) But granting, for the sake of argument, that real and profound resemblances did often come to light in the development of the religions we have just considered; granting that some points of contact can be shewn to have existed in the growth of Bráhmanism and Hebraism on one side, and of Buddhism and Christianity on the other; granting even, as one writer has of late contended, that there is as much in the records of Hindú systems 'of what was parallel, as of what was antagonistic to the Gospel[2];' let us test these suppositions in a different way, and measure the alleged affinities by following out the principles from which they are believed to flow into their logical consequences and their practical results. Now Bráhmanism, as understood by all philosophers, was uniformly striving to obtain exemption from the liability to repeated births: its ultimate effort was to give such kinds of knowledge to its votary as enabled him to say, 'I am Brahma,' 'I am All that is.' As soon as ever this exalted standing has been gained, the transmigration of the spirit ceases; but exactly at the point where the resemblances to Christianity might be expected to

[1] Tertullian *Apologet.* c. XLII. The whole passage is remarkable: 'Sed alio quoque injuriarum titulo postulamur, et infructuosi in negotiis dicimur: quo pacto homines vobiscum degentes, ejusdem victus, habitus, instructus, ejusdem ad vitam necessitatis? Neque enim Brachmanæ, aut Indorum gymnosophistæ sumus, sylvicolæ et exules vitæ. Meminimus gratiam nos debere Domino Deo Creatori [cf. 1 Tim. iv. 3, 4]; nullum fructum operum ejus repudiamus: plane temperamus ne ultra modum aut perperam utamur.'

[2] Prof. Jowett, *Epistles of St. Paul*, &c. II. 385, 386. Lond. 1855. 'The living, perfect truth has points of tangency for the one-sided forms of error; though we may not be thereby enabled to put together the perfect whole from the scattered and repellent fragments.' Neander, *Life of Christ*, p. 41.

attain their fulness, the divergence is most fundamental and entire. The act of reabsorption, every Bráhman argues, will destroy the personality of the human subject; his mental and moral organisation is utterly subverted, superseded, and dissolved. 'Annihilation, therefore, as regards the individual being is in Bráhmanism as much the ultimate destiny of the soul as it is of the body, and "Not to be" is the melancholy result of the religion and philosophy of the Hindús[1].' And if the end of all their mighty speculations be thus cold and desolating, what shall be our judgment of the younger system of philosophy, which, affecting to restore and purify the ancient creed, reduced it to more dismal blanks, and lengthened out the awful series of negations? The common cry of Buddhism was: 'It is transient; it is wretched; it is void.' With these reflections on the emptiness of all around him, the philosopher was labouring to appease the hunger of the human spirit; or if he ventured to discourse of future recompence and liberation from the evil of our present lot, the goal to which he ever pointed is the state where all the elements that enter into our idea of being will be utterly exhausted and burnt out. The heaven of philosophic Buddhism is *nirvána*. 'The mighty efforts of science in the ancient world have only issued in the forming of a vast and universal abstraction. They gave birth to Buddhism, a system in which there is no longer more than one sole existence, the Absolute, and in which this same existence is the infinite Void resembling non-existence. Here, then, is the furthest bound that could be reached by science, when applied to spiritual and divine things; it is the deification of Nothing[2].'

On the other hand, we cannot fail to notice how revealed religion, with each phase of its development, had grown more positive in its form, and brought men better tidings. It was eminently hopeful and constructive. It unfolded the great truth, that man is in the present life preparing for his ultimate condition; that he now begins to be what he will be for ever. It preaches more and more distinctly of the sacredness of human nature, as restored and glorified in Christ; it lays new stress on the material part of man, as wedded to his individual spirit, and as destined with that spirit to live on for ever; and thus, while Buddhism plants us in a sepulchre and extols *it* as our place of refuge from all human sorrows and all burdens of the flesh, the Gospel rolls away the stone from the door of the sepulchre; it

[1] Prof. Wilson, *Lectures*, p. 65.
[2] Gabriel, *Théodicée Pratique*, p. 84. Paris, 1855.

makes us free indeed, and points us to the ultimate 'redemption of the body' and the glorification of our whole humanity.

It is far, however, from my wish, in charging Buddhism with those fearful consequences, to deny or question the amount of social benefit resulting from its propagation in some parts of central and eastern Asia. Popular Buddhism, intermingled, as it is, with older maxims and more positive traditions, is far better than the nihilistic Buddhism of philosophy: and, accordingly, in this, as in some other cases where the territory invaded by the new religion was before in the possession of a ruder and more sanguinary creed, it may have doubtless proved an engine for exalting the character of millions who embrace it, and, to some extent, may have prepared a way for Christianity[1]. But that far more powerful agencies are still required among them is apparent, from the utter inability of Buddhism[2], even where it most predominates, to satisfy the reclamation of man's conscience, and to banish the hereditary demon-worship and the vulgar deprecation of the serpent[3].

(4) There is one more special point of view in which the truths of Christianity may be most forcibly contrasted with the best and brightest products of eastern speculation. All these varied products, estimated at their highest value, were but faint approximations to the sum of living and life-giving verities transmitted to us from the Founder of the Christian Church. When brought into comparison with the Gospel, they are poor and meagre, partial and one-sided. He who watches some of the more mighty fluctuations of the Hindú spirit, in its effort to escape from speculative difficulties and solve the awful riddles

[1] Upham has the following note on a passage in the *Sacred Books of Ceylon*, II. 54, which inculcates the greatest tenderness in treating animals: 'Although the present state of Buddhism properly excites our strongest interest and exertions to turn its followers from the blindness and selfishness of its modern tenets to the brightness of the Christian revelation: yet, in this passage, as well as in the simple offerings of fragrant perfumes and flowers, *contrasted with the cannibalism and serpent and demon-rites* it supplanted, the Buddhist doctrine must be esteemed to have been a great blessing and amelioration.' Wuttke, in like manner, rejoices to record the humanising influence of Buddhism when introduced, in connexion with other creeds, among the brutal hordes of Chingiskhan (I. 248). Tennent makes the same admission in reference to all the countries of eastern and central Asia. He says (*Christianity in Ceylon*, pp. 203, 204) that it was 'an active agent in the promotion of whatever civilisation afterwards enlightened those races by whom its doctrines were embraced.'

[2] 'Die Hülle ist geblieben, der Geist gewichen: der Buddhismus ist jetzt eine Mumie.' Wuttke, II. 590.

[3] *e.g.* Tennent, as above, p. 232.

by which it is oppressed, will see it here and there approaching, if not touching, a great line of thought, which, when pursued, might possibly have issued in the scriptural solution; yet ere long the cheering hopes which progress of this kind might foster are all doomed to disappointment. The speculator seems to be diverted from his proper object by the intervention of some fresh chimera or some puerile conceit; he loses his mental balance, and the fruit of all his metaphysics is a maimed or transcendental theory of the universe repugnant to his moral instincts. Thus, how much soever we may be disposed to chafe at these phenomena of heathenism, the fact remains indisputable, that if we add together and combine all single truths elicited by the profoundest thinkers in the various schools of Bráhmanic philosophy, such contributions are all very far from making up the circle of Christian theism; they cover only some few corners of the field of revelation[1].

For example, He whom Christians worship is a Being higher far, and far more truly God-like, than the worthiest of Hindú conceptions. These, indeed, are not unwilling to recognise the main distinction drawn in Holy Scripture between the subject and the object,—the finite and the infinite. They all regard the perfect extrication of material from immaterial as the end and aim of true philosophy. While rejecting or ignoring the idea of created spirits[2], as distinct from emanations, they are all in favour of the doctrine of a great and universal Soul,—*the* substance, *the* reality. Some, moreover, have contended that this Great Soul is one, or simple; others, that it is resolvable into parts, and therefore multiform and manifold; yet all of them agree in treating it as the original and self-dependent Something, over and beyond which is no other entity; they are alike desirous to exalt it far above the possibility of future contact with the transient and phenomenal. To this supreme and all-embracing Spirit the Védántins assign not only an eternal subsistence, but also many of the specific properties which enter into our idea of personality, as intelligence, volition, and the like.

[1] Cf. Dean Trench's *Hulsean Lectures* (1846), p. 58: 'And thus each of the great divisions of the Gentile world had but a fragment, even in thought, of the truth: the Greek world, the exaltation of manhood; the Oriental, the glorious humiliation of Godhead: and thus, each of these, even as a speculation, was maimed and imperfect. These systems, so far from providing what men needed, had not satisfactorily and on every side even contemplated what he needed; much less had they given it.'

[2] See *Aphorisms of the Yoga*, ed. Ballantyne, Part I. p. 63.

Yet here the many points of similarity between their system and the Christian are exhausted, and we enter on a startling contrast. The Védántins[1], on the one hand, labour to identify the glorious Spirit of the universe with His own production, and, in order to effect this, question the reality of the external world, and treat it as illusive; on the other hand, they totally repudiate the idea of individual existence, or of personality attaching to all rational creatures, and securing to each man the power of self-determination. A second school, or the Nyáya, recognises the personal character of God more fully; it ascribes to Him such attributes as will, activity, and intelligence; but no account whatever is taken by it of His moral government, His fatherhood, His providence, His justice, or His mercy. In this school, again, where true subsistency is granted to the world of matter, and where finite souls are recognised, the origin of both is carried backward to eternity, while all the mental and corporeal faculties possessed by human beings in one stage of their existence are in no case held to be essential parts of them, and, as such, infinite in duration. The Sánkhya system, as we saw already, occupied, in some particulars, a middle place among the jarring tenets of Hindú philosophers. It regarded matter as a real aggregate of qualities; it recognised a spiritual essence gifted with a species of volition; it pleaded even for the personal distinctness of all human souls; yet, on the other hand, it went so far as to attribute the government of the world entirely to the operation of physical agents, and made Spirit, whether human or Divine, a mere spectator in some gorgeous and gigantic drama. Indeed, the one school of Hindú philosophy among whose tenets the idea of a Divine providence was clearly and consistently developed, is the latest modification[2] of the Sánkhya system; and even this, I should again remark, might be indebted for its higher characteristics to some intercourse with Christianity.

Another instance of the general inability of Hindúism to contemplate religious truth under more than one of its manifold aspects was furnished by the *Bhagavad-Gítá*; which, when its large and comprehensive spirit is remembered, might be deemed the least of all amenable to this censure. I have before alluded to the stern and naked Pantheism which it preaches; but the want of balance in its author is no less strikingly apparent in discussing moral questions. So long as he is aiming merely to

[1] See a recent article in the *North British Review*, No. 49, p. 224.
[2] Above, p. 153.

destroy the errors of an older creed,—so long as he exposes the narrowness, the spiritual pride, the dreamy indolence, and inefficiency of the Yoga-system, his criticism is often most acute, his logic overwhelming; but as soon as ever he attempts to cure the evil he complains of, it is manifest that the remedy is utterly inadequate: it is a tissue of self-contradictions, a huge mass of unrealities. The genuine devotee, the *Karmayogin*, is to suffer and to act in every case without emotion and without regard to consequences. He must pluck up all within him that may serve to foster the illusions of the human and that interferes with the development of the divine: affections, be they pure or impure; instincts, whether high and noble or unworthy and corrupted; sympathies, inwoven though they be with all the innermost fibres of his being; and when at last he yields assent to the unnatural conclusion that the real dignity of man consists in utter abnegation of self-consciousness, he rises to the fulness of his ultimate condition,—absorbed in breathless calm and frigid apathy, a stranger to the impulses of nature, dead to all the duties and enjoyments of religion.

But, further, it is prominently brought before us in the annals of Hindúism, that the highest minds have always been most prone to drift away from the positions of their own acquiring, and have gradually relaxed their hold on the more spiritual portions of the ancient creed. For instance, all the loftier thoughts of God were once connected with a special veneration of the first member of the Hindú triad. Sacerdotal Áryans stood in a peculiarly close relation to Brahmá; they were esteemed the privileged offspring of his head; and, therefore, if the great idea of unity was ever to be vindicated from the ravages of Polytheism, the natural way to such a restoration was by passing upward from the Bráhman to Brahmá, and thence to Brahma, the pure Spirit of the universe; the lower emanation serving as an index to the higher, and this again directly guiding to the Source of all created being and the simple Origin of all things. But so far were Bráhmans, as an order, from desiring such recovery, that they gradually abandoned their belief in one divine Administrator of the world[1]; and, instead of seeking refuge in the worship of Vishńu, whose

[1] Elphinstone's *India*, pp. 90, 101. 'The opinion of the vulgar,' he remarks, 'is more rational than that of their teachers: they [the vulgar] mix up the idea of the Supreme Being with that of the deity who is the particular object of their adoration, and suppose him to watch over the actions of men, and to reward the good and punish the wicked.'

milder incarnations were attracting to his altars the more gentle souls of the community, the members of the sacerdotal class selected for their patron-god that very inmate of the pantheon who had long been dreaded as the primary cause of desolation, and is worshipped as the animal[1] divinity of modern Hindústán. The Bráhman is, in other words, the special votary of Śiva,—of him who is invested by popular imagination with most hideous and appalling attributes,—of him who is described in their Puráńas[2], 'wandering about, surrounded by ghosts and goblins, inebriated, naked, and with dishevelled hair, covered with the ashes of a funeral pile, ornamented with human skulls and bones, sometimes laughing, sometimes crying. I should also add, for the completion of this melancholy picture, that the votaries of Śiva, and still more of Déví, his consort, who is singly venerated by a large proportion of the people in Bengal, are ready to undergo excruciating tortures in honour of their divinity. 'Some stab their limbs and pierce their tongues with knives, and walk in procession with swords, arrows, and even living serpents, thrust through the wounds; while others are raised into the air by a hook fixed in the flesh of their backs, and are whirled round by a moveable lever, at a height which would make their destruction inevitable, if the skin were to give way[3].'

(5) But, turning from these dark and ghastly spectacles, which seem to be among the ripest products of the pagan mind of India, it is most consolatory to reflect that there is still within our reach the grand corrective and the sovereign antidote.

While heathen systems are unequal to the work of rectifying the infatuations of the human spirit and of cancelling human guilt,—while, even at the best, the authors of those systems can only here and there find out some fragmentary truth, but are all powerless in determining its precise relation to other verities or binding them together in one definite body of belief, the Gospel has at length successfully encountered the great problem; it has furnished what must ever be regarded,

[1] This peculiarity is sufficiently indicated by the fact that Śiva, since the 8th or 9th century of our era (cf. above, p. 134, n. 1), has been worshipped under the symbol of the phallus (or *linga*), intimating perhaps that his destructive powers have always reference to some future reproduction.

[2] Elphinstone, p. 89. It is also very remarkable that Śiva-worship, notwithstanding the apparent incompatibility, has in later times been found in close alliance with Buddhism: Stuhr, I. 209.

[3] *Ibid.* p. 90.

even from a 'rational[1]' point of view, the only fitting and profound solution.

It does not, indeed, profess to clear away all shades of intellectual difficulty: the imparting of a merely speculative satisfaction was never made a primary object in the plan of its great Author. It is even ready to acknowledge, by the lips of an Apostle, that, if measured not by present, but ulterior standards of illumination, we see only 'through a glass,' while that which we behold is still encompassed with 'enigmas' (1 Cor. xiii. 12). Yet, compared with all the previous legacies of God, the Gospel is a boon immeasurably vast, incalculably precious. On the one side, it has clearly taken into its account of man, not some, but *all* the factors of his complex being, and, in harmony with this conception, it asserts, as no anterior system had been able to assert, the primal dignity of human nature, and, still more, the permanence of human personality. On the other side, the Gospel harmonizes and collects together in one focus all the scattered and enfeebled rays of truth concerning God and His relation to the creature. It produces them in their original unity and fulness, not as fragments isolated from the other truths which are essential to their rightful action and their just interpretation, but as one coherent, living, and organic whole. In this, indeed, we recognise a leading aim and characteristic of the Gospel. It is far from seeking to establish the reality of spirit by denying the reality of matter. It is far from elevating human souls in such a way as to annihilate the human body. In the world of thought it does not so insist on the objective as to question or deny the subjective. It does not so discover God in nature as to miss Him in the province of the supernatural or exclude Him from His temple in the mind and heart of man. It does not so maintain the power and privileges of the corporate as to cripple or suppress the action of the individual. It never so proclaims the monarchy of God as to deprive the human agent of his self-determination, and thus make him irresponsible. It never so expatiates on the details of the future kingdom as to dazzle our imperfect understanding or blind us to the duties of our present lot. There is, in other words, a marvellous and majestic balance in the doctrines which the Gospel has been authorised to bring before us; and the point round which that balance is effected, or as seen from which all other elements in the Christian system

1 That this view of Christianity is neither novel nor unworthy, may be seen in the *Ars Generalis* of the excellent Raymund Lull, the philosophic missionary of the 13th century; on whom see Neander, *Ch. Hist.* VII. 83 sq.

have derived their mutual fitness, is the glorious truth[1], announcing how the Word, who is with God and is God, has verily assumed our human nature, and how God in Him is 'reconciling the world unto Himself, not imputing unto them their trespasses.' The Incarnation, while it forms the turning-point of universal history, is more especially the life and marrow of all Christian dogmas. Wheresoever it has been distinctly apprehended by the reason and digested in the soul of man, there is an end of creature-worship. Those ineradicable instincts of our nature which had driven so many of the pensive spirits of the ancient world to fashion for themselves elaborate theories of transmigration, and, through consciousness of their demerit, to persist in torturing out the remnants of their evil passions, find in Christ their proper object and their permanent satisfaction. He whose life is 'hid with Christ in God' is able to approach the throne of grace with holy confidence; he looks forward to the world invisible with awe indeed, but with no abject shrinking, and no slavish terror; his unswerving hope is to be there 'accepted in the Beloved,' who has gone as our Forerunner to the inmost glories of the sanctuary; 'who ever liveth to make intercession for us.' 'Taking to Himself our flesh, and by His incarnation making it His own flesh, He hath now of His own, although from us, what to offer unto God for us[2].'

'In him dwelleth all the fulness of the Godhead bodily; and ye are filled up in Him.' Thus argued the great Doctor of the Gentiles, who, in writing to the Phrygian Church (Col. ii.), was under the necessity of checking one of the most early manifestations of that ethnic spirit which ere long expanded into Gnosticism, and threatened to degrade the Gospel of his heavenly Master into one of the effete philosophies. The object of the misbeliever at Colossæ was not, perhaps, so definite as this; he may have merely sought to blend with Christianity a number of Judaical observances, whose meaning had been swallowed up in evangelic institutions. Yet his aim was also to resuscitate the past and reinaugurate the reign of shadows. He was anxious, in a spirit of assumed humility, and as the fruit of visions claimed especially for himself, to introduce the worship of the angels and of other finite emanations, like the Indian *dêvas;*

[1] 'We say that the divine ideas which had wandered up and down the world, till oftentimes they had well-nigh forgotten themselves and their origin, did at length clothe themselves in flesh and blood: they became incarnate with the Incarnation of the Son of God. In His life and person, the idea and the fact at length kissed each other, and were henceforward wedded for evermore.' Dean Trench, *Hulsean Lectures* (1846), p. 20.

[2] Hooker, *Eccl. Pol.* v. li. 3.

while, to finish the incongruous compound, he was pleading for a class of disciplinary tenets which, in the rigour of their asceticism, would lift him almost to a level with the self-destroying *yogin* of the East.

But how, in such a case, did the Apostle combat the pretensions of 'philosophy and vain deceit'? He reasoned with still greater urgency for the transcendent Headship of the Word Incarnate—for that 'truth of truths' which, lying at the very core of Christianity, was the first to suffer from attacks of the confirmed believer in a spurious Gnosis[1]. So it was at Ephesus, where, not many years after, a denial of the Incarnation was more openly united with unchristian dread of all material forms of being, and commended to the undiscerning by extreme asceticism of life (1 Tim. iii. 16—iv. 5). The fautors of that early error were, accordingly, warned by the Apostle of the consequences that were sure to flow from their attempted intermixtures. They were taught how every project for combining with a supernatural revelation the theosophy of the Essene, or the self-torture of the Hindú hermit, was derogatory to the honour of our blessed Lord, was utterly at variance with the genius of the perfect system He had planted. They were taught how Christians had been raised, by fellowship with Christ, far higher than the shadowy ordinances of the old œconomy, and, still more, could have no need of supplementary illumination from extraneous sources. They were taught how Christians, cleaving to the Head, could never be dependent on the intercession of created spirits, nor on aught so secondary and so intermediate. They were taught how the ascetical extravagances to which they had been tempted were but 'elements of the world'; traditions emanating not from heaven, but from the breast of unregenerate man, and, therefore, alien to the Law of Christ. They were admonished, most of all, (and would that such an admonition may be echoed on to every period of the Church beset by like temptations!) that, as Christ, and Christ alone, is the Fulfilment of all ancient hopes, the Substance of all ancient shadows, so all Christian *progress*, whether in the apprehension by the Church of things revealed to us already, or in wider publication of good tidings to the heart-sick millions still 'without,' must have its origin, its root, and its sustaining principle in Him 'from whom all the body, having nourishment ministered and knit together by the joints and bands, increaseth with the increase of God.'

[1] Thiersch, *Ch. Hist.* I. 139.

APPENDIX I.

The Nisháďan *or* non-Áryan *Tribes of Hindústán, and some account of their Religion.*

It is now admitted on all hands that certain primary strata of population, by whatever name they may be called, had long extended over all parts of India, when they were attacked and gradually dispersed by the incursions of the Áryan settlers. Remnants of such original population are still found in all the various mountain-tribes, and more especially among the natives of the Dekhan, to the south of the great Vindhya-chain. In the age of Manu, or rather at the time when laws and institutes which bear his name were promulgated, the Áryan had not been able to push further southward than the 22nd degree of north latitude, and beyond him lay a mass of human beings, who are there described as 'barbarians living in forests, and speaking an unknown tongue.' (See *Journal of the Asiatic Society*, XIII. 277, 278.) Abundant traces of their presence have been also brought to light by the publication of the Védas. In these ancient documents, one ordinary name for all who ventured to resist the onward march of the invaders, or the men of 'Áryan colour,' is that of 'Dasyus' (cf. above, p. 133, n. 1). The same uncouth and 'irreligious' tribes are also characterized as *anagnitra:* 'those who do not tend the fire,' or 'fail to worship Agni.' Another appellation of a similar import, is *kravyád*, or 'flesh-eaters,' (κρεοφάγοι). In the following period, as represented in the literature of the Bráhmańas, the aboriginal population are thrown into the 'same category with thieves and criminals, who attack men in forests, throw them into wells, and run away with their goods' (Prof. Max Müller in Bunsen's *Univ. Hist.* I. 346). In the Puráńas 'the inhabitants of the Vindhya mountain,' called Nisháďas, are said to be 'characterized by the exterior tokens of depravity' (*Vishńu Pur.* ed. Wilson, p. 100). 'The Matsya says, there were born outcast or barbarous races, Mléchchas, as black as collyrium. The Bhágavata describes an individual of dwarfish stature, with short arms and legs, of a complexion as black as a crow, with projecting chin, broad flat nose, red eyes, and tawny hair; whose descendants were mountaineers and foresters. The Padma has a similar description, adding to the dwarfish stature and black complexion a wide mouth, large ears, and a protuberant belly. It also particularizes his posterity as Nisháďas, Kirátas, Bhillas, Bahanakas, Bhramaras, Pulindas, and other barbarians, or Mléchchas, living in woods and on mountains.' 'These passages intend,' continues Prof. Wilson (*Ibid.* p. 101, n.), 'and do not much exaggerate, the uncouth appearance of the Goands, Koles, Bhils, and other uncivilized tribes, scattered along the forests and mountains of central India, from Behar to Kandesh, and who are not improbably the predecessors of the present occupants of the cultivated portions of the country. They are always very black, ill-shapen and dwarfish, and have countenances of a very African character.' To these must also be applied the language of Herodotus, where he speaks of black and savage Indians (cf. Lassen, I. 389).

As the Áryans by the force of conquest gradually extended their original frontiers, they would either subjugate the old inhabitants entirely and reduce them to the state of Śúdras, serfs and menials, or else would push them all into the mountain-fastnesses, or lastly drive them forward to the southern part of the Peninsula.

1. In the first case, the position of the rude Nisháda's would become most wretched and humiliating. As early as the laws of Manu (ch. x.) it was ordained that—

> Their abode must be outside the towns.
> Their property must be restricted to dogs and asses.
> Their clothes should be those left by the dead.
> Their ornaments, rusty iron.
> They must roam from place to place.
> No respectable person must hold intercourse with them.
> They are to aid as public executioners, retaining the clothes, &c. of the criminals.

A class of serfs, who answer in the main to this description, still exist in almost every province of Hindústán: and the following contrasts, for which we are indebted to the pen of General Briggs (*Journal of the Asiatic Society*, XIII. 282, 283), may serve to indicate how widely the aborigines had always differed from the Áryan conquerors.

1. Hindús are divided into castes.
   The aborigines have no such distinctions.
2. Hindú widows are forbidden to marry.
   The widows of the aborigines not only do so, but usually with the younger brother of the late husband—a practice they follow in common with the Scythian tribes.
3. The Hindús venerate the cow and abstain from eating beef.
   The aborigines feed alike on all flesh.
4. The Hindús abstain from the use of fermented liquors.
   The aborigines drink to excess; and conceive no ceremony, civil or religious, complete without.
5. The Hindús partake of food prepared only by those of their own caste.
   The aborigines partake of food prepared by any one.
6. The Hindús abhor the spilling of blood.
   The aborigines conceive no religious or domestic ceremony complete without the spilling of blood and offering up a live victim.
7. The Hindús have a Bráhmanical priesthood.
   The indigenes do not venerate Bráhmans. Their own priests (who are self-created) are respected according to their mode of life and their skill in magic and sorcery, in divining future events and in curing diseases: these are the qualifications which authorise their employment in slaying sacrificial victims and in distributing them.

8. The Hindús burn their dead.
The aborigines bury their dead, and with them their arms; sometimes their cattle, as among the Scythians. On such occasions a victim ought to be sacrificed to atone for the sins of the deceased.
9. The Hindú civil institutions are all municipal.
The aboriginal institutions are all patriarchal.
10. The Hindús have their courts of justice composed of equals.
The aborigines have theirs composed of heads of tribes or families, and chosen for life.
11. The Hindús brought with them (more than three thousand years ago) the art of writing and science.
The indigenes are not only illiterate, but it is forbidden for the Hindús to teach them.

2. But although a great majority of aborigines in northern India had been thus imperfectly blended with the Áryan strangers who subdued them, others have retained a large amount of savage independence in the mountain-fastnesses to which they had retreated (*e.g.* the Bhils, the Mirs, the Khulis, the Goands: cf. Prichard, *Researches*, IV. 166 sq.). Every year is adding to our knowledge of their general habits as well as of their language and religion: and it is gratifying to notice that the best informed of modern writers on the subject are more and more agreed as to the oneness of the stamp impressed on all the aborigines of India, however multiform and scattered at the present day. That general stamp is said to be 'Mongolian' (Prof. Max Müller, as above, p. 348). The various tribes appear to have issued, like their Áryan successors, from the northern parts of Hindústán, and to have all spoken a language belonging to the Tamil (or Turanian) as distinguished from the Sanskrit (or Indo-European) stock. Recent occurrences have brought the English government into collision with one of these hill-tribes, the Sontáls, who are scattered over the country in considerable numbers from Cattack to Bhagalpur (see *Journal of the Asiatic Society*, as above, p. 285): but the most copious and interesting account of the religious character and condition of the whole group, is furnished in a memoir by Captain (now Major) S. C. Macpherson (*Ibid.* pp. 216—274). The title of his paper is *An Account of the Religion of the Khonds in Orissa* (*i.e.* Uria-desa, 'land of the Urias,' lying between the eastern mountains of the Dekhan and the sea-coast). After citing numerous legends in illustration of the doctrines there current, Major Macpherson has exhibited the main features of the Khond religion in the following summary (p. 273): 'The Supreme Being and sole source of good, who is styled the God of Light [Boora Pennu or Bella Pennu], created for himself a consort, who became the Earth-Goddess [Tari Pennu or Bera Pennu] and the source of evil: and thereafter, he created the earth, with all it contains, and man. The Earth-Goddess, prompted by jealousy of the love borne to man by his Creator, rebelled against the God of Light, and introduced moral and physical evil into the world. The God of Light arrested the action of physical evil, while he left man perfectly free to receive or to reject moral evil,—defined to be "disobedience towards God, and strife amongst men." A few of mankind entirely rejected moral evil, the remainder received it. The former portion were immediately deified; the latter were condemned to endure every form of physical suffering, with death, deprivation of the immediate care of the Creator, and the deepest moral degradation. Mean-

while, the God of Light and his rebel consort contended for superiority, until the elements of good and evil became thoroughly commingled in man and throughout nature.

'Up to this period the Khonds hold the same general belief, but from it they divide into two sects, directly opposed upon the question of the issue of the contest between the two antagonist powers.

'One sect holds that the God of Light completely conquered the Earth-Goddess, and employs her, still the active principle of evil, as the instrument of his moral rule. That he resolved to provide a partial remedy for the consequences of the introduction of evil, by enabling man to attain to a state of moderate enjoyment upon earth, and to partial restoration to communion with the Creator after death. And that, to effect this purpose, he created those classes of subordinate deities, and assigned to them the office—first, of instructing man in the arts of life, and regulating the powers of nature for his use, upon the condition of his paying to them due worship; secondly, of administering a system of retributive justice through subjection to which, and through the practice of virtue during successive lives upon earth, the soul of man might attain to beatification. The other sect hold, upon the other hand, that the Earth-Goddess remains unconquered; that the God of Light could not, in opposition to her will, carry out his purpose with respect to man's temporal lot; and that man, therefore, owes his elevation from the state of physical suffering into which he fell through the reception of evil, to the direct exercise of her power to confer blessings, or to her permitting him to receive the good which flows from the God of Light, through the inferior gods, to all who worship them. With respect to man's destiny after death, they believe that the God of Light carried out his purpose. And they believe that the worship of the Earth-Goddess by human sacrifice, is the indispensable condition on which these blessings have been granted, and their continuance may be hoped for; the virtue of the rite availing not only for those who practise it, but for all mankind.'

In addition to these human sacrifices, which still continue to be offered annually, in order to appease the wrath of Tari and propitiate her in favour of agriculture, there is a fearful amount of infanticide among the Khond people. 'It exists in some of the tribes of the sect of Boora to such an extent, that no female infant is spared, except when a woman's first child is female; and that villages containing a hundred houses may be seen without a female child' (*Ibid.* p. 270).

3. But, in addition to the wild and barbarous mountaineers whose creed is sketched in the foregoing extract, there was always a large body of Nishádan, or non-Áryan, tribes of India who retained their former hold on nearly all the southern part of the Peninsula, and ultimately, with the aid of Áryan influence, reached a high degree of civilization. 'We find the Dekhan occupied entirely by aboriginal races, with only a small and late sprinkling of Bráhmanic blood. Civilization there is Bráhmanic, and the native languages are full of Sanskrit vocables; but the grammar has resisted, and language has thus retained its independence' (Prof. Max Müller, as above, p. 432). Mr. Caldwell, in his able work entitled *A Comparative Grammar of the Drávidian* [Tamil], *or South-Indian Family of Languages*, Lond. 1856, has disputed some of the current theories respecting this section of the non-Áryan races of India. He doubts whether the Drávidians were in origin identical with the Áryanised Súdras of Northern Hindústán (p. 70), and is inclined to

argue, from 'the difference which appears to exist between the Drávidian languages and the Scythian under-stratum of the northern vernaculars,' that 'the Drávidian idioms belong to an older period of the Scythian speech—the period of the predominance of the Ugro-Finnish languages in Central and Higher Asia, anterior to the westward migration of the Turks and Mongolians.' He is also convinced that the 'Drávidians never had any relations with the primitive Áryans but those of a peaceable and friendly character; and that, if they were expelled from Northern India, and forced to take refuge in Gondwana and Dánda-Kárńaya, the great Drávidian forest, prior to the dawn of their civilization, the tribes that subdued and thrust them southwards must have been Pre-Áryans.'

Mr. Caldwell, however, does not wish to disguise the fact, that even if the Drávidians had not sunk as low as the Puráńas seem to intimate, when branding them with the name of rákshasas, or monkeys, or vile sinners who ate raw meat and human flesh, they were for a long time 'destitute of letters and unacquainted with the higher arts of life' (p. 77). In their religious worship, also, these Drávidians differed widely from the creed and usages of the Bráhmans: and, what is especially worthy of our notice, Mr. Caldwell has distinctly shewn the similarity between the former and the practices observed for ages among the Scythian tribes of Northern Asia.

'The system which prevails in the forests and mountain-fastnesses throughout the Drávidian territories, and also in the extreme south of the Peninsula amongst the low caste tribes, and which appears to have been still more widely prevalent at an early period, is a system of demonolatry, or the worship of evil spirits by means of bloody sacrifices and frantic dances. This system was introduced within the historical period from the Tamil country into Ceylon, where it is now mixed up with Buddhism. On comparing this Drávidian system of demonolatry and sorcery with 'Shamanism'—the superstition which prevails amongst the Ugrian races of Siberia and the hill-tribes[1] on the south-western frontier of China, which is still mixed up with the Buddhism of the Mongols, and which was the old religion of the whole Tartar race before Buddhism and Mohammedanism were disseminated amongst them—we cannot avoid the conclusion that those two superstitions, though practised by races so widely separated, are not only similar but identical.

'I shall here point out the principal features of resemblance between the Shamanism of High Asia and the demonolatry of the Drávidians, as still practised in many districts in Southern India.

'(1) The Shamanites are destitute of a regular priesthood. Ordinarily the father of the family is the priest and magician; but the office may be undertaken by any one who pleases, and at any time laid aside.

'Precisely similar is the practice existing amongst the Shánárs and other rude tribes of Southern India. Ordinarily it is the head of the family, or the head-man of the hamlet or community, who performs the priestly office: but any worshipper, male or female, who feels so disposed, may volunteer to officiate, and becomes for the time being the representative and interpreter of the demon.

[1] In E. T. Turnerelli's work on *Kazan*, II. 116 sq., we have some account of the Tchouvash and other aboriginal tribes of the neighbourhood. They were said to be of Finnish origin. They recognise two principles, of good and evil; the good Genius requiring no worship, and rarely receiving any, the evil Genius (Keremet) being constantly appeased by sacrifice (p. 133). Their chief priest (Jomza) unites in his own person the offices of priest, soothsayer, sorcerer, and physician.

'(2) The Shamanites acknowledge the existence of a supreme God; but they do not offer him any worship. The same acknowledgment of God's existence and the same neglect of his worship characterize the religion of the Drávidian demonolaters.

'(3) Neither amongst the Shamanites nor amongst the primitive un-brahmanized demonolaters of India is there any trace of belief in the metempsychosis.

'(4) The objects of Shamanite worship are not gods or heroes, but demons, which are supposed to be cruel, revengeful, and capricious, and are worshipped by bloody sacrifices and wild dances. The officiating magician or priest excites himself to frenzy, and then pretends, or supposes himself, to be possessed by the demon to which worship is being offered; and after the rites are over he communicates, to those who consult him, the information he has received.

'The demonolatry practised in India by the more primitive Drávidian tribes is not only similar to this, but the same. Every word used in the foregoing description of the Shamanite worship would apply equally well to the Drávidian demonolatry; and in depicting the ceremonies of the one race we depict those of the other also.'

APPENDIX II.

Coincidences between Lamaism and Mediæval Christianity.

Mr. H. T. Prinsep, in his recent work on *Tibet, Tartary, and Mongolia*, 2nd ed. Lond. 1852, has, with the aid of MM. Huc and Gabet's *Voyages dans la Tartarie*, &c., revived a question of some importance touching the origin of various parallelisms between Buddhism, as organized in those districts, and certain forms or usages of Mediæval Christianity. Some, at least, of these phenomena had excited the astonishment of Latin missionaries as far back as the middle of the thirteenth century, who explained them on the supposition that Lamaism was not so much one phase of Buddhism as a remnant of the influence exercised in those remote districts by the missions of the 'Nestorian' Church[1]. In 1661, two Jesuits, Grueber and Dorville, on their return from China, penetrated far into Tibet and brought accounts of extraordinary resemblances between the faith of Lassa and of Rome. Mr. Davis still more recently drew attention to them in his *Remarks on the Religion and Social Institutions of the Bouteas* (Roy. Asiat. Soc. II. 491 sq.), selecting for particular comment 'The celibacy of the clergy and the monastic life of the societies of both sexes; to which might be added, their strings of beads, their manner of chanting prayers, their incense, and their candles.' Other writers have again insisted on the strong resemblance between the hierarchy of the Lamas and that of western Christendom, particularly as we find it in the Middle Ages; the resemblance extending even to minor points of discipline and articles of dress. But such topics appear to have assumed no great importance in the eyes of Europe until Volney, and others like him, resolved to find in them a novel engine for subverting Christianity.

The question was then asked, By what hypothesis can we explain the striking correspondence between two systems which appear to be in other respects so totally independent? Is it the result of actual intercourse, or is it merely an extensive specimen of the way in which internal affinities of thought and sentiment will often clothe themselves in forms analogous if not identical? When the number, the variety, and

[1] The resemblances were afterwards explained on the hypothesis of diabolical counterfeits. 'Father Bury, a Portuguese missionary, when he beheld the [Chinese] bonzes tonsured, using rosaries, praying in an unknown tongue, and kneeling before images, exclaims in astonishment, There is not a piece of dress, not a sacerdotal function, not a ceremony of the Church of Rome, which the devil has not invented a copy of in this country.' Kesson, *The Cross and the Dragon*, p. 185, Lond. 1854. Medhurst (*China*, p. 217, Lond. 1857) points out the coincidences between Romanism and Chinese Buddhism in respect of ceremonial. He also mentions the image of a virgin ('queen of heaven'), having a child in her arms and holding a cross.

the minuteness[1] of the parallelisms in question are duly weighed, the latter hypothesis will hardly commend itself to the acceptance of historical critics; and accordingly I shall adopt the former. But here again, it must be asked: Did Buddhism, in this matter, borrow from Christianity or Christianity from Buddhism? Let us first hear Mr. Prinsep's answer. Starting from the fact, that Gautama Buddha flourished long anterior to the propagation of the Gospel, and asserting further, on what authority I know not, that the principles of Buddhism were quite familiar in some parts of western Asia, not to say of Europe, under the guise of Pythagoreanism or Mithraism; this writer is prepared to argue that the early Christians were indebted to Buddhist converts for no small part of their ecclesiastical organisation.

'To a mind,' he says, 'already impressed with Boodhistic belief and Boodhistic doctrines, the birth of a Saviour and Redeemer for the western world, recognised as a new Boodh by wise men of the east, that is, by Magi, Sramanas, or Lamas, who had obtained the Arhat sanctification, was an event expected, and therefore readily accepted, when declared and announced. It was no abjuration of an old faith [!] that the teacher of Christianity asked of the Boodhists, but a mere qualification of an existing belief by the incorporation into it of the Mosaic account of the creation, and of original sin and the fall of man. The Boodhists of the west, accepting Christianity on its first announcement, at once introduced the rites and observances which for centuries had already existed in India. From that country Christianity derived its monastic institutions, its forms of ritual and of Church-service, its councils or convocations to settle schisms on points of faith, its worship of relics, and working of miracles through them, and much of the discipline, and of the dress of the clergy, even to the shaven heads of the monks and friars.' Now if Christianity were thus fused with Buddhism 'on its first announcement,' we might surely have expected to find some definite notice, in the early Christian writers, of so marvellous an amalgamation; but instead of any single whisper on the subject, the tone in which these writers reprehend *all* forms of heathenism, is rigorous and uncompromising, and St. Paul (as we have seen) had warned the Phrygian converts in particular against the least indulgence of a spirit such as that here contemplated.

The present view is also strengthened by our survey of the fundamental principles involved in Buddhism and in Christianity. Those principles are quite incapable of intermixture: they are mutually repulsive and annihilative. I am accordingly disposed to think that during all the time that Christianity was warring against Gnostic errors, or in other words until the doctrines taught by the Apostles were completely vindicated and established, it was totally impossible for a system such as Buddhism to affect in any sensible degree the institutions of the primitive Church. The jealousy with which she guarded the deposit of the faith would surely have impelled her to resist all compromise with heathenish observances, associated as they must have been at first with heathen doctrines. That such jealousy, however, was relaxing in the fourth century of our era is too plainly

[1] The points of resemblance specified by the French missionaries are, the use of the cross, the mitre, the dalmatic, the hood, the office of two choirs, the psalmody, the exorcisms, the censer of five chains, the benediction of the lamas by placing the right hand on the head of the faithful, the rosary, celibacy of the clergy, spiritual retirement, the worship of saints, fasts, processions, litanies, and holy water. Prof. Wilson in *Journal of As. Soc.* XVI. 263.

manifest in the writings of the period; and I think it therefore not improbable, that together with the rapid growth of the ascetic and monastic spirit may have come a disposition to accept some portions of the rites and ceremonies which pre-existed in the heathen monasteries of the East[1]. The same remark may possibly be extended to some other usages, as processions of images, worship of relics, pilgrimages, indulgences, and the like, which always have their root in ethnic rather than in Christian modes of thought. But whatever may be ultimately determined with regard to the precise development of these conceptions in the bosom of the Christian Church, it is, I think, extremely probable that some at least of the minute resemblances between the Buddhism of Tibet and Mediæval Christianity are directly traceable to the effect of Christian missions. Although the rise of Buddhism was very long anterior to the earliest of those missions, and although many of its peculiarities are far more ancient than the origin of Christianity itself, that form which we entitle Lamaism[2] is found to be comparatively modern,—not older than the 13th century of the present era. Buddhism, it is true, had been propagated in Tibet six hundred years before (Wuttke, II. 559); but it was only under Kublai-Khan (A. D. 1260) that the adherents of that system were reduced under the dominion of a regular hierarchy by the appointment of the first Grand Lama, and the transfer of the spiritual government of Buddhism to his hands (*Ibid.* I. 215 sq., II. 591: Abel-Rémusat, *Mélanges Asiatiques*, I. 136, 137, Paris, 1825). At this juncture, when the ancient forms and usages might naturally be made to undergo extensive alterations and be invested with a pomp befitting the inauguration of the new hierarchy, we know for certain that Tibet had been brought into immediate communication with teachers of Christianity and also with the ritual system of the Western Church. The Khans had at their court not only Jews, Muhammadans, and Buddhists, but Latin and Nestorian missionaries (see, for example, the graphic account in the *Travels of Marco Polo*, ed. Wright, pp. 167, 168, Lond. 1854; and other evidences in Neander, *Ch. Hist.* VII. 70 sq.): and in the fourteenth century of our era, the arrival of a strange Lama, who came 'from the far west,' is said to have actually wrought such changes in the aspect of religious worship in Tibet[3]. Wuttke (II. 559) conjecturing, after Huc and Gabet, that this very Lama was himself a Christian, remarks with reference to him: 'Er änderte an den Grundlehren des Buddhismus nichts, verschärfte aber die Disciplin, änderte den Kultus und führte neue Liturgien ein; und die katholischen Missionäre Huc und Gabet fanden die Ähnlichkeit mit dem katholischen Kult höchst auffallend.' The special processes by which these innovations *might* have been in almost every case effected are admirably sketched by Abel-Rémusat, as above, pp. 138, 139: 'A l'époque où les patriarches bouddhistes s'établirent dans le Tibet, les parties de la Tartarie qui avoisinent cette contrée étaient remplies de chrétiens. Les Nestoriens y avaient fondé des métropoles et converti des nations entières.

[1] Lassen, in the third volume of his *Indische. Altert.* pp. 441, 442 (Leipzig, 1857), expresses himself in favour of this view. He concludes: 'Ein Einfluss des Buddhismus ist ferner nicht zu verkennen in der bei den christlichen Priestern gebräuchlichen Tonsur, so wie in dem Gebrauche der Glocken, welcher bei den Buddhisten viel älter ist, als bei den Christen und in dem Gebrauche von Rosenkränzen, da es feststeht, dass die Inder bei ihren Gebeten sich der *axamâlâ* genannten Kränze bedienten.'

[2] Lama = 'a superior,' from *la* (bla) 'above.' The more accurate form would be *blama*. Schott, p. 32, n. 2.

[3] This Lama was the preceptor of Tsong Kaba, who founded the monastery of Khaldan, near Lhassa, in 1409, and introduced the new ritual, after he had overcome the scruples of the Grand Lama. See Wilson, *Journ. of the As. Soc.* XVI. 263.

Plus tard les conquêtes des enfans de Tchingkis y appelèrent des étrangers de tous les pays ; des Géorgiens, des Arméniens, des Russes, des Français, des musulmans, envoyés par le khalife de Bagdad ; des moines catholiques, chargés de missions importantes par le souverain pontife et par St. Louis. Ces derniers portaient avec eux des ornemens d'église, des autels, des reliques *pour veoir*, dit Joinville, *se ils pourraient attraire* ces gens *à nostre créance.* Ils célébrèrent les cérémonies de la religion devant les princes tartares. Ceux-ci leur donnèrent un asile dans leur tentes, et permirent qu'on élevât des chapelles jusque dans l'enceinte de leurs palais. Un archevêque italien, établi dans la ville impériale par ordre de Clément V., y avait bâti une église, où trois cloches appelaient les fidèles aux offices, et il avait couvert les murailles de peintures représentant des sujets pieux. Chrétiens de Syrie, romains, schismatiques, musulmans, idolâtres, tous vivaient mêlés et confondus à la cour des empereurs mongols, toujours empressés d'accueillir de nouveaux cultes, et même de les adopter, pourvu qu'on n'exigeât de leur part aucune conviction, et surtout qu'on ne leur imposât aucune contrainte. On sait que les Tartares passaient volontiers d'une secte à l'autre, embrassaient aisément la foi, et y renonçaient de même pour retomber dans l'idolâtrie. C'est au milieu de ces variations que fut fondé au Tibet le nouveau siége des patriarches bouddhistes. Doit-on s'étonner qu'intéressés à multiplier le nombre de leurs sectateurs, occupés à donner plus de magnificence au culte, ils se soient approprié quelques usages liturgiques, quelques-unes de ces pompes étrangères qui attiraient la foule; qu'ils aient introduit même quelque chose de ces institutions de l'Occident que les ambassadeurs du khalife et du souverain pontife leur vantaient également, et qui les circonstances les disposaient à imiter? La coïncidence des lieux, celle des époques autorisent cette conjecture, et mille particularités, que je ne puis indiquer ici, la convertiraient en démonstration.'

These observations of Abel-Rémusat, it will be noticed, are all intended to apply especially to points of ritual; and so far we may agree with him in thinking that an imitative people were at such an epoch not unlikely to adopt the usages of western missionaries: but when other writers, following in his footsteps, argue on this ground that *all* external resemblances whatever between the pagan East and Christian West are similarly due to Latin and Nestorian missions of the Middle Ages, they enter, as it seems to me, upon a hopeless undertaking.

PART III.

RELIGIONS OF CHINA.

RELIGIONS OF CHINA.

'Behold, these shall come from far; and lo, these from the north and from the west; and these from the land of Sinim.'

A REVIEWER of the second Part of 'CHRIST AND OTHER MASTERS' put on record his conviction that 'the very centre of the controversy' now waging between the Christian faith and its assailants is the point I have been hitherto attempting to elucidate. 'Discussions of particular doctrines are,' he argues, 'secondary to this deeper question,' touching the main relations of the Gospel to other ancient systems, and the cogency of claims, which it advances, not as a philosophy among philosophies, but rather as the living and life-giving 'Word of God,' which offers a continuous attestation of its supernatural origin by working mightily in them that believe (1 Thess. ii. 13). Assured that all solutions of this problem, which deserve the name of rational and philosophic, must materially depend upon the clearness of our insight into the distinctive genius of each system, or, in other words, involve an accurate knowledge both of what it really was and what it actually achieved, I shall endeavour in the following pages to conduct the reader through a fresh department of heathendom, selecting for review those wild and multifarious creeds which flourished in localities remote from the original haunts of man, and in all likelihood completely foreign to the sphere of Hebrew influence. When the mind is once familiarized with characteristic principles of such outlying systems, we shall find ourselves more able to discuss the several points of correspondence which are said to have resulted from long years of intercourse between the earlier Hebrews and Egyptians on the one side, or the later Hebrews and the Medes and Persians on the other.

As I cannot hope to furnish satisfactory reports from all the single provinces of ancient heathendom, my plan is to devote one special chapter of this Part to China, a second to Mexico, and a third to some of the more dominant islands of the Eastern and Southern Oceans, in the hope that by so doing the important phases of religious sentiment will each in turn have been submitted to the reader for reflection and comparison.

If ever it be possible to ascertain the independent workings of the natural heart of man, such knowledge may especially be sought in regions now before us. There whatever forms of civilisation have existed seem the native and, as one might think, spontaneous products of the soil. The glimmerings of tradition are more faint and more unsteady. They who knowing God refuse to glorify Him as God, are eventually abandoned to their own devices; and amid the anxious gropings after truth which follow that terrific obscuration of the moral consciousness, we see a fresh exemplification of the sacred story, where the younger son, having gathered all together, takes his journey into a far country; yet too often when the land of his adoption has been stricken by some 'mighty famine,' none is found to answer his despairing cry for bread, nor fill the aching void within him.

There are still, indeed, sufficient indications in the darkest depths of heathendom, that man is everywhere the self-same being, open to the same appeals, and giving utterance to the same emotions, conscious of incurable discord in the elements of his moral nature, lifting up his heart to heaven, and yearning after some emancipation from the iron yoke of evil. Hence it is that in all creeds whatever certain points emerge where natural and revealed religion seem to touch, and where they almost promise to embrace each other. Yet on close examination nearly all the chief suggestions which they offer in the hope of healing and exalting our depraved humanity are found to be divergent, not to say antagonistic. They proceed from very different thoughts of God, of man, and of the universe; and therefore differ both as to the meaning and the method of redemption. If I here abstain from dwelling largely on these numerous contrasts and divergencies, the reader who possesses any adequate knowledge of Christianity will hardly fail, in passing, to remedy the defect. For such a class of persons, it should be remembered, I am now engaged in writing. It is not my leading object to conciliate the more thoughtful minds of heathendom in favour of the Christian faith. However laudable that task may be, however fitly it may occupy the highest and the keenest intellect of persons who desire to further the advance of truth and holiness among our heathen fellow-subjects, there are difficulties nearer home, which may in fairness be regarded as possessing prior claims on the attention of a Christian advocate. My aim, accordingly, will be to shew by strict analysis of ancient systems that as none of these could possibly have given birth to Christianity, so neither does the knowledge thence derivable of what has been attained by man's unaided efforts warrant a presumption that any merely human agent could originate that system of harmonious mysteries, whose life and centre is the Crucifixion of the 'Lord from heaven.'

I may also be allowed to add, that in the present chapters the more thoughtful reader will not fail to recognise the proper tendency of certain current speculations, which are recommended to us on the ground that they accord entirely with the last discoveries of science, and embody the deliberate verdicts of the oracle within us. Notwithstanding all that has been urged in their behalf, those theories are little more than a return to long-exploded errors, a resuscitation of extinct volcanoes; or at best they merely offer to introduce among us an array of civilizing agencies, which after trial in other countries have been all found wanting. The governing class of China, for example, have been long familiar with the metaphysics of Spinosa[1]. They have also carried out the social principles of M. Comte upon the largest possible scale. For ages they have been 'what people of the present day are wishing to become in Europe[2],'—with this difference only, that the heathen legislator who had lost all faith in God attempted to redress the wrongs and elevate the moral status of his subjects, by the study of political science or devising some new scheme of general sociology: while the 'positive' philosopher of the present day who has relapsed into the same positions is in every case rejecting a religious system which has proved itself the mightiest of all civilisers, and the constant champion of the rights and dignity of man. He offers in the stead of Christianity a specious phase of neo-paganism, by which the nineteenth century after Christ may be assimilated to the golden age of Mencius and Confucius; or, in other words, may consummate its intellectual freedom, and attain the highest pinnacle of human progress, by reverting to a state of childhood and of moral imbecility.

[1] Cf. Hegel, *Phil. of Hist.* p. 69, Lond. 1857.

[2] Huc, *Le Christianisme en Chine*, &c. I. 358, Paris, 1857.

CHAPTER I.

Religions of China.

'Die Chinesische Religion ist eine schlechterdings selbstgemachte des natürlichen Menschen, so ungestört von fremden Einflüssen, wie keine andere. Wir dürfen uns daher auch nicht wundern, wenn wir in ihr merkwürdige Berührungs-punkte mit den Lehren eines modernen Heidenthums unter christlichen Völkern finden.'

Antiquity of Chinese civilization: its permanence and diffusion. Isolation of the Chinese: their characteristics: contrast with the Hindú. Their traditions: religious phases.

§ 1. *Confucianism. The sacred books:* Yih-king; Shoo-king; She-king: Le-ke. *Intellectual activity. Influence of Choo-he. The Emperor: king, priest, and penitent. Worship of heaven, and of earth: of genii and demons: hero-worship: goddess-worship: worship of ancestors. Idea of God. Was the oldest creed of China theistic, or worship of Nature? Ethics and politics. Philosophy of the Absolute. Dualism:* Le *and* Ke; Yang *and* Yin. *Theory of man. Antagonism to Christianity.*

§ 2. *Tao-ism, or School of the Fixed Way. Lao-tse: supernatural attributes ascribed to him: primitive account of him: his travels. The* Tao-te-king. *Real meaning of the Tao. How far resembling the God of Christians. Alleged doctrine of the Trinity. Moral system. Book of Rewards and Punishments. Actual condition of the Sect.*

§ 3. *Fo-ism, or Chinese Buddhism. Introduction of Buddhism into China. Varieties of Buddhism. Fo-ism, and Lama-ism. How far Buddhism prevails in China. Why the primitive Buddhism was unacceptable. Monasticism in Tibet. Fo-ism without a regular hierarchy. Hierarchy of Tibet. Lama-ism and Mediæval Christianity. Doctrine of hereditary incarnations. Divergence of Fo-ism and Lama-ism from primitive Buddhism. New theology in Nepál and Tibet. Fo-ist objects of worship: Manju-śrí: Kwan-shi-in: O-me-to. Apparent resemblance to Christianity. Civilizing power of primitive Buddhism: its ethical character. The last hours of Hiuan-Thsang; contrasted with the last hours of Bede.*

If China were regarded simply as one spacious hive of human beings, all proceeding with instinctive art and order to fulfil the various tasks prescribed by the superior powers, the investigation of successive phases in its mental history might well attract the interest and excite the musings both of statesmen and philanthropists. They see unrolled before them the eventful annals of an empire whose prodigious population far outnumbers that of all the Indo-European family.

But inquiries such as we are prosecuting in these chapters will have stronger and more sacred claims upon the sympathies of every philosophic Christian. China, he remembers, is the birthplace of the oldest institutions known to history, the centre of the most enduring civilisation in the world. However much of wild pretension has in course of time been pruned away by critics from the semi-legendary archives of most other countries, those of China, it is still conceded even by the more sagacious of our modern scholars, have not suffered in their passage through the literary ordeal. There is reason to believe that portions of her present territory were the seat of thriving and of fully organised communities not less than two thousand years before the Christian era[1]. It is true, indeed, that of surviving records none may in their extant form be much anterior to the birth of Herodotus. It may be questioned also whether the Chinese have ever had a series of regular annals stretching to a more remote antiquity than the commencement of the Greek Olympiads or the first Assyrian conquests in the Holy Land; but inasmuch as all accounts which have been left us, from that epoch downwards, bear a perfectly historic impress, it is probable that fragmentary notices of ancient China which profess to have come orally from very primitive ages, are, at least in all their broader outlines, worthy of the credit which has been awarded to them by the modern Sinologue. Before the name of the Middle Kingdom had been ever uttered in the learned halls and avenues of the Athenian Academy; before the eagle of the Roman legions, thirsting after universal sway, had tried its earliest flight across the Central Apennines; before the English of that ancient world, the colonising merchants of Phœnicia, had unfurled their sail upon the waves of the Atlantic, and trafficked in the precious metals on the coasts of Albion and Ierne,—large communities of settlers stretching far across the plateau of Upper Asia were already living under the patriarchal rule of great and powerful princes. Chinese ports

[1] See, for instance, Prof. Neumann's paper in the *Journal Asiatique* (1834), tome XIV. pp. 50 sq.; and Prichard's *Researches*, IV. 476—480. Gutzlaff, in like manner, dates the commencement of the historical period from the accession of the Hëa dynasty B.C. 2207: *Chinese History*, I. 75.

were even then frequented by adventurous traders from Ceylon, from India, from the Persian Gulf. A knowledge of Chinese astronomy found its way beyond the mountains and took root in northern Hindústán[1]. The products of the almost fabulous industry of China had established their reputation in countries lying farther to the west; nay, cups of Chinese porcelain, inscribed with her peculiar symbols, had been buried in the ancient sepulchres of Egypt[2]. Or, looking from our modern point of view, we find that ages after the distinctive nationality alike of Egypt and Phœnicia is obliterated, or absorbed in that of their oppressors; when both Nineveh and Babylon are swept away, and other races strange in tongue and stranger still in spirit are exploring the vast pile of ruins and are bent on disinterring one by one the trophies of the former masters of the eastern world, few changes have come over the ideas, the habits, or the institutions of the Middle Kingdom. China is China still. Her arts, her laws, her customs, the more sacred and more classic portion of her writings, most of all her marvellously characteristic language in its various dialects, continue to be everywhere diffused[3]; while far beyond the proper limits of her empire she impresses the peculiar genius of her policy and civilisation, from the borders of Siberia to the snowy chain of Shang-gan-Alin and the easternmost extremity of Japan. It is computed that the circle of Chinese influence at the present day embraces a population of not less than four hundred millions of human beings.

We cannot urge, indeed, that China has been utterly exempted from all foreign perturbations. The great wave of Huns, which propagating itself beyond the Don and Danube, had ultimately, under Attila, produced confusion in the capital of the Roman world, originated in the upper valley of the Hoangho, from whence it had been forced in new directions by the vigorous unity of Chinese rulers; and at last, when their dominions were invaded, and in part subdued, by hordes of

[1] Lassen, *Ind. Alterth.* I. 742.

[2] Gfrörer, *Urgesch. des menschlichen Geschlechts*, p. 214, Schaffhausen, 1855, in his allusion to this fact, exclaims most naturally, 'Welcher Blick in die graue Urzeit öffnet sich uns hier!' The subject is discussed at length in Sir John F. Davis's *China*, II. 72 sq. Lond. 1841.

[3] A few mountaineers, however, still continue to hold out against the civilisation of the great mass of the Chinese: Prichard, IV. 487 sq. According to Duhalde, there cited, the unconquered Miao-sse 'have not adopted the religion of the Lama, but still remain devoted to the superstition which appears to have been the primitive one in all eastern Asia, namely, that termed *Shamanism*:' see above, pp. 261, sq.

Mongols and Mandshurs, it is remarkable that like the Visigoths and Lombards, who ravaged all the fairest plains of southern Europe, the invader found the reigning civilisation far too strong for him; he was himself led captive; he bowed before the ancient language and majestic institutions of the very nation he had spoiled. The Chinese empire has moreover experienced the disturbing influence of religious controversy, and a large proportion of the people have been fascinated by a creed whose birthplace was in central India: yet here again the genius of the Chinese state-religion proved itself so dominant that no sensible changes have been thus effected in any part of the political or social machinery.

And corresponding to the wide extent of China, to the permanence of her institutions, and the consciousness of her superior rank among the Asiatic tribes, has been her tendency to look on others with indifference or contempt, and her unconquerable isolation. Long before the inroads of the Tatars made it necessary to protect her people by building the Great Wall, a spiritual barrier was in process of erection. China grew into a kind of homogeneous world within herself: the China-man was virtually cut off in sympathy from every other nation, just as much as if his lot were cast in some distant planet. The Middle Kingdom was and is to him the centre of the universe; all others, they of the 'Great Western Ocean[1]' not excepted, being mere extremities or pendants. Hence had sprung not only the distinct and thoroughly national character of almost everything which called itself Chinese, but also the monotonous air pervading every single feature of that nationality. Arts, manners, and religion in so far as it is really indigenous, appear to have been cast in precisely the same mould. As in the physical characteristics of the nation, the old traits almost universally recur, the same dark eye with its oblique expression, the same black hair, the same tawny skin, so in their mental temperament and moral qualities the uniformity is no less manifest. As a people the Chinese are shrewd and clever, calculating, sordid, plodding, and prosaic[2], enterprising,

[1] A specimen of Chinese impressions respecting Europeans (who are called the people of 'Ta-se-yang,' = 'the Great Western Ocean,') may be seen in Prof. Neumann's *Preface* to his version of the Chinese *History of the Pirates*, pp. xxii. sq.

[2] 'A partir de l'époque historique, on ne rencontre plus que ce qu'on pourrait appeler de la prose, et du sens commun.' Pauthier, *Chine*, p. 43, Paris, 1839.

fraudulent, and gambling, strong in worldly wisdom, wanting in religious fervour and in moral sensibility; while, in spite of the unparalleled extent of popular education, all the higher intellectual faculties, with very rare exceptions, have remained from age to age imbecile and inert.

These properties of the China-man are best appreciated on contrasting him for a moment with his Hindú neighbour[1]. In the Áryan race, as early as their first descent on northern India, the imagination is ever asserting its predominance. Their favourite mythes are all of a peculiar wildness and exuberance; they revel in the vague, the vast, the allegorical, the shadowy, the mysterious. In China, on the contrary, imagination exercises very little influence. Relics of the early poetry, in which, if ever, we might hope to trace the operation of this class of faculties, are seldom more than tame and frigid representations of ordinary life. Excepting one important school[2]

[1] We have a curious account of the Chinese and their ancient civilisation, written by one of themselves (in the *Vie et Voyages de Hiouen-Thsang*, pp. 230, 231; ed. Julien, Paris, 1853):

The Buddhists of India wished to detain this pilgrim, urging that the Buddha was not born in China, and that the Chinese were *Mie-li-tch'e* (Mléch-chhas, 'barbarians'). It was also added, that 'les vues des habitants sont étroites et leurs souillures profondes.' Then comes the answer of the China-man:

'Le roi de la loi [*i.e.* the Buddha] a fondé sa doctrine pour qu'elle se répandit en tous lieux; quel est l'homme qui voudrait s'en abreuver tout seul et délaisser ceux qui ne l'ont pas encore reçue? Or, dans ce royaume (en Chine), les magistrats sont graves et les lois sont observées avec respect. Le prince se distingue par sa haute vertu et ses sujets par leur loyauté; les pères par leur affection, les fils par leur pieuse obéissance. On y estime l'humanité et la justice, et l'on place au premier rang les vieillards et les sages. Ce n'est pas tout: la science n'a pas de mystères pour eux; leur pénétration égale celle des esprits; le ciel leur sert de modèle et ils savent calculer les mouvements des sept chartés (du soleil, de la lune et des cinq planètes). Ils ont inventé (toutes sortes) d'instrumens, divisé les saisons de l'année et découvert les propriétés cachées des six tons de la musique. C'est pour cela qu'ils ont pu expulser ou soumettre les animaux sauvages, toucher et faire descendre les démons et les esprits, calmer (les influences contraires du) *In* et du *Yang* [the male and female principles in nature, the harmony of which is essential to the well-being of creation], et procurer la paix et le bonheur à tous les êtres.' In the *Laws of Manu* (x. 43, 44) the *Chínas* are reckoned among those Kshatriyas, who had been debased through their neglect of sacred rites and through their want of intercourse with Bráhmans.

[2] This school, the *Tao-sse* (respecting whom, see below, § 2) had a mythology in many points resembling that of the Greeks and Romans. A judicious writer on Chinese institutions in the *Nou-*

whose Indian tastes and predilections are continually betrayed, the Chinese have no primitive mythus, corresponding to the vivid and romantic imagery in which different tribes of man had veiled their worship of external nature, or idealised the legends of their simple forefathers. All in China is more commonplace, more tangible, more practical, more real. 'What the Chinese cannot comprehend with the natural understanding exists not for them, and is an object of their derision.' Hence the Bráhman comes to be esteemed by learned followers of Confucius a mere dreamer and fanatic; while in his opinion they are abject and plebeian spirits, selfish, sordid, and materialistic. He disparages the world around him on the plea that it is only an illusion, acting as the transient mirror of the supernatural and enduring: they as absolutely yield themselves to the dominion of the seen and temporal; they long for nothing higher.

On proceeding to investigate the early history of 'these utilitarians of the ancient world,' their own traditions[1] uniformly point us backward to the mountains of the west,—the sources of those mighty streams that fertilize the whole of central China, and the spot to which the memory afterwards reverted as the paradise of primitive man and as the cradle of all natural and preternatural being[2]. When the Chinese issued from their native highlands they appear to have first occupied the numerous valleys of the Kwan-lun, and most writers on the subject have conjectured, from the simple genius of their language, its monosyllabic forms, its want of organisation, and its very limited affinities with foreign idioms[3], that their isolation from the rest of men was dated from a very distant period. In the earliest dawn of history, we see them like the other shepherd-tribes of central Asia, wandering onward with their eyes directed to the pastures of the south and east; yet in the meanwhile little higher in the scale of civilisation than the

veau Journal Asiatique (1854), v. série, tome IV. p. 314, says that he has read some of the Tao-sse dramas, and found in them the fable of Epimenides, the fable of Niobe, the fable of Venus issuing from the sea after Saturn had thrown into it a magical composition, the representation of Neptune armed with a trident, &c.

[1] Prichard, IV. 478 sq.; Gfrörer, pp. 217 sq. The latter is of opinion that the Chinese have all sprung from a Turanian stock.

[2] Cf. above, pp. 211 sq. on the Mahá-Méru of the ancient Áryans, corresponding to this legend. Other features of the Chinese paradise will be found in Lüken's *Traditionen*, p. 67, Münster, 1856.

[3] Prichard, IV. 481: cf. the 'Introduction,' prefixed to M. Biot's edition of the *Tcheou-Li*, Paris, 1851, pp. v. sq.

Bushmen of the present century[1]. Their dress consisted of the skins of animals; their food of roots and insects. From this depth of barbarism the legends tell us how they finally emerged at the command of early emperors,—a representation savouring, it is true, of ages when the state-machinery was fully organised, but well adapted to convey the notion, that material progress flowed in their case from administrative ability. When due allowance has been also made for some of the ideal excellencies ascribed to early kings and statesmen, it is obvious that the march of ancient China in acquiring all the arts of settled life was most extraordinarily rapid. The whole empire seems as if it sprang directly from a savage to a civilised condition by one mighty bound; but, having exhausted all its elasticity in this single effort, had been afterwards reduced as rapidly into a stiff and spiritless automaton. The borders of the Chinese empire were at first indeed comparatively narrow. In the seventh century before Christ they had extended only so far as to embrace five out of the present eighteen districts; while beyond them and around them lay a multitude of barbarous people whom it was their object to subdue and humanize. As early, however, as the second century of the Christian era, the huge system of Chinese administration had received its finishing touch. The emperor was everywhere regarded as the centre and moving principle of the whole machinery: government-schools, which had been planted long before, were now enlarged and multiplied in every quarter: while literary merit, tested by competitive examinations[2] in a number of accredited books, became the single passport to promotion in the public service.

With these cursory observations on the state of ancient China, I proceed to notice the peculiar forms and phases under which religion has been there diffused among the people.

The number of such forms is three:

1. The State-religion, as re-modelled by Confucius.
2. Tao-ism, or School of the fixed Way.
3. Fo-ism, or Chinese Buddhism.

§ 1. *Confucianism.*

The civilisation of ancient China, as of other Eastern states[3], is founded mainly on one class of writings, which are held to be

1 Gutzlaff, I. 124 sq. Pauthier, pp. 33 sq.

2 Meadows, *The Chinese and their Rebellions*, pp. 402 sq. Lond. 1856.

3 Differing, in this respect, from

deserving of especial honour. These the China-man entitles *king*, or, with peculiar emphasis, 'the books.' As might perhaps have been predicted from the general texture and constitution of his mind, he never thinks of God as of a Being who reveals Himself objectively to man, and therefore manifests no faith in any kind of supernatural religion. Yet the Chinese seldom fail to draw distinctions between the authority of the *king* and every other class of ancient writings. The 'holy man[1]' (*shing-jin*) is said to have possessed instinctively the power of diving to the bottom of metaphysical discussions, and of yielding a spontaneous obedience to the promptings of the pure and perfect nature he inherited in common with the rest of men. His teachings therefore on their first enunciation are all absolutely true: they rank far higher than the works of those who are entitled 'sages' (*heen-jin*), but who only rise to full perception of religious truth, and practise all the higher virtues, after painful and assiduous cultivation.

In this chain of 'holy men' the foremost link was Fuh-he, the reputed founder of Chinese civilisation and author of the oldest of the 'sacred' books,—the *Yih-king*[2]. It is not my purpose to insist at present on the legend where Fuh-he, escaping from the waters of a deluge, re-appears as the first man at the production of a renovated world, nor on the fact that he is there attended by *seven* companions, his wife, his three sons, and three daughters[3], by whose intermarriage the whole circle of the universe is finally completed. His work is even more mysterious than his personal history. 'The wisest among the Chinese have entered this labyrinth, but only to come out of it

Greece and Rome, where, in the absence of 'sacred' books, there was a much freer development of human thought. Pauthier seems to be of opinion that the *king* bear a strong resemblance to the *Védas* in the general character of their contents ('non pour le contenu mais pour l'espèce du contenu'); and adds that this conformity 'n'est peut-être pas purement due au hasard.'

[1] Meadows, as above, pp. 347, 348.

[2] The best edition 'ex interpret. Regis' is that of Mohl, Stuttg. 1834—1839. This annotator was Wăn-wang, 'the literary prince' and founder of the Chow dynasty, who during his imprisonment (B.C. 1144—1142) arranged the diagrams of Fuh-he on different principles. His rearrangement and expositions, as completed by his son, Chow-kung, became the text of the earliest of the Chinese sacred, or canonical, books.

[3] See Mr. Mc Clatchie's paper in the *Journal of the Asiatic Society* (1856), XVI. 403, 404, where it is contended that in Fuh-he and his family we may recognise Noah and the second parents of the human race: cf. Gutzlaff, I. 129, 130, Wuttke, II. 100, 101.

more bewildered.' It may be described as an expanded form of ancient and recondite speculations on the nature of the universe in general, the harmonious action of the elements and periodic changes of creation. These ideas were primarily expressed by means of eight peculiar diagrams (*kwa*), which constitute the basis of natural philosophy as well as of religion. Yet the work professing to unriddle all the mysteries which are believed to have been latent in those venerable signs, was treated as a series of enigmas in the classic age of Chinese literature; and so capricious were the expositions to which the *Yih-king* was submitted, that instead of being as at first a cosmological essay it became eventually a standard treatise on ethical philosophy.

The second of the Chinese 'sacred' books is called the *Shoo-king*[1], which, as more historic and intelligible than its predecessor, has been everywhere esteemed the chief authority in tracing out the spiritual development of the Middle Kingdom. It commences with the reign of Yaou, one of the very earliest emperors, and stretches onward to the life-time of Confucius: while the moral and political maxims it contains have formed the text on which the ingenuity and erudition of the native commentators have been exercised for ages. The vast importance of the *Shoo-king* in directing the national mind of China was never more evinced than in the desperate efforts to suppress it during the reign of Che-hwang-te, the scourge of the barbaric Huns and the projector of the Great Wall (about 240 B.C.). This able tyrant, anxious to uproot the old traditions and to render everything Chinese dependent on his beck, had spared the copies of the enigmatical *Yih-king;* but all other books, both secular and sacred, had, with very rare exceptions, been committed to the flames[2].

The *She-king*[3] is the third authoritative document that serves to illustrate the general course of Chinese civilisation. It comprises 311 odes and other lyrics, for the most part moral in their tone, and sometimes breathing in the midst of tender sentiments and deep regrets a freshness and simplicity entirely characteristic of the earliest ages of mankind. The ancient bard appears more conscious than the modern China-man of

[1] See *Le Chou-king*, ed. De Guignes, Paris, 1770; and *Livres Sacrés de l'Orient*, par Pauthier, Paris, 1842. Gutzlaff, speaking of the *Shoo-king*, says that 'it forms the great text-book, upon which all Chinese literati have expatiated:' (I. 127).

[2] Gutzlaff, I. 223, 224: Meadows, pp. 333, 334.

[3] See *Chi-king, sive Liber Carminum*, ed. Mohl, Stuttg. 1830.

some corruption cleaving to the human family as a whole; and here and there we trace an ardent aspiration after some more lofty stage of being, which, as time went over, was completely stifled by the growing love of pelf, and the incurable self-sufficiency engendered in the heart of the Chinese.

Inferior only in authority to works already mentioned, is the Chinese book of rites and manners, *Le-ke*[1], which, prescribing as it did for all relationships of life and all the various orders of society, established everywhere unnatural stiffness and fastidious decorum. Other writings[2], nearly if not altogether standing on the same superior level, might be added to this series; but in it we have the principal monuments of the older race of 'holy men,' and therefore the great bases of all Chinese history and ethics, politics, philosophy, and religion.

It appears, however, highly probable that several changes were effected in the ancient creed of China during the fifth and sixth centuries before the promulgation of the Gospel. In Kong-fu-tse (a name which missionaries from the west have Latinized into Confucius), we behold the 'prince' of Chinese 'wisdom,' or the second founder of the state-religion; and as all the ancient documents were then submitted to inspection and revision[3], it is rather to Confucius than to Fuh-he, or to other ancient worthies, that the ruling forms of civilisation in the Middle Kingdom must be ultimately referred.

The labours of Confucius constituted a fresh epoch in the mental progress of the Indo-Chinese world. He comes upon the theatre of history soon after the demise of a reformer, who in various points is most unlike him. Śákya-muni died, as we saw reason to believe[4], in 543 B.C.: Confucius was born in 551

[1] See *Le Li-Ki, ou Mêmorial des Rites*, ed. Callery, Turin, 1853.

[2] It is usual to speak of the four works above noticed, together with the *Tsun-tsew*, (an historical composition of Confucius), as the Five Sacred writings (*Woo-king*): see Mohl's *Pref.* to the *Yih-king*, pp. 79 sq. But the *Ta-hëo* (or 'great doctrine,' ed. Pauthier, Paris, 1837), the *Chung-Yung* (ed. Abel-Rémusat), the *Lun-yu* (ed. Schott), and the *Hi-tse*, all emanating directly from the school of Confucius, though not always written by himself, are held to be co-ordinate authorities in favour of the state-religion. Next in order stand the works of Mencius (Meng-tse), who died about 317 B.C. His various treatises are edited by M. Stanislas Julien, Paris, 1824.

[3] Meadows, p. 332, who remarks: 'It is well known that he expressly repudiated portions of the ancient literature, as containing doctrines adverse to the views which he held and strove to diffuse. The names only of some celebrated ancient books, one dating from the times of Fuh-he himself, have been preserved.'

[4] Above, pp. 154, 155.

B. C. Addicted in his early boyhood to the study of the ancient records[1], he acquired a habit of contrasting the disorders and demoralisation of his age with the ideal pictures they presented of the primitive line of Chinese kings. The heavenly maxims of a Yaou, the stern and simple virtues of a Shun, the perfect system of administration that had characterised the golden age of Yu, these all excited the unbounded admiration of Confucius; and at the early age of three-and-twenty he conceived the thought of leading back his fellow-subjects to the ancient models. It was the predominant force of this idea that afterwards impelled Confucius during his long life to visit several courts of Chinese princes, among whom the country had been subdivided, and in some few cases he was actually allowed to try his grand experiment as a political and social reformer. But his course as he advanced was very far from prosperous. The importance given to virtue as the proper basis of good government exposed him to the scorn of some and the malignity of others. The last words he uttered savour not of hope and exultation, but of bitter disappointment. During his life, however, an enthusiastic band of followers had begun to cluster round him; and after rearing his modest tomb upon the banks of the Soo river, they proceeded with untiring industry to methodise his principles and circulate his writings. 'My doctrine' he had constantly declared[2] 'is that which all men ought to follow. It is the doctrine of Yaou and of Shun. As for my way of teaching, it is perfectly simple. I cite the patterns left us by the ancients. I counsel men to read the sacred books (*king*), and I require them to form the habit of reflecting on the various maxims there preserved.' Accordingly the principal ground on which Confucianism has ever rested its appeal is narrow, and the ruling spirit of the system cautious and conservative. It promised that the old traditions of the country should be sacredly collected and as sacredly embalmed; and very much of the success it ultimately won is due to its profession of respect for social and political precepts current in the governing class, and the effectual aids it thereby rendered in maturing and consolidating the nationality of China.

But although the fashion was to eulogize the founder of this system as the last and brightest of the Chinese 'holy men,' and

[1] See the ample sketch of his life and writings in Pauthier's *Chine*, pp. 121—186. The collected works of Confucius were published, with an English translation, by Marshman at Serampore, in 1809; and with a German translation at Berlin (1826-1832), under the editorship of Dr Schott.

[2] In Pauthier, p. 134.

though an obvious tendency of all the 'reformations' he promoted was to deaden the activity of the human intellect, and make the future ages a mere reproduction of the past, we are not justified in arguing that the mind of the Chinese did actually subside at once into a state of apathy and torpor[1]. On the contrary it seems as if the fluctuations of religious thought were not less numerous in Peking than in the eastern capital of the Cæsars.

Taking no account of those great movements which ran counter to the state-religion, and as such will be considered separately, we find that under the nineteenth or Sung dynasty (extending from A.D. 960 to A.D. 1279), the general tone of Chinese 'orthodoxy' had experienced an important modification. As the earlier changes synchronized with various tokens of activity in the western world, Confucius being the contemporary of Pythagoras and his greatest follower Mencius the contemporary of Aristotle, so the epoch that beheld the first advances of the Christian schoolmen and the growth of speculative Judaism in writers like Maimonides, was also that in which the doctors of the Middle Kingdom laboured to evolve a definite and coherent system of philosophy from the writings of their ancient sages. Whether traceable, as some conjecture[2], to the agency of printing which had been invented and established with imperial sanction as early as the middle of the tenth century; or whether, as might also be conjectured, some at least of the new impulse was communicated to the governing classes by the rapid growth of Buddhism and the consequent infusion of a Hindú spirit, there can be no doubt that China was producing a new race of scholars marked by greater aptitude for metaphysical speculations. Their philosophizings, it is true, were based on the received traditions of the ancient writers, with whom at every turn they claim a spiritual fellowship[3]; yet all

[1] Prof. Neumann's remark is perhaps exaggerated, but there is no reason for doubting its substantial truth: 'Das Mittelreich zeigt nicht weniger *geistige* und politische Revolutionen als andere Theile der Welt.' See his valuable contribution on 'Die Natur- und Religions-philosophie der Chinesen,' in Illgen's *Zeitschrift für die historische Theologie* (1837), VII. 19.

[2] *e.g.* Meadows p. 334, who remarks: 'The originative capacities of many minds, which would otherwise have lain dormant in unlettered ignorance, must have been brought [by the cheapening of books] into fruitful action in the fields of philosophical speculation and historical inquiry.'

[3] The following clear testimony is from the philosopher, Choo-he (Tschu-hi), translated by Neumann, as above, p. 21: 'Kong [Confucius], Meng [Mencius], Tsching und Tschang [both of whom flourished 1000 years after Christ] sind die

had grown more conscious that in order for the state-religion to retain its old supremacy and crush or counteract the innovations now rampant in all quarters, it must coin a more scholastic terminology, must grapple with a harder class of questions, and must speak out far more plainly not on matters of finance, economy, and etiquette, but on the nature of the world and its inhabitants, and the true relation of the seen and temporal to the Absolute and All-embracing.

The philosopher who guided this great movement to a prosperous close was Choo-he, termed by European scholars the Aristotle of the Middle Kingdom, and revered by all the governing class of China as 'the prince of sciences.' The commentaries he has left behind on all the Chinese classics are a fraction only of his multitudinous writings; yet in them especially it was that Choo-he shaped the course which Chinese thought has very generally followed from his day to our own[1]. All statements on religious subjects which are not supported by appeals to his authority are branded as injurious and heretical; and since the millions who present themselves as candidates for office under government are constantly employed in learning his works by heart, it is most obvious that the influence he still exercises, whether as a guiding or a cramping agent, is incalculably vast. If the intelligence of China only reached its prime when first awakened by Confucius, it was passing through the phase of manhood, if not verging to a state of absolute senility, when Choo-he breathed his last in A.D. 1200.

What, then, may be deemed the leading features in the practical working of Confucianism, a system planted, there is reason for believing, in the twilight of the world's history but perfected as late as the concession of our Magna Charta?

In that system, as administered in every age, the emperor of China is the foremost object. Mounted on the 'dragon throne,' as it is called, he is the mainspring of the whole machinery, whether his empire be regarded as a civil or religious institution. The laws indeed distinguish very clearly between the private and official status of the emperors; for as

vier berühmten Stützen unserer Lehre. Die Weisheit und die Untersuchung des Grundes aller Dinge ruht auf diesem festen Fundament: alle jene andern Lehrer haben sicherlich geirrt. Nur diese vier verehrt man als die Grundpfeiler der Weisheit; ihre Entfernung [in der Zeit] von Fohi [Fuh-he] will wenig sagen: *sie verbindet das gleiche Princip.*'

1 See Neumann, as above, pp. 22 sq., Meadows, pp. 335 sq., and Mc Clatchie in *Journal of As. Soc.* (1856), XVI. 433.

individuals they enjoy a privilege, granted also, with conditions, to their subjects, of choosing for themselves a second or subordinate creed, and emperors have at different times made very different choices[1]. But as every father of a Chinese family is constrained to recognize the state-religion by some special acts of homage, so the emperor himself, officially considered, must be always 'orthodox,' devoted to the maintenance of the sacred books, as well as to the vindication of all ancient usages. These jointly form the rule according to which the various functions of the government must be directed; and so long as any emperor abstains from innovations in performing his public duties, he is honoured as the 'Son of Heaven,' the source and champion of established order, the exponent of mysterious principles which underlie the course of nature, and the organ of some powerful but impersonal energy that lingers round about us and above us. Heaven itself is present in him: he becomes in virtue of that presence a celestial potentate, not only the great chieftain of the Middle Kingdom, but a pattern of ideal excellence for every member of the human family.

It should also be observed that ever since the patriarchal times of Yu[2], the emperor has been invested with a twofold character. He is king and also priest of China: standing in the latter capacity at the head of a peculiar cultus, and declaring of himself in that relation, 'I am one man,' *i.e.* the only being of my kind[3]. As such he only has the privilege of uttering some hereditary form of prayer, and offering a more costly and more potent sacrifice than any other mortal[4]. The large group of mandarins, who form his agents in the task of government, have also, it is true, been each invested with a quasi-sacerdotal power; yet the objects whom they have the right to worship are esteemed of lower dignity,—as genii of the soil, the streams, the mountains; or malignant demons, haunting this or that

[1] Thus, at the present day, the emperor as a private person adheres to Buddhism, which (so to speak) had mounted the imperial throne of China, as far back as the Ming dynasty: while under the Sung monarchs, the Tao-ists were equally in the ascendant. See an interesting article on Chinese institutions in the *Nouveau Journal Asiatique* (1854), IV. 292 sq.

[2] Gutzlaff, I. 142, 143.

[3] See Mr. S. C. Malan's recent volume entitled *Who is God in China?* pp. 186, 187.

[4] 'L'empereur a le droit de sacrifier au Ciel et à la Terre: les seigneurs sacrifient aux dieux tutélaires de l'empire,' &c.' *Li-ki*, ed. Callery, p. 16. It also would appear as though fresh solemnity were given to the imperial sacrifice by offering on some occasions *in the open country*. *Ibid.* pp. 47, 60, 62, 119.

locality; or elements and atmospheric agencies regarded in their nudest form, of wind, of drought, of rain, of lightning or of tempest. Accessories of the mandarinic worship also correspond to this idea of fundamental subordination and derived authority. The emperor, for example, sacrifices at the seat of government in temples which have been devoted to that special use: the mandarins officiate, on the contrary, in the provincial temples. The emperor is attired in sacerdotal vestments of peculiar hue and texture, and embroidered with numerous symbols of the sun, the moon, the planets, to betoken his exalted mission as the Heaven-born pontiff; while the mandarins in acts of public worship still preserve their ordinary dress. To sacrifice aright it is contended that the emperor must undergo a special course of training: he must fast on three consecutive days; he must abstain from every kind of sensual gratification, and in order, as it seems, to check the least intrusion of a secular spirit, he must during those days take no part in the administration of public justice. On the contrary, the mandarins are bound by no such stringent regulations: they appear to act as civil rather than as sacerdotal functionaries. The disparity again is noticeable in the different kinds of sacrifices they are authorised to offer. When the emperor once a year, or in some grand emergency, comes forth to sacrifice, the victim chosen is a goodly ox, and not this merely, but an ox submitted to a searching process of purification[1], with a view, it is believed, of marking more distinctly the exalted nature of the rite and the superior dignity of the object in whose honour it is consumed: while in the various branches of the mandarinic cultus, incense and libations are the common offerings, or if otherwise, anxiety is seldom felt to offer up the costliest victim of its kind.

Yet even where the rites of China are most solemn and most obviously religious in their purport, it is difficult to trace in them a particle of zeal or fervour, least of all the consciousness of personal demerit[2]. The heart-broken ejaculations of

[1] 'Il est assez curieux' says M. Callery (*Li-ki*, p. 63, n. 2) 'que les anciens Chinois aient admis, dans cette circonstance, la nécessité d'une purification, eux qui n'ont jamais attaché à rien aucune de ces idées *de souillure légale si communes chez les peuples sémitiques et chez les Hindous.*'

[2] 'In China trennt keine Sündenschuld die Menschheit von Gott; das menschliche Geschlecht ist nur in vereinzelten Erscheinungen abgewichen; und der Mensch ist ja seinem Wesen nach mit Gott eins, hat kein selbstständiges Dasein Gott gegenüber, ist noch nicht wahrhaft persönlicher Geist, der als solcher auch sündigend von Gott sich lösen könnte.'—Wuttke, II. 63.

the Hebrew penitent, gazing through his tears on symbols of the temple-worship which announce the unapproachable holiness of God and whisper also of His love and placability; the spectral gloom of the ascetic, pining year by year beneath the shadow of some Indian fig-tree, in the hope of torturing out the remnant of his earthly passions, and so hastening the hour of ultimate reabsorption;—these are things entirely foreign to the cold and callous nature of the Chinese. Whenever their great model, the imperial pontiff, offers up the yearly sacrifice to Heaven, it savours less of awe and adoration than of pride and self-complacency: it publishes the fact that harmony continues to subsist as heretofore between celestial and terrestrial powers: it certifies the oneness of the emperor in act and interest with the unseen spirit which pervades the universe and is directing all the fortunes of the Middle Kingdom. An exception to this general statement does exist, however: for, on one or more occasions in the lifetime of an emperor, we see him driven to adopt the lowly posture of the suppliant, and offer a more genuine sacrifice to Heaven. An army of barbarians, for example, hover on the frontiers; or an earthquake threatens to engulf some fertile district; or a pestilence is raging in the capital; or famine rouses and inflames the angry passions of the populace; rivers overflow their margin, crops are blasted, heaven and earth appear at enmity; or, worst of all, some brilliant comet, the precursor of dynastic changes, sheds a baleful light across the firmament. Excited and dismayed by these portentous incidents, the ruler of the Middle Kingdom seems to hesitate for once respecting the validity of his claim to be entitled 'Son of Heaven:' he fears lest, owing to some former negligence or present incapacity, his high commission is about to be withdrawn[1]. The only refuge open to him is in bowing to the terrible scourge by which he is chastised: 'he humbles himself before Heaven and his subjects, by publishing those self-accusatory and repentant documents, which Europeans peruse with surprise and ridicule, but which are wrung from his pride by his fears, and are earnest, trembling efforts to avert the execution of Divine justice[2].'

But the sacrifices offered up to Heaven were not the only rites in which the Chinese emperor was seen invested with pontifical authority. A second temple where he had been long accustomed to officiate was dedicated in honour of the Earth,

[1] Meadows, p. 18.

[2] *Ibid.* p. 19: cf. *Chou-king*, ed. De Guignes, pp. 141, 142.

the great correlative divinity of ancient China. Hope, and joy, and gratitude, were periodically awakened in all quarters by the contemplation of the genial processes of nature. 'Earth,' men felt, 'is bearing in her lap whatever is found needful to our life: as Heaven suspends the luminaries overhead. From Earth we gather riches; to Heaven we look for good examples. It is fitting therefore to evince respect for Heaven, and pay a tribute of gratitude to Earth[1].' In other words, as we shall see hereafter, the Chinese have learned to worship two great Powers or Principles, the former ruling in the active and paternal province of creation, the second in the passive and maternal; and thus constituting, in popular phraseology, the Father and the Mother of all things.

Passing by the manifold objects of religious worship which originated in the non-official creeds of China, we discover that Confucianists have also been accustomed from very early times to offer prayers and sacrifices to a multitude of minor deities. The parent-gods, or Heaven and Earth, were, so to speak, resolved into their various elements, in such a manner that the populace, who felt no inclination to adore them as a whole, might choose some favourite aspect or some special energy of nature, and so concentrate on it the principal share of their devotion.

In this pantheon it would seem as though the highest place, in theory at least, had been allotted to a class of spiritual or quasi-spiritual intelligences, like the genii and the demons of other heathen systems: but the period when such modes of worship took their rise it is impossible to determine. The *Shoo-king*, as edited by Confucius, is not wanting in examples where the early emperors[2] of China sacrificed to spirits of the hills, and rivers, as well as to the shining host of heaven;—thus intimating that the usage may have been a remnant of the old 'Turánian' creed which lingers still as devil-worship, under many of its most appalling aspects, on the plains of upper Asia and apparently among a handful of the Chinese mountaineers. So deeply rooted was it in the heart of the people that Confucius was unable, or unwilling, to dislodge it[3].

But popular as every kind of spirit-worship is in China, she

[1] *Li-ki*, Ch. x. ed. Callery, p. 16.

[2] Gfrörer, pp. 277 sq. Gutzlaff, I. 134.

[3] Medhurst's *China*, pp. 193, 194, Lond. 1857: "When one of his disciples asked him how he was to serve spiritual beings, he replied: 'Not being able to serve men, how can you serve spirits?'" In other words, he chose to speak exclusively on different subjects.

is even more addicted to the worship of departed men. This superstition forms a very prominent article in the creed of the Confucianist. Originally suggested by the feelings of respect, of admiration and of gratitude, it issued in the deification of each man who had stood foremost in promoting the diffusion of some useful art, or who communicated some extraordinary impulse to the intellect of China by the fruitful produce of his pen. Confucius was himself an instance of the latter kind of deification. 'His fame,' writes one of his devoted followers[1], 'overflowed all China like a deluge, and extended to the barbarians. Wherever ships or carriages reach, wherever human strength penetrates, wherever the heavens cover and the earth sustains, wherever the sun and moon shed their light, wherever frost or dew falls, wherever there is blood and breath, there were none who did not approach and honour him: therefore, he is equal to Heaven:' *i.e.* co-ordinate and on a level with the very loftiest form of being. The whole empire is at present dotted over with temples sacred to the memory of Confucius, and a very large number of animal sacrifices (more than sixty thousand) are provided annually by the government for immolation to his manes, in addition to the multitudinous offerings brought by earnest individuals. Similar feelings are betrayed in the devotions which the more accomplished China-man perpetually addresses to Kwan-yu, the model of fidelity, of courage, and of magnanimity: and every age contributes a fresh stock of inmates to the crowded pantheon[2], or displaces this or that divinity whose worship had been general in the age preceding.

Another feature of Chinese mythology, if such it can be called, is the comparative absence from it of licentious stories and revolting rites, like those already noticed[3] in the old religion of Phœnicia, and in fact pervading, more or less, all other dualistic creeds. The goddess-worship of *modern* China (for to

[1] Medhurst's *China*, p. 192. Dr. Medhurst adds: 'Thus have these atheistical people deified the man who taught them that matter was eternal, and that all existences originated in a mere principle.'

[2] See *Li-ki*, ed. Callery, p. 114. A very remarkable instance, shewing that this kind of apotheosis still goes on among them, will be found in the native *History of the Chinese Pirates*, translated by Neumann. We there read (pp. 43, 44) of a brave man, Shaou-yuen, who was killed A.D. 1809, while engaged in defending the citadel of Lanshih: 'The villagers were greatly moved by his excellent behaviour; they erected him a temple, and said prayers before his effigy. It was then known what he meant [when he said] that he should be glorified in the course of the year. Now that twenty years are passed, they even honour him by exhibiting fireworks.'

[3] Above, pp. 69, 70.

this alone our evidence refers) has mainly found expression either in the deification of chaste wives or else in that of virgins. It is stated[1] even that the worship of one particular virgin, who is made the tutelary goddess both of women and of sailors, is the dominant superstition into which the heathenism of China is subsiding at the present day. How far such modification of religious thought may be connected with some slender knowledge of the Roman-catholic version of Christianity, I do not pause to determine.

But the phase of creature-worship, which from very ancient times has constituted the special characteristic of heathenism in China, is the worship of departed ancestors. According, it would seem, with those ideas of clanship and those strong domestic instincts which have ever operated with peculiar force upon the spirit of the China-man, the custom of preserving some memorial of his forefathers grew at last into the custom of paying them religious honours. It was felt that 'as all created beings owe their origin to Heaven,' which is accordingly an object of the deepest veneration, 'so man owes his existence to his ancestors,' and ought to give them worship for this reason[2]. To restore and justify the practice, which had previously been falling to decay, was one of the earliest reformations[3] attempted by Confucius: and at present it has been so universally recognised in China, by the learned and unlearned, by adherents of the state-religion and of non-official creeds[4], that we may point to it as to a common principle which more than any other penetrates the moral life of all Chinese society. 'Building a tomb

[1] The French writer in *Nouveau Journal Asiatique*, as above, p. 295, is of opinion that this worship of the virgin, Kwan-yin, is more popular than any other. A mysterious reverence attaches to her name, and she is said to be the tutelary goddess of women. Her 'nativity' and 'assumption' are both celebrated. Gutzlaff (in the *Journal of the Asiatic Society*, XVI. 79, 80) distinguishes between Kwan-yin, the goddess of mercy, who is thought to be of Hindú origin, and Ma-tsoo-poo, 'the holy Mother,' of Chinese origin. The worship of the latter was introduced, he writes, 'some centuries ago. She is so strikingly akin, in her whole character and figure, to the Virgin [of the Roman-catholic Church], that the Chinese at Macao call her *Santa Maria de China*. The sailors make her especially an object of adoration; and there are very few junks that have not an image of her on board. She is also accompanied by very dismal satellites, the executors of her behests.'

[2] *Journal Asiatique*, as above, p. 298.

[3] Pauthier, *Chine*, p. 127. The same practice, we may have occasion to remark hereafter, is also found in records of ancient Egypt.

[4] 'The Buddhists have taken advantage of this prevailing sentiment, and have grounded on it a variety of superstitious services.'—Medhurst, p. 212.

in the form of a horse-shoe, they inscribe thereon the name of the deceased, erect a tablet to his memory in the hall of his ancestors, and repair annually to the graves, in order to prostrate themselves before the manes and to offer victuals to those hungry spirits[1].' The precise intention of the sacrificer has been differently estimated by different writers. All agree, however, that no reference is made by him to moral guilt or to the reinstatement of departed souls in a position of primeval innocence. On the contrary, they are addressed as beings capable of giving aid and counsel to the meritorious of their progeny, and also of inflicting vengeance on the fallen and unworthy[2]. To their own they occupy the place and wield the high prerogatives of the Supreme Being. The vulgar seem, indeed, to fancy that the appetite of the deceased is really gratified by feeding on the subtler portions of the food presented at his grave ; and notions equally absurd appear, in later times at least, to be profusely indicated by the offering of a species of gilt-paper, covered with figures of houses and utensils, which becomes, on passing through the fire, available as the currency of the unseen world[3]. But other and more philosophic minds have uniformly repudiated this debased interpretation of their ancient customs. For example in the *Le-ke*, or authorised ritual of Confucianism, it is declared that the oblations to the manes should be understood *symbolically*, as meaning, 'That we ought to keep the dead before our eyes, and honour them as if they were still living[4].' On earth the father and mother were re-

[1] Gutzlaff, I. 60, 61. On the ancient ceremonial, see the *Li-ki*, ed. Callery, p. 42.

[2] *Chou-king*, ed. De Guignes, pp. 106, 179. At other times, however, nothing is said of their immortality and present influence: they are commemorated or deplored as beings altogether of the past.

[3] *e.g.* Medhurst, pp. 213, 214, who adds: 'Besides transmitting money to the distressed and indigent spirits, the Chinese think it necessary to provide their ghostly friends with clothes, and other articles, adapted for their use in the shades below. With this view, they cause coats and garments to be delineated on paper, which pass through the fire, as certainly and as regularly as the paper-money, into the abodes of spirits.'

[4] *Li-ki*, ed. Callery, p. 121. Wuttke (II. 65, 66) has the following remarks on the rationale of this strange custom of offering gold and silver paper: 'Falsch ist es, dass diese Sitte an die Stelle früherer Menschenopfer getreten wäre, oder dass man den Seelen der Gestorbenen durch das Verbrennen die auf dem Papier gezeichneten Dinge zum Gebrauch im Jenseits verschaffen wolle, wenn auch zur Zeit der Mongolen, welche den Todten Menschen und Thiere nachsandten, solche für das chinesische Bewusstsein ungereimte Dinge vorgekommen sein mögen......Das Gold- und Silber-papier mit seinen Bildern bedeutet dann den Reichthum, und das Verbrennen des Papiers ist dann

vered by all the members of their family, who saw in them an image of the two divine Principles in nature; and similarly on their removal hence they were regarded as the chosen deputies and ministers of Heaven, as watching with affectionate interest all the varied fortunes of their progeny, and urging them along the beaten road of duty to a higher and a happier stage of being. These relations with the world invisible were not unnaturally held to be most real in the case of the emperor himself, who as the Son of Heaven and father of his people had become an object of especial favour and solicitude to all his royal predecessors; yet the humblest China-man believes, and has believed from ages out of memory, that his welfare both in this world and the next is made to hinge almost entirely on the due discharge of filial obligations, and the offering up of periodic sacrifices to the manes of his ancestors.

From this account of the external aspects of Confucianism as a religious system, I pass forward to a more minute investigation of the primary article of faith and of ideas which had been silently moulding the established forms of worship. Ever since the western missionaries came in contact with the literati of the Middle Kingdom, two important questions have been agitated in reference to these subjects. It was asked, in the first place, Do Confucianists believe in the existence of a Supreme Being? and, secondly, What words or phrases in the Chinese language form an adequate rendering of the 'God' of Christianity? Upon the latter question[1], though hardly separable

freilich *die verdünnteste und abgeflachteste Weise des Opfers*, welche ein prosaisches, den Besitz leidenschaftlich liebendes Volk ersinnen kann.'

[1] The principal word selected by the early Roman-catholic missionaries as equivalent to אֱלֹהִים and Θεός, was the Chinese *Teen*, which means, however, nothing more than 'Heaven,' the visible and invisible 'Heaven,' as construed in its broad indefinite sense. To give a greater personality to the idea intended by it, the word *Choo* (= 'Lord') was subsequently added by authority of the Inquisition; and the phrase 'Teen-Choo,' 'Heavenly Lord,' or 'Lord of Heaven,' became the recognised appellative of God for all Romish converts in the empire. Among the Chinese missionaries of other communions who rejected *Teen*, the general practice was to render the biblical name of God either (1) by *Shin*, or (2) by *Shang-te*, both of which have found a number of determined advocates, especially since the missionary conference held at Shanghae, in 1847. It is contended on the one side that *Shin* is not a faithful rendering of Θεός, because it is really a collective noun, is never used with a numerical affix, and therefore cannot possibly mean *one* Shin. (See Mr. S. C. Malan's recent volume, entitled *Who is God in China?* He pleads earnestly and learnedly in favour of the phrase *Shang-te*.) On the other hand it is maintained with equal earnestness

from the first, I shall decline to enter; feeling that the only persons who can claim to speak about it with any semblance of authority are those who have acquired a competent knowledge of Chinese. It is somewhat different with regard to the more general subject of inquiry, 'Are the governing class of China atheistic?' for the right solution of that problem is derivable not so much from the discussion of particular terms, as from the main complexion of her history and sacred literature. Yet rich as the materials are for such investigation, and accessible as they have now become to ordinary scholars, the difficulties experienced in turning them to good account are of no common magnitude. The ardour of the Christian missionary, who in this case as in others proved himself the pioneer of art and science and philosophy as well as of the Gospel, not unfrequently propelled him into serious errors and exaggerations; and owing to the way in which he has misread the monuments of eastern paganism and overcoloured both its truths and untruths, the first duty of dispassionate students is to subject his reports to close and rigorous criticism, by going back, wherever it is possible, to the original authorities.

When Ricci headed the first regular mission of the Jesuits in China, opening his great campaign at Nanking in 1590, it became a leading feature of his project to disarm the opposition of the governing class[1] by making common cause with them against the popular forms of misbelief. To justify this questionable measure, and so facilitate the arduous work of the

that *Shang-te* is an ethereal ψυχὴ κόσμου, 'not a personal Being distinct from matter;' and warnings are accordingly held out to the effect that by sanctioning the worship of *Shang-te*, we should be virtually dethroning the Great Self-existent Spirit, whom the Hebrew and Christian have equally worshipped under the adorable name Jehovah. (See, for instance, Mr. McClatchie's paper on *Chinese Theology*, in the *Journal of the Asiatic Society*, XVI. 427 sq.) As far as I can judge, the verbal controversy is at last resolvable into a question of metaphysics, 'Have the Chinese any conception of a pure spirit, or of incorporeality in the Christian sense?'

[1] 'Il était en quelque sorte de mode d'être son partisan et son apologiste. Les lettrés en particulier n'hésitèrent pas à se déclarer pour lui, parce que, dans ses discours, il attaquait avec un succès complet les doctrines des bonzes [*i.e.* of the Buddhist monks] et des docteurs de la Raison (Tao-Sse), et que, d'autre part, il professait toujours un profond respect et une grande admiration pour les enseignements de Confucius. Le docteur européen était à leurs yeux un vrai membre de la corporation des lettrés, un Confucéen, un partisan de leur doctrine, un ennemi des superstitions des bouddhistes et des rêveries des sectateurs de Lao-Tze.' Huc, *Le Christianisme en Chine*, &c. II. 154, 155.

evangelist, he uniformly pleaded that Confucius was the brightest luminary of the ancient world,—a genuine philosopher, whose tenets harmonised in almost every point with those transmitted in the sacred family from antediluvian times, and consequently that the Gospel, so far from advocating any kind of novelty, was in substance a revival of the primitive faith of China. The missionary at the same time ventured to take part in sacrifices offered to Confucius, on the ground that honours thus awarded to the great philosopher of China were all purely civil[1]. It was felt indeed by Ricci, as by many of his coadjutors, that a meeting-place might be established between the Gospel and the authorised religion of the Middle Kingdom by laying stress upon the doctrine of one infinite, all-embracing Spirit[2], whom the China-man appeared to worship as *Teen*, or *Shang-te*. The two great temples at Peking, in which, as we have noticed, the emperor himself was in the habit of sacrificing to Heaven and Earth respectively, were held to be alike the sanctuaries of this one eternal Spirit: the Creator and Conservator of the universe was merely worshipped under different titles[3]. On the contrary it was alleged with equal firmness by a learned member[4] of the same fraternity (the Jesuit Longobardi), that many statements of his predecessors on this subject were devoid of all foundation. According to his view the Chinese literati had never during the historic period worshipped one supreme and spiritual Intelligence,—a God whose being is entirely independent of the visible and sensible universe: and notwithstanding all the fervid eulogies which, half in ignorance and half in malice, have attempted to exalt the 'wisdom' of the Middle Kingdom to equality with that of Palestine, the verdict of Longobardi is continually corroborated by the disquisitions

[1] *Le Christianisme en Chine*, II. p. 155. Other missionaries of a kindred spirit, and professing the same admiration for Confucius, travelled about the country in the disguise of watchmakers, astronomers, artists, and engineers.

[2] We are told of Ricci in particular: 'Negabat religionem, quæ unum sine consorte Deum doceret, peregrinam esse. Hanc probabat fuisse a Sinensibus philosophis et eorum principe Confucio traditam, sed obliteratam paulatim temporum vitio.' Hardwick's *History of the Reformation*, 3rd ed., p. 408, n. 3. It was even pretended in some quarters that the Christian doctrine of the Holy Trinity had been anticipated by three horizontal lines, made use of in the *kwa* of Fuh-he (above, p. 280), to represent Heaven; or else by the triplication of *Shang-te* into Heaven, Earth, and man.

[3] See *Nouveau Journal Asiatique* (1854), tome IV. p. 300.

[4] His essay, first printed at Madrid in 1676, was translated into French, in 1701, with the title *Traité sur quelques points de la religion des Chinois*, par le R. Père Longobardi.

of our modern sinologues. They hold that, theoretically at least, the followers of the Chinese state-religion are all atheists to a man[1]. However much the instincts of their moral nature must rebel against this blank and desolating creed; however much they are impelled when bending under some disastrous visitation to take refuge in the thought of a superior *Teen*, or 'heaven,' and recognise in him the attributes of justice and of mercy, of fatherhood and special providence, the highest efforts of their reasoning faculties all stop at the conception of an 'unintelligent and will-less principle,' from which the universe, its laws and its inhabitants, have been eternally projected or evolved.

How long these modes of thought and feeling have been prevalent in China; whether as one class of writers are disposed to argue they may be regarded as the earliest product of a national mind absorbed entirely in the love of pelf, or whether they resulted gradually from the adoption by the learned orders of a system of philosophy akin to that which we entitle 'naturalism,' it is not easy to determine. In the *Shoo-king*, which Confucius (we have seen) remodelled out of older documents, allusion is made as many as eight-and-thirty times[2] to some great Power or Being, called *Shang-te*. The name itself imports 'august' or 'sovereign Ruler.' As there depicted he

[1] See, for instance, Meadows, p. 361. Prof. Neumann, whose opinion as a very accomplished Chinese scholar is peculiarly valuable, had already expressed himself with even greater emphasis: 'Nie und nimmermehr ist dem Chinesischen Volke ein Gott erschienen; von einer Offenbarung ist keine Spur bei dieser prosaischen Nation. Die Wörter *Gott*, *Seele*, *Geist*, als etwas von der Materie ganz Unabhängiges und sie willkürlich Beherrschendes, *kennt die Chinesische Sprache gar nicht*. Ein einziges Band umschlingt, nach den Ansichten der Weisen dieses Landes, alles Seyende, das Reich der Natur und das Reich des Geistes; der Bruch, die Störung der angemessenen Thätigkeit eines Gliedes bringt Unordnung in die ganze Kette des Seyenden. Die geistigen und moralischen Kräfte gebieten aber den physischen; wer Tugend und Sitte beleidigt, stört die glückliche Ordnung der Elemente, er bringt Unheil über die Gesellschaft und ist ihr desshalb verantwortlich. *So innig ist dieser Ideengang mit der Sprache selbst verwachsen, dass es unmöglich ist, den ersten Vers der Genesis ohne weitläuftige Umschreibung ins Chinesische so zu übersetzen, dass er wirklich Chinesisch ist.* Denn *hoa*, das Wort für *schaffen*, bedeutet eigentlich auf eine spontane, unbewusste Weise vom Nichtseyn zum Seyn übergehen; und *tsáo*, welches in der Bibelübersetzung von D Morrison vorkommt, wird von den Chinesen bloss in der Bedeutung von anders machen aus einem Etwas, nie aber in dem Sinne von *schaffen, dem Machen aus einem Nichts*, gebraucht.' *Naturphilosophie der Chinesen*, as before, pp. 11, 12.

[2] Malan, *Who is God in China?* p. 167.

possesses a high measure of intelligence, and exercises some degree of moral government: he punishes the evil, he rewards the good. To him especially is offered the sacrifice *Loöe;* while other ceremonies are performed in honour of 'the six Tsong, the mountains, the rivers, and the spirits generally[1].' These beings of inferior rank appear to constitute the court, or retinue, of the celestial Ruler; and elsewhere he is attended by 'five heavenly chiefs, members also of his council, who are set over the presidents of heaven, of the earth, and of the sea. These, in turn, range in the world of *shin* (or spirits of the air), of *kwei* (souls of the deceased), and *ke* (spirits of, or from below, the earth)[2].' It is again expressly stated in the *Shoo-king,* and perhaps with reference also to the nature of *Shang-te:* 'Heaven is supremely intelligent: the perfect man imitates him (or it): the ministers obey him (or it) with respect: the people follow the orders of the government[3].' And, finally, it is enjoined[4] by fresh authorities that, on these sacred grounds, the 'people shall not hesitate to contribute with all their power to the worship of the sovereign Lord of Heaven, *Shang-te,* to that of celebrated mountains, great rivers, and of the *shin* of the four quarters.'

On the other hand, a second class of writers have contended, that in the very oldest products of the Chinese mind no proper personality has ever been ascribed to this supreme and all-embracing Power. Heaven is *called* the Father of the Universe, but only in the same way as Earth is called the Mother[5].

[1] *Le Chou-king,* ed. De Guignes, pp. 13, 14. The editor is unable to determine accurately what is meant by the six *Tsong* (='worthy of respect'). They seem to be different kinds of spirits. As for the sacrifice *Loöe,* it is explained by Choo-he (in Neumann, as above, p. 64) to mean the sacrifice of the inexorable death, 'because Heaven and Earth feel no pity.'

[2] Malan, as before, p. 166. On the *five* chiefs here alluded to, as relieving *Shang-te* in his administration of the world, see the *Notice de L'y-king,* appended to the *Chou-king,* as before, p. 432. May they not correspond to the *five* planets of ancient China? See above, p. 276, n. 1.

[3] *Le Chou-king,* pp. 124, 125. One of the native commentators there cited (n. 3) says that 'Heaven is simple, intelligent, just, spiritual and all-seeing.' And another adds: "To be able to chastise the bad, to recompense the good, to be truth itself, to be a spirit incomprehensible, immutable, permanent, just, devoid of passion,—all this is contained in the two Chinese characters (*Tsong-ming*), which in this passage signify 'supremely intelligent.'"

[4] *Le-ke,* ch. VI. (quoted by Mr. Malan, p. 185). Mention is also made of sacrifices to ancestors and to the tutelary gods of the empire (p. 28, ed. Callery).

[5] *Le Chou-king,* p. 151. '*Heaven,* therefore, has no higher meaning than *Nature.*' Hegel, *Phil. of Hist.* p. 138.

Both of them are said to live, to generate, to quicken: yet neither to have life inherent in itself. They both are made the objects of solemn prayers and sacrifices. Both may also be described as 'spiritual'; yet only in so far as spirits[1] of which they are in some sort the aggregate expression are diffused in every form of animated nature. 'Heaven' is in particular (these writers argue) a personification of the ever-present Law, and Order, and Intelligence, which seem to breathe amid the wonderful activities of physical creation, in the measured circuit of the seasons, in the alternation of light and darkness, in the ebb and flow of tides, in the harmonious and majestic revolutions of the planetary bodies. 'Heaven,' in other words, so far from being personal, or spiritual, or self-conscious, is a blind necessity inherent in all forms of life, a Law and not a Legislator, a Power without volition, and a Guide without intelligence[2]. Nay, many of these writers have gone so far as to contend that *Shang-te* himself, of whom the highest and most god-like qualities are predicable, is really no more than a great 'Anima mundi[3],' energising everywhere in all the processes of nature, and binding all the parts together in one mighty organism, exactly as the soul of man pervades and animates the body: and in accordance with this notion they remind us how the *Le-ke*[4] had decided, that 'if we speak of all the *shin* (or spirits) collectively, we call them *Shang-te*.'

After threading my way as far as possible among this tangled, and in many points conflicting, evidence, I am led to the conclusion that in China as elsewhere had lingered from primeval ages the conception of one living, bounteous, and paternal providence, whose earthly shadow[5] was believed to sit exalted far above his fellows on the throne of the Middle

[1] 'Wenn man sagt: Himmel und Erde haben keinen Geist, so heisst diess so viel: Himmel und Erde *haben nur in so weit* Geist, als daraus die vier Jahreszeiten und alle Dinge hervorgehen.' Tschu-hi (Choo-he), translated by Neumann, as before, p. 61. The whole of the dialogue on 'Heaven and Earth' is well worth perusal.

[2] Thus in the *Hi-tse* ascribed to Confucius (IV. 4, appended to *Yih-king*, ed. Mohl) the author avows that while the sages act freely, it is different with the primary elements of the universe, the male and female principles in nature, or, in other words, the Godhead of ancient China. The action of these results from forces inherent in their very being.

[3] See the passages collected by Mr. McClatchie, as before, pp. 390 sq.

[4] *Ibid.* p. 401.

[5] *Le Chou-king*, p. 151: 'Le Ciel a établi un Roi pour conserver les peuples et pour les instruire. Ce Roi est le Ministre du Souverain Seigneur (Chang-ti), pour gouverner paisiblement et avec douceur l'Empire.'

Kingdom; but that ultimately this conception was broken and obscured, until the unity of God no longer formed the basis of the Chinese creed. Philosophy then came forward as in other countries, and attempted to recover the idea of unity. 'Heaven' was made by the more thoughtful of philosophers a verbal representative of all the energies in nature: all were *said* to flow originally from it, as from the common source of life, and common principle of order: all were *said* to have been recapitulated and embraced in it as in the animating soul and ruling spirit of the universe: while, in the worship of the many, 'Heaven' was ordinarily confounded with the firmament itself, the blue ethereal canopy above our heads, the shining and the burning heavens[1].

But whatever may be thought of the preceding summary, no one will deny that the absence of distinct allusion in the writings of Confucius to a God at all resembling the God of Christianity is very strange and startling. The few scanty notices which they afford are barely recognitions of some powerful and indefinite Heaven (*T'een*),—a cold abstraction of the logical faculty, whom the philosopher does not dream of clothing with moral and spiritual attributes, or of propounding as an object of man's love and adoration. He seems, in fact, to have been wavering more than once respecting the existence of this great abstraction; for when questioned on the subject by his followers, he either evaded the inquiry or else reprimanded them for prying into matters unconnected with their duties to society and lying far beyond their depth[2]. To him a personal Deity, the Maker, the Redeemer, and the Sanctifier, was theoretically superfluous. "You find yourself," he argued, "in the midst of a stupendous, yet most orderly piece of mechanism. That mechanism, so far as we can tell, is self-originating, self-sustaining. Change there is, but no creation: all things from eternity existed and were subject to a flux and reflux, in obedi-

1 '"Whom do you worship?" I asked. "I worship Heaven just as you foreigners do," he replied. "Who is the Heaven you worship?" "Why, Shang-te, of course," said he. "Can you *see* Shang-te or not?" I inquired. "Why," replied he, looking at me with surprise at my ignorance, and leading me to the door while he pointed up to the sky, "there he is!" "What!" said I, "do you mean that *blue sky* up there?" "Of course," said he, "that is Shang-te, *the same as your Jesus!*" I have never yet asked the above questions without receiving *precisely the same answers;* for *all* classes of Confucianists in China consider Shang-te to be the animated material heaven.' M[c] Clatchie, as before, p. 397.

2 Cf. *Journal Asiatique* (1834), XIV. 57.

ence to initial laws impressed upon them, how and why we know not, by some stern necessity. Be warned and guided by this principle: devote yourself no longer to the fruitless study of theology: it brings, and can bring, with it no practical advantage. Seek not to explore the doctrine of final causes: rather, if you speculate at all, confine your thoughts to the discussion of phenomena and the laws of phenomena. Such alone are useful and legitimate subjects of inquiry. It is possible indeed that laws may be connected somehow with the demons of the air, or else with other forms of spiritual agency: we cannot absolutely say that they are not. You may continue, therefore, on this ground, to follow the established ritual of your ancestors. 'Sacrifice *as if* your sacrifice were a reality: worship *Shin* as if *Shin* were really present[1].' But meanwhile your chief concern is with the visible and palpable universe, and with the homely tasks of life. You constitute one little member in some mighty organism; you stand as part of some great moral order: strive to act on all occasions as such a being should act. Far from pausing to bemoan your weakness or unworthiness, remember that 'he who offends against Heaven has no one to whom he can pray[2].' The past is gone and is irrevocable. Be more vigilant in time to come. Endeavour so to rule yourself, according to the sacred maxims, that you may be fitted first tc rule a family, and lastly may attain the highest point of your ambition,—an office under government. To practical men the theatre of this present life gives ample scope for enterprise: it teems with stern realities and all-engrossing cares: perhaps[3], too, it may prove your last, your sole possession. Be thoughtful, therefore, be industrious: make the most of what you have: be modest, sober, grave, decorous; cultivate the qualities which mark the men of 'the due medium[4];' more particularly aim at that which forms the crowning excellence of all, be scrupulous in your devotion to the emperor, the Son and representative of Heaven. For is not he in very truth the father of his people?

[1] See above, p. 292, n. 1; and Malan, *Who is God in China?* p. 14. Abel-Rémusat, *Chung-Yung*, c. XVI. § 3, compares the language of Confucius on these subjects with the corresponding language of Spinosa, of whom he thinks the Chinese a worthy precursor.

[2] Medhurst, p. 186. In another passage there cited, Confucius declares: 'Imperial Heaven has no kindred to serve, and will only assist virtue.'

[3] See Wuttke's investigation of this article in the Confucian creed, II. 40 sq.

[4] This is the meaning of *Chung-Yung*, the title of the Confucian treatise on the duties and transcendant dignity of the 'holy man,' who identifies himself completely with the fixed order of Heaven.

and as filial piety has ever been the source of joy and blessing to the single household, and as reverence for the memory of departed kinsmen is the glory, hope, and safeguard of survivors, so to venerate the emperor of the Middle Kingdom is to aid in regulating the whole course of nature; every comfort which you prize or long for is involved in it,—domestic peace and social order and the safety of the commonwealth. And if," Confucius seems to have concluded, "if you wish to place your institutions on the very surest basis, educate the young, diffuse intelligence in every quarter; most of all insist upon the study of that science which surpasses every other, as enabling you to turn all other kinds of knowledge to a practical account,—I mean, the science of political economy[1]."

Vast, however, as the influence of Confucius was in moulding the institutions of his country and imparting that distinctive air of regular animation which pervades the social life of China at the present day, he could not draw men off entirely from the deeper questions touching their connexion with supernatural powers and their relation to the world invisible. The human heart *must* muse and speculate on these momentous questions; for the plodding and prosaic China-man himself was not entirely dead to their importance. What then was the drift of 'orthodox' philosophy in reference to the subjects which Confucius had comparatively disregarded? The answer is furnished in the numerous works of Choo-he[2], whom we saw abundant reason for esteeming the approved expositor of Chinese metaphysics and theology. According to the views propounded by him, and in part at least transmitted from preceding ages, there is underlying all phenomena, however mixed and manifold they seem, a fundamental unity, of which the common name is *Tae-keih*, the Absolute, or literally the 'Great Extreme.' Beyond it, as the highest 'pinnacle of heaven,' the one ultimate power, the entity without an opposite, no human thought whatever is capable of soaring. Itself incomprehensible, it 'girdles' the whole frame of

[1] 'It is rather extraordinary that political economy constitutes the first science which all Chinese boys are taught.' Gutzlaff, I. 198. It was the wish of Confucius himself that his disciples should all become state officials, and therefore, as in the *Lun-Yu*, 'he confined his instructions to political economy, to which he reduces all the duties of life.' *Ibid.* p. 196.

[2] My knowledge of his writings is derived chiefly from Prof. Neumann's translations, above cited. I have also profited by the recent work of Mr. T. T. Meadows, who devotes a chapter (ch. XVIII.) to the subject of Chinese philosophy; and also by the paper of Mr. McClatchie, as before cited, on 'Chinese Theology.'

nature, animate and inanimate. From it alone as from the fountain-head of being issued every thing that is[1]. 'Creation' is the periodic flowing forth of it. 'The Absolute is like a stem shooting upwards: it is parted into twigs, it puts out leaves and blossoms: forth it springs incessantly, until its fruit is fully ripe: yet even then the power of reproduction never ceases to be latent in it. The vital juice is there; and so the Absolute still works and works indefinitely. Nothing hinders or can hinder its activity, until the fruits have all been duly ripened, and activity gives place to rest[2].'

It is, meanwhile, acknowledged by the great philosophers of China that this thought of one efficient Cause, or rather of one causative power and principle, was quite unable to retain its true ascendancy in opposition to the seeming contradictions of the outer and the inner world. The vision of the soul, the eye of faith, was gradually bedimmed, and hence those higher intuitions which had prompted Hebrew patriarchs to hold communion with the Self-existent, who converts all agencies whatever into means for carrying on His moral government, were lacking in the ordinary China-man. The God whom he adored was rather an ideal being than the living God of nature. 'All things in the world,' says Choo-he[3], 'seem as to their primary tendencies to issue from the One: the One, however, is not really in a condition to bring them forth;' the meaning of

[1] Tschu-hi (Choo-he), as above, pp. 46, 47. In reply to the question 'What is the Absolute?' it is there answered (p. 46): 'Das Absolute ist die höchste, erhabenste, äusserste, grösste Fundamental-Normalurkraft; alle Menschen sind durch das Absolute und alle Dinge sind durch das Absolute.' In another passage (p. 72) it is said that *Tae-keih* itself springs out of something higher, out of *Wu-keih* 'the Illimitable.'

[2] *Ibid.* p. 50. The following passage (also quoted from Choo-he, by Mr. McClatchie, p. 381) forms a good illustration of the Chinese theory respecting a succession of similar worlds: "Being asked, 'From the opening and spreading out (of the world from chaos) to the present time, is not 10,000 years; how was it *before* that time?' He (the philosopher) replied, 'Before that there was another (world) similar to the present one.' Being asked, whether Heaven and Earth are capable of being annihilated, he replied 'No, but it is my opinion that *when men completely depart from correct principles*, then the whole will become chaos, and men and things will cease to exist, and then there will be a *new commencement*.'"

[3] *Ibid.* p. 71. The question had been asked, 'Ist die Einheit Grund (*causa efficiens*) des Lebens?' To which it was replied, quoting Hong-Khiu: 'Das Eins bleibt...immerdar das Fundament, auf dieselbe Weise, wie der Zehner in 100, 1000, und 10,000; das Zwei kann durchaus nicht als dasjenige betrachtet werden, wodurch ein Ding wird; es ist bloss der Grund des Hervortretens.' Choo-he then adds further explanations of his own.

which is probably that while our reason points us back to the hypothesis of unity, our senses are too apt to lead us in a different direction: multiplicity is everywhere apparent and so constitutes for us the law of the phenomenal universe. In other words, the Chinese speculator found himself impelled to the conclusion that although the proper basis of all life is one, and though such unity may still by some mysterious process form the ultimate principle of rest and motion, yet duality is the active visible cause of all advancement, the foundation of the present order of the world[1]. It thus resulted that in spite of the idea of abstract unity which lingered as an echo of some old tradition in the background of their metaphysical system, the Chinese philosophers were all addicted to the theory of two principles. Their ordinary speech was *dualistic.* They rested on two entities or essences, the one a power or cause, the other a more passive something where that power or cause could operate[2]. The former may be styled the ultimate *immaterial* element of the universe (*Le*); the second (*Ke*), consisting as it does of matter most ethereal in its texture, may be styled the ultimate *material* element of the universe. *Le* is, therefore, only another name for *Tae-keih;* it is the Absolute regarded in association with material essences, and manifesting itself in virtue of such association as the cause of organisation and of order. Both these elements as to their essence are held to be eternal; and so inseparably united that one is necessary to the true subsistence of the other. 'If there were no *Ke*, then *Le* would not have anything to rest upon[3].' The predicates of *first* and *second* are inapplicable to all such cases: but if we must speak of order and priority, the immaterial element is worthy of the foremost place[4]: particularly since this element is the basis of all things viewed abstractedly, as destitute of form and figure; while *Ke*, the primary matter, acts as the substratum on which things endued with form and other qualities all take their stand, or out of which they have been gradually evolved.

1 'Tschi-hiang sagt: Das Eins ist der Lebensgrund, so wie es die Ursache ist der Bewegung und der Ruhe; seine Grenze ist deren Grenze; das Zwei ist *die Ursache des Werdens*, so wie der vollendeten Bewegung und der darauf folgenden Ruhe, eben so der vollendeten Ruhe und der darauf folgenden Bewegung.' *Ibid.* p. 72.

2 Meadows, p. 68.

3 See this and other extracts in McClatchie, p. 384. The thought of necessary interdependence between *Le* and *Ke* had sometimes led men to speak of the primary matter as identical with the Absolute: *ibid.* p. 383.

4 Choo-he, as before, pp. 32, 33.

But *Ke*, again, if duly analysed, is found to be not singular but dual, not simple but compounded. The resolution of this primary matter into its constituent elements[1] gives birth to two opposite essences, to *Yang* and *Yin*, which therefore may be treated as the phases under which the Ultimate Principle[2] of the universe displays itself in the phenomenal world. As early as the *kwa*, or diagrams of Fuh-he, the symbolic mode of representing them was a broken and black line for *Yin*, a white and continuous line for *Yang*. The popular account of this duality, in which it was intended to express the parting asunder of the one chaotic *Ke* and the production of Heaven and Earth, is all the more remarkable, because it reappears not only in the story-books of other Chinese sects[3], but also, we shall see hereafter, in the ancient mythus of New Zealand. *Yang* and *Yin*, thus generated by the 'Great Extreme' of the Chinese theology when separating himself from unformed matter, are called the two *Ke*, and may be represented either by the names of positive and negative essences, or else in a more concrete form, as the paternal and maternal principles of nature. From the constant evolution and interaction of these opposite essences[4] resulted every species of formal matter and the mixed phenomena of the world. According to the different proportions in which *Yang* and *Yin* are blended is the character of every grade of creaturely existence. Every thing is *Yang* and *Yin* together. For the highest actual manifestation in which *Yang* preponderates we look to Heaven itself, which is accordingly to be esteemed the aptest image cognisable by the senses of the ultimate and all-embracing Principle. Earth is, on the contrary, the highest form of *Yin*. The same duality where one or other of the factors operated, either for the purpose of transforming or uniting, issued in the first production of the innate essences, which constitute the Five Elements of water, fire,

[1] '*In* und *Yâng* gehen aus der Urmaterie hervor; sie sind beständig in gegenseitigem Kampfe, und sie müssen immer im Kampfe seyn; daraus entsteht das Gute und das Böse, daraus der Ursprung des Verschiedenen:' *ibid.* p. 78.

[2] 'Der Ausdruck: das *Absolute* (Tai-Ky), ist gleichbedeutend mit dem Worte *Urkraft* (Ly):' *ibid.* p. 42.

[3] *E.g.* of the followers of Taoism, who say that 'after chaos was settled, heaven and earth divided, and human beings were born:' in Medhurst, p. 198. Mr. McClatchie also notices (*Journal of As. Soc.* XVI. 386) the affinity between this representation and that of the Chaldean Bel, who was said to form light and darkness, &c. by *cutting himself in two.*

[4] 'It is here,' as Mr. Meadows well remarks, 'that Chinese philosophy slips over the much discussed, hitherto unsolved, and apparently unsolvable question of the existence of matter:' p. 344.

wood, metal, and earth[1]. 'A transcendental union and coagulation now takes place of the Ultimate Principle, the Two Essences and the Five Elements. The Positive Essence becomes the masculine power, the Negative Essence the feminine power—conceived in which character the former constitutes the Heavenly Mode or Principle, the latter the Earthly Mode or Principle: by a mutual influencing, the two produce all things in the visible, palpable world; and the double work of evolution and dissolution goes on without end[2]:'—*Yang* evincing its peculiar force in every kind of progress, *Yin* in every kind of retrogression: *Yang* determining commencement, *Yin* completion: *Yang* predominant in spring and summer, and the author of all movement and activity, *Yin* more visible in the autumn and the winter, passive, drooping, and inert.

These dualistic speculations on the constitution of the universe in general are consistently adopted in the framing of the Chinese theory of man. In popular phrase it was the marriage of Heaven and Earth, the male and female principles in nature, that give rise to the production of the human species: or in other words, since *Yang* and *Yin* must always coexist as the material ground on which the Ultimate Principle takes effect, they enter into the composition of rational as well as of irrational beings. Man, however, in addition to his physical framework, is endowed with Five qualities or Virtues, corresponding to the Five Elements of the Chinese cosmogony. These constitute his mental and moral nature[3]. They unite him to the Absolute, the *Le*, from which proceeded all ingredients both of rationality and order, and with which the spirit of man

[1] Choo-he, as before, p. 43, pp. 82 sq.

[2] Meadows, p. 345.

[3] They are '*Jin*, *E*, *Le*, *Che*, and *Sin*, which are called the Five *Tih*, or Five Virtues: *tih* being a word that, like our English *virtue*, signifies first, qualities or characteristics generally, whether of man or of things; and then, collectively, the best qualities of man, or Virtue as opposed to Vice. In accordance with the dictionaries, *Jin* is usually rendered by *Benevolence* (or Charity in its widest sense); *E*, by Righteousness [Uprightness]; *Le*, by Propriety; *Che*, by Wisdom; and *Sin*, by Sincerity. But sinologues will perceive that as the Five *Tih* embrace the *whole* of what we consider the better side of man's nature, it is not certain that these five English words are exhaustive.' *Ibid.* p. 346.

In the *Li-ki*, ed. Callery, p. 45, the question is stated differently: 'L'homme émane (pour le moral) de la vertu du Ciel et de la Terre; (pour le physique, il émane) de la combinaison des (deux principes) *In* èt *Jañ;* (pour la partie spirituelle, il émane) de la réunion des esprits et des dieux; et (pour la forme qui lui est propre, il émane) de l'essence la plus subtile des cinq éléments.'

is strictly one and consubstantial. As the Chinese speculator had evaded the great problem touching the origin of primary matter, so he offers no intelligible explanation of the rise and growth of evil. He affirms indeed that every man is at his birth in the possession of a nature radically good. Itself an efflux from the source of Order, it gives proof of this celestial origin by moving in obedience to the general laws on which all other things are founded. 'Human nature,' says a great Confucian authority[1], 'is good, just as water has a tendency to flow downwards; men are universally inclined to virtue, just as water invariably flows downwards.' And the only qualification which the author offered of this startling language is appended in the following extract: 'Water, by beating, may be made to splash over your head, and by forcing may be made to pass over a mountain; but who would ever say that this is the natural tendency of water? It is because violence is applied to it. Thus men can be made vicious: but it is by no means their nature.' Vice, in other words, is in the system of the Chinaman a rare and casual deviation from the path of rectitude, produced by strong solicitations of the outer sensible world, to which the culprit, for some cause or other, finds himself attracted. And in manifest accordance with this pantheistic principle, evil is there said to punish itself, or rather it is punished by the necessary operation of the order which it dares to violate. With sin, as it involves a painful consciousness of guilt, or evil in the biblical sense of the expression, we very seldom meet; for in the Chinese system, evil-workers are not viewed as persons gifted with moral freedom, and sin is never represented as ingratitude, or even as rebellion against a personal and holy God. We cannot say of evil that it ought not to be; it is a something that must be. It enters, and must enter, into a concatenation of causes and effects originating from eternity: it is the shadow which gives harmony and contrast to the picture of the universe: it is the *Yin* of the moral world, as good is the *Yang*[2]. The root of both is in the primary material essence. They are both the necessary modes in which the Absolute comes forward

[1] Mencius, quoted in Medhurst, p. 196.

[2] Choo-he says expressly, as before, p. 76: 'Das bewegende Princip [*Yang*] ist das Gute und das ruhende Princip [*Yin*] ist das Böse, wie diess oft genug die Vollkommenen und Weisen gesagt haben; denn aus der aufrecht stehenden absoluten Urkraft erfolgen die zwei Entgegengesetzten, gegenseitig in nothwendiger Beziehung Stehenden, und daraus erfolgt nun Jegliches, das einem Jeden Eigenthümliche.'

into being, and conducts his operations in the region of phenomena. And as moral guilt is thus unknown to the Confucianist, so neither does he manifest a wish or craving after spiritual regeneration. He has no 'word of prophecy that shineth in a dark place until the day break and the day-star arise in the heart.' He offers up no sacrifice for sin, in order to restore relations between man and God, which are subverted by iniquity. He lives exclusively within the sphere of nature: his home is there, and he is wholly satisfied with his condition and his prospect. He believes in no futurity, excepting, it may be, some reproduction of the present forms of life and matter. What he worships are the tutelary gods of China, or creation contemplated in its twofold character of Earth and Heaven, or else, succumbing more completely under the dominion of the seen and tangible, his worship is degraded into hero-worship; he deifies humanity itself[1].

How many are the points in which Confucian tenets are opposed to Christianity it were superfluous to enumerate. The opposition in respect of doctrines is entire and fundamental. It is the opposition of nature and of grace, of unregenerate and regenerate principles, of sight and faith, of earthy and of heavenly. And how vast will therefore be the revolution in the moral nature of the China-man if he shall ever learn to practise the unworldly lessons of the Gospel, or to echo those heroic sentiments which more than once have been propounded in his hearing by the ardent and devoted missionary! 'I have had no home,' exclaimed Capillas to the implacable mandarins, when they consigned him to the executioner in 1647, 'I have had no home but the world, no bed but the ground, no food but what Providence has sent me day by day, and no other object but to do and suffer for the glory of Jesus Christ, and for the eternal happiness of those who believe in His Name[2].'

[1] According to Renan (*Etudes d'Histoire Religieuse*, p. 200, Paris, 1857) the Chinese were of all people the least supernaturalist, which may (he thinks) explain 'the secret of their mediocrity.' It is not unworthy of notice that M. Comte, of whom we are continually reminded in our study of Confucianism, has recently announced a new scheme of man-worship, which he ventures to predict will supersede Christianity, and form a kind of bridge to persons who are passing across the gulf between Theism and Atheism. The title of the tract is *Culte Systématique de l'Humanité*, Paris, 1850. All the benefactors of mankind are to be the objects of this cultus: Moses, Solomon, St. John, St. Paul, Buddha, Confucius, Muhammad; but, strange to say, the name of our blessed Lord does not appear in the catalogue!

[2] See the narrative in Mr. Kesson's work entitled *The Cross and the Dragon*, p. 112.

§ 2. *Tao-ism, or School of the Fixed Way.*

Although the tenets of the governing class appear to have accorded with the calculating and materialistic genius of the Chinese nation, individuals were never wanting in whose spirit the religious sentiment was ineradicably fixed. If the adherents of the state-religion frequently remind us of the sceptical and self-complacent Sadducee, we find existing side by side with them another Chinese sect whose mystic creed and fervid temperament especially resemble those of the Essene. The Chinese spiritualists had learned to recognise a head and champion many years before the origin of the Confucian movement: for Lao-tse, the founder of Tao-ism, seems to have been born as early as 604 B.C., and therefore was already hastening to the close of his career when the reformer of the state-religion entered on his first appointment as inspector of the corn-marts of his native province. Confucius shewed himself at every turn a politician and a sociologist, proceeding, it is true, on strictly moral grounds, yet hoping to recover and cement the unity of China most of all by the assiduous cultivation of political economy and by proficiency in general state-craft. Lao-tse, however, manifested an entirely different bias. He had always been a scholar and recluse, alive to the reality of the world invisible and to the presence of superior powers; of ardent and imaginative temper, subtle, penetrating, spiritual, unambitious; the unwavering preacher of inaction and retirement[1], and as such exposed to the reproach of inculcating apathy and moroseness, and of cherishing among his followers a dislike of human kind, and a contempt for the well-ordering of Chinese society. In other words, the genius of Confucianism was cold and worldly, that of the Taoists was more earnest, soaring, and contemplative: the first inclined to scepticism, the second to superstition: in the judg-

[1] The Chinese themselves were not slow in perceiving the real bent of his philosophy. Thus Choo-he, as before, p. 27, declares: 'Die Satzungen des *Lao-tse* zielen durchaus auf das Leere; auf die Ruhe und Unthätigkeit. Die Aufgabe des Lebens besteht (nach ihm) in einer tiefen Selbstbeschauung.' And in the 'Notice Historique,' supplied by M. Stanislas Julien's edition of the *Tao-te-king*, p. xxi., we have the following native criticism: 'Ceux qui étudient la doctrine de *Lao-tseu* la mettent au-dessus de celle des lettrés; de leur côté, les lettrés préfèrent Confucius à *Lao-tseu*. Les principes des deux écoles étant différents, il est impossible qu'elles puissent s'accorder entre elles. Suivant *Lao-tseu*, si le roi pratique le *nonagir*, le peuple se convertit; s'il reste dans une quiétude absolue, le peuple se rectifie de lui-même.'

ment of the former, man is bound to make the most of the present life, while in the latter the chief aim was to subdue all earthly appetites, and deepen a desire for the unfading and immortal.

As we saw already in the case of Śákya-muni, the oldest narratives[1] respecting Lao-tse agree in representing him as a man and a philosopher: exalted, it is true, but all the while a being subject to the ordinary conditions of humanity, and therefore such as men might hope to imitate. His ignorant disciples have, however, added large embellishments to the original story. Anxious to place their master high above the rank of mortals, and so gain themselves the power of competing with a host of foreign emissaries, who deified the founder of the Buddhist system, the Tao-ists had begun as early as the fourth century of the Christian era to assert for Lao-tse a supernatural origin. They celebrated the stupendous marvels of his birth[2]: they worshipped him as later Bráhmans worshipped the mysterious

[1] This subject has, for the first time, been critically discussed by M. Julien, as above. Even the *Légende Fabuleuse de Lao-tseu* denies (p. xxv.) that he was 'a divine and extraordinary being.' It adds, however: 'Dès le moment de sa naissance, il reçut une pénétration divine et fut doué d'une intuition profonde. La vie dont le ciel l'anima ne ressemblait point à celle des hommes ordinaires; il était destiné à devenir le maître et le propagateur du *Tao:* c'est pourquoi il put être protégé par les esprits du ciel et commander à la multitude des immortels.' (p. xxvii.)

[2] 'Quelques auteurs disent que *Lao-tseu* est né avant le ciel et la terre; suivant d'autres, il possédait une âme pure émanée du ciel. Il appartient à la classe des esprits et des dieux. Certains écrivains racontent que sa mère ne le mit au monde qu'après l'avoir porté dans son sein pendant soixante et douze ans [others say, 81 years]. Il sortit par *le côté gauche de sa mère.* En naissant il avait la tête blanche (les cheveux blancs): c'est pourquoi on l'appela *Lao-tseu* (l'enfant-vieillard). Quelques autres disent que sa mère l'avait conçu sans le secours d'un époux.'....*Légende Fabuleuse*, as above, p. xxiii. This legend is extracted by M. Julien from a Chinese 'History of the gods and the immortals,' by Ko-hong, who wrote about A.D. 350. It is most remarkable that the same story is in substance told of Śákya-muni by his later followers. St. Jerome, and after him Ratramnus, mention the story as current in their day (cf. Lassen, *Ind. Altert.* III. 370, 406, 411), and as early as the *Lalita Vistara* (assigned by M. Foucaux and Prof. Wilson to about 150 B.C.), Śákya-muni is said to have been miraculously born *from the side* of his mother, Máyá, who died seven days after his birth; see *Journal of the As. Soc.* (1856), XVI. 243. The feeling which gave rise to this peculiar theory of incarnations,—a wish to represent the incarnate one as free from all hereditary taint of matter and of evil,—was shared by Valentinian heretics, and in the 16th century by our Joan of Kent: see Hardwick's *Hist. of the Reformation*, 3rd ed. p. 257, and n. 2.

Krishńa, on the ground that he was one of many *avatáras*, the 'exalted, precious, and most venerable Prince,' identical with him, who under different aspects is the 'incomprehensible Non-being.' 'Lao-tse inhabited,' according to a popular legend, 'the abode of matchless purity; he was, in other words, the great progenitor of the subtle and primordial elements (of creation): he was the basis of the earth and of the shining heaven. Before the dawn of the great beginning, he had taken root in the bosom of supreme repose and in the deepest void. It was he, and he alone, who from the height of his imperial throne distributed the subtle elements of air and gave transparency to ether. He extended and transformed both heaven and earth, to bring about, in cycles of incalculable period, the production and the death of all created forms. His person was transfigured (by assuming a mortal body); he submitted to the various conditions of this soiled and dusty world; yet meanwhile bearing small resemblance to the crowd with whom he came to sojourn. He appeared to men as an illustrious sage. The good and evil of successive generations were all noted by him: and his doctrine had been shaped according to the times. He was the great instructor of the generations: he inculcated his principles with due measure. He attained unto the nine heavens: he stretched himself as far as the four seas. Since the period of the three kings, the emperors and potentates of all successive generations have bowed down before him and embraced his teaching[1].' As the story runs, however, in the oldest version, disengaged from wild and fabulous after-growths which thickened with the lapse of ages, Lao-tse is found to be an eminent Chinese sage, of whom it was recorded that he 'loved obscurity,' and who by dint of self-renunciation was believed to have attained the highest point of moral and religious eminence (or, in a word, to have acquired the *Tao*). His early studies lay among the royal archives of his native province, which were placed under his immediate custody: but as the troubles of the age increased and deepened his dissatisfaction with the men and things around him, he appears to have at last retreated altogether to 'the passage of Han-ku[2],' in order that he might devote the evening of his days exclusively to philosophic speculations.

Owing to the mystery in which that period of his life has

[1] Translated in Pauthier's *Mémoire sur l'origine et la propagation de la Doctrine du Tao*, Paris, 1831, pp. 20, 21.

[2] *Notice Historique sur Lao-tseu*, prefixed to M. Julien's edition of the *Tao-te-king*, p. xx. The district to which he retreated was in his native province of Ho-nan.

been enveloped, Lao-tse is thought by many writers to have travelled out of China into countries lying westward, and either to have learned or taught in them the leading articles of his creed[1]. The chief authority in favour of this statement specifies[2] not only Hindústán and Parthia, but also districts bordering on the western or Caspian sea, and even kingdoms of Ta-thsin (the Roman empire), as alike included in the regions then explored by the Chinese philosopher. It is doubtless true that such external intercourse would best enable us to account for some points of contact which exist between the doctrines commonly ascribed to Lao-tse, and those which in the same eventful era occupied the thoughtful spirits of India and of Greece[3]. We also find in it a possible explanation of some Aryan and Hellenic mythes[4] which reappear in various dramas of this Chinese sect, but are unknown to others. We may further trace with some degree of probability the origin of contradictions which are said to have existed from early times between historic legends of Confucianists and of Tao-ists, with reference to the founding of the Chinese empire and its ancient civilisation[5]. If Lao-tse had actually braved the perils of a journey to the far-off borders of the Mediterranean, and had really drawn his knowledge from a channel which was also open to the other doctors of the ancient world, we are prepared at once to recognise in such community of origin the ground of all the family-likeness which has been detected in the speculations of the East and West. But, on the other hand, the evidence in favour of this connexion is exceedingly precarious, and will never stand the test of rigorous criticism. The legend where the story first appears[6], so far as we

[1] Abel-Rémusat, *Mélanges Asiatiques*, I. 92, Paris, 1825.

[2] See the *Légende Fabuleuse*, as before, pp. xxx. xxxi.

[3] Abel-Rémusat (*ibid.* p. 95) says, in speaking of the 'sublime reveries' of Lao-tseu, that they present 'une conformité frappante et incontestable avec la doctrine que professèrent un peu plus tard les écoles de Pythagore et de Platon.' Pauthier in like manner concludes, 'avec une espèce de certitude,' that 'les doctrines, les croyances des sectateurs de Lao-tseu sont des doctrines, des croyances empruntées de l'Inde.' He then goes so far as to determine that the Chinese philosophy is to be connected with the Sánkhya and Védantine schools (*Mémoire*, as above, p. 49), and even (as he elsewhere argued) with the theorisings of the Gnostics and Neoplatonists, and last of all with those of Schelling.

[4] Above, p. 276, n. 2.

[5] See Prichard, IV. 486. According also to Prof. Neumann (as there quoted) the Tao-ists frequently charge Confucius with rejecting usages and ignoring facts that told against his own system.

[6] See M. Julien's 'Introduction' to the *Tao-te-king*, p. ix.

have any present means of judging, is taken from a mythological account of Chinese gods and heroes, not earlier than the fourth century after Christ; *i.e.* eight hundred years, and more, after the demise of Lao-tse. It also makes the great philosopher allude to his intention of visiting the Roman empire[1], long before the deposition of the Tarquins and the planting of the first republic: and what is still more noticeable as bearing on the foreign derivation of Tao-ism, it is said expressly that Lao-tse composed his principal work, 'consisting of something more than 5000 words,' *not* after his return from western countries, but upon the eve of the departure for his unknown resting-place.

That work, however, still remains (the *Tao-te-king*) the monument of his extraordinary power and penetration: for even if we hesitate to echo all the praises of an able sinologue, who finds in Lao-tse 'a genuine philosopher, a judicious moralist, an eloquent divine, and a subtle metaphysician[2],' there is ample reason for assigning him a place indefinitely higher than the mass of his contemporaries, and superior also to the greatest of his disciples.

What, then, was the substance of his teaching on the central truth of all religion,—the nature and the attributes of God? In other words, what is the meaning of the *Tao*, which among Tao-ists very soon supplanted both the *T'een* and *Shang-te* of the previous period? It were idle to insist on the resemblance of this appellation either to the *déva* of the Bráhmans, or the θεός of other countries. The primary meaning of the word, as given by Morrison and others, is 'a way,' or 'the fixed Way.' Its secondary meaning is 'a principle; the Principle from which heaven, earth, man, and all nature emanates.' Among Confucianists the word was chiefly used in its untechnical sense, but still with indirect allusion to the orderly course of human conduct. 'The way (*Tao*),' said Confucius himself, 'is not frequented: I know why. Intelligent persons go beyond it, while the ignorant fall short of it[3].' As soon, however, as the term

[1] Perhaps one of the earliest instances in which China manifested her acquaintance with the Roman empire, occurred in the time of Vespasian and Domitian, when a Chinese army marched victoriously as far as the eastern coast of the Caspian. Their own writers say that the leader of this expedition meditated an attack on the Ta-thsin (Romans), but that on the advice of the Persians he changed his mind: Humboldt's *Cosmos*, II. 185, 186, Sabine's ed.

[2] Abel-Rémusat, *ibid.* p. 93.

[3] Quoted in M. Julien's 'Introduction' to the *Tao-te-king*, p. x. I am indebted largely to the work of this distinguished scholar for the views here advocated on the subject of Tao-ism.

had been adopted by Lao-tse and his disciples, many writers have supposed that *Tao* at once became a synonym of 'the primordial Reason, the Intelligence, which having formed the world, still rules it as the spirit rules the body[1]:' and accordingly such writers are accustomed to describe Tao-ism as the 'rationalism' of China. But the recent publication of the sacred book on which the whole of that religion is believed to hinge goes very far to modify the old hypothesis. The *Tao* of Lao-tse in its exalted meaning is declared to be entirely void of thought, of consciousness, of judgment, of activity, of intelligence[2]. It is the deification of that one transcendant *Way* by which all beings came at first into existence: it is fixed, impassible, eternal; and in proportion as mankind are more devoted to the doctrines of apathy and inaction, they are said to walk directly in the *Tao*, to approach the *Tao*, and eventually to gain the *Tao*[3]. 'This Way,' writes a native commentator[4], 'whose level is high above the world, has neither colour, form, nor appellation. If you seek it with the eyes, you do not find it: if you listen, you do not hear it. The reason is, that it is not susceptible of utterance

[1] *Ibid.* p. xii. 'Ce mot me semble,' wrote Abel-Rémusat, 'ne pas pouvoir être bien traduit si ce n'est par le mot λόγος, dans le triple sens de *souverain être*, de *raison* et de *parole*. C'est évidemment le λόγος de Platon, qui a disposé l'univers, la *raison* universelle de Zénon, de Cléanthe et des autres stoïciens,' etc. Pauthier goes still further, and connects the doctrine of Christianity itself with Tao-ism (*Chine*, page 114). He says that the attributes given to the *Tao* are those 'qu'ont donnés à l'Etre suprême toutes les doctrines spiritualistes de l'Orient, transmises à l'Occident *par une voie juive et grecque;* par les thérapeutes et les esséniens, dont Jésus, le fils de l'homme, fut *le révélateur et le représentant;* doctrine dont les gnostiques furent aussi les représentants à l'état philosophique.' He then continues, in a passage full of misrepresentations as to the real genius of Christianity: 'Tous ces théosophes, les esséniens, qui étaient en quelque sorte les stoïciens de la Judée, comme Lao-tseu et ses premiers sectateurs l'étaient de la Chine; les thérapeutes, qui menaient en secret une vie contemplative et réglée sur une morale austère; les gnostiques, qui furent les révélateurs et les continuateurs de la *philosophie orientale*, au dire de Clément d'Alexandrie [!]; tous, ou presque tous, partaient du principe "qu'il faut dégager l'âme des entraves et des influences de la matière;" principe appelé *zoroastrien* par les écrivains des premiers siècles de notre ère, parceque ce furent les écrits de Zoroastre qui le transmirent de l'Asie orientale et centrale dans l'Asie occidentale, où, après avoir été interprété et appliqué de mille manières, il devint *le principe chrétien en Europe*' [!].

[2] *Tao-te-king*, ed. Julien, 'Introd.,' p. xiii.

[3] *Ibid.* p. xv.

[4] *Ibid.* p. 121, where a distinction is clearly drawn between the ordinary *Tao*, 'the way of justice, of rites and of prudence,' and the sublime *Tao* of Lao-tse.

by the human voice, nor of being designated by the help of names.' The 'nameless' being is, however, styled by Lao-tse 'the origin of Heaven and Earth[1],' since all things are the fruit of its self-manifestation. 'O how profound the *Tao* is! It seems to be the patriarch of all existences...I cannot tell whose son it is: it seems to have preceded the master of the Heaven[2].' 'Behold the nature of the *Tao:* it is vague, it is invisible...Inside it, lies a spiritual essence. This spiritual essence is profoundly true...It gives birth to all beings[3].' 'Man imitates the Earth: the Earth imitates the Heaven: the Heaven imitates the *Tao:* the *Tao* imitates his own nature[4].' Yet the *Tao*, in a certain sense, is represented as the fitting guide and model for all human beings. 'He that imitates not the *Tao* will die prematurely[5].' 'A prince that rules his empire by the *Tao* is exempted from the malice of the demons[6].' 'The *Tao* is the refuge of all creatures: (being universally diffused) it is the treasure of the virtuous man, the ultimate resource and resting-point of the unholy[7].' In a word, the *Tao* is the most exalted and most estimable being in the universe.

I feel disposed to argue from these various passages and others like them, that the centre of the system founded by Lao-tse had been awarded to some energy or Power resembling the 'Nature' of modern speculators. The indefinite expression *Tao* was adopted to denominate an abstract Cause, or the initial Principle of life and order, to which worshippers were able to assign the attributes of immateriality, eternity, immensity, invisibility. They also felt that human happiness was in some way or other connected with assimilation to its likeness: without, however, rising to a clear conception of its personality,

[1] *Ibid.* p. 1, p. 122.

[2] *Ibid.* p. 7.

[3] *Ibid.* pp. 29, 30, 165. In p. 174 we have the supplementary idea of preservation. 'Il nourrit,' says a commentator, 'tous les êtres comme une mère nourrit ses enfans.' Elsewhere it is *Virtue* that nourishes what the *Tao* has produced (p. 75).

[4] *Ibid.* p. 37.

[5] *Ibid.* pp. 45, 83, in both of which passages, however, the non-imitation of the *Tao* is explained by the context to mean no more than 'waxing old and impotent,' and by the commentators, 'placing oneself in opposition to the *Tao*' (p. 187).

[6] *Ibid.* p. 89. The gloss upon this passage (pp. 246, 247) gives us some of the chief characteristics of the perfect prince who governs by the *Tao:* 'Le Saint emploie le vide et la lumière (c'est-à-dire se dépouille de ses passions et dissipe leurs ténèbres) pour nourrir sa nature, la modération et l'économie pour subvenir aux besoins de son corps, la pureté et l'attention la plus sévère pour fortifier sa volonté, le calme et la quiétude pour gouverner son royaume.'

[7] *Ibid.* pp. 93, 251.

volition, or intelligence, much less of those peculiarly moral attributes, as goodness, mercy, justice, which the sacred family were uniformly taught to predicate of the Supreme Being[1]. The will-less, unintelligent *Tao* of ancient China was thus something very different[2] from the personal God of revelation, very different also from the Logos of St. John, and from the Living 'Way' of Christians.

Not content with offering violence to the words of Lao-tse, in order at all hazards to establish such affinity, some writers have gone further still, and have discovered in the 'doctrine of Reason' (as they term it) the anticipation of one high and central mystery of the Gospel,—the doctrine of the Holy Trinity in Unity. 'The principal object of the *Tao-te-king*,' a modern Chinese scholar has declared, 'is to establish a particular knowledge of one Supreme Being in Three Persons. Numerous passages so clearly speak of a Triune God, that no one who reads this book can any longer doubt that the mystery of the Most Holy Trinity was revealed to the Chinese more than five centuries before the advent of Jesus Christ[3].' It was expected that a deeper knowledge of this singular resemblance would, as furnishing points of contact with the heathen mind, contribute largely to the spread of Christianity in China, and accordingly the triad of Lao-tse continues to assume importance in the publications of the present day[4]. One writer even goes so far as to discover in the Chinese triad the three principal characters which enter into the formation of the ineffable name of God,—or the JEHOVAH of the ancient Hebrews; and from hence he has

[1] M. Callery (*Li-ki*, pp. 142, 143) has some judicious annotations on the same subject. While conceding that the *Tao* of Lao-tse is properly rendered the 'Way,' and is sometimes described as actually possessing the qualities of a way, he thinks that the philosopher was led to the adoption of this term chiefly because it was general and obscure, in order to bring out more clearly the difficulties he experienced in giving any denomination to the Ultimate Principle of all things.

[2] 'Die Idee des christlichen Gottes ist das reine Gegentheil jener leeren Einheit, ist die lebendige Fülle alles Lebens selbst; und diese positivste aller Ideen wird wahrlich nicht durch blosse Verneinungen errungen:' Wuttke, II. 79.

[3] Montucci, *De Studiis Sinicis*, p. 19, Berolini, 1808 (quoted by Julien, *Tao-te-king*, p. iv.). The motive of this writer may be gathered from what follows: 'Studium ergo et vulgatio hujus singularissimi textus, *missionariis utilissima*, evaderent ad messis apostolicæ peroptatam coacervationem feliciter provehendam.'

[4] *e.g.* Wiseman's *Lectures on Science and Revealed Religion*, p. 402, Grant's *Bampton Lectures*, p. 268, Lond. 1844. The former says with great confidence: 'The doctrine of a Trinity is too clearly expounded in his (Lao-tse's) writings to be misunderstood.'

not only argued for some actual intercourse between philosophers of Eastern and Western Asia, but has also found in the supposed transcription of the Hebrew name 'indisputable traces of the route which the ideas we call Pythagorean and Platonic had pursued on their migration into China[1].'

The only passage of the *Tao-te-king* which supplies a warrant for these grave conclusions is the following: 'You look for the *Tao*, and you see it not: its name is *I*. You listen for it, and you hear it not: its name is *Hi*. You wish to touch it, and you feel it not: its name is *Weï*. These three are inscrutable, and inexpressible by the aid of language; we are therefore in the habit of combining (or confounding) them into one (the three all seem to meet in one single quality,—voidness or incorporeity). Its upper part is not enlightened: its lower part is not obscure (*i.e.* the properties of this entity are the same throughout)......It is called a form without form, an image without image. It is vague and undefinable. Go before it, and you see not its face; follow after, and you see not its back[2].'

I give this memorable passage exactly as it stands in the translation of one of the most illustrious living sinologues; but the reader will have scarcely failed to notice that, when so translated, there is little left in it to justify phantastic theories of which it was the strongest and the most explicit basis. I should also add, that so far from the three syllables (*I*, *Hi*, *Weï*) enshrouding any special mystery, like that ascribed to them by this hypothesis, they all are terms well known to China, and were all expounded by disciples of Lao-tse before the Christian era. The first imports the absence of colour; the second, the

[1] Abel-Rémusat, *Mélanges Asiat.* I. 95, 96, and more fully in his *Mémoire sur la vie et les ouvrages de Lao-tseu*, pp. 43 sq. He affirms that the essential, or articulated, letters of יְהוָֹה are I, H, V, and that these were combined into a Chinese trigram I-Hi-Weï, of which, he thinks, the several characters have no meaning in the Chinese language, and therefore a meaning for them must be sought elsewhere. This he readily finds in Judæa.

[2] *Tao-te-king*, p. 19, ed. Julien, and notes, p. 147. The version of Dr. Wiseman, who follows Abel-Rémusat, is different in some particulars. For instance, one passage is made to say: 'These three are inscrutable, and, being united, form only one. Of them the superior is not more bright, nor the inferior more obscure.' In a second passage of the *Tao-te-king* (p. 65) we read: 'The *Tao* produced one; one produced two; two produced three: three produced all beings:'—which is explained by the native commentators to mean, first, the self-manifestation of the *Tao* as unity, then, the separation of this unity into the male and female principles (*Yang* and *Yin*), and thirdly, the production of harmony between these two (p. 211).

absence of sound or voice; the third, the absence of form or body[1]; they are, therefore, all most fitly used to characterise the great 'Unnamed,' who is the ultimate Principle of Tao-ists.

But the moral teaching of this school is even more remarkable than the stress which it has laid upon the thought of some transcendant unity in nature. The genuine convert or 'holy man,' as he is called, was ever anxious to conserve his primitive simplicity. He shrank from every kind of luxury, of bustle, and of competition. His leading aim was to 'make void the human heart;' to drain away from it whatever ministered to passion, to cast off the bondage of 'particular affections,' and convert his principal occupations into virtual inactivity[2]. He was anxious also to perform good deeds without the slightest sense of satisfaction or even with entire unconsciousness[3]. Each holy man who thus preserved the *Tao*, by destroying or ignoring self, was finally exalted into a model, and perennial source of blessing, for other members of the human family[4]. The man of a superior virtue is like water, of which one excellency is that it does good to all creatures. Water also does not strive (it flows into the empty spaces and avoids the full). Its home is in localities which have no charm for crowds (a proof of self-abasement). Therefore does the sage approach still nearer to the *Tao*. He is content with the lowliest positions. His heart is struggling to become as deep (and tranquil) as an abyss. If he distribute favours, his aim is to excel in humanity (his tenderness is not confined to individual favourites). If he speak, his actions do not afterwards belie his promise. If he govern, his desire is to establish peace. If he work, he shews capacity and aptitude. If he change his calling, he adapts himself completely to the times. He strives with no one: hence it is that he incurs no blame[5].' 'I possess three precious things,' is the assertion of Lao-tse himself: 'these I hold and guard as I would guard a treasure. The first is called affection (tenderness for living creatures); the second is called economy (frugality and moderation); the third is called humility, which prevents me from wishing to become the first man of the empire. I have affection, and hence it is I am courageous. I have economy, and hence it is that my expenditure is large. I

[1] *Tao-te-king*, 'Introd.' pp. vii. viii.

[2] *Ibid.* pp. 5, 7, 9.

[3] *Ibid.* p. 58.

[4] *Ibid.* p. 31. It was not, however, contemplated that all persons were capable of understanding and appreciating the doctrine of the *Tao*: some would of necessity deride it as enveloped in darkness (p. 63).

[5] *Ibid.* p. 11, and notes, p. 136.

dare not be the first man of the empire; hence it is that I have power to become the chief of all men[1].'

But besides the moral truths occasionally enunciated in the 'Book of the Way and of Virtue' (the *Tao-te-king*), we have other and more copious means of understanding the ethical system of Tao-ism. The members of that sect have long been in the habit of printing by subscription, and circulating as a matter of religious duty, the collection of moral maxims known as the *Book of Rewards and Punishments*[2]. Each maxim is followed by a gloss or commentary, and in almost every case elucidated by appropriate tales and anecdotes. The high repute in which this volume stands is further indicated by the circumstance that the authorship has been in modern times attributed to Lao-tse himself, in his capacity of deified and 'venerable Prince' or incarnation of the *Tao*[3]. 'Every wise man,' writes a commentator[4], 'ought to be full of respect for this book: he ought to believe sincerely all the maxims it delivers, and ought to practise them faithfully, regardless of all obstacles, and without suffering the zeal he had evinced at the commencement to diminish at the close of his career. He ought every morning to read it aloud, and to meditate on every phrase with serious attention. Let him redouble his efforts to perform good works, and his anxiety and ardour to correct past failings. Then will happiness spring up within himself to recompense his merits; and his end will be advancement to the rank of the immortals.' While the general tone of this production harmonises with the older treatise, it bears frequent witness also to the presence of a more eclectic and accommodating spirit. There was no sympathy whatever between Confucius and the founder of Tao-ism. The contemplative philosopher was in the eyes of the more practical and bustling sociologist a very 'dragon[5], who rises high above the clouds and floats in ether:' and Confucius had no wish to understand him or to follow his example. But this work of the disciples of Lao-tse, while it condemned some other forms of misbelief and of malpractice, recognised as true the doctrine

[1] *Ibid.* p. 101.

[2] *Le Livre des Récompenses et des Peines*, ed. Julien, Paris, 1835.

[3] See above, p. 308. The *Livre des Récompenses* itself attributes the composition to *Thaï-Shang*, another name for Lao-tse. It is, however, in reality a compilation (how modern we cannot say) of sentences drawn or imitated from the *king* of the Confucianists, the *Tao-te-king* and other philosophical and moral treatises: cf. M. Julien's 'Avertissement,' p. x.

[4] *Livre des Récompenses*, &c. p. 519.

[5] See the version of this well-known story in the *Tao-te-king*, 'Introd.' p. xxix.

taught by all the 'three religions[1],'—that which had been long in the ascendancy, and those which had been simply tolerated at the date of its compilation. And in one single passage a commentator actually makes the author of Tao-ism add the worship of the god *Fo* (or Buddha) to a list of other meritorious actions[2]. The original conception of the *Tao* had now indeed been gradually obscured, and ran the risk of being quite obliterated. In this later treatise, the great business of man's life is not to master his affections and escape from everything that tends to agitate his soul, or binds his spirit to the earth, but rather, as we saw in Buddhism[3], to accumulate the largest possible stock of merits. It is the duty of the 'three counsellors[4],' or, elsewhere, of the 'god presiding over life,' 'the prince of spirits[5],' to register the bad actions of all men; and according to the measure of their turpitude, as grave or venial, 'to cut off twelve years or else a hundred days from the duration of human life. When the allotted period is exhausted the man dies; but if, at the hour of death, a crime remains unexpiated (or, in other words, if no sufficient compensation has been made), it causes the transmission of unhappiness to his children and his grandchildren[6].' Urged by this regard to the well-being of himself and his posterity, every genuine Tao-ist labours hard to regulate his wishes and to purify his intentions[7]. He must set his own heart right and then attempt to influence others[8]. He must be humane, abstaining even from all cruelty to the minutest animals[9]. He must practise filial piety, must be affectionate as a brother, and respect his seniors[10]. He must pity the orphan and the widow[11]; he must sympathise with the afflicted[12], and rejoice with all who prosper[13]. He must help the needy, and take part in rescuing those who are in peril[14]. He

[1] *Livre des Récompenses*, p. 422.

[2] *Ibid.* p. 517.

[3] Above, p. 168.

[4] *Livre des Récompenses*, p. 13. 'These are names given by the Chinese to six stars, placed two and two, which correspond to ικ—λμ—νξ of the Great Bear.'

[5] *Ibid.* pp. 13, 502.

[6] *Ibid.* p. 502. The possibility of repentance and its efficacy, as here glanced at, are both recognised more fully in p. 514.

[7] *Ibid.* pp. 328, 512. 'Nous devenons coupables dès le moment que nous avons formé ce désir. Si l'homme peut rectifier son cœur lorsqu'il est seul et désœuvré, il pourra le conserver pur et intact au moment du danger.'

[8] *Ibid.* p. 65.

[9] *Ibid.* pp. 51, 73. In the latter passage, it is added: 'Si vous les blessez, vous n'imitez point la bonté du Ciel et de la Terre, qui aiment à donner la vie aux créatures.'

[10] *Ibid.* p. 56.

[11] *Ibid.* p. 68.

[12] *Ibid.* p. 74.

[13] *Ibid.* p. 77.

[14] *Ibid.* pp. 79, 83.

is not to boast of his superiority, nor divulge the imperfections of other men[1]. He is to act from kindly motives without waiting for a recompence; and, finally, he must not murmur against Heaven[2]; while they who fail to act according to these noble principles, are said to 'violate the duties which society imposes on them, dishonour their ancestors, stifle the germs of virtue which Heaven has planted in them, and corrupt public manners[3].'

In the system of Confucius we are seldom able to detect the slightest reference to a pure and righteous God whose moral law is broken by iniquity. The same remark must be extended also to Tao-ism. Once or twice indeed the doctors of the 'Way' incite us to the imitation of Heaven and Earth, who manifest their gentle nature in dispensing life to all the creatures; but the check imposed on evil thoughts and evil actions is more commonly the fear of giving umbrage not to God, but to the spirits of earth or heaven, who are affected, it is urged, by all the works of men, and have the power to punish or reward according to their quality[4]. The good man's pathway is encompassed by a host of these invisible agents, who are all continually engaged for his protection[5]; and in one remarkable passage, where a Chinese scholar had been strongly tempted to unchastity, the tempter fled, confounded by his reference to the supersensuous world, and the proximity of purer beings: 'the spirits of heaven and earth,' he argued, 'encircle us on every side; how then could one think of sinning in their presence[6]?'

We have scarcely any means of ascertaining the amount of influence exercised by this religion in the centuries immediately succeeding the death of Lao-tse. In later ages many of his opinions were disseminated far and wide, not only in China proper, but in Cochin-China, in Tonquin, and in Japan[7]. As early, however, as the reign of Woo-te, the sixth of the Han

[1] *Ibid.* pp. 91, 93.

[2] *Ibid.* pp. 107, 372.

[3] *Ibid.* p. 328.

[4] *Ibid.* p. 1.

[5] *Ibid.* p. 126. On the contrary the demons are said to stand aloof from him through terror and respect (p. 124).

[6] *Ibid.* p. 331: cf. pp. 489, 490.

[7] Julien's 'Avertissement' to the *Livre des Récompenses*, p. viii. The same writer in his 'Introduction' to the *Tao-te-king* (p. xi.) has pointed out a serious error in some current statements on this subject, according to which Tao-ism was said to have been once extensively propagated in Tibet and northern Hindústán. The mistake arose from confounding *Tao-sse*, followers of Lao-tse, and *Tao-jin*, followers of Śákya-muni—a name given to the Chinese Buddhists before they were called *Seng* or 'Doctors.'

dynasty who mounted the imperial throne, 140 B.C., a very large accession is recorded to the ranks of the Tao-ists[1]. The fear of death had fallen with unwonted power on many who were filling high positions in the Chinese empire, and unable to find peace or comfort in the tenets of Confucius, crowds of them resorted to the schools of his more spiritual opponent. But Tao-ism, as presented to us in this later stage of its development, had passed into a very different phase. Proceeding, it appears, on the hypothesis that 'holy men' are so completely identified with the *Tao* as to have acquired a perfect mastery over natural forces, which are still, however, fettering ordinary mortals, the Tao-ists grew most ardent in their cultivation of theurgy and various forms of magic[2]. They became, in some degree, the Neoplatonists of China. Their talk was now of spells, of amulets, of gifts of second sight, of charms, of incantations, of specifics in the very handwriting of the prince of demons; and affecting most of all to tranquillise the apprehensions of their votaries, they sought to manufacture an elixir of such potency, that all who drank it would be rescued from the grasp of death himself[3].

Henceforth the school of Lao-tse, in spite of all its early promise, occupied itself far too exclusively in the pursuit of these phantastic and debasing superstitions. To the Christian missionaries of the seventeenth century, the Tao-ists seemed the most 'abominable' sect of China, living only to corrupt and fascinate the populace by magical performances, in which they still are said to figure, at one time as mere jugglers, at another as physicians, at a third as fortune-tellers, at a fourth as gifted

[1] Gutzlaff (I. 235) attributes this accession to the influence of the empress, who was addicted to the creed of Lao-tse, 'and considered the heartless doctrines of the Chinese sage [Confucius], as the greatest enemy to the mystical system of her beloved master.'

[2] Thus in the *Livre des Récompenses*, &c., where magic is condemned whenever it is used for exciting social tumults (p. 422), there is no doubt expressed as to the 'supernatural powers' of some Tao-ists: see, for instance, the 'Histoire' in p. 423, where a magician of the sect was said to have brought down, for immoral purposes, 'toutes les déesses du Ciel et celles du mont Wouchan.'

[3] No traces of this 'elixir vitæ' are found in the *Tao-te-king*. It is said, however, that as early as 209 B.C. a Chinese expedition was sent across the Eastern sea into Japan to seek for such a medicine (Prichard, IV. 493). The idea may possibly have been derived from the *amrita* (=ambrosia) of ancient India (see above, p. 127, n. 2). From the East it travelled into Egypt, where Ptolemy Philadelphus, in possession of the secret, could declare ὅτι μόνος εὕροι τὴν ἀθανασίαν: Athenæus, Lib. XII. c. IX. (p. 536 E, ed. Casaubon).

with the power of drawing secrets from the world invisible, through intercourse with those who are possessed by demons. They are notwithstanding held in high repute by nearly every class of the Chinese: the ordinary appellation of their chiefs is that of 'heavenly doctors,' and the arch-chief of the sect, resembling in consideration and magnificence the Grand Lama of Tibet, is commonly believed to exercise, as the incarnate *Tao*, absolute dominion in the sphere of the invisible. 'He appoints and removes the deities of various districts, just as the emperor does his officers; and no tutelary divinity can be worshipped, or is supposed capable of protecting his votaries, until the warrant goes forth under the hand and seal of this demon-ruler, authorising him to exercise his functions in a given region[1].'

How remote are all such representations from the glorious facts of Christianity, and from the cheering visions of the Christian Apocalypse! 'Fear not: I am the first and the last: I am He that liveth and was dead, and, behold, I am alive for evermore, Amen; and have the keys of hades and of death' (Rev. i. 17, 18).

§ 3. *Fo-ism*[2], *or Chinese Buddhism.*

The sad experience of five centuries had gradually suggested to reflecting China-men, that neither of the two religious systems heretofore exposed could extricate the human spirit from perplexities in which she found herself involved, nor satisfy the wants and longings of our moral nature. One of these religions had succeeded doubtless in imparting form and animation to Chinese society, but meanwhile pushed into the background every question which affected our relationship to God and to the world invisible. Its chief concern was with the present life. The other, mystic and imaginative in its whole complexion, had run wild as it grew older; it was rapidly transforming the ideas of Lao-tse into a system of most abject demonology,—little if at all distinguishable from the ancient superstitions, whose main object was the deprecation and disarming of malignant principles.

While brooding over these momentous topics, and it may be, half despairing for himself as well as for his people, an intelligent emperor, Ming-te, about the sixtieth year of the Christian era, is reported to have had a most remarkable vision.

[1] Medhurst, pp. 200 sq.

[2] *Fo* or *Foĕ* is the first syllable of *Foĕ-t'a* or *Fu-t'a* = *Buddha*.

According to one account[1] there stood before him a resplendent figure, of gigantic size, and with a glorious nimbus round the head; and when his ministers of state were all consulted as to the most probable meaning of this dream or apparition, one of them replied that the description of it corresponded to a story he had heard of some great genius in the western country, who might therefore be intending to solicit the notice of the emperor. Another version of the legend is, that in the maxims of Confucius himself, was one affirming that the 'Holy Man' is in the west[2], or will hereafter issue from the west; and that impressions which this oft-repeated sentence left on the imperial mind could never be obliterated. In either case the sequel of the story is precisely the same. A deputation of mandarins proceed across the western mountains in the hope of learning fresh particulars respecting this mysterious personage; and on returning home they are accompanied by a Hindú teacher, bringing with him a large stock of books, and, as a present to the emperor himself, the portrait of Śákya-muni.

Thus the Buddhism of the Middle Kingdom rose at once into the rank of a 'religio licita;' its formal recognition occurring in the very year when the Apostle to the Gentiles passed in chains to the prætorium of the Cæsars, 'thanking God and taking courage' (Acts xxviii. 15). Buddhism, it is true, has never been allowed to interfere with the administration of the Chinese empire, nor been able to dethrone the old religion of the country. It was more or less contemned by the Con-

[1] Pauthier's *Chinè*, p. 256.

[2] Gutzlaff, I. 250. Some of the early missionaries in China, who gave currency to this legend, (*e.g.* Duhalde, *De la Chine*, &c. I. 360 sq. Paris, 1735), were of opinion that Confucius actually intended to point out the birth of Christ, and that the Chinese envoys actually started on a journey into Palestine to hail the advent of the Great Redeemer. On their way they encountered certain Buddhist missionaries coming from India, whom mistaking for true disciples of Christ they carried back as teachers of their fellow-countrymen. 'Thus,' says the translator of Schlegel, *Philosophy of Religion*, p. 136, note, 'was this religion introduced into China, and thus did this phantasmagoria of hell intercept the light of the Gospel.' No one has, however, been able to detect the saying here ascribed to Confucius in any of his extant writings. The passage most likely to have suggested the current story is one in the *Chung-Yung*, c. XXIX. §§ 3, 4: yet there even no allusion whatever is made to a country *in the west*. It is only declared with reference to the true sage: 'Il conforme ses actions aux lois du Ciel et de la Terre, et il n'éprouve aucun trouble; il se règle sur les intelligences supérieures à l'homme, et son esprit n'éprouve aucun doute: *il est cent générations à attendre le saint homme*, et il ne se dément jamais.'

fucianists, as foreign, innovating, and seditious. Patronised by one prince, it was sometimes roughly handled by another[1]; and in the century after that which witnessed the establishment of Christianity in the great metropolis of the west, the Chinese Buddhists, now attaining some numerical importance, were exposed to very bitter persecutions. Edicts from the prince of Wei not only authorised the demolition of their temples and the burning of their sacred books, but also instigated a general massacre of the Buddhist monks[2]. In the succeeding reign, however, dating from A. D. 452, the triumphs of their cause grew visible in almost every part of China. Cloisters rose again with marvellous facility, and multiplied so fast, that at the end of the next fifty years the total number of such buildings had been swollen, it is said, to thirteen thousand[3]. At the same time frequent intercourse with India, some account of which is happily preserved to us in records of the pilgrimages of Fa-hian[4] in the fourth, and of Hiuan-Thsang[5] in the seventh century after Christ, resulted in the importation into China of Buddhist pictures, books, and relics, and in the enlistment of a host of fresh auxiliaries, all burning to diffuse a knowledge of the law, or *Dharma;* till, won over by the zeal of Hindú

[1] Pauthier, p. 257.

[2] Gutzlaff, I. 291: Schott, *Über den Buddhaismus in Hochasien und in China*, p. 19, Berlin, 1846. Until this period it seems as if the new religion had made very little progress in China: cf. *Tao-te-king*, 'Introd.' p. x.

[3] Schott, as before, p. 20. The same kind of activity is just now visible in Birmah, where new temples and monasteries ('kyums') are daily springing up, even in the districts under British authority: Wilson, in *Journal of As. Soc.* XVI. 260.

[4] Translated by Abel-Rémusat, Paris, 1836.

[5] Translated by M. Julien, Paris, 1853. This latter pilgrim spent seventeen years (A. D. 629—A. D. 645) in countries situated to the west of China. In one passage (p. 26), he thus describes the object of his travels: 'J'étais vivement affligé de voir que les livres sacrés étaient incomplets, et que leur interprétation offrait de fâcheuses lacunes. Oubliant alors le soin de ma vie et bravant les obstacles et les dangers, j'ai fait serment d'aller chercher dans l'occident la *Loi* [Dharma] que le Bouddha a léguée au monde:' cf. p. 44, where he says that on his return to China he will translate and circulate the sacred books, and 'beat down the thick forest of errors.' 'Ensuite j'interrogerai la multitude des maîtres, et de leur bouche je recevrai l'enseignement de la droite *Loi.* Une fois de retour (en Chine), je traduirai les livres, je répandrai au loin des vérités inconnues; j'abattrai la forêt épaisse des erreurs, je détruirai les artifices des fausses doctrines, je réparerai les lacunes de *la doctrine de l'éléphant* [the translator (p. 467) corrects this into '*la doctrine des images*'] (la doctrine bouddhique), et je fixerai la boussole de la *porte mystérieuse* (de l'enseignement religieux).'

doctors (*Fan-seng*)[1] and ascetics (*shamans*)[2], a large portion of the Chinese populace were numbered with the followers of this foreign creed; nay, emperors themselves, the sons of Heaven, were not unwilling to lay down their sceptres, if they might but pass the evening of their lives beneath the shadow of a Buddhist monastery[3]. The culminating point of these successes was the fall of the Mongol dynasty in 1368.

I may have hitherto appeared to speak of Buddhism as of one organic system, animated by a definite creed, directed by a common hope and purpose, and binding all its converts to one centre of administration. But such inference is unquestionably incorrect. What Buddhism was when it put forth its earliest aphorisms, the 'undeveloped' *sûtras*, we have seen[4] already, while engaged in tracing the career of Gautama and analysing the first principles of his philosophy. Yet exactly in proportion to the wondrous elasticity of the system he had founded, and its marked superiority to those distinctions which had long been severing man from man and one people from another, is the freedom and the ease with which it commonly allied itself to pre-existing forms of heathenism, until the thoughts and symbols proper to it have been well-nigh buried in a motley crowd of foreign and conflicting elements. Buddhism once prevailed, or is prevailing, not only in Hindústán[5] the birthplace, and Ceylon the sacred island of the creed, but also in Tibet and Tatary, in China and Japan, in Cochin-China and Tonquin, in Siam and the Birman empire, to say nothing of its ancient rule in Java, and the remnant of it now surviving in Bali, an islet of the Indian archipelago, and possibly in regions still more distant and diverse[6]. Of all these heterogeneous populations none so truly represent the genuine forms of Buddhism, none so cordially agree together, as the natives of Ceylon, of Birmah[7], and

[1] *Fan*-seng (='doctors out of *India*') has been represented in other languages under the form of *Bonzen* or *Bonzes*.

[2] See above, p. 169, n. 3.

[3] Schott, p. 20.

[4] See above, p. 157.

[5] Even after the general expulsion from India small bands of Buddhists were still found in particular localities as late as the 12th century: and Jainism, which may be regarded as the surviving twin-sister of Buddhism, continued to produce effects at a far later date; for instance, modifying the ethical spirit of the Tamil literature: see Caldwell, as above, pp. 86 sq.

[6] 'Ob noch weitere Verbreitung des Buddhaismus nach *Polynesien* oder gar nach *Süd-Amerika* hin stattgefunden habe, wie man vermuthet hat, darüber fehlt vor der Hand noch jeder sichere Anhaltspunkt: jedenfalls hat sich daselbst nichts davon direkt erhalten.'—Weber, as above, p. 66.

[7] In Sangermano's *Burmese Em-*

Siam, whose sacred books almost entirely correspond, because translated not as in the other cases from Sanskrit, but from Páli. In those countries also images are numerous, yet with the exception of subsidiary figures, which are never worshipped, such as dragons and lions, they are 'all of the same character, representing Gautama or his disciples, generally in a sitting posture with the legs crossed, and the hands in the act of prayer or benediction[1].' On the contrary, as one result of the accommodating character of this creed, amalgamations are elsewhere so numerous that in spite of the original identity of the books disseminated, it requires no ordinary effort to understand wherein consists the family-likeness of the different sects[2]. They all, in general terms, are *Buddhist;* but the main conceptions of their votaries are divergent, nay, in many points are fundamentally opposed.

Perhaps there is no readier and more profitable way of representing this vast disparity than by contrasting some of the chief features of two neighbouring and related systems—the Fo-ism of China, and the Lama-ism of Tibet: for in so doing I may dissipate objections to the Gospel which have long been drawn from the alleged consistency of Buddhism, its compactness and numerical predominance. The new religion was extensively adopted in both those countries at nearly the same date; they both together inherited the sacred texts according to the same recension; yet so very inefficient was Buddhism in curbing and subduing the more wayward nationalities with which it came in contact, that, except in isolated cases, the Chinese, who have adopted what they call 'the customs of India[3],' are scarcely in their general character to be distin-

pire, ed. Tandy (Or. Tr. Fund, 1833), p. 83, it is stated that the only Buddhists recognised as orthodox by the inhabitants of that empire are the Buddhists of Ceylon.

[1] Prof. Wilson, in *Journal of As. Soc.* XVI. 253.

[2] 'In its migrations to other countries, since its dispersion by the Bráhmans, Buddhism has assumed and exhibited itself in a variety of shapes. At the present day, its doctrines, as cherished among the Jainas of Guzerat and Rajpootana, differ widely from its mysteries as administered by the Lama of Tibet; and both are equally distinct from the metaphysical abstractions propounded by the monks of Nepál. Its observances in Japan have undergone a still more striking alteration from their vicinity to the Syntoos; and in China they have been similarly modified in their contact with the rationalism of Lao-tseu and the social demonology (?) of the Confucians...But in each and in all the distinction is rather in degree than in essence.' Tennent's *Christianity in Ceylon*, pp. 206, 207.

[3] *Catechism of the Shamans*, ed. Neumann, p. 117.

guished from the vulgar followers of Confucius and Lao-tse. The only genuine Buddhists[1] are the monks and mendicants. They only can be said to recognise a common symbol, or confession of faith; they only have initiatory rites; they only form a separate and sacred corporation. Others who are known as worshippers of Fo, and constitute one half, or possibly two-thirds[2], of the enormous population of the Middle Kingdom, are rather tolerated than approved by the authorities of the sect. They are expected to confess the general excellence of their religion, to confide in some particular Buddha, or to worship one or other of the numerous Pusas (*Bódhisatwas*); to abstain from all the grosser forms of vice, to venerate the sacred writings of their predecessors, and the topes, or *sthúpas*, in which some reliquiæ of a departed Buddha are interred; and finally, to aid by contributions from their substance in supporting the *shamans*, monks, ascetics, and devotees[3]. The strict fulfilment of conditions such as these entitles them, it is believed, to higher spheres of being after death, but does not raise them to the dignity of the 'enlightened,' nor facilitate their passage to *nirvána*, the goal of genuine Buddhism. In Tibet this utter laxity of principle has never been so fully and so openly avowed; yet even there the old divinities are not dethroned entirely, and the poorer classes make their offerings, with the public sanction of the Lamas, to genii of the hills, the woods, the rivers, and the valleys[4].

The difference in the measure of amalgamation which took place in these two countries, is attributable to the different

[1] Gutzlaff, in *Journal of As. Soc.* XVI. 89.

[2] The same writer (*Ibid.*) conjectures that two-thirds of all the religious edifices in China are nominally Buddhist: but as Schott observes (*Über den Buddhaismus*, &c. p. 23, and 'Zusätze,' p. 127), statements of this kind are only true in a certain sense, *viz.* as implying that the eclectic polytheism of the Chinese populace extends itself so far as to include Buddhas and Bódhisatwas among the objects of common worship.

[3] Schott, *Ibid.* p. 17. The extreme laxity of Fo-ism is never shewn more vividly than in the fact, that the Chinese have little or no scruple on the subject of destroying animal life (cf. above, p. 161). They are said to be 'an omnivorous race; few living beings escape being made food for men, and are slaughtered and eaten without the least scruple. But to shew some regard for life, notwithstanding, they now and then dedicate some pigs to Buddha, which are permitted to live their natural space of life, and are never killed' (*Journal of As. Soc.* XVI. 84). The Shamans, on the contrary (*Catechism*, as above, p. 124), are directed to be extremely careful in this matter: they are not even to use *dry* wood in cooking, lest they should destroy insects in it.

[4] Major Cunningham's *Ladák*, p. 366, Lond. 1854.

tempers of the people, and the circumstances under which the new religion had been introduced. It is recorded[1] of Śákyamuni himself, that on observing no immediate prospect of success among a nation like the China-men, so long at least as the missionaries attempted to communicate his metaphysical doctrines, he suggested the employment of some other means more calculated to effect his purpose. The *Dharma* was to follow gradually upon the track of secular propagandists, who were smoothing the approaches to the Chinese mind, by giving lessons in arithmetic and astronomy. Others might be won by an appeal to the emotional province of their nature; but the China-man by working on his reason and self-interest. Whatever degree of credit we assign to statements of this kind, they are most useful as implying the strong repugnance which the China-man would always feel to a religious system like that of unadulterated Buddhism. His social instincts were opposed to its monastic rigour, his active habits to the indolence in which it seemed to thrive and revel. More than other men, he proved himself a firm believer in the reality and permanence of the present universe. The Buddhist *sútras*, on the contrary, proclaim[2] the absolute nothingness of all within us and around us: all is treated as an empty show: its origin is from nothing; its destination is to nothing; nay, the very core and essence of creation is declared to be non-being. Human life itself, so precious to the China-man, is in the creed of Gautama compared to single 'dew-drops, trembling on the leaf of the lotus.' Hence, indeed, arose the ardour of the primitive Buddhist in discoursing about the emptiness of human joys, and calling men to a complete renunciation of themselves and of the world. So far from meddling with the common business of society, they were each to seek a quiet refuge in the cloister, or attired in a peculiar dress, the cowl upon their head, the rosary suspended from their girdle[3], to go forth and urge their fellow-men to bow before the majesty of the *Dharma*.

[1] Schott, p. 42. The parallel in modern times is unmistakeable: 'Es sind hier offenbar Arithmetik und Sternenkunde (nebst Sternendeutkunst) gemeint, also gerade diejenigen Zweige des Wissens, welche auch *den römischen Glaubensboten im 17ten und 18ten Jahrh. bis ins Innerste des kaiserlichen Palastes Eingang verschafften.*' Precisely the same course had been pursued in the 16th century, with a view to counteract the Reformation in Bohemia.

[2] Above, pp. 162 sq.

[3] See Appendix II. above, p. 263; for in these and other points the monasticism of China resembles that of Tatary and Tibet. In the *Catechism of the Shamans*, as edited by Neumann, the second Part consists of the 'Regulations,' or direc-

In Tibet, where Buddhism was appealing to an ignorant, a pastoral, a simple-hearted race, it seems to have at once produced a very deep impression. Its actual development is far more nearly that which might have been predicted from a knowledge of its general principles. Disgusted with the 'epicurean atheism[1]' which heretofore prevailed throughout the districts on the Indian frontier, the Tibetians of Ladák had eagerly embraced the offers of the Buddhist missionaries at an early period; and since the middle of the seventh century after Christ, with only one important interruption[2], Buddhism under somewhat different aspects was enthroned as the religion of the whole country. Hence resulted the distinctive character of its dogmas, the apparent fervour of its moral tone, and the severity of its discipline. The mild Tibetians have for centuries been threatening to become a nation of religious mendicants. At the present day, the traveller is amazed by the ascendency of the *lamas*,—monks, or literally 'superiors,' carrying each one in his hand the 'prayer-cylinder[3]' or 'precious and religious wheel,' a revolution of which is held to be equivalent to the recitation of a roll of prayers. In every family one at least of several children is devoted to the service of the cloister, so that the assemblages of monks and nuns, who flock to the *viháras* in hundreds and in thousands, constitute no inconsiderable part of the entire population. Owing probably to this enormous increase in the number of the *lamas*, the common law of Buddhism, by which mendicants are sternly interdicted from the exercise of all mechanical arts, is totally rescinded, and the *lamas* both of Tibet and of Tatary are permitted to support themselves by various handicrafts, while living in the convents.

But another point in which the Fo-ism of the Middle Kingdom has diverged still more considerably from the Lama-ism of the adjacent regions is the absence from it of a regular and

tions touching the manners and customs of priests (or rather monks) after initiation. The editor remarks (p. 138): 'They so much resemble the monastic rules (Regula Monastica) of the Middle Ages, that one might be supposed to be copied from the other:' cf. Medhurst, p. 217.

[1] This, according to Major Cunningham, *Ladák*, p. 357, was the religion of the 'Bons' or 'Pons,' connected with the Sanskrit *Punya* ='pure.' Hence 'Pons'=Puritans, or Cathari.

[2] *Ibid.* p. 359.

[3] Major Cunningham has shewn (*Ibid.* pp. 375 sq.) the very high antiquity of this device. So efficacious is it thought to be, that 'cylinders, about one foot in height, are placed in rows around the temples, and are turned by the votaries before entering. Larger ones are turned by water, which keeps them perpetually revolving day and night.'

graduated hierarchy. When the creed of Śákya-muni finally won its way into the palaces of China, it was only raised to the position of a secondary (non-official) creed. As such the advocates of Buddhism were content to see it left. They urged that it was merely the completion[1], not the contradiction, of anterior systems. In their teaching, they adhered as closely as possible to the language of the sacred writings (*king*); they left the education of the masses in the hands of the imperial government; they recognised the excellence of the Confucian morality, although Confucius was himself esteemed inferior to Śákya-muni, and no fitting object of men's worship[2]; but in order most directly to secure their hold on the affections of the Chinese populace, they cordially accepted current maxims on the duty of sacrificing to departed ancestors[3], nay, freely acquiesced in the established worship both of good and evil spirits[4]. Thus, the continuity of old traditions remaining undisturbed, the 'Son of Heaven' was under no immediate apprehension of losing his supremacy by the admission of the foreign creed. His vast authority, exceeding in religious matters the prerogatives enjoyed by many an autocratic emperor of Byzantium, enabled him to regulate and curb all classes of his subjects, the compliant Buddhists not excepted. The Grand Lamas of Tibet were, on the contrary, the sole depositories both of temporal and spiritual power. Until comparatively recent times they were the masters of large tracts of country, which they governed in the spirit of the Roman Pontiff during the palmy days of Innocent III. They corresponded with the 'Sons of Heaven' on terms of brotherhood and of equality; and even now, when China has by force of arms obtained possession of Tibet, their claim to jurisdiction, as lords spiritual, continues to be freely recognised, as well in their own neighbourhood as in the hordes of barbarous Calmucks roving from the marshes of the Volga to the ruins of Samarcand. In some respects, indeed, these powerful Lamas and their agents are unlike the lordly pontiffs of western Christendom. Their theory of toleration[5] is

[1] Schott, as before, p. 22.

[2] Thus, in the *Catechism of the Shamans*, it is directed (p. 92): 'You shall not stay in a temple of the followers of Confucius and Lao-tse.'

[3] See above, p. 290.

[4] In the *Catechism*, as above, p. 102, the priest (or monk), taking the food at dinner in his left hand, is ordered to pray and say: 'O ye bad and good spirits, I now offer you this. May this meat be spread out for all bad and good spirits unto all the ten quarters [?] of the world.'

[5] When a Franciscan missionary of the XIVth century was describing the state of religion in China, he adverted to this characteristic

most comprehensive. As examples of a system of belief which thrives wherever men are lapsing into pantheism or utter atheism, they hold that each religion of the world has in it all the elements of necessary truth, and consequently that every one 'shall be saved by the law or sect which he professeth.'

Yet meanwhile outward forms of Lama-ism are often strikingly akin to rites and customs of Mediæval Christianity. 'The use of the cross, the mitre, the dalmatic, the hood, the office of two choirs, the psalmody, the exorcisms, the censer of five chains, the benediction of the lamas by placing the right hand on the head of the faithful, the rosary, celibacy of the clergy, spiritual retirement, the worship of saints, fasts, processions, litanies, and holy water[1];' such are specimens of the minute coincidences still adduced by Roman-catholic missionaries in proof of the amalgamation which Buddhism had effected in some districts with the ritual system of the Christian Church[2]. In what way soever the liturgical affinities in question are most satisfactorily explained; whether we regard them as genuine imitations rising out of some actual intercourse, or whether they exhibit no more of real sympathy than is implied in the fortuitous resemblance of the ape to man[3],—it is remarkable

laxity in the following terms: 'In isto vasto imperio sunt gentes de omni natione quæ sub cœlo est, et de omni secta; et conceditur omnibus et singulis vivere secundum sectam suam. *Est enim hæc opinio apud eos*, seu potius error, *quod unusquisque in sua secta salvatur.*' Raynald. *Annal. Eccl.* ad an. 1326, § 31. Marco Polo, in like manner, ascribes a similar declaration to Kublai-Khan (Bk. II. ch. ii.): 'There are four great Prophets, who are reverenced and worshipped by the different classes of mankind. The Christians regard Jesus Christ as their divinity; the Saracens, Mahomet; the Jews, Moses; and the idolaters, *Sogomom-bar-kan*, the most eminent among their idols. I do honour and shew respect to all the four.' Instead of the corrupt expression here italicized, read *Śákya-muni Burchan* ('Burchan' being the Mongolian word for 'Buddha').

[1] See *Journal of As. Soc.* XVI. 263.

[2] Cf. above, pp. 265 sq., where this subject is considered in detail.

[3] 'The enemies of Christianity, since the time of Voltaire, have not failed, at the name of Bonzes, to throw out many malicious epigrams against religion. The similarity here observed is not real, but is that caricature resemblance the ape bears to man, and which has led many naturalists into error; for the ape has with man no real affinity, no true internal sympathy in his organic conformation, but merely the likeness of a spiteful parody....We may lay it down as a general principle that the greater the apparent resemblance which a false religion, utterly and fundamentally different in its spiritual character and moral tendency, externally bears to the true, the more reprehensible will it be in itself, and the greater its hostility to the truth.' F. von Schlegel, *Phil. of Hist.* p. 134.

that only a few of them exist beyond the confines of Tatary and Tibet; while in respect of general organisation, passing downwards step by step from the Grand Lama to inferior orders of the hierarchy, China can as yet present us with no parallels whatever. The communities of Fo-ists in that empire seem to be all virtually independent; they are barely held together by the recognition of common precepts, and the bond which keeps them all in due subordination to the officers of the state-religion.

Again, the Lama-system differs fundamentally from that of Chinese Buddhism in the doctrine of hereditary incarnations. The great thought of some intelligence, issuing from the Buddha-world, assuming the conditions of our frail humanity, and for a time presiding over some one favoured group of Buddhist monasteries, had been long familiar to the natives of Tibet. The founder of the confraternity of *red* Lamas[1], dating as far back as the eighth century after Christ, is said to be an instance of this self-humiliation. In the following centuries the practice was for monks or mendicants of particular tribes to choose a kind of 'chief-abbot[2],' in the hope of thus preserving the continuity of their order for successive generations. Of such distinguished potentates we have examples in men like Tsong Kaba[3], who founded the great monastery of Khal-dan near Lhassa, in 1409, and by whose influence, it is said, a multitude of changes were effected both in the administration and the ritual system of Tibetian Buddhism. Still no progress seems to have been made, until the latter half of the same century, in ripening the idea of *perpetual* incarnations. Then it was that one chief-abbot, the 'perfect Lama,' instead of passing, as he was entitled, to his ultimate condition, determined for the benefit of mankind to sojourn longer on the earth and be continuously new-born[4]. As soon as he was carried to his grave in 1473, a search was instituted for the personage who had been destined to succeed him. This was found to be an infant, who established its title to the honour by appearing to remember various articles which were the property of the Lama just deceased, or rather were the infant's own property in earlier stages

[1] Cunningham's *Ladák*, p. 367. This Lama (Urgyan Rinpoche), who was invited into Tibet, is said to have been an incarnation of the Buddha Amitábha, the fourth of the celestial Buddhas of that region. He is viewed as an incarnation either of Amitábha or of Manjusrí. His tutor was the strange Lama 'from the far west,' who may possibly have imported Christian ideas: above, p. 265; and *Journal of As. Soc.* XVI. 263.

[2] *Ibid.* p. 369.

[3] Also written Tsong Khapa.

[4] Cunningham, as before, pp. 368, 369.

of existence. When the proofs of such identity were deemed irrefragable, the new candidate was formally promoted to the vacant chair: and in the fifth abbot of this series originated the famous hierarchy of the Dalai-Lamas (in 1640). So fascinating grew the theory of perpetual incarnation, that a fresh succession of rival Lamas (also of the *yellow* order) afterwards took its rise at Teshu-lambu, while the Dalai-Lamas were enthroned in Lhassa; and at present[1] every convent of importance, not in Tibet only, but in distant parts of Tatary, is claiming for itself a like prerogative. Each confraternity believes that the departed abbot is still actually present with his subjects though enshrouded in a different body. Conscious of the dark malignity of demons, quivering at the thought of men who practise demoniacal arts and lead astray by their enchantments, these Tibetians are 'in bondage to fear;' their only refuge is the presence and superior holiness of one who, by his mastery over all the adverse forces[2] of creation, is believed to rescue his true followers from the rage of their oppressor. The religion of Tibet is thus from day to day assuming all the characteristics of man-worship[3]. Anxious cravings after some invincible protector there impel the human spirit to fashion for itself a novel theory of salvation; and the sight of one who styles himself incarnate deity excludes all living faith in God and in the things invisible.

From these remarks on characteristic differences between the Fo-ism of China and the Lama-ism of other regions, I pass forward to examine some fresh points which serve no less directly to evince the fluctuating and elastic genius of the creed we are reviewing. Buddhism then, as extant both in China and Tibet, is not the Buddhism of Śákya-muni, nor the Buddhism of the earliest race of his disciples. Primitive Buddhism, there is little or no cause for doubting, was entirely atheistic[4].

[1] *Journal of As. Soc.* XVI. 254.

[2] 'The Lamas in Tatary are constantly exorcists and magicians, sharing no doubt very often the credulity of the people, but frequently assisting faith in their superhuman faculties by jugglery and fraud:' *Ibid.* p. 264. This use of magic seems, however, disallowed in some other districts: for the *Catechism of the Shamans*, ed. Neumann, p. 111, prohibits the Buddhist monks from studying 'the works of Lao-tse' on demonolatry, &c.

[3] 'Durch diese vielen leibhaften Gegenstände der Andacht ist die buddhaistische Religion in Tibet *ein wahrer Menschen-Cultus* geworden, indem besonders ihre geistlichen Ober-häupter wahrhaft *göttlicher Verehrung* sich erfreuen. Auch werden die irdischen Überreste jedes Ober-Lama's als Reliquien aufbewahrt und angebetet:' Schott, as before, p. 33.

[4] Cf. above, pp. 162 sq.

As such its primary tenet led directly to the thought of ultimate annihilation. There was nothing to receive the spirit of man on her eventual extrication from *sansára*, the world of appearance; and therefore instead of being absorbed as in the old Bráhmanical theology, and so escaping through absorption from the fatal liability to repeated births, the elements of life were all declared by early Buddhist doctors to be literally 'burnt out,'—the spirit passed at length into extinction, or *nirvána*[1]. Atheism was thus attaining its most dismal consummation in proclaiming an abyss of universal void.

On the contrary, there often lingered in the mind of northern Buddhists the idea of some great Being separable from this frail and shadowy world, superior also to the highest of created entities, and constituting in himself the only source of ultimate felicity. The very Buddha who persisted in ignoring the Creator and the Judge of men was sometimes elevated to this dignity; while the *nirvána* of his early followers, far too cold, too dreary, and too abstract, was ere long invested by the popular imagination with a different class of attributes, nay, changed into a paradise of inexhaustible enjoyment. In Nepál, and portions also of Tibet, we find the traces of a still more definite and systematic theology, yet there it had been borrowed, we have reason to believe, from the adjacent Bráhmanism[2]. By five spontaneous acts of wisdom and reflection, the self-existent Ádi-Buddha has projected from his own essence five intelligences of the first order ('The celestial Buddhas'); which in turn, by their exertion of corresponding energies, give birth to other five intelligences of the second order ('the Bódhisatwas')[3]. These become creative agents in the hands of God, or serve as links uniting him with all the lower grades of creaturely existence. But to other countries lying within the circle of Buddhist witchery this doctrine of spontaneous emanations is utterly unknown. The Buddhas are, in every case, 'enlightened' men, advancing upwards by the natural force of merit from one stage of greatness to another, till at last they are exempted altogether

[1] This point has also been recently discussed by Mr. Max Müller, *Buddhism and Buddhist Pilgrims*, pp. 45 sq. Lond. 1857. See above, p. 165, and n. 4.

[2] Prof. Wilson, in *Journal of the Asiat. Soc.* (1856), XVI. 255, 256. The intermixture is still further illustrated in the numerous elements derived by Buddhists of Nepál and of Tibet from the mystical system of the Hindú Tantrists. Thence, for example, came the 'filthy theory of the Buddhist Sáktis,' or the female energies of the Dhyání Buddhas: Cunningham's *Ladák*, pp. 366, 384.

[3] See Abel-Rémusat, *Mélanges Posthumes*, p. 48, Paris, 1843.

from the sad contingencies of human life. The Bódhisatwas (or, in Chinese, *Pusas*)[1] are, again, incipient Buddhas; they are all accredited competitors, approaching the possession of like immunities and like distinctions; they are rising by self-sacrifice and through the salutary influence they exert upon their fellow-men to that which forms the summit of all human efforts. Yet this very goal which Buddhas have attained, and Bódhisatwas are attaining, is to be the final destination of all sentient beings. Every age produces an array of Bódhisatwas, and hereafter at the winding up of universal nature, when its mighty revolutions are complete, *sansára* will have been utterly depopulated by the gradual drafting of its tenants to the Buddha-sphere, *i. e.* by their annihilation, in the language of philosophy, or by their deification, in the language of the simple and unlettered. In this system, therefore, it is plain that the idea of God, though not expressly and in terms excluded, has been robbed of all its force, its meaning, and its vitality; and hence, in spite of rapturous invocations now and then addressed to a superior Buddha, as identical with a supreme Intelligence, the Fo-ists of the Middle Kingdom can be hardly said with any measure of propriety to know or fear, to love or worship God. Their ethical writings[2] are devoid of reference to His being: they contain no single precept on the duties which men owe to Him.

But is it then to be concluded that the Chinese Buddhists are without a definite object of religious worship? On the contrary, the empire is now thickly studded with their temples: 'they combine irreconcilable principles of atheism and polytheism,' insomuch that it is easier 'to find a god than a man in China[3].' Towering high above the other images are three colossal forms which re-appear in almost every temple. These are either representations[4] of a Buddha and two of his chief dis-

1 'Bódhisatwas' = *Pu-ti-sa-ta*, then *Pu-ti-sa* and finally *Pu-sa*. In the estimation of the ordinary Fo-ist a *Pusa* is a god, one inmate in the crowded pantheon: Schott, p. 23.

2 *e. g.* the *Catechism of the Shamans*, passim. The Buddhist monk when called to his devotions by the sound of the wooden bell is to utter a wish that it may 'glorify the religion,' and that 'all living creatures may become enlightened' (p. 101): but there is no mention of any duty which men owe to God. The most that we can say of the 'God-like nature' is, that it dwells 'in an atmosphere of eternal complacency and repose; no greater sympathy [being shewn] with good than with evil, no displeasure against sin, no manifestation of approval of virtue.' Sir J. Bowring, *Kingdom and People of Siam*, I. 294. Lond. 1857.

3 Medhurst, p. 219.

4 Wilson, as before, p. 253. Abel-Rémusat (*Mélanges Posthumes*, p. 26) has cited a prayer where he thinks that worship is

ciples; or else of three Buddhas past, present, and future; or in other cases they are meant to symbolise the primitive Buddha, Śákya-muni, as allied with *Dharma*, the religion he had founded, and with *Sangga*, the community or confraternity of religious men. It is, however, most remarkable, as again exemplifying the multiformity of Buddhism, that the 'Three Precious Ones' of modern China are not identical with the 'Three Supremacies' of somewhat earlier generations. Śákya-muni has indeed his constant votaries not only as the Shakya-Thubba of Ladák, and as the Kodom or Gautama of other regions, but also as the Shekia and the Fo of Chinese Buddhism. Yet his fame appears to have been long declining even where the solemn sacrifice of flowers and perfumes still continues to be offered; and hereafter, on the expiration of five-and-twenty centuries from the present time[1], he is expected to be absolutely superseded by a fresh and more benignant Buddha, called *Maitréya* or *Mi-le.* It was probably a consequence of this foreboding as to his eventual deposition that led in China and in some adjacent districts to the worship of three other objects, scarcely inferior to Gautama himself, yet all of them unknown to the original Buddhists[2]. Such are Amitábha (O-me-to[3]), Avalókitéśwara (Kwan-shi-in[4] or Padma-páńi), and Manju-śrí[5] (Jámya or Jam-

rendered to Buddha as *the first member of a triad.* The form is this: 'Adoration à *Bouddha*, adoration à *Dharma*, adoration à *Sangga*,' to which is annexed the Bráhmanical *Ǒm.* See above, p. 195.

[1] Schott, p. 13; Bowring's *Siam*, I. 305; Sangermano's *Burmese Empire*, p. 85.

[2] Wilson, as before, pp. 241, 242. Two out of the three are first noticed in the account of the pilgrimage of Fa-hian (at the close of the 4th century): Cunningham's *Ladák*, pp. 362, 363.

[3] The Chinese modification of the Sanskrit *Amitábha* (= 'unmeasured, infinite Light').

[4] Kwan-shi-in = 'world-inspecting *Sound*,' a mistaken rendering of the Sanskrit *avalókita-íswara* = 'world-inspecting *Lord.*' The mistake arose from not perceiving the fusion of *a* + *í* into *é*, and so reading *swara* 'sound' for *íswara* 'lord.' The other title *Padma-páńi* is also pure Sanskrit (= 'lotus in his hand,' or 'lotusbearer'), and is said to accord in signification with the Tibetian name *Chakna-padma*: Schott, p. 30, n. 1. Major Cunningham, on the contrary, identifies *Avalókitéśwara* with the Tibetian *Chanrazik*, and regards Padma-páńi as a different and still later Bódhisatwa: *Ladák*, pp. 362, 363, 383.

[5] Another form, also of Sanskrit origin, is *Manju-gósha.* The first seems to indicate a being of 'mild or gentle majesty;' the second a being of 'mild or gentle voice:' Schott, p. 40, n. 1. The Chinese corruption of *Manju-śrí* is *Wen-choo;* while the Tibetian form is *Jam-pal.* According to one version (Lassen, III. 777) *Manju-śrí* was a veritable man, by whom the conversion of Nepál to Buddhism had been originally attempted, in the tenth century after Christ.

pal). The last, though chiefly occupied, as men believe, in the diffusion of religious truth, and in such office bearing in his hand a naked sword, the symbol of his power and his acumen, has not hitherto absorbed so large a share of popular devotion[1] as the two with whom he is immediately associated. His province is the world of intellect; while Kwan-shi-in, the second of these three divinities, is the author of all joy and happiness in the family-circle, and has even been deputed to administer the government of the whole earth. In many districts of Tibet, which seems to claim his more indulgent patronage, he is incarnate, under the name of Padma-páṅi, in the person of the Dalai-Lama: and perhaps no cry so often strikes the ear of travellers in that country as *Om! Mani-padme! Húm*, 'Glory to the Lotus-bearer, Húm[2]!' Both there and in Mongolia, this far-stretching potentate is represented sometimes with innumerable eyes and hands, and sometimes with as many as ten heads, all bearing crowns and rising conically one above another[3]: but in every part of China the imagery employed is far less cumbrous and ornate; and what is more remarkable, this single tenant of the Buddha-world, in violation of a law by which distinctions as to sex are not perpetuated in the most exalted stage of being, is invested with a female figure, and with feminine decorations[4].

High above the head or heads of Padma-páṅi, and so forming the very apex of that sacred cone or pyramid, is seen the visage of his great superior, Amitábha, who, radiant with the glories of a perfect Buddha[5], is perhaps the most revered of all the objects worshipped in the Fo-ist temples. It is probable

[1] Schott, p. 41.

[2] *Mani-padme* is a misreading or corruption of the Sanskrit *Padma-páṅi*. The whole of this invocation, alluding to the way in which Padma-páṅi was first revealed, is said to have been suggested directly from heaven, as the bearer of innumerable blessings to the human family: Abel-Rémusat, *Mélanges Posthumes*, p. 403: 'Neubekehrte Fürsten der Mongolei lernten vor Allem diese Formel beten, vermuthlich damit der heilige Schauer, den sie ihnen einflössen sollte, das Feld ihres Glaubens desto fruchtbarer machte; und noch heutzutage ist sie in beiden Ländern [Tibet and Mongolia] dem Laien eben so geläufig als dem Geistlichen, und behauptet sich neben seinen anderen vorschriftsmässigen Gebeten.' Schott, p. 61.

[3] Schott, p. 45; Wilson, as before, p. 242.

[4] *Ibid.* Perhaps this notion may be borrowed from the theory of Buddha-śaktís, or female energies, which is, and has been for some ages, current both in Nepál and in Tibet: see Cunningham's *Ladák*, p. 364.

[5] 'Den Chinesen ist nun A-mi-ta, (O-me-to) ein vollendeter Buddha, wie Sâkjamuni, aber von diesem bestimmt geschieden:' Schott, p. 49.

that he was once regarded only as an image of the absent Śákya-muni, who on finishing his salutary work is thought to have retreated for a while into some deep abstraction, without absolutely ceasing to exist. Amitábha may thus have been to the originator of the Buddhist creed exactly what his offspring and co-regent, Padma-páni, will in course of ages be to him. So great, however, is the present dignity of Amitábha, that all the other gods of China are apparently outstripped by him, and well-nigh thrown into the shade[1].

To him the Fo-ist looks for grace, for mercy, for deliverance from all kinds of evil. Starting like the previous Buddhas from a low position, he has worked his way, it is believed, through a succession of new births into the loftiest sphere of the invisible regions. There he sits enthroned for ever on a lotus, his celestial court comprising an array of *Pusas* (or advanced competitors for Buddha-ship), and closer still in place and honour to his own unrivalled majesty, appearing his chief-minister and disciple, the co-regent Padma-páni[2].

The main features of this paradise of Amitábha are deserving of a more extended notice, partly on the ground that they are altogether irreconcilable with the early creed of Buddhism[3], and partly as suggesting a comparison with images that sometimes meet us on the page of sacred prophecy. 'This paradise includes within it every thing most noble and most sumptuous; and the city of the gods is all constructed of gold and precious stones, arranged with perfect art. The atmosphere is ever redolent of spices, and resounds with blissful harmonies. The streams again move forward like a tender strain of music. Round about are stately trees of silver with branches of pure gold, all covered by a rich variety of precious stones and the most gorgeous fruits. The spaces also are occupied by trees of eight different sorts,

[1] 'Mit seinem *unendlichen Lichte* [the meaning of Amitábha] hat er Sâkjamuni selber fas ganz verdunkelt.' *Ibid.*

[2] *Ibid.* p. 50.

[3] Schott, who has translated largely from a Chinese work intended to excite men's faith in the *Tsing-t'u* (or paradise of Amitábha), says with perfect truth that very much of the description, and the whole theory respecting this Buddha, is in direct contradiction to the creed of Gautama. 'Amitábha soll ein vollendeter Buddha sein, obschon ein Solcher nicht einmal vom Himmel aus an dem Erlösungswerke ferneren Antheil nimmt. Er und die seligen Bewohner seines Reiches sollen *ewig leben*, obschon dies einem Axiome des Buddhaismus geradezu widerspricht. Die im Tsing-t'u Wiedergebornen leben dort...mit Pusa's zusammen, sind im Besitz derselben Gaben, im Genusse derselben Vortheile, und doch keine eigentlichen Pusa's.' (p. 57.)

consisting each of two different jewels, on whose leaves and on the lotus-flowers there growing in the midst, innumerable seats have been provided for the Buddhas. A golden vault responding to the breath of every zephyr in celestial harmonies extends its shadow over all the trees, and at their feet flows forth in gentle murmurs many a copious stream of water, holy, living, wonder-working. The tenants of this paradise are all without distinction of rank or sex[1]; they all are equal, glorious in form and aspect, and exempted from the possibility of future births into a world of misery. In the centre of the region is a grove consisting of the goodliest trees; where peerless in his beauty and resplendent as the evening sky reposes the great Buddha Amitábha, a peacock and a lion forming the supporters of his throne. His right hand, the dispenser of his grace, is white, and rests upon his lap: while in his left hand, he is holding a dark vase of holy water. Round about him sit the Bódhisatwas, his elect, who offer up their prayers for the well-being and conversion of all creatures[2].'

The possession of this supreme felicity is said to have resulted in all cases, not as in the primitive Buddhism[3] from ascetic habits painfully acquired by free submission to an almost endless series of new births, but simply from unbounded trust in Amitábha, and unceasing prayer to him in his capacity of champion and rewarder. He swore, it is believed in China, that 'if any being in all the ten worlds should, after repeating his name, fail to attain life in his kingdom, he would cease to be a god[4].' The process of salvation was now represented, in accordance with the earth-ward tendency of men addressed, as something far more easy and indulgent than was commonly imagined. 'It requires no whole day, but only a few instants every morning. What it asks for is, one prayer [*O-me-to Foě*, or 'Amitábha Buddha'], ten times repeated. It is, therefore, burdensome to no man: it will interfere with no man's social

[1] In a different description of the paradise of *O-me-to* (Amitábha) communicated in Medhurst's *China*, p. 207, it is said that 'there are no women; for the women who live in that country are first changed into men.' The legend then continues: 'The inhabitants are produced from the lotus-flower, and have pure and fragrant bodies, fair and well-formed countenances, with hearts full of wisdom, and without vexation,' &c.

[2] Translated from a Mongolian source in Schott, pp. 52, 53. The Chinese legends on the subject, which, as he observes, are very numerous, preserve the same general outlines, but, as might have been anticipated from the genius of the people, all the details are less florid and grotesque.

[3] Cf. Schott, pp. 57, 58.

[4] Medhurst. *Ibid.*

duties, nor his worldly business......Yes! it is the work of an instant every morning, and nevertheless it brings advantages that are to last for all eternity[1].' Faith, however, is imperatively needed in the human subject ere this saving work can be achieved. Without it there ensues no movement in the right direction, just as when the will refuses to exert its force upon the bodily organism. 'A Buddha can deliver all creation, yet is powerless in respect of men who have no faith[2].' The vilest sinner, on the contrary, who is possessed of this most efficacious principle, will rise at once superior to the fear of death, and will be rescued from the pains of hell. If at the hour of dissolution he have strength enough to supplicate the mercy of *O-me-to*, and can repeat the supplication ten times, 'the images of hell are sure to be transformed into a lotus; and the sinner, snatched from ruin, will obtain admission into paradise. The Buddha,' it is added, 'can effect all this, because his mercy and his wonder-working power are both indefinitely great[3].'

The reader may be tempted to infer, on meeting with this very remarkable language, that the authors of the documents in question were not altogether strangers to Christianity itself, whose tenets they appear to be adopting and distorting. And in favour of such interpretation is the fact, that their idea of absolute faith in one divinity as *the* condition of deliverance from all forms of evil, was unknown to every other creed of heathendom, until, in times comparatively recent, it was also manifested in the Krishńa worship of the Bráhmans, and perverted by them into pretexts for unbounded laxity and self-indulgence[4]. Every one, moreover, is disposed to grant that the Chinese conception, as here indicated, is quite foreign to the ethics and religion of Śákya-muni, and in truth was a production of far later ages[5].

[1] Translated by Schott from the *Tsing-t'u-uen*, as before, p. 65.

[2] *Ibid.* p. 81.

[3] *Ibid.* p. 94. A discussion follows as to whether the intercession of the living is available for the comfort or recovery of the dead. 'In den *Sútras* steht geschrieben: "Die verdienstlichen Handlungen, welche Andere nach seinem Tode für den Menschen thun, erwerben nur eins von sieben [*i.e.* the harvest is disproportionate to the seed sown]; was aber der Mensch *für sich selbst bei seinen Lebzeiten thut*, das wird ihm tausendfaltig vergolten." Warum also wartet man bis an seinen Tod, und bittet Andere, statt seiner zu beten?'

[4] See above, pp. 182, 234; and the more recent consideration of the subject in Weber's *Indische Skizzen*, pp. 92 sq. He is now even more persuaded that Christianity was at the bottom of those thorough changes in the old beliefs of India (p. 94).

[5] Schott, p. 58, who refers these modifications to a period, 'in

Possibly, when some adventurous heralds of the Gospel, in the seventh and following centuries after Christ, began 'to turn their faces towards heaven, and, travelling with the Book of Truth[1],' surmounted the vast obstacles that severed China from the western world, the influence they exerted in the presence of a creed so flexible as Fo-ism, was more deep and lasting than is generally believed. Or it may be that in still later ages, when the courts of the Great Khan were thronged by ardent representatives of all known religions; when the Christian preachers in particular were 'commanded to attend him and bring with them their Book[2];' and when, as the result of this indulgence, both the Latins and Nestorians dared to plant their missions even in Peking itself, the eastern capital of the empire, some of the vibrations thus excited in the Chinese mind had led to an occasional adoption of Christian phraseology, analogous to what is happening in the *Tae-ping* rebels of the present day.

But whatever be the true account of the phenomena to which I have adverted, it is obvious that the actual changes in the Fo-ist system did not penetrate below the surface. Faith in Amitábha bears the slightest possible relation to faith in Christ the Righteous. The phantastic paradise of Amitábha has no common ground with that which Christians see prefigured on the glowing page of the Apocalypse. In both those heathen parallels the most essential element is one that has receded most of all into the background. Holiness of heart and life is not proclaimed in them as the concomitant of genuine faith, nor as the one condition of eventual blessedness; but, on the contrary, the novel tenet has been there adopted with the plain avowal that by it mankind will be exonerated altogether

welcher man selbst den Geistlichen keine grossartige Selbstverläugnung und keine angestrengte Meditation mehr zutrauen konnte.'

[1] This phrase occurs in the famous Syro-Chinese inscription, the genuineness of which has been disputed for more than two centuries: see, on the one side, Abel-Rémusat, *Nouveaux Mélanges Asiat.* II. 189 sq., and on the other, Prof. Neumann, in the *Jahrbücher für wissenschaft. Kritik* (1829), pp. 592 sq. Mr. Kesson, *The Cross and the Dragon*, pp. 16 sq. Lond. 1854, and (more in detail) M. Huc, *Le Christianisme en Chine*, I. 48—93, have reviewed the whole question. But, however that particular controversy may be settled, there is no doubt that soon after A.D. 782 (the date of the inscription) Christianity did find its way as far as China through the wide-spread influence of 'Nestorian,' or Syrian, missionaries (Huc, I. 98 sq.).

[2] See the narrative in Marco Polo, Bk. II. ch. ii. (p. 167, ed. Wright) and Huc, I. 367 sq. The title of M. Huc's chapter is 'Le Catholicisme à Péking pendant le treizième siècle.'

from the stern injunctions of the moral law. On sifting all such specious but entirely hollow approximations to the doctrine of our blessed Lord, one is continually reminded of the daring counterfeits disseminated far and wide by the abettors of the earliest heresies. The solifidianism of Hindústán and China is the solifidianism dissected and denounced by the believing Irenæus[1]. It is alien from the spirit of pure and Catholic Christianity. Attempts to mix what is incapable of admixture, were accordingly resisted and defeated here and there upon the very threshold. Men discovered that they could not 'sew a piece of new cloth on an old garment:' concord or consistency was felt to be impossible: 'the new piece taketh away from the old, and the rent is made worse.'

It is, indeed, the clear opinion of those modern writers who have had the largest opportunity of tracing out the principles of Buddhism to their practical results, that while it has appeared to flourish most in Birmah and Siam, its course in China has for centuries been one of retrogression and decay. The very monks of Fo-ism, who are nominally bound by far more stringent regulations than the rest of the community, are said to go beyond their pupils in the puerility of their superstitions and the immorality of their lives. 'The ignorance, selfishness, chicanery, mendacity, mendicancy, and idleness of the bonzes cannot be exaggerated,'—such is the deliberate judgment of one[2] who spent his days in China, chiefly in the hope of elevating the moral and religious status of the Chinese people. And even if

[1] 'Quapropter nec ulterius curarent eos [*i.e.* prophetas] hi, qui in eum [Simonem] et in Helenam ejus spem habeant, et ut liberos agere quæ velint: secundum enim ipsius gratiam salvari homines, sed non secundum operas justas.' Iren. *Contra Hæreses*, Lib. I. c. XXIII. § 3 (ed. Stieren).

[2] See Gutzlaff's communication, which he sent to Europe not long before his death, in the *Journal of the As. Soc.* XVI. 73 sq. His testimony is echoed on the whole by that of Sir John Bowring, who cannot be charged with disparaging Buddhism in order to exaggerate the importance of Christianity. He writes (*Kingdom and People of Siam*, I. 297, Lond. 1857): 'The real and invincible objection to Buddhism is its selfishness.... A bonze seems to care nothing about the condition of those who surround him: he makes no effort for their elevation or improvement. He scarcely reproves their sins, or encourages their virtues. He is self-satisfied with his own superior holiness, and would not move his finger to remove any mass of human misery.' Wuttke, by a different process, comes to a result substantially the same: 'Thatsächlich hat der Buddhismus in China allen Geist verloren, ist faul und dumpf geworden: ein ganz mechanisches Formel-wesen, dem Chinesen so natürlich, hat die Stelle der gewaltigen Ideen eingenommen.' (II. 84.)

it be contended that the Christian zeal of men like Gutzlaff caused them here and there to overcolour their descriptions of the blindness and the inefficiency of Fo-ism, no one will deny that its material strength has long been rapidly declining, and the outward glory of the system vanishing from day to day. The Fo-ist temples 'are now mostly deserted, and in a state of ruins; the votaries fewer and fewer, and the offerings very sparing[1].' What may be the future of this mighty empire, what the changes that may supervene hereafter on the agitation of the present times, it were not easy to conjecture. The Christian missionary may have still occasion to sit down and cry despairing on the frontier, 'O that the everlasting gates of rock would open!' but one fact appears to have been well established, that in this particular 'China during the last twenty or forty years has undergone a very great change, and is still verging to a more important crisis[2].'

I am far, however, from contending, with some Christian writers, that the vast dissemination of Buddhist tenets was in former days so utterly adverse to the higher interests of humanity. To say of this religion that its votaries are people 'whose business is to do nothing, to think on nothing, and to live as much as possible on nothing[3],' is a representation meagre, hasty, and one-sided. When Buddhism started on its northern missions, full of youthful hope and unextinguishable ardour, we behold it shaping many a savage horde into a peaceful confraternity; it quenched the violence of domestic strife; it sheathed the scimitars of the bloodthirsty Mongols, who were bent on carrying desolation to the very heart of Europe; it planted convents, and therewith conventual schools and libraries in regions heretofore oppressed by every kind of demonolatry and darkness; it carried some imperfect elements of Hindú civilisation far across the sandy wastes of Tatary, and shed some glimmerings of a higher light within the borders of Siberia; and even if the proselytes it made have far too frequently relapsed into their old condition, and so proved the utter impotence of Buddhism to effect a permanent and radical change[4], the partial

[1] Gutzlaff, as above, p. 91.

[2] *Ibid.* How far the struggles now proceeding may affect the ultimate position of Chinese Buddhism is also matter of deep interest to those who watch the fortunes of the Middle Kingdom: for it is well known that the rebels have invariably betrayed a most decided hostility to Fo-ism, its doctors, and its images.

[3] Neumann, *Pref.* to the *Catechism of the Shamans*, pp. xxiii, xxiv.

[4] See above, pp. 168, 249.

benefit resulting from its propagation ought on no account to be forgotten. Buddhism should in fact be measured, not by Christian, but by heathen standards; and when so regarded, it will, in its palmier days, appear almost to justify the startling eulogy bestowed upon it by a modern writer, when he speaks of Buddhism as the 'Christianity of the East[1].' The stress which it originally placed on ethics in their social and political aspect; its contempt for principles which long created an impassable gulf between the different orders of Hindú society; its fuller recognition of the rights of woman; its mild and inoffensive spirit, its equanimity under suffering, its forgiveness of injuries, are some of the peculiar features which adorn its moral code. Instead of ministering[2] to all the grosser passions, like the theories of Islam, it carried its appeal directly to the intellectual and contemplative province of man's nature; instead of finding its chief stimulus in struggles after fame and in the offer of material prosperity, it preached the vanity of earthly goods, the hollowness of human approbation; instead of teaching man to hoard the produce of his industry, it not unfrequently suggested the devotion of superfluous treasure to the founding of a refuge for the blind, the destitute, the crippled, the diseased. Some kings are mentioned[3], who, starting from the worship of the

[1] 'On a désigné le bouddhisme par le nom de *Christianisme de l'Orient*, et, à la convenance près, cette exagération exprime assez bien l'importance des services qu'il a rendus à l'humanité:' Abel-Rémusat, *Mélanges Posthumes*, p. 237.

[2] See the *Dharma* contrasted in this particular with the *Kurán* by Major Cunningham, *Bhilsa Topes*, pp. 53, 54.

[3] The following picture of a model Buddhist king is well worth transcription. It is taken from the *Vie et Voyages de Hiouen-Thsang*, ed. Julien, pp. 204, 205: 'Suivant la tradition, le trône était occupé, il y a soixante ans, par un roi nommé Kiaï-ji (*Cîlâditya*): il était doué de grands talents et possédait de vastes connaissances. Il était humain, affectueux, bienfaisant et dévoué pour le bonheur du peuple. Il était plein de respect pour les Trois Précieux [the *Buddha*, the *Sangga*, or assembly of religious, and the *Dharma*, or Law]. Depuis son avénement au trône jusqu'au moment de sa mort, nulle parole inconvenante ne s'échappa de sa bouche, et la colère ne rougit point son visage. Jamais il n'eut l'idée de faire du mal à ses sujets ni de tuer une mouche ou une fourmi. Dans la crainte de causer la mort aux insectes qui vivent dans l'eau, il ne permettait pas d'en donner à boire aux élèphants ou aux chevaux avant de l'avoir soigneusement filtrée. Quant aux hommes du royaume, il leur défendait sévèrement de tuer des animaux. De là vient que les bêtes féroces s'attachaient aux hommes, les loups oubliaient leur fureur; la paix régnait dans l'intérieur des frontières, et des présages de bonheur éclataient chaque jour.' Another king of the same name,

'Three Precious Ones,' had carried their philanthropy and tenderness for every kind of animal life to most absurd extremes, and even were accustomed to dole out in alms not only the immense accumulations in the royal coffers, but the whole of their personal ornaments.

It would, perhaps, be difficult to single out a Buddhist of any period in the range of history who manifested such a high and generous nature as the pilgrim, Hiuan-Thsang, to whom I have before alluded. The best portion of his life was all consumed in perilous wanderings, undertaken with the aim of rescuing the *Dharma* from the errors which had overgrown it, and of recommending it on every side to the affections of his fellow-men. In these researches he was able to collect a multitude of sacred writings, which on his return to China he translated, in concert with a band of his disciples, into the language of his native country. When the hour of death was fast approaching, he commanded all his worldly goods to be distributed among the poor; he caused the votive statues to be fashioned; he required the brethren of his convent to recite the usual prayers. At last his friends are all invited to assemble round his couch and take a joyous leave of his 'impure and despicable body,' which, after having played its part, is lost to him for ever. 'I hope,' he adds, 'that all the merits I have gained by my good works may now accrue to the advantage of other people. My wish is to be born with them into the heaven of the *Touchitas* (the blessed), to be admitted into the family of *Mi-le* (Maitréya), and to serve this Buddha of the future, who is full of tenderness and of affection. When my fate is to descend afresh into the world, and undergo another series of existences, I hope at every new birth to do my duty towards the Buddha with unwearying zeal, and ultimately to arrive in turn at the supreme Intelligence.' He then gave utterance to his deep regrets on feeling that the world was fast receding from his grasp; but at the very moment of dissolution, when his pupils asked him, 'Master, have you really obtained the

and contemporaneous with the traveller himself, was in the habit of convoking general assemblies, and there distributing all his wealth among his subjects. On one occasion he gave away in alms the whole of his royal ornaments. 'Maitenant que j'ai pu (par l'aumône) les déposer dans le *champ du bonheur*, je les regarde comme conservées à jamais. Je désire, dans toutes mes existences futures, amasser ainsi d'immenses richesses pour faire l'aumône aux hommes, et obtenir les dix facultés divines dans toute leur plénitude. (p. 256.)

right of being born into the assembly of *Mi-le?*' his quivering lips responded 'Yes;' and so he yielded up the ghost[1].

A spectacle resembling this in many of the outward circumstances, yet presenting also many a deep and touching contrast, was beheld soon afterwards within the walls of a secluded convent in our own Northumbria. It was the death-scene of the Venerable Bede. He also was the brightest luminary of the sphere in which he moved; for though his creed may in some few particulars have been alloyed by elements of thought and feeling at variance with the genius of primitive Christianity, his heart was ever true in its allegiance to our heavenly Father, and he died receiving as the end of his faith the crown of glory that fadeth not away. The days and years of Bede, like those of Hiuan-Thsang, had been devoted mainly to the spread of sacred literature, and when his strength was failing and his peaceable career was gliding to its close, we see him in a crowded

[1] 'Puis il leur dit: "Le moment de ma mort approche; déjà mon esprit s'affaisse et semble me quitter. Il faut promptement distribuer en aumônes mes vêtements et mes richesses, faire fabriquer des statues et charger des religieux de réciter des prières." Le vingt-troisième jour, on donna un repas aux pauvres et l'on distribua des aumônes. Le même jour, il ordonna à un mouleur nommé *Song-kia-tchi* d'élever, dans le palais *Kia-cheou-tien*, une statue de l'*Intelligence* (Bódhi); après quoi, il invita la multitude du couvent, les traducteurs adjoints et ses disciples "a dire joyeusement adieu à ce corps impur et méprisable de *Hiouen-Thsang* qui, ayant fini son rôle, ne méritait plus de subsister longtemps. Je désire, ajouta-t-il, voir reverser sur les autres hommes les mérites que j'ai acquis par mes bonnes œuvres; naître, avec eux, dans le ciel des *Touchitas;* être admis dans la famille de *Mi-le* (*Maitréya*) et servir ce *Bouddha* plein de tendresse et d'affection. Quand je redescendrai sur la terre pour parcourir d'autres existences, je désire, à chaque naissance nouvelle, remplir avec un zèle sans bornes mes devoirs envers le *Bouddha*, et arriver enfin à l'*Intelligence transcendante* (*Anouttara samyak sombódhi*)." Après avoir fait ces adieux, il se tut et entra en méditation; puis, de sa langue mourante, il laissa échapper d'amers regrets, en sentant qu'il ne jouissait plus du *monde des yeux* (de la faculté de voir), du *monde de la pensée* (de la faculté de penser), du *monde de la connaissance qui naît de la vue* (de la connaissance des objets sensibles), du *monde de la connaissance qui naît de l'esprit* (de le perception des choses spirituelles), et qu'il ne possédait point la plénitude de l' *Intelligence.*' The 'Master of the Law' then uttered two *gáthás*, aspirations to *Maitréya tathágata.* For some time he continued motionless and took no food. At last, 'au milieu de la nuit, ses disciples lui demandèrent: "Maître, avez vous enfin obtenu de naître au milieu de l'assemblée de Mâitrêya?" "Oui," repondit-il, d'une voix défaillante. A ce mot sa respiration s'affaiblit de plus en plus, et, au bout de quelques instants, son âme s'évanuit.' *Ibid.* pp. 344 sq.

circle of affectionate pupils, eager to imbibe the treasures that continued to pour forth from his capacious memory. Among his brother-presbyters he also parted the small remnant of his worldly substance, 'giving with much love and joy what he had previously received from God.' The tears of the bystanders were at length beginning to flow fast; for each of them perceived that Bede, the master-spirit of their thriving confraternity, had girded up his loins to die; yet sorrow was in their case all transmuted into joy, when they remembered that the spirits of the just are in the hands of the Omnipotent, and Christ the risen Lord of dead as well as living. 'They rejoiced,' is the account of an eye-witness, 'when he said, "It is time that I returned to Him who made me, who created me, and formed me out of nothing. I have had a long life upon the earth; the merciful Judge has also been pleased to order for me a happy life. The time of my departure is at hand, for I have a desire to depart and to be with Christ." And with many such like remarks he passed the day until eventide. Then the boy, whom we have already mentioned, said to him, "Still one sentence, dear master, remains unwritten." He replied, "Write quickly." After a little while, the boy said, "Now the sentence is finished." He answered, "You have spoken the truth—it is indeed finished. Raise my head in your hands, for it pleases me much to recline opposite to that holy place of mine, on which I used to pray, so that, while resting there, I may call upon God my Father." And being placed upon the pavement of his cell, he said, "Glory be to the Father, and to the Son, and to the Holy Ghost"—and as soon as he had named the name of the Holy Spirit, he breathed out his own spirit, and so departed to the kingdom of heaven[1].'

[1] Beda died A.D. 735, about seventy years later than Hiuan-Thsang. The most accurate version of this narrative of Cuthbert will be found in Mr. Stevenson's 'Preface to Beda,' pp. xv. sq. Lond. 1853.

CHAPTER II.

Religions of America, particularly the Mexican.

'Darin besteht eben die Bedeutung der Amerikanischen Religionen, dass sie mehr als andere, wenigstens mehr als andere Religionen von Kulturvölkern, das primitive und unabgeschwächte Heidenthum darstellen.'

Vagueness of American traditions. Languages. Origin of the Tribes. Proofs of foreign influences. Two classes.

§ 1. *The wild Tribes. Fetishism. Worship of the heavenly bodies. Pantheism. Doctrine of a Great Spirit. The system really dualistic. The worship chiefly deprecative. Its gloomy aspect. Doctrine of Manitoes.*

§ 2. *The demi-civilised Tribes, especially the Mexican. Ancient civilisation. General character of Mexican influence. Monotheism. Teo-tl. Traces of a Supreme Spirit. Tezcatlipoca. Huitzilopochtli. Meanings of the Serpent-symbol. Terrible aspect of Aztec worship. Human sacrifices. Alleged resemblance to Hebraism. Sacred Triad. Quetzalcoatl. Symbol of the cross. Traditions of a Deluge.*

It is now established that the eastern promontories of the New World were sighted by the storm-tost Greenlander, and trodden by the sturdy foot of the adventurous Northman long before[1] the last 'discovery' of that continent in 1497. Yet little or no definite information resulted from such voyages beyond the fact that certain media really existed for connecting the barbarians of Labrador, of Nova Scotia, and of Massachusetts, with the people on the coasts of Scandinavia, and the consequent possibility of transporting thither some vague knowledge of white

[1] See the interesting revelations in Rafn's *Antiquitates Americanæ*, Hafniæ, 1845, and Humboldt's *Cosmos*, II. 234 sq. Sabine's ed. The first recorded view of the American coast was obtained in 986. In 1000, Leif actually landed with thirty-five companions on a point which he called Helluland, identified with Labrador. From thence one of the party penetrated further south to what they called Vinland (from the wild vines growing there).

men and some few germs of Christianity[1]. Nor do any of the frequent narratives sent home to Europe by the first 'Conquistadores' throw much light upon the primitive traditions of the various tribes whom they subdued. Intoxicated by their lust of gold, devoting all their wondrous energies to the extension and consolidation of their empire, many of them were deaf not only to the pleas put forward by the native in behalf of his hereditary freedom, but also to the war-songs and the legends that continued to give utterance to his baneful superstitions. Other Spaniards in a frenzy of fanaticism were instigated to destroy[2] the only archives, by the light of which we could have hoped to track with any certainty the course pursued in the migrations of the 'civilised' families of America; while in reference to the Indians proper, the historical materials then as now surviving are no better than a mass of wild hyperboles; they tell of 'nations creeping out of the ground—a world growing out of a tortoise's back—the globe reconstructed from the earth clutched in a musk-rat's paw, after a deluge[3].' Hence the difficult nature of the problems which confronted the ethnologist when he proceeded by more scientific methods to determine the mutual relations of the tribes and peoples of America, to penetrate still further into mysteries connected with their past condition, and educe some elements of light and order from the midst of that far-spreading chaos, which had, in the judgment of the superficial writer, hopelessly enveloped the history of the New World.

The first great generalisation thus obtained had reference to the physical characteristics of the native population. It was found that, on eliminating a subordinate class of 'singular and inexplicable diversities[4],' the people of that continent, in all their geographical distribution, from the Arctic Ocean to Cape Horn, may be described as homogeneous, or the scions of one parent stock. The squalid Esquimaux, at one extremity of the

[1] Some white men appear to have remained in America at an early period, and in 1121 we find a Greenland bishop making a voyage to Vinland: cf. Münter, *Kirchengesch. von Dänemark*, &c. I. 561, Leipzig, 1833.

[2] 'The strange, unknown characters inscribed on them [the picture manuscripts] excited suspicion. They were looked on as magic scrolls; and were regarded in the same light with the idols and temples, as the symbols of a pestilent superstition, that must be extirpated:' Prescott, *Conquest of Mexico*, p. 32, Lond. 1854.

[3] See *History, Condition and Prospects of the Indian Tribes*, ed. Schoolcraft (recently compiled for the Government of the United States), Part I. p. 13.

[4] There is still some difference of opinion among ethnologists respecting the extent and value of these 'diversities;' see Prichard, V. 290 sq.

chain, the polished Aztec, or Peruvian, at the other; agriculturists, and hunters, and canoe-men; tribes frequenting the shores of the great northern lakes, or scattered in the dense savannahs of the South; the stunted Chayma, the athletic Caraib, and the half-clad native of the Land of Fire, exhibit the same general lineaments, and constitute together one distinct variety of the human species. They 'possess alike the long, lank, black hair, the brown or cinnamon-coloured skin, the heavy brow, the dull and sleepy eye, the full and compressed lips, and the salient and dilated nose[1].' But in the course of wide and patient investigations which have issued in this grand result, another class of facts were sometimes felt to wear a very different aspect and to point in very different directions. So far was the explorer of American antiquities from meeting with a common language, or one group of kindred dialects, that varieties of human speech were found to be almost innumerable; each narrow tract of country being occupied by tribes continually at war with each other, esteeming every stranger an enemy, and possessing few, if any, of the ordinary means of intercommunication.

Here again, however, science has contributed her timely aid in filling up the blanks of primitive history. It has been shewn, entirely to the satisfaction of all competent philologers, that if, as in the former case, we make a few exceptions, capable of being explained on the hypothesis of accidental or colonial intercourse with foreign countries, the discordant languages of America are all held together by common and peculiar principles of construction, pointing to a primitive centre, and acknowledging the plastic influence of one mother-tongue. These languages are neither monosyllabic, like the Chinese, the primitive Malay, and other kindred idioms; nor dissyllabic, like a second class of ancient languages related to the Hebrew; nor analytical, like the tongues of modern Europe, which are substituting, or have substituted, for the old inflections a vast number of auxiliary particles. The proper description of the American dialects, as spoken for the last three hundred and fifty years, is *polysynthetic*[2], meaning that their organisation is so flexible, so arti-

[1] Morton's *Crania Americana*, quoted with other testimonies to the same effect in Squier's *American Archæological Researches*, No. 1. pp. 23, 24, New York, 1851.

[2] The credit of working out this idea belongs to Mr. du Ponceau: see Prichard, v. 305 sq., who has added (pp. 313 sq.) some judicious observations on the probable causes of the vast dissimilarity in the words themselves. This may be referred, partly to the isolation of the various tribes, partly to the

ficial, and so highly complex, as to make them far more capable than any other dialects of combining a large assortment of ideas and various shades of meaning into one polysyllabic term. In other words, however manifold those languages may be as to their vocabulary, their structure and grammatical forms are all peculiarly related,—so peculiarly, that traits of family-likeness and the same distinctive physiognomy are seen pervading the whole group.

But harder questions in the meantime have been agitated by American archæologists, with reference to the ultimate affinities of the native population; and while one school are persuaded that nothing whatever has transpired which can be fairly thought to militate against received ideas of aboriginal unity; a second, in proportion it would seem to their belief in the specific oneness of the 'American race,' have manifested a desire to disconnect the Old and New Continents entirely. They assert not only that the measure of civilisation attained by some of the American tribes is altogether underived, but (which is a distinct and totally independent theory) that the race itself is strictly autochthonic, and is therefore a new *species* of human beings[1]. As writers of the last century were sometimes ready to contend that *every thing* American had been imported from the shores of the Old World, these champions of the autochthonic theory must needs assume an attitude no less defiant, and a phraseology no less emphatic: they affirm accordingly that *nothing* has been so derived.

Now difficult, or even, with our extant means, impossible as it may be to single out the parent stock, in which the fathers of the New World had their origin, I hold the multiplication of productive centres, both in this and other cases, to be absolutely unnecessary, and, in the present state of ethnological science, to be utterly unjustifiable[2]. If no ray of light whatever could be

wonderful richness of their first vocabulary, partly to the feverish activity of their imagination and rhetorical faculty, which are ever coining new expressions; but resemblance is perhaps most of all destroyed by certain current principles of truncation and agglutination, impelling the American Indians to cut off the beginning and the end of polysyllables almost without limit, and to form other words by merely aggregating a number of such fragments into new compounds.

[1] Pott, who seems to be himself influenced more especially by philological reasons, has collected (in his *Die Ungleichheit menschlicher Rassen*, Lemgo, 1856, pp. 242 sq.) the main arguments of those who are led by the perplexing phenomena of the New World to deny the derivation of the human family from a single pair.

[2] See Part I. ch. II. *On the Unity of the Human Race*, above, pp. 34 sq.

thown upon the questions which concern the primitive population of America; if no analogy to their case had existed in the spread of the Malayo-Polynesian tribes across the islands of the Eastern Archipelago and the Pacific Ocean; if the speech of the Americans had absolutely no affinities with any other human dialects; if their traditions, meagre as these are, had hinted nothing of a distant home and of a perilous migration; if insoluble enigmas were presented by the physical structure of Americans, or if their moral powers and mental capabilities were such as to exclude them from a place in the great brotherhood of men; if, lastly, no resemblances were found, I will not say, in primary articles of belief, but in the memory of specific incidents and in those minor forms of human thought and culture which will hardly bear to be explained on the hypothesis of 'natural evolution,' we might then, perhaps, have cause to hesitate in our decision, or to treat the peopling of America as something more exceptional than had been hitherto supposed.

But no necessity whatever has been shewn for the adoption of such theories. There is literally nothing, say our ablest writers, either in the bodily structure or psychology of the American tribes to prove an independent origin, or even to beget suspicions touching a plurality of human 'races'[1].' In the limits of the American family, and notwithstanding the mutual resemblances which it unquestionably offers, we can find varieties of human beings, passing, there as elsewhere, one into another by graduated shades of difference; while the Esquimaux, who are as genuine members of that family as the Aztecs or Algonquins, link it on, by speech as well as by traditions, to the natives of the sister-continent. Again, if the diversities of language could be fairly cited as conclusive of the absolute distinctness of the whole American people, they would prove with equal force that every single tribe is also autochthonic. The loss of primitive vocables in one case would remain as wondrous and inexplicable as in the other. The development of any primitive speech into the finished and elaborate forms presented by the living dialects of America is antecedently not less improbable than the first deflection of the polysynthetic family from one original type of language. Neither is the want of correspondency between the speech of the Old and New Continent so absolutely universal as had once been represented. Without affecting to pronounce a judgment on the merits of particular controversies,—as, for instance, that relating to the

[1] Prichard, v. 541.

Othomi of Central America, whose language[1] has been held to be monosyllabic and akin to the Chinese,—I may remark that writers adverse to the theory of unity are sometimes driven to admit the known existence of as many as one hundred and eighty-seven words[2], which are the common property of the Old World and the New. But more convincing proofs of some great exodus from Asia to America are furnished by the vague traditions of the early emigrants. The tide of population in the New Continent is always said to have been propagated from the west and north-west. If credit be conceded to the stories of the Mexicans and others, they all issued from that very region; in one case they had crossed the water, in a second they had marched along some frozen pathway. They were previously acquainted with white men; they were accustomed to the representations of animals familiar to Asiatics, but unheard of, during the historic period, in America itself[3]. The picture or mnemonic writing[4] of the Old World reappears in different latitudes of the New. The practice of erecting huge pyramidal temples, corresponding not in general structure only, but also in minute and arbitrary details, has been common to the demi-civilised tribes alike of Asia and America[5]. Arguing therefore

[1] Cf. Pott, as above, pp. 252 sq., and Ampère, in the *Revue des Deux Mondes*, 1853, Tome IV. pp. 93, 94.

[2] Squier, as above, p. 26. Of these words, it is remarked, 'one hundred and four coincide with words found in the languages of Asia and Australia, forty-three with those of Europe, and forty with those of Africa.'

[3] These and many other points are dwelt upon by Wuttke, whose chief conclusion is as follows (I. 346): 'Alle diese Erscheinungen lassen uns an der asiatischen Abstammung der halbgebildeten Völker von West-Amerika nicht mehr zweifeln. Die bestimmten bei den verschiedenen Indianerstämmen sich wiederholenden Sagen von einer Einwanderung aus Westen über ein Meer oder eine Strasse, die nachher zugefroren,—Sagen, welche mit den erwähnten sibirischen von einer Auswanderung nach Osten übereinstimmen [p. 157], verstärken das Gewicht der mexikanischen Überlieferung noch mehr.'

[4] See above, p. 50, n. 2. Niebuhr (*Lect. on Ancient Hist.* I. 49, 50) points out the approximation made in some districts of Central America to the 'hieratic' mode of writing practised by the Egyptians. The use of *Knotenschnüre* (knot-strings) as an aid to the memory was common, both in America and in almost every other part of the ancient world (Müller, p. 359), anterior to the introduction of the art of writing.

[5] Squier, as above, p. 83. 'What striking analogies exist,' cries Humboldt (as there quoted), 'between the monuments of the old continents and those of the Toltecs, who, arriving on Mexican soil, built several of these colossal structures, truncated pyramids, divided by layers, like the temple of Belus at Babylon. Whence did they take the model of these edifices? Were

from coincidences such as these, which are in every case more likely to have been the fruit of some external intercourse than of mere accident or of spontaneous growth in disconnected regions, I incline to the opinion that the old inhabitants of America had either crossed by Behring's Strait, or else along the way of the Aleutian islands, which in fact supply a bridge between the two continents. Such primitive colonists might be an early offshoot from the stock of nations which was rapidly propelled across the steppes of central Asia, and who, lapsing more and more completely into barbarism, had finally escaped through various channels into islands of the Eastern and Southern Seas. Regarded thus, the primitive people of America belong to a great section of the human family which is entitled the 'Turanian:' they are ultimately one with the Malays; they are a part of that mighty stream of population which under the name of Tshud and Turk and Scythian was diffused throughout the whole of upper Asia, was pushed forward by the growing vigour of the Chinese empire, was displaced by the triumphant progress of the Áryans in the vast peninsula of Hindústán. Or it may be, that the peopling of America resulted from a long succession of such movements, and that ruder tribes were subsequently intermixed with others[1] more advanced in civilisation and more capable of gaining that ascendency which some of them had finally enjoyed. Objections, I am quite aware, have been directed against both of these hypotheses, and in the present state of knowledge it may be impossible to give a satisfactory answer to every one of such objections. Yet on looking at the problem as a whole, I am persuaded that the vast preponderance of testimony is favourable to the idea of Asiatic immigration, not only as accounting for the presence of materials out of which the 'civilised' communities were framed, but also

they of the Mongol race? Did they descend from a common stock with the Chinese, the Hiong-nu, and the Japanese?'

[1] This is the conclusion of Mr. Schoolcraft, who closes his careful summary of the ante-Columbian traditions (Part I. pp. 19 sq.) in the following passage (p. 26): 'Thus we have traditionary gleams of a foreign origin of the race of the North American Indians, from separate stocks of nations, extending at intervals from the Arctic Circle to the Valley of Mexico. . They point decidedly to a foreign, to an oriental, if not a Shemitic, origin. Such an origin has from the first been inferred. At whatever point the investigation has been made, the eastern hemisphere has been found to contain the physical and mental prototypes of the race. Language, mythology, religious dogmas,—the very style of architecture, and their calendar, as far as it is developed, point to that fruitful and central source of human dispersion and nationality.'

as affording the best clue to many a mystery connected with the barbarous tribes themselves.

As soon as we approach the subject of American religions, it is most essential on the very threshold that we realise the force of a distinction here indicated between the 'civilised' and savage populations who occupied the New World when it was first explored by Europeans. The former class comprise[1] the Mexicans and Peruvians, together with the intermediate families of Mayans, and Muyscas of Bogota, who, planted on that side of the continent which looks directly towards Asia, were each an independent centre of civilisation in the midst of wild and barbarous hordes[2]. The second class may be distributed into (1) the Red Indians of North America, (2) the Indians of the Great Antilles, (3) the Caraibs or Carribees, (4) the Indians on the Eastern coast of South America. These two varieties of men, though generally like each other in physical conformation, and though speaking similar and cognate tongues, were intellectually in almost opposite conditions. The half-civilised American had even worked his way above one group of tribes and nations on the Old Continent; he was superior to the Finn, who represented the best phase of culture in the 'Scythian' family; he took precedence also of the Mongol, who at nearly the same period flashed from time to time across the theatre of general history, and then relapsed into the darkness of his native steppes. The barbarous American was, on the contrary, as destitute of all the higher forms of culture as the wild man of New Zealand or Kaffraria: his delight was to retard the intellectual progress of his fellows, and intent on what is called 'a nameless principle of tribality,' to foster habits which could hardly fail to issue in the utter disintegration of society.

§ 1. *The wild Tribes of America.*

My observations on this class of men will be restricted within very narrow limits, partly because the members of it are seldom or never likely to provoke comparison with Christians,

[1] In this distribution, I follow Dr. J. G. Müller, whose *Geschichte der Amerikanischen Urreligionen* (Basel, 1855), though far from satisfactory in some respects, has the great merit of being well arranged.

[2] It should, however, be remembered that the area of North American civilisation had once been far more extensive than it was in the age of Columbus; as may be inferred from the ruins which are being constantly brought to light, for instance, in the valley of the Mississippi: *Ibid.* pp. 45 sq., Schoolcraft, Part II. pp. 84 sq.

and partly because the leading principles of their religion are the same as will be found in tribes of every age and climate, so long as they continue standing on the same moral level. In the old 'Turanian' creed of China we observed how prominent was the place awarded, first, to spirit-worship,—understanding by that term not only adoration or deprecation of local genii and demons, but commemorative offerings made in honour of departed ancestors; and secondly, to worship of the powers or laws of nature, and especially the element of light itself as centred in the host of heaven. Now both these forms of primitive heathenism recur at every turn among the Indians of North and South America. Their religion, speaking generally, consists of two great factors; spirit-worship, which is found to be more deeply rooted in the higher latitudes, and element-worship, which appears to have exerted a peculiar witchery in countries lying nearer the equator. In America, however, as in China, the two phases of belief are seen existing side by side, and not unfrequently are made to touch and interpenetrate each other. Excepting the manes of departed ancestors[1], which ought perhaps to constitute an independent class, the spirits worshipped by the heathen of America are not unfrequently embodied in specific forms or objects, corresponding to the *fetishes*[2] alike of Greenland, Africa, Australia, and Siberia. Some particles of true divinity are thus believed to tenant the thing worshipped, which accordingly ceases to be regarded as the beast or brute matter it really is, and rising far above the character of a type, or emblem, is identified completely with the thing it represents[3]. One object of this kind becomes *the*

[1] Compare the following account of Mr. Schoolcraft, Part I. pp. 38, 39, with the remarks already made (above, p. 289) on the similar custom of the Chinese: 'The periodical offering of cakes, libations, flesh, or viands at the grave to ancestors.....is seen to be an idea incorporated into the practice of the American, at least the Algonic Indians. These Indians, believing in the duality of the soul, and that the soul sensorial abides for a time with the body in the grave, requiring food for its ghostly existence and journeyings, deposit meats and other aliment, at and after the time of interment. *This custom is universal*, and was one of their earliest observed traits.' The same remark is applicable to the Caraibs and Brasilians: Müller, p. 73. The same superstitious ideas prevail through the whole of the country north of the Zambesi: see Livingstone's *Researches in South Africa*, p. 434.

[2] The word 'Fetishism,' which has now obtained general currency as descriptive of one early stage in the religions of heathendom, is derived from the Portuguese *fetisso*, 'a magical charm' or 'spell.' It was adopted from thence by the Negroes of Western Africa: cf. the Chinese *joss* and the Portuguese *dios*.

[3] Müller, p. 52. The same

god, the patron-spirit of the fascinated savage: it he carries constantly about with him, or treasures as the glory and the safeguard of his wigwam; so that, notwithstanding the very partial exercise of the imagination and reflective faculty which seems to be implied in every form of spirit-worship, the worshipper is always under the necessity of localising the object of his special adoration and of bringing it directly under the cognisance of the senses. On the other hand, the more conspicuous and commanding objects of external nature, as the sun, the moon, the planets, are not worshipped barely as material and inanimate substances. The wild man of America, like other heathen, both of civilised and barbarous races, has been long accustomed to the thought that all the heavenly bodies are possessed of animation, and even gifted with some measure of intelligence. To each, accordingly, has been ascribed one independent, vitalising soul. The sun-god, for example, is the living sun itself, and worship is never paid to it symbolically, as though it were the representative of some invisible or absent spirit, but because it is an actual depository of the supersensuous, an embodiment of the Divine.

The two main lines of thought exemplified in spirit-worship, and in deification of the elements and heavenly bodies, may have thus been gradually blended into one. The subtle spirit is corporealised; the higher forms of matter are each tenanted and consecrated by the energy of some appropriate spirit. If the term 'God' be chosen to express the aggregate of all such spirits, it may be affirmed with equal truth that ultimately God is every thing, and every thing is ultimately God. The wild man of America is in fact a worshipper of all above him and around him. As the skies, the woods, the waters are his books, they also form his oracles and his divinities. Pervaded by some spiritual essence, every leaf that rustles in the forest, quite as much as the great orbs that move in silent majesty across the firmament, conveys to him a message from the unseen world. The threatening cloud, the genial shower, the lightning, thunder, and *aurora borealis*, flowers of every hue and animals of every shape and species, are alike regarded as instinct with supernatural virtue, and as fitted to enkindle in the

writer says truly (p. 75): 'Das Thier, das als Fetisch verehrt wird, ist nicht Symbol dieser oder jener göttlichen Naturkraft, sondern überhaupt ein göttliches Wesen wie jedes andere.' Mr. Theodore Parker is, therefore, in error when he talks of the visible object being in Fetishism a *type* of the Infinite Spirit: *Discourse*, pp. 32 sq. Lond. 1850.

human heart the sentiments of awe or love, of adoration or of deprecation.

In systems where it is admitted by all writers that principles like these are ever active and predominant, we naturally fail in the attempt to vindicate a proper standing-ground for any doctrine bearing close resemblance to Christian theism. Passages exist, indeed, in which the wild man of America expresses a belief in some Great Spirit[1], manifesting itself not only as the root and basis of all being, but at one time in the light of a beneficent Creator, at a second as the sun-god, at a third as the great God of heaven, and not unfrequently in more appalling aspects as the god of battle and of death. At first the European missionaries[2], in their zeal to seize all possible points of contact with the old beliefs of those whom they were seeking to recover, had unconsciously diverged into the track of infidels, who represented the natural religion of the wild man as almost on a level with the highest truths of Christianity, and, after labouring to explain away his human sacrifices, anthropophagy and the like, waxed eloquent in praising the unrivalled purity and spirituality of his worship. In the present day, however, when inquiries of this kind are prosecuted is a far more critical temper, it is generally agreed that all approximations to monotheism observed among the tribes of the New World are little more than verbal. Their Great Spirit is at best the highest member of a group[3], the brightest inmate of a crowded pantheon; as the sun-god of their system, quickening, gladdening, fructifying; a personification of the mightiest of all natural energies, but not a personality distinct from nature, and controlling all things by his sovereign will.

[1] Thus, Mr. Schoolcraft (*passim*) thinks this doctrine 'at the base of their theology,' although he argues that in practice they were polytheists to a man. Mr. Prescott (*Conquest of Peru*) begins his third chapter with a similar statement: 'It is a remarkable fact, that many, if not most, of the rude tribes inhabiting the vast American continent, however disfigured their creeds may have been in other respects by a childish superstition, had attained to the sublime conception of one Great Spirit, the Creator of the universe,' &c. He also adds, however, that these elevated ideas 'do not seem to have led to the practical consequences that might have been expected.' On the ideas current in South Africa, respecting a Supreme Being, see Livingstone, pp. 641, 642.

[2] Müller, who adduces many proofs of this position (pp. 99 sq.), affirms: 'Diese Ansicht ist nicht bloss bei Englischen und Französischen Deisten und Populärphilosophen, sondern auch bei Reisenden und Missionären sehr verbreitet.'

[3] Cf. Wuttke, I. 91, 92, Müller, p. 102, pp. 114 sq.

The greatest Spirit of the Indian is accordingly declared to be the offspring of an evil mother[1], subordinate to some inexorable Fate, the victim of some will-less and unchanging Principle by which his rule is ever liable to interruption and reverse. But, what is more observable, that Spirit is devoid of every thing which constitutes the glory of the God of revelation. In spite of all his grandeur, goodness, and ubiquity, he exercises no control upon the lives of individuals, or the government of the world. 'There is no attempt by the hunter, priesthood, jugglers or powwows, which can be gathered from their oral traditions, to impute to the great merciful Spirit the attributes of justice, or to make man accountable to him, here and hereafter, for aberrations from virtue, good-will, truth, or any form of moral right[2].'

The passing illustrations thus afforded of the old American theology enable us to understand some other of its characteristic principles. With the idea of one inscrutable necessity ever present in the background, the more prominent features of the system were all rigorously *dualistic*[3].

Minor gods, whose operation was regarded as beneficent, were ranked in one special series, with the sun-god as their glorious chief. In him, the great dispenser of all radiance and fertility, 'the being by whose light and heat all living creatures were generated and sustained,' the various tribes of the New World had uniformly recognised the highest pitch of excellence; and even where, transformed into a god of battle, he was worshipped with horrid and incongruous rites, or fed by human hecatombs[4], the sun-god never ceased to occupy the foremost rank among the good divinities. His titles were the 'father,' the 'sustainer,' the 'revivifier;' and to be at last translated to the sun, or his attendant stars, was deemed the summit of felicity. On the other hand, the rude American was haunted by the thought of some coequal and coordinate array of hostile deities, who manifested their malignant nature by creating discord, sickness, death, and every possible form of evil. These

[1] Müller, p. 149. This writer shews, in discussing the religion of the Caraibs, the identity of their supreme Mother with Fate and the Principle of evil (p. 230).

[2] Schoolcraft, I. 35.

[3] 'Everywhere our Indians have upheld this idea of a duality of gods, giving one good, and the other evil, powers, with its ancient developments of subordinate polytheisms.' *Ibid.* III. 60. The same antagonism was even more strongly manifested among the Caraibs, and on the eastern coast of South America: Müller, pp. 260, 261.

[4] See Müller, pp. 141 sq., and below, on the human sacrifices offered to the great Mexican divinities.

were held in numerous cases to obey the leadership of the moon[1], which, owing to its changeful aspects, had become identical with the capricious evil-minded Spirit of American Indians. It especially, as in their creed the parent of misfortune, many of them were ever anxious to propitiate and disarm. In it is found the chief divinity of all the warlike races, more especially the Caraibs[2]; and everywhere the worship of the Indian was mainly occupied in deprecating powerful and malevolent spirits, demons, spectres, fiends, hobgoblins, whose errand was to poison human joys and aggravate the load of human wretchedness. If only the American could turn away their anger, and evade or disappoint their malice, he had realised the principal aim of his religion. Hence his constant dread of some unearthly apparition. Hence the meaning of his fetishes, his amulets, his charms, his exorcisms, his trembling and convulsive efforts to explore the secrets of the past or future, his wild cries, and frantic dances. Hence again the vast ascendency obtained by seers and witches, payés, jossakeeds, and medicine-men, with other dark and nameless instruments of heathen sorcery.

It is true the wild man of America was not entirely lost to his original destination. He dreamed of having once been master of some purer language, of a world divided from the present by some dire catastrophe, of service rendered by his ancestors to milder and more powerful chieftains[3]. Whether pushing his rude canoe across the waters, or chasing the buffalo amid the depths of his primeval forests, he would muse at times, as did the Aztec in his massive temples, on the advent of a gracious Spirit, condescending, under various shapes of man or animal, to battle with a legion of hideous monsters[4], who were said to have delighted most in the enslaving of the human species. Yet in spite of all such happy memories, and such vague presentiments of something higher and more satisfying, the wild tribes of America were commonly overwhelmed

[1] Müller, p. 53, p. 170, p. 272. Livingstone (p. 235) found moon-worship prevalent among some tribes of South-Central Africa.

[2] 'Wahrend indessen anderswo gewöhnlich der Sonnendienst an der Spitze dieser höhern Naturverehrung steht, herrscht bei den Karaiben der Mond vor, ähnlich wie bei einzelnen nordischen Wilden und Grönländern,' *etc.* p. 218.

[3] Schoolcraft, I. 16. The current story of some mighty deluge will be considered in discussing the religion of Mexico.

[4] The mytho or legend of Manabozho (Müller, pp. 126 sq., Schoolcraft, I. 317—319), as held among the Algonquins, has its parallel in many other tribes, most of all, perhaps, in the Mexican account of Quetzalcoatl.

by gloom, anxiety, and terror. Their habitual 'notions of the spirit-world exceed all belief; and the Indian mind is thus made the victim of wild mystery, unending suspicion and paralysing fear......Not to be in misery from these unnumbered hosts is to be blessed[1].' The whole religion, writes another high authority, 'is the religion of fear, which even among cultivated nations so predominates in the religious character of the heathen, that Lucretius (VI. 23) could describe Epicurus, the subverter of religion, as one who had also made an end of fear. Daring as the Indian is at other times, in facing visible dangers under the impulses of passion; firm and self-collected as he shews himself in bearing the most poignant tortures, he is notwithstanding always full of awe, of fear, of horror, at the thought of the invisible spirits who hold rule in nature; and as soon as he is once mastered by this feeling, he becomes the most timid creature upon earth[2].'

We seldom see the darker traits of his religion so distinctly, as when brought together in the doctrine of *Manitoes*, which constitutes, it has been thought, the nearest approximation he has ever made to some originality of conception[3]. The word *Manito*, or Manedo, itself appears to signify 'a spirit:' hence the foremost member in the series of good divinities, the Great Spirit of the old American, is called in various tribes Kitchi or Gezha Manito[4]; the name of the evil-minded Spirit being

[1] Schoolcraft, I. 16. Compare Livingstone's account of the African tribes: 'Their religion, if such it may be called, is one of dread. Numbers of charms are employed to avert the evils with which they feel themselves to be encompassed. Occasionally you meet a man, more cautious or more timid than the rest, with twenty or thirty charms round his neck:' p. 435. 'There is nothing more heartrending than their death-wails. When the natives turn their eyes to the future world, they have a view cheerless enough of their own utter helplessness and hopelessness. They fancy themselves completely in the power of the disembodied spirits, and look upon the prospect of following them as the greatest of misfortunes. Hence they are constantly deprecating the wrath of departed souls, believing that, if they are appeased, there is no other cause of death but witchcraft, which may be averted by charms.' (p. 440.)

[2] Müller, p. 83. The same conviction is repeated (p. 260) with reference to the Indians of *South* America: 'Man sieht, dass auch hier das Schauerliche und Furchterregende vorherrscht; Furcht ist ja das Grundgefühl, das durch das Vernehmen des Göttlichen auch bei diesen Naturmenschen erregt wird; die ganze Natur ist von einer Unzahl von Geistern erfüllt, die bei Tag und bei Nacht, beim Schlafen und beim Wachen, Welt und Seele mit Angst und Schauder erfüllen.'

[3] Schoolcraft, I. 34, 35.

[4] These names vary considerably: see a collection of them, Müller, pp. 104 sq.

Matchi Manito. But, when employed without such epithets, this title is restricted to a minor emanation from the Great Spirit, which, revealing itself in dreams to the excited fancy of the youthful Indian, and inviting him to seek its efficacy in some well-known bird or beast, or other object, is selected by him for his guardian deity, his friend in council, and his champion in the hour of peril. He believes, however, that other Manitoes may prove far mightier and more terrible than his own, and consequently he is always full of apprehensions lest the influence granted preternaturally to his neighbour should issue in his own confusion. Add to this the prevalent idea, that Manitoes intrinsically evil are ever exercised in counterworking the beneficent, and that the actual administration of the world, abandoned to these great antagonistic powers, is the result of their interminable conflicts, and we cease to wonder at the moral perturbations which mark the character of the wild man. The fever of intense anxiety is never suffered to die out; until at length he either passes to another world, the simple reproduction of the present, or migrates into viler forms of animal existence, or, as in the case of the most highly favoured, is emancipated altogther from an earthly prison-house, and rescued from the malice of his demoniacal oppressors.

§ 2. *The demi-civilised Tribes, especially the Mexican.*

Although the barbarous population of the New World had always far outnumbered those who in the age preceding the discoveries of Columbus were struggling up the lower slopes of intellectual culture, it is rather in the creed of the minority, as indicating more of genius and reflection, that we seek for any definite resemblance to the facts and institutions of the Bible. There is reason to believe that some of these advances towards civilisation should be dated from a very high antiquity, especially in Yucatan and other parts of Central America, in which the Mayan family[1] had risen far above the intellectual level of their neighbours; but the Mexicans, who settled in a savage state upon their northern border, will at present be selected as the type of demi-civilised heathenism in the New World, partly because our fund of information respecting Mexico is comparatively copious and exact, and partly because an opportunity is there presented of watching a late phase in 'the religion of humanity' associated in the end with no small progress in

[1] Prichard, v. 339 sq., Müller, pp. 452 sq., and Fancourt's *Hist. of Yucatan*, pp. 114 sq. Lond. 1854.

political organisation and in many of the higher arts of life. That Mexicans had borrowed largely from the Mayan builders, who, already in the dawn of history, erected towns and palaces and pyramid-temples, rivalling those of Egypt in area and magnificence, is now conceded both by European and American archæologists. That numerous elements of faith and worship had been also gradually derived from the more cultivated Mayans, whom they conquered or displaced, as well as from the Toltecs[1], their own kinsmen and immediate predecessors on the soil of Anahuac, is a statement likely to receive continuous illustration from researches of the present day. But much as Mexico might profit by the early dissemination of intelligence and the creations of artistic skill upon the confines of her empire, it is certain that when studied by the Spanish conquerors, the various factors in her social and religious life had all been moulded into one harmonious system: veils of allegory, woven partly if not altogether by her own imagination, were thrown over many a wild tradition of her simple ancestors; her creed, her laws, her ritual, and administrative principles, had all assumed a very definite and distinctive character. The Aztec, in his general policy, became the Roman of the New World; and, after crushing and absorbing minor states, in virtue of his martial prowess and fanaticism, had suceeded in building up an absolute monarchy upon the basis of a terrible superstition, which reminds us, in its dark and sanguinary spirit, of the Siva-ism of Hindústán, and of the Baal or the Moloch-worship of western Asia.

[1] It is in tracing the fortunes of the Toltecs that we first obtain a tolerably close approximation to historical exactness. The traditions of them handed down by the Aztecs, or Mexicans proper, inform us that they migrated from an unknown country called the primitive Tlapallan about 544 of the Christian era, and, advancing southwards, settled in Mexico about 648 (see Prichard, v. 328; Prescott's *Conquest of Mexico*, ch. 1). It is also worthy of notice that the epoch 544 corresponds with the ruin of the Tsin dynasty in China, which occasioned many violent commotions beyond the limits of the Chinese empire, and may have been instrumental in propelling a new race of colonists as far as North America (cf. Wuttke, I. 349). The Mexicans proper, issuing from the far north, did not reach the borders of Anahuac till the beginning of the 13th century, and only fixed their habitation near the principal lake in 1325. 'At the beginning of the sixteenth century, just before the arrival of the Spaniards, the Aztec dominion reached across the continent from the Atlantic to the Pacific; and under the bold and bloody Ahuitzotl, its arms had been carried far over the limits already noticed as defining its permanent territory, unto the farthest corners of Guatemala and Nicaragua.'

On proceeding to discuss the central tenets of the ancient Mexicans we are confronted by a question which deserves to rank the foremost in this species of investigation—'What were their ideas respecting a Supreme Intelligence, the one, true, living God?' In Mexico, as in most heathen countries, very different answers have been given to such inquiry; some writers declaring that the Mexicans, in spite of their two hundred objects of worship, were ultimately and in truth monotheists; while others, who regard the term monotheism as importing no less that Christian theism, have repudiated the interpretations put on Mexican phraseology, and ranked the ancient Aztec with the nature-worshippers of other parts of heathendom. It is worthy of notice that the Mexican name for god[1] is *teo-tl*, which, on separating the termination from the root, approaches nearly to *θεός*, *dêva*, *deus*, *tius*, and other kindred forms, as well as to the *tao*[2] of China and the *tua*[3] of the South-sea islanders. It is deserving also of consideration that the term *teo-tl* was not inherited from the Toltecs, and was not imported into the land of Anahuac by the Mexicans themselves, but gradually adopted from the aboriginal population skirting them upon the southern frontier of their new dominions[4]. If it should eventually be established that the Mayan race who occupied this frontier were an Asiatic colony, forming the centre and the nucleus of American civilisation, the presence of a word like *teo-tl* will undoubtedly assume a higher importance than has hitherto belonged to it. But until historical media have been fully ascertained, it is presumptuous to advance a theory on the strength of merely verbal resemblances, which in some other cases can be shewn to have been altogether accidental.

[1] This word was accordingly employed by the early missionaries as the equivalent of *Dios*, not, however, without exciting disputes like those already noticed in reference to the Chinese *Shin* and *Shang-te*.

[2] See above, pp. 311 sq.

[3] Russell's *Polynesia*, p. 68, Lond. 1852. The fullest form of this Polynesian word is, however, not *tua* but *atua*, the *a* being, it would seem, a component part of the title. (Shortland's *Traditions, &c. of the New Zealanders*, p. 61. Lond. 1854.) Other persons, on similar grounds, have maintained the original identity of *Votan*, the serpent-god of the Mayans, with the *Odin* and *Woden* of Teutonic heathenism, and even with the *Buddha* of eastern Asia. But all such attempts at identification are merely fanciful, or at the best exceedingly precarious.

[4] Müller, p. 472. In Nicaragua, which received the names of its divinities neither from the Toltecs nor the Aztecs, the word *Teot* (pl. *Teotes*) was in common use, and was applied equally to the superior gods and to the Spaniards.

The word *teo-tl* was, however, used with epithets and adjuncts that forbid us to dispute the grandeur of the object it was meant to designate. The Mexicans beheld in him the being[1] 'by whom we live,' 'omnipresent, that knoweth all thoughts and giveth all gifts,' 'without whom man is as nothing,' 'invisible, incorporeal, one God, of perfect perfection and purity,' 'under whose wings we find repose and a sure defence.' This Being also had been worshipped by some elevated spirits, without image, sacrifice, or temple. He was called the 'Cause of causes,' and the 'Father of all things.' He was reverenced as the parent and productive principle in nature; he was actually identified with the sun-god, which on this account was designated *the* Teo-tl. In proportion also as the Aztecs had invested the chief powers and spirits of their ruder ancestors with human shapes and attributes, the reigning tendency to anthropomorphism might have led them to ascribe a human will and personality to the supreme Spirit. On the other hand, it is more probable that this only God of Central America was a conception far too vast and glorious for the ordinary intellect. To such he was a vague, impersonal abstraction: he was never worshipped by the many[2]; no attempt was made to circulate a knowledge either of his being or his character; and practically the administration of the world was not referred to Him, but to inferior spirits, good and evil, ruling each in his own single providence, and presiding over this or that peculiar energy of physical creation. In effect, the only difference to be traced between the popular theology of wild and demi-civilised Americans, is that which we have traced already in describing the Áryan of the Véda and the Áryan of the second, or 'heroic,' period of Hindú history and religion. All the beings worshipped in the former case are spirits, demons, genii, with no definite shape in the imagination of the worshipper, haunting every form of nature, animate and inanimate; while in the second stage of natural religion, the divinities are far more generally humanised, assuming forms in which, amid a number of grotesque embellishments, the features of humanity are ever struggling to obtain expression and predominance. The amulets and fetishes of the American Indians are seldom, it is true,

1 Prescott, p. 19, Lond. 1854.

2 'The idea of unity—of a being with whom volition is action, who has no need of inferior ministers to execute his purposes—was too simple, or too vast, for their understandings; and they sought relief, as usual, in the plurality of deities, who presided over the elements, the changes of the seasons, and the various occupations of man.' Prescott, *Ibid.*; cf. Müller, p. 474.

abandoned altogether, but are moulded into human effigies minute in form[1] and occupying the subordinate rank of *lares* and *penates*. The sacred corner of the wigwam, where the ancient fetish was reposited, or the sacred mound on which the wild man, writhing under some calamity, offered his best victim to the sun-god, has been superseded by a group of splendid temples ('houses of God,' or *teo-calli*), crowning a gigantic pyramid, and glittering with the costliest decorations. Seers and medicine-men have given place to regular priests and priestesses, the fountains of all popular education; the frantic shrieks of former generations have been softened into measured chants, their lawless rites into a pompous and elaborate liturgy; while holidays, originally restricted for the most part to the annual commemoration of departed ancestors, have multiplied so fast that 'every week, nay almost every day, is set down in their calendar for some appropriate celebration[2].'

Standing at the head of thirteen[3] chief divinities, whom ancient Mexico has learned to worship, either jointly or in rotation, is Tezcatlipoca, whose rank appears to be 'inferior only to that of the Supreme Being.' Several writers, who have earnestly endeavoured to make out affinities between the Old Testament religion and the creed of Mexico, and by this process to connect the Aztec tribes with the Semitic family of western Asia, go so far as to recognise the One God of the ancient Hebrews in Tezcatlipoca; and in aid of their conjectures they adduce a long array of epithets, investing him with every species of divine perfection. According to this view he was represented as the 'merciful and long-suffering,' and yet 'the stirrer-up of strife,' a god of vengeance and of battles; the 'Creator of all things,' and the 'Giver of life,' and yet requiring the blood of sacrifice to flow for ever on his altars; pardoning the guilty only in consideration of the blood of the innocent; supreme and unapproachable, and yet enlisting numerous fellow-workers in the government of the universe. He was 'the Holder of all things in his hand,' 'the Giver of inspiration, who laughs at human wisdom:' 'the Trier and Prover of hearts, who

[1] Müller, p. 571. They are called the 'little ones' (*tepitoton*).

[2] Prescott, p. 24.

[3] The special number *thirteen*, in reference to the greater gods of Mexico, appears to be connected either with a monthly division of the calendar (cf. Müller, p. 94), or else with the very peculiar cycles of the Mexicans, which included fifty-two years (13 being a quarter), years of eighteen months, months of twenty days, half decades, and half lunations of thirteen days: see Prichard, v. 353, 355.

made man in his own likeness,' 'the Acceptor of vows,' 'the Forgiver,' 'the Enjoiner of charity[1].' But the force of such expressions is materially abated when we view them in relation to others of no less authority. These latter seem to have connected, if not absolutely identified, Tezcatlipoca with the ancient sun-god of the New World. In the remarkable address, for instance, of the Mexican high-priest, the language runs as follows: 'We entreat that those who die in war may be graciously received by thee, our Father, the Sun, and our Mother, the Earth, for thou alone reignest[2];' and in a subsequent passage, the place of happiness, reserved by him for warriors slain in battle, is declared to be the sun itself. The name Tezcatlipoca, being interpreted, is the 'Shining Mirror;' on the monuments and in the paintings he is often represented as encircled by the disc of the sun[3]. His proper home is in the heavens[4]; from thence he came, descending on a spider's web, to persecute Quetzalcoatl, the benignant deity of the Toltecs; and in strict accordance with such representation, his choicest influence seems restricted to the world of the invisible; his face is covered with a mask; he is declared to be inpalpable as 'night and air;' he has the power of granting immortality, and reigns supreme in all the regions of the dead.

Upon the whole, that view seems preferable which makes Tezcatlipoca the deified impersonation of the generative powers of nature. As such, he was united to the primitive goddess and first woman of the Mexicans, Cihuacohuatl, the 'female serpent[5].'

[1] These and other like epithets are collected and expounded in Lord Kingsborough's *Antiq. of Mexico*, IX. 179, who concludes his summary by remarking, that 'all the attributes and powers which were assigned to Jehovah by the Hebrews, were also bestowed upon Tezcatlipoca by the Mexicans.'

[2] Squier's *American Archæological Researches*, p. 162, New York, 1851; Müller, p. 620. This prayer contemplates him chiefly in his character of 'god of death, and of the dead.'

[3] Squier, p. 163.

[4] See Müller, p. 614.

[5] Much as Mr. Squier may ridicule 'the error of the bigots,' who discovered an allusion to Eve and the Tempter of our first parents in the representation of the Great Mother, Cihuacohuatl, always giving birth to twins, 'bequeathing the sufferings of childbirth to women, as the tribute of death,' and uniformly accompanied by a snake, or feather-headed serpent,—I would suggest that there is in such resemblances abundant matter for grave philosophising. 'In all this,' writes Mr. Prescott, 'we see much to remind us of the mother of the human family, the Eve of the Hebrew and Syrian nations' (p. 464). Cf. Wuttke, I. 263, Lüken, *Traditionen*, &c., pp. 121, 122, the latter of whom declares, after comparing the legend with others: 'Auf die merkwürdige Uebereinstimmung der Sage in so vielen Theilen mit der Bibel brauche ich den aufmerksamen Leser wohl nicht hinzuweisen.'

As such, his highest type and aptest emblem was the sun; as such, he was occasionally entitled Tonacateucli ('embodied lord sun')[1]. As such, he bore the semblance of a handsome man, endowed with inexhaustible vigour, and rejoicing in the periodic renewal of his youth. As such, the costliest sacrifice of all was offered annually in his temple, during the arid month of May[2], when vegetable nature seemed expiring, and when fears began to be expressed for the well-being of the harvest. Then it was that pontiffs singled out one human being, in the spring of life, and of unblemished beauty, to personate, and suffer for and with, the highest member of their pantheon. When the day of this great sacrifice arrived, and the career of mirth and revelry assigned to the unhappy victim was completed, his heart, still palpitating under the murderous knife, was lifted up towards the sun and cast before the image of Tezcatlipoca, while the crowd below were bending breathless in the act of adoration.

If ever this divinity could justly claim to be compared with the all-holy God of revelation, he had forfeited his primal glory and descended altogether to the heathen level, when Mexico was first explored by Europeans, and her baneful idols put to flight by the advance of Christianity.

But Tezcatlipoca, though appearing to receive unbounded worship from the later Mexicans, was not their national divinity; recourse was never had to him as to the oracle, the leader, and the special patron of the Aztec tribes. That post from ages out of memory had been allotted to the still more terrible Huitzilopochtli[3],—a name compounded, it is said, of two words, importing 'humming-bird,' and 'left,' and illustrated by the fact that his gigantic image always bore some feathers of the humming-bird on the left foot. The reason of this etymology is found in certain peculiarities of the bird in question; its rich and brilliant plumage serving to dazzle the imagination of the Aztecs, while its frantic courage, as compared with its minute proportions, rendered it a favourite symbol of their own

[1] Squier, p. 161. This etymology is not, however, absolutely certain.

[2] Cf. Müller, p. 618, Prescott, pp. 24, 25.

[3] From *Huitzilin*, 'a humming-bird,' and *opochtli*, 'on the left hand:' cf. Müller, pp. 591, 592. He is also of opinion that in earlier ages, before the growth of anthropomorphism, this same divinity was called *Huitziton*, 'a little humming-bird,' and worshipped under that simple form, as a god of the air and firmament (p. 596). Prichard seems to prefer a different etymology, treating Huitzilopochtli as an historical personage (Huitzitoc), raised after his death to the 'left hand' of the god Tezcatlipoca (v. 365).

warlike, daring and indomitable temper. Accordingly, whatever may have been the primary idea suggested by the name Huitzilopochtli, or whatever may turn out to be the true interpretation of the marvellous story of his birth[1], it is indisputable that he grew ere long into the Śiva and the Mars of Central America. Another of his titles (Mexitli) had been transferred in early times to Mexico itself; and one of the first structures raised by Aztec builders on the table-land of Anahuac was the sanctuary of this, their guardian deity. His image was of a colossal bulk, erected on a blue stone, quadrangular in form, and with a snake, or serpent, issuing from each corner; the chains or collars about the idol's neck were ten human hearts, all made of gold; his girdle also consisted of a great golden serpent. Some at least appear to have regarded this ferocious war-god as the brother of Tezcatlipoca[2]; the largest temple of the Mexican metropolis was their common property; and in the costly and grotesque embellishments of both we always find the symbol of the mystic serpent more or less conspicuous.

There is ample reason for believing that ideas embodied in this representation were substantially the same in Europe, Asia, Africa, and America[3]. Unable though we are to specify that one interpretation of the Ophite symbol which explains and harmonises all the rest, it is remarkable that many different views had coexisted in the same locality. The serpent was at one time treated merely as a type of primitive matter; at a second, it became the image of superior knowledge, cunning, and sagacity. The periodic casting of its skin suggested the adoption of this reptile as an emblem of returning life, of spring-tide, of fertility, of rejuvenescence; and, regarded in the same peculiar aspect, the 'great century' of the Aztec tribes was represented as encircled by a serpent grasping its own tail: while other facts appear to indicate no less distinctly that, in both the Old World and the New, the serpent was employed to symbolise the highest forms of being, as the sun-god, the great

[1] The story is as follows: 'The mother of Huitzilopochtli was a priestess of Tezcatlipoca (a cleanser of the temple, says Gama), named Coatlicue. She was extremely devoted to the gods, and one day, when walking in the temple, she beheld descending in the air a ball, made of variously coloured feathers. She placed it in her girdle, became at once pregnant, and afterwards was delivered of Mexitli, or Huitzilopochtli, full armed, with a spear in one hand, a shield in the other, and a crest of green feathers on his head.' Squier, p. 195, Müller, pp. 601, 608.

[2] Müller, p. 615.

[3] *Ibid.* pp. 484 sq., 611 sq., and authorities cited above, pp. 216 sq.

mother of the human family, and even the First Principle of all things[1].

But though serpents were for reasons of this kind exalted into objects of religious worship, and venerated both in heathen countries and by various sects of Christian misbelievers as the primary source of intellectual illumination, it is also true that many primitive nations looked upon those reptiles with religious awe and horror, recognising in them a personification of the Evil Principle, or emblems of malignant energies, in both the physical and moral world[2]. The victory gained by Krishna in his arduous struggle with Káliya was held to have been frequently repeated in the wilder tribes of North America,—for instance, where the arrow of the philanthropic Manabozho had been guided to the heart of the Great Serpent, Meshekenabek, at the same time striking terror into an enormous brood of demons by which he was attended; and in Mexican paintings a huge serpent is sometimes exhibited in the act of being cut in pieces by the great divinity, Tezcatlipoca.

If I mistake not, the predominant idea connected with the serpent-symbol, in the worship more especially paid by Aztecs to their national divinity, was the idea of a terrific and destructive agent. This at least is certain, that the modern world is unacquainted with a system of religious thought whose whole complexion was so dark, so ghastly, so funereal. Everywhere it seemed to breathe of suffering and of death. The numerous altars of Huitzilopochtli reeked continually with the blood of human hecatombs[3], and that in cities where, amid some cheering gleams of moral sensibility, the Conquerers found no lack of goodly structures and of graceful ornaments, to indicate the progress made by the ferocious Aztec in the arts of social life. These desperate efforts to secure the favour of the gods by offering human victims were indeed by no means limited to ancient Mexico; for all the wild tribes of America[4] had been wont from ages immemorial to sacrifice both children of their

[1] This is the view adopted by the rationalistic Mr. Squier, one of the most recent inquirers, in his *Serpent Symbol* (American Archæol. Researches, Part I.). He concludes (p. 243): 'Whether we accept the scriptural tradition of "the fall" in a literal sense, or as an allegory referring to man's departure from the original religion, under the seductions of an unholy superstition, of which the serpent was the emblem,—in either case the antiquity of the symbol is equally established.'

[2] *Ibid.* pp. 227, 244.

[3] Prescott, p. 19. Southey is also quite correct when he speaks of Mexican temples
'Whose black and putrid walls were scaled with blood.'

[4] Müller, pp. 142 sq.

own and prisoners taken in their savage conflicts with some neighbouring people. Acting also on the rude belief, that such oblations would conduce to gratify the animal wants of their divinity, as well as to appease his wrath, they had contracted the vile habit of feasting on the remnant of these human sacrifices, and at other times proceeded to indulge in the most brutish forms of cannibalism. But when the Aztec rule eventually prevailed in every part of Anahuac, the sacrificing of all foreign enemies became a still more solemn duty. We are told that 'the amount of victims immolated on its accursed altars would stagger the faith of the least scrupulous believer[1];' while cannibalism, that dark accompaniment of human sacrifice in almost every country, was in Mexico peculiarly rife, and from the partial efforts to disguise it, had become peculiarly revolting[2].

The character of the national god, to whom each Mexican had solemnly devoted all his strength, reflected, and in turn contributed to fix, the moral characteristics of the nation. Their ruling spirit was severe and sanguinary. Their familiarity with blood begat in them a brutal thirst for carnage. The great drum, composed of serpent-skins, was ever and anon emitting its disastrous challenge from the temples of Huitzilopochtli, and so calling men to arms. Their very wars were undertaken not so much from pride of conquest as in order to bring home fresh victims for the solemn festivals; and imitation of their bloody rites was always rigorously demanded as an indispensable condition of their friendship and alliance.

Of minor points connected with the worship of Huitzilopochtli one appears to be deserving of especial notice. It is recorded how, in all the long migrations of the Aztec tribes, four priests had been accustomed to bear aloft a wooden image of this great divinity[3]; the vehicle on which it rested being called the 'chair of god,' and serving, like the sacred chest of other ancient nations, to remind them of his special favour and his present personality. Some writers have moreover dwelt on these arrangements as supplying what they deem a close resem-

[1] *Ibid.* p. 502. The numbers vary considerably, and some accounts are doubtless much exaggerated (pp. 637, 638); but there is every reason to believe that not fewer than 2500 human beings were offered annually in the Aztec dominions. As many as 136,000 human skulls were found by the companions of Cortés within the precincts of the temple of Huitzilopochtli (Prichard, v. 365; Prescott, p. 26).

[2] Prescott, pp. 27, 28, 49; Müller, pp. 628 sq.

[3] Müller, p. 594; Winer, *Realwörterbuch*, under 'Bundeslade.'

blance to the sacred chest, or ark, of Israel, which was carried by the Levites on their shoulders through the wilderness and even to the field of battle. But the fancied parallelism, like many others of the same description, will be found to vanish on a close analysis. Apart from contradictions which are everywhere discernible in the religious dogmas of the Hebrew and the Aztec, it is obvious that the purpose of the two sacred vehicles in question, and consequently all the main ideas thereby suggested to the people, were completely different[1]. The 'ark of the covenant' had always been the centre and palladium of the Hebrew system, not because it bore within it or without it a material representation of the Unapproachable and only God, or was contributing in any way to bring Him more directly under the cognizance of the senses, but because it was ordained at first as the repository of His Holy Law. Its prominent position ever intimated to the Hebrew that the covenant, in virtue of which he stood so very near to God, was ultimately and entirely moral; that the term of his election depended altogether on his keeping of the commandments; that his mission to the world at large was to assert the unity and vindicate the holiness of God against the mass of errors and corruptions under which those precious truths were ever liable to be lost.

I am unable to discover any proof that Aztecs had arrived at the conception of a sacred trinity, or triad; though attempts have not been wanting[2] to establish such a theory in Mexico as well as in most other parts of ancient heathendom. The object commonly chosen to fill up the third place, thus uniting on a level with Tezcatlipoca and Huitzilopochtli, is the water-god of Central America, entitled Tlaloc[3]. In accordance with this

[1] Bähr, *Symbolik des Mosaischen Cultus*, I. 399—407.

[2] *e.g.* in Lord Kingsborough's *Antiq. of Mexico*, VI. 410 sq., where Acosta declares that 'Satan, in order to increase the majesty of his own worship, has wished, by cunningly introducing the doctrine of the Holy Trinity among the Indians, to abuse it' (p. 411).

[3] Müller, pp. 500 sq. Children were among the victims offered at his altar; and it is worthy of remark that they were immolated during the dry season, in order, if possible, to draw down blessings from the angry water-god. His wife, or female counterpart, was called Chalchiucueje, and to her, the water-goddess, all infants immediately after birth were brought for purification; the rite then practised bearing some vague resemblance to Christian baptism. (*Ibid.* pp. 503, 652.) But, as Mr. Prescott well remarks, with reference both to this and many more affinities, the first race of missionaries 'fastened their eyes exclusively on the points of resemblance,' taking small account of other and essential contrarieties. 'In their amazement

theory, he has been converted into the Preserver, while the gods already noticed were believed to act respectively as the Creator and Destroyer. The truth appears to be, that if the number *three* must be completed, the divinity whose character and influence best entitle him to rank with the chief tenants of the Aztec pantheon is Quetzalcoatl.

As the story of this god is in itself remarkable, and may be found hereafter to involve a series of important questions, bearing more or less directly on our general subject, I propose to give the chief particulars of it somewhat more in detail. Whether we regard the whole as purely mythical, or as belonging rather to the family of historic legends, it is probable that when the Toltecs entered Mexico[1] in the seventh century of the Christian era, Quetzalcoatl was enthroned already as their patron deity. From them it was that all the knowledge of him which is traceable in Anahuac had passed over to the Aztec tribes by whom they were succeeded. The current version of the story is as follows:

Quetzalcoatl (or the 'Feathered Serpent') had been destined to become the high-priest of Tula, the metropolis founded by the Toltecs on their immigration into Mexico. His birth, some writers have asserted, was miraculous[2]; and in proportion as he ripened into manhood it was obvious in how many points he differed from the multitude by whom he was surrounded. His complexion was not red, but fair, his eyes large, his forehead open, his beard thick and flowing. Raised ere long to the position which had been allotted to him by the gods,

they not only magnified what they saw, but were perpetually cheated by the illusions of their own heated imaginations. In this they were admirably assisted by their Mexican converts, proud to establish—and half believing it themselves—a correspondence between their own faith and that of their conquerors' (p. 465).

[1] See above, p. 362, n. 1.

[2] This view is strongly espoused by Mr. Squier, but I confess myself unable to verify some of his statements (pp. 185 sq.). His description of the birth of Quetzalcoatl is as follows: 'The god of the Milky Way, in other words, of Heaven, the principal deity of the Aztec pantheon, and the Great Father of gods and men, sent a message to a virgin of Tulan [Tula], telling her that it was the will of the gods that she should conceive a son, which she did without knowing any man' (cf. above, p. 308, n. 2). According to Mr. Squier, Quetzalcoatl was an intermediate demi-god, or rather a reputed incarnation of the highest god, Tezcatlipoca, and was thus analogous (he thinks) to Buddha, Zoroaster, Osiris, Taut in Phœnicia, Hermes or Cadmus in Greece, Romulus in Rome, Odin in Scandinavia, Votan in Guatemala, Bochica among the Muyscas, &c. But how is such a theory to be reconciled with facts which Mr. Squier, in spite of all his archæological erudition, appears to have

Quetzalcoatl underwent a course of voluntary penance[1]; substituting, it is said, for human sacrifices of the olden times the drawing forth of blood from his own body. He then proceeded, with the help of Huemac[2], the temporal prince of Tula, to instruct and civilise the people round about him. He compiled an equitable code of laws; he introduced a milder and a purer ritual; he arranged the calendar; he set his face against all forms of violence and bloodshed; he encouraged arts of peace, as agriculture, metallurgy, and the like. Beneath his genial influences the Toltecs rose at once into a thriving principality. It was the golden age of Anahuac, when the corn sprang up with such luxuriance that one ear became a burden for a man; when cotton grew of all colours so as to supersede the art of dyeing; and when other products of the soil were so abundant that the life of the community might be described as one perpetual feast. The palaces of Quetzalcoatl were constructed of gold, of silver, and of precious stones; the air was laden with rich perfumes, while the birds in brilliant plumage gladdened every heart with their enchanting music.

But the reign of order and prosperity was not of long duration. The god Tezcatlipoca cast an envious eye upon this earthly paradise; and calling to his aid the powers of magic undertook in various garbs to mar and ruin the great work of Toltec civilisation. He seduced the daughter of king Huemac; from which event was dated the decline of moral purity and the diffusion of a lax and revolutionary spirit. The high-priest himself ere long succumbed beneath the same malignant opposition. He was tempted to purchase immortality by drinking a renowned elixir which the chief divinity presented

completely overlooked? For instance, how would he explain the deadly feud between Tezcatlipoca and Quetzalcoatl, which led to the ejection of the latter and the absolute ruin of the principality?

[1] See Kingsborough's *Antiq. of Mexico*, VI. 177, where these penances are regarded as a species of 'self-sacrifice' (cf. Southey's *Madoc*, Part II. No. X.). Müller, on the other hand, maintains (p. 582) that the self-chastisements of Quetzalcoatl were not *penances*, properly so called,—arising neither from a consciousness of guilt nor from a mystic wish to extricate himself entirely from the fetters of the body,—but were partial oblations of human blood intended as substitutes for the human sacrifices of earlier times. The same writer has justly remarked (pp. 582, 590) that when the worship of Quetzalcoatl was adopted by the Aztecs, they forgot his own strong abhorrence of human sacrifices, and offered such to him as well as to the other gods.

[2] Müller, p. 587, who tries to make out that Huemac and Quetzalcoatl are really the same person, or at least are different names applied to the same personification in different stages of the mythe.

to him in the guise of an old man; but no sooner was the cup exhausted than Quetzalcoatl felt himself impelled to quit the scene of all his former labours and to visit Old Tlapallan, the great cradle of the Toltec race. Upon the eve of his departure he destroyed the costly palaces; the fruit-trees were all smitten with a curse of barrenness; the singing-birds were ordered to accompany him and entertain him on the journey. His path, of which the general tendency was eastward, brought him after some deflections to Cholula, where halting for a term of years he was permitted once again to carry out his great reformatory project, and even to diffuse a knowledge of his principles in countries lying farther to the south[1]. It was in Cholula that some of his enthusiastic followers first proceeded to invest him with divine prerogatives. A temple was there dedicated in his honour, and the ruins, bearing witness to his primitive grandeur, are still classed among the noblest monuments of Mexican heathenism. The final flight or disappearance of Quetzalcoatl is narrated differently in different versions of the story. All, however, represent it as both sudden and mysterious. The received account is, that on his last endeavour to reach Tlapallan he descended to the shores of the Mexican gulf; and as he entered the unearthly bark, composed of serpent-skins, that was to carry him across the ocean, he consoled his followers with the promise that he would eventually return among them and establish his benignant rule in every part of Anahuac. A belief in this return[2] was lingering in the heart of many a Mexican as late as the arrival of the Spaniards. Cortés was himself identified at first with the expected deity; his white and bearded followers were esteemed the progeny of Quetzalcoatl, or revered as 'children of the sun;' and the locality from which they sprang was still believed to be none other than the fabled region of Tlapallan.

Now it is obvious that a narrative like this may be interpreted from very different points of view. We may consider it, for instance, as a genuine mythe,—embodying, under allegorical forms, the rude conceptions that prevailed respecting God and nature at some early period in the annals of mankind; or,

[1] 'Seine Herrschaft dehnte sich aber hier sehr aus, von Cholula aus sandte er Kolonien nach Huaxayacac, Tabasco und Campêche, später rühmte sich der Adel in Yucatan von ihm abzustammen, und *in der neuesten Zeit fand man dort noch Leute seines Namens*, wie in Chiapas Nachkommen Votans.' *Ibid.* p. 579.

[2] On these and other strange prognostics of the coming of the Spaniards, see Prescott, pp. 104, 105, and Fancourt's *History of Yucatan*, pp. 57—59.

secondly, it may be taken as a legend, more or less historic in its subject-matter, setting forth in brilliant colours the achievements of some true philanthropist, whom love and gratitude at length exalted to a place among the gods. According to one method of interpretation[1], the Toltec tribes, long after they emerged from barbarism, had formed the habit of ascribing all their progress as a nation to the work of some ideal hero, whom they designated Quetzalcoatl. He was thus in their eyes a personification of the whole community: its qualities had been transferred to him: whatever it had done was said to have been done by him. For instance, as the principal seats of Toltec civilisation were Tula and Cholula, these were made the theatre on which he acted, and from which his principles had been transmitted to adjacent districts. As the Toltec tribes all vanished, or were driven onward to the south and east, in many cases owing to their dissolute habits, and in others to the violence of some encroaching and more warlike neighbour, the reverses of the nation are all vividly repeated in the life of Quetzalcoatl.

It is felt, however, by the authors of this quasi-mythic theory that the *deification* of the Toltec people, under the disguise of an ideal hero, is inadequately explained on their hypothesis as to the origin and import of the story. They accordingly attempt to trace it farther back into the region of pure mythus. They affirm that long before the age when Quetzalcoatl became the representative of Toltec nationality, a god with whom he was eventually confounded had been worshipped in the cycle of divinities who were supposed to tenant each one his own province in the realm of nature. Quetzalcoatl, as to the original conception, was, in other words, a nature-god, devoid of human form or human properties; and even after a prevailing tendency to anthropomorphism led men to devise for him a novel story, and invest him with exalted attributes befitting the ideal founder of Toltec civilisation, it is urged that frequent glimpses of his genuine character continue to be visible; they witness to the fact that even by the later votaries of Quetzalcoatl he was known to be a mere personification of natural energies. The sphere of action which, according to this view, the primitive world assigned to him had always been the

[1] This is Müller's theory, who remarks (p. 580): 'Eine genauere Ansicht und Kritik dieser Erzählung, die sich auf die Analogie mythologischer Gesetze gründet, zeigt uns zunächst, dass Quetzalcoatl *die euhemerisirte Idee des Toltekischen Kulturvolks in ihrer religiösen Fassung ist.*'

region of the air. The symbols commonly connected with his worship were the sparrow, the fire-stone, and the serpent; all of which the author of the present theory does not hesitate to claim as justifying his peculiar method of interpretation[1]. The god who forms and regulates the currents of the air is welcomed as the god of health and joy, of affluence and fertility. The struggle waging between him and the divinity Tezcatlipoca is resolved into the action of conflicting elements: the breeze of heaven, opposed and vanquished by the fiery sun-god, is compelled to seek a refuge in some distant clime to which the singing-birds all follow him. The ultimate return of the benignant Quetzalcoatl from the east is similarly identified with the recurrence of the trade-winds blowing from that quarter; the idea of him as the great national benefactor having been suggested by the plenteous showers which then descend in periodic blessings on the table-land of Anahuac.

Yet how plausible soever this interpretation of the story may seem at the first glance, it cannot stand the test of thoughtful criticism. Its author seems to have forgotten that Toltec civilisation, rising as it does alone like some oasis in the desert, is a fact demanding an historical explanation; and we naturally ask what better explanation can be given than that which traces known improvements to their ordinary sources,—to the genial impulse first communicated to a multitude by some one master-spirit? He assumes that after a nation has grown weary and ashamed of its barbaric usages, there is a general disposition felt not only to personify itself, but also to bow down and worship such personification, as though it were reality. He assumes still further that a nation at this period of its growth is likely to engraft the worship of ideal heroes on some primitive worship of the elements, thus combining in the process two incongruous mythes, entirely different in their texture, and resting on a different basis.

On the other hand, if we approach the tale of Quetzalcoatl, unencumbered by mythic theories of our own, we cannot fail to be impressed by the remarkable semblance of reality pervading almost every part of it. Embellishments there doubtless are in that, as in most other stories, which have been transmitted

[1] *Ibid.* pp. 593 sq. The employment of a bird to symbolise the air-god is all natural enough; but there is greater difficulty in tracing the fitness of the two remaining symbols. The fire-stone (sometimes black, sometimes green) is supposed to have been originally an aerolith; while the serpent is here viewed under its benignant aspects, as an emblem of rejuvenescence and fertility.

through the same precarious media; but the argument which prompts us to reject it as unworthy of all credit, on the ground that we can never wholly disentangle the historic from the non-historic elements in its composition, would require us also to resolve the brightest worthies of the Middle Age into a series of mythic beings, because some dreamers of the school of Simeon Metaphrastes have, in ministering to the unhealthy cravings of the period, garnished all their 'Lives of Saints' with fables and absurdities. Affected by considerations of this kind, the ablest writers on American heathenism contend for the reality of several of the leading acts ascribed to Quetzalcoatl. He is viewed as an *historic* personage: historic as Confucius, notwithstanding all the myriad temples now devoted to his worship; historic as the Rajah Brooke in Borneo, notwithstanding all the wondrous tales which may, and probably will, be circulated in the Eastern Archipelago by the Dyaks of some future age.

One class of writers[1] have discovered in the Toltec worthy an illustrious priest or prince of Tula, who on the decline of power and civilisation in his own locality had fled in search of his mysterious fatherland; but rallying his attendants for a while had been intrusted with the government of Cholula, and had planted there a sacerdotal principality which long survived as the metropolis of some new system of religion. This method of accounting for the story fails, however, in what seems to me a most essential point. No circumstance has been more uniformly mentioned than the *foreign* air of Quetzalcoatl. He was a white man, wearing a long beard[2]. Such testimony to his strange appearance is remarkably corroborated by the language of the Mexican king[3] as handed down by Cortés. The story is there lifted altogether from the region of pure mythus. Quetzalcoatl is an ordinary foreigner, retiring hostile and indignant far across the waters and expected to return and conquer Mexico in the most literal sense. Nor is it unworthy

[1] Prichard, for example, acquiesces in this view (v. 364, 365).

[2] Müller's only resource in getting rid of these peculiarities is to urge (1) that Quetzalcoatl was said to be of fair complexion, because his *vestments* were white, and (2) that he was said to have a thick and flowing beard, because the Toltec priests were in the habit of wearing their hair very long! Wuttke, on the contrary, is so influenced by these special features in the narrative as to pronounce absolutely on the foreign extraction of Quetzalcoatl: 'Dass die bildende Wirksamkeit eines Mannes von fremdem und *weissem* Stamme die Veranlassung zu der Vorstellung dieses Gottes wurde, ist nicht zu bezweifeln' (I. 262).

[3] *Ibid.* p. 261.

of remark that stories of white men were current in some other districts of America. The arrival of mysterious strangers in the highlands of Peru[1] had given birth to all the civilisation which it finally attained; and this commencement, a great writer has suggested, coincides in point of time with the original 'discovery' of the middle and southern parts of the United States by mariners from the north of Europe[2].

We are not, perhaps, at liberty to gather any definite inference, touching the origin of Quetzalcoatl, from the circular shape of temples dedicated to his worship: yet the presence of the symbol of the cross, embroidered on the long white mantle of his priest and planted here and there upon the shrines of Yucatan, has not unnaturally given rise to the idea that he possessed some meagre knowledge of the Christian faith. The Spaniards all grew confident[3] on witnessing these strange phenomena that the Gospel had been propagated in America long before their own arrival; some appealing for an explanation to the labours of St. Thomas, others clinging to the thought that they had been preceded by the Spanish fugitives who left their country when King Roderic was defeated by the Moors; but all agreeing that the presence of their venerated symbol, in the midst of a revolting form of paganism, arose from the unhallowed commerce of Americans with the prince of darkness. It might far more plausibly have been contended that this hollow approximation to the ceremonies of the Latin Church, if not in every case fortuitous, was due to some extrinsic influence which is known to have been exercised by Quetzalcoatl. We are told, indeed, that in the Toltec districts he himself had introduced the symbol of the cross, and also

[1] The two 'children of the sun' (brother and sister, husband and wife) to whom the Peruvians ascribed their knowledge of civilised life, were called Manco Capac, and Mama Oelle (*Ibid.* p. 305; Prescott, *Conquest of Peru*, pp. 3 sq. Lond. 1854): cf. Squier, as above, pp. 187—192, on other parallels, real or imaginary.

[2] Humboldt, *Cosmos*, II. 298, Sabine's ed.

[3] See Kingsborough's *Antiq. of Mexico*, VI. 418. On the other hand it must be borne in mind that the Spanish conqueror occasionally taught the natives to engraft the symbol of the cross on their abominable ritual. Thus Peter Martyr (of Anghiera, living at the court of Madrid) declares in his *Decades of the Newe Worlde*, Lond. 1555 (Dec. III. fol. 157): 'Owre men gaue them a painted picture of the blessed vyrgine, which they placed reuerently in their temple, and above it a *crosse*, to be honoured in the remembrance of God and man, and the saluation of mankynde. They erected also an other great crosse of wood in the toppe of the temple, whyther they oftentymes resorte togither to honour the image of the vyrgine.'

recommended the practice of adoring it[1]. We learn again that his peculiar principles, whatever these might be, were rapidly diffused beyond the city of Cholula, and survived long after in the sacred colonies which he had placed in Yucatan[2]. Yet, on the other hand, it should be stated that the use of crosses in religious worship might have been at first entirely independent of Christian agencies[3]. The passion for symbolic representations, deeply rooted in the human breast, prepares us to expect that any simple figure like the cross would almost certainly be appropriated in one or other of the heathen rituals of antiquity; and with regard to many parts of Central America, there is reason for believing that this emblem was religiously employed from early and præ-Christian times. Its office there had been to symbolise the god of rain[4]; and, consequently, as a form embodying the ideas of health, of joy, of plenty, it had grown into a common object of popular adoration.

But whatever be the real import of particular features in the legends of Quetzalcoatl, I am satisfied that he presents to us one clear example, shewing the existence of some intercourse in very distant ages between the Old and New continents. Nor is this the only kind of evidence adducible in proof of such connexion. Many a tenet in the general creed of Anahuac bears no small resemblance to the dreams of Eastern Asia, and the cosmogonic theories of other ancient nations. It was held, for instance, quite as firmly in the New World as the Old, that the material universe had passed through a limited number of chronological cycles, each concluded by a grand catastrophe, of which the agent was some one or other of the physical elements. To quote the language of a high authority, we shall find the same traditions in their substance 'reaching from Etruria to Tibet,' and forward to the ridge of the Mexican Cordilleras[5].' The system of the Aztecs and Tibetians is

[1] Müller. pp. 499, 500.

[2] Above, p. 374, n. 1.

[3] So Mr. Prescott seems to think (pp. 464, 465). In speaking of the early missionaries he remarks: 'They could not suppress their wonder, as they beheld the cross, the sacred emblem of their own faith, raised as an object of worship in the temples of Anahuac. They met with it in various places; and the image of a cross may be seen at this day, sculptured in bas-relief, on the walls of one of the buildings of Palenque, while a figure bearing some resemblance to that of a child is held up to it, as if in adoration.' The style in which the whole of this work is executed appears to leave no doubt as to its heathen origin.

[4] Müller, pp. 496—500.

[5] A. von Humboldt, in Prichard, v. 360. See the whole discussion, pp. 357—361. The first age of the Mexicans (the Age of the Earth, or the Age of Giants), corresponding to the Krita or Satya-yuga of

perhaps in one respect at variance with ideas prevailing in the different branches of the Indo-European family[1]; for it is said to recognise as many as *five* such periods in the lifetime of the universe, while they give only *four*: yet even in the case of Mexico, we are assured, there is some want of uniformity as to the number and the order of the different ages.

What appears to be of most importance is the fact, attested by the hieroglyphic paintings of the Mexican as well as by the tales now current in all quarters from the Arctic Ocean to Cape Horn[2], that one of these great periods called 'the Age of Water' closed with a convulsion, the account of which, in all its broader outlines, is remarkably akin to the Mosaic record of the Deluge. It was not, of course, to be expected that discoveries of this kind, eliciting, as they did, from long-forgotten races of the human family a corroboration of the truths of Holy Writ, would be allowed to circulate without a challenge; and accordingly attempts were made in different quarters, either to explain away American legends of a deluge, or resolve them all into a series of 'cosmogonic mythes[3].' They were considered at the very most to indicate a popular belief in some 'creation out of the water and in spite of the water.' Yet so numerous, so minute, and so extremely arbitrary, are the points in which those legends are now found to have approached the sacred story, that some species of affinity between the two is far more generally recognised; excepting

Hindústán, was held to be 5206 years in duration. The human race of this age was destroyed by famine. The second period was the Age of Fire, in which birds only escaped the final conflagration, except one man and one woman, who saved themselves in the recesses of a cavern. The third period was the Age of Wind or Tempests, which two men only had survived. The fourth period was the Age of Water, the duration of which is said to have been 4008 years. The earth was inhabited by men, whose mother was the 'Female Serpent' (above, p. 366, n. 5). Then came the period in the midst of which the world now is: its human population being all descended from one man and one woman, who were rescued from the general calamity at the close of the Age of Water. Some reflections on these subjects, as regarded from a geological point of view, will be found in Mr. Hugh Miller's *Testimony of the Rocks*, Lect. VII. VIII.

[1] See, for instance, above, pp. 214 sq.

[2] Lüken's *Traditionen*, &c. pp. 216—235: Faber's *Origin of Idolatry*, II. 141 sq.

[3] Müller, p. 112. On returning to the subject (pp. 515, 516) he pronounces even more dogmatically: 'In solchen Analogien mit der biblischen Flutherzählung ist weder eine historische Abhängigkeit der Urvölker von einander, noch ein christlicher Einfluss auf die amerikanischen Erzählungen anzunehmen, sondern selbstständige Gestaltungen.'

where an archæologist or schoolman is incorrigibly blinded by his love of system-building. Even the divines of Germany[1], beneath whose shadow every kind of mythic theory has sprung up with rank luxuriance, seem to have been almost reconciled to a belief, that the traditions now and formerly current in America respecting some great deluge, must have all been carried over from the Old Continent.

Instead of dwelling on this subject, I shall ask the reader to examine for himself the following specimens selected almost at random, partly from the wilder tribes, and partly from the more refined communities of North America. The first[2] is still in actual circulation among the Cherokees; yet so peculiar is its form, that efforts have been made in vain to represent it as a recollection of some Christian teaching. In the gifts of speech and prophecy there attributed to the Dog, we are reminded rather of the service rendered to Manu, according to the Âryan legend[3], by the mighty and mysterious Fish. The story of the American Indians has been thus reported from their own lips by an intelligent explorer of every thing connected either with their present or their past condition:

'The water once prevailed over the land, until every person was drowned but a single family. The coming of this calamity was revealed by a dog to his master. This dog was very pertinacious in visiting the banks of a river, for several days, where he stood gazing at the water and howling piteously. Being sharply spoken to, by his master, and ordered home, he revealed to him the coming evil. He concluded his prediction by saying, that the escape of his master and family from

[1] Thus Ewald, in *Götting. Gelehr. Anzeigen*, 1855, No. 69, p. 688, shews a leaning in favour of the common view, which, on this ground especially, refers the peopling of America to immigration from Eastern Asia. With regard to the minute coincidences between the Mexican and Hebrew versions of the Deluge, he declares: 'In solchen wesentlichen Gleichheiten können wir kein zufälliges sich Begegnen finden.' One of the best-informed, and at the same time most dispassionate of American writers on these subjects (Mr. Gallatin) has, in like manner, come to the conclusion that the native legends originated 'in a real historical recollection of an universal deluge, which overwhelmed all mankind in early ages of the world' (Prichard, v. 361).

[2] Schoolcraft, *Notes on the Iroquois*, pp. 358, 359, Albany, 1847.

[3] Above, p. 223. The difference is, however, no less remarkable. In the Hindû story, the Fish who acts as an incarnation of the Deity, is moving in his own proper element, and simply rescues the small remnant he has taken under his especial patronage; while in the case before us, the Dog, according to his true character, is made to die for his master's family in the deluge which he had predicted. Müller, it may be noted, suggests (p. 515) that Coxcox in the Mexican story of the deluge is himself a humanized representation of some ancient Fish-god, corresponding to the Dagon of Syria, &c.

drowning depended upon their throwing *him* into the water; that to escape drowning himself, he must make a boat, and put in it all he wished to save; that it would then rain hard a long time, and a great overflowing of the land would take place.

The dog then told his master to look for a sign of the truth of what he had said, to the back of his neck. On turning round and doing so, the dog's neck was raw and bare, the bone and flesh appearing. By obeying this prediction, the man and his family were saved, and from these rescued persons the earth, they believe, was again peopled.'

The other legends hereunto appended are both silent as to any warning which prepared the human race for the outbursting of the Deluge; but some of the minutiæ there preserved are most remarkable. The account is furnished by A. von Humboldt[1], one of the chief authorities respecting the picture-writings of ancient Mexico.

'Of the different nations that inhabit Mexico, the following had paintings representing the deluge of Coxcox, *viz.* the Aztecs, the Mixtecs, the Zapotecs, the Tlascaltecs, and the Mechoacans. The Noah, Xisuthrus, or Manu of these nations, is termed Coxcox, Teo-Cipactli, or Tezpi. He saved himself, with his wife Xochiquetzatl, in a bark, or, according to other traditions, on a raft. The painting represents Coxcox in the midst of the water waiting for a bark. The mountain, the summit of which rises above the waters, is the peak of Colhuacan, the Ararat of the Mexicans. At the foot of the mountain are the heads of Coxcox and his wife. The latter is known by two tresses in the form of horns, denoting the female sex. The men born after the deluge are dumb. The dove from the top of a tree distributes among them tongues represented under the form of small commas.'

Again:

'The people of Mechoacan preserved a tradition that Coxcox, whom they called Tezpi, embarked in a spacious *acalli* with his wife, his children, several animals and grain. When the Great Spirit, Tezcatlipoca, ordered the waters to withdraw, Tezpi sent out from his bark a vulture, the zopilote, or *vultur aura*. This bird did not return on account of the carcases with which the earth was strewed. Tezpi sent out other birds, one of which, the humming-bird, alone returned, holding in its beak a branch clad with leaves. Tezpi, seeing that fresh verdure covered the soil, quitted his bark near the mountain of Colhuacan.'

[1] A. von Humboldt, *Vues des Cordillères et Monumens de l'Amérique*, pp. 226, 227. This great writer very justly asks: 'Ne doit-on pas reconnoître les traces d'une origine commune partout où les idées cosmogoniques et les premières traditions des peuples offrent des analogies frappantes jusque dans les moindres circonstances?' That the South Sea islands are no exception to this rule may be seen in Ellis, *Polynesian Researches*, I. 387 sq. A very striking instance has been brought to light in the *Mission Field* (July, 1859): it is the Dyak version of the Deluge. 'They say that long ago there was a great overflow of the sea, which drowned the world, and that only one human pair of each of the four races, 'Orang Puteh,' Malays, Chinese, and Dyaks, were saved from destruction, each in their prahus.'

CHAPTER III.

Religions of Oceanica.

'I believe that the ignorance which has prevailed regarding the mythological systems of barbarous or semi-barbarous races has too generally led to their being considered far grander and more reasonable than they really were.'

Discovery and general character of the region. Original unity of the population. Two existing varieties. Probable course of migration.
§ 1. *The Papuan Family. Low state of religious sensibility. Idea of God. Worship of the dead. Veneration of the Waringin-tree.*
§ 2. *The Malayo-Polynesian Family. Ethnological affinities of the Vitians. Their sanguinary spirit. Serpent-symbol. Ndengei. Traditions.—The New Zealanders. Character of the Maori. Religious sensibility. Ideas of God. Mythe of Heaven and Earth. New race of divinities. Nature of worship. Worship of ancestors. The ariki. The tohunga. Form of baptism. Institution of tapu. Story of Mani. Fitness of Christianity: its progress in Polynesia.*

THE name of 'Oceanica' is here employed in its extended signification, as embracing the whole group of human beings who are scattered through the myriad islands of the Eastern and Southern Seas, from Madagascar on the eastern coast of Africa to the western shores of the New World. It seems to have been ordered in the plans of the Almighty, that the natives of this Archipelago should remain almost entirely strangers to the other sections of the human family, until, upon the dawn of that eventful epoch which divides the Modern from the Mediæval life of Europe, all the bearings of the grand discovery could be adequately perceived. The Spaniard had secured his empire in America, and was introducing there some feeble germs of Christian civilisation, when the pride of conquest once again impelled him onward into other spheres of enterprise. A fleet, despatched from Mexico itself, in the third quarter of the sixteenth century, enabled him to plant the Spanish flag on many of the Philippines. The Portuguese, and after them the Dutch, approaching from the opposite side, extended the horizon of man's thoughts and stimulated the new spirit of adventure; while England, now advancing proudly to her place among the maritime powers of Europe, was importing from the Farther East not only the choice products of a tropical soil, but stories tending to beget compassion for 'poor infidels captived by the devil.' The first of her great mariners returned in 1580 from his perilous voyage round the globe.

Henceforward almost every year was serving to lift up the veil that covered some remoter province of the Eastern Archipelago. Another world, as new to Europe as the continent discovered by Columbus, and affording not a few distinct analogies to that remarkable region, was now gradually laid open to the skilful navigator, and explored by men of science, and by heralds of the Christian faith. It stretched on every side in groups of islands, differing in soil and structure, as in geographical distribution; here presenting to the eye a mass of savage and volcanic mountains, towering high into the clouds; there a cluster of low coral reefs that scarcely peer above the surface of the water; here abounding in luxuriant pastures and sparkling like so many 'gems under the sunny sky of the Great Ocean;' there a long succession of untrodden wilderness and sombre forest; here suggesting the idea of an old continent dismembered and in part submerged, and there of one that seems at present only in course of formation.

The inhabitants of this region are at first sight no less various in their aspect than the island-groups on which they have been severally planted; and accordingly the first impressions of the European mariner who touched at several of these groups in succession were commonly adverse to the thought of primitive unity.

He found the natives of different islands and different parts of the same island varying widely from each other in temperament, in physical structure, in habits, and in speech. Yet here, as we have seen already in America, it was rather to a superficial and unscientific gaze that local variations had presented insurmountable difficulties. Fresh inquiry brought to light fresh points of contact between tribes where such affinity was not at first suspected; and so numerous are the common elements of thought and feeling, language and mythology, which after a minute analysis are seen to underlie the startling discrepancies in physical organisation, that ethnologists on merely scientific grounds are more and more disposed to hesitate before pronouncing against the ultimate derivation of the Oceanic islanders from one parent stock. It is remarkable that within the last few years, the speech of the Malays, itself originally monosyllabic, has been grammatically connected[1] with idioms spoken as far northward as the confines of eastern India and western China; thus directing us again to the conclusion, that morally as well as geographically the Indian Archipelago is only a prolongation of the Indo-Chinese world, and Asia the great centre out of which the population of the whole had radiated long anterior to the birth of pagan history. This clear approximation in two languages, of which the seat of one is on the mainland, of the other on the islands, furnishes a fresh and still more definite link of union between Asia and Polynesia,—a link, 'which, even by itself, is strong enough to hold two of the mightiest chains of languages together; the Nomads of the sea extending from the east coast of Africa to the west coast of America; the Nomads of the continent swarming from the south-east to the north-west of Asia.'

Neglecting, for the present, some few tribes of Oceanica[2], whose ethnological affinities are still undetermined, we shall find that all the rest are capable of classification under two great varieties.

The members of the first, and probably the elder of the groups, have very much in common with the Khonds and other primitive people scattered in the mountains and forests of Central India[3], and in some adjacent regions; but they most of

[1] See Mr. Max Müller's 'Last Results of the Turanian Researches,' in Bunsen's *Phil. of Univ. Hist.* I. 403 sq.

[2] *e. g.* the people known by the various titles of 'Arafuras,' 'Alfoers' and 'Alforians' (? Arabic الخرارج). 'Nothing,' says Prichard (V. 255), 'can be more puzzling than the contradictory accounts which are given of their physical characters and manners. The only point of agreement between different writers respecting them is, the circumstance that all represent them as very low in civilisation, and of fierce and sanguinary habits.' Yet even this representation is disputed by D. H. Kolff, *Voyages, &c.*, translated from the Dutch by Mr. Earl (Lond. 1840), pp. 156 sq. Mr. Earl's own account (*The Native Races of the Indian Archipelago, or, Papuans*, pp. 61 sq., Lond. 1853) is probably the most correct. He thinks that 'Alforias' is not a generic term for a particular race of people; 'but was generally applied to the inland inhabitants of these islands, to distinguish them from the coast tribes.' He derives the name from the Portuguese 'Alforias' = 'freedmen' or 'manumitted slaves;' but it would rather seem to have been imported directly from Arabia, and not through a European medium, so that its proper sense would be 'outsiders,' 'persons beyond the influence of the coast settlements.'

[3] See above, pp. 257 sq., where

all resemble the African negroes in the sooty blackness of their skin, their crisped and woolly hair, their broad noses, thick and prominent lips, receding chins and foreheads, and even in their general build[1]. These Oceanic negroes, also termed Negritos, and more properly Papuans[2], have now their stronghold in New Guinea, where indeed they are enabled to retain their old supremacy, as absolute masters of the sea-coast. In other islands, they are found at some distance only from the shore, among the woods and mountain-fastnesses, maintaining their unequal struggles with a different race of settlers, and in spite, as it would seem, of all their physical prowess, destined in the end to melt away. Their utter extirpation in particular islands is matter of authentic history.

The second group of Oceanic tribes and nations, by which indeed those great displacements were effected, is best known as the Malayo-Polynesian family, the brown or copper-coloured race. It seems that long after the Papuans were diffused in nearly all the intertropical islands, a fresh current of emigration had begun to set in that direction from the eastern continent of Asia. Lively, graceful, and in general structure not unfrequently reminding us of Arabs, these new settlers form a pointed contrast to their sullen, savage, and ill-favoured predecessors. Instead of shunning the society of white men, and thus resisting all endeavours to promote their intellectual and religious elevation, few of them have ever yet relapsed entirely to a state of barbarism. They constitute the demi-civilised population[3] of the Oceanic world. It seems most

the earliest or pre-Áryan population of Hindústán are said to be 'very black, ill-shapen, and dwarfish, and to have countenances of *a very African character.*' The Papuans were certainly of the same race with the Semangs of the Malay Peninsula (Earl, as above, ch. IX.), and with the natives of the Andaman islands in the Bay of Bengal (ch. X.). Other woolly-haired tribes are also said to exist at present in the mountain range which traverses the eastern side of the Indo-Chinese Peninsula (*Ibid.* p. 158). To the early influence of this family may be perhaps attributed the fact that many of the ancient idols of the Hindús 'have negro characteristics' (p. 160).

[1] W. von Humboldt, *Über die Kawi-Sprache*, I. p. iv. Berlin, 1836. Some of the full-blooded Papuans have spiral and twisted hair growing in large tufts to a considerable length: others have hair growing in short and closely-frizzled curls: Prichard, v. 4.

[2] 'Pua-pua,' or 'Papua,' means 'crisped,' and as referring to the quality of the hair, has come to be applied to the entire race: Earl, *Papuans*, p. 3.

[3] 'Alle diese Völkerstämme nun besitzen solche gesellschaftlichen Einrichtungen, dass man sie mit Unrecht von dem Kreise civilisirter Nationen gänzlich ausschliessen würde. Sie haben eine fest gegründete, und gar nicht durchaus

probable[1] that after entering the Indian Archipelago, upon their work of conquest or extermination, they alighted first of all in Sumatra and next in Java; thence, like genuine Tatars of the Ocean, they roved onward in their swarming *prahus* to the different coasts of Borneo, to the Cœlebes, and northward to the Philippines,—a group of islands where the traces of them are especially manifested by the regularity and richness of the native speech.

Advancing now beyond the zone of what are termed the pure Malay dialects[2], one section of this copper-coloured family appears to have wandered eastward in search of other territories, and, avoiding for a time all fresh collisions with the powerful Papuans of New Guinea and the neighbouring groups, had found their way to the Ladrones, to the Carolines, and ultimately to the Sandwich Islands on the northern border of the Tropics. From this centre[3] it is not unusual to derive the kindred streams of population, which proceeding southward occupied the clustering islands commonly known as Polynesia Proper, and penetrated even to New Zealand: so that, in the widest meaning of the term, Malayo-Polynesian tribes have been diffused across the whole of Oceanica, and have now become the dominant race, excepting in one narrow circle, where the elder family, as we have seen, with more or less admixture, still continue to preserve their ancient independence.

But before I enter on some points relating to the native creeds of Oceanica, as brought especially to light by recent missionary enterprise, it is important to observe, that in the northern territory, or the part approaching nearest to the

einfache, politische Verfassung, religiöse Satzungen und Gebräuche, zum Theil sogar eine Art geistlichen Regiments, zeigen Geschicklichkeit in mannigfaltigen Arbeiten, und sind kühne und gewandte Seefahrer:' W. von Humboldt, as above, p. iii. On the contrary, few, if any, instances exist in which the Papuans have been known to manifest like qualities: cf. Earl, pp. 94, 111.

[1] See Shortland's *Traditions, &c. of the New Zealanders*, pp. 30 sq., Lond. 1854, and Russell's *Polynesia*, pp. 37 sq., Lond. 1852: where objections on the score of distance and the difficulties of navigation are fully considered.

[2] W. von Humboldt, as above, p. ii.

[3] Shortland, as above, pp. 32, 33. The New Zealanders themselves have preserved traditions of the voyage of their ancestors from Hawaiki, which this writer identifies with the largest of the Sandwich Islands: cf. the full discussions respecting the original 'Migrations of the Oceanic tribes' in Mr. Hale's *Ethnography and Philology of the United States Exploring Expedition*, pp. 117—196, Philadelphia, 1846.

ancient seats of Asiatic culture, there were islands which had been indebted largely for the rudiments of civilisation to other and non-Christian powers, in ancient times to Bráhmanism and Buddhism[1], and in modern times to indefatigable preachers of Islám[2].

The island first and principally affected by these foreign influences was Java, which in turn, as the 'Phœnicia of the East,' became an ever-active agent for disseminating the new opinions through far wider circles[3], among the Batta of Sumatra, in the Cœlebes, and even on the western coast of Borneo. It is more particularly worthy of remark, that not a few of the ideas thus propagated over so large an area had been first imported from Hindústán by peaceful colonies of priests and sages, who without material succours were permitted to fix their residence among the natives, and had gradually instilled the principles which they brought with them, till at length there rose in Java a Malay community so tinctured with the languages, the literature, the mythes and the philosophy of India, as to furnish a most faithful copy of Hindú civilisation. 'Perhaps,' says a great authority[4], 'no second example is to be found of a nation undergoing such a complete infusion of the national spirit of another race, without losing its own independence.' If we fix our thoughts entirely on the province of religion, it appears that at some time or other during the interval between the Christian era and the introduction of Islám in the 14th century, the Javanese had to a great extent

[1] See above, p. 324. As modified into Fo-ism this religion is still being propagated here and there by Chinese traders and colonists, *e.g.* on the coast of New Guinea and in Borneo.

[2] The Muhammadans entered the Archipelago in the 13th century after Christ, when their creed was very generally accepted by the Malays. See, for instance, Mr. Horace St. John's *Indian Archipelago*, I. 42, 274, Lond. 1853. At the present time this creed is again making considerable progress, as, for instance, in the Arru islands, and even on the coast of New Guinea, with which it has been connected by means of some commercial intercourse between that island and the Moluccas.

[3] See W. von Humboldt's investigation of this point, as above, I. 238—254; and Lassen's *Ind. Alterth.* II. 1054.

[4] W. von Humboldt, p. viii. Elsewhere he writes (I. 4): 'Râma, Arjuna, die ganzen Geschlechter Pându's und Kuru's, und die ubrigen Helden der Indischen Vorzeit leben nicht nur noch jetzt im täglichen Andenken des Volks, sondern mehrere von ihnen werden als einheimisch angesehen, und Java selbst gilt für den Schauplatz vieler ihrer oft besungenen Thaten.' Additional light has been thrown upon this very interesting subject by inquiries which have been since made into the literary remains of Bali; see Weber's *Ind. Studien*, II. 124 sq.

appropriated one or more of the indigenous creeds of India. This may be collected, partly from the numerous literary relics of the island which are found to have been based on corresponding works of the Hindús, and partly from surviving images and inscriptions, or from actual ruins of magnificent temples dedicated to the Hindú gods. It does not seem, however, that the new belief of Java was in strict propriety of language either Bráhmanism or Buddhism. The highest object of men's worship was Batára Guru ('the Venerated Teacher')[1], whom his followers had enthroned superior to all other members of their pantheon. The best-supported of the theories respecting him affirms that he was originally a creation of Bráhmans[2], at the crisis when they had been forced into collision with the Buddhists of their native province, and when consequently the necessity arose of putting forth a rival object, worthy to compete with Śákya-muni. The unwonted prominence ascribed to him in Java led to the diffusion of his name in far more distant regions. It is used, for instance, by the Batta of Sumatra to denote the first of three principal divinities[3], and in the Cœlebes Batára is said to mean the eldest son of the Supreme Being[4]. At the time when Hindú colonists and traders first arrived in Java, Buddhism, we have reason for believing, was totally unknown among the native population. It had certainly obtained no footing there as late as A.D. 414,—the year in which a Chinese pilgrim halted on the island for the purpose of investi-

[1] Some writers have connected *batára* with *avatára*, and so discovered an allusion to Vishńu; but the true etymology seems to be the Sanskrit *bhattára* = 'worthy of veneration:' Lassen, II. 1050, Weber, *Ind. Studien*, II. 126, note.

[2] Very different opinions are entertained on this subject, some writers labouring to identify Batára Guru with Gautama Buddha, others with a second Buddha or Bodhisatwa; but I think that Lassen's arguments are fatal to this theory (*Ind. Altert.* II. 1049 sq.). His own view is that the first Bráhmans, who settled in Java long before the arrival of Buddhists, were of the Vaishńava party, *i.e.* members of the Hindú sect which had invested Vishńu in particular with the attributes of the Supreme Being, and had put him forward, in opposition to the Buddhists, as *the* object of men's worship.

[3] These were Batára Guru, Seri Pada and Mangala Bulan; but if we may credit the account of some missionaries, there stood above them a Supreme Father and Creator, Debata Hasi Asi. According to a native composition, some of the chief divinities were named, with obvious reference to Hindúism, Mesewara (Mahéśwara = Śiva), Bisnu, Brehma, Sri, Cala (W. von Humboldt, I. 238, 239).

[4] *Ibid.* p. 249. In Luzon, one of the Philippines, the name also recurs under the form *Bathala*, as denoting the Supreme God, or Godhead in the abstract (p. 251).

gating the religious state of the inhabitants[1]. Eventually, however, Buddhist doctrines seem to have been introduced in very many provinces, and, what is most remarkable, had flourished for a season side by side with one or more[2] varieties of Bráhmanism. To this harmonious coexistence may be traced the startling intermixture of religious dogmas in the extant literature of Java, the confusion of symbolic representations on so many of the works of art, and the uncertainty which now exists, and will most probably continue to exist, respecting all the details of her sacred history.

§ 1. *The Papuan Family.*

Our knowledge is more scanty still as to the character and condition of the native races, anterior to the age when elements of culture were thus brought among them by the colonies from Hindústán. The absence of vernacular words[3], expressing the idea of Godhead in the abstract, has been cited as a proof that the religion of the primitive masters of the Archipelago was mournfully corrupted and debased. This verdict is emphatically true, as it applies to the Papuan family,—a race which constituted the first layer of population in the islands of the Farther East. At no great distance from the tombs and other monuments that serve to illustrate the ancient rule of Hindú civilisation, there are remnants also of this older race of Oceanic negroes, who, retaining all their inextinguishable hatred of the foreigner, have handed down the rudest possible forms of unimaginative superstition. Such, for instance, are the scattered tribes of Semangs[4], who still linger in the northern forests of the Malay Peninsula. They remind us not unfrequently of

[1] See Lassen, II. 1041, 1042. Fahian remained in Java five months, and speaks both of unbelievers and of Bráhmans, but not a word of Buddhists.

[2] The worship of Śiva, in particular, seems to have been intimately associated with Buddhism (cf. above, p. 253, n. 2): W. von Humboldt, I. 280 sq. The effect of this unnatural union was to discountenance and displace the older worship of Vishńu (p. 288).

[3] Even the Javanese *Yŵang*, which was ultimately used by itself to signify the Godhead, does not appear to have had this meaning in the first instance (*Ibid.* I. 102 sq.). The common term for 'god-like' was *batára*, and for 'Godhead' *dévatá*, both of Sanskrit origin. A similar remark, touching the absence of all words which designate the Deity, is also made with reference to the Marian Islanders: Prichard, V. 176. Among the Dyaks of Borneo there are two names for the Supreme God, '*Dewata*,' and '*Tuppa*;' the latter is thought to be the true Dyak name.

[4] H. St. John's *Indian Archipelago*, I. 74.

African negroes; but their creed has also much in common with that of wild Americans, as well as with the Shamanism that now predominates in all the higher latitudes of Asia, and in many of the oldest tribes of Hindústán. In these remote localities, we can discern no more than feeble glimmerings of the true religion. The idea of God has well-nigh vanished from the human spirit; for as often as attempts are made to hold communion with him she is always under the necessity of localising, or dividing, the object of her thoughts, until the great mysterious Power, of which she stands in awe, has been degraded into one or other of the physical elements. A *moral* order and a *moral* Governor of the universe are both of them conceptions too exalted for the dark and narrow faculties of the savage. Hence it is that few, if any, heathen of this class are ever known to pay their acts of adoration to the Being[1] whom in words they will acknowledge as their chief divinity: all worship is in their case nothing more than deprecation; it is ever tending to propitiate hosts of angry and malignant demons.

Other points, in which a family-likeness may be traced between the creeds we are considering, are the periodical commemoration of the dead, and more especially the worship of departed ancestors. For instance, the Ajetas, a Papuan tribe surviving in the Philippines, are still accustomed to assemble annually at the tombs, in order to deposit there fresh offerings of betel and tobacco[2]. At the time of sepulture the favourite bow and arrows of the hunter are suspended over his grave, from a conviction that he still enjoys the privilege of issuing forth at night, and so reverting for a season to his former occupations. Crude and childish as this fancy is, we may discover in it germs of a belief in some futurity, or reproduction of the present life[3].

[1] See above, p. 262, and compare E. T. Turnerelli's *Kazan*, II. 133, respecting the religious ideas of the aboriginal tribes in that neighbourhood.

[2] Earl's *Papuans*, p. 132. Tobacco was also offered up in sacrifice by very many of the wild tribes of America (see Müller's *Amer. Urreligionen*, pp. 59, 86, 92, 130, and elsewhere).

[3] See above, pp. 290 sq., p. 355, n. 1, on the analogous idea of the Chinese and the American Indians; and Livingstone, p. 319, of the negroes of South-Central Africa. The Alforias, on the contrary, appear, at least in some districts, to have no conception of the immortality of the soul (Kolff, *Voyages*, &c., translated by Earl, p. 159). When a man dies, it is related that his friends assemble and destroy all the goods he may have collected during his life: even the gongs are broken to pieces and thrown away.

According to the testimony of recent travellers in Oceanica, the Papuans of New Guinea and elsewhere continue for the most part void, not only of poetic feeling and mythology, but also of those leading elements which enter into the received idea of a religion. 'We could not discover the slightest trace of religion among them,' such is the report of one intelligent writer[1], in speaking of New Guinea. 'The Ajetas,' writes a second[2], 'have no religion, and adore no star.' Yet, on the other hand, it is apparent from the context of these passages that the authors both intended by 'religion' a coherent system of belief and worship governed by a regular hierarchy. Of such there are no traces, either in the wild tribes of America or of the Eastern Archipelago. We ask in vain among those primitive people for the shrines and temples dedicated to the worship of particular deities[3]. We ask in vain for any sacerdotal family, or any institution bearing close resemblance to the Hindú law of caste[4]. The right of sacrificing is there held to be the common property of all, and that in cases where it may be practically restricted either to the head-man of some patriarchal group[5], or else to seers and medicine-men and wizards, who establish their pretension to a mastery in the world of spirits by the frequent use of exorcisms, of incantations, and of magic spells. So far indeed are the Papuans from abjuring *all* religion that we find them everywhere betraying a keen sense of their relation to invisible agents and led captive by a number of most abject superstitions. They believe that the mysterious Power above them is discerpted and diffused in almost every part of nature, animate and inanimate;

[1] Modera's *Reize naar de zuid-west Kust van Nieuw Guinea*, as quoted by Earl, *Papuans*, pp. 49, 50. It is worthy of remark that the same statement had been previously made by Kolff, *Voyages*, &c., p. 158, with reference to the 'Alforias' of the Arru islands.

[2] De la Gironière, *Souvenirs de Jala Jala*, quoted in Earl as above, p. 132.

[3] 'The want of any form of public worship, or of idols, or of formal prayers or sacrifice, makes both Caffres and Bechuanas appear as among the most godless races of mortals...Though they all possess a distinct knowledge of a deity and of a future state, they shew so little reverence, and feel so little connexion with either, that it is not surprising that some have supposed them entirely ignorant on the subject:' Livingstone, pp. 158, 159. A Portuguese account, translated by Purchas, declares that the 'Caphar nation is the most brutal and barbarous in the world, neither worshipping God nor any idol, nor having image, church, or sacrifice,' &c.

[4] This is the more noticeable, because a species of caste-system does prevail in many parts of Polynesia proper.

[5] Earl, p. 85, speaking of the natives of Dory, in New Guinea: cf. above, p. 261.

and selecting some one form in which this power is thought to be especially active, they embrace it as their fetish and their guardian deity. Such fetish is at one time a rude piece of sculpture, as a snake, a lizard, or some other reptile; at a second time it is a bit of bone or mineral; at a third it rises to the dignity of a human figure, small in size and absolutely hideous in expression. This third variety indeed, which in New Guinea is entitled *karwar* (a mean figure carved in wood and holding up a shield), may be regarded as their highest mode of representing or embodying the divine. It occupies a prominent place in every cottage, serving there the two-fold purpose of an oracle and an idol. The persons who consult it are said to 'squat before it, clasp the hands over the forehead, and bow repeatedly, at the same time stating their intentions. If they are seized with any nervous feeling during this process it is considered as a bad sign, and the project is abandoned for a time; if otherwise—that is to say, if they really wish to carry out the proposed object—the idol is supposed to approve. It is considered necessary that the *karwar* should be present on all important occasions, such as births, marriages, or deaths[1].'

Among the few minute peculiarities, which recent enterprise has brought to light, in aid of the endeavour to connect religious thoughts and customs of Papuans with those of continental Asia, there is none perhaps more striking than the veneration paid to the waringin-tree[2], a species of banyan or Indian fig. So strong is their devotion to it that the wilder tribes of Ceram lodge and almost live among its branches; and throughout the aboriginal family of the Archipelago[3], this tree has been no less invested with sacred and mysterious characteristics. A similar kind of veneration, we have seen[4], prevailed in every part of India from a high antiquity. The *vatá* was there absolutely worshipped by the superstitious multitude; beneath its sacred shadow the ascetic wasted his remaining strength in the attempt to consummate his reabsorption into Brahma; and thither, as their favourite haunt, resorted poets and philosophers, all eager to bestow on it their choicest appellations, and rejoicing to behold in its majestic form the 'tree of knowledge and intelligence.' If these coin-

[1] *Ibid.* pp. 84, 85.

[2] *Ibid.* p. 116: cf. p. 160.

[3] *Ibid.* where Mr. Earl adds that the lower classes, at least, of China have imbibed precisely the same ideas, even where they are 'untainted with Buddhism.'

[4] See above, p. 215, and the references there.

cidences do not actually warrant a belief that in the intertropical islands, as elsewhere, the veneration paid to the waringin-tree is a distorted reminiscence of events recorded in the opening chapters of Holy Writ, the general circulation of such a story both in Eastern Asia and in Oceanica will at least supply us with additional hints as to the ultimate and generic unity of the populations there located.

§ 2. *The Malayo-Polynesian Family.*

In passing from the older to the younger family of Oceanic islanders, attention is arrested by one special group, which either from a geographical or ethnological point of view may be regarded as transition-links between the black and copper-coloured races[1]. These are the Fijíans or Vítíans[2], lying midway between the shores of India and America, and on the very confines of the zone of population where Papuans are still intermixed with Polynesians proper. To what extent such intermixture has actually taken place in the Viti islands, may be very difficult to determine, either from the physical structure of the people, or the genius of their native language: but all writers on the subject now agree, that notwithstanding their generally dark complexion, they exhibit much of the plasticity, the animation, and the intellectual power which characterise their graceful neighbours in the Tonga or Friendly islands. With regard, however, to the spiritual condition of the former, the reports of recent missionaries and explorers are both absolutely appalling. Those Vitians who continue strangers to the Gospel, are the Aztecs of the Oceanic world. Their

[1] M. Dumont d'Urville (quoted in Prichard, v. 243, 244) was the first to draw attention to this point, having observed that in many of their characteristic habits the Fíjíans resembled the Malayo-Polynesians more than the Papuans: 'La circoncision,' he continues, 'se pratique généralement parmi les peuples de Viti: le kava est usité chez eux, et le betel ne l'est point, bien que la noiz d'arek se trouve sur leur sol. Ces îles sont donc la *limite commune* de la race cuivrée ou Polynesienne, et de la race noire Océanienne ou Melanésienne.' This intermediate character is said to find a parallel in the natives of Madagascar at the western extremity of Oceanica (*Ibid.* p. 253), who, although belonging to the Malayo-Polynesian family, have numerous points in common with Papuans.

[2] An interesting account of the present state of these people will be found in Dr. Berthold Seemann's *Viti: an Account of a Government Mission to the Vitian or Fijian Islands in the years* 1860—61: Cambridge, 1862. The natives term their islands collectively '*Viti;*' the common designation '*Fiji,*' or '*Feejee,*' comes from the Tonguese, who cannot pronounce the *v*: p. 404.

vigour is expended chiefly on the field of battle, and familiarity with bloodshed, while creating a fanatical depreciation of human life, appears in the majority of cases to be drying up the springs of natural affection. We behold in them, as in the Mexicans, a dark exemplification of the way in which some knowledge of the useful arts may co-exist with almost every species of atrocity[1],—with infanticide, with human sacrifices, with the strangulation of whole families in honour of some fallen chief, with brutish feasts upon the bodies of their foes and even of their fellow-subjects. It may be that very many of these horrible usages were first of all adopted under the influence of the devil-worship, which prevailed, and is prevailing, in every part of heathendom; but the Vitians of the present day are instigated to commit such deeds of darkness, rather by a false idea of immortality than by eagerness to pacify a host of angry and vindictive spirits. Arguing, for example, that the state of man after death[2] will be at first identical in every way with that in which he died, they generally destroy a friend or relative, long before the natural close of his existence. They are guilty also, here and there, of self-immolation; in the hope of thus securing an escape from

[1] The best, and indeed the only full, authority respecting the savage customs of these islanders is Wilkes's *Narrative of the United States Exploring Expedition*, Vol. III. Lond. 1845. The practice of putting widows to death at the funerals of their husbands seemed to W. von Humboldt a proof of Indo-Malayan influence; and, he might have added, that in both cases the future happiness of the victim was thought to be involved in this act of devotion; but among the Vitians, widows are not the only persons so immolated; slaves and even children of the deceased sometimes sharing the same fate. Speaking of the negroes of South-Central Africa, Dr. Livingstone says, that 'when a chief dies, a number of servants are slaughtered with him to form his company in the other world' (p. 318). He then adds, 'As we go north, the people become more bloodily superstitious.' Captain Wilkes's description of the cannibalism of the Vitians is inexpressibly revolting (III. 97, 102): cf. Russell's *Polynesia*, pp. 265, 266; and Seemann's *Viti*, pp. 173 sq. The same horrid usages prevail as extensively among the savage natives of the New Hebrides and New Caledonia (Russell, p. 427).

[2] Wilkes, *Exploring Expedition*, III. 96. He had previously remarked (p. 94): 'This belief in a future state, guided by no just notions of religious or moral obligation, is the source of many abhorrent practices.' The report, however, of Mr. Hale, philologist to the United States Expedition (p. 54, Philadelphia, 1846), is, that according to the general belief of those islanders 'the soul passes through two states or conditions of future existence [the first, of happiness; the second, of misery] before it undergoes its final destiny —annihilation.'

misery and decrepitude in this life and from permanent dishonour in the next. So rife indeed has grown the practice of strangulation or of burying men alive, from one cause or other[1], that only a single instance of natural death came under the observation of Europeans during a protracted stay in one of those islands.

If we now proceed to question the same authorities with reference to specific tenets there prevailing, we discover, as in Mexico and other regions, that the symbol of the mystic serpent has been always made to play a very prominent part. The highest member of the Viti pantheon, and the ruler (as men think) of all the island-world, is Ndengei[2], who, though manifesting himself, it is believed, from age to age in a variety of human forms, is actually worshipped as a mighty serpent; the figure of that reptile being dominant in all the representations, even where it has not been exclusively adopted. Some few glimmerings of moral consciousness are visible in the widespread notion that one class of disembodied spirits, who would fain revert to the immediate presence of the highest god, are constantly repulsed by an enormous giant wielding a large axe[3].

[1] The cause may be, and often is, a real wish to benefit the person immolated; and it constantly happens therefore that a son strangles his parents at their own request. 'Mr. Hunt did all in his power to prevent so diabolical an act; but the only reply he received was, that she was their mother, and they were her children, and they ought to put her to death. On reaching the grave, the mother sat down, when they all, including children, grandchildren, relations, and friends, took an affectionate leave of her. A rope, made of twisted tapa, was then passed twice around her neck by her sons, who took hold of it, and strangled her; after which she was put into her grave, with the usual ceremonies. They returned to feast and mourn, after which she was entirely forgotten as though she had not existed' (p. 95). See also Seemann, *Viti*, pp. 192 sq.

[2] 'The word *Ndengei* is supposed by some to be a corruption of the first part of the name *Tanga-loa* (great Tanga), the chief divinity of Polynesia' (Hale, as above, p. 184); which seems to fall in with the received opinion that the Vitians, if not originally Polynesian, adopted some of the religious tenets, as well as some of the arts, of their Polynesian neighbours.

[3] Wilkes, III. 83. 'Those who are wounded dare not present themselves to Ndengei, and are obliged to wander about in the mountains.' But, as Captain Wilkes continues, 'whether the spirit be wounded or not, *depends not upon the conduct in life*, but they ascribe an escape from the blow wholly to good luck.' A singular coincidence is found in some districts between opinions of the natives and those prophecies of Holy Writ which carry on our thoughts to the great winding up of all things. They hold, 'that all the souls of the departed will remain in their appointed place, until the world is destroyed by fire, and a new one created' (p. 94).

'With this weapon he endeavours to wound all who pass him.' The approach to Ndengei is, however, much facilitated by the mediation of two other Viti deities, the sons of Ndengei, who connect the highest god with a descending series of minor spirits, each the tutelary genius of a single island or a separate tribe[1]. But here, as elsewhere, the benignant spirits are continually thwarted by the arbitrary powers of mischief and misrule, who constitute the gods of the infernal regions[2]. One of these, it is contended, sits upon the brink of 'a huge fiery cavern, into which he precipitates departed spirits.' Another ('the one-toothed lord') is pictured to the warm imagination of the trembling native as inhabiting the figure of a man, with wings instead of arms, and claws to snatch his victims. 'His tooth is large enough to reach above the top of his head: it is alleged that he flies through the air emitting sparks of fire.' The dread of such malevolent beings far outbalances the hope inspired among these tribes by vague ideas respecting the beneficence of other spirits; and as happiness itself is seldom there associated with the presence of moral qualities, either in the judge or in the human subject, but is treated merely as the fruit of chance or of caprice[3], the sentiment of fear is still more terribly awakened whensoever the Vitian, in the hours of silence or of sickness, listens to the beating of his inmost heart, and communes more directly with the world invisible. To the consternation thus excited we may trace the number of the *mbure* ('spirit-houses'), where he stops to deprecate the powers of darkness and present his horrible oblations. On this feeling had been grounded the despotic sway[4] long exercised by the *ambati*, or members of the sacerdotal order, each of whom was venerated as the mouthpiece of a spirit ruling in one single district, and as able by his frantic gestures to ward off impending evils, or extort a favourable answer to the cry of the oppressed.

We may perhaps discover some faint echo of a primitive tradition in the story circulated far and wide among the Viti islands as to the extraction of all human beings from one single

[1] *Ibid.* p. 84.

[2] *Ibid.* pp. 84, 85.

[3] 'At Rewa, it is believed that the spirits first repair to the residence of Ndengei, who allots some of them to the devils for food, and sends the rest away to Mukalou, a small island off Rewa, where they remain until an appointed day, after which they are all doomed to annihilation. The judgments thus passed by Ndengei seem to be ascribed rather to his caprice than to any desert of the departed soul:' p. 85.

[4] *Ibid.* pp. 87 sq.

pair[1]. The first-born of mankind, according to this story, shewed himself unfaithful to his Maker and grew black[2]. The second-born, less biassed on the side of wickedness, was fairer and was better clad. The last in order of production, but the first in virtue and intelligence, were members of the white race. But a more remarkable coincidence is furnished by the legend of some mighty deluge, which, however startling from its close affinity to the sacred narrative, can hardly have been coloured in late years through intercourse with Europeans, since it is alleged that the precedence of one island (Mbenga) is derived entirely from the general currency which this tradition has obtained among the rest.

The story is thus reported to us by a recent hand[3]:

> 'After the islands had been peopled by the first man and woman, a great rain took place, by which they were finally submerged; but, before the highest places were covered by the waters, two large double canoes made their appearance. In one of these was Rokora, the god of carpenters; in the other, Rokola, his head workman, who picked up some of the people, and kept them on board until the waters had subsided; after which they were again landed on the island. It is reported that in former times canoes were always kept in readiness against another inundation. The persons thus saved, eight in number, were landed at Mbenga, where the highest of their gods is said to have made his first appearance. By virtue of this tradition, the chiefs of Mbenga take rank before all others, and have always acted a conspicuous part among the Fíjis. They style themselves *Ngali-duva-ki-langi* (subject to heaven alone).'

It is refreshing to narrate that, in addition to such intimations of original oneness with the rest of men, a nobler proof of the humanity of the Vítían has been found, during the last twenty years, in his religious susceptibility. Those very islands, which were stained from age to age by every species of licence and atrocity, have now become the starting-point of vigorous efforts[4] to disseminate a knowledge of the Gospel on the farthest

[1] *Ibid.* p. 82: cf. Hale's *Ethnography*, &c. *of the Exploring Expedition*, pp. 177, 178, where a similar tradition, long prevalent in the Tonga islands, is explained as 'an ancient mythos, under which the early history of the islanders is veiled, though in the passage of centuries the real parts have been forgotten, and the story has received of late a new application,' owing to the intercourse with Europeans.

[2] Cf. Livingstone's *Travels*, p. 24.

[3] Wilkes, pp. 82, 83. Mr. Hale, as above (p. 55) confirms this statement, and conjectures (in a note) that the whole alluvial plain on the east side of the group of islands might be easily submerged by one of the immense waves that sweep across the Pacific. See also Seemann, *Viti*, pp. 395 sq.

[4] See Russell's *Polynesia*, pp. 264 sq. pp. 420—424; and *Events in Feejee, narrated in recent letters from several Wesleyan Missionaries*, Lond. 1855. Until 1841 the progress of the Gospel was very slow, but in 1846 nine of this group of islands were wholly or mainly

shores of Oceanica. The mariner who touches now at spots where until recently no symptom had been shewn of spiritual improvement, is amazed on finding how the fiercest wolves of heathendom are tamed by Christian agencies, how cannibals have lost their relish for the blood of others, and how brutal and barbaric clans are being fast converted into peaceful confraternities. 'Violence shall no more be heard in thy land, wasting nor destruction within thy borders.'

But the Gospel has been also propagated in some other islands of the Archipelago, and has taken root especially in one distant group, of which the natives seem, with slight admixture, to be genuine Polynesians[1]. If the Viti islanders were made to furnish the best type of mixed or intermediate families, uniting the Papuan to the younger stock of Oceanic nations, an example of these latter, scarcely altered from their primitive condition, might be studied some few years ago among the people of New Zealand. 'The Maori of New Zealand,' we are told[2], 'are one of the branches of the Polynesian family, who seem to have been preserved, to the greatest extent, unmixed

Christian, and twenty-four, including the two large ones, were partially illuminated. The following extract from a letter printed in the *Wesleyan-Methodist Magazine* for 1856, p. 460, is a very remarkable testimony to the further progress of the same great undertaking. This letter is dated Viwa, Feejee, August 23, 1855: 'Thousands,' says the writer of it, 'have within the last few weeks abandoned heathenism, and made a profession of Christianity; and their conduct now presents a delightful contrast to their proceedings during the former part of this year. The first eight months of our residence in Feejee contributed some of the darkest records to the pages of Feejeean history; the most experienced missionaries confessing them to have no parallel. Now a glorious change is effected, by the power of the Spirit, in many towns which a few months ago a missionary or teacher durst not enter, the prevailing practice being war and cannibalism. The people then trusted to their gods and reverenced them, strictly prohibiting admission into their temples: now they crave teachers and books, and are endeavouring to sing the praise of God, and learning to read the Bible.'

[1] Some writers have suspected (Prichard, v. 126 sq.) from the diversities of physical character that the Maori ought not to be considered one race of people but are in reality a mixed nation, consisting (1) of the remains of an aboriginal population (Papuan), and (2) of a Polynesian race who conquered them, and became gradually blended with them by intermarriages. Yet similar varieties exist in all the other Polynesian islands, and as the natives of New Zealand are themselves unconscious of any radical distinction between the various classes of their own community, it is most probable that the existing variations of type result from certain differences of caste, which are extensively recognised among all the islands of the Great Ocean.

[2] Shortland, *Traditions, &c. of the New Zealanders*, pp. 79, 80.

with foreign alloy;' and as the principal superstitions, until lately dominant in those parts, are said to represent with singular fidelity the state of religious feeling which has long obtained 'throughout the great mass of the islands of the Pacific Ocean[1],' the Maori have on this account been here selected for a more particular notice.

It appears to be established that the colonisation of the group of islands called New Zealand is comparatively modern, stretching backwards at the furthest to a period of five or six hundred years[2]. When Cook approached that region in 1769, the natives had already earned a very bad pre-eminence; they were noted for their lack of conscientiousness, as well as for their gross and murderous ferocity; and the reception given to all succeeding visitors, of whom no small proportion fell into the snare of the infuriated savage, only added to the prevalent conviction that the people of New Zealand had become incorrigibly vile, and must in future be entirely abandoned[3]. The low tone, however, of the moral system there prevailing, the weakness of domestic instincts, the decay of parental authority, the desecration of the marriage-tie, the general disregard of human suffering, the perpetuation of a cannibalism, as rife and horrid as in other parts of heathendom,—these all were superadded to an eminent measure of spiritual susceptibility. Like the men of Athens, whom St. Paul attempted to impress with the idea of one almighty and illimitable God, as well as of the common origin and consanguinity of the human species, it was found

[1] Sir G. Grey, *Polynesian Mythology*, p. xii. Lond. 1855; where the resemblance is thought to extend in some measure as far as the 'religious system of ancient Mexico.' It may be definitely asserted that the same general ideas, and very many of the same minutiæ, are, or were till recently, extant in (1) the Navigator Islands, (2) the Friendly Islands, (3) the Society Islands, (4) the Hervey Islands, (5) the Austral Islands, (6) the Gambier Islands, (7) the Low or Dangerous Archipelago, (8) the Marquesas, (9) the Sandwich Islands, the most northerly group of Polynesia; together with a multitude of smaller clusters, and, as the most remote of all the Polynesian settlements, Easter Island, which is at no great distance from the coast of South America.

[2] Shortland, p. 19; Grey, pp. 132 sq. Hale, *Ethnography*, as above, pp. 146 sq. This last writer, while agreeing that the New Zealanders are 'evidently of the pure Polynesian stock' (p. 11), cannot help noticing how, in complexion, form and profile they 'come very near to North American Indians.' Mr. Earl (*Eastern Seas*, p. 277) is similarly struck by 'the extraordinary and almost perfect resemblance' which the Dyaks (a variety of the copper-coloured race) bear to 'those aboriginal tribes of South America, which occupy a similar description of country.'

[3] Russell, *Polynesia*, p. 347.

that Polynesians proper carried their habitual manifestations of religious feeling to a more than ordinary pitch (δεισιδαιμονέστεροι). 'When we compare them,' says an accurate writer[1], 'with the natives of Australia, who, though not altogether without the idea of a God, hardly allow this idea to influence their conduct, we are especially struck with the earnest devotional tendencies of this people, among whom the whole system of public polity, and the regulation of their daily actions, have reference to the supposed sanction of a supernatural power; who not only have a pantheon, surpassing, in the number of divinities and the variety of their attributes, those of India and Greece, but to whom every striking natural phenomenon, every appearance calculated to inspire wonder and fear,—nay, often the most minute, harmless, and insignificant objects, seem invested with supernatural attributes, and worthy of adoration. It is not,' he continues, 'the mere grossness of idolatry, for many of them have no images, and those who have, look upon them simply as representations of their deities, but it is a constant, profound, absorbing sense of the ever-present activity of divine agency, which constitutes the peculiarity of this element in the moral organisation of this people.'

What, then, was the general state of feeling in the heathen of New Zealand, with respect to a most vital point of all religions,—that of one supreme Creator? The reply is, such conceptions of the Godhead were unknown to them, and when at first presented to their notice by the Christian missionary, were received with no small measure of repugnance and contempt[2]. According to the Maori creed the ultimate origin of all things, even of the higher gods themselves, is Night and Nothingness. The wild traditions of that people, dating as they constantly profess[3] from ages long anterior to their settlement in New Zealand, all 'begin with nothing, which produced something, and that brought forth something more, and generated a power of increasing[4].' And as night, in their philosophy, preceded day, the oldest order of the Maori gods are also

[1] Mr. Hale, as before, pp. 16, 17.

[2] Thus Mr. Taylor, in his *Te Ika a Maui*, or *New Zealand and its Inhabitants* (p. 13, note; Lond. 1855), tells us that 'speaking to Te Heuheu, the powerful Chief of Taupo, of God, as being the Creator of all things, he ridiculed the idea, and said, Is there one maker of all things amongst you Europeans? is not one a carpenter, another a blacksmith, another a shipbuilder?' &c. 'And so was it in the beginning; one made this, another that: Tane made trees, Ru mountains, Tanga-roa fish,' &c.

[3] Shortland, p. 42.

[4] Taylor, p. 14, Shortland, p. 39.

gods of darkness; one who has been deemed the prototype of all the rest is there entitled the 'Great daughter of Night,' the goddess of gloom, of solitude, of hades, and of death[1]. There seems, however, to have always lingered in the mind a glimmering of some purer and more noble class of verities; men felt that spirit in its essence is superior to all forms of matter, and that thought must therefore have been pre-existent, planning and directing the formation of the visible world[2]. In this particular, indeed, we recognise a faint approximation in New Zealand to the cosmogonic theories that long absorbed the interest of the speculative China-man. The Absolute of the one[3] is only a more philosophic method of expressing the First Thought of the other. But resemblance is more clearly traceable in the texture of the ancient mythe, in which the moulding of the universe into its present shape has been referred to an abrupt division between Heaven and Earth[4],—the two great powers, or principles of nature, which heretofore were blended into one, or held together by some potent and indissoluble bond. Their names, according to the Maori creed, were Rangi (Heaven) and Papa (Earth)[5]. Till this divulsion, says a native story, the six children born to them were ever musing within themselves as to the difference between light and darkness. Wearied by the long continuance of impenetrable void, they rose eventually into an attitude of wild rebellion; and muttering to each other, asked what should be done with Rangi and Papa. 'Shall we slay them, or shall we separate them?' Tu-mata-uenga[6] said, 'Yes, let us kill them.' Tane Mahuta[7] re-

[1] Her Maori name is *Hine-nui-a-te-po*, which under slight modifications is also found in other islands, as in Tonga, Tahiti, and Hawaii: Taylor, p. 41.

[2] Taylor, p. 14, who styles the first period in their mythological system the 'epoch of thought,' and observes with reference to this branch of their traditions, that they 'mark a far more advanced state' of intelligence than is discernible among the heathen of the present day.

[3] See above, pp. 300 sq. Mr. Taylor, without making any allusion to these coincidences, points out some particulars of dress and manufacture which betoken, to his thinking, a Chinese or Japanese origin: pp. 184, 185.

[4] Above, p. 303.

[5] Grey, *Polynesian Mythology*, pp. 1 sq.; Taylor, pp. 19, 20.

[6] Sir G. Grey explains this word as meaning 'man,' or 'fierce man'; and Mr. Taylor identifies Tu-mata-uenga with Tute-nga-nahau, the third son of Rangi and Papa, and the grand author of evil, who, according to the same story, 'cut the sinews' that united Heaven and Earth.

[7] Tane is the first of living creatures or emanations, and to him has been assigned the work of 'propping up' the heavens. This was his first great duty; afterwards

plied, 'No, by no means, rather let us separate them; let one be placed above and let the other remain below; let the one be like a stranger far removed from us, let the other be near as a father or mother to us.' Five of their unnatural offspring hearkened to this counsel; one alone was strongly opposed to the idea of separation; five decided that their parents should be riven asunder; one only loved them. This affectionate son was Tawhiri-matea, the father of the winds, who, at the close of the catastrophe, determined to chastise his brothers for their foul impiety. Tane, who is viewed as the progenitor of trees, or rather as a tree himself, was shaken and uprooted; Tanga-roa, in like manner, the presiding spirit of the ocean, foamed and quivered under the avenging tempest; and accordingly the universe, as now existing, had been cradled in the midst of elemental wars, of furious conflicts and convulsions.

One result of the great severance between Earth and Heaven was the projection of a second order of divinities,—the rebel sons of Rangi and Papa, who are thus distinguished from the members of the older series as the gods of light. They constitute at present the chief divinities of heathen Polynesia; their place is in the highest and most glorious of the ten heavens [1]. Conjectures have been made to the effect that long before the first migrations of the Polynesian tribes, they were accustomed, as a people, to adore one principal divinity [2], who was, eventually,

we hear of him giving birth to trees and every kind of birds. The other sons of Rangi and Papa, were Tiki or Tii, a (male?) divinity from whom proceeded man (cf. Taylor, p. 23; Hale, *Ethnography*, &c. pp. 23, 24); Tahu, the author of good, but never prominent in this system of mythology; and Tanga-roa, the father of all fish, and the great god of ocean. This last name varying in different parts of Oceanica (as *Tangaloa, Tanaloa, Taaroa*) is thought by some to indicate a self-existent God, 'the creator of the earth, or at least of the islands of the sea, and of the human race' (Hale, p. 22). 'At the little newly-discovered island of Fakaofo, the natives spoke of him with great awe as *Tangaloa i lunga i te langi* (Tangaloa above in the heavens):' *Ibid.*

[1] Taylor, p. 17.

[2] Hale, p. 22. In the mythology of the Tongans, this divinity (Tangaloa) is made to fish up their group of islands and to cover it with fruits and animals, like those of Bulotu (his own special paradise), but perishable and of inferior quality. 'He sent his two sons, Toobó and Váca-ácow-ooli, with their wives, to people it. Váca-ácow-ooli was wise and virtuous; Toobó idle and depraved. Envying the prosperity of his brother, Toobó at length killed him [? Cain and Abel]. Tangaloa, enraged at this, sent Váca-ácow-ooli and his family with prosperous gales to an eastern land, where they became ancestors of the Papalangi, or White People. The descendants of Toobó were condemned to be black, because their hearts were bad [cf. the Vitian legend, above, p. 398]: they remained at Tonga, and are the

on the formation of the mythe respecting the divorce of Earth and Heaven, confounded with a son of Rangi and Papa, the marine god Tanga-roa. It has also been suggested, but with far less probability, that these islanders had originally confined their worship to three leading aspects in the character[1] of the Supreme Being, and had thus arrived at the conception of three grand personifications,—the Creator, the Sustainer, the Revealer. Still, whatever may be thought of these suggestions, it is clearly ascertained that the New Zealander of modern times, in common with all other natives of Oceanica, was in principle as well as practice an avowed polytheist. His pantheon, we have seen, outnumbered that of India or of Hellas. Everything that came within the cognizance of the senses was believed to be the organ of one special god, the offspring of one present and peculiar energy, which the Maori called its 'father[2].' This diffused, discerpted Power was sometimes represented as devoid of form or personality; its mode of manifestation being absolutely identified with startling and mysterious processes of nature, as displayed in meteors, rainbows, whirlwinds, and the like. At other times, such manifestation was restricted to the form of a particular beast, or bird, or reptile, as the dog, the shark, the woodpecker, the rat, the ant, the lizard. Or in cases when the gods[3] assumed distinctly human shapes in the imagination of the Maori, and were consciously invested with human attributes, they always bore, as in the rest of heathendom, a close

present race of inhabitants:' Prichard, v. 107, 108. I am disposed to think that the Orongo, Orono, and Rono of the Sandwich Islanders are only debased forms of Tangaroa; and it is curious to remark, that traditions were there also prevalent respecting visits of White Men as somehow connected with this divinity, insomuch that Captain Cook, like Cortés in America, was actually taken for their favourite god, and reverenced on that account.

[1] *e.g.* Hale, as above, p. 24; who adds, however, that the meaning and application of the three names which he proposes, 'have been much confused.'

[2] See Mr. Taylor's catalogue of some of these 'creative fathers,' pp. 32, 33, note.

[3] 'On nearly, if not quite, all the groups [of Polynesia] there have been, at a very late period, men who have been regarded by the natives as partaking of the divine nature,—in short, as earthly gods:' Hale, p. 20. At the Marquesas the common title of these persons is '*atua*, or gods, who receive the same adoration, and are believed to possess the same powers as other deities' (p. 21). 'At Depeyster's Group, the westernmost cluster of Polynesia, we were visited by a chief, who announced himself as the *atua* or god of the islands, and was acknowledged as such by the other natives' (*Ibid.*). These remarkable phenomena remind us very forcibly of the modern man-worship of Tibet (above, p. 332).

resemblance to their ordinary worshippers; and hence the brightest heaven of this mythology does little more than reproduce the various ills and conflicts of the present life. The history of a god, in other words, is that of some great chief or warrior, frequently disfigured by the grossest of all human vices, and too seldom calculated to suggest one noble wish or stir one generous emotion. These gods 'were cannibals; they were influenced by like feelings and passions with men, and they were uniformly bad. To them were ascribed all the evils to which the human race is subject; each disease was supposed to be occasioned by a different god, who resided in the part affected[1].'

The generic name of a divinity, in the language of New Zealand, is *atua*[2], varied in the other districts of Polynesia to *hotua* and *etua;* but, as might have been anticipated from the character imputed to such beings, they are seldom or never made the objects of religious worship in the Christian meaning of the term. The constant purpose of their votaries was to pacify, to vanquish, to disarm them. In the vast majority of cases, the *atua* was a powerful adversary skilled in supernatural arts, and rendered proof against all ordinary weapons. Hence arose the multitude of charms and rites of divination (*karakias*[3]), forming the chief element in the Maori worship. Every act of grave importance, hunting, fishing, war, the planting or the reaping of the *kumara* (sweet potatoe), was preceded by a multitude of solemn incantations, uttered with the hope of throwing obstacles in the way of some antagonistic power, of binding him by potent and unearthly spells, and so constraining him to waver in his purpose or withdraw his opposition. The same feeling was again predominant whenever the Maori brought his scanty sacrifice to one or other of the gods: he laboured to avert by offerings the displeasure he had previously awakened by the repetition of some mystic formula.

It seems, however, that a closer approximation to our ideas of worship was occasionally manifested in the tribute paid by Maori to the souls of their departed ancestors[4]. These, also,

[1] Taylor, p. 34.

[2] Cf. above, p. 363: to which remarks it may be added, that *tua*, so far from being equivalent to *atua*, means in Polynesia 'back' or 'behind,' and hence a member of the lowest class, a peasant (Hale, pp. 31, 32. 335).

[3] 'They have spells suited for all circumstances—to conquer enemies, catch fish, trap rats, and snare birds, to make their kumara grow, and even to bind the obstinate will of woman; to find any thing lost, to discover a strayed dog, a concealed enemy; in fact, for all their wants:' Taylor, p. 72.

[4] Hegel (*Phil. of History*, Lond.

were included in the multitude of the *atuas;* and on them, indeed, as genii intimately connected with the present race of men[1], the hopes and fears of their posterity were principally fixed. Each tribe, and single family of a tribe, rejoiced in the protection, or was trembling under the disapprobation, of its own *atua.* To that narrow circle he became the chief of the divinities. He issued forth to battle with his kinsmen; he was hovering near them in the hours of gloom, of peril, of privation; and so long as they were true to their ancestral courage, he was ever struggling at their side against an army of invisible assailants. When consulted by the Maori, on occasions of extraordinary moment, the *atua* was believed to give his answer by appearing personally in the sacred house to which his presence was invited, and discoursing there in a mysterious sound, 'half whistle, half whisper[2].' At ordinary times a powerful link between the natural and supernatural was furnished by the head-chief[3] of the tribe (*ariki,* whether male or female)[4], who, as standing in a blood-relation with their patron-deity, was thought to be admitted more than others to a secret knowledge of his will. But, in addition to this higher class of mediators, very many of the principal households of New Zealand had their own *tohunga*[5] (family-priest or 'speaker'), occupied in uttering charms and offering sacrifice on their behalf. Him

1857, p. 99) seems to think this worship of the dead a special characteristic of the African negroes. 'Their idea in the matter is that these ancestors exercise vengeance, and inflict upon man various injuries—exactly in the sense in which this was supposed of witches in the Middle Ages.'

[1] Mr. Shortland (p. 61) seems to think that these were the only *atuas,* who produced any sensible effect on the religious character of the New Zealanders. Mr. Taylor writes in like manner: 'Their ancestors were addressed as powerful familiar friends; they gave them offerings, and if it can be said that any prayers were offered up, it was to them that they were made' (p. 72). The same has been already observed in speaking of the Chinese (above, pp. 290 sq.): cf. Russell's *Polynesia,* p. 69.

[2] Shortland, p. 100, pp. 64 sq.

[3] In many of the tribes visited by Dr. Livingstone in South Africa, there was nothing like a priesthood. He remarks, however, on approaching the mouths of the Zambesi, 'The chiefs in these parts take upon themselves an office somewhat like the priesthood, and the people imagine that they can propitiate the Deity through them:' (p. 581).

[4] Shortland, p. 84, Taylor, pp. 42, 43. The *Ariki* of New Zealand was identical with the *Aliki* and *Arii* of other islands.

[5] Mr. Hale, however (p. 20), is disposed to consider the *tufunga, tohunga, tahuna, tahua,* &c. 'merely as persons appointed by the real priests,—*i. e.* the *aliki,* or chiefs,—to go through the drudgeries of their office, with which they are unwilling to be troubled.'

also a divinity was in the habit of possessing[1], and arousing to so great a pitch of fury, that the multitude who gathered awe-struck round about him were all eager to detect the will of Heaven amid the cries and horrible contortions of the seer.

In some few districts of New Zealand it was thought again that intercourse with the invisible world might be secured or furthered by the use of wooden images[2], resembling the fetishes of the Papuan family. Here, however, the amount of reverence paid to the material object can scarcely be regarded as idolatrous, in the proper meaning of the phrase. 'The natives declare they did not worship the image itself, but only the *atua* it represented, and that the image was merely used as a way of approaching him.'

It is still more worthy of remark, as tending to elucidate our special subject of inquiry, that one sacred ordinance, which seems to have been practised by the Maori long before their intercourse with Europeans, bears at first sight a distinct analogy to Christian baptism[3]. Soon after the birth of a child, the custom was to carry it to the priest, who, at the close of some preliminary forms recited a long list of names belonging to the ancestors of the child, and ended by selecting one of them for it. As he pronounced this name he solemnly sprinkled the child

[1] Taylor, p. 41. The same kind of frenzy has been noted in the wild tribes of America (above, p. 359).

[2] Taylor, p. 73: cf. Hale, p. 26, Russell, p. 69, whose accounts are somewhat different; but these writers seem to agree that there was less image-worship in New Zealand than in most other districts of Polynesia. The absence of regular temples in New Zealand is equally remarkable, although the Maori have a singular tradition respecting some great Red House (*Whare-kura*), which they fancy had once existed among them, and which 'the Christian natives compare to Babel' (Taylor, p. 68).

[3] The practice of circumcision, in the Friendly, the Vití and the Society Islands, has also been adduced as furnishing some possible link of connexion with the Asiatic continent (*e.g.* Russell, *Polynesia*, p. 36): yet, as this writer observes, 'it is not regarded in the South Sea as a *religious ceremony*, but perpetuated merely as an ancient custom of which no account can be given, and for the use of which no reason is assigned.' Examples of the same, or of a similar, usage are recorded in the New World. Thus, the South Americans, in some districts, used to crop the ears of their children soon after birth (Müller, *Amer. Urrelig.* p. 285). Various parts of the body (the ears, the tongue, the breast, &c.) were circumcised among the natives of Central America (*Ibid.* pp. 479, 480), and still more among the Aztecs, where the ceremony was connected with some dedication to Huitzilopochtli (p. 640), and as such might be esteemed equivalent to an oblation of human blood. In the Friendly Islands it was not unusual for the natives to cut off a finger, in the hope of appeasing the gods.

with a small branch of the *karamu* (coprosma lucida): while in other districts of the island, where a somewhat different rite prevailed, the ceremony was always conducted near a running stream, in which the child, when it received its name, was not unfrequently immersed[1]. Yet, notwithstanding this apparent affinity between the heathen and the Christian ordinances, it is not difficult to trace in them a fundamental contradiction. The infant of the Maori was regarded from the moment of its birth as 'an exceedingly sacred object[2],' and as such was to be handled in the first instance only by the sacred few. The Gospel, on the contrary, has taught with emphasis that every one 'naturally engendered of the offspring of Adam' brings into the world a tainted, vitiated, fallen nature, and that baptism was itself appointed by the New Man from heaven, with special reference to the counteraction of that taint and the removal of that moral disability. Hence, while there is not the slightest recognition in the Maori 'baptism' either of sin or guilt or the remissibility of guilt, the Christian sacrament derives its character entirely from the recognition of such doctrines. While the Maori charm was contemplating the dedication of the boy to nothing higher than Tu[3], the god of war, and was invoking on him, as the greatest of all excellencies, that he might 'flame with anger,' and have 'strength to wield a weapon,' the young Christian, on the contrary, has been enrolled under a very different Captain; he is sworn as the soldier of the Cross, to fight manfully against sin, the world, and the devil, and daily to proceed 'in all virtue and godliness of living.'

There is another usage common to the Maori, and to all the Polynesian tribes[4], however distant from New Zealand, which is often thought to be among their most essential peculiarities.

[1] Taylor, pp. 74 sq.; cf. Shortland, p. 121. Sir G. Grey (*Polynesian Mythology*, p. 32) makes use of language calculated to suggest still closer affinities between the heathen and Christian rites; *e.g.* 'hurriedly skipped over part of the prayers of the baptismal service.' On the Mexican custom of dedicating infants to the water-goddess, see above, p. 371, n. 3.

[2] Shortland, p. 122.

[3] Taylor, p. 75, where the *karakia* is given at length. Tu is the god of war in the north of New Zealand; Maru, still more Satanic, fills that office in the south.

[4] Whatever may turn out to be the ethnological position of the Vitians, it is noticeable that they also have the usage of *tapu*, which they call *tambu* (Hale, p. 51). Perhaps they have adopted it from their Tonga neighbours, just as the Muslim was induced to borrow the Hindú theory of caste from the people he invaded. The name for *tapu* in the island of Madagascar is *fady*, but the usage is there also substantially the same: Prichard, v. 208.

This is the institution of *tapu* (taboo), a word employed like many others of the Oceanic dialects, either as a noun, an adjective, or a verb. According to one etymology, it means no more than 'thoroughly marked[1],' and hence may have arisen its ordinary application to sacred things and persons, and restrictive or prohibitory laws. *Tapus*, however, in this latter sense must not be ranked with arbitrary regulations instituted by some ancient legislator for political or social objects. They were uniformly made to rest upon religious ideas; all their sanctions were derived immediately from precepts of religion, and in this respect we may compare them with enactments of the Jewish law,—for instance, that on clean and unclean meats, or that in virtue of which the Hebrew might contract uncleanness by touching a dead body, or most of all, perhaps, with the sabbatical institutions, which under pain of God's displeasure periodically rescued a space of time from secular and common purposes. One principle which forms a characteristic of the Maori system was, 'that if any thing *tapu* [sacred] is permitted to come in contact with food, or with any vessel or place, where food is ordinarily kept, such food must not afterwards be eaten by any one, and such vessel or place must no longer be devoted to its ordinary use[2].' This law, pervading though it did all classes of society, and modifying their most common thoughts and occupations[3], was especially manifested in the case of the *ariki*, or head-chief, whose sacredness in their minds bordered very close on absolute divinity. His house, his garments, everything relating to him was *tapu*. The spot on which he trod, external to his own domain, was consecrated and appropriated by that act[4]. It was believed that persons who partook by accident of any food which had been cooked for the *ariki*, did so at the peril of their life[5]; and though a ceremonial was provided by means of which restrictions of this kind were softened or entirely taken off[6], the Maori was per-

[1] Shortland, p. 81, who says that it 'only came to signify sacred or prohibited in a secondary sense, because sacred things and places were commonly marked in a peculiar manner.' In Mr. Hale's *Polynesian Lexicon*, as before, p. 331, we have the following entry: '*Tapu*, *tabu*, ubiq., sacred, and hence, forbidden,' while *tapui*, in the Samoan, is 'to make sacred,' &c.

[2] Shortland, *Ibid.*

[3] Taylor, p. 57. In these cases the *tapu* was for a time thrown over workmen, employed in some task of great importance to the community at large: *e.g.* 'No one but the priest could pause in front of the party engaged in gathering the *kumara;* those who presumed to do so, would be either killed or stripped for their temerity.'

[4] Shortland, p. 84.

[5] Taylor, p. 56.

[6] Shortland, p. 83. When the *tapu* was taken off, the object be-

petually haunted by the dread of violating the appointed ordinance, and trespassing on sacred ground.

I am disposed to think with one who has bestowed considerable pains on this investigation, that the tapu-system had arisen gradually in Polynesia, in proportion as the theory of religion there prevailing was more fully mastered and developed[1]. When the many were familiarized with the idea that an *atua*, or divinity, resided in some principal chief or priest, it followed that a portion of his spiritual essence was communicated of necessity to all the objects he might touch. It followed also, 'that the spiritual essence so communicated to any object was afterwards more or less retransmitted to any thing else brought into contact with it.' Hence accordingly arose the duty of protecting aught in which that spiritual essence was inherent, or over which its virtue had been temporarily diffused, from every risk of being polluted by contact with articles of food; since the act of eating what had touched a thing *tapu* must carry with it the necessity of eating particles of the sacred essence of the *atua*, from which its own sacredness was all derived[2]. In this way had been formed the mightiest of political engines for exalting the importance of the priest-king of New Zealand, for strengthening his iron arm, and thus investing him with almost supernatural powers for good or for evil.

It were difficult to single out a legend that more fully serves to illustrate the modes of thought and feeling once predominant in Polynesia, than the cluster of wild fables which from time to time have gathered round the primitive story of Maui the Young (*potiki*). He has not unjustly been regarded as *the* mythic hero of the Maori; in some particulars he well deserves to be entitled the Oceanic Baldur; in others, the Prometheus of the Southern Seas. There is no group of islands where he was not held in constant reverence under one or other of his numerous appellations[3]; but New Zealand he was made to

came *noa*, 'free,' or 'common;' *i.e.* was deprived of all the sacredness with which it was before invested.

[1] *Ibid.* p. 82, Hale, pp. 19, 20.

[2] Mr. Shortland adds (but less conclusively): 'If to eat an enemy was the greatest insult to be offered him, how horrible to eat any thing containing a particle of the divine essence.'

[3] Perhaps the oldest, certainly the fullest, form which it assumes is *Mafui*, current in the Navigator (Samoan) Islands. This with a suffix becomes *Mafuike* (? a member of the Mafui family), by means of which we are enabled to arrive at the form *Mafui'e* or *Mafu'e*, and finally at *Maui*. It has been thought indeed that Maui is the primitive form, and was intended to describe the person who first sighted land (*Ma-u-i*; Taylor, p. 29); but, on this hypothesis, what explanation

claim for his own property, the native title of that region importing 'The Fish of Maui,' and so bearing witness to the popular belief that all the island had emerged originally from the depths of ocean through the exercise of his transcendent power.

The stories tell that Maui was the last-born child of Tarahunga or Taranga[1], being descended also, after many generations, from Tu-mata-uenga, one of the unnatural sons of Heaven and Earth[2]. Though finally admitted to the number of the gods, and though at times confounded even with the highest members of the ancient pantheon[3], he is not unfrequently declared to be of purely human origin. His youthful pranks, betokening always an exuberance of life and vigour, and occasionally intermingled with proceedings of more than dubious morality, remind us of the early feats ascribed to the heroic Krishńa[4]; while his struggles with a huge sea-monster (Tunurua) furnish some additional points of contact or comparison with the Hercules alike of India and of Greece. On this account it was that he acquired a lasting hold on the affections of the ancient Maori, and was scrupulously invoked by them as their own tutelary genius on many grand occasions, and especially when they were setting out upon some fishing expedition.

Very many of the strange adventures which are told of Maui indicate his vast superiority over his five elder brothers in strength, in cunning, in good fortune. To astonish or to overreach them he would voluntarily assume the form and other qualities of a bird; and once, in this disguise, appears to have succeeded in gaining admittance to the subterranean world, in which his parents were detained. Ere long, however, it was found that the mysterious visitor was a man, or rather was 'a god,' and when his mother finally beheld in him her own little Maui ('Maui possessed of the top-knot, or power, of Taranga'), her delight at the discovery was rapturous and unbounded.

can be offered of *Mafui?* Besides, it must be borne in mind that Maui was in all probability the offspring of an age long anterior to the first discovery of New Zealand.

[1] See the legend in Sir G. Grey's *Polynesian Mythology*, pp. 31 sq., and in Mr. Taylor's *Te Ika a Maui*, pp. 23 sq. The New Zealand *Taranga* explains the *Ti' iti' i-a-talanga* of other islands, and the *Maui-a-talana* of Hawaii.

[2] Above, p. 402, n. 6.

[3] *e.g.* in the Tonga islands, it is he who supports the earth itself, and causes earthquakes (Prichard, v. 105, 152), just as Tane props up the heavens; and in the same district Maui, and not Tangaloa, was said to have fished up those islands out of the sea with a hook and line. (*Ibid.* p. 106, note; cf. Hale, p. 23.)

[4] See above, pp. 199 sq.

'This,' she exclaimed, 'is indeed my child. By the winds and storms and wave-uplifting gales he was fashioned and became a human being. Welcome, O my child, welcome! by thee shall hereafter be climbed the threshold of the house of thy great ancestor, Hine-nui-te-po (the goddess of the world invisible), and death itself shall thenceforth have no power over man.' With the express intention of achieving the fulfilment of this hopeful prophecy, the hero of New Zealand entered on the last and greatest of his labours. He had noticed how the sun and moon, which he was instigated to extinguish, were immortalised, because it was their wont to bathe in some living fountain: 'he determined, therefore, to do the same, and to enter the womb of Hine-nui-te-po, that is, Hades, where the living water —the life-giving stream—was situated. Hine-nui-te-po draws all into her womb, but permits none to return. Maui determined to try, trusting to his great powers; but before he made the attempt, he strictly charged the birds, his friends, not to laugh. He then allowed Great Mother Night to draw him into her womb. His head and shoulders had already entered, when that forgetful bird, the Piwaka-waka, began to laugh. Night closed her portals: Maui was cut in two, and died. Thus death came into the world, [or rather, in accordance with a second and more congruous version, kept its hold upon the world]. Had not the Piwaka-waka laughed, Maui would have drunk of the living stream, and man would never [more] have died. Such was the end of Maui[1]!'

In the main complexion of this fable, notwithstanding all its wildness and monstrosity, is found the aptest illustration which the mythes of Oceanica will furnish of the spirit there and everywhere engendered by the loss of real faith in God. Religion was debased into a hopeless, loveless dread of physical suffering and disaster. Old presentiments of some exalted Champion, who might silence or suppress the agencies of evil and so glorify together all the members of the Maori household, were eventually abandoned in despair as treacherous and illusive; death, they felt, had triumphed over Maui, and not Maui over death. How cheering, therefore, to a people, prostrate, powerless, terror-stricken, were the tidings of great joy which circulate in every land with the diffusion of the holy Gospel!

1 Taylor, p. 31, Grey, p. 57. The versions of the story are considerably different in different writers. In one case Maui is made the bringer-in of death, through his abortive attempt to deceive the great goddess of Night (Grey, p. 10); in the other, he is only unsuccessful in his vigorous struggle to subdue it.

Here had been revealed the one, all-glorious and all-merciful *Atua*, 'manifest in the flesh,' yea, wedded by the bands of an eternal love to the humanity which He adopted. Hence arose new principles of life and health and blessedness, which, permeating through the various members of the Christian organism, united each to each by reconciling all to Christ, the Head and Saviour of the Body. 'He tasted death for every man.' 'Forasmuch as the children are partakers of flesh and blood, He also Himself took part of the same, that through death He might destroy him that had the power of death, that is, the devil; and deliver them who through fear of death were all their life-time subject to bondage.'

And already there is cause enough for gratitude, as we count up those precious harvests which the messengers of Christ are reaping on the blood-stained shores of Oceanica. The wizards of New Zealand bow at length before the majesty of the Gospel; the expiring voice of every oracle proclaims that Christ, the Son of Mary, is verily Divine[1]. Of Polynesia, as a whole, it may be urged with equal confidence, that she is waking from the death of sin, and stretching out her hands to God, her Refuge and Redeemer. Island after island has been touched, rebuked and quickened by the ministrations of His grace; and with a promptness and expansive ardour that shone forth so brightly in our Anglo-Saxon forefathers, as soon as ever they were folded in the Christian Church, those Polynesians are in turn transmitting onward all the blessings they receive from us. 'Now,' exclaims a chief of Raratonga[2], pleading with his pagan neighbours and extolling the incalculable good that has resulted to himself and to his tribe from a sincere adoption of the Gospel, 'Now we enjoy happiness, to which our ancestors were strangers; our ferocious wars have ceased; our houses are the abodes of comfort; we have European property; we possess books in our own language; our children can read; and, above all, we know the true God and the way of salvation by His Son, Jesus Christ. This alone can make you a peaceable and happy people. I should have died a savage, had it not been for the Gospel.'

[1] When the first missionaries preached the Gospel in New Zealand, the natives consulted their *atua*, as to whether the teaching of the Europeans was true or false. 'It is a remarkable fact,' adds Mr. Shortland (p. 100), 'that wherever the inquiry was made, the answer invariably given declared Jesus Christ to be the true God;'—an answer which in part accounts for the rapid growth of Christianity in those regions.

[2] Russell's *Polynesia*, p. 274.

May the bright and blissful era be approaching, when all Christendom, incited by the proofs of fresh vitality and vigour which come back to us from the antipodes, shall count it her chief glory to assist in adding weight to these grand impulses, and forwarding the consummation of the Gospel-triumph; when the Church of God, no more restricted to particular tribes and nations, but embracing in her bosom all varieties of man,—the white, the red, the black, the copper-coloured,—shall be eager to advance into her ultimate condition, a thrice glorious Church, unblemished, indefectible; when island shall no longer cry to island, 'Come over and help us,' but, 'all shall know the Lord, from the least unto the greatest.'

I conclude this portion of my present task in words more forcible than any of my own, because they are the words of one now toiling at his post amid the far-off isles of Oceanica, and there exhibiting from day to day how zeal and prudence, faith and charity, tenderness and manly vigour may exist in graceful combination, and contribute now, as in the age of Apostolic missions, to enlighten and evangelise the world: 'It is indeed,' writes Bishop Selwyn, 'a great and glorious work, appalling in its vastness, and yet sustained by the fulness of the promise that the prayers of the Son of God will never fail, till the Father has given to Him the heathen for his inheritance, and the utmost parts of the earth for His possession.'

PART IV.

RELIGIONS OF EGYPT AND MEDO-PERSIA.

RELIGIONS OF EGYPT AND MEDO-PERSIA.

CHAPTER I.

Characteristics of Egyptian Heathenism.

Οὐ μόνον δὲ τούτου ['Οσίριδος] οἱ ἱερεῖς λέγουσιν, ἀλλὰ καὶ τῶν ἄλλων θεῶν, ὅσοι μὴ ἀγέννητοι, μηδ' ἄφθαρτοι, τὰ μὲν σώματα παρ' αὐτοῖς κεῖσθαι καμόντα καὶ θεραπεύεσθαι, τὰς δὲ ψυχὰς ἐν οὐρανῷ λάμπειν ἄστρα, καὶ καλεῖσθαι κύνα μὲν τὴν Ἴσιδος ὑφ' Ἑλλήνων, ὑπ' Αἰγυπτίων δὲ Σῶθιν, Ὠρίωνα δὲ τὴν Ὥρου, τὴν δὲ Τυφῶνος, ἄρκτον. εἰς δὲ τὰς τροφὰς τῶν τιμωμένων ζώων, τοὺς μὲν ἄλλους συντεταγμένα τελεῖν, μόνους δὲ μὴ διδόναι τοὺς Θηβαΐδα κατοικοῦντας, ὡς θνητὸν θεὸν οὐδένα νομίζοντας, ἀλλὰ ὃν καλοῦσιν αὐτοὶ Κνὴφ, ἀγέννητον ὄντα καὶ ἀθάνατον.

Eudoxus in Plutarch. *De Iside et Osiride*, c. XXI.

Importance of ancient Egypt. Its connexion with the neighbouring countries. Variety of monuments. Discoveries. Small assistance to the theological student. Civilisation. Parallel case of India and China. Mobility of Egyptian art, language and religion. Difficulties connected with the Biblical chronology. Untrustworthy character of some Egyptian traditions. Manetho's list of Kings. The chronological problem still unsolved. Primitive state of Egypt. Chami and Mizraim. Earliest seat of its civilisation. Discrimination of the early from the Hellenised Egyptians. Neo-Platonist theories respecting the early mythology. Sacred books. Extant sources of information. How far the older heathenism of Egypt was monotheistic. Parallel case of India. Practical polytheism of the system. Its pantheistic basis. Orders of divinities. Ptah. Neith. Pasht. Ra or Phra. Early prevalence of sun-worship. The Pharaohs children of the sun. Kneph. Ammon. Isis and Osiris. Hymns in honour of Osiris. Main ideas in the worship. Parallel in the Adonis-worship of Phœnicia. The Cabeiri: an example of planet-worship. General resemblances between the religions of Egypt and Phœnicia. Animal-worship. Apis. Serapis. Mythology localised in connexion with the Nile. Set, or Typhon. Latest form of the Osiris-mythe.

Ethical aspects of the religion of Egypt. Ignorance and abject superstitions of the many. Power and privileges of the sacerdotal order. Temples. Festivals. Oracles.

Doctrine of sacrifice. Typhonic victims; sometimes human. Worship of ancestors. Doctrine of a future life: its peculiar characteristics: its antiquity. Hindú and Egyptian theories of Transmigration. Interest in the fortunes of the body. Mummification. Judgment after death. Formula of self-exculpation. Fate of the condemned. Privileges of the acquitted.

ON resuming this investigation into the distinctive phases of religious thought among the dominant nations of antiquity, the reader will be next invited to a sphere whose influence on the early march of civilisation it were difficult to overstate. The Valley of the Nile had ever since the oldest Pharaohs been the border-land, or point of confluence, where the African was brought into direct communication with his Asiatic brother, and the East was intermingling with the West. As one of the succession of luminous centres, which, emerging here and there amid the dimness of primeval history, are traceable from the Mediterranean to the utmost bounds of Eastern Asia, Egypt, in some branches of her sacred institutions, will be found to have remarkable traits in common with the Áryan conquerors[1] of the Panjáb; while her monuments, alike in area and in massive grandeur, will remind us also of those primitive ages when the Mayan architect was rearing kindred structures[2] near the rivers of the New World.

But full as such analogies may be of interesting speculation, in reference to the ultimate extraction of the human family from one common stock, our present business is to mark the place and character of Egypt during the historic period, and as standing in more intimate relations to the people of her own immediate neighbourhood. The reputation for superior knowledge once enjoyed by all 'the children of the East country' was believed to be the special heritage of the Egyptian priests (cf. 1 Kings, iv. 30). Their cloisters were the recognised abode of art, of science, of religious mystery. Assyrian sculptors learned at Memphis what with greater or with less precision

[1] See Mr. Kenrick's *Ancient Egypt*, I. 105 sq., Lond. 1850, where, after handling the subject very fairly, he concludes 'that there has been some connexion between the civilisation of Egypt and India, while the nations themselves have as much claim to be considered distinct as any others of antiquity:' cf. Sir J. G. Wilkinson's last publication, *The Egyptians*, Pref. pp. IX. X. Lond. 1857. Baron Bunsen, *Phil. of Univ. Hist.* I. 191, is far less guarded in his phraseology: 'The exploded notion as to an original connexion between India (the youngest child of Asia) and Egypt (the deposit of primitive undivided Asia) is as groundless as it is absurd.'

[2] Above, p. 362.

they have reproduced at Nineveh. The sons of Abraham, who like himself went down in search of shelter from a grievous famine, were constrained by closer contact with Egyptian modes of life to throw aside their old nomadic habits; and at length when they returned victorious to the land of promise, the great host was marshalled by a captain, who had grown to manhood in the court of Pharaoh, and was 'learned in all the wisdom of the Egyptians' (Acts vii. 22). Thither also in the dawn of western civilisation came the young philosophers of Hellas[1], panting for some deep and transcendental lore, or listening with the eagerness and awe of children to the stories which had long been whispered in the learned circles of On, of Thebes, of Memphis; so that he who is desirous of understanding the precise development of human thought, alike in Western Asia and in Europe, in Athens, Rome, or even (some would tell us) in Jerusalem itself, must take up his position at this fountain-head of wisdom, and from thence survey the parting of the mighty stream as it flows forth into contiguous regions[2].

Now the scholar of the present age has many fresh facilities[3] for the successful carrying out of such investigations. The recovery of the hieroglyphic character has given, and is still giving every year, a new complexion to the ancient history of the Valley of the Nile. We can no longer speak of Egypt barely as the 'land of ruins,' or the birthplace of insoluble enigmas; her true title is the land of sculptured monuments,—of monuments again made vocal to the ear of science, and from which their secret must ere long be wrested more completely by the ardent pupils of Champollion. Favoured by the excellence of the material, and the singular purity and dryness of the climate, the colossal tombs and temples, to say nothing of those minor works of art dug out of the sepulchral chambers, have preserved a rich variety of inscriptions, more or less decypher-

[1] The evidence on this point is all collected in Lepsius, *Chronol. der Aegypter*, 'Einl.' pp. 41 sq.

[2] Uhlemann scarcely overrates the influence of Egypt, when, after sketching its position in the ancient world, and its relation both to Greeks and Hebrews, he adds (*Thoth, oder die Wissenschaften der alten Aegypter*, p. 6, Göttingen, 1855): 'Aegypten muss als ursprüngliche Quelle alles dessen betrachtet werden, was in späterer Zeit an diesen beiden und anderen von denselben abhängigen Völkern bewundert und angestaunt wird; ohne eine gründliche Kenntniss dieses Urquells kann Keins von beiden richtig erkannt, beurtheilt und gewürdigt werden.'

[3] 'Egyptian archæology and history have undergone a complete revolution since the commencement of the present century.' Kenrick's *Preface*.

able, and more or less conducing to an accurate knowledge of the past. 'There was not a wall, a platform, a pillar, an architrave, a frieze, or even a doorpost, in an Egyptian temple, which was not covered within, without, and on every available surface, with pictures in relief, and with hieroglyphic texts explaining those reliefs. There is not one of these reliefs that is not history: some of them actually representing the conquests of foreign nations; others, the offerings and devotional exercises of the monarch by whom the temple or the portion of the temple on which the relief stood, had been constructed....There was no colossus too great, and no amulet too small, to be inscribed with the name of its owner, and some account of the occasion on which it was executed[1].' We can easily understand that when the power of reading these inscriptions began to be recovered, men would turn with fresh enthusiasm to the study of Egyptian antiquities. Here, at least, they seemed to argue, we are building on a definite and stable basis. Our materials are no more of doubtful age and questionable reputation. The mind and spirit of that ancient world, with which we long to hold communion, left its impress deeply graven on the face of pyramids which tower, as they have towered for ages, high above the sandy flats of the adjoining desert. There, accordingly, if ever, we may hope to find the master-clue which is to guide us through the intricacies of primeval history, reveal afresh the hopes and fears which then were struggling in the human bosom, and resolve for us, it may be, many an arduous problem which concerns the origin, the early wanderings, and the final destiny of man.

Nor can we say that expectations of this kind have been entirely disappointed. Very large accessions to our knowledge of the ancient East have flowed, and are still flowing, from investigations of the learned Egyptologer. As we gaze for instance on the long array of monumental paintings in our great Museums; as we listen to interpretations of the hieroglyphic texts by which those paintings are accompanied; the daily life of men who were perhaps contemporary with Moses has again been vividly depicted on the dullest imagination. We behold as well the toils, the sufferings, and the pastimes of the many, as the power and luxury of the few. The peasant labours at the plough or tends his cattle, while the lordly owner of the soil is near him in a two-horse chariot. The goldsmith

[1] Osburn, *Monumental History of Egypt*, I. 195, substantially from Lepsius, as above, pp. 36, 37.

and the scribe, the potter and the glass-blower, the boat-builder, the weaver, and the dyer, each is occupied in his appropriate calling. Here we see a group of idlers watching the caprices of a game of ball, or listening in the midst of flowers and perfumes to the music of the seven-stringed harp: while there a countless multitude are shaping the materials of some stately edifice, or pressing a beleagured town, or marching home victorious with a lengthened train of captives.

It seems to be confessed, however, by the great majority of Egyptologers, that notwithstanding the number and minuteness of these revelations, our familiarity with monuments of ancient Egypt has contributed in no proportionate degree to our acquaintance with the inner being of the people. The manners of the Old Egyptian we may thoroughly appreciate: his mental and moral life is still obscurely apprehended. Means are now at hand for studying the grotesque configuration of his gods, and tracing out the smallest details in his pompous ritual; yet the thoughts which underlay those symbols, and found utterance in those sacrifices[1], must be learned, if ever, from a different source and by a different process.

If I venture, therefore, on a fresh discussion of such problems, it is not from any wish to speak with confidence where confidence is really unattainable. I do not purpose to invade the province of the Egyptologer, whose main conclusions are no longer open to dispute; but rather, taking those conclusions for a guide, wherever they are held in common by the learned in each special study, my aim will be to estimate the leading characteristics of Egyptian heathenism, as one of many forms in which the moral wants and instincts of our nature found expression during the first ages of the world. In doing this, however, exception will be freely taken to the crude and arbitrary theories of some modern writers[2], who, not

[1] 'When we endeavour to penetrate into the conceptions which this splendid ritual expressed, we encounter insuperable difficulties:' Kenrick, I. 349: cf. I. 437.

[2] That English critics are not alone in their misgivings with respect to some of Baron Bunsen's generalisations may be gathered from an extract like the following. The author, Dr. Max Uhlemann, is also an Egyptologer of no mean reputation (*Aegyptisch. Alterthumskunde*, III. 12, Leipzig, 1858): 'Bunsen's Untersuchungen sind unbezweifelt und unbestritten ein geistreiches Werk,......aber in der Chronologie enthalten auch sie, wie die aller übrigen Forscher, nur Muthmaassungen und unerweisbare Annahmen, die jedoch durch die Zuversichtlichkeit, mit der sie auftreten, dem *unaufmerksamen* Leser als unzweifelhaft erscheinen dürften, da durch Zahlenveränderungen, durch willkürliche Textverbesserungen, durch Hinzuthun oder Hinwegnehmen

content with 'reconstructing' almost every text which militates against their favourite dream of a society 'existing many thousand years before the date usually assigned to the Creation,' are further bent on sacrificing to a spirit of conjectural criticism the highest of all Christian teachings and the best convictions of the human heart.

The great antiquity which is now commonly attributed to Egyptian culture has in several cases been connected with the thought, that in the Valley of the Nile, the prominent forms of social and religious life had been completely stereotyped at once, and so distinguished in all future ages by an air of absolute immobility.

Now the same conclusion, we must bear in mind, was formerly adopted with respect to India and the regions of the Further East. So meagre was our knowledge of the subject, when presented to us by the earliest race of Oriental scholars, that the Védas and Puránas, for example, were regarded as not only products of the same age, but also as reflecting the same modes of thought, the same archaic aspects of Hindú society. There, however, the unanimous verdict of a riper criticism, while fatal to pretensions of unfathomable antiquity, has certified us that the national spirit both of India and of China had been subject, in the lapse of ages, to extensive fluctuations[1].

And a like remark is equally true of Egypt, even while she bowed beneath the sceptre of the Pharaohs. Her supposed exemption from the law of human mutability is vanishing with every fresh accession to our knowledge. The minute inspection and decyphering of her monumental archives have disclosed to us a series of important transformations, have established the existence of successive strata of development, and thus contributed to make us conscious of distinctive epochs in the lifetime of the whole community[2]. It may be, indeed, that all the principal characteristics of Egyptian culture, had, as in the

von Jahresangaben der Alten schliesslich Alles auf wunderbare Weise vortrefflich zu stimmen und sich wechselseitig zu bestätigen scheint.'

[1] Above, pp. 134 sq., pp. 283 sq..

[2] 'Avant que les dernières découvertes des égyptologues eussent jeté un jour précieux sur la chronologie des premières dynasties, sur les transformations et les altérations qui se sont opérées dans la langue, dans les institutions, dans le culte et les arts des Egyptiens, on se figurait que tout avait été immuable parmi eux. On prenait la vieille Égypte en bloc comme un monolithe historique qu'il fallait tirer du sable dans lequel il était enfoui, et l'on ne distinguait ni les localités ni les époques.' Maury, in the *Revue des Deux Mondes* (1855), Tom. XI. p. 1053.

case of China, been projected with so much rapidity at first, that we can never hope to understand the origin and real infancy of the people[1]. It may further be contended, that the nationality of Egypt, or the genius which distinguished her from African and Asiatic neighbours, was 'very much the same' in earlier and in later times. All statements of this kind if not unduly pressed convey a large amount of truth; they serve to represent the *general* fixity of corporate as of personal idiosyncrasies; and yet we can no longer doubt that after Egypt had begun to print her records on the pyramids of Ghizeh and Sakkarah, she passed through numerous and important changes,—changes which affected not only her political institutions, but the character of art, of language, of religion.

The second province, that of language, where some modifying agency had been at work, I leave for the discussion of the competent Egyptologer[2]. The third will come more properly before us at a future stage of our inquiry; but the point relating to the gradual changes in the quality of Egyptian art it is expedient to consider now, because the epochs thus obtained are thought by some who are most eminently learned in such matters, to agree with main divisions of Egyptian history in the Pharaonic era.

It is commonly admitted that the finest specimens of Egyptian art[3] are those which have the fairest claims to be regarded as the oldest,—those which fall within the period of the 'first twelve dynasties.' The bloom of youth is ever traceable on the productions of the early race of artists; all the statues and bas-reliefs are executed with surprising truthfulness and vigour; and although we must allow that both in purity and finish several works belonging to the close of this great period indicate considerable progress, it is no less certain that

[1] Wilkinson, *The Egyptians* (Lond. 1857), Pref. p. vii. who adds (p. viii.) that 'the *general character* of the people, as of their architecture, had been long established when we first become acquainted with them from their monuments, and continued to be the same till the decline of Egyptian power.'

[2] See the *Revue des Deux Mondes*, as above, pp. 1055 sq. on the recent labours of M. de Rougé in this special province.

[3] See *The British Museum* (Egyptian Antiquities), two volumes in the 'Library of Entertaining Knowledge.' Mr. Osburn, *Monumental History of Egypt*, I. 260 sq. (Lond. 1854), infers from the absence of all crude and 'imperfect' works of art in Egypt that the skill of the primitive artists was a 'portion of that civilisation which its first settlers brought with them when they located themselves in the valley of the Nile.'

the character of the whole is so distinctive as to mark it off completely from the period next ensuing.

In the second stage of art, embracing monuments of 'the eighteenth and nineteenth dynasties,' the fervour and simplicity of earlier times have been succeeded by a large amount of stiffness and conventionality. It is the Middle Age of Egypt; during which the symptoms of deterioration are constantly apparent, even where the vast proportions of the works constructed must excite our deepest admiration of the power and energy of the builders.

With the 'twentieth dynasty' commences a fresh era, the age of revival, when the artists of the Valley of the Nile, reverting to the ancient models, executed their works with far greater freedom; yet this period also was of short duration, and when Egypt was absorbed into the empire of the Ptolemies, and finally of the Cæsars, she retained but little of the old artistic spirit: all attempts to mingle Greek with native methods issued in comparative failure, and hastened the extinction of her pristine glory.

If, however, it be now established to the satisfaction of most writers that transitions of this kind are really visible on Egyptian monuments, far less has been effected in determining the point of primary departure, or the *length of time* to be assigned to each successive period of Egyptian history. I shrink from a minute investigation of the chronological difficulties by which the present subject is confessedly embarrassed. While discussing the religions of ancient India, it appeared to be sufficient for my purpose if I pointed out the general *order* of the changes which had supervened upon the old mythology and habits of the people; and a similar course would be adopted now, if statements were not hazarded in various quarters with the object of discrediting the Bible[1] as a whole, by ridiculing what is called the 'Mosaic chronology.'

[1] See above, pp. 46, 47, where two American champions of human inequality adopt this line of argument. In like manner, the account of the Deluge, which was prevalent both in the Old and New World, is said by M. Bunsen and others to have left no echo whatever in the hieroglyphic legends of Egypt. Their avowed object in reiterating this statement is to shew that the emigration of the Old Egyptians must have been 'ante-Noachian,' and indeed many thousand years before the date ascribed by them to the 'Caucasian' deluge. But the silence which has been alleged in justification of their statement is apparently a mere invention of determined theorizers. Osburn, for example (I. 239, 240), says with reference to objections on this very subject: 'We have no hesitation whatever in stating our conviction,

How far, indeed, the Books of Moses, in their present state, supply materials for constructing any definite system of chronology has long been questioned by the ablest and most reverential of our sacred critics. The important variations of the Hebrew and Samaritan texts on one side, and the Septuagint and certain passages of Josephus on the other, have involved the period reaching from the Deluge to the seventieth year of Terah in comparative obscurity. The whole duration of that period in the Hebrew is no more than 352 years; while in the Vatican manuscript of the Seventy it extends as far as 1172 years[1].

But the indefiniteness arising from this cause will never justify the random guesses of some modern Egyptologers, who, dazzled it would seem by the occasional brilliance of their own discoveries, are carrying back the civilisation of the Valley of the Nile to ages long anterior to the earliest glimpse of history in other regions of the world. Those writers should remember, while demanding our entire belief in catalogues of kings and 'palace-registers,' that in the North of India, where the course of civilisation was most parallel to that of Egypt, we have means of proving the untruthfulness of similar documents, and are able to convict their authors of antedating one event of great importance by as many as twelve hundred years[2]. Those writers should again remember, that the testimony of Egyptian priests is not above suspicion; that Herodotus and Diodorus both derived their information from the same authorities, and yet that while Herodotus extends the number of obscure descendants of Menes to 330, Diodorus limits them to 52; and while the former makes the native monarchy of Egypt to have lasted in all 11,340 years, the calculation of the latter stops short at 4,700[3]. These, and other discrepancies, are so 'enormous and so fundamental as to preclude the idea that they can have been superinduced by lapse of time, and a variety of narrators, on a history originally authentic.'

that Lepsius is mistaken;' and accordingly proceeds to demolish the 'stupendous pile of inferences which are built on this single assumption.' And Uhlemann, in like manner, is completely at variance on this point with Lepsius and Bunsen. He declares (*Aegypt. Altert.* III. 10): 'Die ägyptischen Priester *wussten sehr wohl* von einer Zeit, in welcher nach göttlichen Rathschlusse das sündige Menschengeschlecht vernichtet wurde,' &c.

[1] The sum total for this period, according to the various authorities, is *Heb.* 352; *Samar.* 942; *Septuag.* (Vat.) 1172; *Septuag.* (Alexand.) 1072; *Josephus*, 1002.

[2] Lassen, *Ind. Alterth.* I. 501.

[3] Kenrick, *Ancient Egypt*, II. 84, 85.

And on turning to the works of Manetho, the earliest[1] of native historians, who died in the third century before the Christian era, we find that such of his remains as have descended to us must be taken at third hand. His famous lists of kings commence with gods, with manes and with heroes, who are said to have held sway in Egypt for a period of more than thirty thousand years; and even if it were conceded that a writer of his age, the first Egyptian priest who had been gifted with 'historic consciousness,' was equal to the task of carrying back the annals of his country for three or five thousand years, an obstacle was lying in his way which must have stubbornly resisted all real progress. Vast as may have been the astronomical knowledge of the Old Egyptians, great as was their aptitude in framing chronological cycles[2], they 'do not appear at any time to have reckoned in their public monuments by an *era*, like that of the Olympiads, but only to have dated events, as we date acts of parliament, by the years of the king's reign[3].' If Egypt, therefore, was in early times divided into several petty kingdoms; or if the names of co-regents, of pretenders, of provincial governors, assuming to themselves the royal style, were entered on the lists of dynasties, the sum of all the regnal years obtained by this process would very far exceed the true number. A large exaggeration is, indeed, acknowledged now by all our Egyptologers. It is believed that rulers in the primitive nomes, or cantons, may at first have been entitled kings, and also that the starting-point of calculation coincided in particular cases not with the accession

1 'We hear of no *historical* work of that people before Manetho:' Bunsen, *Egypt's Place*, I. 23. Yet the *History* of this native writer, as distinguished from his *Dynasties*, is now lost: while the latter work (edited afresh in Bunsen, I. 605 sq.) is known to us only through Julius Africanus, and Eusebius, and from them through George the Syncellus, a Byzantine monk of the ninth century; of whom it should be added that he places the Creation 5500 B.C. and arranges all his dates accordingly.

2 Cf. Uhlemann, *Aegypt. Alt.* III. 2, 9. Both he and Lepsius are of opinion that the Sothis-period conducts us back to at least 2782 B.C. Mr. Browne, the learned and laborious author of the *Ordo Sæclorum*, has, however, called in question almost every one of the results obtained by German Egyptologers (see his able papers in Arnold's *Theological Critic*, I. 529 sq., II. 125 sq.). Mr. Browne contends that all the native lists of kings are based on cyclical relations, the different cycles being referred to different epochs. According to his view, the *regular* chronology of ancient Egypt is reducible to one cycle, dating from 1805 B.C. (the reign of Joseph's Pharaoh). The 'reduced chronology' has also found another learned advocate in Mr. Nolan, *The Ægyptian Chronology Analysed*, Lond. 1848.

3 Kenrick, II. 95.

to an undivided sovereignty, but with the time at which some ruler was admitted to the rank of a co-regent: for although the sum of regnal years, commencing from the earliest of the human rulers, and ending with the last of Manetho's dynasties, amounted to at least 5000, the number actually assigned upon the same authority as the duration of the *whole* period was not more than 3555 years[1].

But if despairing[2] of results which rest on this precarious basis, we commence our exploration from the age when Egypt is first drawn distinctly into the general history of the world, and so endeavour to trace out her course in the reverse order, we arrive at early points of synchronism about 972 B.C., when Shishak[3] (Sesonch) of the '22nd dynasty' invaded Palestine, and in the fifth year of Rehoboam 'took away the treasures of the house of the Lord, and the treasures of the king's house' (1 Kings xiv. 25). And as Shishak was the first member of a new dynasty, it follows that a Pharaoh of the previous series was father-in-law of Solomon (1 Kings ix. 16), and that Tahpenes, the sister of the Egyptian queen, had been espoused to Hadad, the Idumæan, as early as the reign of David (1 Kings xi. 19 sq.). On these points, indeed, there is no longer any difference of opinion; but the placing of the Exodus itself, the next event where contact with the annals of the Hebrew nation is undoubted, still continues to present some formidable difficulties; inasmuch as it is found to be entangled[4]

[1] Lepsius is disposed to take his stand on this number, which comes down to us through George the Syncellus (cf. *Kritik der Quellen*, p. 499). See, however, *Quarterly Review*, No. 210 (April, 1859), pp. 396 sq., where it is pointed out that this number 3555 may have come from the 'Old Chronicle' merely, and not from the genuine Manetho. The Egyptian years being reduced would give 3553 Julian years for the duration of the thirty dynasties of Manetho; and this, added to 339 (the year B. C. when the last dynasty expired) would also give 3892 B. C. for the foundation of the monarchy. Uhlemann, on the contrary, persists in dating the reign of Menes, the first king of Egypt, 2782 B. C.

[2] 'The recovery of Egyptian chronology, except by slow degrees, and with intervals of unknown lengths between the reigns that are known, is hopeless.' *Engl. Review* (1846), p. 114; an article on *The Pyramids and their Builders*, attributed to Dr. Hincks.

[3] Browne, *Ordo Sæclorum*, § 513.

[4] See one of the best discussions of this point in Kurtz, *Gesch. des Alten Bundes*, II. 173—203, Berlin, 1855. He advocates the old and very plausible theory that the 'Phœnician' shepherds had invaded Lower Egypt in the period between Abraham and Joseph; and that the new dynasty (corresponding to the 18th of Manetho), who persecuted and enslaved the Israelites, were princes of Egyptian blood who had eventually regained the sovereign power. The only serious objection to this view arises from the thoroughly *Egyptian* aspect of the court in the time of

with a further question touching the expulsion of the Shepherd-Kings, or Hyk-sos, and their previous rule in Lower Egypt.

Nor in passing upwards, from the origin of what is called the New Kingdom, or the first reign of the '18th dynasty,' has greater concord been established among writers who profess to be our guides through the confusion of the period next preceding.

The duration of the three dynasties ascribed to it by Manetho is found to vary in the different systems of Egyptian chronology from 511 to 953 years; while other writers, arguing from the total want of monuments which bear the dates of kings later than the 12th dynasty, and earlier than the 18th, have begun to ask with some show of reason, 'Is the Middle Monarchy a real thing or not[1]?' Whatever be the true answer to this question, it is plain that till far more is known with certainty respecting such important intervals, we have but little hope of framing any rational hypothesis, or of inditing a coherent narrative.

And the same perplexity must haunt us on ascending to the 'Old' division of the Pharaonic monarchy. The names of kings belonging to that era are now extant, it is true, in very great profusion[2]. Monuments commencing with the time of Chufu (Suphis, Cheops)[3], the builder of the Great Pyramid,

Joseph; but Dr. Kurtz has also done very much towards the removal of this difficulty (pp. 199, 200).

[1] Dr. Hincks in *Engl. Review*, as above, p. 117. Mr. Kenrick also admits the fact that 'not a single contemporaneous work of art has been found, from the 13th to the 18th dynasty.' He adds, however, (II. 194): 'These things are not sufficient to make us doubt the fact of the invasion and expulsion of the Hyk-sos; but they may excite a suspicion that the chronology of this period of oppression and confusion is not to be relied on, and that as usual it has been unduly extended.' I ought also to remind the reader at this point that M. de Rougé thinks he has at last discovered an allusion to the Hyk-sos rule on a papyrus relating to a war undertaken by a king of the Thebaid against the shepherd-king Apepi (Aphobis). The shepherds are there treated as enemies of the *gods* of Egypt. *Revue des Deux Mondes*, as before, p. 1063: cf. Brugsch, *Die Geographie des alten Aegyptens*, I. 50 sq. Leipzig, 1857.

[2] Especially in the famous Turin papyrus, which before mutilation must have contained 3 or 400 royal names (cf. Herod. II. 142), with the precise lengths of reign attached to each: see Sir J. G. Wilkinson's *Fragments of the Hieratic Papyrus at Turin* (privately printed, 1851). The same author in his last work *The Egyptians*, &c. (1857), while granting that the high antiquity once assigned to some of the monuments is now 'brought within more reasonable limits' is clearly of opinion that those of the fourth dynasty (the earliest of all) were executed not less than 2400 years B.C. (p. 3).

[3] Kenrick, II. 133. On the identification of the names, see Dr. Hincks, as above, p. 102.

continue to bear witness to the fact that even at the opening of the '4th dynasty' the lower valley of the Nile was tenanted by an ambitious and accomplished people, organised into a regular community, as in the age of Abraham and Joseph, and already in possession of the hieroglyphic character, as well as of the reed-pen and the ink-stand.

Yet in spite of all these interesting revelations, Egyptology contributes very little towards the unriddling of the old question, namely, as to which of the primeval dynasties were contemporaneous, and which of them successive. One distinguished writer (as Bunsen) searches for the missing key among the chronological fragments of Eratosthenes, corrected, however, by his own hand; a second (as Lepsius) manifests no confidence in this auxiliary, and gropes his way alone to very different results; a third (as Mr. Browne, or Mr. Nolan, or Mr. Osburn) would curtail the length of early dynasties far more than either of the previous explorers; so that on arriving at the first event distinctly traceable in the archives of the infant colony,—the founding of Memphis, by the oldest of their mortal kings[1], the 'Romulus of Egypt,'—nearly all our certain knowledge of the epoch when some mighty change was supervening on the population of the Nile-Valley, may be gathered up into the vague conclusion of Josephus; who informs us that 'Menes, who built Memphis, preceded Abraham by many years[2].'

But what, in such a case, may be conjectured of the primitive or pre-historic age anterior to the reign of Menes, and the first migrations of the tribe from which he was descended?

This inquiry is again of vast importance to the proper conduct of the enterprise immediately before us; since the ethnological affinities of heathen nations may justly be expected to throw light on the formation of their mythology.

Some Christian writers have attempted to identify the founder of Egyptian civilisation with Ham (or Cham), the son of Noah; others with Mizraim, one of Ham's descendants: and

[1] The author of the article *Ægyptus* in Smith's *Dict. of Greek and Roman Geography*, thinks that the word *Menes* is itself suspicious: it 'too nearly resembles *Manu*, the *Minyas* and *Minos* of the Greeks, the *Menerfa* of the Etruscans, and the *Mannus* of the Germans [cf. Sansk. *man* "to think"] to be accepted implicitly as a personal designation.' Eratosthenes, however, explains Μήνης as equivalent to Αἰώνιος, which is said to be justified by the Old Egyptian and Coptic use of *men* (μην) in the sense of 'to persevere': Uhlemann, *Aegypt. Alt.* III. 82. On the occurrence of the name upon Egyptian monuments, see Osburn, I. 226 sq.

[2] *Antiq.* VIII. 6, 2, ed. Havercamp.

although the efforts of those writers seem to me extremely infelicitous, the words on which their arguments are principally based will prove, I think, suggestive of more tenable conclusions.

One native name of Egypt is *Chami*[1] (χημι), connected with the Coptic χαμε 'black'; while the appellation almost universally current in Semitic countries is *Mizraim*[2], *Misr*, or *Mezrén*, the fullest of these forms, we should remember, being itself a Hebrew dual noun. And on reverting to the genealogical table transmitted in the family of Abraham (Gen. x. 16), it will appear that in the series of Ham's descendants the first place is there allotted to *Cush* (a common name for 'Ethiopians'); and the second place to *Mizraim* (or the Old Egyptians, occupying the two divisions of the Nile-valley). Attention seems to have been thus directed to the fact that all the earliest layers of population, as well below the frontier-island of Elephantine as throughout the present Nubia and Ethiopia, were originally homogeneous,—a result which is corroborated by Egyptian history and in no wise inconsistent with modern discoveries.

Yet some of these discoveries have, I think, necessitated a fresh hypothesis with reference to the dominant race of Egypt in the period of the early Pharaohs. Like the Áryan conquerors of the Panjáb, they do not appear to be the primitive masters of the soil, but rather a deposit of new-comers, dating from some later epoch. The numerous paintings on the monuments, as well as osteological investigations in the tombs, will hardly suffer us to doubt that the Egyptians proper, even of the earlier dynasties, exhibit few decided characteristics of the woollyhaired or negro race, but constitute in some respects

[1] See above, p. 48, n. 1. Plutarch, *De Iside et Osiride*, c. XXXIII. gives the following account of the word: *ἔτι τὴν Αἴγυπτον ἐν τοῖς μάλιστα μελάγγειον οὖσαν, ὥσπερ τὸ μέλαν τοῦ ὀφθαλμοῦ, Χημίαν καλοῦσι.*

[2] Knobel (*Die Völkertafel der Genesis*, p. 273) is disposed to question the ordinary derivation of this term מִצְרַיִם from the bipartite character of Ancient Egypt (Upper and Lower). He urges that Isaiah (xi. 11) distinguishes Pathros, or Upper Egypt, from Mizraim, the remainder of the country, which could hardly have been the case, if the Hebrews used Mizraim as equivalent to *both* divisions. Knobel has accordingly suggested a fresh origin for the term: 'Dieser Dual gehört zu einem nicht vorkommenden Singular מָצֹר......er bedeutet also eine doppelte oder zweiseitige Einschliessung und bezeichnet Aegypten ganz passend als ein von 2 Seiten eingeschlossenes Land' (p. 274). But the analogy of other duals (such as Jerusalem = ἡ κάτω + ἡ καθύπερθεν, Joseph. *Ant.* v. 2, 2) is in favour of the ordinary derivation.

an independent people[1],—of a type which, ethnologically speaking, is described as intermediate between the Syro-Arabian and the Ethiopic. There is very great uncertainty[2] again as to the point at which the leaders of the second colony effected their original settlement in the Valley of the Nile. If we might argue from the fact that monuments adjudged the very oldest are all found in Lower Egypt, not far from On (or Heliopolis), the city which became in after-times one special centre of religious worship, it would seem most probable that the new race of immigrants crossed over by the isthmus of Suez, or the natural bridge connecting Africa with Asia; yet a contrary hypothesis, which represents the civilisers of the Nile-valley as a band of priests descending from the Ethiopian frontier, has been also able to attract a number of influential supporters.

Whatever be the ultimate decision of that controversy, a belief in some great secondary immigration, such as I have just indicated, is now current in all schools of Egyptology[3], not

[1] Uhlemann (*Aegypt. Alt.* III. 57) is very emphatic on this point: 'Nicht von der Geschichte dieses dunklen Stammes hängt die Geschichte der politischen Entwickelung und Cultur der alten Aegypter ab, sondern vielmehr, wie alle noch erhaltenen Denkmäler beweisen, von einem Stamme ganz anderer Abkunft und Farbe...' Cf. Prichard, III. 227 sq., who infers that notwithstanding considerable diversity in figure and complexion, the Old Egyptians as a body 'had something in their physical character approximating to that of the negro' (p. 230).

[2] This uncertainty is connected with the vexed question as to the course pursued by the early civilisers of the Nile-valley. Did they advance northwards from the Thebaid to Lower Egypt? Such is said to be the general verdict of antiquity (Knobel, as above, p. 275); and Ezekiel in particular (xxix. 14), seems to speak of Pathros (Upper Egypt) as 'the land of their *birth*' (מְכוּרָתָם), the cradle of the whole Egyptian people. Thebes was in like manner taken for the oldest of Egyptian cities: whereas it seems to be the general opinion of living Egyptologers that the southern *monuments* at least (whatever may be said of the people) are far more modern than those of Lower Egypt (Osburn, *Mon. Hist.* I. 211); and that Thebes was really the metropolis of the first dynasties, not of the Old but of the *New* kingdom. Other accounts, however, tend to reconcile these two conflicting theories by pointing out that although historical Thebes is younger than Memphis, the course of civilisation did at first flow northwards; Memphis being itself built by an accomplished prince of Abydos in Upper Egypt. In connexion with this point arises the old inquiry respecting the possible influence of Hindús in shaping the original institutions of Egypt (above, p. 418, n. 1); and also the tradition respecting sacerdotal colonies from Meroë in Ethiopia (Diodor. I. 33: III. 3—6).

[3] *e.g.* Bunsen declares, *Egypt's Place*, I. 443, that the facts established by modern researches into language and mythology give us precisely the same result. 'Both carry us historically back to Asia.'

excepting writers who are driven to ascribe the act itself to an unfathomable antiquity. At first, it may be, while the powerful chieftains, such as Menes, were all struggling to consolidate the primitive tribes or cantons[1] into a regular monarchy, the old inhabitants continued to preponderate as largely as the Gauls in France, who, though succumbing everywhere beneath the arms of Clovis, had been able to preserve the language[2] of their former masters and communicate both it and their religion to the great majority of the Franks. A like amalgamation may have followed in the early centuries of the Pharaonic empire; and subsequently when the Hyk-sos gained possession of all Lower Egypt, and the seat of native power had been transferred to Thebes and to a neighbourhood in which the Cushite spirit still predominated, the great fusion may have been again more rapidly promoted, till at length historians had to deal with a community, consisting, as before, of diverse elements, imperfectly attempered to each other, yet so mixed as to produce what we entitle the specific nationality of Egypt.

[1] These νομοί (thirty-six in number?) into which the valley of the Nile was parcelled out are carried back by Diodorus (I. 54) to the time of Sesostris or Sesöosis (Ramses II.?): yet, as is well remarked, 'they did not originate with that monarch, but emanated probably from the distinctions of animal worship; and the extent of the local worship probably determined the boundary of the nome:' cf. Herod. II. 42.

[2] The most opposite views are still entertained respecting the affinities of the Coptic, or, with slight corrections, of the *Old Egyptian* language. On the one side, it is argued that the syntax of that language, and not a little of the vocabulary also, are related closely to the Hebrew and other members of the great Semitic family. A second class of writers look upon the Old Egyptians as intermediate between the Semitic and Indo-European families. ('The roots of the Egyptian language are, in the majority of cases, monosyllabic, and, on the whole, identical with the corresponding roots in Sanskrit and Hebrew. This is said advisedly:' Bunsen, *Phil. of Hist.* I. 185). A third class utterly deny the alleged connexion between Coptic and Hebrew: *e.g.* "Auch die älteste Sprache der alten Aegypter stand mit den sogenannten semitischen *in gar keiner Verbindung;* erst spätere Verkehrsberührungen haben einige Ausdrücke, besonders von Kleidern, Gafässen, Maassen und Gewichten, aus der ägyptischen Sprache in die orientalischen oder umgekehrt übergehen lassen:' Uhlemann, *Aegypt. Alt.* III. 58. In this opinion of an eminent Coptic scholar acquiesces the present Regius Professor of Hebrew, at Cambridge, who has kindly aided me in the examination of the string of words adduced as parallel by Mr. Birch, *Egyptian Hieroglyphics* (appended to Sir J. G. Wilkinson's *Ancient Egyptians*), p. 251. Professor Jarrett is of opinion that it is impossible to establish any relationship between the Coptic and the Hebrew of a closer kind than that which, ethnologically speaking, may be said to exist between 'a Greek and a Negro.' See Appendix I.

Now of these two factors, one, as in the somewhat parallel case of India, will be here comparatively disregarded. I am not attempting to investigate the characteristics of *primeval* heathenism in the Nile-valley, except so far as it has left its impress on ideas and institutions which belong as properly to the historic period. The remarks already made in sketching the religions of barbaric tribes, wherever scattered on the surface of Asia, of America, of Oceanica, would frequently apply with equal justice to the continent whose people we are now considering,—not to provinces alone in which the black or negro type of man evinced his true humanity by emerging here and there into historical importance, but also in that vast expanse of moral barrenness, which stretches southward from the Mediterranean to the Cape, and eastward from the burning cliffs of Guinea to the pestilent mouths of the Zambesi[1].

Yet even when the sphere of study is thus definitely narrowed, it becomes important to discriminate afresh between the earlier and the later periods of Egyptian history. Our judgment, with respect to the development of religion in that country, should be formed apart from clashing theories which come down to us through Greek writers; for although Herodotus, in spite of the absurd misrepresentations of his dragoman, has furnished a large mass of information which is proved to be trustworthy by according in the main with extant monuments, the other tourists and philosophers who handled the same topics, when the Delta was in part Hellenised, and society most deeply tinctured by the foreign modes of thought, can seldom challenge our assent in the same proportion. The Thebaid, it is true, was still comparatively isolated, and as such continued firm in its profession of the hereditary faith, until the sweeping edict of Theodosius, in A.D. 379; but on the founding of the Hellenic capital of Egypt by Alexander the Great, the country as a whole had witnessed the commencement of a new era, in philosophy as well as in political relations. The adornment of the great Museum of Alexandria with the obelisks and sphinxes of the Pharaonic cities, was itself an emblem of the fresh eclectic spirit, then and there imported into all discussions of the old mythology[2].

One result of such eclecticism has been, that writers (native

[1] See Appendix II.

[2] 'Alexandrie et la cour des Ptolémées étaient surtout le théâtre de ce mouvement syncrétique qui rapprochait la théogonie pharaonique du polythéisme grec systématisé par les philosophes.' *Revue des Deux Mondes*, as before, p. 1072.

and Hellenic) of this later period, and especially the Neo-Platonist champions of expiring heathenism, as Porphyry, or Iamblichus, or Proclus, have at times so spiritualized or sublimated the religion of the Old Egyptian, and assigned such arbitrary meaning to the symbols of his ritual, that the primary ideas which it embodied will as seldom be derivable from their writings, as the first mythology of India can be ascertained from speculations of the school of Kapila, or from the aphorisms of the Védánta. Each of the opposing theories started long ago by this class of writers is reflected in the kindred contradictions of modern philosophers. One, for instance, may be heard contending that the basis of Egyptian mythology was altogether materialistic[1]; another, on the contrary, that it was always an exalted system of pure idealism[2], which taught men to enshrine the highest and most abstract truths beneath the guise of earthly symbols, and to recognise a master-spirit guiding the whole mechanism of physical creation. But there is reason to believe, as we shall see hereafter, that neither of these theories have done justice to the rude conceptions of the old mythographer[3]. He looked at nature with a deep but thoroughly childlike interest, seldom conscious of the metaphysical antitheses which enter into all our modern speculations; and accordingly his power of separating between the natural and the spiritual was very different from our own, or even from the

[1] This was the position actually maintained by Chæremon, the Stoic ἱερογραμματεύς who was chief librarian of the Serapeum in the former half of the first century after Christ. According to his view the chief divinities of ancient Egypt were the seven planets and the twelve signs of the zodiac (cf. Uhlemann's *Thoth*, p. 250). In their mythology he recognises no incorporeal Principle, or unseen Intelligence. Prichard's general leaning is in the same direction (*Egyptian Mythology*, Lond. 1819); for, following in the steps of Eusebius (*Evangel. Præparat.* lib. III. c. 4), he concludes that the 'worship of the Old Egyptians was directed towards physical objects; or the departments and powers of nature' (p. 34).

[2] Thus Porphyry addressing a priest named Anebo inquires as to what the Egyptians really held to be the First Cause,—whether an intelligent principle (νοῦν) or something ὑπὲρ νοῦν (cf. a criticism of this passage in Creuzer, *Symbolik*, II. 269); and is answered by Iamblichus who assumes the name of an Egyptian priest, Abammon (*De Mysteriis*, VIII. 4, ed. Gale, 1678). His solution is that the Egyptians by no means affirm the physical origin of all things; but 'distinguish both the animal life and principle of intelligence from nature itself, not only in the universe but also in man' (cf. Creuzer, as above, p. 270).

[3] This judgment which accords substantially with Creuzer's (p. 276) will be also found in Hegel's *Lectures on the Philosophy of History*, p. 217 (Lond. 1857). He argues that in 'Egypt natural and spiritual powers were regarded as most intimately united.'

corresponding faculty of his descendant, who might strive to systematise his notions, when the mythic age of heathendom was drawing to a close.

In seeking therefore to unite ourselves afresh with that remoter period in the history of Egyptian thought, the natural course is to inquire if any written monuments are extant corresponding to the Hindú Védas and the 'sacred' books of the Chinese. Now Egypt also had a class of writings which may fairly be regarded in this very light. The ancient melodies, which Plato tells us were preserved from age to age as the productions of the goddess Isis[1], point to the existence and diffusion of a 'sacred' literature. The common name applied to all such writings by the Greeks was 'Books of Hermes' (their reputed author being scribe of the gods, or the 'Mercurius' of the old mythology). From Clement of Alexandria[2] we can also ascertain the general character of these Hermetic books; for when he wrote the custom was to have them carried in procession through the temple of Isis by the heathen priests of the metropolis. The whole number (two and forty), comprehending various treatises on secular subjects, as on medicine, astronomy, and the chorography of Egypt, consisted of extensive disquisitions on religion and philosophy[3], and also of minute directions for the 'sealing of victims,' the due oblation of the appointed sacrifices, the observance of solemn feasts, the training of the young, and more especially of members of the sacerdotal class, together with the full routine of duties daily claimed from the Egyptian either by the laws of his country, or by gods whom he believed to exercise especial sway in his own neighbourhood.

These works, however, with perhaps one sole exception, have been long unknown to Egyptologers, and are probably beyond the reach of modern exploration. The exception which there seems at least some valid reason for acknowledging

[1] *De Legibus*, II. 4 (*Opp.* VII. 516, Bekk.): cf. Diodor. I. 53, 72; XVII. 50.

[2] *Strom.* lib. VI. c. 4 (*Opp.* II. 756, ed. Potter): cf. Lepsius, *Chron.* Einleitung, pp. 45 sq., and Mr. Birch, *Egypt. Hieroglyph.* (as before), p. 186, where several titles of Hermetic Books are brought together. Bunsen, who considers the 36 books (excluding the last six on medicine) in five classes—(1) Two Books of the Chanter, (2) Four Astronomical Books of the Horoscopus, (3) Ten Books of the Hiero-Grammatist, (4) Ten Ceremonial Books of the Stolistes, (5) Ten Books of the Prophets (Priests),—has summed up his inquiry by admitting that they 'contained no single section of pure history' (I. 23).

[3] *ὧν τὰς μὲν λϛ′ τὴν πᾶσαν Αἰγυπτίων περιεχούσας φιλοσοφίαν οἱ προειρημένοι ἐκμανθάνουσι. Ibid.*

is the famous *Book of the Dead*, or *Ritual*[1]; portions of it dating backwards, we are told, as far as the '12th dynasty,' and thus preserving to us a considerable fragment of the older Pharaonic times. In one department of our subject,—the supposed condition of the human soul after death, and the religious service rendered by her in the world invisible,—I hope to profit largely by suggestions borrowed from this quarter. With regard, however, to the leading characteristics of the old mythology, all other data now accessible to ordinary scholars are less copious and explicit. They consist of hieroglyphic names, or titles, or genealogies of gods, surviving with appropriate emblems on the various tablets, tombs, and obelisks; of colloquies between the gods and kings; of sacred formulæ, as chants in honour of some divinity, or prayers for the deceased, or exhortations to survivors, each transmitted to us on rolls of papyri, and most of them deriving fresh elucidation from reports of Herodotus, or else from statements drawn by Plutarch out of theological works of Manetho.

The question which, as heretofore, excites our special interest at the very outset of our task has reference to the old Egyptian theories on the central truth of all religion,—the being and attributes of God. Now in replying to this question it is commonly admitted that Egyptians had no single word in use by which to indicate the grand idea of a Supreme Intelligence. It may be that such term had never been unknown to the initiated few, though treated as unutterable in all ordinary circles[2]; yet the statement thus suggested carries with it also the admission that belief in one only God was far from being the established creed of the Egyptian people. And in strict accordance with this fact is the exceeding paucity[3] of

[1] Edited, in hieroglyphs, by Lepsius, with the title *Todtenbuch der Aegypter* (Leipzig, 1842). Mr. Birch, who is at present engaged upon an English translation of the whole, has given a short epitome of this curious volume in *Egypt. Hierogl.* pp. 271 sq. Portions of the work *in extenso* have moreover seen the light through other channels. I may also remark that the followers of the Seyffarth (anti-Champollion) school of interpretation have already access to a German version of the *Todtenbuch* in Seyffarth's *Theolog. Schriften der alt. Aegypter.*

[2] Wilkinson, who leans to the idea of some original monotheism, has suggested this account of the matter. The points, however, which Herodotus declines to publish (*e.g.* II. 62) were of a somewhat different kind. On the reputed ἀπόρρητα of the 'greater mysteries' in Egypt and elsewhere, see Warburton, *Div. Leg.* Bk. II. sect. 4.

[3] 'It is worthy of remark that the worship of the supreme God is scarcely mentioned in the history of the Egyptians.' Prichard, *E. Mythol.* p. 292.

statements and allusions which imply exclusive worship in one district of one sole divinity[1]. The aptest parallel is found, if I mistake not, in the history of Hindú religions. With a vague idea of unity which lingered in the background of his metaphysical system ages after it exerted any practical effect, the Old Egyptian had been fascinated more and more by the mysterious powers and processes of nature, till abandoning the ancient faith in God, he bowed in adoration of the world above, beneath, around him. He was still indeed possessed of phraseology which betokened some original conception of a Power superior to the physical elements, and even was accustomed to transfer to it the properties of spirit, as volition and intelligence, which in himself he felt to be inseparable from the true idea of power. He spoke at times of 'a great builder,' 'a creator of the universe,' 'a creator self-created,' 'a soul of the sun,' 'a lord of the two horizons,' a chief 'father of the gods,' 'a mother' also 'of the gods,' a god who was 'the husband of his mother,' 'a goddess-mother of the highest god,' whose glory was that she 'proceeded from herself'; nay, so completely had these forms of speech been tinctured with monotheism as to lead in many writers to a firm belief that all the various gods and goddesses of ancient Egypt are personifications only of Divine omnipotence, or rather are the issue of an intellectual struggle, which was bent on forming the most worthy thoughts of God, and paying homage in the vast profusion of its titles to one personal Deity.

But strict analysis[2] of all such titles, when conducted in the light which we derive from a comparison of other ancient

[1] See the motto at the head of this chapter, which is the passage generally adduced as evidence of a belief in one supreme God, *Kneph*, the ram-headed god of the Thebaid, 'unbegotten and immortal.' The assertion of Plutarch was not true, however, of any early period known to history; and subsequently *Ammon* or *Ammon-Ra* was far more generally worshipped in that region, if we except the island of Elephantine: see below, p. 444.

[2] 'We can find no sufficient evidence for the opinion that the various gods of Egypt are but symbols and personifications of the attributes and powers of one Being, whom the priests, if not the people, recognised as the only true God:' Kenrick, I. 437. The great Cudworth, who took his ideas of Egyptian theology from Iamblichus and other writers of that school, contended, not unnaturally, that the invisible gods of the pagans are the Divine attributes deified (*Intel. Syst.* II. 237 sq. Lond. 1845). He then proceeds as follows (p. 245): 'The pagan theology went sometimes yet a strain higher, they not only thus supposing God to pervade the whole world, and to be diffused through all things......but also Himself to be in a manner all things. That the ancient Egyptian theology, from whence the theologies of other nations were derived,

systems[1], will be sure to make us hesitate before subscribing to this grand conclusion. Here, as there, it is discovered that so far from such personifications carrying up the mind to a transcendent unity, in which 'all the gods of the Egyptian mythology met and became one,' the opposite result has been more generally apparent. The bright memory of one only God has faded from the human spirit; His functions have been all assigned to a succession of subordinate divinities, who constitute *the* objects of Egyptian worship; and the want of fixity or depth in man's religious conceptions is again betrayed at every turn, by the facility with which he can attribute the same glorious titles to different divinities.

The simplest key to all this vagueness and apparent vacillation is contained in the hypothesis, now frequently adopted, that the primitive form of paganism in Egypt was really pantheistic. Till the process, by which single powers of nature were gradually personified, had issued there as elsewhere, in the *humanising* of the earlier race of elemental gods, it was impossible to fix the line of demarcation by which one was distinguished from the other. The attributes were interchanged, the powers themselves were seemingly confounded, because they all at first were viewed as finite emanations of some all-pervading energy. 'Nature' thus became the highest god of the Egyptian priesthood; while the people brought their offerings to some one or other of the manifold powers of nature. Their divinities in general corresponded to the functions of the different sexes; they were either paternal or maternal, active or passive, generative or productive; now believed to be exerting their specific influence from the loftiest spheres of being; now in beasts that minister to our convenience, or in hideous reptiles that are crawling at our feet; at one time challenging the homage of the Old Egyptian in their simplest form of light or fire, of earth or water; at a second stooping down from his unclouded sky on gracious or malignant missions; at a third descending more completely to the region of the senses, or identified with local objects, and especially with that phenomenon which was and is the crowning wonder of his native valley,—the rise, the overflow, the retrogression of the waters of the Nile.

This rapid survey of the old Egyptian theology receives,

ran so high as this, is evident from that excellent monument of Egyptian antiquity, the Saitic inscription often mentioned: "I am all that was, is, and shall be:" see below, p. 442.

[1] Cf. above, pp. 127 sq.; p. 288.

indeed, most ample illustration as a fuller insight is obtained into the meaning of the ancient monuments. As early as the visit of Herodotus[1], and probably for ages long anterior, the Egyptians were accustomed to distribute all their chief divinities into three special classes, the first consisting of eight, the second of twelve members, and the third, perhaps, of an indefinite number, all of whom were said to have been generated by gods of the previous class, as these owed their existence to the first. Some difficulty, it is true, has been experienced in determining which gods should be admitted to a place in the first of the three orders; and it seems most likely that Egyptians of different provinces[2] would, even in the age of Herodotus, have stated their belief respecting this great ogdoad with considerable variation.

Still if we may argue from the order in the list where Manetho professes to arrange the several gods[3], who were believed to have held sway in Egypt, long before all human dynasties, the foremost rank should be assigned to *Ptah*, the Vulcan of the Latins[4], and Hephæstus of the Greeks. If not the God of all Egypt, he was certainly regarded as supreme within the cycle of divinities who were especially adored at Memphis. One designation of the whole country had moreover been derived in early times from this alleged supremacy: for *Egypt* (Αἴγυπτος) seems to be not only identical with *Kopt*, but also a Greek form of *Kah-Ptah*[5] 'land of Ptah,' the land which recognised in Ptah

[1] II. 145. He is pointing out in this passage that the order of the gods, according to the Egyptians, was very different from the Hellenic view: Ἐν Ἕλλησι μέν νυν νεώτατοι τῶν θεῶν νομίζονται εἶναι Ἡρακλῆς τε καὶ Διόνυσος καὶ Πάν· παρ' Αἰγυπτίοισι δὲ Πὰν μὲν ἀρχαιότατος, καὶ τῶν ὀκτὼ τῶν πρώτων λεγομένων θεῶν· Ἡρακλῆς δὲ τῶν δευτέρων, τῶν δυώδεκα λεγομένων εἶναι· Διόνυσος δὲ, τῶν τρίτων, οἳ ἐκ τῶν δυώδεκα θεῶν ἐγένοντο.

[2] Cf. Lepsius, *Chronol.* Einl. p. 253, note.

[3] 'Primus Ægyptiorum deus *Vulcanus* fuit, qui etiam ignis repertor apud eos celebratur. Ex eo *Sol*,' etc. Manethon. *Dynast.* (printed in Bunsen's 'Appendix of Authorities,' No. II.).

[4] He is Cicero's second Vulcanus (*De Nat. Deorum*, III. 55) 'in Nilo natus, *Phthas*, ut Ægyptii appellant, quem *custodem* esse Ægypti volunt.'

[5] Uhlemann, *Aegypt. Alt.* II. 11, 12, who instances the similar word Ἡφαιστία, which Greek writers applied to Egypt, and also mentions that the Ethiopic name of the country is *Gobzo*. The prefix *αἰ* may perhaps be illustrated by such forms as *αἰγυπιός* which was used by Homer for *γύψ*. Bunsen finds the derivation, or at least the sister-form, of *Ptah* itself in פתח 'to open' (*Egypt's Place*, I. 383, n. 252), so that *Ptah* (he thinks) was primarily the 'great Revealer.' Mr. Osburn, again (*Mon. Hist.* I. 263), discovers *Ptah* in *Phut*, the fourth son of Ham.

her chief divinity. The special functions of this god are indicated by his title of 'creator of the sun and moon.' He is not only, like the Greek Hephæstus, eminent for plastic skill, but also is the proper *demiurgus* of the universe, the shaper of primeval matter, the 'leader of the mundane artisans[1],' or, in the highest and most abstract form of the conception, Ptah is the original force of nature and the world-begetting fire[2].

The oldest representation of him was a child or bandy-legged dwarf, reminding us at once of pigmy statues sacred to Hephæstus, and also of the idols (the *Pataikoi*)[3] carried by Phœnician mariners on the prows of their triremes. But in other, and it seems more recent, representations, Ptah is worshipped under a more perfectly human form. He is entitled 'lord of the gracious countenance' and also 'lord of truth.' As such he is accompanied by a female figure (Truth or Justice) with the ostrich feather on her head[4]. He holds before him in both hands an emblem of stability or duration, the so-called Nilometer[5], which is combined with the symbols of life and the kukufa-sceptre. On his head he wears a skull-cap like the pilos of Vulcan; while the body is completely swathed, in mummy-fashion, so that the hands alone are seen protruding outside the envelope. 'Perhaps the swathed body and protruded hands may symbolise the first putting forth of a creative power in action, which had been previously hidden and quiescent[6].' The same functions are suggested more distinctly by a living emblem, which was specially sacred to the great Egyptian *demiurgus*, viz. the beetle of the Nile (or *scarabæus*). Some indeed have traced the ground of this connexion to different causes[7]; but the instinct which directs the beetle to deposit her egg on the soft wet mud of the Nile, and the astonish-

[1] This is the expression of Iamblichus; cf. Wilkinson, *Anc. Egypt*, 2nd ser. I. 249 sq.

[2] 'Die erste als Urfeuer gedachte zeugende Kraft:' Döllinger, *Heidenthum und Judenthum*, p. 412, Regensburg, 1857. Similarly Eckermann, *Mythologie*, I. 74, Halle, 1848: 'Er ist das Lebensprincip im Universum, die *zeugende Urkraft*.'

[3] Herod. III. 37: see Mr. Blakesley's note. The derivation which he seeks is probably to be found in the Egyptian *Ptah*: whence Παταϊκοί.

[4] Wilkinson, as above, p. 250; Bunsen, *Egypt's Place*, I. 382.

[5] Bunsen, *Ibid.*

[6] Kenrick, I. 380.

[7] *e.g.* It was believed that the Nile beetles were all males, or else were altogether without distinction of sex, and therefore fit emblems of creative power, 'self-acting and self-sufficient.' M. de Rougé (*Revue Archéologique*, VIIIe année, p. 53) has given his sanction to this view of the scarabæus-symbol. He also adds (p. 54) that the idea of divine generation as dwelt upon by Iamblichus 'n'est pas un produit de l'esprit philosophique des derniers temps, mais qu'elle appartient à la portion antique et traditionelle des mystères.'

ing skill with which she frames and finally rolls away 'the ball which is the nidus of her future offspring[1],' are such vivid images of functions everywhere ascribed to Ptah, that I prefer this exposition of the symbol to all others which have been suggested.

It is one of the prerogatives of Ptah in the Memphitic system of mythology, that he combines within himself the properties of both the sexes. He is one of two androgynal divinities. The second member of this class is *Neith*[2], the Greek Athene; Ptah in his exalted rank becoming to the male what Neith is to the female deities: and yet so closely are the functions of the two commingled or confounded in some representations that Neith is really the female counterpart of the great *demiurgus*. He is the primary paternal element in nature, she the primary conceptive element. He is the father of the sun, she is the mother of the same luminary ('the great cow, engenderer of the sun')[3]. He is the primordial fire, while she is the primordial space or chaos, self-producing[4], coeternal with him, and coequal, or in other words the 'feminine ether' everywhere diffused as the material basis of all forms of created being[5].

In proportion, however, as the old Egyptians learned to *humanise* their chief divinity, they seem to have assigned him a more human consort. The 'beloved of Ptah' was Pasht (Bubastis, or 'Diana'), commonly depicted as the lioness- or rather the cat-headed goddess. Like Neith she was occasionally styled the

[1] See Mr. Osburn's minute description, *Monum. Hist.* I. 204, 205.

[2] In Plato's time Neith (whom he identifies with Ἀθήνη) was specially worshipped at Sais in the Delta; and Cicero (*De Nat. Deor.* III. 59) speaking of his second Minerva adds: 'orta Nilo, quam Ægyptii Saitæ colunt;' but, as Mr. Kenrick remarks, it is plain from Herod. II. 59, that her worship also extended through the whole country. Mr. Blakesley, on Herod. II. 100, argues in favour of the old notion respecting the verbal identity of Neith and Athene. Improbable as this may be (Kenrick, I. 387, n. 1), there is no doubt that we discover an early trace of the Egyptian name in queen Nitocris (Neitokr = Ἀθήνη Νίκη). It is also interesting to remark that even Cambyses, who is commonly represented as waging a quasi-religious war in Egypt, was nevertheless extremely scrupulous in making the due offerings 'to Neith, the divine mother of the principal gods of Sais:' see M. de Rougé's paper in the *Revue Archéologique*, VIIIe année, p. 40.

[3] Bunsen, I. 386: Kenrick, I. 390.

[4] Plutarch found this property in her very name, which he interpreted, rightly or wrongly, Ἦλθον ἀπ' ἐμαυτῆς.

[5] Cf. the following language of De Rougé, as above, p. 59: 'Dans la génération des dieux célestes ou secondaires, identifiés avec les astres, je comprends encore le rôle maternel du ciel comme espace, χώρα, et même comme matière, ὕλη, *fournissant une portion de l'éther céleste au démiurge pour nourrir ses germes divins.*'

Great Mother, and as such was represented carrying the emblems of life in her hands. She also was esteemed a great fire-goddess[1], which explains the real ground of her alliance with Ptah; but, notwithstanding, her precise relation to the older series of Memphitic gods is very difficult to determine.

The next divinity, whose claims to be connected with that series are indisputable, is the sun-god of Lower Egypt, *Ra*[2] (or with the definite article *Phra*); the centre of whose worship was at On (the Heliopolis of the Greeks). By some he is promoted to the foremost place[3] in the Egyptian pantheon. He alone in the succession of the highest gods is not accompanied by a female counterpart. He only is invested with a plenary jurisdiction. To his honour it was chanted that, while he, and he alone, is the chief 'source of life in heaven and on the earth, he is himself the unbegotten[4].' We have seen, however, that the luminary thus adored by the Egyptians, is described in other places as the offspring of Ptah; whom he succeeds accordingly in the administration of the world. We also heard him called the offspring of the goddess Neith, of her who, notwithstanding, had been made to publish almost in the same breath: 'I am the things that have been, that are, and that will be; no one has uncovered my skirts[5].'

A simple key to all such enigmatical language will be found, if we remember only that Ptah and Neith are the two great parent principles of the universe, and therefore the creation of the sun, the disentangling of primordial light from darkness, would be naturally regarded as the work of one or both of them, according to the fancy of the different worshippers. The sun, it

[1] See the passage from Brugsch's *Travels*, quoted by Döllinger, p. 412. That eminent Egyptologer is of opinion that Pasht was again superseded in later times by Neith.

[2] Copt. ρη 'sun;' φρη 'the sun.'

[3] Lepsius has of late years warmly advocated this hypothesis in a paper *Ueber den ersten Aegyptischen Götterkreis* &c. read before the *Akademie der Wissenschaften* (1851), and published among their Transactions. His main principle is thus stated (p. 193): 'Es bleibt folglich nur die umgekehrte Annahme übrig, und diese bestätigt sich meiner Meinung nach auf das Bestimmteste von allen Seiten, dass der *Sonnenkult* selbst der frühste Kern und das allgemeinste Princip des ägyptischen Götterglaubens war, welcher vor allen Lokalkulten vorhanden, in allen einen wesentlichen Theil bildete, und überhaupt nie, bis in die spätesten Zeiten, aufhörte als die äusserliche Spitze des gesammten Religionssystems angesehen zu werden.'

[4] See various passages to this effect excerpted by De Rougé, as before, pp. 54, 55.

[5] Mr. Kenrick is undoubtedly correct (I. 389, n. 5) in referring to Deut. xxii. 30 for the explanation of this language. It does not imply the mystery of Neith's being (as De Rougé even seems to think, *Ibid.* p. 59), but the fact of her virginity.

was concluded, like the other objects of external nature, had begun to be, and therefore owed his being to the Ultimate Principles of all things. This consideration will again enable us to understand the mythological language of some ancient hymns[1], in which the worshipper, excluding from his view the functions of the *demiurgus*, and no longer dwelling on the old relation between Neith and Ra, has pictured the diurnal motion of the sun-god, as a species of relapse into his native element. 'Thou sheddest thy beams upon the back of thy mother.' 'Thy mother, the sky, is stretching out her arms for thee.' 'O father of the gods, thou reunitest thyself with thy mother on the western mountain. She receives thee daily into her arms.' 'When thou shinest in the dwelling of Night, thou revisitest the sky, thy Mother.'

It is not indeed unlikely that in very primitive times as well as through the period when such hymns as these were graven on the tombs of Lower Egypt, Ra had been exalted to the highest place in the affections both of king and people. Ramses the Great already sacrificed to him as to 'the lord of the two worlds, who is enthroned on the sun's disk, who moves his egg, who appears in the abyss of the heaven[2].' Ra was thus emphatically *king*[3] of the gods: and mortals who had been entrusted with the government of Egypt were esteemed in some mysterious way his progeny, his favourites, his vicegerents. His own title (Ra or Phra) has reappeared in the official name of *Pharaoh*[4]. None of the Egyptian kings[5], indeed, could be admitted to his office till instructed in the secret learning of the priests, and, where such transfer might be necessary, incorporated with the sacerdotal order: yet as soon as his initiation was completed he assumed a power analogous to that enjoyed of old time by the Incas of Peru and now by Emperors of the Middle Kingdom; he was 'president of the assemblies;' he regulated the whole cycle of religious worship as well as the machinery of the Egyptian state; he was himself the object of one kind of adoration[6];

[1] De Rougé, as before, p. 56.

[2] Bunsen, I. 387.

[3] Lepsius, as before, p. 194.

[4] Dr. Hincks (*Engl. Rev.* as before, p. 101) has also pointed out that the names of the earlier Egyptian kings consisted in almost every instance of the name of the sun, and a simple or compound epithet or qualification: cf. Müller, *Amerik. Urrelig.* p. 305. Similarly Potipherah, priest of Heliopolis, (Gen. xli. 45) has been explained by Phont-Phra, 'priest of the Sun.'

[5] Wilkinson, 1st ser. I. 245, 246, 2nd ed.

[6] Diodorus (I. 90) speaks even more strongly: Διὰ δὲ τὰς αὐτὰς αἰτίας δοκοῦσιν Αἰγύπτιοι τοὺς ἑαυτῶν βασιλεῖς προσκυνεῖν τε καὶ τιμᾶν, ὡς πρὸς ἀλήθειαν ὄντας θεούς.

for in him the gods, or more especially the kings of gods and highest of all potentates, had condescended to exert a more than human energy.

But on passing to the upper province of the old Mizraim, there is far less certainty respecting the true character of her chief divinities. *Kneph*, or Chnubis, who was once regarded as the master-spirit of the system, as in some degree the fountain of vitality for Ptah himself, and *the* immortal, self-begotten deity of the Thebaid[1], is adjudged by Lepsius to be one of the most modern products of the Græco-Egyptian theorising[2]. Only as conjoined with Ra could Kneph be styled 'the highest god,' and worshipped as the formative or spiritual principle. The glorious Ammon, also, who had been invested with a like pre-eminence, inasmuch as the Hellenic writers were accustomed to entitle him the 'Zeus of Egypt,' has been similarly disparaged and dethroned by modern criticism[3]. It is contended that until the seat of native empire was transferred to Thebes, and some amalgamation of the pantheons of Upper and Lower Egypt had resulted there in the projection of a great compound divinity, who bore the title *Ammon-Ra*, the primitive god of Thebes was strictly local in his character, and so upon a level with the vast majority of deities.

The greater gods of Upper Egypt whom Lepsius places at the head of his new series, immediately after Ammon-Ra, are

[1] See the motto prefixed to this chapter. The story of Ptah springing from an egg, which issued out of the mouth of Kneph (? Copt. *nef*, 'to blow or breathe'), is no older than Porphyry; and although we may allow that the peculiar symbol of the mundane egg is very ancient, the use made of it by the Neo-Platonists, in its relation to Kneph, was obviously directed to the establishment of their favourite theory as to the priority of some Intellectual Principle in the old Egyptian system: see above, p. 434. Döllinger says of him with apparent justice: 'Seine Auffassung als göttlicher Lebensgeist oder Weltseele scheint erst der spätesten Zeit kurz vor oder nach Christus anzugehören:' p. 411.

[2] As before, p. 164, n. 1.

[3] *Ibid.* p. 173:......'war bis zur Erhebung Thebens wo er als Lokalgott verehrt wurde, ein untergeordneter wenig genannter Gott.' Bunsen on the contrary maintains that 'he stands incontestably at the head of a great cosmogonic development.' (I. 371.) However this may be, it is now generally conceded that many of the earliest attributes of Ammon were identical with those of Khem, the ithyphallic god, or Pan of Herodotus (cf. *Revue Archéol.* xive année, p. 211). Both have the title 'husband of his mother:' both wear the same badge, or head-dress, of long straight feathers; and both are viewed as more especially gifted with generative and productive power. Mr. Osburn, in accordance with his theory, finds the son of Noah Cham (Ham) in the Egyptian Ammon (Amun); and Noah himself in Kneph.

Mentu (Month) and *Atmu* (Tum)[1]. Yet these again, he thinks, are both to be regarded as derivatives from the sun-god: they conjointly fill the place ascribed to Ra in the mythology of Lower Egypt; they are 'children of Ra,' the one an emblem of his superterranean, and the other of his subterranean power; the one associated with the rising, and the other with the setting or nocturnal sun[2]. In this connexion only is it true that Mentu-Ra became the 'god of both the Egypts'; or that Atmu could be called 'the author of all fecundity.' Another of the Theban gods was *Mue* (or Light), who is depicted here and there not only as a son of Ra, but also as the offspring of the solar deities, whose lineage we have just considered. In like manner *Tefnet*, the companion or feminine counterpart of Mue, whom Lepsius wishes to include among the greater gods of the Thebaid, is entitled with a similar import, 'daughter of the Sun.'

It must, however, be acknowledged by all candid minds that no small measure of uncertainty continues to hang over this attempted distribution of the primitive gods of Egypt. We are barely able to discern the outlines of a systematic classification. The fabric of the old theology, if such it may be termed, was built up gradually into a whole by 'the agglutination of parts having a separate origin[3].' At first, as men relinquished the idea of one great Personal Spirit, ruling all things by His sovereign will, they yielded to the witchery of external nature and bowed down before a concourse of provincial deities: the varying phases of religious thought gave birth to corresponding variations of this first mythology; yet everywhere the felt necessity of relying on a god superior to the many, led afresh to the investment of some member of the pantheon with a relative supremacy; until, upon the union of the several nomes, the greater gods were all more fully merged in two large classes, corresponding to political divisions of the Nile-valley. Such a fusion had moreover been promoted from within by the existence of religious sympathy. A link connecting the mythologies of Upper and Lower Egypt was supplied in all the early stages of their formation by the glorious sun-god, Ra,—the offspring of the oldest gods of Memphis, and identified, as we have seen, with one or more divinities whose native sphere is the Thebaid. Ra was, in like manner, the chief medium for advancing that more

[1] Cf. Döllinger, p. 410. A learned friend suggests the Copt. *ατ-μου* = 'immortal' as explanatory of *Atmu*. In Copt. *μου* signifies 'death;' *μουε* 'light.'

[2] Lepsius, as before, p. 187. On this principle he explains the name 'Sun of Night' applied to Atmu.

[3] Kenrick, I. 363; Döllinger, p. 407.

perfect amalgamation, which begins to be distinctly visible at a later period: for how grave soever be the faults committed by Herodotus in classifying the old mythology of Egypt, the account is unimpeachable where he tells us, that in spite of all existing variations, the common worship of two deities prevailed in every canton of the great community[1].

These potentates were Isis and Osiris, who, as overlying or eclipsing all the rest, stand forth conspicuous, from the mouths of the Nile to Elephantine, and supply a centre both of worship for the multitude and speculation for the priestly order. It is probable that certain compound names, like Ptah-Sokari-Osiris[2], will turn out to be examples of transition from an earlier to a later way of thinking. They may also have borne witness to religious struggles[3] and to compromises effected in particular districts. But the fact itself remains indisputable, that in the whole of what is properly entitled the historic period, Isis and Osiris, with a family-circle of inferior deities, are made to play the principal part in the mythology of ancient Egypt.

What, then, is the true relation of these deities to gods who were confessedly members of the 'first order'? Did they constitute an independent and contemporaneous group? Or did they actually succeed the others in the manner intimated by Herodotus, and so commence, by their ascendancy alike in Thebes and Memphis, a new period of Egyptian history? Now in answering such inquiries it is most important to remember that the name, the emblems, and a few at least of the specific functions of Osiris, have been actually traced on monuments of high antiquity; for instance, on the coffin of Menkeres (or Mycerinus) belonging to the '4th dynasty.' Commencing therefore from such facts as this we soon arrive at the conclusion that Osiris had for ages coexisted[4] with Ptah himself in some departments of the Delta; as Brahmá, the younger god of Hindústán, eventually supplanted Indra, the most prominent of Vaidic deities. The solemn worship of Osiris was at first,

1 *θεοὺς γὰρ δὴ οὐ τοὺς αὐτοὺς ἅπαντες ὁμοίως Αἰγύπτιοι σέβονται, πλὴν Ἴσιός τε καὶ Ὀσίριος, τὸν δὴ Διόνυσον εἶναι λέγουσι*, II. 42.

2 Wilkinson, 2nd ser. I. 253.

3 It is well to keep in mind this possible source of change in the religious symbolism of Egypt. Lepsius, as before, pp. 196 sq., has given a detailed account of one struggle between pure sun-worship and Ammon-worship in the reign of Amenophis IV. of the 18th dynasty. The 'reformatory' labours of that monarch were, however, all undone by the reaction 'of the old national hierarchy.'

4 Such is also Mr. Kenrick's conclusion, I. 358, 359.

however, circumscribed in somewhat narrow limits. In allusion to that fact he is entitled 'lord of This' and 'lord of Abydos'[1] in Upper Egypt; though for centuries anterior[2] to the visits of Hellenic tourists, it is plain that he was raised to a position of unrivalled majesty, approaching far more nearly than the other members of the pantheon to the rank of one almighty and illimitable God. He gathers up into himself the choicer and more god-like attributes of all the male divinities; while Isis may be taken as the general representative of functions belonging to the opposite sex. The two together form a dyad. Osiris is the active, plastic, generative principle; and as such he is most naturally connected with a female counterpart, who, contemplated under different aspects, will be found to have assumed to him the manifold relations of sister and of spouse, of daughter and of mother[3].

There is also reason for concluding that Osiris of Abydos had been gradually identified with Ra, the sun-god of Heliopolis; for such amalgamation is not only implied in the new formula *Osiris-Ra*, but is expressly mentioned in the works of Egyptologers both ancient and modern[4]. Like Ra, Osiris, though occasionally described as 'self-begotten,' had a mythological pedigree assigned to him: he was the eldest son of Seb, (Κρόνος) and of Nut or Nutpe (Ῥέα)[5], to both of whom he is declared superior ('greater than his father and more powerful than his mother'). In one respect alone he differs widely from the older sun-god,—in requiring for the exercise of his specific powers the

[1] Lepsius, as before, pp. 190, 191.

[2] The same writer has offered a very probable explanation of the mistake of Herodotus in placing Osiris among the tertiary, instead of primary, gods of Egypt. (*Chronol.* p. 253.) Wilkinson had long before observed: 'If Osiris was not nominally one of the eight great gods, he in reality held a rank equal to any:' 2nd ser. I. 158, note.

[3] Döllinger, p. 413.

[4] Lepsius, *Ueber den ersten Aegypt. Götterk.* p. 194. This writer denies, however, very positively that there was any *genealogical* connexion between the Osiris-group and other old divinities, either in the Memphitic or the Theban series: cf. Diod. I. 11, where Osiris and Isis are plainly identified with the sun and moon respectively. Plutarch (*De Isid. et Osirid.* c. LII.) has given us substantially the same account; and in the monuments we have a further confirmation of this theory: 'ils nous apprennent en effet que la divinité qui remplit le premier rôle est le Soleil, et qu'Osiris, comme la plupart des personnages divins dont l'Olympe égyptien est si malheureusement encombré, n'est qu'une forme particulière de cette divinité:' *Revue Archéol.* XIVe année, p. 193.

[5] This filiation is authorised in the *Book of the Dead* itself (*Rev. Arch.* as before, p. 202): yet the Copt. ⲛⲟⲩⲧⲉ seems to mean 'god,' and ⲛⲟⲩⲧⲉ-ⲡⲉ 'god of heaven.'

aid of some divinity like Isis, who inherits therefore the peculiar properties of the Great Mother, Neith, while he in virtue of some corresponding interchange with the old fire-god of Memphis reappears on more than one inscription as *Osiris-Ptah.*

Combining thus the several functions of creator, of enlightener, of fructifier, Osiris, in that ancient system of mythology, attracted to himself the homage, love, and adoration of the whole community[1]. Osirian hymns which are at length accessible to almost every student, will bear ample witness to this fact; for most of them are outbursts of religious feeling, stimulated by the thought of his transcendent qualities. Osiris is the 'lord of life,' the 'king of heaven,' 'the prince of gods,' 'the lord of ages,' 'the light of the world,' 'the dispenser of nutrition,' 'the quickener of the dead,' 'the guide,' 'the judge,' 'the leveller,' and 'the avenger.'

But instead of swelling this long catalogue of names, which separately taken have an obvious tendency to misinform the reader by suggesting parallels that have no true foundation, I prefer to give one single hymn, as nearly as I may, in its original completeness. It will further serve to introduce us to some other members of the great Osiris-family, and acquaint us with some other aspects of their mythological character. The text of this remarkable hymn is found inscribed upon a *stele*, which the French translator[2] places in the seventeenth century before the Christian era.

HYMN TO OSIRIS.

"Hail, Osiris! lord of the length of times, king of the gods, of names exceeding many[3], conspicuous for thy holy transformations and myste-

[1] Cf. Uhlemann, *Thoth*, pp. 27 sq., who remarks with more especial reference to his view of the Egyptian cosmogony which he elicits from the *Book of the Dead*, that it has 'viele Aehnlichkeit mit der mosaischen, die *ohne Zweifel* [!] aus ihr hervorgegangen; es findet sich in derselben Nichts von einem ungeordneten Chaos wie bei Griechen und Römern; auch bei Aegyptern ist die Welt aus Nichts geschaffen, Alles Vorhandene aus der allmächtigen Hand der schaffenden Gottheit Osiris hervorgegangen.' But how, on this hypothesis, can we explain the co-existence of *two* cosmogonic principles, Ptah and Neith, Osiris and Isis? see above, pp. 441, 447. It is surely far more probable that the dualistic cosmogony of the Greeks to which Uhlemann here refers was itself of Egyptian origin. Such a supposition, I may add, is entirely borne out by the narrative of Diodorus (I. 7), who speaks of the sun as being itself a product of the element of fire (τὸ πυρῶδες); just as the Memphitic Ra was the child of the fire-god Ptah.

[2] M. Chabas, in the *Revue Archéologique*, 14ᵉ année (1857), pp. 65 sq., pp. 193 sq.

[3] As the translator remarks (p. 195), one chapter of the *Ritual* (or

rious emblems in the temples: exalted dweller in Tattu[1]; chief inclosed in Sokhem; master of invocations in Oer-ti; enjoying happiness in Hon; whose right it is to rule in the place of double justice; mysterious soul of him, who is the lord of the sphere; the holy one of the White Wall; soul of the sun; his body itself reposing in Sûten-si-nen; author of invocations in the region of the tree Ner; whose soul is made for watching; lord of the vast abode in Sesennû; greatest of the beings in Shas-hotep; lord in Abydos of the length of times. The way of his dwelling is in the To-sar[2]; his name is constant in the mouth of mortals. He is a god of the earth, an Atûm[3] who in the midst of gods is showering happiness on the creatures; a beneficent spirit in the place of spirits.

"From him descend the waters of the heavenly Nile. From him proceeds the wind. The air we breathe is (also) in his nostrils for his own contentment and the gladdening of his heart: he airs (or purifies) the realms of space, which taste of his felicity, because the stars that move therein obey him in the height of heaven.

"He opens the grand doors; he is the master of invocations in the southern sky and adorations in the northern; the constellations which move onward are all under his immediate gaze; they form his dwelling-place, as well as constellations which remain at rest[4]. To him, by the command of Seb [his father] sacrifice is offered: gods in the firmament adore him with respect, divine chiefs with reverence, all with supplications. Those who rank among the venerable ones all recognise his high authority; the whole earth gives glory to him, when his holiness engages in a conflict: he is an illustrious Sahû among Sahûs, exalted in position, permanent in empire. He is the excellent master of the gods, beautiful and lovely. All who see him of whatever country respect and love him. All who have enjoyed his condescension exalt his name to the highest rank. He has the power of command alike in heaven and earth. Abundant acclamations are addressed to him on the festival of Ûk; consentient acclamations from the two worlds.

"He is the elder, the first-born of his brothers, the chief of the gods. He it is that executes justice in the two worlds, and plants the son upon the father's seat. He is the praise of his father Seb, the darling of his mother Nû [Nut]. Of mighty arm, he overthrows the impure; invincible, he crushes every foe; he strikes terror into all that hate him; he breaks down the barriers of the wicked; ever fearless, he is ever on the alert; he is the son of Seb, commanding both the worlds. He (Seb) has seen his virtues and directed him to guide the nations by the hand to larger measures of prosperity. He (Osiris) fabricated this world with his hand, the waters and the air, the vegetables, all fowls and winged creatures, all fish, all reptiles and four-footed beasts. The earth pays rightful homage to the son of Nû [Nut]; the world rejoices once

Book of the Dead) enumerates as many as a hundred appellations under which Osiris was adored.

[1] This and the following proper names appear to denote localities especially connected with Osiris-worship.

[2] 'Un lieu que les mânes devaient traverser avant d'arriver à la demeure d'Osiris, l'Hadès égyptien.' Chabas, p. 70, n. 1.

[3] *i.e.* like *Atmu*, the solar deity; see above, p. 445.

[4] 'Nous voyons par notre texte que les Egyptiens se figuraient les *khimou* placés en face du Soleil, qui y faisait ses résidences, c'est-à-dire qui y stationnait tour à tour.' p. 71, n. 1.

again, when like the Sun he mounts upon his father's seat; he shines on the horizon, he diffuses dawn upon the face of darkness; he irradiates the light by his double plume; he inundates the world, like the Sun (which shines) from the highest empyrean. His diadem is conspicuous in the summit of the heavens; and is allied (united) with the stars: he is the leader of all gods. In will and word he is benignant, the praise of the greater gods and the delight of the less.

"His sister [Isis] has taken care of him in driving away her enemies by a triple rout; she sends forth her voice in the brilliance of her mouth[1]; wise of tongue, her word is sure to prosper. In will and word she (also) is benignant. Isis is her name, the illustrious, the avenger of her brother's wrong. She sought him without resting; she walked the circuit of this world, lamenting him; she rested not until she found him; light was given out from her[2]; a wind was produced by [the motion of] her wings: she made the invocation at the funeral of her brother: she carried off the elements [elementary particles] of the god of the tranquil heart: she extracted his essence: she made a child [of it]: she gave the foster-child her arm to suck[3]. The place where that occurred is unknown [to mortals].

"His arm (the child's arm) is become strong in the great dwelling-place of Seb. The gods are overjoyed on the arrival of Osiris, son of Horus, fearless, justified, son of Isis, son of Osiris. The divine chiefs collect around him: the gods recognise in him the universal lord. The lords of justice who are met together to correct iniquity are delighted to pay their homage in the great dwellingplace of Seb to the lord of justice. The reign of justice in that region appertains to him. Horus has found his justification (word of justice): he comes forward crowned with the royal wreath by order of Seb. He has received the royalty of the two worlds: the crown of the upper region is planted on his head. By him the world is judged in that which it contains: heaven and earth are under his immediate presence ('le lieu de sa face'). He rules all human beings, the pure, the race of the inhabitants of Egypt and the foreign (barbarous) people. The sun goes round according to his purpose, who also directs the wind, the river, the fluids, the wood of living plants and all vegetable nature. As the god of seeds, he is the giver of all vegetation, and of the precious *kufi:* he brings forth abundance and dispenses it to all the earth. Mankind are all in raptures, their feelings (bowels) are delighted, their hearts are full of joy, because of the lord of supplications. Every one adores his bounty: sweet is his love in us; his tenderness surrounds the heart; great is his love in all the feelings (bowels).

"We render justice to the son of Isis: his enemy falls beneath his fury, and the fautor of iniquity at the sound of his voice: the violent is hastening to his end: the son of Isis, the avenger of his father, is close by him.

"Sacred and beneficent are his titles: fear (or veneration) finds his place: his laws command immutable respect: the way is open: the foot-paths are open: the worlds are both contented: evil flies before him: and with him as her lord the peaceful earth is waxing fruitful. Justice is established by its lord, who menaces iniquity.

[1] 'Le sens est que la déesse avait le don de l'éloquence.' *Ibid.* p. 75, n. 4.

[2] The meaning of this clause is said to be doubtful. M. Chabas renders: 'elle a fait de la lumière avec ses plumes.'

[3] See Plutarch, *De Isid. et Osirid.* c. XVI.

"Delicious is thy heart, O Ûnnefer (revealer of good), son of Isis! He has assumed the crown of the upper region: the title of his father is recognised for him in the great dwelling-place of Seb. He is Phra when he speaks, he is Thoth in his writings. The divine chiefs are satisfied.

"That which thy father Seb ordained for thee, let it be done according to his word."

Reserving the more ethical aspects both of this and other kindred hymns for independent consideration, it is first of some importance to remark, that the Osiris-group, as here depicted, consisting of Seb and Nut, of Isis and Osiris, together with the offspring of the latter pair, ('Horus, the child'), can scarcely have originated in the deification of purely Egyptian nature. In the present stage of the great mythe, there is no disposition, for example, to identify Osiris with the river Nile. His throne is still exalted high above the heavens: the sun itself is the majestic symbol of his universal sovereignty; from thence he looks resplendent and complacent like the monarch of this sublunary world. He dies indeed, as in the later version of the story, and Isis[1], sorrowing and indignant, searches for him in the double character of spouse and sister, and on finding him conducts his funeral obsequies. Here also he comes forth resuscitated on the mundane theatre of being, in the person of his royal son and representative, who therefore bears the sacred name Osiris. Yet in all such highly coloured pictures there are wanting not a few of those distinctive touches, which had afterwards, as we shall see, connected the Osirian mythus with the empire of the Pharaohs and localised it more completely in the Valley of the Nile.

The primitive worship of all objects like Osiris may be contemplated under two aspects, differing somewhat from each other, but incapable of any rigorous or formal separation. That worship seems to be in some localities directly *solar*. Fortunes of Osiris have been interwoven or identified with those of the great orb of day. His votaries have an eye exclusively to

[1] 'Demeter was naturally identified with the Egyptian goddess [Isis]. As Isis bewailed the lost Osiris, so Demeter bewailed the lost Persephone. The sorrows of the bereaved mother and the widowed wife are, of all human sorrows, the deepest and the most hopeless. Unable to find consolation on earth, the sufferer yearns after heavenly sympathy, seeks and surely finds, among the objects of her worship, one who has borne the like afflictions, and is prompt to pity and to redress. Thus, if the comparison may be made without irreverence and without offence, the Isis and Demeter of Paganism were shadows which suffering humanity created for its comfort, in anticipation of the perfect type which it afterwards found in the Mater Dolorosa.' Clark's *Peloponnesus*, p. 37.

periodic motions of the sun and the vicissitudes of the seasons; not so much in reference to the increase or the decrease of his luminous functions, as to seeming changes in his fructifying, fertilising power. In winter he appears to the imagination of the worshipper as languishing and dying; and all nature, ceasing to put forth her buds and blossoms, is believed to suffer with him: while at other seasons of the year the majesty of this great king of heaven is reasserted in the vivifying of creation and the gladdening of the human heart. There is an annual resurrection of all nature; for the sun-god is himself returning from the under-world,—the region of the dead. Or if we study the same representation in its more *telluric* aspect, what is there depicted as a mourning for Osiris is no longer emblematic merely of prostration in the sun-god: it imports more frequently the loss of vital forces in the vegetable kingdom, as the consequence of the solstitial heat. The earth herself becomes the principal sufferer; and the cause of all her passionate and despairing lamentations is the influence that dries up the fountains of her own vitality.

Now whichever be adjudged the primitive form, or the correct interpretation, of this old Osirian mythe, we must remember that, historically speaking, the substance of the mythe itself is not by any means peculiar to the Valley of the Nile. It recurs in nearly all countries bordering on the Mediterranean. It can often be directly traced to Asia, and as often to the agency of those Phœnician colonists, who, scattered thickly in the islands to the west of Syria, were importing to far distant havens, not their amber only but their civilisation and religious knowledge[1]. In the mother-country of Phœnicia[2], the Osirian worship had its ancient counterpart in mysteries of Adonis[3] and the annual

[1] Movers, *Die Religion und die Gottheiten der Phönizier*, pp. 12, sq. Bonn, 1841.

[2] See especially Lucian, *De Dea Syria*, c. 6 sqq. Among other curious particulars he informs us that some of the people of Byblus, at the foot of Lebanon, where the mysteries of Adonis were celebrated every year, and into which Lucian was himself initiated, were of opinion that those ceremonies had been really instituted for *Osiris*, and that he was buried in their country, not in Egypt: cf. Photius *Biblioth.* cod. 242, p. 343, ed. Bekker. In the hymn to Osiris given above, the translator has conjectured, independently of all discussions like the present, that Byblus was 'the region of the tree Ner,' there mentioned (p. 449) as one residence of Osiris. Since the above was written, I find that Brugsch, in his interesting paper *Die Adonisklage und das Linoslied* (Berlin, 1852), agrees in tracing the Adonis-mythe to Asia (p. 27), and in identifying Adonis and Osiris (p. 31).

[3] *Adonis*, there can be no doubt, is identical with אֲדֹנִי 'my lord': and also equivalent to *Tammuz*,

'weeping for Tammuz,' (Ezek. viii. 14). There, again, the fate of the divinity was rigorously identified with periodic changes in the aspect of external nature. The idea of an Adonis in the prime of life was the most vivid image which the Syrian mind could fashion of all fertilising and benignant powers. At length, however, the divinity sinks down oppressed and overwhelmed; his heart is pierced by some mysterious arrow: he dies, and in the sacred month, 'the month of Tammuz,' when the scorching blasts of summer are well-nigh exhausted, a large crowd of Syrian maids and matrons flock together from all quarters; they bemoan the loss of Tammuz; but their vehement ejaculations are all quickly followed by a series of impure and diabolic orgies: symptoms of returning life in nature are to them a signal for festivity as frantic as their former grief. Vitality is coming back to earth: and in its advent they perceive another 'finding' of their lost Adonis (εὕρεσις Ἀδώνιδος).

Nor is this the only instance of some close affinity between the old mythographers of Egypt and Phœnicia. Mingling with the other progeny of Ptah, or the Egyptian Vulcan, stand the great Cabeirian brothers[1], whose repute and worship were extensively diffused in various provinces of the west. The word *Cabeiri* is itself immediately explainable, if we resort to the Semitic languages: for there it means the 'Great' or 'Mighty Ones;' and thus is pointing in the same direction as the ancient dwarf-gods, which were also sacred images of Cabeiri, and were venerated with a kindred fervour by the rude Phœnician pilot and the polished priest of Memphis. The Cabeiri seem to have been eight in number; or, excluding *Esmûn* ('literally eight'), that one of the fraternity who was regarded as the chief or aggregate expression for the whole, we limit them to seven; which strongly indicates, in the opinion of some writers, an original identity of the Cabeiri with the more conspicuous of the heavenly bodies[2]. In the sacred books of China the 'seven

Ezek. viii. 14, in which passage the Vulg. renders 'ecce ibi mulieres sedebant plangentes *Adonidem*:' see Gesen. *Monum. Phœn.* II. 400. Among the Greeks the close connexion with Aphrodite-worship was still more apparent.

[1] Herod. II. 51, III. 37, and above, p. 440. Their father was also called *Sadyk* or *Sydyk*, which is possibly akin to צדיק. Movers (as before, p. 652) has very naturally expressed his wonder that any one should have doubted the identity of κάβειροι and כבירים (= θεοὶ μέγαλοι): for this identity was well known to the ancients.

[2] Thus Xenocrates, a Carthaginian writer (quoted by Clemens Alexand. *Cohortat. ad Gentes*, c. v. § 66), declares expressly ἑπτὰ μὲν θεοὺς εἶναι τοὺς πλανῆτας; and then adds in reference to *Esmûn* (the 'eighth' of the Cabeiri, Movers, p.

brilliant ones,' deemed worthy of peculiar homage, are the sun, the moon, and the five planets; while the planets, when regarded singly, have been made to bear the corresponding title of the 'five heavenly chiefs[1].' The Greek had similarly his seven θεοὶ μέγαλοι, and the Persian his 'seven ministers of the highest:' examples, which appear to be suggestive of the early spread of planet-worship, if they do not absolutely prove that astronomical principles had entered largely into the construction of all mythic systems,—that of Egypt not excepted[2].

Be this however as it may, there is no longer any doubt that in Phœnicia, more than the adjoining nations, we discover proofs of correspondency and contact with the Eygpt of the Pharaohs. In both countries[3] the foundation of mythology is completely *ditheistic.* The superior gods are ranked in pairs according to the functions of the different sexes: while the votaries of both those systems were familiar with the notion of androgynal, or compound, deities. The Baal of the Old Phœnician found the highest symbol of his vitalising power in the great monarch of the heavenly bodies; and corresponding with this fact, the sun-god, born of chaos and elemental fire, was the most glorious deity of the Old Egyptian. Both had also kept their hold with equal firmness on a mythe in which the changing aspects of the vegetable kingdom were set forth as periodic deaths and resurrections of the highest member of their pantheon. In both countries the ascription of benignant or of other properties to stars and planets, issued first of all in the idea of some inflexible Fate, some necessary Order, and then was culminating in the theory of a *magnus annus,* at the close of which it was expected that the whole creation would be reabsorbed, or would revert at least to its original elements.

These points of contact are indeed so many and so obvious, that explorers, setting out with different objects and as different

651) ὄγδοον δὲ τὸν ἐξ αὐτῶν συνεστῶτα κόσμον: cf. Cicero, *De Natura Deorum,* lib. I. § 34, who also quotes Xenocrates, to the same general effect.

[1] See above, p. 296, and n. 2.

[2] Uhlemann (*Aegypt. Alter.* II. 162 sq., *Thoth,* pp. 33 sq.) is a strong supporter of the 'astronomical principle' as applied to the unriddling of Egyptian mythology: but now and then his arguments appear to me unconvincing. He finds an astronomical reason for fixing the number of the primary gods at eight and of the secondary gods at twelve. Mr. Kenrick, (I. 367, 368), with less desire of systematizing, concedes the general truth of this theory, but adds that 'it is not likely that the whole system originated in any *one* principle.'

[3] On this characteristic of the Phœnician theology, see above, pp. 68 sq.

preconceptions, can hardly fail to meet together in the same conclusion,—a belief that the mythologies of Egypt and Phœnicia were pervaded by the same ideas and radiated from a common centre. Which of them was actually the older system: what had been the links of intercourse by which the two were held together, we are still unable to affirm with absolute certainty or precision. If, for instance, the historical character of the 'Old Monarchy' of Egypt have been fully vindicated by recent explorations, it will follow of necessity that interchanges of religious thought were long anterior[1] to the earliest inroads of the Hyksos or Phœnician shepherds; and the meeting-place will consequently have to be determined by following two great lines of civilisation farther backward, to that cradle of all art and language, of all science, letters and mythology—'the primitive land of Aram and the primitive empire in Babel[2].'

But before I pass to a minute consideration of the latest phase assumed in Egypt by the mythe of Isis and Osiris, or in other words the fullest evolution of the national belief in what may fairly be entitled the historic period, it is most important to recal attention to the creed of other and still earlier settlers in the Nile-valley. When the secondary race of colonists from Asia found their way to Egypt, they encountered there a form of superstition so thoroughly rooted in the heart of the people, that in spite of the political and social changes which passed over them, it always held its ground, and went on flourishing until the overthrow of paganism in Egypt. I am adverting to the *animal-worship* of that country; which deserves to be regarded as at once the most repulsive and most universal of its manifold superstitions. We must not suppose indeed that this idolatrous devotion to brute animals had always been unknown in other countries. Traces of it are detected in the primitive paganism of the Hellenic and Germanic tribes: it seems to have prevailed in every district of America[3], where gods and other spirits were believed on some occasions to 'possess' not only all varieties of living creatures, but the very plants and stones; it had existed, and exists at present, in all negro races, and indeed wherever man continues to be awed by a belief that the divinity he worships is impersonal Power, diffused throughout the universe, and manifested in all possible types of creaturely existence.

[1] Movers, as before, p. 41, is in favour of this hypothesis, considering that the solar and stellar worship was engrafted by the influence of the Hyk-sos on the old animal-worship of the Egyptians.

[2] Bunsen, *Egypt's Place*, I. 444.

[3] See for instance, Müller's *Amerik. Urrelig.* pp. 60 sq., 256 sq., 420.

Yet in Egypt this zoolatry appears in such exaggerated shapes and with such monstrous adjuncts, that to trace at length the stages of its progress and the secret of its perpetuity would fill a most remarkable chapter in the history of civilisation. The contemptuous exclamations of the later Greeks and Romans, on witnessing the coexistence of abstruse philosophy and artistic beauty with the worship of brute creatures, are familiar to all persons interested in this study. An admirer and apologist of the Egyptian creed was fully conscious of the reasons which had given birth to such opprobrious criticisms; for he confesses plainly that the multitude did not stop short at merely relative worship, but adored the animals themselves[1] (αὐτὰ τὰ ζῶα). I must not, however, leave unquoted the remarkable passage of Clement of Alexandria, with reference to this question, because it shews as well the sanctity with which the animals were all invested by Egyptians, as the feelings which zoolatry was then exciting in the minds of most spectators whether Christian or heathen. After dwelling on the costliness and splendour of Egyptian temples and directing our attention to the veil inwrought with gold by which the adytum was curtained off from the rest of the building, he continues[2]: 'But if you pass beyond into the remotest part of the enclosure, hastening to behold something more worthy of your search, and seek for the image which dwells in the temple, a *pastophorus* [shrine-bearer], or some one else of those who minister in sacred things, with a grave air singing a Pæan in the Egyptian tongue, draws aside a small portion of the veil, as if about to shew us the god; and makes us burst into a loud laugh. For the god you sought is not there, but a cat, or a crocodile, or a serpent sprung from the soil, or some such brute animal, which is more suited to a cave than a temple. The Egyptian deity appears,—a beast rolling himself on a purple coverlet!'

We might deduce the very high antiquity of this practice from the fact that many of the animals so worshipped had been always sacred only in particular nomes[3]; and though the final consolidation of the monarchy and the comparative fusion of religious tenets which resulted from it, had secured a universal reverence for the ox, the dog, the cat, the hawk, the ibis and two kinds of fish, there was no period when, with these excep-

1 Plutarch. *De Is. et Osir.* c. LXXI. As contrasted with the Egyptian notions he considered the Greeks entirely orthodox (λέγουσιν ὀρθῶς) in their dedication of particular birds and reptiles to particular divinities.

2 *Pædagog.* lib. III. c. 2: cf. Juvenal, *Sat.* xv. 7.

3 Cf. above, p. 432, n. 1.

tions, sacred animals of one nome were not treated as a common article of food in others, and not liable, on every outburst of fanaticism, to be assailed with open violence or contempt[1].

Conspicuous at the head of the zoolatry of Egypt stands the worship of the great Memphitic bull, Apis (Hapi)[2], which is carried back, in its more elementary condition, as far as the '2nd dynasty[3].' In the reign of Ramses II., the great bull is made to bear the title 'second life of Ptah[4],'—a fact which intimates that he was then regarded as the living shrine, or incarnation, of the chief god of Memphis; and a similar exaltation is suggested in the title 'image of the soul of Osiris[5],' which has elsewhere been awarded to him. Viewed in this light Apis was to the Egyptian worshipper a present or incarnate deity. The luxuries deemed appropriate to the highest earthly monarch were all lavished on his service. He was fed with a religious scrupulosity. He was anointed with the choicest unguents. Mates of spotless beauty were provided for him[6]. At death he was embalmed and swathed: his funeral was performed with a magnificence unrivalled in the case of men: a sumptuous monument which still attracts the admiration of all artists was erected in his honour. And since mortals after death were thought to be in some mysterious way united with Osiris, the dead Apis also was entitled for this cause *Osiris-Apis* (Ὀσοράπις), or *Serapis*[7]; and as such was worshipped with supreme devotion

[1] On the various theories respecting the rationale of this kind of worship, see Kenrick, II. 2 sq., Uhlemann, *Aegypt. Alt.* III. 210 sq.

[2] According to Uhlemann (p. 208), the Coptic *hap* means 'the judge' [or rather, 'judgment']; perhaps with reference to the functions of Osiris in the under-world. Of three other bulls admitted to the foremost rank of animal-worship one was Mnevis of Heliopolis, who bore the title 'the resuscitated sun.' The worship both of Apis and Mnevis extended far beyond the cities where they were especially honoured.

[3] Osburn, *Mon. Hist.* I. 247.

[4] *Revue des Deux Mondes*, as before, p. 1074. On the alleged preternaturalness of the birth of Apis, through the agency of a generific beam of light, see Herod. III. 28, and Mr. Blakesley's note.

[5] Plut. *De Is. et Osir.* c. xx.

[6] Wilkinson and others have denied that still worse abominations were connected with the animal-worship of the Egyptians (see Diod. I. 85; Herod. II. 46); but allusions like that in Lev. xviii. 23 agree too closely with the statements of the Greek historians: cf. Döllinger, pp. 226, 227.

[7] That this is the true account of Serapis has been lately proved by M. Mariette, *Mémoire sur le Sérapéum*, to whose labours Lepsius was looking hopefully when he wrote his own Appendix on 'Serapis' in the *Götterkreis* &c. p. 213. Respecting the Greek version of the fetching of the god Serapis from Sinope by order of Ptolemy Soter, and the consequence of identifying Serapis with the Greek Dionysus, see Bunsen, *Egypt's Place*, I. 431, and Maury, *Revue des Deux Mondes*, as before, p. 1073.

in the interval which elapsed before the birth or 'manifestation' of a new calf,—the vehicle to which the soul of the departed Apis was believed to be immediately transferred.

While animal-worship had been thus amalgamated more and more with adoration of the elements and of spirits ruling in the heavenly bodies, the important change to which I have before alluded had been also passing over the complexion of the mythe which centred in the greatest pair of national divinities. There might indeed be no express intention either on the part of priest or people to relinquish the conclusions of the old mythology. In Osiris they might recognise, as heretofore, the ultimate source of all vitality, and as such might find the highest and most adequate symbol of his functions in the great orb of day. They might continue also to associate Isis with him as the counter part of his productive powers, and discerning an appropriate emblem of that goddess in the moon or in the earth, might still, in words, attribute all the higher phenomena of life to the harmonious action of these two divinities. But such is far from being a true account of the religion of the many, or the popular theology[1] of Egypt, in the later Pharaonic period. Owing to a general want of fixity in men's religious tenets, the ingredients of the mythe had been so altered, its area so contracted, its connexion with the world at large so broken and obscured as to have rendered it an almost novel version of the primitive story. The Egyptian mind is seen descending more and more entirely from the worship of the heavenly bodies to the contemplation of the marvellous agencies at work in its immediate neighbourhood. In earlier times Osiris was enthroned upon the sun; but now the Nile itself is substituted for that glorious luminary. Then the spouse of the great sun-god was the mother and the nurse of universal vegetation; now she is the single land of Egypt fructified and gladdened by the Nile. Then Osiris was a nature-god, a verbal representative of forces active in the varied processes of nature: now he has been moulded into the great civilising hero of Mizraim, binding men together in a fixed society, teaching agriculture, and subduing nations not by force alone but by the charms of eloquence and music. Then his death was the suspension of all vital power without the least distinction of locality; now it coincides precisely with

[1] Thus Plutarch (*De Is. et Osir.* c. XXXIII) carefully distinguishes between the people and the more enlightened of the priests: *Οἱ δε σοφώτεροι τῶν ἱερέων, οὐ μόνον τὸν Νεῖλον Ὄσιριν καλοῦσιν...ἀλλὰ Ὄσιριν μὲν ἁπλῶς ἅπασαν τὴν ὑγροποιὸν ἀρχὴν καὶ δύναμιν, αἰτίαν γενέσεως καὶ σπέρματος οὐσίαν νομίζοντες.*

that season of the year in Egypt when decay and barrenness are everywhere ascendant through the Valley of the Nile.

The reason of this gradual localising of the story,—this confusion, one might call it, of the sun with the Egyptian river,—is hardly to be sought in the prevailing fancy that the Nile and sun were wont to meet together at the western horizon, and after plunging down into the under-world came forth again together from the caverns of the east[1]. An explanation, simple in itself and serving also to account for other kindred stories, is suggested by the fact that the Egyptian had been gradually tempted to associate every genial, fertilising power in nature with the annual overflow of his great river. In one meaning of the phrase Herodotus was right, when he declared that Egypt is 'the gift of the Nile[2].' 'My river is mine own' was the ungodly boast ascribed to Egypt in the vision of the Hebrew prophet (Ezek. xxix. 3, 9), 'my river is mine own, and I have made it for myself.' 'Turn the course of the Nile,' it has been said, 'and not one blade of vegetation would ever arise in Egypt.' And the more intelligent of modern travellers, no longer open to the potent witcheries which nature once exerted on mankind, but recognising the almighty hand of God Himself throughout this 'annual miracle of mercy,' are still awestruck by the grand phenomena presented to them as the river bursts afresh into its ancient channels. 'All nature shouts for joy. The men, the children, the buffaloes, gambol in its refreshing waters; the broad waves sparkle with shoals of fish, and fowl of every wing flutter over them in clouds. Nor is this jubilee of nature confined to the higher orders of creation. The moment the sand becomes moistened by the approach of the fertilising waters, it is literally alive with insects innumerable[3].'

Nor are these the only changes introduced into the primitive mythe of Isis and Osiris. Though the mother of both is still Rhea (Nut or Nutpe), doubts have been suggested touching the true name of their father; while the chief progenitors of the gods are now distinctly represented as giving birth to a second pair, which rank in some respects upon a level with the former. Set, or Typhon, is the brother of Osiris[4]; and, accompanied by his spouse and sister Nephthys, he is placed in a position of direct antagonism to the benevolent divinities, to

[1] Osburn, I. 420.

[2] Herod. II. 5.

[3] Osburn, I. 13.

[4] Preternaturally born, however, Plutarch says (c. XII); *μὴ καιρῷ, μηδὲ κατὰ χώραν, ἀλλ' ἀναῤῥήξαντα πληγῇ διὰ τῆς πλευρᾶς ἐξαλλέσθαι*: cf. above, p. 308, n. 2.

Isis and Osiris, and especially to the younger Horus, their child and champion; while a definite character has also been attributed to Thoth[1], the ibis-headed Hermes of Egyptian worship, the inventor of letters, the depository of primeval wisdom, 'the president of the reasoning faculty,' the teacher, counsellor, and secretary of Osiris himself.

The greatest of the difficulties experienced as we analyse these fresh developments of the Egyptian mythology is connected with the origin and import of the evil-minded Typhon. Some of the chief names by which he was at first distinguished are *Set, Seti, Sutech;* but in the course of modern explorations, it has come to light that he was also identified[2] at least on one inscription with the great Phœnician Bel or Baal: and in confirmation of this interesting fact we are enabled to establish that when the Hyk-sos made their grand descent on Egypt, they had recognised in Typhon their own national divinity, had chosen him for their sole leader, and had fought and conquered always under his immediate patronage[3]. With their ascendancy in Egypt, Typhon also had become supreme.

It is quite possible, indeed, that in far earlier times[4] he held a high position in some districts as the elemental god who

[1] The place of this ibis-headed god, 'lord of Shmun' (Hermopolis), appears to be in what is called the secondary series of Egyptian divinities. Bunsen styles him (I. 393) the 'most important of all the Cabeiri' (corresponding to *Esmûn*, above, p. 453). As connected with the Osiris-group he is sometimes entitled 'begotten of Osiris' himself; but the relation indicated in the text is that which he sustains far more frequently. Mr. Kenrick observes of Thoth (*Anc. Egypt*, I. 428), that 'with a name nearly similar, *Taut*, he appears also in the Phœnician history, and in the same character of the inventor of letters.'

[2] See Lepsius, *Götterkreis* (as before), p. 206, who adds: 'Dieser Begriff des *Set* oder *Sutech* als des *ausserägyptischen* Gottes dürfte überhaupt den Schlüssel zu der räthselhaften Natur desselben und seiner zu verschiedenen Zeiten verschiedenen Auffassung darbieten.' This inquiry has since been ably followed out in the *Revue Archéologique*, XIIe année, pp. 257 sq. The original connexion between Baal and Typhon may, I think, be also traceable in the compound Baal-Zephon (צְפוֹן) of Exod. xiv. 2, 9, Numb. xxxiii. 7; which may again have been identical with the *Αὔαρις* or *Ἄβαρις* of Manetho and Josephus; for this border-city of the Hyk-sos, identified by Lepsius with Pelusium (? *Pelishtim*, city of the Philistines), is described by them as *πόλις κατὰ τὴν θεολογίαν ἄνωθεν* Τυφώνιος. There is, however, some difficulty in ascertaining the original relation of Typhon to the hideous monsters of the primitive world, whom Greek writers, from Homer downwards, designated Τυφάων, Τυφωεύς, Τυφώς.

[3] Brugsch, quoted by Döllinger, pp. 421, 422.

[4] Lepsius, p. 204, Bunsen, I. 426.

struggled periodically with the elder Horus, in the conflict ever waged by different atmospheric agencies, as light and darkness, rain and drought, production and decomposition[1]. Studied under this peculiar aspect, Typhon may have seemed to the Egyptian of the older period a terrific but not always a malevolent divinity; just as Nephthys, 'mistress of the house,' and female counterpart of Typhon, was at first almost identical with Isis, and to some extent associated with kindly and maternal properties. But after the expulsion of the hated Hyk-sos, Typhon was no longer tolerated in a single canton of the Nile-valley: his name was chiselled out of all the monuments[2], where it had previously been ranked with those of kings and of superior gods: and in the future period of Egyptian history, Typhon was the synonym for 'evil genius;' he became the great personification of corrupting and disorganising forces, the author of disease, of impotence, of death itself. His symbol was a human form, surmounted by the head of some fabulous animals; while the brutes especially 'possessed' by him were those which the Egyptian either feared or hated, as the incarnations of stupidity, of malice, or of violence—the ass, the crocodile, the hippopotamus, and the bear.

I think, however, that the latest form assumed by this Typhonic mythe admits of easy explanation, as soon as we have learned to see distinctly imaged forth in it the main peculiarities of Egyptian nature. While Osiris was the fertilising river, the fruitful land of Egypt was his spouse. But Typhon his malignant brother, born like him of Rhea, was the enemy of Egypt, and as such allied with its mischances whether physical or political[3]. At one time he is nothing but the sea, which swallows up the waters of the Nile and circumscribes the empire of the Pharaohs; but more commonly the Typhon whom they dreaded was the glowing, scorching, and mephitic blast, the south-wind from the desert. For this reason Nephthys, who had once been merely a personification of the world unseen, as Isis of the visible hemisphere, is now transmuted into the desert itself, the birthplace of all joylessness and utter destitution; thus completing the dark series of antagonisms which

[1] *Revue Archéol.* as before.

[2] *Ibid.* pp. 267, 268: cf. above, p. 446, n. 3, for a similar attempt to suppress Ammon-worship.

[3] In this connexion it is worth remarking that Typhon when expelled from Egypt was believed to have fled on the back of an ass for seven days, *καὶ σωθέντα γεννῆσαι παῖδας Ἱεροσόλυμον καὶ Ἰουδαῖον* (Plutarch, *De Is. et Osir.* c. XXXI): cf. Lepsius, as before, p. 210.

parted Egypt from surrounding nations, and which formed the very essence of the popular theology.

The reader will be now in a position to appreciate the full-blown story of Osiris, which I give with some occasional condensation in the words of Plutarch's treatise[1]; written, it should be remembered, to the chief of the Thyades at Delphi, who herself had been initiated by her parents into the Egyptian mysteries:

"Rhea [Nut] having secretly united herself with Cronos [Seb], the Sun, who was indignant, laid upon her a curse, that she should not bring forth in any year or month. Hermes [Thoth], however, who was also a lover of Rhea, playing at dice with the moon, took away the seventieth[2] part of each period of daylight, and from these made five new days, which are the ἐπαγόμεναι, or intercalary days. On each of these five days Rhea bore a child. On the first was born Osiris, the son of the Sun, at whose birth a voice was heard proclaiming that the Lord of all was coming to light: or, according to another version, a certain Pamyles drawing water, at Thebes, heard a voice from the temple of Jupiter, which charged him to proclaim that a great and beneficent king Osiris was born. On this account Pamyles was intrusted by Cronos with the nursing of Osiris, and hence the festival of the Pamylia, and a kind of *phallephoria* [as in the Bacchic orgies]. On the second day was born Arueris, son of the Sun, whom they call Apollo and the Elder Horus. On the third was born Typhon, not in the usual course, but bursting out with a sudden stroke from the side of Rhea. On the fourth day was born Isis[3]; on the fifth Nephthys, who was called Teleute and Aphrodite[4], and according to some, Nike. Osiris and Arueris were sprung from the Sun, but Isis from Hermes, and Typhon and Nephthys from Cronos......This last pair were married to each other. Isis and Osiris united themselves even before their birth, and their son was called, according to some[5], Arueris, the Elder Horus, and the Apollo of the Greeks.

"Osiris being king at once proceeded to civilise the Egyptians; he taught them agriculture; he enacted laws for them; he taught them to worship the gods, and afterwards traversed the world on the same civilising errand, subduing the nations not by force but by persuasion, and especially the charms of music and poetry: on which account the Greeks concluded that he was identical with Dionysus[6]. In his absence Isis

[1] *De Iside et Osiride*, c. XII—c. XIX.

[2] A round number for 72, the fifth part of 360: cf. LXX as applied to the Seventy-Two translators of the Hebrew Bible.

[3] The text of Plutarch adds ἐν πανύγροις ('in very damp places'); but the reading is doubtful.

[4] This title brings Nephthys into parallelism with Astarte, the female counterpart of Baal, and the Aphrodite of Semitic tribes: see above, p. 70.

[5] The common story was, however, that the child of Isis and Osiris was the Younger Horus, or else Harpocrates.

[6] The conception of Osiris has probably an historical basis in the conquests ascribed to Sesostris; just as the Mexican mythe of Quetzalcoatl (above, pp. 372 sq.) had embodied the traditions of the populace respecting the labours of some true philanthropist. In Diodor. I. 19, it is affirmed that the civilising expeditions of Osiris extended

administered the regency so wisely, that Typhon was unable to create any disturbance; but on his return he conspired against Osiris with seventy-two men and the Ethiopian queen Aso[1]; and having secretly obtained the measure of Osiris, caused a coffer splendidly adorned to be brought into the banqueting-room, promising to give it to the guest whom it should fit. Osiris put himself into it to make the trial; and Typhon and his associates immediately pegged and soldered down the case, and set it afloat on the river. It floated into the sea through the Tanitic mouth, which on that account Egyptians of later days regarded with abhorrence. These things were done on the seventeenth of the month Athyr, in which the Sun enters Scorpion[2], and in the twenty-eighth year of the reign, or as some said of the age, of Osiris. The Pans and Satyrs who lived about Chemmis hearing of this tragedy and being agitated by it, sudden terrors of the multitude acquired the name of *panics;* while Isis cut off one lock of her hair and put on mourning, at the place where she first heard the news, which accordingly obtained the name *Coptos*[3] ......Wandering to and fro disconsolate she finally met with some children who told her whither the coffin had floated, and hence the Egyptians deem the words of children to carry with them a prophetic power......She also learned that Osiris had inadvertently united himself with her sister Nephthys......and went in search of the child which had been put away as soon as it was born through fear of Typhon. This she found after great trouble by the guidance of a dog, who afterwards became her champion and attendant, with the name Anubis......

"She now ascertained that the chest had been floated as far as Byblus [in Phœnicia] and cast ashore, and that the plant *erica* had grown up about it and entirely enclosed it in the trunk, so that the king of the country, amazed at the vast proportions of the tree, gave orders for it to be cut down, and made of it a pillar[4] to support the roof of his palace. Isis guided, as they say, by a divine monitor came to Byblus[5], and sitting

ἕως Ἰνδῶν καὶ τοῦ πέρατος τῆς οἰκουμένης: and it is further worthy of remark, as intimating a certain affinity between the mythe of Osiris and the history of Sesostris, that the latter on his return from his foreign conquests narrowly escaped death by fire at the hands of his brother (Herod. II. 107).

[1] 'The co-operation of a queen of Ethiopia in the plot against his life is significant of the national hostility of that people against the Egyptians, and the prevalence of female dominion:' Kenrick, I. 413.

[2] The 17th of Athyr would correspond with the middle of November (1st Athyr=Oct. 28); and therefore the disappearance of Osiris took place in autumn, just before the sowing-season of the Egyptians, and at the time when darkness was proceeding on its triumph through the months of winter.

[3] The modern *Keft*, the principal city of the nome Coptites in the Upper Thebaid. It is noticeable that the same Greek word κόπτεσθαι 'to lament for the dead,' was of such ill omen in the mind of a Greek, that Herodotus (II. 132, 171) shrank from naming Osiris, a deity analogous to the Apollo of his own traditions and a deity of the upper regions, in connexion with it or with a ceremony that indicated woe.

[4] Here again, as Mr. Kenrick observes (I. 413), we have an historical allusion, *viz.* to the use of Osiride pillars in Egyptian architecture.

[5] On the mythological affinities here implied, see above, p. 452, n. 2.

down at a well, wretched and in tears, was there accosted by the queen's maidens, and on giving proofs of supernatural virtue, was entrusted with the nursing of the infant prince. She fed this child by giving it her finger to suck: she likewise put him every night into the fire to consume those portions of him which were mortal, and transforming herself into a swallow, hovered round the pillar and bemoaned her widowhood. At length, on making herself known, she was allowed to carry off the pillar, and taking out the enclosed sarcophagus of Osiris, she set sail for Egypt. Arriving at a desert place she opened the coffin and embraced the corpse of her husband with bitter tears......She brought it now to Egypt, and while going on a visit to her son Horus, who was being nursed at Butos, she deposited the corpse in secrecy. But Typhon, hunting by moonlight, happened to meet with it, and recognising the body of Osiris, he divided it into fourteen pieces, which he scattered about the country[1]. Isis, on learning this set out in quest of the remains, sailing over the marshy districts in a *baris*, made of papyrus, and as soon as she found one of the members she buried it there. All were ultimately recovered but one (τὸ αἰδοῖον); for it had been thrown into the river and devoured by the fishes, *lepidotus*, *phagrus*, and *oxyrhynchus;* which were afterwards held in abomination. In the room of it, she made an emblem, to which the Egyptians still pay honour (in the φαλληφόρια[2]). Osiris afterwards came back from the under-world, and Horus, aided by the presence of his father, carried out the plan for vanquishing Typhon, and after a fight of many days took him prisoner. Isis, however, loosed his fetters and let him go; at which Horus was so enraged that he tore off his mother's diadem; but Hermes [Thoth] supplied its place by a helmet in the shape of a cow's head......In two more battles Typhon was completely mastered. Harpocrates, being sprung from the union of Isis and Osiris after the death of the latter, his birth was untimely and he had a weakness in his lower limbs[3]."

We should form however an imperfect judgment of the Old Egyptian theory of religion, if we failed to contemplate it also from a different point of view. As hitherto regarded, the chief god Osiris was either confounded with the elemental processes of nature, or, according to the best appreciation of him, was en-

[1] This story of the discerption of the body was meant to explain the circumstance 'that the honour of his interment was claimed by so many different places.' (Kenrick, I. 413.)

[2] In this feature of the mythe we easily discover the same desire to give a quasi-historical account of an existing usage. Phallic emblems are very common in the earlier mythology of Egypt, as in the later Śiva-worship of Hindústán: the object being in both cases to symbolise the generative and reproductive power of nature. This tendency in Egypt was perhaps most fully manifested in *Khem* (the Pan of Herodotus, II. 46), who became a kind of Priapeian Osiris.

[3] Plutarch's observation at the end of the mythe implies that a kind of reverence for the great Egyptian divinities induced him to suppress other particulars still more revolting: Ταῦτα σχεδόν ἐστι τοῦ μύθου τὰ κεφάλαια τῶν δυσφημοτάτων ἐξαιρεθέντων· οἷόν ἐστι τὸ περὶ τὸν Ὥρου διαμελισμὸν καὶ τὸν Ἴσιδος ἀποκεφαλισμόν. (c. XX.)

gaged in regulating natural agencies for the peculiar benefit of the land of Egypt. But existing side by side with this conception of Osiris was another, more exalted and more ethical; implying in its turn a larger measure of religious sensibility. The foremost member of the pantheon was to many of the Egyptians a personification of the good principle. As such, in his own person, or by means of the invincible spear of Horus, he had pierced and crushed the serpent Apap[1]. He was worshipped, therefore, as the friend of right, the enemy and vanquisher of wrong, the author of the blessings which now circulate among the living, and the judge and sovereign of the dead. Osiris was the 'sun-god' in the very loftiest meaning of such phraseology. Exalted far above this sublunary sphere, his piercing vision, as he rode majestic through the heavens, had made him cognisant of human actions; and returning to the under-world in which he was believed to join his mother, and to reign supreme, the Pluto of Mizraim, with no further dread[2] of the malignant breath of Typhon, he presided over a judicial process which should fix the lot of all Egyptians in the world beyond the grave.

It is desirable to consider this more ethical aspect of the creed of Egypt in two separate divisions, as affecting human conduct, (1) in the present, and (2) in the future lifetime of each individual member.

1. Now it is certain that in spite of the monstrosity pervading the whole structure of his mythological system, the Egyptian, as compared with some of his more western neighbours, was preeminently religious. He had ever borne the yoke of a most irksome superstition with alacrity befitting a far worthier cause. The time, the zeal, the treasure he would lavish on the building of his multitudinous temples, or the sustentation and the sepulture of sacred animals, was constant

[1] See *Revue Archéol.* XIVe année, p. 194; Kenrick, I. 421. The letting loose of Typhon by the woman, Isis (Plutarch, c. XIX. where also it is noticeable that an ὄφις appears), might not unnaturally be construed as giving free scope to the powers of evil, and might so have a remote relation to the sacred narrative of the Fall. Movers (pp. 522 sq.) distinctly connects the Typhon both of Phœnicia and Egypt with the Hebrew צִפְעוֹנִי, 'a basilisk,' or 'viper,' *e.g.* Isai. xi. 8; lix. 5; Jerem. viii. 17: and although in the Egyptian mythology the ill effects produced by Typhon were mainly viewed as *physical*, there was certainly no absolute limitation to that class of evils, (cf. Plutarch, c. L.).

[2] 'In dem Todtenkulte trat *Set* erklärlicher Weise mehr zurück. Daher fehlt er in den Götterlisten der Königsgräber; *im Reiche des unteren Osiris hatte er keine Macht.*' Lepsius, *Götterkreis*, &c. p. 207.

proof of his intense devotion to the service of his gods; nay, rather than devour or damage one such animal he was content to suffer all the worst extremities of destitution or disgrace. He seemed again to be continually oppressed by a conviction that divine or supernatural powers were everywhere diffused around him. Nothing is more clearly traceable on papyri which accompany the mummies of the Old Egyptian than his firm belief in the reality of the world invisible,—belief which generating awe and dread became in him the ruling sentiment that hourly cast its shadow on his pathway and that haunted him at every turn[1]. The warmth of his religious feelings was betrayed, and may have also been augmented and embittered, by diversities of worship in the different nomes and by collisions more or less fanatic[2], which arose from such diversities. It has been urged indeed that the Egyptian was not always of a temper so morose and gloomy as some writers had formerly imputed to him; and perhaps there is sufficient ground for this correction; but in reference to the dominant genius of the popular religion, nothing in the ancient world can be regarded as more sombre and dejected. The one national air of Egypt was the Maneros[3],—a threnody upon the death of Osiris. While the tourist could remark that the Hellenic gods were fond of gaiety and dances, those of Egypt were most gratified by demonstrations of an opposite kind, by dirges and a flood of tears. At banquets even it was not unusual to

[1] Osburn, *Mon. Hist.* I. 411. Herodotus (II. 37) begins his description of the ritual observances with the statement: Θεοσεβέες δὲ περισσῶς ἐόντες μάλιστα πάντων ἀνθρώπων: cf. Döllinger (p. 406), who affirms 'Ihre religiösen Gefühle waren wärmer, zäher zugleich und leidenschaftlicher als die der Griechen und Römer.' On this question as to the general temperament of the Egyptians, it is curious to observe that modern writers differ from each other *toto cœlo*. Thus, the author of the article *Ægyptus* in Smith's *Dictionary* considers the old Egyptians a serious people, of a gloomy, meditative genius: and finds in this circumstance an explanation of the fact that the whole of Egypt, after the introduction of the Gospel, was dotted over with convents which gave birth to the wildest Lives of Saints. Whereas Sir J. G. Wilkinson in his last work (*Ancient Egyptians*, pp. 7 sq. p. 13) affirms the very contrary: 'They were the reverse of a serious people; and while their philosophers gave their attention to grave abstruse studies, the rest of the community appreciated a merry life, and were remarkable for a love of excitement, quite consistent with the scenes of buffoonery and the talent for caricature so often displayed in the paintings.'

[2] Kenrick, II. 26.

[3] Explained by Brugsch (*Die Adonisklage*, p. 24) as = *mââ-ne-hra*, 'come to the house,' 'come home again,'—the passionate cry of the 'sister,' 'spouse,' and 'mother' of Osiris.

send round a small model of a mummy, to remind the guest in his more joyous moments that his tenure of the present life was fleeting and precarious[1].

Whether this peculiar state of feeling was a product of peculiar ignorance on sacred subjects we may still be unable to determine with absolute precision; but there seems good reason for concluding that in no country of the ancient world, with the exception of India[2], were the chasms so numerous and so wide between the different orders of society. Egypt was the land of esoteric dogmas and exclusive institutions. Egypt was the home and nursery of that spirit of eclecticism which had promoted the formation of the early Gnostic sects; and Egypt was accordingly a stronghold of the stoutest opposition which was offered to the primitive heralds of the Gospel by the cold and haughty advocates of human inequality. The natural consequence had been that in no country were the masses kept in greater darkness or more intellectually degraded[3]. Much as Plutarch wished to prove that the original aim of their mythology was high and elevating[4], he was driven to acknowledge the failure of the system when his eye was fixed on some of its more popular developments. 'The Egyptians,' he wrote[5], 'at least, the greater part of them, by adoring the animals themselves, and caring for them as for gods, have crammed their ritual full with subjects of laughter and opprobrium. Nor is this the least evil which results from their stupidity. A dangerous notion is implanted, which drives the weak and simple-minded into the worst forms of superstition, and the shrewder and more daring into atheism and beast-like speculations.'

So exclusively was any higher knowledge which they might possess confined to one special order, that the Pharaoh, as we saw already, was esteemed but little more than a divine administrator of the kingdom in the service of the other priests[6]. He ruled as the chief member of the sacerdotal college; while to them had been committed not a few of the most onerous functions of the state. They were the legislators, and the judges, as well as the physicians, the astronomers, the architects, and

[1] See other examples collected in Döllinger, p. 444.

[2] See above, pp. 144 sq.

[3] Wilkinson, who may be fairly reckoned among the numerous apologists of Egyptian heathenism, avows, notwithstanding, that 'the people were left in utter ignorance of the fundamental doctrines of their religion,' (2nd ser. I. 164); and that 'every one was not only permitted, but encouraged, to believe the real sanctity of the idol, and the actual existence of the god whose figure he beheld,' (p. 175).

[4] *De Isid. et Osir.* c. VIII.

[5] *Ibid.* c. LXXI.

[6] Cf. Uhlemann, *Thoth*, p. 11.

the instructors of the youth; and only through their instrumentality as organs of the gods, or as exponents of the will of holy animals, could secrets be extracted from the world invisible, or answers be returned to the inquiries of the doubting and desponding.

We are no longer, it is true, at liberty to urge, like many of our predecessors, that Egyptians were all rigorously distributed into a series of hereditary classes[1], corresponding to the permanent castes of India after she had been completely Bráhmanised. No *absolute* division of this kind appears to have been taught in reference even to the present life; while in the future it was held that all, on passing to the grand tribunal of Osiris, would be placed in a position of complete equality. The fact, however, still remains indisputable that class-distinctions did exist with more than usual tenacity, and that the power of the Egyptian priest had always been enormous. There was no period in the history of Egypt, as inscribed upon her monumental records, when such priesthood was not duly organised[2], and when the hopes and fears of the remaining classes were not vitally connected with its absolute ascendency. The system thus compacted and administered was full of gorgeous and punctilious rites; the temples, glittering with a vast profusion of gold and foreign marbles and distributed into holy and more holy places (as the πρόναος, the σηκός, and the ἄδυτον), were thickly planted[3] in all cantons of the Nile-valley; fes-

[1] Wilkinson has abandoned his former views on this subject (see *Ancient Egyptians*, p. 129), chiefly, it would seem, in consequence of M. Ampère's paper in the *Revue Archéologique*, v[e] année, pp. 405 sq., where the monuments are shewn to indicate that there was no invariable custom nor any rigorous law, prescribing that the religious, military, or civil functions should in Egypt always be assumed as the result of family-inheritance.

[2] See Uhlemann, *Aegypt. Alt.* II. 182 sq.; *Thoth*, pp. 89 sq.

[3] *Ibid.* II. 188 sq., where attention is drawn to some resemblances between the arrangements of Egyptian temples and the Hebrew tabernacle: but see Bähr, *Symbolik*, I. 218. The magnificence of the Egyptian temples is explained at once by the enormous gifts and revenues conferred upon them by some of the more powerful monarchs. Thus the *Annals of Thothmes III.* (of the 18th dynasty), translated by Mr. Birch, in the *Archæologia* (1853), Vol. XXXV. pp. 116 sq., are full of instances in which the bounty of the prince was lavished on the great temple of Ammon-Ra, at Thebes, as the result of aid afforded to him by his tutelar deity during a successful attack on certain places in Palestine. 'Slaves, probably negroes, to open the doors; three fortresses of the Ruten [the Canaanitish enemy], —just as the Lake Mœris and the town of Anthylla supplied the pin-money of the queens of Egypt; linen of various sorts, gold, silver, lapis lazuli, copper, brass, iron, lead, colours for the monuments,

tivals[1], arranged throughout the year according to a systematic calendar, gave rise to frequent pilgrimages and processions; while the oracles[2] of Egypt long enjoyed the highest reputation, and, like 'mysteries' of which she was acknowledged the inventor, furnished models to the imitative genius of her western neighbours.

It is always in the sacrificial rites of a religious system that we trace the consciousness in man of his dependence on the powers above him, or of his estrangement from the source of life and blessedness. And Egypt, as we might anticipate, is no exception to this universal law. There, also, to omit the merely eucharistic[3] class of sacrifices, man had ever indicated his persuasion that he was no longer what he ought to be, nor what he knew he might eventually become. He felt that one or all the gods were standing to him in the posture of hostility, and therefore trusted by piacular offerings to avert the outburst of their indignation and alleviate the burden of his sin. With this conception, animal sacrifices seem to have been offered on Egyptian altars during the whole of the historic period. 'Without shedding of blood there is no remission.' Here had culminated the idea of heathen as of other sacrifices[4]: and in the case of Egypt it was put on record that the offerer sometimes manifested more than common sensibility as to the thoughts which underlie this branch of his symbolic ritual. He was accustomed to bewail the sufferings of the victim he had stretched upon the altar; and when it sank beneath the sacrificial knife he turned and smote himself[5].

bread, loaves of various kinds of food, cattle, geese, gazelles of different kinds, incense, wine, frankincense, offerings to the statues, to the obelisks; fields, meadows, and ponds, stocked with cattle, water-fowl, and pigeons, complete the long list of donations' (p. 154). Many of these provisions went for the daily banquet of the god and of his priests, which took place at sunset.

[1] Herodotus, who thinks that all religious pilgrimages and processions were devised in Egypt, describes six of the principal feasts (II. 59 sq.); but these were a small portion only of such public celebrations: see Uhlemann, *Aegypt. Alt.* II. 200 sq.

[2] *Ibid.* pp. 216 sq. From Herodotus (II. 57, 58) we also learn that the method of divining from victims (τῶν ἱρῶν ἡ μαντικὴ) was of Egyptian origin.

[3] Cf. above, pp. 226 sq. Such offerings as wine, oil, or other liquid, or any single gift, as a necklace, a bouquet of flowers, a bunch of vegetables, and the like (Wilkinson, 2nd ser. II. 338) come under this description. They were generally the expressions of gratitude for benefits received, or, as in India, may have sometimes been connected with a fancy that the minor gods at least were actually delighted by human articles of food and dress.

[4] Wikinson, 2nd ser. I. 146, 147.

[5] Lucian, *De Sacrificiis* (Opp. p. 187, B, Paris, 1615): αἱ δὲ θυσίαι

A prayer[1] was also offered on more critical occasions that 'if any calamity were about to befall either the sacrificer or the land of Egypt, it might all be concentrated on the victim's head;' which was accordingly not eaten by the worshipper but thrown as a devoted thing into the Nile, or else was sold to foreign traders.

The oblation of such sacrifices was the more remarkable in Egypt, owing to the number of the sacred animals there worshipped and the depth of the reluctance which was felt to the effusion of their blood. It must indeed have been the memory of some older teaching, and the force of irresistible impulse thus communicated, which constrained the worshipper to sacrifice not merely geese and other birds, but also his choice oxen and the male calves of the herd. We trace, again, the consequence of struggles which had long been waged between the obligation to offer animal victims, and the obligation to preserve those brutes which he had deemed especially sacred, in the fact that cows and heifers were at length excluded altogether from the list of offerings, and that consequently to offer them was 'to sacrifice the abomination of the Egyptians[2].' It is further noticeable, as supporting this conjecture, that a large proportion of Egyptian sacrifices were selected from the class of animals, which men had learned to call *Typhonic*, so that the thing offered was no more the choicest property of the sacrificer, but a creature hostile both to him and all the tutelar gods of Egypt[3]. An exemplification of such offering is presented in the custom of choosing *red*[4] oxen for oblations, on the ground that Typhon was himself entirely of that colour. And the same idea is also still more closely intimated in the ancient practice of sacrificing what were called Typhonic men, or red-haired strangers[5], at the tomb of Osiris. Attempts, indeed,

καὶ παρ' ἐκείνοις αἱ αὐταί· πλὴν ὅτι πενθοῦσι τὸ ἱερεῖον, καὶ κόπτονται περιστάντες ἤδη πεφονευμένον.

[1] Herod. II. 39.

[2] See Exod. viii. 26, 27, and Wilkinson, 2nd ser. II. 347, 348.

[3] Plutarch, *De Is. et Os.* c. XXXI.: *θύσιμον γὰρ οὐ φίλον εἶναι θεοῖς, ἀλλὰ τοὐναντίον, ὅσα ψυχὰς ἀνοσίων ἀνθρώπων καὶ ἀδίκων εἰς ἕτερα μεταμορφουμένων σωμάτων συνείληφε.*

[4] Herod. II. 38; Diodor. I. 18. If a single black hair was found on the ox, it was sacred to Epaphus (Apis), and as such was accounted 'unclean,' or no proper subject for sacrifice.

[5] Diodor. I. 88. Porphyry, *De Abstinentia*, II. 55, and Plutarch, *De Is. et Os.* c. LXXIII., both quote Manetho as the authority for this inhuman practice, which, he says, was abandoned by a king named Amosis, who substituted a waxen image for the live victim. Herodotus, however, denies (II. 45) that this practice, which had been abolished long before his time, had ever existed; asking, if the Egyptians were so scrupulous about offering animals, *κῶς ἂν οὗτοι ἀνθρώπους θύοιεν;*

are made continually by some writers to discredit the account, which comes to us from Manetho, in reference to this horrible distortion of the rite of sacrifice; but the existence of such usages appears to be unquestionable, attested as it is distinctly by a native priest, and illustrated by the constant practice of most other demi-civilised communities in both the Old World and the New. The very seal made use of in historic ages to denote the fitness of a given victim bore the figure of a man kneeling, with his hands bound behind him, and a sword pointed at his throat[1]. In this unnatural act of bringing to the altar of the gods a victim capable of perfect sympathy with the sacrificer, there is always visible, amid the glare of selfish and vindictive passions, the stern truth that nothing short of human blood was deemed an adequate offering to the highest gods of Egypt, or sufficient for the liquidation of the penalty entailed from time to time by human disobedience.

But the sacrifice which the Egyptian offered to his gods was followed, as in other parts of heathendom[2], by sacrifices for and to the spirits of departed ancestors. His dedication of himself to Ptah, to Ammon-Ra, or to Osiris, was the first and principal act of homage; but the next[3] consisted in the dedication of his own heart to his buried mother, and included a long series of funereal rites by means of which he strove to pay due honour to the 'authors of his body.' Offerings of this class appear to have especially evoked the better feelings of the Old Egyptian; and the prayers which he addressed to his departed ancestors, as well as to Osiris in their favour, prove, if not the moral elevation of his creed, at least the freshness and the strength of his domestic instincts.

2. It is, however, in the views presented of the Old Egyptian in the world beyond the grave that we discover the foundation of his ethical system. Principles of action which had guided him in this life are reflected with peculiar vividness and fulness in the judgment-scenes belonging to the next. The chief authorities for statements on the fortunes of the soul in hades are derived from extant Rituals of the Dead, rolled up in a cylindrical form and not unfrequently discovered in sarcophagi of different periods. As this class of documents, in one shape or other, may be carried back into the earlier

[1] Kenrick, I. 442; Döllinger, p. 442; Uhlemann, II. 191. This scene, however, may possibly allude to the *vicarious* nature of the sacrifice.

[2] See, for example, above, pp. 290, 355, 391, 405, and Appendix II. at the end of this Part.

[3] *Revue Archéol.* XIVe année, p. 194.

dynasties,—supplying to the disembodied soul of every age a kind of guide-book for her pilgrimages in the train of Osiris through the regions of the under-world,—it is indisputable that the Old Egyptian was no stranger to the cardinal truths connected with the prolongation of man's being after death, his conscious and unwearying exercise of functions proper to humanity, and his exposure to the scrutiny of supernatural agents on account of 'things done in the body[1].' Of the hundred and sixty-five chapters which fill up the most remarkable of these Rituals, one is entitled, 'On the life after death;' and the volume, notwithstanding all its mystic names and undecypherable images, is found to be pervaded by the same idea of individual immortality. The vividness of such conceptions is particularly manifested in the fact that nearly all conditions of the present life, in their most earthy and unspiritual shape, had been transferred into man's theory of the life which is to come. At an Egyptian funeral, common articles of food and dress, and certain implements of war, of business and of pleasure, were deposited with or near the corpse: the scenes of daily life were pictured on the mummy-cases, not so much in order to express the piety of survivors, as to gratify and stimulate the dead: a string of prayers and other formulæ were also buried with him for his constant admonition, and as passports through the unknown world to which he had been destined; and at length, when he was entering the 'dark place' itself, the popular belief assigned him 'bread and drink, and slices of flesh off the table of the Sun; when he peregrinates the fields of the blessed, corn and barley are given to him, for he is as provided as he was upon earth[2].'

It has been held indeed, on the authority of Herodotus, that the Egyptians were the *first* people of the ancient world to inculcate this doctrine of the immortality of the human soul;

[1] Mr. Osburn is at one with all Egyptologers when he says (*Mon. Hist.* I. 424): 'The truth that man will be judged after death was brought into Egypt by the first settlers, and universally received by their posterity.'

[2] *Todtenbuch* in Birch's *Egypt. Hierog.* p. 272: cf. Döllinger, p. 432, who traces the origin of this kind of phraseology to a principle which recurs in almost every heathen system, *viz.* a belief in the quasi-materiality of the human soul. It was not regarded as a purely spiritual essence, 'sondern als eine körperliche, nur feinere Substanz, welche im jenseitigen Leben durch mancherlei Wanderungen hindurchgehe, bis sie geläutert—als solche dargestellt in der Form eines Sperbers mit Menschenkopf zur vollen Anschauung des göttlichen Sonnenlichts sich emporschwingt.'

and doubtless the habitual and unfaltering affirmation of it was to some extent *Egyptian*, and was that which gave their highest charm to the Osirian tenets in the eye of other nations: but the language of the Greek historian, properly expounded, means[1] no more than that Egyptians were the first people, who, cherishing the thought of some ulterior existence, had imparted to it novel characteristics by presenting it in the form of a theory of transmigration. In thus embracing the idea of changes from the human to the bestial and the meanest even of all reptile forms, the Old Egyptians occupied the same position as Hindús throughout the second, or Bráhmanic, period of their history. In both those countries we have seen how the religion of the choicer few, as well as of the populace itself, was ultimately pantheistic; and in both accordingly the dogma of transmigration had been strengthened, if not first of all suggested, by the reverence men were taught to feel for each of the innumerable varieties of animated nature. Transmigration was, however, viewed in both these systems as a dire calamity; and therefore to obtain exemption from its fatal law became in both the foremost duty of their genuine votaries. Each pursued this object in a different spirit and by methods of his own devising. The Hindús of every school, the Bráhman and the Buddhist also, shrinking as far as possible from contact with material forms, and casting off as evil all that ministered to the idea of personal immortality, contended that emancipation could be only found amid the loftiest peaks of human knowledge; and accordingly pushed forward, in the one case to complete identification with Divinity itself, and in the other, to the dismal void of utter non-existence.

The Egyptian, on the contrary, had no such fundamental dread of matter and experienced no temptation to accept a theory fatal to the prolongation of his individual being. He was rather prone to speculations which distrusted or depressed the spiritual part of man. The conservation of the body, he imagined, was essential to the vigour and felicity of the soul. Attempts were, therefore, made in Egypt from an early period to exalt, and in one sense immortalise[2], the body by the well-

[1] After telling us (II. 123) that the Egyptians look upon Dionysus and Demeter (Osiris and Isis) as the rulers of hades, he continues: Πρῶτοι δὲ καὶ τόνδε τὸν λόγον Αἰγύπτιοί εἰσι οἱ εἰπόντες· ὡς ἀνθρώπου ψυχὴ ἀθάνατός ἐστι, τοῦ σώματος δὲ καταφθίνοντος ἐς ἄλλο ζῶον αἰεὶ γινόμενον ἐσδύεται· ἐπεὰν δὲ περιέλθῃ πάντα τὰ χερσαῖα καὶ τὰ θαλάσσια καὶ τὰ πετεινά, αὖτις ἐς ἀνθρώπου σῶμα γινόμενον ἐσδύνειν: the term of these transmigrations being 3000 years, *i.e.* one Sothis-period.

[2] This interpretation of the custom of embalming has come down

known system of embalming. Let the bodily organs, it was felt, be saved from putrefaction, and the spirit also will have something left on which to lean for help as her companion and receptacle. In virtue of the strength afforded to her by this union with the former cause of her vitality, she will continue to subsist in some analogous condition; disembodied, it is true, but still associating with her previous tenement, and still in some mysterious fashion living by its life.

The vast importance of such interaction had impelled the Old Egyptian worthy to lavish his chief skill and treasure on the building and adornment of his tomb. He made it capable of defying the malignity of Typhon and the wildest fury of the elements: he covered it with pleasant pictures, the mementos of a happy life on earth; he called the sepulchre itself, his dwelling-place and 'everlasting home[1].' His mummy, in like manner, was entitled 'habitation of Osiris[2];' on the type supplied by the arch-mummy of that god, all others had from age to age been scrupulously moulded; prayers were also offered to Osiris for the purpose of securing their incorruptibility[3]; and as the principal organs of the body were all deemed essential to the rightful actings of the spirit, every limb was now consigned to the protection of one single deity; while Seb, the father of Osiris, was himself entrusted with the guardianship of edifices where the mummy was enshrined.

But while conceding that some minor difficulties continue to embarrass the solution of this problem with respect to the precise intention of embalming, as well as to the limits placed by the Egyptian creed upon the metensomatosis of one class of

to us through Servius (*ad Æneid.* III. 67); and has certainly the advantage of accounting for many practices connected with the burial of the dead. But we have now abundant reason for concluding that the *perfect purification* of the body, and not its conservation merely, was at the root of the ideas expressed in every act of mummification. Thus in Brugsch's edition of the *Saï An Sinsin* (p. 25), it is said, 'Dein Leib ist nun rein durch Wasser und Laugensalz, kein Glied an dir ist unrein; geläutert von allem Uebel und allem Schmutz kommst du zum Richterstuhle...dein Herz ist nun das Herz des Ra, deine Glieder sind die Glieder des grossen Horus.'

[1] Diodor. I. 51: *ἀϊδίους οἴκους προσαγορεύουσιν, ὡς ἐν ᾅδου διατελούντων τὸν ἄπειρον αἰῶνα.* Wilkinson (2nd ser. II. 445) seems to think that this care of the dead body intimated a belief in its eventual resuscitation; but, as Prichard long ago remarked (*E. Mythol.* p. 198), if this doctrine 'was really prevalent among the Egyptians, we must suppose that they took extraordinary care to conceal it, since not the slightest hint respecting it has reached our times:' cf. Müller, *Amerikan. Urrelig.* p. 402.

[2] Osburn, I. 427.

[3] See examples in Döllinger, p. 432.

disembodied spirits and their wanderings through 'the cycle of necessity,' it is impossible to doubt that, in the later periods of Egyptian independence, every spirit was believed to pass at once from this life to *Amenthe*, the dim region of the underworld, in which account was solemnly taken by Osiris of its actions and its words. In this belief, so universally diffused, we see the clearest and most urgent motive to a course of upright living which the Old Egyptian had been made to feel. The duties which he recognised as proper to the gods, his neighbour and himself, may all be gathered from the judgment-scenes enacted at the great tribunal of Osiris.

On examining the pictures thus transmitted to us, we discover that not a few of the more heinous sins remaining to be expiated in a future life consisted of deflections from a long array of merely ceremonial precepts. Every thing in ancient Egypt, not excluding the most ordinary avocations and most trivial pastimes of the people, had been thrust beneath the iron yoke of arbitrary legislation. As the Nile, for instance, was a sacred river, and as such invoked in the Egyptian hymns[1] among the foremost of the national gods, whatever bore directly on the culture of the soil and the succession of the crops in every district of the Nile-valley was enforced among the duties claimed from husbandmen by that divinity. 'To brush its sacred surface with the balance-bucket at a forbidden time was a crime equal in atrocity to that of reviling the face of a king or of a father[2].' The spirit, therefore, which presided over all the social institutions of the Pharaonic empire was akin to that which we have watched already shaping the national character of the Chinese; it was exclusive[3], cramping, isolating, stern, prohibitive, despotic. And corresponding to this general estimate is the discovery that the virtues there imputed to the Old Egyptians are nearly always of a negative kind. The spirit at the bar of judgment ever struggles to evince her own integrity,—'to justify herself'—and is accordingly most earnest in proclaiming her habitual abstinence from open vice and from all possible breaches of the ceremonial institute. She can declare, indeed, on some occasions, that she

[1] A stanza of one such hymn is given by Mr. Birch, as before, p. 268.

[2] Osburn, I. 435.

[3] Thus in the deprecations of a spirit on approaching the judicial balance, she is made to protest 'I have not changed the customs, neither have I enacted foreign abominations.' (*Ibid.* p. 432.) Hence the violent hatred of all strangers which was highly characteristic of the Old Egyptians: see Hengstenberg, *Dissertations on the Pentateuch*, II. 458, Edinb. 1847.

has 'given bread to the hungry, water to the thirsty, garments to the naked, and asylum to the wretched outcast[1],' as well as proper victims to the gods and the funereal offerings to the manes; but her language in the great majority of recorded judgment-scenes is rather that of confident *disavowal;* while confessions of innate depravity, or appeals to the forgiving mercy of the judge, appear to find no echo in Egyptian Rituals.

The deceased is, in those Rituals, pictured, first of all, as undergoing a long series of preliminary transformations in order to evade the malice of infernal demons, and 'obtain his heart.' He enters the bark of the Egyptian Charon[2], and crosses over to the 'Hall of the Two Truths;' the title of which is borrowed from the goddesses of Truth and Justice, who assist in all determinations of Osiris. Ever since the mythic death ascribed to this divinity, it is believed that he has sat in judgment on the souls of men; and every spirit on admission finds him ready at his post, attended by Anubis, 'the director of the balance,' by Horus waiting to conduct acquitted mortals to the nearer presence of Osiris, and by Thoth, the great recorder, with a tablet in his hand. The heart of the deceased, which after various struggles has been rescued from the demons of the under-world, is now submitted to the fatal balance. Formulæ of exculpation[3] are presented to him; and although he is supposed to meet the reckoning solely in his own strength and to escape the crisis only when assured of personal innocence, some friendly guidance is upon his own petition administered by Thoth, the Mercury of the Egyptian hades. Of the formulæ[4] here mentioned one consists of deprecatory addresses to the gods of the Hall of Judgment, the divine assessors of Osiris. In the second a long catalogue of sins are, one by one, denied or disavowed, before the 'two-and-forty avengers,' who as the personifications of the sins themselves are represented waiting for the adverse inclination of the balance, in order to inflict their torments on the soul of the condemned.

I give the former series at full length, because it tends far more than any others to exhibit the religion of the Old

[1] *Revue Archéol.* xive année, p. 194.

[2] According to Diodor. I. 96, the word *Charon* is itself Egyptian (χαρω='silence'): cf. Uhlemann, *Thoth*, p. 62. Rhadamanthus, in like manner, is by some connected with the Egyptian *Amenthe*.

[3] It is worth while to compare the protests of the Old Egyptian as recorded in his *Ritual* with those contained in the 31st chapter of the Book of Job. The points of similarity and of contrast are equally instructive.

[4] They are translated from the *Todtenbuch* by Mr. Osburn, I. 430 sq.

Egyptians in a favourable light, and illustrates the nature of that secret and self-judging law, which everywhere in spite of intellectual aberrations is still active, in the cause of truth and righteousness, among the inmost fibres of the human heart:

1. I have neither done any sin, nor omitted any duty to any man.
2. I have committed no uncleanness.
3. I have not prevaricated at the seat of justice.
4. I have not spoken lightly.
5. I have done no shameful thing.
6. I have not omitted [certain] ceremonies.
7. I have not blasphemed with my mouth.
8. I have not perverted justice.
9. I have not acted perversely.
10. I have not shortened the cubit.
11. I have not done that which is abominable to the gods.
12. I have not sullied my own purity.
13. I have not made men to hunger.
14. I have not made men to weep.
15. I have done no act of rapine[1].
16. I have not accused of rapine falsely.
17. I have not revived an ancient falsehood before the face of man.
18. I have not forged the deeds of sluices, houses, or lands.
19. I have not forged any of the divine images.
20. I have not withheld the seven linen garments due to the priests.
21. I have not committed adultery.
22. I have not polluted the purity of my divine land (*i. e.* my tomb).
23. I have not been avaricious.
24. I have not forged signet-rings.
25. I have not cut down on my mother's land (*i. e.* my maternal inheritance) the timber that grows thereon.
26. I have not falsified the weights of the balance.
27. I have not withheld milk from the mouths of the infants.
28. I have not driven away the flocks from their pasturage.
29. I have not netted [the] ducks [of the Nile] illegally.
30. I have not caught [the] fishes [of the Nile] illegally.
31. I have not [unlawfully] pierced the bank of the river when it was increasing.
32. I have not separated for myself [clandestinely] a channel (*lit.* arm) from the river when it was subsiding.
33. I have not extinguished the perpetual lamp (*lit.* hourly lamp).
34. I have not added anything to any of the sacred books.
35. I have not driven off any of the sacred cattle.
36. I have not stabbed the god (*i.e.* sacred animal), when he comes forth [from his shrine].

Wherever the Egyptian failed to pass this ordeal, and the second not unlike it, he incurred a dark succession of

[1] The besetting sin of the Old Egyptian appears to have been *theft*, for which he had obtained a special notoriety, as well as, it would seem, a kind of legal indulgence (Herod. II. 121; Aulus Gellius, xi. 18; Diodor. I. 80).

tremendous penalties. The hapless spirit, banished from the presence of Osiris, who inclines his sceptre in token of disapprobation, is now hurried back to earth by ministers of vengeance in the hideous form of apes. She migrates from the human to the bestial sphere of being, and commencing with some animal shape[1] to which indeed she had contracted an affinity by former habits, she proceeds from year to year, from century to century, now rising and now sinking in the scale of creaturely existence, till at last the destined cycle is completed by the winding up of all things. The most abject stage in this rotation seems to be the lowest region of *Kar-Neter*, the Phlegethon of the Greeks. 'None of the dead can endure it; the waters being of flame and waves of fire of the most intense and unconquerable heat; while the thirst of the dead in it is unquenchable; and they have no peace in it, because it is filled with weeds and filth[2].'

But on the contrary the human spirit who has stood the various tests applied to her at the tribunal of Osiris, passes on with the permission of the demons, and moves freely through the joyous halls of *Aahlu* (Elysium). Her body also purified at length, by its evisceration[3], from all properties which rendered it offensive to the gods, has been assimilated by the mummifying process to the actual form of Osiris. The whole man, according to the later representations, has become *Osirianised;* the name of the great sun-god is combined, without distinction of age or calling, with the name of the departed

[1] Wilkinson, as above, p. 447. It is rarely, however, as Mr. Kenrick remarks (I. 480), that we find 'among the funereal monuments of Egypt anything which relates to the metempsychosis;' the reason, perhaps, being that every embalmed corpse, duly interred, was *presumed* by the survivors to have passed the scrutiny of the infernal judge, and so was in a state of permanent felicity.

[2] Birch, as above, p. 275.

[3] See the remarkable passage in Porphyry (*De Abstinentia*, IV. 10), where is preserved the invocation addressed by the embalmers to the sun in the name of the deceased; at the end of which he is made to say, 'If I have committed any other fault during my life, either in eating or drinking, it has not been done on my own account, but on account of these;' pointing to the chest containing the viscera. Such passages (cf. above, p. 142) remind one of St. Augustine's statement respecting himself while he continued a Manichæan: 'Adhuc enim mihi videbatur, non esse nos qui peccamus, sed nescio quam aliam in nobis peccare naturam,' (*Confess.* V. 10). It is also worthy of remark that while expressions such as those just cited have a *Manichæan* aspect, overlooking or denying the freedom of the creature, the general tendency of the religions of Egypt, of Phœnicia and of Babylonia, was rather towards a *Pelagian* estimate of human sinfulness.

mortal; he attains to a subordinate stage of deification; he acquires a faculty of self-translation and self-transformation[1], just as the condemned are driven onward by some irresistible fate into the forms of animal life; he issues forth at will into the upper regions; he soars high above the earth with the alertness of the hawk or ibis; he revisits the sepulchre in which his body is preserved, and thence derives a fresh accession to his vital powers. He inherits the two-fold life of the divine Osiris; all his happiness consists in tracking that illustrious sun-god, in addressing adorations to him, and in sailing with him through his daily circuits, in the barge employed by him to circumnavigate the firmament, or 'waters of the heavenly Nile.'

In other words, the Sun which to Egyptians had for ages been the grandest symbol of their deities, and not unfrequently the glorious home or vehicle of Deity itself, was also the most lofty image they could form of pure and ultimate enjoyment. The reward of all acquitted spirits was translation from the sacred Valley of the Nile, its joys and sorrows and mutations, to the one unchanging source of brilliance and fertility. 'This great god speaks to them and they speak to him; his glory illuminates them in the splendour of his disc, while he is shining in their sphere[2].'

[1] Döllinger, p. 434: cf. above, p. 214, n. 2; where a similar faculty is said to have entered into the Hindû conception of original 'perfectness.'

[2] Rosellini, in Kenrick, I. 487.

CHAPTER II.

Alleged Affinities between the Hebrew and Egyptian Systems.

Κατὰ τὰ ἐπιτηδεύματα Αἰγύπτου, ἐν ᾗ κατῳκήσατε ἐπ' αὐτῇ, οὐ ποιήσετε, καὶ κατὰ τὰ ἐπιτηδεύματα γῆς Χαναάν, εἰς ἣν ἐγὼ εἰσάγω ὑμᾶς ἐκεῖ, οὐ ποιήσετε, καὶ τοῖς νομίμοις αὐτῶν οὐ πορεύσεσθε. τὰ κρίματά μου ποιήσετε, καὶ τὰ προστάγματά μου φυλάξεσθε, καὶ πορεύεσθε ἐν αὐτοῖς. ΕΓΩ ΚΥΡΙΟΣ Ο ΘΕΟΣ ΥΜΩΝ. LEVIT. XVIII. 3, 4. (LXX).

Influence of Egypt on the Hebrews. Improbability that heathenish ideas were adopted in Hebraism.

§ 1. *Ritual resemblances. General nature of ancient symbolism. Character of the Mosaic institute.* (1) *Circumcision existed in distant countries: how related to the Abrahamic institution. Specific differences between the Hebrew and all other rites.* (2) *Cherubim. Compound symbols in other countries. Real nature of the Cherubim. How connected with man's redemption. Relation to the Sphinx.* (3) *Holy and most holy places. Real import of the Hebrew sanctuary. Egyptian contrasts.* (4) *Urim and Thummim. Alleged parallelism. Thummim and Thmei. Probable meaning of the Hebrew symbol.* (5) *The Red Heifer.* (6) *The Scape-goat. Minor points of resemblance. Who or what was Azazel?*

§ 2. *Doctrinal contrasts. Hebrew monotheism and Egyptian polytheism. Ethical character of Hebrew monotheism.*

The moral sensibility of the Hebrew contrasted with the moral dulness of the Egyptian. Man's relationship to God not recognised in Egypt. Bestial incarnations. Doctrine of a future life, universally diffused; not necessarily connected with sublime ideas of God. The Egyptian dogma. The Christian doctrine. How treated in the Old Testament. The Babylonish exile the penalty of indulging heathenish notions.

THAT some examples of external correspondency, more marked and less fortuitous than any we have hitherto detected, can be traced between the ritual codes of the Egyptian and the Hebrew, is no longer questioned even by the warmest advocate of supernatural religion[1]. These affinities, however, as we

[1] Thus Witsius, in his *Ægyptiaca*, p. 4, Basil, 1739, declares expressly 'magnam atque mirandam plane convenientiam in religionis negotio veteres inter Ægyptios atque Hebræos esse,' and adds: 'Quæ cum fortuita esse non possit, necesse est ut vel Ægyptii sua ab

might at once anticipate from the absorbing interest of the points involved, give birth to a variety of conflicting interpretations. Some, for instance, have contended that as early as the age of Abraham, the priests of Lower Egypt were induced to borrow from him certain portions of the patriarchal creed, as well as to accept instruction at his hands in secular and useful learning. Others, on the contrary, affirm that Abraham himself and his descendants in the time of Moses had not scrupled in particular cases to incorporate the riper wisdom of the land of Egypt with their own hereditary laws and their most cherished institutions. While a third class, arguing from the fact that both these peoples radiated from a common centre, would refer the numerous points of similarity which they exhibit to the influence of a purer and more primitive generation, when the fathers of the Hebrew race still[1] recognised the sacred character of worthies like Melchisedek, and communed with them as with 'priests of the most high God.'

The feelings also which suggest the different theories on this subject are as widely different as the theories themselves. On the one side stand the writers both of earlier and later ages, who are actuated by a strong conviction that we had almost 'as well not worship God at all as worship Him by rites which have been employed in paganism[2].' The presence in the Bible of some element of faith or worship, known to have been actually borrowed from the primitive faith or worship of the circumjacent heathen would in their view silence or invalidate all arguments in favour of a special Revelation; and accordingly they feel concerned to demonstrate that 'images of truth,' wherever such exist in Gentilism, were merely due to the refracted rays of supernatural light whose proper sphere was in the bosom of the sacred family. Others, unrestrained by

Hebræis, vel ex adverso Hebræi sua ab Ægyptiis habeant.' And Hengstenberg, in our own day, makes a similar admission: 'He [Spencer] sets out with an assertion—in the main correct, but pushed by him to an extreme—that many parts of the Mosaic ceremonial law present a striking agreement with the religious usages of heathen nations, particularly of the Egyptians.' *Dissertations on the Genuineness of the Pentateuch*, I. 4, Edinb. 1847.

[1] See above, p. 69, n. 2.

[2] This is Warburton's characteristic way of putting the case of his opponents: cf. *Div. Leg.* II. 312 sq. Lond. 1846. A similar class of scruples have occasionally peeped out in discussions of the post-Reformation period on the subject of ecclesiastical vestments and other ceremonies: *e.g.* at the Hampton Court Conference, where objections were urged against the surplice, on the ground that such a dress was worn of old time by priests of Isis.

feelings of this kind, nay, anxious even, it would seem, at all hazards to multiply the points of sympathy between the Hebrew and the heathen systems, find their only possible justification of the ceremonial law of Moses in assuming its profound dependence on the institutes of the Egyptian law-givers. While particular branches of that ritual were (say they) intended to condemn or counteract the grosser vices of polytheism, the general object was to gratify a multitude of childish prejudices[1], which the Hebrew had contracted in the course of his long residence in Egypt. Customs and ideas of heathenish extraction were engrafted on the Law, and that by the express authority of God Himself, in order to amuse the fancy, and preoccupy the spirit of the Israelitish people, who might else, through their incorrigible love of superstitious imagery and impatience of all purely spiritual truth, have been seduced into apostasy. One school of modern writers has, however, accepted this position so far only as to grant that several usages commanded in the Law of Moses were in fact adapted from the ritual code of the Egyptians; but instead of finding in that circumstance a reason for disparaging the ceremonial system of the Hebrews, they proceed to build on their admission a fresh argument in favour of the early date and high authority of the Pentateuch[2].

[1] Spencer's work, *De Legibus Hebræorum ritualibus*, is pervaded by this strange idea. As Bähr expresses it (*Symbolik des Mosaischen Cultus*, I. 41, Heidelberg, 1837), God appears in his theory 'as a Jesuit who makes use of bad means [Spencer himself says *ineptiæ tolerabiles*] to bring about a good result.' In some respects the legal institute might justly be regarded by the Christian Fathers as a kind of *condescension* to the wants and weaknesses of man, and consequently as a συγκατάβασις or *accommodation* to the actual status of its Jewish subjects (cf. Acts xiii. 18); but Spencer's theory is a coarse and violent perversion of this philosophic principle. Instead of looking on the law of Moses as a lower and symbolic form of true religion, possessing therefore an internal fitness, and a definite place in the grand scheme of man's redemption, he could see in it nothing more than a huge 'apparatus of ceremonies,' having 'no agreement with the nature of God.' Perhaps the closest of patristic approximations to his standing-ground occurs in one of the letters of Gregory the Great (Bed. *Hist. Eccl.* I. 30): with which may be compared the startling assertions of Mr. D. I. Heath, *Exodus Papyri*, pp. 103 sq. Lond. 1855.

[2] This, for example, appears to be the moving principle of Dr. Hengstenberg in his *Die Bücher Mose's und Aegypten*, Berlin, 1841, where the points of outward similarity are unduly multiplied. His own avowal is: 'Je ursprünglicher, selbstständiger und einzigartiger die israelitische Religion in Bezug auf den Geist war, desto weniger hatte sie es nöthig, mit scheuer Aengstlichkeit jede äussere Berührung mit den Religionen anderer Völker zu vermeiden' (p. 153).

Now, if we try to disembarrass our minds as far as possible from any mere presumptions, it is evident that contradictory theories in vogue with reference to alleged resemblances between the Hebrew and Egyptian systems are in almost every case extravagant or superficial or one-sided. We are bound, for instance, to acknowledge on the threshold, that some very deep impressions had been made upon the sons of Abraham by their continued sojourn in the empire of the Pharaohs. From the nature of the case the Hebrews must have been disciples and not doctors. Going down a handful of mere nomades to that country of the ancient world whose institutions had been longest organised, they could not fail to have experienced the transforming influence everywhere implied in such an altered mode of life. We know, indeed, for certain that the land of Goshen proved the nursery of their national spirit, and the training-school in which they gradually imbibed some elements of art, of agriculture, and of civil polity. We know, again, that during their abode in Egypt, the majority of Hebrews proper,—to say nothing of the 'great mixed multitude,' who having learnt to share their fortunes were blended with them at the Exodus,—contracted more and more a fondness for Egyptian thoughts and customs, utterly at variance with the creed inherited from their fathers[1]. The same vicious predilection had moreover gained such stubborn hold upon them that in after-ages it was constantly evincing its importance, and could scarcely ever be eradicated.

Nor have these considerations been sufficiently answered by the plea that all the popular bias on the side of Egypt, active as it was before the promulgation of the Law, had constituted an additional reason why the Lawgiver should abstain from every thing which countenanced or confirmed it: since, according to the framers of the theory of accommodation, it was politic in Moses to recognise and so to consecrate, as far as might be, what the present temper of the Hebrew people rendered him unable to displace. Nay, ask these writers, might not Moses be induced to grant some measure of indulgence to his weak and sense-bound followers by his own experience of the real strength of their temptations, or the real good which might have been deducible from heathen customs? Educated from his earliest childhood in the court of the Egyptian monarch, and, it may be, actually initiated[2] into the

[1] On their religious condition while in Egypt, see Kurtz, *Gesch.* II. 38—42.

[2] Cf. Uhlemann's *Thoth*, p. 6.

sacred circles of the priesthood, was he not (say they) both skilled in the symbolic ordinances of Egyptian worship and enabled to discern the hidden truths which lay enveloped in the midst of it? If many of the oldest Greek philosophers, as Thales or Pythagoras[1] or Plato, who had sojourned there a shorter period, could return exulting from the land of Egypt laden with a rich variety of intellectual spoils; if through their visits many a germ of mathematical science and the outlines of a purer system of ethics and theology were rescued from comparative oblivion; if the principle of distributing their pupils into outer and inner classes, an enlarged conception of the grandeur of the universe, or a more fascinating list of dogmas, such as that of transmigration and the like, had all been widely spread along the shores of the Mediterranean, why should not the foster-child of Pharaoh's daughter have been equally imbued with reverence for ideas and institutions of his adopted country[2], or at least inclined to tolerate in others what to lofty spirits like his own may have been radiant with the light of true philosophy?

Now let it be conceded, in reply to these surmises, that the 'human learning' of the Hebrew legislator was from first to last *Egyptian*. Let it also be conceded that the fondness of his subjects for Egyptian ritualism was such as to have baffled all the wisest schemes designed to counteract it; and enough will yet remain to make us hesitate before subscribing to this novel phase of the accommodation-theory. If the Books of Moses be accepted as our guide (and other guidance in this region we have none), is it consistent either with their letter or their spirit that the Law, as authorised at such a crisis by God Himself, could carry with it any sanction of things *purely heathenish* in their nature? Was it not pervaded by indignant

[1] The prohibition by Pythagoras of *all* animal food and *all* animal sacrifices (adduced by Uhlemann, *Thoth*, p. 12, as an illustration of his Egyptising) has rather a Hindú aspect; and of later years, indeed, it has grown fashionable to speak of the founder of Pythagoreanism as a kind of Buddhist missionary; his name or title (Pythagoras = 'Buddha-guru') being quoted as confirmatory of such hypotheses. Others, however, dwell upon his supposed *Phœnician* origin, and so make him the depository of Semitic, if not Biblical, traditions; while many of his ascetic principles are clearly traceable among the Palestinian Essenes.

[2] Miss Martineau, *Eastern Life*, p. 104, tells us that Plato came to Egypt, 'and sat, where Moses had sat, at the feet of the priests, gaining, as Moses had gained, an immortal wisdom from their lips:' but when she adds that Moses learned to become 'a redeem-legislator,' as Plato a 'spiritual philosopher,' I confess my utter inability to understand her meaning.

protests against heathenism as such? The call of Moses, the appointed legislator, was as critical and peremptory as the call of the Apostle of the Gentiles: it was also followed by a like inversion and revulsion in the spirit of the 'chosen vessel.' He too had been sent to 'bear the name of God before the Gentiles and kings and the children of Israel,' and to suffer for that Name's sake (cf. Acts ix. 15, 16). He learned at starting on his mission, and he kept engraven ever on his mind, a clear idea of the 'complete and absolute distinction of the Jewish faith from that of any other ancient nation[1].' This distinctness of position and belief, proclaimed no more through hieroglyphs intelligible only to the few, but in the ordinary writing of the Hebrew people, was exactly in accordance with the destiny marked out for them as conservators of the true religion. The whole genius therefore of their institutions was distinctive, separative, incapable of compromise, impatient of amalgamation; so distinctive, so peculiar, that the wonderful vitality of Hebraism in after-times can only be explained on the hypothesis that men's devotion to it had been supernaturally produced, and ever since the childhood of the nation had been growing upward with their growth. Or if advancing from these general probabilities we study some of the first chapters in the national records of the Israelites, we shall again perceive at every turn the traces of antagonism between their own and the Egyptian system. In the Exodus itself, which led the way to the formation of the legal institute, we have to witness no mere secular emancipation from the yoke of a new line of Pharaohs, but the mightiest of religious victories which the ancient world had seen. Designed to vindicate the personality and holiness of God, as well as the distinctness of His chosen people, it was ushered in by a succession of stupendous acts which tended to rebuke and stultify the nature-worship of Mizraim: it was consummated in that moment, when the Hebrews, flushed with hope and exultation, were all forward in responding to the grateful anthem of their leader: 'I will sing unto the Lord, for he hath triumphed gloriously....The Lord is my strength and song, and He is become my salvation' (Ex. xv. 1, 2). As, therefore, in the parallel case where Christianity is struggling hand to hand with some bewitching or besotting form of heathenism, it is most needful to protect her neophyte against all risk of fresh contamination by decrying or discountenancing customs which may serve, remotely even, to perpetuate modes

[1] Cf. Dr. Donaldson's *Christian Orthodoxy*, p. 117, Lond. 1857.

of thought and feeling adverse to the rightful exercise of her transforming influence; so the Pentateuch evinces a continual jealousy lest peradventure the old thirst for heathenish vices should be stimulated through the medium of unhallowed associations. Intermarriage, for example, with the neighbouring heathen is most sternly interdicted both by Moses and by Joshua whenever it is likely to involve among its fruits the imitation or adoption of heathen customs. The redeemed community have ample warrant for believing that they are no more a friendless band of foreign shepherds, mingled and well-nigh confounded with the meanest subjects of the Pharaohs, but 'a kingdom of priests, a holy nation, a peculiar treasure unto God above all people' (Ex. xix. 5, 6); and because the ground of such election, owing to the nature of God Himself, is ultimately and entirely moral, the elected race is under a proportionate obligation to exhibit in the sight of the surrounding world its moral superiority: 'After the doings of the land of Egypt, wherein ye dwelt, shall ye not do: and after the doings of the land of Canaan, whither I bring you, shall ye not do; neither shall ye walk in their ordinances. Ye shall do My judgments, and keep Mine ordinances, to walk therein: I am the Lord your God.' (Lev. xviii. 3, 4.)

The question, therefore, as to the transmission of religious thoughts and usages from the Egyptian to the Hebrew is discovered to be far more complicated than at first sight may appear. It is a question little likely to be solved, as many writers have of late attempted, by adducing an array of bare presumptions on the one side or the other. To discuss it we must enter on a rigorous examination of the facts themselves; and with a view to such investigation, I shall here arrange all possible affinities in two separate classes[1]: (1) the minor points of ritualism which may have been inherited in common, or externally derived from one system to the other, without implying any true internal sympathy; and (2) the cardinal points of doctrine which must ever have determined the character of those systems, and have proved the real secret of their weakness or their strength.

§ 1. *Ritual Resemblances.*

Before entering on the criticism of any particular instances, it is important to recall attention to remarks already[2] made in

[1] All inquiries into merely civil and political arrangements are passed over as not directly bearing on the present subject.

[2] Above, pp. 74 sq.

reference to the offices discharged by symbolism in the religions of antiquity. The lack of any clear ideas on this point has tended more than other causes to becloud the whole of the discussions opened in the present chapter. I have urged that since the ancient Hebrew was in temperament, as also in the measure of his intellectual training, not unlike the native of surrounding countries, symbolism of some kind or other was most needful in that early period to the planting of religious truth and its development within him. He was far less capable than his remote descendants of all abstract and unearthly contemplation; he was living more than they in the impressions made upon the eyesight; and accordingly it was the part of wisdom in obtaining from him the acceptance of a supersensuous truth to represent, or, one might say, embody it in concrete shapes, to clothe it in more visible and sensuous drapery, and enforce it by suggestive actions and symbolical institutions. Here, as in the case of teaching by parable or allegory, a pure thought has been invested in expressive forms which bring it more directly under the cognisance of every human mind endowed with the most elementary of religious intuitions. Symbol was, in other words, a species of primeval language: the symbolic institutions were the illustrated and illuminated books, in which the early generations of the human family might learn the rudiments of true religion: and, aided as it was among the Hebrews by a series of collateral expositions ever guarding it from misconstruction and reverting to the spiritual principles on which it had been framed, the ritual law was one of God's chief agents in the education of the elder Church. It deepened in man's heart the consciousness of his dependence and degeneracy; it taught the need of a redemption and foreshadowed the Redeemer; while by it the grand conception of one holy God had been associated with the homeliest of man's actions, and diffused 'into the very midst of the popular life.' Compared with Christianity, indeed, that ritual system of the Hebrew was unripe and rudimentary; it was made up of 'weak and beggarly elements;' it proved itself a Pædagogue and not *the* Teacher; the result to which it ever pointed the aspirations of its worthier subjects was not actually achieved until 'the fulness of the times had come,' until the Incarnation of the Son of God and the effusion of the quickening Spirit: yet in reference to the stage of progress then attainable by man, it offered an effectual apparatus for evoking and conserving the religious principle; and when at last the sentence of abrogation was pronounced, the law of ordinances fell, as scaffolding falls off, because the edifice it served to rear had reached the full proportions, and because a system not inglorious in itself has 'no glory in this respect by reason of the glory that excelleth.'

If, then, sacred emblems of the ancient world were thus peculiarly significant; if symbolic institutions were a species of necessity arising out of the capacities and condition of the human mind, and so were common to the rituals both of Jew and heathen, all objections to the Bible which depend upon the *mere existence* of resemblances between these rituals, irrespectively, that is, of the ideas therein embodied, fall entirely to the ground. It would be equally presumptuous to disparage or reject the doctrines of the Gospel, prior to all scrutiny of its contents, because these doctrines are transmitted to us in the ordinary characters made use of in the printing of the other writings of antiquity, or else because particular forms of speech are found to be employed alike by the Apostle of the Gentiles, and the orators, the poets or the moralists of ancient Greece. The same outward act or emblem might continue to embody the same primitive truth and so be equally innocuous in both systems, which are made the subjects of comparison. Or, upon the other hand, it might be gradually connected in the lapse of ages with divergent if not opposite and contradictory ideas[1]. But wherever any emblem had been consciously transferred from one ancient people to another, care would doubtless be employed to rescue it from all supposed perversions then attaching to it, so that in its fresh position it might harmonise instead of jarring with the other members of the ritual system. Let this only be effected, and a symbol used extensively in heathen countries for the representation of a thing reputed holy might

[1] The following observations of Kurtz (*Gesch. des Alten Bundes*, I. 310), though not expressing the exact view here advocated, are well worthy of attention: 'In der hohen Blüthe ägyptischer Weisheit, Cultur und Industrie hatte Israel die beste Schule menschlicher Bildung, deren es für seine künftige Bestimmung bedurfte; durch die Bekanntschaft mit der tiefen Anschauung der Aegypter, die das ganze Leben mit allen seinen Aeusserungen und Verzweigungen unter religiösen Gesichtspunkt stellte, konnte selbst Israels *religiöse* Anschauung mehrfach bereichert werden, und in der Symbolik des ägyptischen Cultus fand es schon eine völlig ausgebildete *Form* des religiösen Lebens vor, die, weil *aus nothwendigen und allgemein gültigen Anschauungs- und Denkgesetzen des menschlichen Geistes hervorgegangen*, nicht ausschliesslich nur zum Träger des ägyptischen Pantheismus anwendbar war, sondern, von dem specifisch-israelitischen Princip beseelt, verklärt und umgestaltet, auch dem Cultus des israelitischen Theismus zum willkommnen Träger dienen konnte.'

be also chosen as an apt exponent of a thing more lofty and more holy still; the freedom of the symbol from profane associations facilitating the adoption of it, and imparting to it an especial fitness for its new office.

It is, therefore, highly probable that if the Hebrew legislator, acting here as always under the supreme direction of Jehovah, were induced to sanction rites and ceremonies current in the land of Egypt, or in other nations of antiquity, he was influenced by no wish to gratify the merely 'puerile superstitions' of his followers, but by reasons more exalted in themselves and more befitting his exalted character. He engrafted them into the legal institutions either because they were the uncorrupted heirloom of the patriarchal age, or else because, from their inherent fitness and expressiveness, they were commended to him as at once convertible in aid of the great project he was called to carry out.

The number of these ritual correspondencies is stated with considerable variety by different writers. Some[1], however, I shall scarcely glance at; first, because the facts on which it is attempted to support them are extremely vague and problematical, and, secondly, because those facts, when fully ascertained, admit of a more simple and more rational explanation. In selecting the examples here subjoined for more minute analysis, I take the points which have been universally esteemed the most important of the series, and which century after century have furnished his main arguments to the impugner of the Books of Moses.

[1] Thus, the division of the Hebrews into twelve tribes, alleged by some writers as analogous to the territorial divisions of Egypt, naturally resulted from the number of Jacob's children. The distinction between clean and unclean meats, was pre-Mosaic and patriarchal, reaching backward to the Deluge. Hence may also be explained the strong repugnance felt to *swine* among the Israelites as well as the Egyptians, and the feeling of contempt with which they both regarded swineherds. The Levitical hierarchy had, moreover, several points of close resemblance to the various orders of Egyptian priests; yet most important differences are also traceable; for instance, in the perpetual exclusion of the Hebrew priesthood from all grants of territory. (Cf. Prichard, *Egypt. Mythol.* pp. 409 sq.) In this class of merely accidental correspondencies I am inclined to place the 'holy women' of the Israelites, a kind of nuns or female Nazarites, distinct from priestesses, but nevertheless devoted to ascetic modes of life (Ex. xxxviii. 8; 1 Sam. ii. 22): with whom may be compared the holy women of Egypt and Phœnicia (Herod. II. 54, 56).

CIRCUMCISION.

(1) The rite of circumcision, though practised by the Hebrews from an earlier epoch, was perpetuated in the ritual system of their legislator, and, as raised by him into a national institution, takes its place among the subjects handled in this chapter. Now that some such rite was also common in the land of Egypt, where Abraham himself had sojourned prior to its introduction into his own family, is definitely stated in a well-known passage of Herodotus[1]. He there informs us that the custom was native with Egyptians and Ethiopians, as also with the Colchians, who, according to his version of the matter, were an old deposit of Egyptians reaching backward to the conquests of Sesostris. He then adds that circumcision was derived from Egypt by the Syrians of Palestine and the Phœnicians. In the absence of all mention of the Jews, as well as of the Ishmaelites who, Abrahamic also in their origin, had practised the same rite, we may conjecture[2] that the information of Herodotus, which may have been derived exclusively from traders, was restricted to the *coast* of Syria. Still there is no reason for suspecting the general truth of the account, that centuries before the date of his travels some conformity in this respect existed between the Hebrews and Egyptians. The 'reproach of Egypt,' as adverted to by Joshua (v. 9), is capable of two or more interpretations; but if taken to mean 'that which Egypt would herself have stigmatised[3],' the phrase will intimate that as early as the

[1] II. 104; see Diodor. I. 28, and the abundant literature on the whole subject in Winer, *Realwört.* s.v. 'Beschneidung.' Sir G. Wilkinson affirms (Rawlinson's *Herod.* Vol. II. p. 171) that the rite was common in Egypt itself 'at least as early as the 4th dynasty, and probably earlier, long before the birth of Abraham.'

[2] See Mr. Blakesley's note on Herodotus, as above. The difficulty connected with 1 Sam. xviii. 25; 2 Sam. i. 20, etc., where 'Philistines' are distinguished as the 'uncircumcised,' Mr. Blakesley meets by remarking that 'subsequently to the time of Saul a great change took place in the population of the Philistine cities, and that a considerable Egyptian element [practising circumcision] had probably been introduced.'

[3] See Rosenmüller, *in loc.*, who refers to Ezek. xvi. 57; xxxvi. 15; Ps. xxxix. 9, in illustration of the Hebrew phraseology. Yet other texts appear to justify the passive rendering, 'that which exposes Egypt to reproach;' viz. uncircumcision (cf. 1 Sam. xvii. 26), or else idolatry (cf. Ezek. xx. 7), with which the Hebrews had been previously infected. New difficulties arise from the examination of Jer. ix. 25, 26, where both the Hebrew and Vulgate (as expounded by St. Jerome, *in loc.*) are quoted to prove that many persons in Egypt and Edom, as well as Ammonites and Moabites, *did* practise circumcision, though strangers to the true faith: cf. Ezek. xxxi. 18; xxxii. 24, 29, 30, 32.

period of the Exodus the lack of circumcision[1] had been held disreputable in Egypt; and although it may be now successfully contended, more especially from a profusion of extant mummies[2], that the practice had been far from universal, its prevalence in the age of Moses may be urged with some show of reason.

The remote antiquity of the practice is again suggested strongly, if not absolutely proved, by its existence far beyond the area both of Hebrew and Egyptian influence. Traces of it have been found not only in the Cushite race of Ethiopians proper, and in Troglodytes[3] whose haunts were chiefly on the confines of the Red Sea, but far away at the extremity of the African continent[4], among the distant isles of Oceanica[5], and even, there is reason for supposing, in the very heart of the New World[6]. Yet if phenomena like these transport us backward to a period long before the call of Abraham or the adoption of the usage in his household, there is nothing in the language of the sacred penman which can fairly be regarded as at variance with such a supposition. The peculiar terms, indeed, in which the ordinance of circumcision was prescribed to him at first (Gen. xvii. 10) would rather indicate that the

[1] Cf. Ex. iv. 24 sq., which implies that, for some cause or other, the rite had been at first omitted, even in the household of Moses, although the obligation to administer it was known to Zipporah, his wife. Its subsequent suspension in the wilderness appears to have rested altogether upon *moral* grounds; the people 'who obeyed not the voice of the Lord' were for a season placed in the condition of the excommunicated, and therefore were thrust back into the standing-ground of the unclean (cf. Josh. v. 5—7).

[2] 'From the examination of the mummies it appears that the practice was very limited, not extending to one in fifty; but it must be remembered that a large proportion of these are not of very high antiquity.' Kenrick, I. 450.

[3] Diodor. III. 32, who remarks that they acted παραπλησίως τοῖς Αἰγυπτίοις, though it is not altogether improbable that the Troglodytes were of Arabian lineage, and might thus derive the practice from Ishmael. It is still not uncommon in Abyssinia (cf. Uhlemann, *Aegypt. Alt.* II. 257), but whether adopted from the heathen natives or the Judaizers of the Early Church is matter of dispute.

[4] *e.g.* Dr. Livingstone writes (pp. 146, 147): 'All the Bechuana and Caffre tribes south of the Zambesi practise circumcision (*boguera*), but the rites observed are carefully concealed.' He thinks, as there practised, it was 'only a sanitary and political measure,' and further suggests that, owing to the want of 'a continuous chain of tribes practising the rite,' it 'can scarcely be traced, as is often done, to a Mahometan source' (p. 149). Prichard (*Researches*, III. 287) believes it 'a relic of ancient African customs, of which the Egyptians, as it is well known, partook in remote ages.' The practice is still common in Æthiopia.

[5] Above, p. 407, n. 3.

[6] *Ibid.*

idea itself was older and was not unknown to him. The elevation of an ancient symbol to the rank of a Divine ordinance exactly corresponded to the change effected in a second ancient rite,—the practice of lustration, where the element of water, naturally associable with ideas of purity, was chosen by our blessed Lord in His initiatory sacrament, to symbolise, and by the working of His Spirit to convey, the highest form of purification,—the remission of sins.

What then may be said to constitute the special and distinctive differences between the heathen and the Hebrew rite of circumcision? It is not, I think, unlikely that this usage was connected first of all with the idea of generative purity, and so of a transcendent fitness for religious service, and the higher culture of the intellect. As such it had continued to be prized in Egypt by the members of the hierarchy[1], even though neglected or disparaged by the bulk of the people; among whom, indeed, on losing its original significance, it came to be regarded merely as an ancient custom or a sanitary and prudential regulation[2]. It might also in some districts be corrupted, with corruptions of religious thought, into a species of bloody offering[3], or might even as a substitute for human sacrifices be administered in every case with the intention of propitiating an angry god, like Moloch or Huitzilopochtli. But whatever had become the heathen version of this symbol, no one will deny that when the Hebrew father circumcised the members of his household, he both acted with a definite purpose and was animated by a spirit thoroughly religious. There the rite was not to be administered, as once it was in Egypt, at the age of fourteen and upwards 'when reasons of health or purity might prompt it,' but as soon almost as the recipient of it was a sharer in the blessings of existence,—on the eighth day after birth. As such it formed a strictly *national* solemnity, embracing not the favoured classes of society to whom it gave

[1] Origen distinctly affirms this (*in Ep. ad Roman.* lib. II. c. 13; Opp. V. 138, 139, ed. Lommatzsch), adding that men of science were subjected to the rite of circumcision, and that no persons uncircumcised were allowed to study the sacerdotal or hieroglyphic characters.

[2] Cf. Herod. II. 37, and above, p. 491, n. 4.

[3] Above, p. 407, n. 3. Döllinger (*Heidenthum und Judenthum*, p. 790) appears to have adopted this theory: 'Erinnert man sich, dass auch in Rom und bei den Galliern frühere Menschenopfer durch eine leichte Wunde, ein Ritzen der Haut und Vergiessen einiger Blutstropfen ersetzt wurden, so ist es wohl denkbar, dass auch die Beschneidung ein solcher stellvertretender Opfer-Ritus gewesen sei:' cf. Kurtz, *Gesch. des Alt. Bund.* I. 185.

admission to the higher forms of intellectual greatness, but extending always to the lowliest member of the Hebrew commonwealth. And corresponding to the freedom of its spirit and its equal operation was the grandeur of the end for which it was appointed. Like the rest of the Mosaic institute, that symbol was profoundly ethical. Translated into words, the meaning of it was 'Be ye holy, for I am holy.' 'The Lord appeared to Abram, and said unto him, I am the Almighty God; walk before Me, and be thou perfect; and I will make my covenant between Me and thee, and will multiply thee exceedingly' (Gen. xvii. 1, 2). The rite of circumcision, as the narrative proceeds to tell us, was the seal and 'token' of this covenant (ver. 11). Outward in the flesh, and so according with the sterner genius of the old economy, it imprinted on the mind of every Hebrew the peculiar closeness of his own relations to the pure and perfect God, and the necessity therein implied of fearing and of loving Him, and circumcising more and more 'the foreskin of the heart' (Deut. x. 12—16).

CHERUBIM.

(2) Another instance where it is imagined that the symbolism of heathen countries has been reproduced among the legal institutions is the figure of the cherubim, compared with the Egyptian sphinxes of the Pharaonic times. No question of this kind has been more frequently discussed, and few, it might be added, to so little profit. There is now indeed far less uncertainty than heretofore about the shape and meaning of the ancient sphinx. It was in Egypt of three kinds: 'the *andro-sphinx*, with the head of a man and the body of a lion; the *crio-sphinx*, with the head of a ram and the body of a lion; and the *hieraco-sphinx*, with the same body and the head of a hawk[1].' The first of these, which from the nature of its composition is most capable of being brought into comparison with the Hebrew cherub, is now regarded as a symbol of the union, in a fabulous shape, of mental and of physical energy[2]; the wisdom and intelligence of the man, combining with the courage and the brute force of the lion. Where a sphinx was planted by the Old Egyptian in the neighbourhood of the

[1] Wilkinson, 2nd ser. II. 200. This writer justly observes that the head of the human being in the first division is never feminine, much less virginal, as Bähr (*Symbolik*, I. 358) has incorrectly reasserted.

[2] Wilkinson, *Ibid.* Hengstenberg, *Die Bücher Mose's und Aegypten*, p. 159.

throne, the special properties which it was meant to symbolise were all attributed to the king himself; but where, as still more frequently happened, the position was in front of some Egyptian temple, it was rather meant to celebrate a union, in the deity[1] there worshipped, of the same exalted and commanding powers.

When we turn, however, to the Hebrew symbols which are often deemed in close analogy to this, and strive to ascertain their real form and meaning, it is most important to observe that such compounded representations had never during the historic period been exclusively Egyptian[2]. On the contrary, they seem to have abounded in all regions of the ancient world, in which the monuments of sacred art have been transmitted to our times. It has been stated, for example, that 'in the earliest Assyrian monuments, one of the most frequently met with is the eagle-headed human figure. Not only is it found in colossal proportions as sculptured upon the walls or guarding the portals of the chambers, but it is also constantly represented among the groups on the embroidered robes. In other cases, the head of the bird occurs united with the body of a lion, under which form it is the same as the Egyptian hieraco-sphinx[3].'

One definite parallel to representations of this kind has been suggested in the griffin of the Greek mythographers, which was avowedly an importation from some eastern system; but the specious theory, framed by Herder[4] for connecting griffins by a

[1] This reference to a deity is denied by Wilkinson, who thinks that all sphinxes, wherever placed, were 'types or representatives of the king:' but the theological import of such at least as were placed before temples was known to Plutarch (*De Is. et Osir.* c. IX.), and is maintainable on other grounds: cf. Rawlinson's *Herodotus*, Vol. I. p. 633, on the Man-Lion and the Man-Bull, as symbols of two Babylonian divinities.

[2] See the numerous examples of the contrary collected in Bähr, I. 357, 358, who declares with reference to the compound figures of ancient Egypt, that he cannot find a single instance possessing any true affinity to the Hebrew cherubs. The nearest approach to any actual resemblance, viz. a combination consisting of the heads of *four* creatures (a lion, a man, an ox, and an eagle), seems to be among the emblems of Hindûism (p. 352). Wilkinson, 2nd ser. II. 275, was most reminded of the Hebrew cherubs and their position in the tabernacle, by two figures of the goddess *Thmei* (or Truth) overshadowing by their wings the sacred beetle of the Sun.

[3] Vaux, *Nineveh and Persepolis*, p. 32, Lond. 1850: cf. pp. 293, 294.

[4] See the ample refutation of it in Bähr, I. 350 sq. Dr. Donaldson, *Christian Orthodoxy*, p. 354, has somewhat extended the dimensions of this theory by connecting the Greek *harpies*, 'which Homer de-

second link with cherubim of Holy Scripture, though revived from time to time by the more daring of philologers, is destitute of all internal probability as well as of historic basis. Cherubim, as they occur in representations of the Bible from its earliest chapters to the closing visions of St. John, are *not* mere guards, or watchers, blocking the approach to some forbidden object. In the text (Gen. iii. 24), which more than others will at first sight favour such interpretation of their functions, it is not asserted that the cherubim were placed *outside* the garden; neither is it said that they were planted on that sacred soil to 'watch' it merely; for if 'watching' was in any sense ascribed to them, as well as to the sword-like flame, the word employed will shew that they were watchers only as the first man was a watcher; they were doing there what he had signally failed to do (ii. 15). And in like manner the position of those emblems in the Hebrew tabernacle had never been upon the threshold of the holiest place, nor even before the mercy-seat, but in immediate contact and connexion with the throne of God Himself (Exod. xxv. 18). A careful survey of these facts will be sufficient to repel the notion that the cherubim were emblems only of exclusive and prohibitory power; and if we seek, as we are bound, the fuller illustration of their form and import in the copious visions of Ezekiel, and especially among the wonders of the great Apocalypse, it is evident that, whatever may turn out to be their true relation to the sphinx, they differed from the griffin absolutely and entirely. Both indeed were composite in structure, though the figures which make up the symbol were unlike in the two cases: and with this mere shadow of approximation ceases all affinity whatever.

How then, following in the steps of Holy Scripture, may we characterise the Hebrew cherubim? Each cherub was a group of figures, or was rather one compounded figure, consisting of four parts. The leading or most prominent shape resembled a human being, while the rest were like some portions

signates as stormy winds,' and the Greek *Kerb-erus*, 'which barred the entrance to Hades,' with the sphinx of Egypt, which, he says, 'watched over the sepulchres,' and the כְּרוּב of Holy Scripture, which he characterises, first, as 'the harpy or seizer,' and, then, by a transition hard to follow, as 'symbolical of the Divine presence,' and a 'sign of warning to forbid a rash or profane approach to the shrine of inaccessible sanctity' (p. 355). It may seem presumptuous to disbelieve or controvert the etymology of *cherub*, here suggested; but Dr. Donaldson knows, as well as I do, that a multitude of other guesses, quite as plausible, have been in turn examined and rejected by Hebrew lexicographers.

of the ox, the lion, and the eagle. The whole emblem, it is true, might have been somewhat different at the different points of Hebrew history[1]; but two or more of these distinctive elements had always been the recognised members of cherubic combinations. Now we gather from Ezekiel that the fundamental thought embodied in such emblems was the property of *life:* they were emphatically the 'living ones[2];' they represented, therefore, several of the noblest forms of creaturely existence, each excelling in its province, each contributing to the production of a group, in which the human form[3] predominated, and the four together constituting an ideal image of all animated nature.

So interpreted we readily understand not only their position in the sacred garden, but their office in the sanctuary of God on earth and also their proximity to God Himself in visions of the blessed. The planting of the cherub on the ground, which man had once inherited but failed ere long to cherish for his best possession, was suggestive of the truth that he and all whose fortunes had been linked with his had still, in virtue of some gracious mystery, a part and interest in Eden. The appearance of the cherub in the holiest of all was further proof of such an interest; it prolonged the hopeful pledge afforded to the Hebrew by traditions of his forefathers; it told him that the representatives of man and of creation generally had still their place allotted to them on the mercy-seat of the Most High; and in the glowing scenes of the Apocalypse when Adam's family have re-assembled round the throne of God to sing the praises of the great Redeemer, the same mystic creatures shew the ardour which that anthem has excited in their bosoms, by a rapturous 'Amen' (Rev. v. 14).

Whatever, therefore, may be urged in proof of some external correspondency in the Mosaic age between the cherub as already known to members of the sacred family and the

[1] Bähr, I. 314. Hengstenberg (as before, p. 162), who, differing from Bähr, argues in favour of the original connexion between the sphinx and cherub, is of opinion that in the time of Moses the cherubic emblem consisted of two members only, the man and the lion, and refers, in proof that such a double representation was occasionally continued in far later times, to Ezek. xli. 18—20. He urges also, from Exod. xxv. 20, that the Mosaic cherub had only *one* aspect.

[2] Ezek. i. 5, 13 sq.; x. 17. The LXX render ζῷα, which is also the word made use of in the Apocalypse, iv. 6, and generally.

[3] 'Out of the midst thereof came the likeness of four living creatures. And this was their appearance: they had the likeness of a man.' Ezek. i. 5.

sphinx as sculptured in approaches to Egyptian temples, there can be no doubt that the two emblems were associated in those two systems with very different thoughts. The one might serve to symbolise the best conceptions which a pagan mind could form of properties possessed by favourite kings or by some nobler inmates of his crowded pantheon; while the other was designed to be a complex image of created nature in its highest, most ideal form, yet always bowing in distinct subordination to the great Creator, and as such ascribing 'glory and honour and thanks to Him that sat on the throne, who liveth for ever and ever' (Rev. iv. 9).

HOLY AND MOST HOLY PLACES.

(3) It has again been frequently remarked that the division of the Hebrew sanctuary into a holy and most holy place was made to follow the Egyptian model; the idea in both those cases being that the special residence of the Divinity should form a kind of inner shrine, or adytum, secreted from the popular gaze by some mysterious curtain. Now the fact that the Egyptian temples *did* contain what was entitled a 'most holy region[1],' as well as various courts conducting to it, is no longer open to dispute; yet with this solitary mark of outward correspondency, possessed in common by most other nations of the ancient world[2], the parallelism in question seems to be exhausted[3]. As the Hebrew sanctuary was one, in order to symbolise the absolute unity of God, so all arrangements there established had an eye to the surpassing purity and spirituality of His nature. There, as everywhere, the genius of the Hebrew system vindicated its true honour, as entirely and profoundly ethical. The migratory tent as well as the elaborate temple on Mount Moriah was a pledge to Israelites that God Himself, no mere abstraction, but a present, living, reigning God, had entered into fellowship with His elect, and though the heaven and the heaven of heavens were his (Deut. x. 14),

[1] Uhlemann, *Thoth*, p. 7, and above, p. 468.

[2] Bähr, I. 219.

[3] I have already called attention to the seeming parallelism between the 'ark of the covenant' and the sacred chests, or boats, of heathen nations, while discussing a ritual peculiarity of the Mexicans (above, pp. 370, 371); and the same remarks may be applied at once to the Egyptian ceremony entitled 'the procession of shrines,' and described at length by Wilkinson, 2nd ser. II. 271 sq. The few external resemblances will only serve to bring out more clearly the internal contradictions. Cf. Orcurti, *Catalogo Illustrato dei Monumenti Egizii* (Torino, 1852), pp. 91, 92.

had condescended to develope their religious sentiment by tabernacling in the midst of them. 'I will dwell among the children of Israel, and will be their God; and they shall know that I am the Lord their God, that brought them forth out of the land of Egypt, that I may dwell among them: I am the Lord their God' (Exod. xxix. 45, 46). The sanctuary had thus for them the kind of meaning which the Incarnation now possesses for the storm-tost spirit of the Christian; it presented to them one fixed point amid the fluctuations of the universe; it was the index of God's kingdom upon earth; it brought the infinite within the limits of the finite, it was raised into the meeting-place of human and Divine, and so became the feeble prelude to the mightiest of all facts. And as the holy-place was that to which the Israelite had access by his sacerdotal representatives, and where through them he could perform his ministry in the sight of God, so in the holy of holies, whence they all were equally excluded, there was imaged out the truth that even for the best of Israelites the way into the inmost presence of Jehovah 'was not yet made manifest.' Veils and barriers intercepted their approach to Him, whose glory, shining forth between the cherubim, was high above the mystic covering of the Ark; yet the admission of one single priest with the appointed offerings on the Day of Atonement was sufficient indication to the Hebrew who was truly bent on finding out 'the wonders of the Law,' that the condemnatory witness there deposited in the Ark might still be silenced and averted altogether by some absolute propitiation, symbolised in the arrangements of that annual solemnity.

It were superfluous to point out in detail how completely such ideas were absent from the goodliest temple of Mizraim, where the grovelling inmate of the holiest place was one or other of the sacred animals; and where the worship rendered by fanatic swarms of votaries was often no less gross and bestial than the object!

URIM AND THUMMIM.

(4) Greater confidence has sometimes been expressed by theorisers on this subject as to the Egyptian origin of the mysterious symbol which the Hebrew commonly entitled the *Urim and Thummim.* We collect from Diodorus and other writers[1] that in Egypt the chief judge engaged in listening to

[1] See Wilkinson, 2nd ser. II. 28, and a fuller discussion of this point in Mr. Tomkins's *Hulsean Essay*, (1850) pp. 80 sq. Hengstenberg argues for the identity of the two customs, while Mr. Kenrick (II. 53,

the cases brought before him wore about his neck a chain of gold and precious stones to which had been attached a small image of *Thmei*, the goddess of truth or justice, and that when the depositions of the litigants were heard, his practice was to touch the successful person with the image in token of the truth or justness of his cause. The drift of this Egyptian symbol is immediately apparent. It impressed on the administrator of public justice[1] that impartiality ought always to preside at his decisions, and the same idea of strict integrity was further hinted by the fact that Truth herself was pictured with closed eyes, and that the judges, in funereal rituals found at Thebes, were also represented 'without hands.' There is, however, far greater difficulty in ascertaining the precise complexion of the Hebrew usage which is frequently compared with this. The narrative respecting the institution of it will be found in Exod. xxviii. 30: 'And thou shalt put in the breast-plate[2] of judgment [*or*, righteousness] the Urim and the Thummim; and they shall be upon Aaron's heart, when he goeth in before the Lord: and Aaron shall bear the judgment of Israel upon his heart before the Lord continually.' We read again (Numb. xxvii. 21) that on the designation of Joshua to the leadership which had been previously enjoyed by Moses: 'He shall stand before Eleazar the priest, who shall ask [counsel] for him, after the judgment of Urim before the Lord;' implying that the wonderful emblems here connected with the

n. 1) seems to take the opposite view.

[1] Diodorus (I. 48) mentions as a common interpretation that the ἀρχιδικαστής, who appeared on the tomb of Osymandyas with closed eyes and with the figure of truth suspended from his neck, was bound πρὸς μόνην βλέπειν τὴν ἀλήθειαν: cf. Ælian, XIV. 34. Hengstenberg, *Die Bücher Mose's und Ägypten*, p. 156, is almost alone in maintaining that the primitive signification of this emblem was rather 'promissory' than didactic, pointing to some special presence and inspiration of the goddess of Truth in the Egyptian courts of justice. He refers in illustration to Deut. xxxiii. 8, 9.

[2] It has been urged (for example, by Mr. Tomkins, p. 83), as an admissible rendering of the Hebrew וְנָתַתָּ אֶל־חֹשֶׁן that 'these two mysterious names (Urim and Thummim) were *no visible part of it* (the breast-plate) *at all*, but attributes assigned to it emblematical of high moral qualities.' Yet as precisely the same phrase occurs in Exod. xxv. 16, 21, where the allusion is to the placing of the two Tables within the ark, we can hardly doubt that the Authorised Version is here correct, and that the Urim and Thummim were something superadded, and materially separable from the breast-plate: cf. Bähr, II. 108, 109. In Lev. viii. 8, it is said expressly, 'And he put the breast-place upon him; also he put in the breast-plate the Urim and the Thummim.'

breast-plate of the high-priest were meant, as being one with it, to serve the purpose of an oracle, whatever be the right interpretation of the method in which responses were detected and delivered (cf. 1 Sam. xxviii. 6).

The intimations, therefore, of a common parentage for the Egyptian and the Hebrew symbols, are restricted chiefly to the circumstance that both may be described as solemn badges, and that some *judicial* characteristics are attributed to their possessors in the two cases respectively. The chief judge, among his other decorations, wore about his neck the chain of office, with a precious seal, or effigy of truth, suspended from it: the chief priest, in asking guidance from Jehovah, wore the breast-plate of righteousness, containing in the precious stones of which it was composed an emblem of collective Israel; and armed with it he was directed to 'go in unto the holy place for a memorial before the Lord continually.' But the statement of this semblance of external approximation, or rather of remote affinity in the *uses* of the two solemn symbols, is enough to make us thoroughly conscious of their general dissimilitude. The Aaronic breast-plate, for example, was not worn in any court of human judicature; it had no reference to the ordinary business of the individual Hebrew, but to special difficulties connected with the fortunes of the whole sacred corporation; neither was it meant to quicken in the spirit of the wearer a conviction of his personal frailty, or his need of more than ordinary watchfulness in executing his high office.

Whence, then, grew the prevalent notion that some very close affinity existed between the emblems now in question? It is clearly traceable to the rendering, which had been adopted in the Septuagint[1], of the expression *Thummim*. That Hebrew word has there been made equivalent to 'Truth' (ἀλήθεια), and as the great Egyptian goddess, who presided over

[1] Urim (אוּרִים) is rendered δήλωσις in LXX, and (more literally) φωτισμοί in Aquila. The plural form is best explained as a plur. majest., so that it points to the idea of *Divine* illumination. The same account must be given of the plural form in Thummim (תֻּמִּים) which the LXX, and Philo after them, have rendered ἀλήθεια, and Aquila (more literally) τελειώσεις. Wilkinson, who seems to accept the rendering of the LXX, thinks that the 'dual or plural word' (Thummim) corresponds to the Egyptian notion of the 'two truths,' (cf. above, p. 476), or two similar figures, marking a double capacity of the goddess (2nd ser. II. 28, 29). He also gives a drawing of a breast-plate, where both Ra (the Sun) and Thmei are represented together; which is doubtless a still closer parallel to 'Lights' and 'Perfections.'

the courts of law, and aided the decisions of Osiris in the under-world, had also borne the name of Truth (*Thmei*), it was conjectured that the traces of a radical connexion between *Thmei* and *Thummim*, or in other words between the Hebrew and Egyptian customs, had been half-unconsciously attested by the Alexandrine version of the Pentateuch. But this conjecture has been seriously weakened, if not overthrown entirely, by other considerations: first, that 'Thummim' is a regular Hebrew form, grammatically unconnected with the Coptic *Thmei*; secondly, that in rendering 'Thummim' into Greek, the Seventy have departed from the letter of the Hebrew text and so confounded qualities which really differ; and thirdly, that the error introduced by them may probably have had its origin, like others of the same description, in their strong Egyptian bias.

I may add that when the glorious properties of light and of perfection had been thus ascribed emphatically to the Hebrew breast-plate by affixing to it the significant symbols of the Urim and Thummim, the high-priest was made to bear the whole of the 'oracular apparatus' with him as 'a memorial before the Lord.' If, therefore, in accordance with some other texts of Holy Scripture the inserted emblems may be construed[1] as uniting into one the highest moral qualities ascribable to God Himself, it is no idle fancy to conclude that Aaron, so adorned and bearing on his heart the names of the children of Israel, was to them a vivid image of the law of mediation (cf. Numb. xvi. 47, 48), and to us a luminous shadow of '*the* Mediator between God and man,' who having in the fulness of the times obtained a more excellent ministry, has gathered up into Himself the various functions of the mediatorial office.

THE RED HEIFER.

(5) In the law prescribed through Moses (Numb. xix.) for the cleansing of those Hebrews who had been defiled by touching a dead body, there is special mention of the colour of the victim to be offered up on such occasion; that its ashes, mingled with the lustral water, might conduce to the removal of the disability contracted, and so 'sanctify to the purifying of the flesh' (Heb. ix. 13). The victim was to be a *red* cow or heifer, without spot; and as no other valid reason seemed to be

[1] See this point well drawn out in Mr. Tomkins's Essay (as above) pp. 84 sq.

suggested[1] for the naming of one definite colour, fresh recourse was had by certain writers to the ancient usages of Egypt in the hope of thence extracting the desired elucidation. We have noted in the last chapter[2] that red was the Typhonic colour, and therefore, if full credit may be given to the account of Plutarch, the Egyptians 'never sacrificed any but perfectly red cattle.' It is plain, however, that if any foreign reference was intended, the idea of counteracting[3], not of copying the Egyptian custom is involved in the selection by the Hebrews of a cow or heifer in the place of the more usual ox (Lev. iv. 14); since both those animals, as we have seen already[4], were invested with peculiar sacredness throughout the Valley of the Nile. The truth will probably turn out to be, that the adoption of the red colour in both cases corresponded only because of its inherent fitness to express the thought which it was made to symbolise in each community. It was the colour of *blood*[5]; and while in Egypt this idea was readily connected with the deadly, scathing, sanguinary powers of Typhon, it became in the more ethical system of the Hebrews a remembrancer of moral evil flowing out into its penal consequences, or an image of unpardoned sin (cf. Isa. i. 15, 18).

THE SCAPE-GOAT.

(6) A further instance of supposed affinity to the Egyptian ritual is discovered in the ceremonies appointed for the Hebrew nation on the greatest of their annual celebrations,—the Day of Atonement (Lev. xvi). It is there provided that the high-priest of Israel, after making atonement for himself and for his house, shall take two goats, and when they had been solemnly presented shall cast lots upon them; 'one lot for the Lord and

1 Maimonides wrote a special treatise *De Vacca rufa*, and the subject has been handled with singular frequency in all ages; yet the Hebrew doctors admit that even Solomon, who knew most other things, was in ignorance respecting the red heifer.

2 Above, p. 470.

3 This view is strongly urged by Spencer, whose work contains a very full discussion *De Vitula rufa Deo immolanda*; but Hengstenberg, as before, p. 182, while conceding the partial truth involved in it, has suggested that the offering was feminine to make it accord more fully with the common Hebrew word for sin, which is also of the feminine gender.

4 Above, p. 470.

5 Hengstenberg, *Ibid.* p. 188. Bähr adopts a different view: 'Das Thier war...Antidotum gegen den Tod und die Todesgemeinschaft, und musste eben darum auf den Begriff Leben hinweisen; das geschah nun schon durch sein Geschlecht, noch mehr und bestimmter aber durch sein Aussehen, es trug die Lebensfarbe' (II. 500).

the other lot for the scape-goat [*or*, Azazel]. And Aaron shall bring the goat upon which the Lord's lot fell, and offer him for a sin-offering: but the goat, on which the lot fell to be the scape-goat [*or*, on which Azazel's lot fell], shall be presented alive before the Lord, to make an atonement with him, and to let him go for a scape-goat [*or*, to Azazel] into the wilderness.' And in the following verses of the same chapter, where the ceremony in question is minutely sketched, we gather the additional information, that the high-priest was to 'lay both his hands upon the head of the live goat and confess over him all the iniquities of the children of Israel, and all their transgressions in all their sins, putting them upon the head of the goat, and shall send him away by the hand of a fit man into the wilderness.'

The practice of transferring, emblematically, the sins of the offerer to the innocent victim chosen by him as their representative had doubtless its analogy[1] among the Old Egyptians, who, in some at least of their oblations, prayed over the head of the victim that evils then impending might be all averted upon it; but there is no necessity whatever for supposing that a practice so graphic and so natural in itself was specially Egyptian, and not rather as primeval as the earliest dawn of the idea which prompted substitutionary offerings.

It is urged, however, that apart from any minor proofs of correspondency, the whole conception of the *two* goats as there appointed, and the seeming dualism connected with their mode of treatment, indicate still deeper tinges of Egyptian influence[2]. On minute inquiry this interpretation of the Hebrew ceremonial will be found to rest on the assumption that *Azazel* in the passage just recited is another name for Satan, and therefore that the final driving of the goat into the desert is, in Hebrew phraseology, a solemn renunciation of the powers of darkness, in the name of the whole reconciled community of Israel; or, in accordance with Egyptian forms of speech, a sending back of evil to the favourite haunts of its Typhonic author.

[1] Herod. II. 39; Kenrick, I. 443, 444. Wilkinson, referring to this practice, argues from the negative evidence of the sculptures that it was no more than occasional and exceptional.

[2] Spencer, II. 450 sq., has advocated this view in his usual manner, contending that while the Hebrew practice of sending away the second goat partly recognised the heathen theory of sacrifice, the whole rite was calculated to impress the truth that sin-offerings are due to God only, while the evil spirit, which he found in Azazel, was to be regarded as unclean, and as an object of abhorrence: cf. Bähr's criticism of these ideas, II. 693—695.

Now the meaning of the word *Azazel* is confessedly involved in very great obscurity[1]. One ancient derivation, as attested by the version of the Seventy (ἀποπομπαῖος), makes the name equivalent to scape-goat ('hircus emissarius'); but how, it was demanded, passing by some other disputable matters, could the goat as mentioned in v. 10 be sent *to* or *for* Azazel, if Azazel were the goat itself? The force of this consideration led directly to the notion that Azazel meant either a person or a place; and as the parallelisms between some incidents, relating to Jehovah and to it, appeared in favour of the *personal* rendering, the alleged connexion of the word with evil spirits, or with Satan, came at length to be more generally accepted. Azazel was explained[2] as equal to 'the segregated,' 'the apostate,' 'the unclean;' and although the title is not found elsewhere in Holy Scripture[3], nor the doctrine thus suggested capable at first sight of reduction into harmony[4] with its severe monotheism, this bold interpretation of the chapter of Leviticus is on the whole perhaps more justifiable than any other which has been proposed.

[1] See the different interpretations of it in Winer, *Realwört.* s. v.

[2] Thus Hengstenberg, as before, p. 166, note; who revives the derivation of Bochart, according to whom the root of Azazel is עזל = عزل = 'semovit,' 'dimovit,' &c. Ewald, who formerly espoused the Satanic theory in reference to *Azazel*, has of late years explained the word to mean 'das Unreine, Unheilige (eigentlich das Getrennte, Verabscheute), die Sünde' (*Ibid.* p. 176); but is there not something very harsh and unintelligible in saying, as v. 10 would then be made to say, that the second goat was sent forth as its destination *to sin*, or unholiness? On the contrary, the relation in which *Satan* here stands to the desert has some analogies in Matt. xii. 43, Luke viii. 29, Rev. xviii. 2.

[3] *Azalzel* and *Azael* were, however, quite familiar to the later Jews in the sense of 'evil spirit' or 'fallen angel' (see Eisenmenger, *Entdecktes Judenthum*, II. 155); and from them, perhaps, the word was handed over to Muhammadans.

[4] Bähr, it must be acknowledged, has stated his objections to this view with very great ability. After urging that the vindication of the Divine Unity was the leading, ever-prominent aim of the Mosaic system, he adds: 'Offenbar würde aber der so strenge Mos. Monotheismus gänzlich aus seiner Konsequenz fallen, wenn er an dem heiligsten und wichtigsten Festtag, bei einer religiösen Feierlichkeit, in der der ganze Cultus kulminirt, den Teufel so neben Jehova gestellt hätte, wie es nach dieser Deutung v. 8—10 der Fall wäre' (II. 687). He forgets, however, such revelations as those contained in Gen. iii., and still more in Zech. iii., which latter passage also brings together, in the closest juxtaposition, Jehovah, Satan, and the high-priest. Bähr's own solution of the difficulty is to derive Azazel, as above, from עזל, and to render 'zu völliger Hinwegschaffung' (II. 668), but in attempting to construe the entire passage on this hypothesis, the difficulties appear to be only multiplied.

If therefore, the identity of Satan and Azazel be conceded, what is here revealed as to the true relation of Satan to Jehovah? How shall we explain the casting of lots upon the two goats, and the devotion of the second to the powers of darkness? That no actual sacrifice to Satan *could* have been intended by the Hebrew ceremony, we may gather most conclusively from the next chapter of Leviticus (xvii. 7), where all offerings made to demons are strongly interdicted. Nor will such a startling version of this incident be needed when the passage has been duly weighed. The *two* goats, it will be seen, were equally chosen to assist in the performance of the one sin-offering; and as both were solemnly presented to Jehovah at the door of the tabernacle, both were recognised by priest and people for His special property. He it was who guided the lot by which the one was destined to be offered, and the other sent unoffered and alive into the dreary desert. It is also most observable that the goat which was symbolically destined to bear away the *pardoned* sins of Israel, and so to bury them out of sight, had been already 'presented alive before the Lord,' and *in idea* had been offered like the other goat 'to make atonement with him' (v. 10); so that the duality of the offering was most probably ordained to represent two different aspects, or to carry on two separate stages, of the same remedial process[1]; one of the twin victims dying in the usual manner, and the second being spared to shew the Hebrews in a striking figure, that iniquities remitted by Jehovah on the Day of Atonement were for ever hidden from their eyes,—remanded to the sphere of the unclean Azazel, or the 'land not inhabited' (v. 22). The most important truths, however, which the vivid ritual of that grand solemnity had served to inculcate, were first and chiefly the remissibility of human sin, and secondly the consequent call for its entire renunciation: and as truths like these were lying at the core of the Mosaic system, it alone of all religions had its Day of Atonement.

§ 2. *Doctrinal Contrasts.*

On passing forward from this necessarily brief examination of particular features, which are said to characterise alike the Hebrew and Egyptian rituals, we shall find that the alleged resemblances which meet us on the surface are succeeded by a contrast far more absolute and unmistakeable. 'With respect

[1] Hengstenberg, as before, p. 171.

to theology,' it is remarked by one[1] who proved himself as quick as others in discovering indications of ritual sympathy, 'with respect to theology, no two systems can be more directly opposed to each other than the Mosaic doctrine was to that of the Egyptians.' If resemblance to the latter *must* be sought among contiguous nations of the ancient world, there is no question, after what has been advanced in the preceding chapter, that the country whither we should bend our footsteps is Phœnicia[2], or the primitive land of Canaan. Yet as every fundamental tenet of the Hebrew had been always diametrically at variance[3] with the tenets of his Canaanitish neighbours, it will follow that so long as he was true to his own principles, he stood in no more friendly attitude to the theology of Egypt. I shall make this point more clearly manifest by choosing one or two examples, where it might have been presumed that we should trace, if not the positive marks of friendly interchange, at least the general vestiges of common ancestry.

(1) Now both in Egypt and Phœnicia, during the historic period, we shall look almost in vain for recognitions[4] of the power and presence of one only God, the spiritual Principle of the universe, distinct from all material forms, and guiding by His legislative will the life and final destiny of all creation. Both countries, it is true, had long retained some glimpses of this grand idea in their knowledge, and some echoes of it, broken and confused by human passions, are still audible amid their wild ejaculations to Baal and Osiris, or are lurking here and there in epithets, by which they thought to honour their great female gods, as Neith or Astarte; but practically a belief in the Supreme Intelligence was disappearing from the earth, when Abraham received his summons from 'the God of glory' to set forth upon the wondrous pilgrimage which brought him as a witness for the truth delivered to his fathers from the eastern bank of the Euphrates. There his family were lapsing with the multitude and 'serving other gods' (Josh. xxiv. 2). They also, peradventure, learned to gaze upon the sun when it shined, or the moon walking in brightness, and their heart was secretly enticed and their mouth kissed their hand (cf. Job xxxi. 26, 27). And when descendants of the patriarch were

[1] Prichard, *Egypt. Mythol.* p. 406.

[2] Above, pp. 452—455.

[3] Above, pp. 68 sq.

[4] Kenrick, speaking on this point (I. 438), goes further still, and while admitting that the highest order of monotheism was 'the clear doctrine of the Hebrew Scriptures,' urges that it cannot be traced in any pagan speculations older than the school of Anaxagoras.

similarly 'called' out of Egypt, their high mission was connected with the spread and conservation of the same great verity. The challenge which struck terror into their idolatrous enslavers was a proclamation of the sovereignty of God: 'Against all the gods of Egypt I will execute judgment: I am the Lord:' exactly as in later ages, one of the most haughty of the Pharaohs, glorying in the vast profusion of his foreign conquests and presuming on his godlike[1] strength, was doomed, by the chastising breath of the Omnipotent, to utter and immediate ruin: 'The land of Egypt shall be desolate and waste, and they shall know that I am the Lord; because he hath said, The river is mine and I have made it' (Ezek. xxix. 9).

No account can here be taken of the 'esoteric' doctrines, which are said to have been handed down in Egypt by the help of her more sacred 'mysteries.' I speak of the religious creed of the Egyptian, either as inscribed upon his public monuments, or as recorded in funereal papyri of the many, or expounded by the treatise of an honest advocate like Plutarch; not as it was represented to us in the transcendental speculations of the Neo-Platonists, who breathing the fresh atmosphere of Christianity had often borrowed all their choicer and more spiritual ideas from the Gospel they were striving to uproot. That popular creed of Egypt, we have seen already, was in substance nothing higher than a deification of the various energies of nature; and in form was one of the least spiritual of the old polytheisms. 'Worship was paid in its turn to almost every object that revolves in the heavens, and to every creature which is possessed of locomotive powers on the earth[2].'

What contrast, therefore, could be greater than the pure and absolute monotheism instilled into the mind of all the Hebrews? Far from being a mere sublimation of the pagan system, it was based throughout on the most opposite conceptions; it was penetrated by another spirit. God in it was everywhere revealed and worshipped as the one invisible Creator and Sustainer, as the only supramundane spirituality. I subjoin a single passage from the Pentateuch, in proof of this assertion; and the passage, beautiful and touching in itself, is worthy of particular notice here, because it furnishes the most explicit condemnation not of stellar worship merely, which was shared by other Gentile nations both of East and West, but also of the vile zoolatry which flourished with portentous rankness on the soil of ancient Egypt:

[1] Cf. Herod. II. 169. [2] Prichard, as before, p. 407.

'Take ye, therefore, good heed unto yourselves (for ye saw no manner of similitude on the day that the Lord spake unto you in Horeb out of the midst of the fire) lest ye corrupt yourselves, and make you a graven image, the similitude of any figure, the likeness of male or female, the likeness of any beast that is on the earth, the likeness of any winged fowl that flieth in the air, the likeness of any thing that creepeth on the ground, the likeness of any fish that is in the waters beneath the earth: and lest thou lift up thine eyes unto heaven, and when thou seest the sun and the moon and the stars, even all the host of heaven, shouldest be driven to worship them, and serve them, which the Lord thy God hath divided unto all nations under the whole heaven. But the Lord hath taken you, and brought you forth out of the iron furnace, even out of Egypt, to be unto Him a people of inheritance, as ye are this day' (Deut. iv. 15—20).

But God as represented to us in the Hebrew Scriptures has not only been invested with an absolute mastery in all the realms of physical creation, which is therefore said to constitute 'His robe of glory' and to be 'expended in His service.' The few verses just recited lead at once to the idea of still more God-like characteristics. The Jehovah of the Hebrews is holiness itself. He is no expression fabricated by philosophy to denote the aggregate of all mechanical forces, active in the different provinces of nature; but the living, personal, holy God: and with a view to the diffusion of His holiness on earth, He chooses a peculiar people, who become the favoured nursery of religious truth, until, endued with power from on high, the germs of life and godliness deposited with them may fructify in every land and issue in the universal 'healing of the nations.' And the soul of the Mosaic system, which was meant to act as one of the more elementary exponents of God's will, is eminently ethical. It ever deals with man as with a free and strictly moral agent. Passing over all the speculative riddles, which perplexed the intellect or charmed the fancy of the Old Egyptian sages, it proclaims that God above us is our very King and Father, and as such constrains us to obey Him. Its grand purpose is, in other words, to cultivate the human *will*, to draw it into harmony with the Divine; and hence the key to all the homeliest of the Hebrew symbols will be found in the magnificent inscription, 'Holiness unto the Lord.' Here also I extract one single passage from the Pentateuch, to show that all the ethical system of the ancient Hebrews was erected on their firm belief in the immaculate holiness of God, that holiness attracting to itself the homage, love, and adoration of a free and grateful people:

'And now, O Israel, what doth the Lord thy God require of thee, but to fear the Lord thy God, to walk in all His ways, and to love Him, and to serve the Lord thy God with all thy heart and with all thy soul; to keep the commandments of the Lord, and His statutes, which I command thee this day for thy good? Behold, the heaven and the heaven of heavens is the Lord's thy God, the earth also, with all that therein is. Only the Lord had a delight in thy fathers to love them, and He chose their seed after them, even you above all people, as it is this day. Circumcise therefore the foreskin of your heart, and be no more stiffnecked. For the Lord your God is God of gods and Lord of lords, a great God, a mighty, and a terrible, which regardeth not persons, nor taketh reward: He doth execute the judgment of the fatherless and widow, and loveth the stranger, in giving him food and raiment. Love ye therefore the stranger: for ye were strangers in the land of Egypt. Thou shalt fear the Lord thy God; Him shalt thou serve, and to Him shalt thou cleave, and swear by His name. He is thy praise, and He is thy God, that hath done for thee these great and terrible things, which thine eyes have seen. Thy fathers went down into Egypt with threescore and ten persons; and now the Lord thy God hath made thee as the stars of heaven for multitude' (Deut. x. 12—22).

(2) In such a system of religion, where the spotless character of God Himself and the original goodness of the world which He had called into existence are beheld in their most perfect contrast to all that which had *become* evil, sin is in the same proportion a profound reality[1]. Grounded in that system on the moral freedom of the creature, it attains its true importance; it is recognised as flowing from perverted wills of personal beings, or rather every act of disobedience is the absolute refusal of the human will to stand in a receptive, creaturely relation to the Author and the Giver of all good. The fruit of this conviction had been ever manifested by the Hebrew; on the one side, in his abject self-renunciation and the frequent bitterness of his repentance; on the other, in his trembling hope of ultimate forgiveness. There is no period in the history of his race[2], how dark soever be the clouds that menace the theocracy, how keen soever his own sense of personal shortcomings, when he ceases to take refuge in the thought, that in some latter day 'a fountain shall be opened to the house of David and to the inhabitants of Jerusalem for sin and for uncleanness' (Zech. iii. 1). The feeling of imperfect reconciliation in the present makes him yearn more deeply for the 'times of refreshing' and the bringing-in of true atonement.

But in Egypt we discover few, if any, traces of a similar aspiration. There the want of clear conceptions with regard to the surpassing holiness of God was followed by comparative

[1] Cf. Hävernick, *Introd. to the Pentateuch*, p. 100.

[2] Above, pp. 100 sq.

deadness of the moral intuitions. Sin was losing its inherent turpitude, because the standard of integrity, which should have been the holy character of God Himself, was lowered with the gradual obscuration of that character. Most true it is that sacrifices had continued to be offered on the altars of the Old Egyptian, and that some at least of these oblations corresponded in their outward form and import to sin-offerings of the Hebrew; but we gather no less clearly from the Rituals of the Dead and from abundant disavowals of the spirits for whose benefit those Rituals were compiled, that the prevailing consciousness of guilt was very superficial: man was gradually arriving at the thought that while obedience on the one side was no arduous or impracticable task, all disobedience would *inevitably* issue in the transmigration of the erring spirit; and the offerings to the gods must, therefore, have degenerated into mere routine, instead of quickening the perception of demerit, or of leading up the soul to God in acts of genuine self-devotion. The indifference of the Old Egyptian to this deeper view of sacrifice as well as the unspiritual tone pervading all his moral precepts, may remind us of the frigid self-complacency which we have witnessed in the temper of the ancient China-man. We cannot say that it was merely the outsideness of ritual worship, or the legal pressure by which it was enforced, wherein those nations differed so completely from the Israelite; he also, in accordance with the *literal* genius of the old œconomy, was required to fix his eye upon the *body* as well as on the soul of his religion: the chief difference had consisted rather in the clearness of the spiritual insight, which enabled all the members of the sacred family to perceive the true relation even of the poorest of their ritual actions to the holy will of God, by whom they were commanded.

Their belief in such relationship to that exalted Being had again been vivified by what they knew of their own lofty origin. They were created in the image of God; in that connexion therefore they could see the basis both of present growth in habits of obedience, and of restoration, through some mediatorial system, to the likeness which they felt to be most grievously impaired. But this conviction of man's primal dignity had well-nigh faded from the sensuous spirit of the Old Egyptian. He could dream of dynasties of gods who occupied the earth anterior to his own creation; yet the human sovereigns he believed could never spring from such; the natures of the two had no points of contact, or the fortunes of the two could not be linked together; and accordingly the annals of the human period in Egyptian history open, it has been remarked[1], with kings of purely human lineage, and contain no reminiscence of primeval virtues or of times when God and man were fully reconciled. And corresponding to this lack of faith in the harmonious meeting of the human and Divine is the remarkable absence from the Old Egyptian creed of the idea of incarnation. There was no reluctance, it is true, to welcome the chief gods as dwelling in the bestial Apis or in other sacred animals[2], just as in the earlier *avatáras* of the Bráhman, Vishńu is beheld descending to the abject level of the fish, the boar, the tortoise: but in Egypt we shall find no counterpart of the exalted Krishńa, stooping for a season to the semblance of a human body and the mean 'condition of the threefold qualities,' that he may help in the uplifting of mankind in general or reveal some method of escape from the necessity of repeated births. The only faint approximation to this thought of sympathy with human kind is traced in periodic conflicts of the irresistible Horus with the scorching blasts of Typhon; yet while all advantages derived to man from such encounters are entirely physical, Horus also acts throughout as an unmixed divinity; he never stands invested with a human form in order to become the champion of the human species. Hence, indeed, it is that when the disembodied spirit of the Old Egyptian fights her way as far as the tribunal of Osiris, she has there no mediator and redeemer; and although she has the prospect of escaping and of floating with the glorious sun-god in celestial regions, it is only after she makes good her claim, as in some earthly court of justice, to the sentence of deserved acquittal.

(3) But is there not one point,—the doctrine of a future life,—in which the creed of Egypt was confessedly superior to

[1] Lepsius, *Chronol.* pp. 26, 27, who also urges with more or less propriety: 'Hier ist kein inniges Wechselverhältniss zwischen Gott und den Menschen, *wie im Alten Testamente*, kein Herabzaubern Olympischer Götter durch Dichter und Künstler unter die Heroen eines jugendliches Volkes, wie das der Griechen, noch auch nur ein zwitterhaftes Gemisch von menschlichen und dämonischen Gestalten einer trüben Phantasie, wie bei den Babyloniern und Chinesen:' cf. Herod. II. 142.

[2] Wilkinson, who mentions it as a merit of the Old Egyptians that they did not *humanise* their gods, has added (2nd ser. I. 176) that 'their fault was rather the elevation of animals and emblems to the rank of deities.' The heroes (ἡμίθεοι) of the Old Egyptians were consequently not demigods in the Greek sense (*i.e.* having one divine parent) but *gods* of an inferior rank: yet in the age of Manetho there was a disposition (Kenrick, I. 352, II. 92) to Hellenise on these points.

the teaching of the Books of Moses? This has often been asserted; and instead of pausing to appropriate the admission as an argument in favour of the independence of the Hebrew system, I proceed to ascertain how far the excellence ascribed to Egypt was possessed of real value. Now in seeking a true answer to the question, we should bear in mind that almost every tribe of man, wherever scattered or however brutalised, has had distinct conceptions of a life beyond the present; and the vividness with which such feelings are expressed is sometimes in inverse proportion to the intellectual culture of the people,—greatest in the savage, least in the philosopher. The Chayma, or the Esquimaux, the unimaginative Papuan, or the wildest rover in the forests of Central Africa, has never doubted that the spirits of departed ancestors still linger near the place of sepulture, retained in close connexion with the body they had once enlivened, and subsisting more or less upon the offerings made by the survivors. It need scarcely, therefore, be esteemed a matter of surprise, if the idea of an ulterior stage in man's existence, stretching far beyond the term of natural life, was quite familiar to the Old Egyptian. Such idea was but a primary intuition which belonged to him as *man*. Yet, as this doctrine in most regions had existed side by side with every phase of devil-worship, and without involving any definite notion either of a moral order or a moral Governor of the world, the simple fact of its existence in the Valley of the Nile can furnish no legitimate proof of spiritual elevation[1]. Nor on analysing the accounts of the Egyptian dogma, as presented to us by its warm admirers, are we justified in treating it as something either special or abnormal. The Egyptian seems to have imagined, when he introduced the custom of embalming, that the progress of death itself might finally be arrested and the past condition of the man be closely imitated in all future time; and when with this idea of simple prolongation, and the offerings to the dead as prompted by it, was connected the more ethical doctrine of a future judgment, for the grosser crimes which man had perpetrated in his previous lifetime, the acquitted spirit, freed at length from the necessity

[1] It is interesting to observe that De Wette, Vatke, and others (quoted by Hengstenberg, *Dissertations*, &c. II. 460, 461) have begun to acknowledge that an entire silence respecting the doctrine of immortality may belong to a higher point of view than the belief in immortality where it exists only in this crude, unspiritual state. Such concessions undermine the cavils of the older race of Deists, who attempted to degrade the Mosaic religion below all forms of heathenism whatever.

of migrating to other animals, attained no higher destination than was commonly awarded to her by the wild tribes of America[1]; her heaven was the resplendent sun himself, conceived of, it may be, as personal, but certainly as undistinguished from the centre of physical illumination.

Now, I grant, that these conceptions of futurity have no existence in the Books of Moses. They are foreign to the genius of revealed religion[2], and accordingly when urged in a malignant spirit by the later Hebrew sceptics they were all repudiated by our blessed Lord Himself as proving ignorance 'of the Scriptures, and the power of God' (Matt. xxii. 29). He told the captious Sadducee how some conditions and relations of the present life would *not* be simply and at once transferred into the future stage of being: just as the Apostle in discussing the objections of Hellenic sophists has proceeded to throw further light upon the mystery of our constitution, and has taught us how the resurrection-body will be very different from a bare resuscitation of the body once committed to the ground. 'It is sown a natural, it is raised a spiritual body' (1 Cor. xv. 44).

Part, indeed, of the transcendent excellence of Christianity, as compared not only with all heathen systems, but with Hebraism itself, consisted in the deep reality which it alone has given to *both* worlds. It never leads man to disparage his position and neglect his duties here, by preaching that the visible world is empty and illusive. Neither does it fashion for him a new sphere of being, modelled on the present life and reproducing all his animal enjoyments. Neither does it, in the third place, so restrain the human soul within the limits of the mundane as to shade off many a motive to exertion which is furnished by our clearer knowledge of the things invisible. The Gospel has brought life and immortality *to light;* and blessedness, as there revealed, is both the prolongation and transfiguration of our present blessedness. How just soever be the statement that the germ of man's future self is lying in his present self, the ripening and unfolding of that germ so far exceeds our comprehension that we measure it only

[1] Above, pp. 358 sq.

[2] It has been reserved for Mr. D. I. Heath to discover (*Exodus Papyri*, p. 203) that 'with respect to the great subject of man's futurity, our present views in Europe are identical in principle, though not in detail, with those which were held by the *actual opponents* of Moses'! The true doctrine, according to Mr. Heath, (and here, he avers, is 'the one really distinguishing feature of Christianity') consists in proclaiming 'the human resurrection of each human being to a human kingdom of mutual human remission of sins'! (p. 103).

by reflecting on the way in which the Gospel has in fact transcended the best visions of the old œconomy, or by noting how the Pattern-Man Himself received unspeakable accessions to His human dignity when, rising from the lowliness of earth, He was 'crowned with glory and honour.' But as life with Christ in glory must have always for its precondition the accordance and assimilation of the human will to God's, the training of that will must also be the first necessity in the education of mankind. 'To walk *with* God' is that which ever constitutes the basis of translation *to* God (Gen. v. 24). The true value, therefore, of belief in immortality arises from the ethical spirit of the system upon which it is engrafted, and the nature of the Person in whom it has subsistence. Where that Person is the living, loving and Almighty God, there is revealed in every glimpse of His exalted character a strong assurance of continuous being[1] to His genuine worshippers. As many as believe that God truly is, believe that He is also 'a rewarder of them who diligently seek Him.' They *must* repose their confidence in Him for present and for future. Unto such He never can have been 'the God of the dead, but of the living.'

Now it was the primary aim of the religion of the Hebrews to plant deeply in man's heart, and that by painful and protracted discipline, the grand conception of God's perfect truthfulness and the unswerving justice of His rule; and never till this object was attained could faith in immortality, as now unveiled to us by Christ and the Apostles, have been fostered in the Church of God to any salutary purpose. The Hebrews, it is true, like other nations of antiquity, were never left in total darkness with respect to the existence of the human spirit after death. Some intimations of their knowledge[2] on that

[1] 'That the Sadducees did not recognise this [the almightiness of God], our Lord marks as the root of their unbelief in the resurrection. In the theology of the Pentateuch this hindrance is fully overcome. He who created the world out of nothing—for whom nothing is too wonderful—death cannot obstruct *Him*, if He wills to preserve the soul. But in the theology of the Pentateuch, His will is pledged equally with His power. The God of the Pentateuch is love; He who reveals Himself so full of grace to His people, and enters into the most intimate communion with them, in doing so declares that He will preserve them to eternal life. To this foundation of the doctrine of the resurrection in the Pentateuch our Lord Himself refers (Matt. xxii. 31, 32).' Hengstenberg, *Ibid.* p. 469: cf. above, p. 71, n. 1.

[2] For some valuable remarks on this point, I would refer inquirers to a recent Essay by Mr. T. T. Perowne, *The Essential Coherence of the Old and New Testaments*, pp. 84 sq. Camb. 1858.

subject are discovered even in the earliest of their sacred writings; and accordingly the absence of allusion to a future stage of being where as Christians we should have expected such allusion, or the vague and joyless terms in which a future life is sometimes mentioned, where as Christians we should use a more explicit phraseology, can only be adduced to shew that Hades was to them more shadowy than to us, or that ideas of immortality had been remanded to the background in the admonitions of the Hebrew doctors. And the explanation of this difference, as of others like it, will be found in what has been already more than once suggested,—the elementary condition of the people. Their chief thoughts must all be concentrated for a time upon the law of temporal, visible retribution, as dispensed through the arrangements of a theocratic system, in order that when this idea was deeply rooted, faith in the invisible and future retribution might spontaneously grow up. The Israelitish worthy, confident that God was with him, had been meanwhile going forward on his earthly pilgrimage, in a condition, as to intellectual certainty, like that of Abraham himself, who, under the immediate eye of an unfailing Benefactor, started on his journey to the land of Canaan, 'not knowing whither he went.'

Before I bring these observations to a close, it may be well to glance a moment down the stream of Hebrew history, and ascertain the feelings of the sacred writers at the period of the Babylonish exile with regard to the admissibility of foreign notions into their hereditary creed. An apt example may be found among the visions of Ezekiel, who more than other prophets was accustomed to revert for imagery to the days of the Exodus and to events which followed closely in its train. He thus becomes a species of transition-link from Egypt to Babylon. The flower of the two tribes who had been rescued from the scourge of the Assyrian spoiler were now smitten by a like calamity; and, refusing to be comforted, had hung their harps upon the trees that lined the banks of the Chebar, when a prophet, the partaker of their sad mischances, was commissioned to point out the moral agencies which had precipitated this catastrophe. How dark the contrast to a mind like his, between the coming up from Egypt and the going down to Babylon! There he saw a youthful people full of hope and ardour, marching with the Lord Jehovah at their head to occupy the soil which He had promised to their fathers. Here he sees them broken, joyless, and forlorn, a nation of mourners and of captives, driven from the homes which had been long preserved to them as by a miracle of mercy, and succumbing under the terrific curse which lighted on the wandering Cain. As contemplated by Ezekiel, the whole Hebrew race were going backward; they were exiles in a moral desert, in the 'wilderness of the people;' they were forfeiting the vantage-ground on which their fathers had been planted, and, abandoned to the grasp of a blaspheming power, were melting fast away into the heathen multitudes by whom they were surrounded. And the cause of this disastrous retrogression was declared to be the preference which the Israelite himself had manifested for all heathenish modes of thought. His craven wish had been to lose his sacred nationality, and so to be commingled and confounded with the world. 'We will be as the heathen, as the families of the countries, to serve wood and stone' (xx. 32).

To make Ezekiel more entirely conscious of the evils that were eating out the national life, he is transferred in spirit to the precincts of the Hebrew sanctuary (ch. viii.), the spot on which, if ever, might be found the lingering vestiges of unadulterated truth. But no: in rivalry or feigned alliance with the altar of Jehovah, he beholds 'the image of jealousy.' A nature-god of Canaan, viewed as Baal, the producer, or as Moloch, the destroyer, stands enthroned upon a level with the God of Abraham. 'Son of man,' is the inquiry, 'seest thou what they do, even the great abominations that the house of Israel committeth here, that I should go far off from my sanctuary?' And then, as if to indicate the depth of the corruption now contracted by the Hebrew Church, Ezekiel has to witness, one by one, the other great idolatries, which, in despair of God and of her own religion (v. 12), she had borrowed from the heathen nations round about her. First of all he sees the grovelling rites of Egypt, imaged under 'every form of creeping things and abominable beasts.' The seventy elders of the house of Israel, faithless representatives of those who once had followed Moses to the holy mount (Ex. xxiv. 1) as witnesses of the more secret glory of Jehovah, are now impiously attempting to change that 'glory of the incorruptible God;' they stand before the image of Egyptian reptiles 'every man with his censer in his hand.' Another vision is unfolded to the prophet; he beholds in a fresh quarter of the sacred precincts that the old Phœnician worship of Adonis, the original type of the Osirian mysteries, has threatened to efface the purity of earlier generations. Women are assembled at the temple of

Jehovah, to bemoan the loss of Tammuz, as the prelude to licentious revelry and diabolic orgies. Last of all the prophet's eye is fixed upon the inner court of the Lord's house, to which the priests alone have access, and which priests no longer blush to desecrate and to deride. It does not seem enough that the community at large are superadding the zoolatry of Egypt to the foul abominations of Phœnicia: men of priestly rank, the 'princes of the sanctuary,' though kneeling on the sacred threshold, have each turned his back upon the holiest of all, and, like the Old Parsee, whose superstitions they are now adopting, 'worship the sun toward the east' (v. 16). 'Then He said unto me, Hast thou seen this, O son of man? Is it a light thing to the house of Judah that they commit the abominations which they commit here? for they have filled the land with violence, and have returned to provoke Me to anger; and lo, they put the branch to their nose. Therefore will I also deal in fury; Mine eye shall not spare, neither will I have pity; and though they cry in Mine ears with a loud voice, yet will I not hear them' (vv. 17, 18).

CHAPTER III.

Characteristics of Medo-Persian Heathenism.

Μάγοι δὲ καὶ πᾶν τὸ Ἄριον γένος, ὡς καὶ τοῦτο γράφει ὁ Εὔδημος, οἱ μὲν τόπον, οἱ δὲ χρόνον καλοῦσι τὸ νοητὸν ἅπαν καὶ τὸ ἡνωμένον· ἐξ οὗ διακριθῆναι ἢ θεὸν ἀγαθὸν καὶ δαίμονα κακὸν, ἢ φῶς καὶ σκότος πρὸ τούτων, ὡς ἐνίους λέγειν. Οὗτοι δὲ οὖν καὶ αὐτοὶ μετὰ τὴν ἀδιάκριτον φύσιν διακρινομένην ποιοῦσι τὴν διττὴν συστοιχίαν τῶν κρειττόνων· τῆς μὲν ἡγεῖσθαι τὸν Ὠρομάσδην, τῆς δὲ τὸν Ἀρειμάνιον.—Damascius, *De Primis Principiis*, c. cxxv. (p. 384, Kopp).

Ancient Persia: related to India. Religious differences one cause of the separation between Indo-Áryans and Perso-Áryans. The reputed founder of Zoroastrianism. Ormazd-worship older than the reign of Darius. Magism, and its propagation. Intermixture of Ormazd-worship with foreign elements. The Avesta*: its relation to the original sacred books of Persia: probable order of its composition. The* Yasna. *The* Vendidád. *The* Yeshts. Zervána-akarana. *Ultimate belief in some one Primal Essence. Probable connexion of Zervan with the Bel of Babylonia. The Parsee belief in unity; not traceable in the Avesta. Ormazd and Ahriman. Amshaspands: their probable origin in light-worship. Dualism. Iran and Turan. The homicidal serpent. Devs, the antagonists of Amshaspands. Manichæism: its relation to Zoroastrianism. Mythe connecting Zervan with Ormazd and Ahriman. Moral import of such mythes. Largeness of spirit, a distinguishing feature of the Ormazd-religion. Ideas of purity. Practical character of the old Persian. King-worship.*

If the object of the present work had been to trace the early growth of heathenism, without regard to the contemporaneous fortunes of the sacred family or the possible interchanges of religious thought between the Hebrew and other systems, the true place of the discussions opened in this chapter would have doubtless been immediately after the religions of Hindústán[1].

[1] This remark appears to have been called for by complaints of an intelligent and not unfriendly critic in the *Colonial Church Chronicle*, who, in common with some other reviewers of Part III., lost sight of the original intention of the present writer as expressed in the title-page of his work. Let it be again repeated that these chapters do not pretend to furnish a complete and systematic history of ancient heathenism; but rather to exhibit the chief points of correspondency or contrast between heathenism and revealed religion.

For though it be impossible by means of extant monuments to carry back the civilisation of Persia to the same remote antiquity[1], much less to rank her with the great primeval empires of Babylon, of Egypt, or of China, facts are now at our command which will determine the exact position of the Persians proper in the ancient family of man. The region known as Persia (*Parasa* in cuneiform inscriptions) was a leading province of the 'pure Iran,' whose frontiers, reckoning eastward from the Caspian gates, extended to the very foot of the Hindú Alps; and therefore, as the name[2] itself will testify, the population which at length predominated was an off-shoot from the Áryan stock, who, after settling in the region of the Five Rivers, were the undisputed lords of Árya-vartta, and diffused their influence to the southernmost extremity of the Hindú Peninsula.

The proofs of this connection have been strengthened at all points by late researches and inductions of comparative philology. The language of the ancient Persian, or at least that one of many current languages, the Zend, in which the earliest of his 'sacred' books were written, is found to be most intimately related to the Sanskrit of the Védas: it deserves to be entitled second, if not eldest of the sister-tongues which form the Indo-European family. So close, indeed, is the affinity both in structure and in actual words, that we are justified on purely philological grounds in urging the protracted intercourse[3] of Persians and Hindús; who clung together as a great community ages after the migrations of the Celt, the Teuton, and the Slave across the bounds of eastern Europe.

Fresh and still more definite information is reflected on this subject from the ancient books of the Hindús. The names of certain gods and heroes, who were strangers, it would seem, to the mythology of other kindred tribes, continued to be held in equal reverence by the Áryan on the Sutlej and his brethren on the Persian Gulf. The memory, for example, of a Hindú sun-god with the title *Vivaswat* is lingering[4] in the Zend

[1] 'The true historic period does not commence till five generations before Darius Hystaspis (or about B.C. 680), when Achæmenes founded a kingdom in Persia Proper.' Rawlinson, *Journal of As. Soc.* XV. 252.

[2] See above, p. 122, n. 1, and the references there. The form *Iran*, which has been already detected on coins of the Sassanian period, is undoubtedly equivalent to *Ariana*, *Airya*, and *Airyana*.

[3] M. Müller's 'Last Results of the Persian Researches,' as reported in Bunsen's *Phil. of Univ. Hist.* I. 112; Spiegel, *Avesta*, I. 5, Leipzig, 1852.

[4] Lassen, *Ind. Alt.* I. 518, 519.

Vivanghwat, whom the Persian honoured as the father of the mighty Yima, first and best of human rulers; and although in stories of the Indo-Áryan, Vivaswat had *two* sons, Manu and Yama, each invested with transcendent dignity, and so inheriting a separate empire, one within the sphere of the living and the other of the dead, it is impossible to doubt the common parentage and ultimate identity of Yima and Yama. In like manner, the mysterious *soma* of the Védas, treated there not only as the best of sacrificial plants, but also as a true divinity[1], had been reflected in the sacred *homa*[2] whose enlivening juices, first expressed by Vivanghwat, were celebrated with a kindred fervour in the earliest of the Zendic hymns.

But facts, which have thus tended to authenticate the old connexion of the Persians and Hindús, may also be adduced to illustrate the grounds of their eventual separation. It is not material for our present purpose to consider in what part of Asia the divergence had originated; whether (as some think) in the locality which formed the cradle of the human race, and so anterior to the first dispersion; or whether (as is far more probable) that schism was consummated at a period when the Áryan character was fully formed beneath the glowing skies of India. But be this as it may, we have now ample reason for concluding that the final rupture in that primitive population was in part[3] at least connected with religious differences. Rebelling, it would seem, against the 'wild-grown nature-worship' which had characterised the earlier period of their history, or dissatisfied, perhaps, with the account there given of conflicts which they felt to be proceeding in the outer and the inner world, one section of the Áryans fell away from the

[1] Above, p. 127, n. 1; pp. 130, 226.

[2] Burnouf, *Études*, in the *Journal Asiat.* (1844), p. 475, and Spiegel, *Avesta*, I. 8. This change of a Sanskrit sibilant into a Zendic aspirate is of constant occurrence: *e.g.* the geographical name *hapta hendu* of the Avesta is the *sapta sindhu* of the Véda; both referring to the north of India, or the land of the 'Seven Rivers' (*i. e.* the Five of the Panjáb, together with the Indus and the Saraswati). The word Saraswati itself is also traceable in Haraqaiti. Rawlinson (*Journal of As. Soc.* XV. 251, n. 1), who mentions this example, adds: 'The proper names of men, too, both in the Vendidad, in the cuneiform inscriptions, and even in the Greek notices of Persia, are in many cases Vedic or Puranic, and can almost always be referred to a Sanskrit etymology, thus authenticating the connexion of the races.'

[3] 'Es finden sich nun auch Spuren, welche darauf schliessen lassen, dass die Trennung der beiden Völker *zum Theile wenigstens*, aus religiösen Gründen erfolgt sei.' Spiegel, *Avesta*, I. 9.

society of their brethren, and in close analogy with later times and distant countries left the traces of the feud engrained in their religious phraseology. Thus, the Sanskrit name for god, *déva,* bearing witness to the ancient worship of the element of light[1], is plainly kindred to the Zend *daéva;* and yet this latter tongue had ceased to use it of divinities in general, and confined it to a class of hostile genii following in the train of the great Evil One. The highest also of the Vaidic gods, the glorious Indra[2], whom the warm imagination of the early Áryan had been wont to picture as diffusing genial showers upon the earth, or chasing from the clouds the various ministers of evil, had become in Persia, as in later stages of Hindú mythology, a spirit of inferior rank; yet with the noticeable difference, that the Perso-Áryans had proceeded to invest their Andra with malevolent attributes. In further proof of this revulsion in men's thoughts, it is contended by some writers[3] that the first of good divinities among the Persians, viz. *Ahura,* or *Ahura-mazda* (Ormazd), is etymologically connected with *Asura* in the mythology of the Old Hindú; who was accustomed to employ the title as descriptive of the multitudinous demons dreaded by himself, or by his household, though it seems to have been treated by the earliest of the Vaidic poets as a word of no ill-omen.

Every fresh investigation into the degree of these divergences, as well as the distinct formation and consolidation of the Perso-Áryan creed, is fitly prefaced by a question as to the antiquity and origin of its reputed founder. Not long after the Christian era[4] it was usual to ascribe the planting of the sacred system of the Persians to an individual teacher, whom they designated Zarathustra (Zoroaster); and the scanty remnants of that people, who have found a shelter from the

[1] Above, p. 126, n. 1.

[2] Above, pp. 123, 127.

[3] *e.g.* Spiegel, I. 9, followed by Dr. Donaldson, *Christ. Orthod.* p. 128: but cf. Burnouf, *Commentaire sur le Yaçna*, I. 78, Paris, 1833.

[4] See a list of the conflicting testimonies with respect to his age in Dr. John Wilson, *The Pársí Religion*, pp. 398—400, Bombay, 1843. Döllinger, *Heidenthum*, p. 352, staggered by these contradictions, has revived the theory of more than one Zoroaster, or at least distinguishes between Zarathustra the Perso-Áryan prophet and the Zoroaster, Zarades, or Zaratus of Greek writers, who was really, he thinks, a type, or mythical creation, representing a totally different (Hamitic) form of heathenism, but ultimately confounded with the historic Zarathustra, when the fame of the latter had extended to Western nations: cf. Westergaard, *Zendavesta*, 'Pref.' pp. 16 sq. Copenhagen, 1852—54.

fury of the Muslim, in the towns of western India, or the wilderness of Yezd, look up with reverence to the same Zartúsht as the great prophet of Parseeism[1]. There is also evidence to shew that in the judgment of at least some Persians, he had flourished in the reign of king *Vístáspa*[2], or (according to a common change) *Gustásp;* and other writers[3], starting from this incident, have not unnaturally referred the ministry of Zoroaster, and the earliest publication of the Zoroastrian tenets, to the lifetime of *Hystaspes*, father of the great Darius.

Now if it be meant that Zoroaster, a contemporary of Darius, was the actual author of the system of religion, in which *Ahura-mazda* (Ormazd) became the principal object of men's worship, we have reasons the most cogent and conclusive for rejecting such interpretation. Ormazd had long been reverenced as 'the god of the Áryans[4],' when Darius wrote the history of his exploits upon the rock of Behistun: indeed some passages in that magnificent inscription will not suffer us to doubt that the great movement headed by Darius was essentially *religious*[5], aiming at the restoration of an ancient faith which had been threatened, and in part subverted, by the influence of the Magus. The first care of the victorious prince

[1] Dosabhoy Framjee, *The Parsees*, pp. 238 sq. Lond. 1858.

[2] See Spiegel, *Avesta,* I. 41 sq. who quotes the traditional account of the Bombay Parsees. A regular history of their 'legislator,' the *Zartusht-Námah*, written in the 13th century after Christ, has been translated from the Persian by Mr. Eastwick, and is appended to Dr. J. Wilson's *Pársí Religion.*

[3] Ammianus Marcellinus (Lib. XXIII. c. 6), of the 4th cent. after Christ, is most explicit on this point. He also says that Zoroaster was a Bactrian, that he made additions to the creed of the Magi, deriving these additions 'ex Chaldæorum arcanis;' and further, that he visited the north of India, and reaching a secluded spot among forests, conferred with members of the Bráhmanical order. The testimony of Agathias (of the 6th cent. after Christ) is more valuable (II. 24), because he professes to give the opinions of the Persians themselves; yet while repeating the story that Zoroaster lived at the court of Hystaspes, he added, as the view of the Persians, that it was very doubtful whether this Hystaspes was the father of Darius (εἴτε καὶ ἄλλος οὗτος ὑπῆρχεν Ὑστάσπης.)

[4] 'The Median engravers, who executed the Scythic version of the great inscription of Bisitun (Behistun), so well understood the difference between Áryan Dualism and Scythic Magism, that when they had to speak of Ormazd in connexion with other gods, they interpolated after the name the distinctive epithet of "god of the Áryans."' Rawlinson, *Jour. Asiat. Soc.* XV. 249.

[5] See Rawlinson's *Herod.* App. Bk. I. Essay V.; App. Bk. III. Essay II.

was 'to rebuild the temples which Gomates had destroyed, and to restore to the people the sacred chants and worship, of which Gomates had deprived them[1];' and, as indicating both the nature and extent of the corruption, he declares expressly that 'the *lie* had become abounding in the land, both in Persia and in Média, and in the other provinces[2].' Supposing, therefore, the age of Zoroaster to have been the fifth or sixth century before Christ, we are reduced to the necessity of concluding that his mission had been rather to restore and purify, than to initiate the sacred system which was afterwards connected with his name. He must have been, as he indeed is sometimes represented, nothing more than one important member in a series of 'ancient *Persian prophets*[3].'

But the tendency of modern criticism, with only few exceptions, is to carry back the age of Zoroaster into prehistoric times, or representing him as the 'Vyása' of the Perso-Áryans, to invest him with the dubious, half-impersonal character, which attaches to his Hindú prototype, the so-called author of the earliest Véda. While some (as Lassen[4]) have declared it utterly impossible to fix the period when he lived and so abandoned the inquiry in despair, Sir H. Rawlinson has lately started an hypothesis[5] which finds in Zoroaster the personification of an old religious system, or in other words, the sacred eponym of an adjacent, but non-Áryan race. To understand this view we must remember[6] that three different populations coexisted from an early date upon the plain of the Tigris and Euphrates, one descended from a Scythic, Cushite or Turanian stock; a second cognate with the Babylonians and Assyrians, or, in other words, Semitic; and the third consisting

[1] *Behist. Inscr.* (as given, among other places, in the above work, Vol. II. p. 595); where Darius adds, 'As (it was) before, so I restored what (had been) taken away. By the grace of Ormazd I did (this).'

[2] *Ibid.* p. 593.

[3] Thus in the '*Desátír* or sacred writings of the ancient Persian Prophets,' translated by Mulla Firuz Ibn Kaus (Bombay, 1818), Zirtúsht is the 13th prophet in the series, and the fifth Sassan (contemporary with the emperor Heraclius) the last. But the historical value of this work, which seems to have been fabricated as late as the 16th century, is very small indeed. It seems to have issued from the syncretistic movement, of which Akbar was the leading spirit: cf. Spiegel, *Avesta*, I. 49, and Wilson, *Pársí Religion*, pp. 411, 412.

[4] 'Seine Zeit zu bestimmen wird nie möglich seyn.' *Ind. Alt.* I. 754.

[5] See his paper entitled *Notes on the Early History of Babylonia*, in the *Journ. As. Soc.* XV. 215—259, and the still more recent discussion of the subject in Rawlinson's *Herod.* as referred to above, p. 522, n. 5.

[6] Cf. above, pp. 51 sq., and Rawlinson, as above.

of the Medes and Persians proper who were members of the Indo-European family. Neglecting for the present the effects produced by the Semitic element, it seems that Scyths, the aboriginal owners of the soil, were strongly intermixed with Áryans in the whole of ancient Media, and that, owing to the higher civilisation of the Scyth or to the witchery exerted by some features of his thaumaturgic system, the new-comers almost universally adopted the religion there established[1]. This, according to the present view, was genuine Magism,—the primeval faith associated far and wide with the time-honoured name of Zoroaster, and at length erroneously ascribed to early 'Persians,' by Herodotus[2], who represents it as 'purely and entirely elemental,' or a nature-worship of the simplest form, expressed in adoration of 'the sun and moon, of fire, of earth, of water, and of winds.' The same ideas, it might be not unreasonably contended, found acceptance in some parts of Persia proper; and when Cyrus was at length supreme in every province of Iran, he seems to have conciliated his Scytho-Median subjects by his patronage of Magi, and by placing Magism[3] on a level with the worship of the great Ormazd and other Áryan deities. This statement rests, indeed, on the authority of the *Cyropædia;* yet whatever value be assigned to it, there is now ample reason for concluding that such lenient measures were at once reversed on the accession of Cambyses, who, impelled by a fanatic spirit bordering upon frenzy, had extended his religious warfare into the Valley of the Nile. It is accordingly narrated that the old adherents of the Magian faith, emboldened by the absence[4] of the despot in the west, attempted to recover their importance by intriguing in behalf of the Pseudo-Smerdis; and as soon as the pretender had been planted on the throne proceeded to the extirpation of

1 'The Medes not only adopted the religion of their subjects, but to a great extent blended with them, admitting whole Scythic tribes into their nation. Magism entirely superseded among the Medes the former Áryan faith,' &c. Rawlinson's *Herod.* Vol. I. p. 430.

2 I. 131.

3 Xenoph. *Cyrop.* VIII. 1, § 23, and Creuzer, *Symbol.* I. 189, n. 1. The conduct here ascribed to Cyrus will receive some illustration from what Herodotus states respecting Xerxes, who, departing from the policy of Cambyses, and to some extent of his own father, did not scruple to consult the Magian soothsayers (VII. 19, 37). It was probably much later when the Magi as a body were installed as priests of Ormazd; for 'their name *Magu* occurs only twice in all the extant Zend texts.' Westergaard, 'Pref.' p. 17.

4 *Behist. Inscr.* (Rawlinson's *Herod.* Vol. II. p. 593).

established forms of worship. The avenging of this impious wrong became, as we have seen, a leading object in the policy of Darius. He declares repeatedly that 'by the help of Ormazd' he had confounded all the schemes of the insurgents, had abolished the reign of lies, had reared afresh the temples that were ruined by the Magians, had restored the several branches of the ancient liturgy. To this indeed we may ascribe the fact that king Darius was regarded by succeeding ages in the light of a religious reformer; hence the honourable mention of Gustasp (Hystaspis) in the sacred books of Persia; hence the feeling of respect with which his memory was long cherished by all classes of the Old Parsees.

It must be granted that the difficulties attaching to this theory of Zoroastrianism are neither few nor inconsiderable; and yet some theory of the kind appears to be almost necessitated by the force of modern evidence, especially of that discovered on the cuneiform inscriptions. In favour of it is the circumstance that the religion of early 'Persia,' as described by Herodotus, has scarcely aught in common either with the religion of Persian monuments or Persian sacred books; and therefore we are driven to suppose that his remarks apply to Magism, which may still have flourished in the western provinces, and not to the religion of Ormazd as patronised and practised at the court. In favour, also, of this theory, is the argument, that if the creed of the Magi had been merely a provincial variation of Ormazd-worship, no intelligible account is given of the religious movement strangled by Darius, and his own abhorrence of the Magian faith.

Yet, on the other hand, we have an almost equal difficulty in understanding how the Perso-Áryan people could in after-times have been induced to reverence the memory of Zoroaster, to accept a mere personification of Magism as the favoured organ of their own beneficent deity, and elevate what has been called the 'old heresionym of the Scyths' into the teacher of Gustasp, whose son became a champion of the Áryan gods[1]. This difficulty is relieved perhaps by taking into account the

[1] 'Under the disguise of *Zarathushtra*, which was the nearest practicable Áryan form, *Ziraishtar* (or the seed of Venus) became a prophet and lawgiver, receiving inspiration from *Ahuramazda*, and reforming the national religion.' Sir H. Rawlinson, *Journ. As. Soc.* xv. 254. This learned writer has elsewhere (p. 246) sought to justify his explanation of the word *Zarathushtra;* but does not seem to have noticed the verbal affinity of *Ishtar*, *Asteria*, and *Astarte* (this last representing the Aphrodite of Semitic tribes).

flexible and imitative genius of the ancient Persians, which extended also to religious matters[1]; and as positive proof will be adduced of minor amalgamations between the creed of Persia and other systems, it is possible that some such fusion was gradually effected on a larger scale, and that on the subsiding of the storm in which the festival of the Magophonia had originated, 'a mongrel religion grew up, wherein the Magian and the Aryan creeds were blended together[2].'

But whatever might be the precise complexion of that older system it received its death-blow[3] at the period of the Macedonian occupation, or at least amid the sanguinary struggles of the Parthian conquest. From the former, we must date a large infusion of Hellenic thoughts and customs; while the latter was a fresh uprising of the Scythic population, banished or held down in bondage from the time of Cyrus.

Owing to the strong persistence of these foreign agencies, the sacred language of the Perso-Áryan was depressed, neglected, and well-nigh extinguished; the old worship of Ormazd gave place again to Magism[4], tinctured, it may be, with some Hellenic speculations; nor when Scyths were finally ejected by the daring of the native or Sassanian monarchs, and hurled back on one side into Georgia, and on the other to Afghanistan, could the religion of Cambyses and Darius be restored to its original purity. Henceforth it bore the frequent traces of its intercourse with foreign creeds. Its sacred writings were indeed recovered, but no evidence survives to tell us, whether they were then collected and restored from extant manuscripts or from oral tradition. A new tongue (the Pehlevi or

[1] Herod. I. 131, 135.

[2] Rawlinson's *Herod.* Vol. I. p. 431. The vitality of Magism was evinced for ages after, in a form analogous to that already noticed (above, p. 455) in discussing the animal-worship of the Old Egyptian, *viz.* by transfusing one of its more cardinal doctrines into the very soul of the new creed. This peculiarity consisted in the adoration of the element of *fire.* Hence the name 'fire-temples' and the title 'fire-worshippers.' I may mention that Mr. Dosabhoy Framjee (*The Parsees*, pp. 256 sq.), affecting to believe, like other Anglicised Parsees, that the religion of their own sacred books is pure theism, 'repels with indignation' the idea of worshipping any of the material elements. A Parsee, he says, while engaged in prayer, is merely 'directed to stand before the fire, or to direct his face towards the sun, as the most proper symbols of the Almighty.' But disclaimers of this kind are not easily reconciled with the express assertions of Parsee authorities; as indeed may be seen at length in Dr. Wilson's *Pársí Religion*, pp. 194 sq.

[3] Spiegel, *Avesta*, I. 16, 17.

[4] Sir H. Rawlinson, as before, p. 255.

Huzváresh) was adopted as the vehicle of public worship, and the badge of the new dynasty; and since the Greek, the Jew, the Buddhist, and the Christian had all from various quarters penetrated to the banks of the Tigris and Euphrates, it is not so difficult to understand how the 'reformers, teachers, prophets' who sprang up with this fresh outburst of Persian nationality, should have all departed widely from the older standards, or should, speaking generally, have 'formed their language and the whole train of their ideas on a Semitic model[1].'

And if the general history of the Medo-Persian were thus chequered and eventful, we shall be prepared to find no small variety in the tone of his religion and the texture of his sacred books. The whole collection of such writings, or at least of parts which have come down to us, is known as the *Avesta*, literally the 'Text[2].'

One chief result of modern exploration in this region of philology has been to demonstrate, that whether as preserved in the original, or as translated by Parsees, the treatises of the Avesta *in their present shape* can date no farther back than the Sassanian revival, in the time of Artaxerxes, or the third century of the Christian era (A.D. 226). Another of those results has tended to confirm and justify suspicions with regard to the antiquity of several writings which are commonly adduced as high authorities by modern Parsees. Of one important work (the *Bundehesh*) we may affirm with certainty that it had never existed in the Zend, or older dialect of Persia, but was first compiled in the court-language of the restoration-period; while some others (as the *Dabistán* and *Desátír*) may be rejected absolutely as fabrications of far later centuries. Such criticisms are not, of course, intended to deny that many chapters of the Persian sacred books are capable of being carried back to a most venerable antiquity. Whole works may have been actually committed to writing as early as 400 B.C., for 'books of Zoroastrians' are related[3] to have perished at the time of Alexander's expedition. Many also of the sacred chants and ceremonial precepts may, as now existing, have originated at the epoch of the first migrations. Yet, while

[1] Max Müller, as before, p. 118; Renan, *Hist. des Langues Sémitiques*, I. 77, 78, Paris, 1858.

[2] Spiegel, p. 45: 'bei den späteren Parsen stets gebrauchte Bezeichnung für den Text der heiligen Schriften.' *Zand* or *Zend* properly means 'commentary' or 'translation' (*i. e.* of ancient texts): see Westergaard, *Zendavesta*, 'Pref.' p. 1.

[3] Cf. Westergaard's *Pref.* p. 18.

granting this, our ablest scholars seem to be persuaded more and more that works which have been brought together in the Avesta, are not only the productions of different ages, but have all been modified and modernised by the intrusion of fresh matter. They stand, in other words, to primitive documents of the Ormazd-religion in substantially the same relation as the Prayer-Book to the Use of Sarum.

In attempting to refer the several parts of the Avesta to the different epochs which produced them, Spiegel, the most competent of living writers on this subject[1], draws attention to three separate stages of progression or development. The earliest stage, he thinks, is represented by the second part of the *Yasna,*—the liturgy or sacrificial service of the Persians, consisting of invocations to the 'pure' Ormazd, to elements and energies of nature, to the spirit of the worshipper himself, and also to beneficent genii whose abodes are in the world invisible. The mode of handling theological topics is there characterised by a remarkable absence both of order and precision: every thing accounted pure and brilliant, beautiful and salutary, is the object of half-conscious homage and unreasoning worship, so that early invocations of the Yasna may be justly brought into comparison with the oldest hymns of the Rig-Véda. The next stage of that religion, according to the same authority, is represented by the Vendidád, or 'Law Given,' in which, besides a most incongruous list of remedies for earthly ills, has been narrated the creation of the 'sixteen holy places,' the origin and growth of evil and its partial overthrow as the result of Zoroaster's mission; all communicated in the form of a dialogue between that prophet and the great Ormazd. As the theology of Persia has become at this stage far more definite and distinctive, bearing witness to the presence of the main ingredients which compose the 'Zoroastrian' system, the transition may perhaps be illustrated from the course pursued by Hindú thought in passing from the simplest form of nature-worship to the cultivated Bráhmanism of the heroic age. The third and most important step in the development here indicated led to the production of the first part of the Yasna, and the multifarious hymns and prayers collected in the *Yeshts.* The gods and genii of the Persian creed have now been classified in parallel ranks, according to their different properties: the

[1] Spiegel's first notice of these points was published in Weber's *Ind. Studien* (1850), I. 313 sq., and he has since extended the inquiry in his edition of the *Avesta* and elsewhere, arriving at the same result.

attributes of each are clearly separated and dogmatically fixed: the system known as Zoroaster's has attained its full proportions; its whole 'character is unmistakeable:' while the martial and intolerant spirit of Sassanian princes breathing in their sacred books will frequently remind us of the terrible Śiva-ism of later Hindústán, which, after scourging and extruding the disciples of the Buddha, left its dark and bloody trace on the Bráhmanical religion.

No sooner have we entered on a more minute investigation of the Perso-Áryan dogmas than allusions meet us, here and there, to a mysterious Being of transcendent dignity, yet one whose place in the construction of that system is most difficult to ascertain; enveloped as it is in clouds and controversies, which have long continued to obscure the character and parentage of Zarathustra himself. I am referring to a deity entitled *Zervan* or *Zervána-akarana*, who, strange to say, had sometimes been not only associated but identified[1] with Zoroaster, and described as both 'the origin of the Medians and the father of the gods.' The old opinion was, that in this member of the Persian system proofs might be discerned of a conception bordering on the pure and spiritual monotheism inherited by members of the sacred family. *Zervána-akarana* was held to designate a personal god, to whom was given the appellation, 'Time without Bounds,' or 'Uncreated Time[2].'

[1] As, for instance, by Moses of Chorene, a writer of the 5th century (Wilson's *Pársís*, p. 128). According also to this Armenian authority, the people of the East identified Zervan with Sim or Shem (cf. Rawlinson, in *Journ. As. Soc.* XV. 245, n. 2).

[2] While there is considerable unanimity in rendering *Zervan* either 'Old' or 'Time' (=Κρόνος), the precise meaning of the adjective *akarana* is still matter of dispute. Anquetil Duperron, the first translator of the *Avesta*, rendered the word by 'sans bornes;' but, as Schlottmann observes, against Spiegel (Weber's *Ind. Stud.* I. 378), it is not derivable from the Pehlevi root קנאר, which gave rise to the old interpretation 'boundless.' It is rather (he thinks with Roth and others) to be explained by reference to the Sanskrit *akarana*, 'uncaused,' 'uncreated' (from *karana* 'cause'). That the Perso-Áryans were not only familiar with such epithets, but were in the habit of applying them to the heavenly bodies, is obvious from a remarkable hymn of the Yasna, which Burnouf translates as follows (*Comment. sur le Yaçna*, p. 559): 'J'invoque, je célèbre et ces lieux et ces pays, et les parcs des bestiaux, et les maisons, et les lieux où se gardent les grains, et les eaux, et les terres, et les arbres, et cette terre et ce ciel, et le vent pur, *les astres, la lune et le soleil, lumières qui sont sans commencement, incréées*, et toutes les créations de l'être saint et céleste, ceux et celles qui sont purs, (génies) maîtres de pureté.' It has been suggested to me that as one meaning of the Sanskrit

Philosophy had also learned to speak of him as 'universal Being,' as the grand personification of eternity, as the primordial and illimitable void from which creation in its varying aspects is successively evolved. He was the basis of all other forms of being, whence conflicting powers of the phenomenal world had each derived its origin, and whither it was destined to revert on the expiring of the present strife, and the completion of the present cycle of existence. Zervan was, in other words, the Absolute, or primal essence, like the *Tae-keih* of the Confucianist, the Bythos of the early Gnostic, or the Ὂν of Neo-Platonism. Like them he was believed to have existed long before the contrariety of good and evil had been manifested in creation; and accordingly the practice was to represent him rather as a 'metaphysical abstraction'[1] dwelling in impenetrable void, than as an active and presiding deity; he was said to have been neither 'endowed with self-consciousness' nor 'possessed of moral perfections.' But here, as in some other cases[2], a more critical knowledge of the language, and a juster estimate of the antiquity, of sacred documents has modified the first conclusions of speculative philosophy. It is found, for instance, that so far from Zervan standing out conspicuous in the creed of ancient Persia, the allusions to him in her sacred writings are extremely few, as well as cursory and indistinct. Thus, in the principal passage cited from the *Vendidád*[3] in reference to this subject, Zarathustra, when the words are accurately rendered, has been merely made to say: 'What the holy-minded One (*i. e.* Ormazd) created, he created in the *boundless* (or, the uncaused) *Time*.' And in a subsequent verse, which forms the second important passage bearing on the character of Zervan, the favoured servant of Ormazd is bidden to 'invoke the self-created firmament, the *boundless* (or, the uncaused) *Time*, and the breeze that works in the high places[4].' On a careful scrutiny of these and other like expressions, it appears that only one of two inferences is really justifiable, either, that some elementary substratum was here said to have existed from eternity, and so to have preceded the formation of

karana is 'the time occupied by the moon in passing through a small part of her orbit,' *a-karana* might possibly have meant 'undivided.'

[1] *e.g.* Gibbon, ch. VIII.

[2] See above, pp. 311 sq., on the nature of the Chinese *Tao*.

[3] Farg. XIX. § 33 (*Avesta*, I. 245, ed. Spiegel). The original here is: 'dathat. çpentô. mainyus. dathat. zrvânê. akaranê.'

[4] *Ibid.* § 44: cf. § 55, and Spiegel's essay in the *Zeitschrift der Deutschen morgenländ. Gesellsch.* (1851), v. 228, 229.

the visible universe, or else, that 'uncreated Time' had been regarded as a species of *material*, in and out of which was formed that definite period of duration, which, according to the Perso-Áryans, was allotted for the lifetime of the present world. Such language does not, therefore, warrant the hypothesis that Zervan was the principal god of Persia, in the judgment of those writers who compiled her sacred books.

It is again remarkable that the name of Zervan is never found upon the cuneiform inscriptions of Darius Hystaspis. Everything beneficent is there ascribed distinctly to the grace and succour of Ormazd,—a circumstance which, owing to the constant repetition of the formula, could hardly fail to have impressed on the explorer his belief in the 'radical and irreconcilable' divergence between Zervan-worship and the genuine system of the Perso-Áryans. Still there is no reasonable ground for doubting that in subsequent centuries, when the feeling after unity was re-awakened in the human spirit, and when men were anxious to revert, in thought at least, to something permanent, illimitable, uncreated,—some existence underlying and reducing into harmony the painful contradictions of the visible universe,—a string of texts like those surviving in the *Vendidád* were eagerly appropriated by more philosophic thinkers, till with such the name of *Zervan* was the recognised expression of belief in some great Primal Essence. I subjoin one extract from a later Parsee writing[1] of considerable repute, in which this theory of Zervan has been formally developed. The opening sentence strikes me as containing an allusion to the passage of the *Vendidád* above recited:

'In the religion of Zoroaster, it is to this effect declared, that God (*Khudá*) created every thing from time; and that the Creator is *Time*. And for *Time* no limit has been made, and no height has been made, and no root has been made. And it always has been, and it will always be. He who has intelligence even will not be able to tell whence it has been made. So great is its glory that there is no other being who can be called Creator, because the creation was not then made. Afterwards, fire and earth were created; and from their union *Hormuzd* (Ormazd) was created. *Time* was the Creator, and this Lord has guarded the creation he has made.'

Nor is the theory of Zervan, as here advocated, inconsistent

[1] The work entitled *I'lmá-i-Islám* was composed about A.D. 1126, and contains the replies of a Parsee doctor to a Muslim inquirer: see the original in Wilson's *Pársís*, pp. 135, 136.

with a second, which has recently proceeded from a different quarter, *viz.* that this god. whose worship had in later times been made to rest on rare and dubious texts of the Avesta, was in fact an early importation from some foreign and non-Âryan system. We have reason for supposing that the name of Zervan is related to the *ziru-banit* of Assyrian monuments[1]. The title there comes forward as an ordinary epithet of Bel, the βῆλος ἀρχαῖος of Babylonian mythology, and therefore intimately connected with the thought of *time*[2]. It is accordingly conjectured, that the knowledge of this great divinity, who, under the descriptive name *Bel-itan*, or 'Old Bel,' was once supreme in ancient Babylonia, had passed over to the Scythic magi, at a period when the different populations of that region were extensively intermingled. Thence the Zervan-dogma may have penetrated into Media, so that the divinity, connected by Herodotus[3] with 'the cycle of the heavens,' and incorrectly represented by him as of 'Persian' origin, might really correspond with the great Bel of ancient Babylonia; and at length, when the amalgamation was completed in the Magian and Persian creeds, and it was necessary to adjust the relative functions and positions of such gods as Zervan and Ormazd, a further precedent might be derived from the traditions of the Babylonian Semites, who had learned to venerate not only a supreme divinity (the Βῆλος ἀρχαῖος), but also a reflection of him, called the Βῆλος δεύτερος, or the 'Assyrian Hercules[4].'

In any case we are at liberty to argue that faint glimmerings of one only God,—inert, indeed, if not impersonal, but still the Primal Cause of all things—are discernible here and there in the remains of Medo-Persian heathenism; and certainly such a dogma, whether viewed as the reanimation of some patriarchal

[1] See Sir H. Rawlinson's paper in the *Journ. As. Soc.* xv. 245, n. 2.

[2] The word *Zervâna*, according to Spiegel, I. 271, signifies *old* (not 'time' merely), and so would be a fair translation of the Semitic איתן, which is found distinctly in Bel-itan, or Old Bel. Spiegel in this matter has arrived at very much the same result as Rawlinson, but by a different process. He contends especially for the Semitic origin of the Zervan-dogma, from the fact that the name *Zerovanes* itself has been preserved in Berosus among the fragments of the Babylonian mythology.

[3] I. 131, where Mr. Blakesley suspects that the historian is following the 'account of some person who confused the genuine Persian with a Median [*i. e.* Magian] ritual.'

[4] 'Beide, der erste und zweite Bel, eben so wie Zarvan und Ormuzd, werden in einer Beziehung identificirt und in der andern unterschieden. Ahuramazda als der Absolute, Ewige, Ueberweltliche gedacht...ist der Zarvan-akarana.' Schlottman, in Weber's *Ind. Stud.* I. 378, 379.

tenet, or as due to interchanges of religious thought with Scythic and Semitic tribes, or as the product of a speculative yearning to resolve all contrarieties of the visible world into an ultimate and higher unity, is often traceable in the literature of modern Parsees[1].

Yet, on the other hand, so long as our chief guides into this region are the sacred books of ancient Persia, and the monuments belonging to the age of Darius Hystaspis, we are no less under the necessity of urging in reference to *Zervána-akarana*[2], that his worship was unknown to all the early generations of the Áryan settlers. He must therefore be eliminated from discussions of the Perso-Áryan theology; and the rather, since his name, whenever first admitted in that system, had produced in it no sensible effect. *Zervána* was from first to last a colourless abstraction, which Parsees are even now accustomed to esteem the mere equivalent of 'eternity.'

If we, accordingly, neglect this foreign and intrusive element, we find that the theology derivable from the pages of the Avesta[3] is, in form at least, completely *dualistic*. A belief in two great principles, of rival power and contradictory functions, is

[1] The following extract from Mr. Dosabhoy Framjee's work *The Parsees*, pp. 250, 251, will remind some readers of the strong assertions made by Ram-mohun Roy and other half-Christianized Hindús as to the primitive theology of the Védas: 'The religion propounded by him [Zoroaster] is a simple form of theism, recognising but one God, the Creator, Ruler, and Preserver of the universe, without form, invisible. To Him is assigned a place above all, and to Him every praise is to be given for all the good in this world, and all the blessings we enjoy. Zoroastrianism does not require any image of God to be made for the purpose of worship, as to Him is attributed no form, shape, or colour. He is an immense light, from which all glory, bounty, and goodness flow. He is represented as the mightiest, the most just, and the most benevolent. His mercies are as boundless as His being. The adoration or worship of any other object is blasphemous.' The author of such language would most probably explain the countless 'invocations' addressed in the Yasna to the various forms of created nature as no more than picus remembrances of high and noble objects: cf. Wilson, *Pársí Religion*, pp. 265 sq.

[2] Rawlinson and Spiegel are quite at one on this point. The latter writes (*Avesta*, Exc. I. 271): 'In dem ganzen persischen ursprüng-lichen Religionssysteme ist diese Lehre ein Misston.'

[3] The monuments are not included in this statement, because, with one exception where the 'god of lies' is glanced at, they contain no traces of the Persian dualism. Their silence, however, with regard to Ahriman is well explained in Rawlinson's *Herodotus*, Vol. I. p. 427, n. 4, where we are reminded that 'the public documents of modern countries make no mention of Satan.'

conspicuously set forth in every portion of those writings, or at least in all the portions where the language of the worshipper does not betray the influence of incurable polytheism. The rival principles of Medo-Persia are *Ahura-mazda*[1] (Ormazd), the good divinity, and *Ağra-mainyus* (Ahriman), the 'Evil-minded.'

Now with reference to Ormazd, it must be granted that he is not only, in accordance with his title, 'god of the Áryans,' but has also been at times invested with high honours and prerogatives which suffice almost to lift him to the rank of the Supreme Intelligence. He is the sovereign Judge, the sovereign excellence, the sovereign knowledge: 'greatest, best, most beautiful, the strongest, most intelligent, most graceful, and most holy[2].' Everything, so far as it is elevated in its aim and noble in its nature, was the product of his hand: he is the 'Maker of the pure creation;' more exalted than the brilliant, fertilising Mithra, ruler of a spacious province and gifted with ten thousand eyes; superior also to the holy Sraŏsha, the author of abundance, bearing in his hand the instruments of vengeance to chastise a multitude of evil spirits[3]. One example taken from the Yasna[4] will exhibit all these varied characteristics in a single group: 'I invoke and celebrate the creator Ahura-mazda, luminous, resplendent, best and greatest, excellent in strength and in perfection, most intelligent, most lovely, eminent in purity, possessing the good knowledge, source of pleasure, who created us, who fashioned us, who feeds us, most accomplished of intelligent beings.'

In the train of this divinity, or at times associating with him as possessors of the same exalted nature, are six other spiritual beings, genii of the world of light. The common name 'amshaspand' (*amesha-spenta*, or the 'immortal holy one') is equally applied to all these seven intelligences; each has special days in every month devoted to his honour; though

[1] On the various etymologies of this word, see Burnouf, *Commentaire sur le Yaçna*, pp. 70 sq.; Wilson, *Pársí Religion*, p. 110. Another name or title of Ormazd, viz. *Spento-mainyus*, 'the Holy-minded,' brings him into more direct antagonism with the 'Evil-minded.'

[2] *Vendidád*, Farg. XIX. § 47.

[3] *Ibid.* §§ 51—53: cf. Spiegel's *Studien*, in *Zeitsch. Deutsch. morg. Gesell.* V. 223, 224. In a passage there translated from the *Minokhired* (a work of the Sassanian age) we notice an endeavour to establish some original co-operation between Ormazd and Zervána-akarana: 'Der Schöpfer Ormazd erschuf diese Welt und Creaturen und Amschaspande und den himmlischen Verstand *aus seinem eigenen Lichte* und mit dem Jubelrufe *der unendlichen Zeit*.'

[4] Burnouf, *Comment.* p. 146.

expressions, we must also grant, are never wanting where Ormazd is ranked indefinitely above the others, and regarded as the luminous chief and 'lord of the amshaspands[1].' It is probable, as hinted in a previous chapter[2], that this frequent limitation of the 'holy ones' to *seven* has reference to the primitive worship of the heavenly bodies, the sun, the moon, and the five planets. Light, in its most elemental form, had fascinated the imagination of the early Áryan, and at first, perhaps as the appropriate symbol of the Godhead, had suggested the generic name of his divinities[3]. The sun-god (Savitri) was celebrated by the Hindú poet in the oldest of the Vaidic hymns; and consequently, when his kinsmen paid their homage to the gorgeous sky of Persia, it was not unlikely that they all continued to associate some ideas of the invisible world with the more brilliant of the heavenly bodies. The great lord of light, proceeding on his course in peerless dignity and beauty, was the 'eye' of Ormazd himself; the lesser lights were his attendants, shining by his splendour and executing his behests; and thus, in spite of all the systematising of the first mythology which resulted in the formal 'dualism of Zoroaster,' the old practice[4] of ascribing personality to sun and moon and stars, and so exalting them to objects of religious worship, was perpetuated in the Persian system to the close of its existence.

But as physical light appears to be involved in deadly strife with physical darkness, so the glory of Ormazd was ever liable to diminution and eclipse beneath the shade of Ahriman, his lying, 'evil-minded,' and corrupting adversary. In the strength imparted to such contrasts by the Medo-Persian creed consists its grand peculiarity[5].

We must not suppose, indeed, with some living writers, that dualism was utterly unknown in all other heathen countries. Typhon's place in reference to Osiris was in many points analogous to that of Ahriman, the rival of Ormazd[6].

[1] Wilson, as above, p. 129. On the names of the *amshaspands*, see Burnouf, as before, pp. 147—174.

[2] Above, pp. 453 sq.

[3] Above, p. 126.

[4] The following is M. Burnouf's version of a hymn in the *Yasna* (*Comment.* p. 375): 'Je célèbre, j'invoque Ahura et Mithra, élevés, immortels, purs; et les *astres, créations saintes et célestes;* et l'astre Taschter (Tistrya), lumineux, resplendissant; et la lune, qui garde le germe du taureau; et le soleil, souverain, coursier rapide, *œil d'Ahura-mazda;* Mithra, chef des provinces.'

[5] Sir H. Rawlinson has gone so far as to conjecture that it was the rise of this 'dualistic heresy' which led to the original disruption of the Áryan tribes.

[6] Plutarch, *De Iside et Osiride*, after describing the malignity of

The Bráhman, also, could discourse of deep and irremediable antagonisms between the laws of matter and of spirit; and in some of the non-Áryan tribes of India[1], to say nothing of American and other distant parallels, the two great members of the pantheon are the Sun, or light-god, and his wife, the Earth; the latter being adverse to the former as evil to good, yet both of them esteemed the fitting objects of religious worship. Still the shape assumed by Persian dualism is so peculiar, the antagonistic forces are so nearly balanced, and the contrast has been carried out so rigorously in its details, that we are justified in treating this as a distinctive feature in the history of religious thought.

In Persia also, even more than Egypt[2], the relations of the two chief gods reflect the physical circumstances of the country and the struggles of the early population. While their brethren on the Sutlej were invoking Indra and his host to aid in the expulsion of the dark-complexioned 'Dasyus,' the first settlers in Iran were waging a like contest with the 'hostile ones,' the *Tuîryas*[3] (Turanians). Every inch they rescued from the natives was a triumph won from Ahriman by timely succours of Ormazd; while in the lengthened fluctuations of that contest they beheld an image of the warfare ever raging in the spirit-world, where powers of good and evil, moral light and moral darkness, had alternate mastery. As from the fiat of Ormazd proceeded all the good things of creation, Ahriman had the terrific privilege of *creating* and transmitting evil[4]. Every thing that tended to impede the propagation of life and purity and light, or interrupted the benignant flow of order and pros-

Typhon, proceeds (c. XLVI.) to speak of Zoroastrian dualism as something akin to that of Egypt: but Mr. Kenrick (*Anc. Egypt*, I. 419) argues that the contrast was less definitely established in the Egyptian system; for if not 'we should find other gods whose attributes are beneficent assailed by other Typhons.'

1 See the extracts from Major Macpherson's paper on the religion of the Khonds, above, pp. 259 sq.

2 Above, pp. 460 sq.

3 Spiegel, in *Zeitsch. Deutsch. morg. Gesell.* v. 223. The Vaidic equivalent is *túrya*, 'hostile.'

4 Thus in the opening Fargard of the *Vendidád*, as soon as it is mentioned that Ormazd had created any pure locality, the addition uniformly follows: 'Dann schuf eine Opposition desselben Aĝramainyus, der voll Tod ist.' After statements such as this, continually repeated in his own sacred books, it is difficult to understand how an intelligent writer like Mr. Dosabhoy Framjee (*Parsees*, p. 255) can argue that Ahriman 'should be taken in an allegorical sense, to denote the cause of the temptation under which man often falls into evil.' The *personality* of Ahriman is quite as clearly stated as the personality of Ormazd.

perity, was imputed to the envious rage of the arch-demon, ever battling from a species of necessity within the borders of his rival. One of these co-ordinate powers was thus an object of desire and reverence, and as such received the willing homage of all worshippers, the frequent prayer, the grateful offering; while, on turning towards Ahriman, the object of men's dread and horror, prayer itself was changed to abject deprecation, and sacrifice became no better than a weapon or a charm for warding off calamity[1]. To illustrate the old ideas on this subject, I may mention that a hideous serpent, which in Egypt was connected with Typhonic malice[2], was in Persia also the peculiar agent of the Evil-minded. Hence, indeed, arose the fancy that of salutary effects believed to flow in primitive times from the great homa-sacrifice the foremost was the generation of a warrior who might slay 'the homicidal serpent, with three necks, with three heads, with six eyes, and with a thousand forces,—that remorseless god, who destroys purity, that sinner who ravages the worlds, whom Ahriman created the chief foe of purity, in the existing world, for the annihilation of the purity of the worlds[3].'

Exactly as the projects of Ormazd were carried out by six immediate ministers or colleagues, Ahriman ere long was made the centre of a circle of malignant spirits, sons of darkness; six of whom, the *devs* (*daēvas*), stand arrayed in deadly strife against the luminous *amshaspands*. The two orders had thus formed so many pairs of strong antitheses: they personated in the one case high and salutary properties, as life and goodness,

1 Plutarch, as before, c. XLVI. Among the other multitudinous objects invoked in the *Yasna*, frequent mention is made of the *Izeds*, a class of gods or genii which at times are scarcely distinguishable from the *Amshaspands*. They are saluted as 'the most worthy of the masters of purity, the most praiseworthy, the most pervading, the delight of the master, the pure master of purity.' The highest member of this order would appear to have been Mithra. We have again considerable difficulty in determining the precise nature and functions of another class of spirits mentioned in the Yasna, *viz.* the *Fervers* or *Fravashis*, which, although reminding us of guardian angels and good genii, are more properly considered as ideal prototypes of actual intelligences (cf. Wilson, *Pârsî Religion*, pp. 130, 131). Every thing in nature, up to Ormazd himself (*Vendidâd*, XIX. 46), has its own special *Ferver*: and occasionally such model beings were supposed to form a vast spiritual army fighting on the side of the good Principle, passing also between earth and heaven, and carrying the devotions of 'pure' men to the feet of Ormazd (Döllinger, *Heidenthum*, p. 362).

2 Above, p. 465, n. 1.

3 Translated by Burnouf, *Études*, 'Le Dieu Homa,' in *Journal Asiat.* (1844), IV. 493.

truth and plenty, and the element of fire itself considered as a source of happiness; they personated in the other case destruction, malice, lying, penury, and elemental fire that shrivels and devours.

The question now is, Are we justified in speaking of the Persian form of dualism as absolute and eternal? Were the powers in conflict so equipotent, the elements of good so hopelessly and so inextricably blended with the elements of evil, that mankind must ever groan between the terrible contrariety?

Such is often said to be the character of genuine 'Zoroastrianism;' and little or nothing, I am bound to mention, is detected in the ancient books of Persia that necessitates an opposite conclusion. In those writings, the two kingdoms almost uniformly stand in harsh and absolute antagonism; on one side there is primal Good producing and reviving good, and on the other, primal evil, which, possessed of a co-ordinate power, is working, and must ever work, disorder and decomposition. It appears, moreover, that belief in this most rigorous form of dualism had been perpetuated in a Persian sect entitled Magusæans, while the influence which it once exerted is perhaps still more distinctly to be traced in the projection of the Manichæan heresy.

Máni, we should here remember, lived and taught at Babylon in the third century after Christ, and in the mythic names attributed to his pupils (Buddas[1], Thomas, Hermas) may be found not only proof of his reputed influence, but allusion to particular systems of belief which he attempted, not long after the Sassanian revival, to amalgamate with the Ormazd-religion.

It is foreign to our purpose to inquire in what degree the Buddhist, Christian, and Hellenic elements were intermixed[2] by him with genuine 'Zoroastrianism;' but as none of those foreign systems can be charged with teaching the dogma of two opposite and co-eternal principles, we may conclude that in the view of Máni, who insisted ever on such dogma, it was held to be a genuine heirloom of the ancient Persian worthies. On the other hand, as Máni himself is said to have been barbarously put to death upon the charge of falsifying the pure religion of

[1] The old reading *Addas* is now corrected into *Buddas* (Lassen's *Ind. Alt.* III. 406).

[2] F. C. Bauer, *Das Manichäische Religionssystem*, followed, in the main, by Lassen, contends that in those particulars where Manichæism separated itself from the 'doctrine of Zoroaster,' it came nearer to Hindú systems and especially to Buddhism. On the strange way in which Zoroaster (Ζαράδης), Buddha, Christ, and Máni were associated on a level by some of the Mediæval Manichæans, see above, p. 25, n. 2.

Zoroaster, we are not at once entitled to draw positive inferences as to the early character of that religion, from accounts which have descended to us of the Manichæan heresy.

It must, indeed, be granted that so far as our particular question is concerned, the language used by Persians in the fifth century after Christ again implied a prevalent disposition to reduce all contrarieties of the physical and moral world into an abstract unity. For that Zervanism was then at least a primary article of their faith, the following extract from the proclamation[1] of a Persian general (A.D. 450) will abundantly establish:

"Before the heavens and the earth were, the great god Zruan (Zervan) prayed a thousand years, and said, 'If I, perhaps, should have a son named *Vormist* (Ormazd), who will make the heavens and the earth.' And he conceived two in his body, one by reason of his prayer, and the other because he said *Perhaps*. When he knew that there were two in his body, he said, 'Whichever shall come first, to him will I give over my sovereignty.' He who had been conceived in doubt passed through his body and went forth. To him spake Zruan: 'Who art thou?' He said, 'I am thy son Vormist.' To him said Zruan: 'My son is light and fragrant breathing; thou art dark and of evil disposition.' As this appeared to his son exceedingly harsh, he (Zruan) gave him the empire[2] for a thousand years. When the other son was born to him, he called him Vormist. He then took the empire from Ahriman, gave it to Vormist, and said to him, 'Till now I have prayed to thee, now thou must pray to me.' And Vormist made heaven and earth; Ahriman on the contrary brought forth evil."

[1] The author of it was Mihr Nerseh, grand vizier of Iran. It was addressed to the Armenians, and has been preserved in the *History of Vartan* by an Armenian bishop Elisæus (pp. 11, 12, translated by Neumann, Lond. 1830). The account respecting Zervan and the two derived intelligences (Ormazd and Ahriman) agrees substantially with that transmitted by another Armenian writer of the 5th century after Christ: see the *Réfutation des Sectes*, par Eznig, pp. 75 sq. (translated into French by De Florival, Paris, 1853). Döllinger (p. 360, note) has also pointed out distinct allusions to the same mythe in Theodore of Mopsuestia, who says, in speaking of Zervan (*ἀρχηγὸν πάντων*), that while making a libation (? of the homa-plant), *ἵνα τέκῃ τὸν Ὁρμίσδαν, ἔτεκεν ἐκεῖνον καὶ τὸν Σατανᾶν*.

[2] The priority of birth and empire here attributed to the Evil One has a most striking parallel in the dualistic system of the Bogomiles (of the 12th century after Christ): see Hardwick's *Middle Age*, pp. 303 sq. There also Satanael is the first-born, and is entrusted for a season with the chief administration of the world.

In accordance with the hopeful spirit that gave being, both to this and other kindred mythes, the reign of the good Principle, though subsequent in point of time, was represented as far mightier and more lasting than the reign of evil. Ahriman, the child of doubt, shall be hereafter superseded[1]. On the expiration of some dark millennium, he shall cease to be the terror of all pure and upright beings, while his rival, raised to the administration of the kingdom, shall create a second order of superior spirits, or at least initiate some remedial process, by which all things now existing may revert to their original condition. In other words, the ancient Persian could descry beneath the manifold contradictions of the actual world an aboriginal unity, nay, could hear amid them all the promise of some blessed restoration.

Faint, indeed, and broken were the whispers of that promise. Often the mere echo of instinctive longings under which the heart of man had ached in every region of the ancient world, it was devoid of all historic basis, and was pointing onward to no definite fulfilment; yet in spite of its intrinsic weakness, and in spite of all the clouds in which it was involved by desperate speculations on the origin of evil, a belief in some such promise,—a belief in the superior majesty of truth and her eventual triumph,—had been always lingering in the Persian mind. We may hereafter have occasion to observe that under the Sassanian monarchs, some at least of the more popular traditions on this subject bore no slight resemblance to the Messianic prophecies transmitted in the Hebrew Church.

As special virtue had been constantly ascribed to *words* of Ormazd, it was by these, as parts of his offensive armour, that the good man was commissioned to do battle with the swarming hosts of darkness. For example, when the Evil One demanded[2] of Zarathustra 'By whose word wilt thou smite, by whose word wilt thou destroy?' the 'holy man' is said to have replied: 'A

[1] These peculiarities of the later Persian creed are fully established in passages brought to light by J. Müller, in 1843, and subsequently considered by Spiegel, in the *Zeitschrift der Deutsch. morgenländ. Gesellschaft* (1851), v. 225. One of such passages affirms in reference to Ahriman: 'Aber es wird eine Zeit sein, wo sein Schlagen aufhört.' And in a second, after describing the effects of the Evil Principle, it is added: 'Es war (eine Zeit), da er nicht war in diesen Geschöpfen, und es wird sein (eine Zeit), da er nicht sein wird in den Geschöpfen.' The same idea of Ahriman's eventual overthrow occurs in Plutarch, *De Isid. et Osir.* c. XLVII.

[2] *Vendidâd*, XIX. 28—32, where I follow Spiegel's version: cf. x. 25, sq. In § 28 we are told 'Dies sind die Worte, welche alle Daevas schlagen.'

mortar and a bowl, the *homa* and the words which Ormazd has spoken, these are my best weapons.' Nor did victory over Ahriman consist in mere escape from present physical suffering, and in larger and more sparkling cups of temporal prosperity[1]. Here the Persian, of historic times at least, was far superior to his kinsman whose importunate prayer for cows and horses and the like was heard pervading all the oldest invocations of the Véda. In the measure of her moral sensibility, Persia may be fairly ranked among the brightest spots of ancient heathendom.

The 'holy man,' indeed, of the Avesta, is often a mere synonym for 'worshipper of Ormazd,' yet excellence, it should not be forgotten, is confined no longer to descendants of a priestly class dissevered by impassable gulphs from all below them: not to the possessor of recondite knowledge, and the lordly founder of some philosophic school; not even to the ardent devotee recoiling from the din and business of the world, and seeking in the silence of the jungle a sure refuge from its perils and seductions. Purity is there made possible for all: in all it is connected with incessant warfare, and in all dependent on exact conformity to the Ormazd-religion, 'in thought, in word, in deed.' Deflection from its precepts is the only cause of permanent disaster. Servants of Ormazd, unfortified by prayer and sacrifice, may yield to the temptations of the Evil One, and as the fruit of their misdeeds may undergo a lengthened term of penance. The body also must in every case eventually succumb beneath the iron yoke of death, the ruthless minister of Ahriman, and then communicate a portion of its own 'impurity' to all who come in contact with it. Still so long as any man was held to have continued in the number of the 'pure,' it was believed that saving efficacy issued to his spirit from the law of Ormazd; that law 'taking away all the evil thoughts, words and actions of a pure man, as the strong fleet wind purifies the heaven[2].

A cursory glance at precepts and prescriptions of the *Vendidád* will serve, however, to convince us that in Persia, as in Egypt, the idea of 'purity' had always been extremely superficial and unspiritual. It involved but little more than a punctilious compliance with established rites and ceremonies. Starting from the thought that every thing in nature was intrinsically either 'clean' or 'unclean,'—a production either of Ormazd the good divinity, or else of the impure arch-demon,—the Old Persian was at least as anxious to escape from bodily defilement[3],

[1] Cf. above, p. 128.

[2] *Vendidád*, III. 149.

[3] On this subject, see, for instance, *Vendidád*, VII. 193—196.

or from contact with material things possessed by Ahriman, as to exemplify the higher moral qualities of which that Evil One had introduced the hideous negations. On the other hand, it is apparent that the consciousness of an unceasing conflict in the spirit-world had kept alive the habit of discriminating between moral light and moral darkness, and produced in many hearts a deep abhorrence of the evil, and a resolute yearning after good. The Persian had been commonly one of the least compromising, if not also the most active and most truthful, nations of antiquity[1]. Accustomed to regard the universe in general as one mighty battle-field, the genuine worshipper of Ormazd had also tenanted his own immediate sphere with foes innumerable: his mission was to aid in counteracting the unwearied malice of the *devs*, to vindicate the cause of right and truth against the advocates of wrong and falsehood; and the stern intolerant spirit breathed by despots like Cambyses indicates the natural product of that system of religion, when directed by unflinching hands.

Indeed the Persian monarchs may be fitly taken as at once the visible centres and the highest practical illustrations of the Medo-Persian theology. Unchecked alike by the intrigues and admonitions of a dominant priesthood, such as that which flourished at the ancient court of Oude, or Thebes, or Memphis, they stood forward the supreme reflections, if not actual incarnations, of the glory of Ormazd[2]. The warm and flexible polytheism of their subjects had been earnestly directed towards them[3]. They seemed to be entrusted with the sole administration of the light-kingdom, as the Pharaohs of an earlier period were the children

Rhode (*Die heilige Sage des Zendvolks*, pp. 453 sq., Frankfurt, 1820) in discussing such passages attempts to establish an absolute identity of view in the Avesta and the Old Testament: but whatever may be urged with regard to some particulars, there is certainly not a word in the Books of Moses to justify the supposition that any creature is *essentially* unclean, or that certain animals are produced by the creative energy of an Evil Principle.

[1] Burnouf, *Études*, in the *Journ. Asiat.* (1840), p. 324, regards the importance assigned to the 'sentiment of human personality and morality' as the best feature of 'Zoroastrianism.'

[2] Thus, when Themistocles (Plutarch, *Them.* c. xxvii.) wished to be presented to the king, he was told by the Persian Artabanus that he must first submit to offer worship 'to the image of god the preserver of all things' (*i.e.* of Ormazd). Curtius (VIII. 5) in like manner says expressly, 'Persas reges suos inter deos colere:' see Hengstenberg, *Genuineness of Daniel*, pp. 103 sq., Edinb. 1847.

[3] Arrian, *Alex.* IV. 11, mentions a report that this *προσκύνησις* began with Cyrus: *Λέγεται τὸν πρῶτον προσκυνηθῆναι ἀνθρώπων Κῦρον καὶ ἐπὶ τῷδε ἐμμεῖναι Πέρσαις τε καὶ Μήδοις τήνδε τὴν ταπεινότητα.*

of the Sun[1]. Their court was an inferior copy of the court of Ormazd: on grand or critical occasions they convoked a solemn council, the idea of which, in form and number, had been borrowed from the brilliant circle of divine amshaspands; and as 'words of Ormazd' himself were deemed most sacred and oracular, the law of ancient Persia had been taken from the lips of her great despot, who by placing his own signet on the harshest of decrees could render them irrevocable.

[1] Above, p. 443.

CHAPTER IV.

Alleged Affinities of the Medo-Persian Creed to Hebraism and Christianity.

Οὕτω λέγει Κύριος ὁ Θεὸς τῷ χριστῷ μου Κύρῳ, οὗ ἐκράτησα τῆς δεξιᾶς... Ἐγὼ Κύριος ὁ Θεὸς, καὶ οὐκ ἔστιν ἔτι πλὴν ἐμοῦ θεός. ἐνίσχυσά σε, καὶ οὐκ ᾔδεις με. ἵνα γνῶσιν οἱ ἀπ' ἀνατολῶν ἡλίου καὶ οἱ ἀπὸ δυσμῶν, ὅτι οὐκ ἔστι θεὸς πλὴν ἐμοῦ. ἐγὼ Κύριος ὁ Θεὸς, καὶ οὐκ ἔστιν ἔτι. ἐγὼ ὁ κατασκευάσας φῶς, καὶ ποιήσας σκότος, ὁ ποιῶν εἰρήνην, καὶ κτίζων κακά. ἐγὼ Κύριος ὁ Θεὸς, ὁ ποιῶν πάντα ταῦτα. Isa. xlv. 1—7. (LXX.)

The Great Captivity: its causes, and effects. With what form of heathenism were the Hebrews brought in contact? General character of Babylonian mythology. Resemblances between the Hebrew and Persian systems. State of religious feeling in the early Christian centuries. Influence in Persia of Jews, of Christians, and of early heretics. Were the Hebrews guilty of corrupting their old religion?

§ 1. *The Fall of Man. The primitive Bull. Meshia and Meshiane; their temptation, and fall. The form of the Tempter.*

§ 2. *Doctrine of the Evil One. Satan and Ahriman; how differing. Scriptural notices of the Tempter; how understood by Jews, and Christians. Heathen testimony.*

§ 3. *Doctrine of Holy Angels. Attributed to heathen influence. The Sadducees. Rabbinical testimony. Early traces of angelic orders. Amshaspands and archangels. Number of archangels.*

§ 4. *Doctrine of the Resurrection of the Body. Not traced in the Avesta. Two theories of the Body. The Hebrew doctrine ante-Babylonic.*

§ 5. *Doctrine of a Benefactor and Mediator. Sosiosh. Persian eschatology. Early place and character of Mithra: a Mediator. Substitution of Mithra for Ormazd. Post-Christian representations of Mithra. Mithraic mysteries. Opposition between Mithraism and Christianity.*

THE second period in her lifetime when the Hebrew Church was forced into more lasting and direct communication with the heathen of surrounding countries must be dated from the middle of the eighth century before the Christian era. As the prelude to a general deportation of the Ten Tribes, the settlers in the Trans-Jordanic province had been carried captive to Assyria under Tiglath-Pileser (2 Kings xv. 29); and at length, about the year 600, a large portion of the feeble remnant, stricken by a like calamity, had run the risk of being quite extinguished under the tremendous despotism, which formed in every age a vivid type of the ungodlike and unchristianlike,—Babylon the Great.

The exile was itself, however, the effect[1], and not the cause, of cravings after 'all the abominations of the heathen.' From the period of the Exodus the leaders of the Hebrew nation had been ever struggling with this downward, retrogressive tendency. 'The Lord God of their fathers sent to them by His messengers, rising up betimes and sending...but they mocked the messengers of God and despised His words and misused His prophets, until the wrath of the Lord arose against His people, till there was no remedy' (2 Chron. xxxvi. 15, 16). Yet penal though it was, the isolation of the Hebrews in the 'wilderness of the nations' had been also meant as a corrective discipline, and actually conduced by visible stages to the culture and the exaltation of the Church. Henceforth, as Jew and Christian have alike acknowledged, there was far less disposition to relapse into the bondage of the old polytheism. Closer contact with the creed and institutions of his heathen taskmasters had wakened in the spirit of the Hebrew exile a more deep and passionate longing not for Salem only, but the worship of his fathers' God. He bowed no more in adoration of the graven image, nor of elements and heavenly bodies: he no longer substituted a personification of recurring processes in animal or vegetable nature for the 'God of the spirits of all flesh.' It is again observable that the trying period of captivity, when the Hebrew could no longer celebrate the ritual worship of his fathers, was selected as the aptest time[2] for inculcating lessons of Divine wisdom on the subject of a new œconomy and a truer service of the heart: while prophecies of the Messiah, in accordance with the law of progress and expansion which obtains in all their earlier stages, had been now detached more plainly from the thought of national triumph or disaster, and invested with their fullest form and their most spiritual expression.

But while sacred writers on the one hand trace that exile to the heathenish temper of the chosen people, and attribute on the other hand the restoration of the Hebrews to a signal act of mercy following their profound repentance, the assailants of revealed religion have persisted in affirming that the sojourn of the Jews in Babylonia was the time when, most of all, they had deflected from the creed of Abraham and David, when the priest and prophet also, equally besotted by the popular love

[1] See above, pp. 515 sq. [2] Above, pp. 108 sq.

of heathenism, had joined in the adulteration of the choicest truths committed to their keeping. With the sole exception of a faithful remnant, whose descendants must be sought for (it is now discovered) in the sect of the Sadducees, the great community returned from Babylon, so infected with the superstitions of the foreign despot, that the doctors of the subsequent period (not excepting Christ and the Apostles) had been all unable or unwilling to shake off the dominant delusion. As the traces of Egyptian heathenism were freely pointed out, by this class of critics, in the ritual institutions of the ancient Hebrew, they proceed to argue that a worse corruption in respect of doctrine had resulted from his long familiarity with the Zendic literature of Medo-Persia.

Now in estimating this momentous question it is doubtless of the first importance to observe that any influences exerted on the Hebrews by the votaries of the Ormazd-religion must have always, in the period of the exile, been extremely slender and indirect. The principal scene of transportation was *not* Persia Proper; and although the natives of some Median cities where those exiles were dispersed might then have been, in part at least, related ethnologically to their Perso-Áryan neighbours, the religion which prevailed in Media[1], before the accession of Darius Hystaspis, and perhaps still later, was the element-worship of the Scythic Magi,—not the formal and elaborate dualism connected with the name of Zoroaster and proclaimed at large in the Avesta. It would further seem that actual conquerors of the Hebrew nation, the Assyrians or Chaldæo-Babylonians, *not* the Medo-Persians, are the people to whose creed we should most reasonably turn in searching for an explanation of the change alleged to have passed over the theology of the conquered. Is there, then, enough of general similarity in the ideas of ancient Babylonians and of Hebrews after the Captivity, to warrant us in carrying this investigation far into details? I answer, that no contrast could have well been greater. The mythology of Babylonia from the oldest period to the Achæmenian conquest[2] will exhibit scarcely any trace of dualism, which forms,

[1] See above, pp. 524 sq.

[2] Its main identity at very different periods is affirmed by Sir H. Rawlinson, *Journ. As. Soc.* xv. 253, n. 3. In a special Essay on the subject (Rawlinson's *Herod.* I. 584 sq.), the absence of all trace of dualism is more distinctly pointed out. Perhaps one of the most remarkable features of the Babylonian mythology is the high rank there awarded to the Moon-god: see above, p. 359, where moon-worship, as exemplified in old religions of America, *is* connected with the thought of some great evil principle.

as we have seen, the most distinctive property of the Persian system, and which Hebrews are supposed to have eventually adopted. That religion, on the contrary, had ever been 'a very gross polytheism,' which is said in general grouping to have borne no small resemblance to 'the mythological systems of Greece and Rome [1];' and therefore must have differed *toto cœlo* from the creed of the Old Testament, alike before and after the Babylonish captivity. I shall accordingly dismiss at once the oft-repeated fallacy which professes to connect the Hebrew exiles with the advocates of the Ormazd-religion, or, despairing of this pretext, throws together[2] into one the motley tenets of Magi, of Perso-Áryans and of Babylonians, gives the general name of 'dualism' to the incongruous compound, and concludes by arguing that the Jews who 'spent the long years of their captivity' in the midst of it 'returned not unimbued with the superstitions of their masters.'

The unfairness of such arguments must not, however, tempt us to deny the fact that striking parallelisms do really exist between traditions now surviving in the sacred books of Persia and some doctrines of the Hebrew and Christian Scriptures. What may be the real ground of such resemblances, the age when they are first apparent, and the aspect they are calculated to assume in reference to the character and claims of Christianity, are questions calling for minute investigation: but since no competent scholar is prepared to say that the Avesta *in its present shape* is clearly traceable further back than the third century after Christ, and since the fact is growing more indisputable every year that a variety of Semitic, if not Christian, elements were intermingled with the faith as well as with the language and literature of the Sassanian period, we are surely not at liberty to urge, before a strict examination of particulars, that traces of revealed religion which exist in sacred books of Persia must be treated as in every case original, and as proving the existence of an imitative spirit only in the Jewish nation. It is antecedently as probable that the Persian borrowed largely from the Hebrew as that the Hebrew borrowed from the Persian.

If resemblances in question should be found too many or too

[1] Rawlinson's *Herod.* I. 586.

[2] This is done, for instance, in Dr. Donaldson's *Christian Orthodoxy*, p. 102, where, unconscious, it would seem, of the confusion, he informs the reader that 'dualism was the creed of the Medes, Persians, and *Babylonians*.' If by 'creed of the Medes' we are to understand pure 'Magism,' the assertion is still further incorrect.

minute to be regarded as entirely accidental,—such, that is, as men might, under similar circumstances, have originated independently of each other,—three suppositions can alone be urged in explanation of the strange phenomena. We may hold that the traditions common to the Persian and Hebrew (1) are equally a portion of 'original truth,' which both alike inherited from fathers of the human family: or (2) the Persians, at the period of the exile, and still more in later and post-Christian times, when their own system reached its full proportions, were conversant in some degree with Hebrew and Christian learning: or (3) the Jewish doctors in the course of their dispersion at, and after the Captivity, contracted an unnatural fondness for the sacred books of Persia.

(1) The first of these three suppositions may of course be held concurrently with the second; yet by many Christian writers of our own and foreign countries, it alone has been regarded as the key to the affinities we are considering. When the genuine works of the Avesta, and still more the *Bundehesh*[1] itself, a Pehlevi compilation, were first brought to light by the adventurous Duperron, men were startled by the suddenness and brilliance of the grand disclosure. They beheld in it a series of most venerable relics, each at least coeval with the Persian monarchy. Nor at present, when it is completely ascertained that some of the results to which Duperron pointed with especial satisfaction were due to his inaccurate version of the sacred texts he had assisted in recovering, is there any lack of Christian writers who affirm that the traditions of the Avesta are well-nigh commensurate with those of the Old Testament. 'Of the King of Heaven' it is asserted[2] 'and the Father of eternal light,

[1] See above, p. 527.

[2] F. von Schlegel, *Phil. of History*, pp. 173, 174, where it is added: 'That with all these doctrines much may have been, or really was, combined, which the ancient Hebrews, and even we, would account erroneous, is very possible, and indeed may almost naturally be surmised; but this by no means impairs that strong historical resemblance we here speak of.' Dr. Mill (*Christ. Adv. Publ.* for 1841, p. 62), in alluding to the preservation of original truth in various parts of heathendom, agrees with Schlegel in ranking Persia far above most other regions: 'Such we find in nations most infected with polytheistic error: and much more we might well conceive to exist in one by which the grosser forms of idolatry were ever held in peculiar abhorrence: a nation whose greatest Prince is signally honoured by Divine prophecy [cf. the motto at the head of this chapter] in being named as the future restorer of God's people to their ancient seat: and whose sages were summoned from afar, before the great and wise of Israel, to adore the infant Redeemer.'

and of the pure world of light, of the eternal Word by which all things were created, of the seven mighty spirits that stand next to the throne of Light and Omnipotence, and of the glory of those heavenly hosts which encompass that throne; next, of the origin of evil and of the Prince of darkness, the monarch of those rebellious spirits—the enemies of all good; they [the Persians] in a great measure entertained completely similar, or at least *very kindred*, tenets to those of the Hebrews.' We may see hereafter that all statements of this kind are both exaggerated and overcoloured; yet no student of the question who considers the proximity of Persia to the cradle of the human race and the existence of a similar cluster of traditions[1] in the kindred tribe of Indo-Áryans, will be likely to relinquish the belief that there, as well as in the darker depths of gentilism, the echoes of primeval truths had lingered ages after they had lost all practical effect.

(2) The next hypothesis accounting for those common elements of thought and worship was at first supported mainly by insisting on the synchronism of Zoroaster and the Hebrew prophets of the Captivity; a further supposition being that if Daniel and Zoroaster had not actually communicated with each other, as doctor and disciple, the reputed author of the Avesta had at least been versed in 'sacred writings of the Jewish religion[2].' It was felt by the adherents of this view, especially when regard was had to the minute disclosures of the *Bundehesh*, that many representations so closely resemble 'those of the Hebrew Scriptures, as to leave no doubt of their real origin, through whatever channel ideas so analogous, or almost identical, can have been derived. The analogy is not of that kind which may be attributed to a similar derivation of tradition from a common source. It is more precise, and evidently belongs to a period not very remote[3].' So long, however, as the history of Zarathus-

[1] See above, pp. 207 sq.

[2] See, for instance, Prideaux, *Connection*, I. 216, Lond. 1718, who adds that the whole system was extracted thence; 'only the crafty impostor took care to dress it up in such a style and form, as would make it best agree with that old religion of the Medes and Persians, which he grafted it upon.' It is curious to observe, in connection with the prophet Daniel, and his influence on the heathen world, that persons are not wanting who identify him with the Hindû Buddha, and ascribe the appearance of Buddhism in Central India to the captivity and dispersion of the Jews. (*Journ. As. Soc.* XVI. 233.)

[3] Prichard, *Researches*, IV. 45, where, however, the so-called 'mythus of the Zendavesta' is taken chiefly from Rhode's uncritical work entitled *Die heilige Sage des Zendvolks* (Frankfurt, 1820).

tra is involved in the obscurity thrown over it by recent criticism, we are unable to refer the introduction of Semitic thoughts among the Medo-Persians to supposed effects of his communication with the Hebrew exiles. Like uncertainty is felt when we compare some striking texts of the Avesta with the kindred language of the Old Testament; for owing to the numerous gaps in Persian history and the changes which the Persian writings have undergone, there is good reason for suspecting the antiquity of certain passages on which our predecessors had implicitly relied. If, on the other hand, we start from the idea that many of the Persian stories which resemble Hebraism were not the product of remote ages, but obtained their earliest credit in the first three centuries after Christ, the history of the period will be found in many different ways to favour such hypothesis.

That age was characterised far more than all before it by a spirit of religious syncretism, an eager thirst for compromise[1]. To mould together thoughts which differed fundamentally, to grasp if possible the common elements pervading all the multifarious religions of the world, was deemed the proper business of philosophy both in East[2] and West. It was a period, one has lately said, 'of mystic incubation, when India and Egypt, Babylonia and Greece, were sitting together and gossiping like crazy old women, chattering with toothless gums and silly brains about the dreams and joys of their youth, yet unable to recall one single thought or feeling with that vigour which once gave it life and truth. It was a period of religious and metaphysical delirium, when everything became everything, when Máyá and

[1] Cf. above, pp. 22, 23.

[2] Speaking of Eastern Syria, Uhlhorn remarks (*Die Homilien und Recognitionen des Clemens Romanus*, Göttingen, 1854, p. 411): 'Kein Land war der Religionsmischung so gelegen wie dieses. Hier haben sich von den ältesten Zeiten an die verschiedensten Völker gedrängt, berührt und vermischt. Judenthum und Parsismus, der noch in den ersten Zeiten der christlichen Zeitrechnung sich stark nach Westen zu verbreitete, wie seine zahlreichen Anhänger selbst in Kleinasien beweisen, berührten und vermischten sich hier. Dazu war griechische Bildung gekommen, selbst Einflüsse des Buddhaismus erstreckten sich bis hieher, wie solche später in Manichäismus wohl kaum bezweifelt werden können. Auf diesem Boden erstarkte nun das Christenthum rasch und brachte eine mächtige Gährung hervor. Dazu kamen dann nach dem Untergange des jüdischen Staates die aus Palästina auswandernden Juden und Judenchristen, welche die Keime der Zersetzung mit hinüberbrachten. So schoss hier eine reiche Saat von Sectenbildungen, die alle mehr oder minder einen Mischcharakter an sich tragen und in denen wir überall wieder unsern Homilien ähnelnde Elemente erkennen, die ein näheres oder ferneres Verwandtschaftsverhältniss bezeugen.'

Sophia, Mithra and Christ, Viráf and Isaiah, Belus, Zervan and Kronos were mixed up in one jumbled system of inane speculation, from which at last the East was delivered by the positive doctrines of Muhammad, the West by the pure Christianity of the Teutonic nations[1].' Out of this remarkable ferment of the human spirit issued both the *Bundehesh* and the *Minokhired*, which, though strongly Persian in their tone, are also strongly tinctured by Semitic and Hebraic notions. For Jews[2] on the destruction of the holy city planted some of their chief schools in Babylonia, and even were at times promoted to high places in the Persian court; in learned centres, like Edessa, were discussed the various tenets of all known religions, Christianity in the number; and the Gnostic Bardesanes, writing from that city in the time of Marcus Aurelius, draws attention to the early progress of the Gospel[3], not in Parthia and in Media only, but in Persia Proper and in Bactria. Passing by the other traces which the new religion left behind it in those far-off regions, we may notice as of vast importance the long-thriving sect of Manichæans, who accepted Christianity as the groundwork of their composite belief: while stress may equally be laid upon the fact that one favourite writing of the later 'Zoroastrians' is only a Parsee adaptation[4] of the apocryphal or quasi-Christian work entitled the *Ascension of Isaiah;* where the prophet, on recovering from his rapture, narrates a journey to the 'seventh heaven,' in which his eyes were gladdened by the vision of Christ and of the Holy Spirit, and beheld inscribed upon a roll the wondrous story of the birth and passion of the Saviour.

(3) In exact proportion to the strength of the hypothesis just mentioned is the weakness of a third account which has been rendered of resemblances between the Persian and the Biblical traditions. Assuming even that the captive tribes were brought into familiar intercourse with the Ormazd-religion; assuming also that the Hebrew people as a body, still unweaned from old

1 M. Müller's 'Last Results of the Persian Researches,' as before, p. 119; although I cannot acquiesce entirely in some of the expressions.

2 Spiegel, *Avesta*, I. 17, 25.

3 Euseb. *Præpar. Evangel.* VI. 10 (Vol. II. pp. 92, 93, ed. Gaisford): cf. Neander, *Ch. Hist.* I. 111.

4 See the comparison between the two works (the *Arda-viráf-náme* and the Ἀναβατικὸν Ἡσαίου) in Spiegel, as before, pp. 21 sq. His closing remark is: 'Die Verwandtschaft der beiden Bücher wird wol Niemand ablengnen, doch scheint die christliche Gestaltung die ältere zu sein. Die Lehre von sieben Himmeln ist nicht parsisch, die spätere Parsenlehre kennt blos drei, über ihnen ist der *Gorothmán*, die Wohnung Ahura-mazdas.'

corruptions, had come back to Zion lusting after 'their fathers' idols;' in other words, assuming two positions which both militate against a long array of well-authenticated facts; we notwithstanding offer violence to all the probabilities of the question by supposing that Hebrew doctors, such as Daniel or Ezekiel, in whose eyes the exile was itself a penalty provoked by heathenish tendencies, should slide away into the superstitions either of their patrons or their taskmasters. The sentiment possessing them had always been: 'How shall we sing the Lord's song in a strange land? If I forget thee, O Jerusalem, let my right hand forget her cunning;' and notable instances may be adduced where men of constancy like theirs could brave the fiercest rage of Babylon, the lions' den, the blazing furnace, rather than renounce their sacred nationality or 'worship any other god.'

But with the view of justifying this main inference more completely, I propose to shew, by strict examination of particulars, that where a truly old relationship exists between the Hebrew and Persian systems, it is naturally explained on the hypothesis of aboriginal unity; and that in other cases there is either no true parallelism at all, or else that points of doctrine, said to be imported by the later class of sacred writers, had been actually current in the Hebrew Church for centuries anterior to the Babylonish exile.

§ 1. *The Fall of Man.*

According to the 'Persian Genesis' (the *Bundehesh*), the earliest representative of animal creation[1] was the primitive Bull (Goshurun), from whose right shoulder, as he fell beneath the stroke of the malignant Ahriman, proceeded Kaiomorts, the first of human beings. This grand prototype of men,

[1] The different passages of the *Bundehesh* relating to this point are brought together in Rhode, *Die heilige Sage*, etc., pp. 383 sq.: cf. Döllinger, p. 367. It is also worthy of remark, that in the Persian story the account of man's fall is intimately connected with the cosmogonic theory which pervaded most other countries of the ancient world both Old and New (see above, pp. 379 sq). In Persia (at least according to one version of the matter) we have first a cycle of 3000 years, when Ormazd is absolute (cf. however, above, p. 539); then, a cycle of the same period, when Ahriman commences his attack upon the light-kingdom, but, abashed by the exceeding purity of the *fervers* of holy men (above, p. 537, n. 1), falls back into the dark abyss, and lies quiescent during 3000 years. At the expiration of this time, Ahriman becomes more bold and active; and in the fourth period of 3000 years, completing the 'magnus annus' of the later Persians, Ahriman is, on the whole, ascendant and predominant.

including in himself the properties of both the sexes, was in turn assaulted by the Evil One, and finally destroyed by machinations of the *devs;* but from the vital force inherent in him there sprang up a plant which yielded as its fruit the true progenitors of the human family (Meshia and Meshiane[1]), or at least became the author of their bodily framework; for the soul itself was held to draw its origin directly from nothing short of heaven. Endowed with noble qualities, man was bidden to approve himself the lord of this lower world, by cultivating 'purity' in thought, in word, in action, and by keeping up a constant warfare with his enemies the *devs.* At first the parents of mankind were humble, and, devoted to the service of Ormazd, were innocent and happy; they were destined also to enjoy more perfect happiness; but Ahriman, the sleepless enemy of man and 'purity,' descending earthwards in the fashion of a serpent, plotted their corruption, and ere long by means of fruit derived from his own province of creation, he seduced them from their true allegiance: they declared that all they saw was Ahriman's, and therefore grew, it is narrated, as wicked as himself.

Without dwelling[2] on the obvious kinship which exists between this story and the sacred narrative, it is worthy of especial notice that one form attributed in Persia to the Evil Principle, or at least one favourite organ used by him for man's undoing, is the serpent, of whose guile and malice traces are continually recurring in the farthest wilds of gentilism[3]. Nor is this representation only to be met with in chapters of the *Bundehesh:* in genuine works of the Avesta also, the great 'homicidal serpent[4]' is the object of men's dread and horror:

[1] With these names compare the Sansk. *mánusha*, the Germ. *mensch*, and the *mannus* of Tacitus, *German.* c. 2 ('Tuisconem deum, *terra editum*, et filium Mannum'). On the Egyptian *Menes*, and other similar forms, see above, p. 429, n. 1, and Diefenbach, *Vergl. Wörterbuch der goth. Spr.* II. 32, 33, Frankfurt, 1851.

[2] I deem it quite superfluous, now that we can speak more positively about the age and origin of the *Bundehesh*, to answer such objections as those of Rhode and the older Rationalists, who used to affirm not only that the Mosaic version of the Fall was unintelligible without the Persian commentary, but also that the Hebrews had derived their knowledge of the whole tradition from a Persian source. Precisely the same kind of hardihood was shewn by Holwell and other sceptics, when they ventured to derive both Hebraism and Christianity from the 'Hindú scriptures': see above, p. 120, n. 1.

[3] See, for instance, the *Prose Edda*, § 34 (Mallet's *North. Antiq.* p. 423, Lond. 1847), where the second child of *Loki* (the Ahriman of Scandinavia) is the Midgard serpent, and the third Hela (Death).

[4] Above, p. 537.

while the Evil One himself is sometimes called 'the Serpent, in direct allusion to his power of counteracting the Good Principle. Thus, Ormazd is heard declaring in the *Vendidád*[1]: 'I am Ahura-mazda, I am the giver of good things. When I formed this dwelling-place, the beautiful, the brilliant, the note-worthy, saying, I will go forth, I will go over, then the Serpent beheld me. Thereupon the Serpent Ağra-mainyus, who is full of death, created, with an eye to *my* creation, nine sicknesses, and ninety, and nine hundred, and nine thousand and ninety thousand.'

§ 2. *Doctrine of the Evil One.*

This extract brings us to a question of very grave importance: Is the doctrine of a personal, superhuman Tempter, as now current in all branches of the Christian Church, the product of religious intercourse which Hebrews had maintained with their enslavers at the time of the Captivity? Is the Satan of the Old and New Testament, in other words, a modern copy of the Ahriman of the Avesta? In replying to this question I shall not survey afresh the main historical probabilities arising on the one side from the nature of the Babylonic (as distinguished from the Medo-Persian) creed, and on the other from the stern, uncompromising spirit of the Hebrew worthies who were sharers in the exile of their nation. On internal grounds alone I hold it to be far more likely that the Persian dogma, as it stands conspicuous in the *Vendidád*, was the corruption and distortion of a primitive truth bequeathed by the first parents of the human family. For no one who is able to discriminate at all, will question that under the more obvious features of resemblance there is lying also a most vital contrariety between the Hebrew and Old Persian theories on the nature of the Evil One.

As Satan in our sacred books is far from being the seductive spirit of the world, or of man's lower nature, 'conceived of in concrete personality[2];' so neither is he there

[1] Farg. XXII. §§ 1—6, where Spiegel's note is: 'Dass Ağra-mainyus eine *Schlange* genannt wird, kann nicht befremden, da er ja bekanntlich auch im Bundehesh unter dieser Form erscheint.'

[2] See Dr Mill's masterly sermons 'On the Temptation' (Camb. 1844), especially Serm. III.: in which the place and power of the arch-fiend are accurately determined. On the contrary, Dr. Donaldson's work, entitled *Christian Orthodoxy*, is devoted in no small measure to the maintenance of a theory, which involves our Lord Himself, and with Him the whole Christian community of

esteemed an absolutely evil being, like the Ahriman of the Avesta, coeternal and coequal with the Good, and like the Good an independent centre of creative energy. Satan is a fallen *creature*, his fall involved like man's fall in impenetrable mystery, and yet a fall which in results which it entailed on the creation has its dark analogy in the first great fall of man, as well as in that fiendish satisfaction which the fallen still experience in communicating their own misery to others. In neither case, however, is the sovereignty of God at all impugned by the existence of ungodlike passions in the creature, and the partial triumph of the powers of evil. Jew and Christian, equally possessed by a belief that there is One, and only one, true Principle of Existence, would alike recoil with horror from the notion which exalted the arch-demon to equality with the supreme and unapproachable Jehovah. The feeling of them both, in later as in earlier times, has been, that Satan is a 'murderer' and a 'liar,' *not* because he is the necessary antithesis of God, but simply because 'he *abides not* in the truth[1]' of his original creation (St. John viii. 44).

A most ample opportunity for testing both the genuineness and depth of this conviction had been offered on the rise and early progress of the Manichæan heresy. No countenance was given in East or West to figments of the Persian misbeliever. Then it was that St. Augustine, who amid the moral and intellectual tempests of his youth had learned to fathom the abyss of human depravity, stood forward to unmask the sophistries beneath which Mani sought to introduce into the Church the dogma of Two Principles; and worthy of our special notice is it, that the arm which levelled the proud system of Pelagius when he ventured to extenuate the malignity of moral evil, was uplifted with the same gigantic

every period, in the charge of swerving from the old (or ante-Babylonic) doctrine of the Hebrew Church in reference both to fallen and unfallen angels (cf. above, p. 72, n. 1). The same tendency (strange to say) is manifested at the same time by the intelligent Parsee writer, above quoted (p. 536, n. 4); who in the teeth of the most cogent evidence is able to declare that the Ahriman of his forefathers was really impersonal, or, as some scholastics would express it, 'was merely the evil of the world *hypostasised*' (precisely Dr. Donaldson's own position with regard to Satan).

1 See Dean Alford on this passage, who remarks that it is 'one of the most decisive testimonies for the *objective personality* of the devil. It is quite impossible,' he continues, 'to suppose an accommodation to Jewish views, or a metaphorical form of speech, in so solemn and direct an assertion as this.'

vigour for the overthrow of Faustus, the great champion of the Manichæans[1].

Turning, then, directly to the books of Holy Scripture, what can we detect in it to justify the charges of its modern adversaries? Is there any discernible variation in the language used at different periods with regard to the existence of diabolic agents and the personality of the Tempter? Now I find no difficulty whatever in admitting, just as when the elementary conceptions of a future life were made the subject of discussion[2], that a steadier light may have been gradually thrown upon this question in successive stages of the Church's growth. The revelations of the Old Testament, and therefore more particularly of the earlier portions of it, were not absolute and ultimate. As centuries went over, many large accessions may be clearly dated in the measure of man's sacred knowledge. It is found accordingly that truths pertaining to the spirit-world have also gained a greater prominence and greater clearness of expression in 'the fulness of the times,' nay, even in the latest writings of the New Testament[3]. It was our blessed Lord Himself, who in delivering the grand parable of the wheat and tares has singled out, for His direct antagonist, *the* wicked one; who told us also in His exposition that this wicked one is the Devil (St. Matth. xiii. 39), and the reapers holy 'angels.' In like manner, one chief object of the Saviour's mission is declared to be the 'stripping from Himself of principalities and powers,' (Col. ii. 15)—the subjugation of those more than human adversaries, with which the Christian in his turn is summoned to do battle (Eph. vi. 12). 'The Son of God was manifested that He might destroy the works of the Devil' (1 St. John iii. 8),—the works of that 'old serpent, which is the Devil and Satan' (Rev. xx. 2). It is true that reasons might exist alike in the prevailing tendencies of Asiatic thought, and in the moral status of the Hebrew Church itself, explaining the comparative absence of allusion to such topics in the early writings of the Bible; 'till the mightier power of

[1] See, especially, the treatise *Contra Faustum, Manichæum* (Opp. x. 221 sq., Bassani, 1807), where several of the Manichæan arguments are also given at length.

[2] Above, pp. 511 sq.

[3] 'In the spiritual world, where the lights are brightest, the shadows are deepest; and instead of hearing less of Satan, as the mystery of the kingdom of God proceeds to unfold itself, in the last book of Scripture, that which details the fortune of the Church till the end of time, we hear more of him [Satan], and he is brought in more evidently and openly working than in any other.'—Dean Trench, *On the Parables*, p. 84, Lond. 1844.

good was revealed we were in mercy not suffered to know how mighty was the power of evil[1]:' yet to say that nothing is recorded of Satanic influence till the period of the Babylonish exile is the arbitrary assumption of determined theorisers, aided in this matter by a rude and vulgar spirit of destructive criticism, which, guiding in old time the hands of Mani, could not rest till it had torn away the passages, and even books, of Holy Scripture[2] where resistance had been offered to his shameless innovation.

In pointing to the earlier intimations of some diabolic agency, I need not touch again[3] upon the ancient passage in Leviticus (xvi.), where *Azazel* is commonly believed to be another name for 'demon,' and is so indeed interpreted by modern writers, who, as soon as the admission has been made, resolve that being into 'a liturgical idea.' Neither shall I urge at length that he who finally bore the title of 'adversary' and 'calumniator' of the human race is called '*the* Satan,' and invested with peculiar guile and malice, in the opening of the Book of Job (i. ii.), no less than in the kindred vision of Zechariah (iii.), which belongs, unquestionably, to the age succeeding the Captivity. My present stand is rather on the sacred narrative of the Fall, which few, if any, even of our most daring critics, venture to bring down as low as the sixth century before the Christian era. Now if the true meaning of that narrative can be determined by consentient verdicts of Jewish and Christian writers, in all ages, it imports that man, through the extraneous solicitations of a personal seducer, and not merely through the motions of inborn concupiscence, was urged to the commission of the first dark sin which wrought

[1] *Ibid.* p. 83.

[2] Thus St. Augustine aptly remarks (*De Utilitate Credendi*, c. 7), just after his own extrication from Manichæan errors: 'Nunc vero postea quam mihi sunt exposita atque enodata multa, quæ me maxime movebant, ea scilicet in quibus illorum plerumque se jactat, et quo securius sine adversario eo effusius exsultat oratio, nihil mihi videtur ab eis *impudentius dici*, vel (ut mitius loquar) *incuriosius* et *imbecillius*, quam Scripturas divinas esse corruptas; cum id nullus in tam recenti memoria extantibus exemplaribus possint convincere. Si enim dicerent, eas sibi *penitus accipiendas non putasse*, quod ab his essent conscriptæ, quos verum scripsisse non arbitrarentur, esset utcumque tergiversatio eorum rectior vel error humanior.' He then goes on to mention that they did reject the whole of the Acts of the Apostles, not for any critical reasons, but *because* the account there given would not square with their notions about the descent of the Holy Ghost on Mani: cf. Tertull. *De Præscript. Hær.* c. xvii., where allusion is made to the arbitrary additions and subtractions of heresy, 'ad dispositionem instituti sui.'

[3] See above, pp. 503 sq.

disorder in himself, his children, and his species. That the visible agent of man's ruin was an *agent* merely in the hands of the great Evil One, St Paul has plainly intimated where he writes that the serpent who beguiled our first mother was the subtle, self-transforming potentate who is still active in the Christian Church (2 Cor. xi. 3, 14); and when the same Apostle turned with ardent hope to the eventual triumph of the Woman's Seed, his comfort flowed from a conviction that 'the God of peace will bruise *Satan* (not the serpent) under our feet shortly' (Rom. xvi. 20).

But excluding once again both these and other Christian testimonies, all of which, it is pretended by the modern sceptic, have been deeply tinctured with foreign superstitions, I appeal to universal heathendom itself in favour of the ancient exposition of the sacred record. There is found to be a singular consent[1], in East and West, in North and South, in civilised and semi-barbarous countries, in the Old World and the New, not only to the fact that serpents were somehow associated with the ruin of the human family, but that serpents so employed were vehicles of a malignant, personal spirit, by whatever name he was described.

As, therefore, the Old Persian is but one of a large cluster of cognate stories, it were surely far more rational to explain them all on the hypothesis of common parentage anterior to the primitive migrations, than to argue, *first*, that Hebrews only had been left without traditions on this subject till comparatively modern times; and *secondly*, that the age in which they finally contracted their belief in Satan and his angels, and so consummated, in the view of the objector, their portentous lapse into the eastern dualism, was, strange to say, the age, when, as a body, they are known to have imbibed far stricter tenets on the unity and monarchy of God.

§ 3. *Doctrine of Holy Angels.*

The spirit which impelled some modern writers to explain the scriptural notices of Satan, the great Tempter, by referring to the influence exercised upon the Jew by Persian dualism, is shewn afresh in their impatience of all statements with respect to the existence of the 'holy,' or unfallen, angels. These also we are told 'belong to a class of conceptions no longer possible in the world[2],' and *therefore* (such is the conclusion of

[1] See, for instance, above, pp. 216 sq.; 369, 553.

[2] Dr. Donaldson's *Christ. Orthod.* p. 349 (following Schleiermacher).

philosophy) they must all of them be proved to have originated in some thoroughly pagan system. The abettors of this startling argument have had recourse especially to effects supposed to have been wrought upon the Hebrews by the 'Zend religion of the Persians[1];' and they point triumphantly, in confirmation of their view, to the existence of the Sadducees[2], a high and philosophic order, who are thought to have preserved the purer creed of earlier generations with remarkable fidelity,—in so far at least as they dissented from the superstitions of the Pharisees, in confessing neither angel nor spirit. Efforts have again been made in this particular instance to support the theory of extensive amalgamation between Hebrews and Babylonians by adverting to the fact that various forms of error and exaggeration in the sphere of angelology *did* spring up, as it would seem, spontaneously among both Jews and Christians of succeeding times.

The chief reliance has been placed, however, on one definite testimony of the Jerusalem Talmud. In that passage[3], it is written: 'R. Simeon Ben-Lachish saith, The names of angels went up by the hand of Israel out of Babylon. For before it is said, "Then flew one of the seraphim unto me:" "The seraphim stood before him," Isa. vi.; but afterward, "the Man Gabriel" [Dan. ix. 21] and "Michael your prince" [Dan. x. 21].' Now whatever else may be implied in such assertions, we are doubtless pointed by them to a circumstance, which cannot fail to have arrested the attention of all Biblical scholars, viz. that after the great exile, *personal appellations* had begun to be assigned in some few cases (Michael, Gabriel, Raphael, Uriel) to the ministering angels of the Hebrew Church. But

[1] Here Dr. Donaldson accepts the dictum of Strauss without the least qualification: *Christ. Orthod.* p. 137.

[2] The author of *Christian Orthodoxy*, p. 372, affirms that 'their disbelief in angels and devils is passed over [by New Testament writers] in guarded silence, as far as any censure is concerned.' He then adds, 'In many respects our Lord seems to have approved and recommended their views;' and again (p. 373), 'It is difficult to resist the impression that Jesus [our blessed Lord] and His brother James, being known by the characteristic title of this sect, openly allowed many of the fundamental doctrines of the Sadducees'! Such language has not unnaturally exposed its author to the animadversions of the last Bampton Lecturer (Mr. Mansel), who, after pointing out the real origin and affinities of Dr. Donaldson's hypothesis, declares that 'by this method of exposition,' according to which our Saviour lent His high authority to the dissemination of religious falsehood, 'Christian Orthodoxy may mean anything or nothing' (p. 419).

[3] Lightfoot's *Heb. and Talmud. Exerc. upon St. Luke* (ch. i. v. 26): *Works*, xii. 24, ed. Pitman.

equally apparent is the fact that these angelic designations are in no way borrowed from the titles of gods and genii which abound in writings of the Medo-Persians, as indeed of every other ancient people; they have no apparent relation, etymological or otherwise, with the element-worship of the East; in thought as well as grammar they are all of them the purest Hebrew; *Michael*, for example, signifying 'who is as God?' and so protesting in its very form against approaches to polytheism[1].

On looking, therefore, with a critical eye upon the question now before us, we discover that the chief external evidence in favour of supposing that the angelology of the Hebrews was of heathen parentage, is totally unconnected with the point at issue; for I feel no obligation to analyse the many wild conceits, which, in the dotage of the Hebrew nation, urged men to 'intrude into the things not seen,' and build their visionary systems of 'celestial hierarchies.' The questions[2] fairly brought

[1] See Dr. Mill's examination of this very point in his *Christ. Adv. Publ.* for 1841, pp. 55, 57. Hengstenberg, *Genuineness of Daniel*, p. 138, remarks with justice that 'both Gabriel and Michael [the two names peculiar to Daniel] occur only in such visions, as from their dramatic character demand the most exact description possible of the persons concerned, and the bringing of them out into stronger relief.'

[2] I cannot, for example, be expected to discuss the general question, opened more than once by Dr. Donaldson, as to whether angels, in the *Christian sense*, are ever mentioned in the old (or ante-Babylonic) Scriptures. Dr. Donaldson seems to be persuaded (*Christ. Orthod.* p. 348) that the received doctrine of good angels is somehow incompatible with the doctrine of the Holy Spirit. He may well, on such hypothesis, be anxious to get rid of what he feels to be a horrible superstition; but surely the argument which he employs is equally fatal to belief in *all* intermediate agencies whatever; for example, in the institution of a Christian ministry, who, like the angels, act in God's behalf, and by authority derived from Him. All theories apart, I cannot help expressing my amazement how any person of average ability can study the Old Testament without discovering at every turn the flattest contradiction of Dr. Donaldson's assertions. Were the two angels, for example, who had been despatched to Sodom other than personal beings, acting as the veritable messengers of the Most High God Himself? They say expressly, 'The Lord hath sent us to destroy it' (Gen. xix. 13). Dean Milman (*Hist. of Christ.* I. 70, Lond. 1840), who also traces the systematising of Hebrew angelology to the residence in Babylon, is notwithstanding ready to admit that 'the earliest books of the Old Testament fully recognized the ministration of angels.' It is, indeed, remarkable that the *only* historical books of the Old Testament where such allusions do *not* appear, are exactly those which were written *after* the Babylonish captivity,—the books of Ezra and Nehemiah.

into the present investigation will relate, (1) to a distinction between higher and lower angels, *i. e.* the existence of orders or *gradations* in the spirit-world; and (2) to the specific number of intelligences who occupy the loftiest rank in these angelic orders.

Now that some distinction of the sort existed long before the Babylonish exile can be satisfactorily evinced from the magnificent passage in the sixth chapter of Isaiah. There the prophet's eye is riveted upon the glory of the six-winged seraphim, who constitute the 'angel-princes' of that early period, and as such are stationed foremost in the ministry of heaven; while one of them by issuing forth (vi. 6, 7) upon a message to Isaiah, and so offering proof of independent personality, enables us to answer the absurd objection that the primitive angels were but passive vehicles or manifestations of God Himself. The vision of Micaiah, in like manner, brings before us in still older times 'the Lord sitting on His throne, and all the host of heaven standing by Him on His right hand and on His left' (1 Kings xxii. 19—22). Nay, traces of angelic orders, such as meet us in the New Testament and later writings of the Old, are pointed out as early as the age of Moses and of Joshua; for the 'prince,' or captain of the Lord's host (Josh. v. 13—15), who then comes forward to conduct the family of God into the land of promise, has been held to correspond[1] with the created angel (Exod. xxxiii. 2, 3), who replaced the glorious Angel of the Presence (Exod. xxiii. 20—23) in administering the Sinaitic dispensation, after Israel had most grievously offended in the matter of the calf. But be this as it may, the close affinity that exists between the language of the book of Joshua and descriptions of the prince of angels, who, as Michael, reappears for the protection of the Israelites in visions of the book of Daniel, may be fairly pleaded as a proof that the familiarity of the Hebrew Church with such conceptions is not due to her reputed intercourse with the Ormazd-religion.

[1] This subject also is discussed at considerable length by Dr. Mill, as above, pp. 92—99. The rival theory is, that the Angel in Josh. v. was none other than the Second Person of the Blessed Trinity,—identical, therefore, with *the* Angel of the Lord, in Exod. xxiii. 20—23, and other places: see Ode, *Commentarius de Angelis*, pp. 1032 sq. Traject. 1739; who, with many modern critics, goes farther still, identifying Michael himself with the uncreated Word of God; while others add again to these supposed identifications by representing the *Gabriel* of the prophet Daniel as a reappearance of the created, or inferior, angel of Exod. xxxii. 34.

It was easy to foresee that the amshaspands of the Persian system[1] would be quoted as the nearest parallel to the archangels of the Holy Scriptures. Those beings, we have learned already[2], were six in number; or, including Ormazd himself, who also is invested on some rare occasions with the title of amshaspand, the whole number may be raised to seven[3]. We saw, moreover, that the probable origin of such specification must be sought in the primeval worship of the heavenly bodies, when the shining multitude above were substituted by man's vain imagination for the Lord of hosts Himself: and as the influence of that ancient superstition was far from being peculiar to the Persians, the allusion to 'seven' principal objects of esteem and worship is continually recurring in all parts of heathendom[4]. It is, however, a mistake to argue that the later Hebrew people, and much less the Hebrew prophets of the exile, manifested any disposition to deify the orbs of light. There is indeed one solitary passage in the book of Tobit, where the speaker, Raphael, describes himself as of the number of the '*seven* holy angels who enter in before the glory of the Holy One' (xii. 15; cf. Rev. viii. 2); but, according to a

[1] *e.g.* the author of *Christian Orthodoxy* declares (p. 135) with reference to the Book of Daniel: 'In this book we find the celestial hierarchy of amshaspands fully recognised.' Other speculators of the same school have sought to bring the *fervers* of Persia into connection with the 'guardian angels' both of Jews and Christians (see St. Matth. xviii. 10; Acts xii. 72; and Dean Alford on the former passage): but the Persian *ferver*, where we are not forced to understand it of the *spirit* of the individual man, was rather the ideal prototype or archetype of some actual being; see above, p. 537, n. 1. With regard to the conception of angels, specially allotted to watch over the affairs of particular *nations*, Hengstenberg (*Daniel*, p. 140) affirms that no trace of it occurs in the Avesta, except that Bahman, the first of the amshaspands, 'who stands in about the same relation to Ormazd as Gabriel here does to the angel of the Lord,' is called the 'protector of all animals' who are there said to constitute his people (Rhode, p. 323), while Ormazd himself is the patron of men. The version of the LXX. in Deut. xxxii. 8, will perhaps bear witness to some old tradition of the Jews with respect to the allotting of particular nations to particular angels: *ὅτε διεμέριζεν ὁ ὕψιστος ἔθνη, ὡς διέσπειρεν υἱοὺς Ἀδάμ, ἔστησεν ὅρια ἐθνῶν κατὰ ἀριθμὸν ἀγγέλων Θεοῦ*, where the Hebrew is לְמִסְפַּר בְּנֵי יִשְׂרָאֵל: cf. Prof. Selwyn's *Notæ Criticæ*, 'Deuteron.' p. 65, Cantab. 1858.

[2] Above, p. 534.

[3] Rhode, p. 365; Mill, as before, p. 59.

[4] Above, pp. 534, 535, to which examples may be added the seven *rishis* of Hindústán, who, at least in the Puranic period, were represented as 'seven primeval personages, born of Brahmá's mind and presiding, under different forms, over each Manwantara.'

different method of enumeration, the archangels of the Hebrew are more frequently reduced to *four* (Michael, Gabriel, Raphael, and Uriel), each presiding over one of the four armies of ministry who sing praises to the Holy and the Blessed[1]. Still if we had higher reasons for accepting the account of Tobit as an illustration of the general state of knowledge on this subject at the period when he wrote, it would be running counter to the sacred usage, both of the Old and New Testament, to argue that the number *seven*, as there employed, contains the slightest reference to the worship of celestial luminaries, or to any phase whatever of gentile superstition[2]. 'Seven,' alike before and after the Captivity, had its own specific import for all members of the Hebrew Church. It was the signature of fulness, union, manifoldness, perfection; and therefore the 'seven spirits of God' in the Apocalypse (i. 4; iv. 5) are understood as pointing us directly to the diverse operations of the One all-gracious Spirit[3]; while the 'seven stars' are the 'angels of the seven churches,' and the 'seven candlesticks' a grand collective symbol of the whole Christian body (i. 20).

§ 4. *Doctrine of the Resurrection of the Body.*

To foster a belief in the awakening of man's body from the sleep of death, and in the final glorification of his whole humanity, was a primary object in the teaching of St. Paul and of apostles generally. In their view 'the redemption of the body' at the re-appearing of our Lord and Saviour, was the crowning-point in a succession of stupendous acts which dated from His own ineffable assumption of our weak and dying flesh. Yet writers are not wanting who assure us that the doctrine of the resurrection, so specifically and profoundly Christian, is a relic only of primeval barbarism which passed into the Hebrew creed, like others of the same description, at

[1] See the passage from the *Pirke* of Rabbi Eliezer (who, according to Fürst, *Bibliotheca Judaica*, I. 232, flourished about A.D. 70), in Dr. Mill's work, as before, p. 58, n. 10. Dr. Donaldson (p. 136) breaks through this difficulty at once by urging that when the Jews limited the number of 'attendant spirits' to *four*, they did so 'probably from some confusion between the amshaspands and the seraphim of Isaiah on the one hand, and the four creatures of Ezekiel on the other'!

[2] Cf. Bähr. *Symbolik*, I. 189 sq.

[3] Hengstenberg, *Die Offenbarung des h. Johan.* I. 91, 92, Berlin, 1849.

the period of the Babylonish exile[1]. Observing, it would seem, that fuller light is thrown upon the mystery of our future being, in proportion as the 'mystery of godliness' itself was gradually unfolded, those irreverent critics have not scrupled to conjecture that instead of such ulterior light proceeding from the supernatural source, it must have had an earthly origin among the ancient votaries of Ormazd.

And here, as in some other cases, the supposed 'discovery' of the doctrine in the Zendic books had been facilitated by the mistranslations of their first editor. It is since established by more competent scholars[2], that in passages where Anquetil Duperron rendered 'till the resurrection,' the words really signify 'for ever,'—an important rectification, which, as soon as it is generally made known, will silence not a few of the objections borrowed from this quarter. Like results have also followed from the critical examination of some other Zendic texts; until at present all who are entitled to pronounce a judgment on the question may be heard affirming that no glimpses of a resurrection of the body can be traced in extant books of the Avesta.

Still that Persians did not long continue strangers to the thought of some ulterior re-embodying of the souls departed, may be argued with great shew of reason from the testimony of the historian, Theopompus[3], who died about the year 300 B.C.

1 *e.g.* Wegscheider does not blush to affirm that this opinion unquestionably grew up 'e notionibus mancis et imperfectis hominum incultiorum,' and that it finally passed over to the Jews from the school of Zoroaster (quoted in Mr. Mansell's *Bampton Lectures*, 1858, pp. 417, 418).

2 Burnouf, *Études*, in *Journ. Asiat.* (1840), pp. 7 sq., was the first scholar who pointed out this mistake. His conclusions have been since corroborated by Spiegel, *Zeits. Deutsch. morg. Gesell.* (1847), I. 260, 261; *Avesta*, I. 15, 248, n. 2. According to the *Vendid.* Farg. XIX. 89 sq., as there translated, the good or 'pure' spirits are removed on the *third day after death* to a place of perfect happiness, and the bad spirits to a place of torment: cf. Wilson's *Pársí Religion*, pp. 337, 338.

3 The testimony of this writer has been examined at some length by J. G. Müller, *Theol. Studien und Kritiken* (1835), pp. 482 sq. in an article entitled 'Ist die Lehre von der Auferstehung des Leibes wirklich nicht eine alt-persische Lehre?' The discussion turns in a great measure on the force of ἀναβιοῦν in the following passage: Θεόπομπος, ἐν τῇ ὀγδόῃ τῶν Φιλιππικῶν, καὶ ἀναβιώσεσθαι, κατὰ τοὺς Μάγους, φησὶ τοὺς ἀνθρώπους καὶ ἔσεσθαι ἀθανάτους (in Diogen. Laert. 'Proœm.' § 9). The other passage of importance is preserved in Plutarch, *De Iside*, c. XLVII. the chief words being: τέλος δ' ἀπολείπεσθαι τὸν ᾅδην, καὶ τοὺς μὲν ἀνθρώπους εὐδαίμονας ἔσεσθαι, μήτε τροφῆς δεομένους, μήτε σκιὰν ποιοῦντας.

He has declared that in accordance with the Persian creed, as soon as the great struggles of Ormazd and Ahriman are all exhausted, Hades will become a void; and that mankind attaining to true happiness will then 'require no nourishment and will cast no shadows.' And elsewhere his language is still more explicit; for he says that if we may believe the Magi, men will come to life again and be immortal:—both which statements fairly indicate that at the close of the 'great year' of Persia, every thing, it is believed, will have reverted to the primitive condition, and that the human body, no exception to this general law, will have itself experienced the refining and exalting process.

There are reasons, it is true, for urging[1] that two different lines of thought existed in the schools of ancient Persia: one, proceeding from a rigorous form of dualism[2], akin to that of Mani, and so, as in the convents of northern India, making of the human body a mere prison-house in which the soul was doing penance for her past misdeeds; the other mourning over the dissolution of the body as a victory won by Ahriman, and so including the idea of re-embodiment among the blessings that would ultimately flow from the subversion of his empire. But the testimony of Theopompus may be viewed as an expression of the 'orthodox' belief, especially when we bear in mind that subsequent language of the *Bundehesh*[3] is strikingly in favour of the resurrection theory.

On the other hand, assuming, as in previous instances, that Hebrew prophets would have seen no difficulty in borrowing novel tenets from the creed of their enslavers, it appears to me indisputable that the doctrine of the resurrection of the body was believed to some extent among the members of the sacred family long before the period of the Babylonish exile. I shall lay no stress at present on debateable texts[4]; of which, however, it is no exaggeration to affirm that while incapable of *proving* that the doctrine of a resurrection was fully or definitely held, they nevertheless bear witness to the fact that the idea of resurrection had never been repugnant to the feelings of the ancient Israelite, but rather coincided with the expectations that arose in him from a belief in God's redemp-

[1] See Döllinger, *Heidenthum*, p. 381.

[2] Above, p. 538.

[3] The passages are collected in Rhode, as before, pp. 465 sq.; but, as Spiegel remarks, a correct and critical edition of the *Bundehesh* will doubtless modify the old assertions on this point also.

[4] Cf. Fairbairn's *Ezekiel*, pp. 356—359.

tive and restoring mercy. It will here suffice to mention that the words which Daniel is said to have indited under the inspirations of the Medo-Persian system are in perfect unison with declarations of Isaiah two centuries before. For instance, if the prophet of the Captivity was pointing onward to a crisis when 'many of them that sleep in the dust of the earth shall awake' (Dan. xii. 2); the jubilant prophet of the reign of Ahaz had already comforted his audience by the promise that the Lord 'will swallow up death in victory' (Is. xxv. 8); nay, the words which, in a second passage, are employed by him have found their literal echo in the words of Daniel just recited; for Isaiah also has proclaimed in no ambiguous language 'Thy dead men shall live, together with my dead body shall they arise; awake and sing, ye that dwell in dust' (xxvi. 19).

§ 5. *Doctrine of a Benefactor and Mediator.*

(1) Connected with the re-awakening of the dead, at least in some of the more recent, or post-Christian, writings of the Persians, there is frequent mention of a glorious hero-prophet, by whose ministry, as one chief organ of Ormazd, the empire of the *devs* shall be subverted, earth herself shall be restored to something of her pristine glory, and the wrongs of man redressed. The name of this expected champion of the Perso-Áryan race is Sosiosh (*Saŏshyańs*[1], 'the Benefactor'). He is first of all presented to our notice in a passage of the *Vendidád*[2], which, if the new translation of it be accepted, is found to run as follows: 'Zarathustra gave warning to Ağramainyus (and said): "Base Ağra-mainyus! I will smite the creation, which is fashioned by the *devs*; I will smite the *Nasus*, whom the *devs* have fashioned. I will smite the *Pari* whom men worship (?), until Sosiosh the Victorious is born out of the water *Kańsaŏya*, from the eastern clime, from the eastern climes.'"

The meagre hint of Sosiosh, thus communicated in the early part of the Avesta, was expanded and embellished in the works of the Sassanian epoch and especially in the *Bun-*

[1] Spiegel, *Avesta*, I. 244, n. 1, informs us that the root of the word is *su* ('to profit'), to which it is related as the future participle: hence 'der nützen werdende' 'der Helfer.' It was not, however, a proper name nor limited to an individual worthy, but rather marked a series or *class* of benefactors, and as such it occurs also in the plural number.

[2] Farg. XXI. 16—19: cf. *Zeits. Deutsch. morg. Gesell.* (1847), I. 261, 262, where the old translation was first corrected.

dehesh[1]. That benefactor was from first to last a *man;* and like two other beings, his precursors, now associated with him in the work of liberation and each reigning in succession for a thousand years, he was distinctly held to be the offspring of the holy Zoroaster; yet the name of Sosiosh alone, as greatest or as last in order of the hero-prophets, was the rallying-point where Persians were accustomed to find refuge from the miseries of their present lot. The time assigned for his appearance (say the authors of the story) is the time when evil and impiety of every kind have grown to an appalling magnitude. Approaching with a noiseless step, he will evince the greatness of his mission by destroying death itself, and by recalling all the dead to life. The first to rise again will be the prototype of men (or Kaiomorts), and after him the earliest pair of human beings (Meshia and Meshiane); then, in seven and fifty years, the long array of their descendants. All of these have been appointed to receive the gift of immortality by drinking of the sacred *homa.* Next will follow a grand separation of the pure and impure, of the righteous and unrighteous; friend will lose the sweet companionship of friend, the husband will be severed from his spouse, the sister from the brother. They who stand the sifting of that day are borne aloft to the peculiar dwelling of Ormazd: the rest are driven back to the abodes of misery and torment which had also been their portion from the third day after death. The change, however, thus effected is not destined to be ultimate. A blazing comet (Gurzsher), hitherto held in fetters by the moon, will break away from his confinement, and, rushing wildly on the earth, will be converted into the agent of Ormazd for purging out the dross that now adheres to all created nature; Ahriman himself will vanish in the flames,

[1] See the passages in Rhode, pp. 465 sq. Spiegel (*Avesta*, I. 32 sq.) has also drawn attention more especially to the full-blown eschatology of the Persians and compared it with that of the later Jews, which, in his opinion, it strongly resembles (p. 35). The main points, according to his representation, are as follows: 'Die Erwartung eines sowol *weltlichen* als geistlichen Herrschers, der sowol sein Volk zum herrschenden macht, zum Regenten über alle seine Bedrücker, der aber auch die Religion wieder reinigt. Dass das Reich *tausend Jahre* dauern soll, ist überall bestimmt ausgesprochen:'—points indeed which may remind us not only of the Messianic tenets prevalent among the later Jews, but also of the modified Judaism which in the form of Chiliasm (or sensuous Millenarianism) was current more or less in various branches of the early Christian Church, and only repressed with great difficulty: see Neander, *Ch. Hist.* II. 395—401.

and hell, the dark abyss of Duzakh, with its godless tenants, being purified and renovated by the final conflagration, the whole family of man will be assembled on the new-born earth to sing the glory of Ormazd and the amshaspands.

(2) But the latter history of religious thought in Persia introduces us to one more being who has not unfrequently been placed in close comparison with the Founder of Christianity. His name is *Mithra;* and so paramount are claims which he advances, in the estimation of some modern writers, that the Gospel is itself pronounced by them a branch of Mithraism[1]. No small confusion, it is true, exists among the older notices of Mithra even in the Persian sacred books[2]; yet there, as elsewhere, the prevailing image represents to us a wakeful and beneficent divinity[3], 'lord of life and head of all created beings,' active, luminous, fertilizing, purifying, and invincible. His place and functions in relation to the highest god appear to have resembled those of the Greek Apollo; and at periods when Ormazd sinks back into comparative quietude, the old connexion with the creature-world and the administration of the light-kingdom, are dependent on the energy of Mithra, who is thus the living and abiding link between the visible and the invisible. Associating intimately and well-nigh upon a level with Ormazd[4] himself, this secondary principle of good is also from his very nature the antagonist of the Evil One. He

[1] This, for instance, was one of many self-contradictory views propounded by Dupuis in his *Origine des tous les Cultes* (above, p. 27, n. 1): and even Creuzer, while rejecting the theory with something like contempt (*Symb.* I. 238, n. 2; cf. p. 341), is induced to look favourably upon another oft-repeated story which ascribes the origin of some ecclesiastical usages (*e.g.* the institution of the Christmas festival) to the influence of Mithraism (*Ibid.* p. 261). Christ, according to this notion, was, in a spiritual sense, the *Sol Novus*, and His birth was therefore celebrated at the period of the year, which Mithraism assigned to the new birth of the celestial luminary. See, on the general question of Mithra-worship, Von-Hammer, *Mémoire sur le culte de Mithra*, Paris, 1833.

[2] The same remark applies equally to the Greek writers: for Herodotus (I. 131), in speaking of the imitative genius of the Persians, is thought to be guilty of confusing the Venus of Assyrian mythology, *Mylitta*, with the Persian *Mithra* (cf. Xenoph. *Cyrop.* VIII. 13, § 12). The real representative of Venus in the later Persian system was Anahita (Anaitis); Mithra and Anahita corresponding in the main to Baal and Astarte: see Rawlinson's *Herod.* I. 271, 272; Döllinger, *Heidenthum*, pp. 384, 385; Burnouf, *Sur le Yaçna*, pp. 351 sq.

[3] For instance, in the *Yasna* (Burnouf, p. 222), 'J'invoque, je célèbre Mithra qui multiplie les couples de bœufs qui a mille oreilles, dix milles yeux,' &c.

[4] See the passage from the *Yasna*, quoted above, p. 535, n. 4.

marshals the bright army of beneficent genii[1] in their conflict with the *devs;* in him the soul departed finds her best conductor to the bridge of Chinevad; while bodies of the dead, though captured by the prince of darkness, are the objects of his sympathy and care.

It may have been the service rendered to the votary of the Ormazd-religion in the daily war with Ahriman, that made the later Greek of Plutarch's[2] age assign to Mithra the peculiar title 'Mediator' (*μεσίτης*); for although a somewhat similar class of functions was awarded to other beings, as Sraŏsha and Ráshne-rást[3], who both were thought to superintend the great judicial process after death, in order that the soul of man might then receive her fitting recompence, 'not a hair too little nor too much,' it was to Mithra, most of all, that subjects of the light-kingdom were instructed to address their homage. Some were even ready to contend that if the first man had sung the praise of Mithra, or had ever named that name, his soul would forthwith have ascended to the mansions of ultimate felicity.

In proportion as Ormazd himself receded from the active visible sphere of being, or, in different language, was abstracted more and more from his connexion with the Sun, that luminary was appropriated as the home or symbol of his younger representative. Originally placed, as it would seem, midway between the sun and moon, and so perhaps identified on some occasions with the planet Venus[4], Mithra was ere long a potent and invincible sun-god[5], author of the light, dispeller

[1] Hence his rank as chief of the *Izeds;* above, p. 535, n. 4.

[2] *De Isid.* c. XLVI. Plutarch himself seems to regard Mithra as partaking of the natures both of Ormazd and Ahriman (*μέσον δ' ἀμφοῖν*): cf. Dr. Donaldson's *Christ. Orthod.* p. 131, and Creuzer, I. 292, the latter of whom supposes that Mithra was a kind of chemical mean or 'Liebesfeuer,' harmonising two antagonistic Principles.

[3] Spiegel, *Avesta*, I. 31; Burnouf, *Sur le Yaçna*, p. 200.

[4] See above, p. 568, n. 2.

[5] Strabo is the first Greek writer who says this expressly: Πέρσαι... *τιμῶσι δὲ καὶ ἥλιον, ὃν καλοῦσι Μίθρην* (XV. 13). *Ἀπόλλωνα δὲ ἥλιον τὸν περιπολοῦντα εἶναι νόμιζε, γονὴν ὄντα τοῦ Διός, ὃν καὶ Μίθραν ἐκάλεσαν.* *Homil. Clem.* III. 50, ed. Dressel. It is further worth noting that the name does not occur on the Achæmenian inscriptions until the reign of Artaxerxes Mnemon (Rawlinson's *Herod.* Vol. I. p. 272, note): yet there can be no doubt as to its ancient usage in connection with the *Sun*, in both the branches of the Áryan family. To pass by Medo-Persian names *Mithradates* (or Μιτραδάτης, Her. I. 110), as importing 'given by the Sun' (cf. *Hormisdates* 'given by Ormazd'), we have continual examples in the Rig-Véda, where *Mitra* is used as the equivalent of *Áditya*, 'the sun,' or one at least of twelve per-

of the darkness; and in subsequent stages of the mythe, he rose completely to the rank of a supreme divinity, corresponding in the vastness and the splendour of his attributes to the Osiris of the later Pharaohs. Mithra was *the* sun-god of the Medo-Persian system. Drawing his existence no longer from Ormazd, of whom in the Avesta he was ever made a creature and a tributary, he is pictured to us in post-Christian writings as the preternatural offspring of a rock, or of the soil[1]. According also to the numerous sculptures of him still surviving he has been invested with distinctly human properties. He is a young man, clothed with a tunic and a Persian cloke, and having on his head a Persian bonnet or tiara. He kneels upon a prostrate bull; and while holding it with the left hand by the nostrils, with the right he plunges into its shoulder a short sword or dagger. The bull is at the same time vigorously attacked by a dog, a serpent, and a scorpion. The ideas embodied in the suffering animal are at once elucidated when we call to mind[2], that in the old mythology of Persia all organic life, the human and the bestial, issued from the shoulder of the primitive bull; and therefore astronomic and other symbols here employed are probably to be expounded of the action of the sun-god on created nature, his far-piercing beams awakening all its latent energies, opening the fresh veins of life and drawing thence a large supply of fructifying virtue. The key, however, to Mithraic mysteries, all of which are said to have been celebrated in a species of 'cave,' was not entrusted to the vulgar and unlettered, but reserved, as in the other kindred rites and orgies, for the few who underwent a solemn initiation. Here indeed the worship of the Persian sun-god lost all traces of its old resemblance to the creed of the Avesta. It fell off into the whirl of mystic and ascetic faiths, wherein the laxer party, such as Commodus and monsters like him, reconciled the adoration of Serapis and of Mithra with the foulest violations of the law of conscience; while the genuine devotee was eagerly accepting the severe prescriptions of the mystagogue[3], who told him that by passing through a length-

sonifications of the Sun corresponding to the signs of the Zodiac.

[1] St. Jerome, who followed a history of Mithra by Eubulus (now lost), informs us (*Adv. Jovinian.* Opp. IV. col. 149, ed. Bened.): 'Narrant et Gentilium fabulæ Mithram et Erichthonium, vel in lapide, vel in terra, de solo æstu libidinis esse generatos.'

[2] Above, p. 552.

[3] 'At the time of the final agonies of Paganism, the only portions of the old religion which retained any vitality, at least among those of Greek race and language, were the mysteries. Here alone persons agitated by

ened ordeal of torture and privation, he was able to escape from the necessity of repeated births, and consummate his union with the glorious Mithra, 'his god and his crown.'

There is no doubt that while the visions of the *Bundehesh* derived their colouring, and in part their substance also, from Semitic or from quasi-Christian influences, the advocates of Mithra-worship in the earlier centuries of our era were engaged with more or less of system in retarding the triumphant march of Christianity[1]. At a period when the claims of our religion were put forward with an irresistible charm alike in the unspotted lives and the heroic deaths of its true-hearted converts, many of the heathen, still unwilling to embrace it, so far yielded to vibrations it excited in all quarters, as to recognise in it the hidden working of a supernatural virtue. We discern this tendency amid the swarm of startling heresies that sprang up in its track; for most of them were anxious to embody one or more dissevered doctrines of the Gospel with their wild and heathenish speculations; and others have been also charged with mimicking the smaller details of its ritual system[2]. We discern this tendency still more in one particular instance, bearing on the present theme, for 'almost every thing that Zoroaster taught of Mithra' was perpetuated in the school of Mani, with the noticeable difference that the Persian misbeliever did not scruple to transfer it all directly to his Christ[3].

religious hopes and fears, distracted by doubt, oppressed with a sense of sin, found pleasing excitement in dark riddles and symbolic rites, and consolation in the promised immortality.' Clark, *Peloponnesus*, p. 112.

[1] This is one of Von Hammer's conclusions, in which Creuzer (I. 329) apparently acquiesces, extending the remark to other heathen 'orgies' and 'mysteries' of the post-Christian period. Yet, as various writers have complained, there was occasionally a disposition in apologists of the early Church to lay undue stress on some points of resemblance between Mithraism and Christianity.

[2] *e.g.* Tertullian (*De Præscript. Hær.* c. XI) alludes to such apparent mimicries in speaking of Mithraism itself: 'Sed quæritur, a quo intellectus intervertatur eorum, qui ad hæreses faciant? A diabolo scilicet, cujus sunt partes intervertendi veritatem: qui ipsas quoque res sacramentorum divinorum in idolorum mysteriis æmulatur. Tingit et ipse quosdam, utique credentes et fideles suos [referring to the ceremony of initiation when water was poured by the mystagogue on the aspirant's head]: expositionem delictorum de lavacro repromittit: et si adhuc initiat Mithra, signat illic in frontibus milites suos; celebrat et panis oblationem' (referring perhaps to a kind of Parsee communion, where bread was blessed by the priest and eaten, in conjunction with draughts of the homa-plant: cf. Döllinger, p. 373).

[3] Neander, *Ch. Hist.* II. 177.

And, strange though such an issue may appear, not Mani's system only, but the heathen form of Mithraism as well, was able, in the breaking up of old religions, to attract unto itself a multitude of followers both in East and West. It flourished in alliance with some kindred systems in the mother-city of the Roman empire: it was planted, by the ardour of the foreign legionaries, in the Roman capital of Britain[1].

Vain, however, and unfruitful was the zeal put forward in transplanting these fantastic shadows of exhausted paganism. The western world, excited by the general 'shaking of the nations,' was now yielding to the voice of the celestial Charmer: it was gazing on the silent march of that obscure yet glorious, of that suffering yet majestic system, to whose birthplace the inquiring Magi came of old, the first-fruits of the Gentile harvest. 'When they saw the young child, with Mary His mother, they fell down and worshipped Him.' And Christians of all future times have counted it their highest glory to prolong that wondrous act of love and adoration. They are conscious that in Christ are fully satisfied the cravings of a spiritual hunger which religions of the world may stimulate but have no power to appease. While Bráhmans, in despair of all the helpers whom their own imagination had created, were still dreaming of some future and more permanent *avatára;* while the Buddhist, equally in north and south, abandoned the original Buddha and sought comfort now in picturing to himself the distant paradise of Amitábha, 'the unmeasured Light,' and now in praying for the gracious intervention of some Buddha of the future; while the primitive vision of the helper Sosiosh, dim and fluctuating at the best, was blotted from the Persian mind entirely, or was fading under the augmented brilliance of the younger Mithra;—Christ and Christ alone, expected in the old œconomy and made manifest in the new, the living, reigning, and historic Christ, the brightness of the Father's glory and the 'first-born' of a human brotherhood, was everywhere imprinting on the world an image of His love, which neither time nor space

[1] See Wellbeloved's *Eburacum*, pp. 80—86, York, 1842; and, for some very curious matter with regard to this and kindred subjects, *An Essay on the Neo-Druidic Heresy in Britannia* (ascribed to the late Mr. Algernon Herbert), pp. 29 sq. Lond. 1838. The 'Druidizing Mithriacs,' referred to in this essay, are supposed to be an offshoot from 'a sort of magical association' that 'had grown up in the eastern parts of the Roman dominions, founded upon the doctrines and mysteries of the Persian Magi.'

could deaden. He 'lighteth every man' by shining down into the heart. He is the true Sun, of which all heathen mediators are but transient and confused *parhelia*; for while Mithra, once his mighty rival and as such rejoicing in the Name of 'the Invincible,' has left no traces, save in monumental sculptures, of the homage rendered to him in the early centuries of our era, Christ, the sovereign Lord of all, is going forward on His peaceful conquest of the nations, 'the same yesterday and to-day and for ever.'

APPENDIX I.

Alleged connexion between Coptic and Hebrew.

(See above, p. 432, n. 2).

Through the kindness of my friend, Professor Jarrett, I am now in a position to supply the following brief comparison of ordinary words in Coptic and Hebrew. It seems to shew that so far as *vocabulary* is concerned, the relationship between the two languages can hardly be established.

Comparison of common words in Coptic and Hebrew.

	Numerals.				
			60	ⲥⲉ	ששים
1	ⲟⲩⲁ	אחד	*70	ϣⲃⲉ	שבעים
*2	ⲥⲛⲁⲩ	שנים	*80	ϩⲉⲙⲉⲛⲉ	שמנים
3	ϣⲟⲙⲧ	שלש	90	ⲡⲓⲥⲧⲁⲟⲩ	תשעים
4	ϥⲧⲟ	ארבע	100	ϣⲉ	מאה
5	ⲧⲓⲟⲩ	חמש	1000	ϣⲟ	אלף
6	ⲥⲟⲟⲩ	שש		Nouns.	
7	ϣⲁϣϥ	שבע	Father	ⲓⲱⲧ	אב
*8	ϣⲙⲟⲩⲛ	שמונה	*Mother	ⲙⲁⲩ	אם
9	ⲯⲓⲧ	תשע	Brother	ⲥⲟⲛ	אח
10	ⲙⲏⲧ	עשר	Sister	ⲥⲟⲛⲓ	אחות
20	ϫⲱⲧ	עשרים	Son	ϣⲏⲣⲓ	בן
30	ⲙⲁⲃ	שלשים	Daughter	ϣⲉⲣⲓ	בת
40	ϩⲙⲉ	ארבעים	Man	ⲣⲱⲙⲓ	אדם, איש
50	ⲧⲁⲓⲟⲩ	חמשים	Woman	ⲥϩⲓⲙⲓ	אשה

Head	ⲁⲡⲉ, ⲁⲫⲉ, ϫⲱ, ϫⲱϫ	ראש
Eye	ⲃⲁⲗ	עין
Mouth	ⲣⲟ	פה
Tooth	ⲛⲁϫϩⲓ	שן
Nose	ϣⲁ	אף
Beard	ⲙⲟⲣⲧ	זקן
Neck	ⲕⲉⲛϩⲉ	ערף
and	and	
Shoulder	ⲙⲟⲧⲓ	שכם
Arm	ϣⲱⲃϣ	זרוע
Hand	ⲧⲟⲧ, ϫⲓϫ	יד
*Finger	ⲧⲏⲃ, ⲑⲏⲃ	אצבע
Belly	ⲑⲏ, ⲛⲉϫⲓ	בטן
Heart	ϩⲏⲧ	לב
Knee	ⲡⲁⲧ	ברך
Foot	ⲫⲁⲧ	רגל
Ear	ⲙⲁⲁϫⲉ	אזן
Flesh	ⲁϥ	בשר
Skin	ⲁⲛⲟⲙ	עור
Day	ⲉϩⲟⲟⲩ	יום
Night	ⲟⲩϣⲏ	לילה
Light	ⲟⲩⲱⲓⲛⲓ	אור
Darkness	ⲕⲁⲕⲉ	חשך
†Water	ⲙⲱⲟⲩ	מים
†Sea	ⲓⲟⲙ	ים

Fire	ⲕⲗⲱⲙ, ⲕⲣⲱⲙ	אש
Wind	ⲛⲓⲃⲉ	רוח
†River	ⲓⲁⲣⲟ	נהר, יאר
Tree	ϣϣⲏⲛ	עץ
Leaf	ϫⲱⲃⲓ	עלה
Ox / Cow	ⲉϩⲉ	בקר, פר
*Sheep	ⲉⲥⲟⲟⲩ	צאן, שה
Horse	ϩⲧⲟ, ϩⲑⲟ	סוס
Ass	ⲉⲱ	חמור, אתון

Verbs.

See	ⲛⲁⲩ	ראה
Hear	ⲥⲱⲧⲉⲙ	שמע
Eat	ⲟⲩⲉⲙ, ⲟⲩⲱⲙ	אכל
Drink	ⲥⲉ	שתה
Go	ⲓ, ⲙⲟϣⲓ, ⲛⲁ, ϣⲉ	הלך, יצא
Run	ⲡⲏⲧ	רוץ
Take	ⲁⲙⲟⲛⲓ, ϭⲱⲡⲓ	לקח
Give	ⲙⲁ, ⲙⲏⲓ, ⲙⲟⲓ, ⲧⲏⲓ	נתן
Do	ⲉⲣ	עשה
Say	ϫⲉ, ϫⲱ	אמר
Love	ⲙⲉⲣⲉ	אהב
Hate	ⲙⲉⲥⲧⲉ	שנא
Touch	*ⲙⲁϣ, ϣⲓ, ϫⲱϩ	משש נגע

(1) Of the above words those marked † are *identical:* יְאֹר being used of the Nile.

(2) The words marked * have considerable resemblance, which *may* point to a common origin.

(3) The remainder, a vast majority, appear to have no connexion whatever.

The following is a short list of accidental *resemblances which have also occurred to Professor Jarrett (the Coptic words meaning the same as the words set against them):*

ⲥⲁⲃⲉ = sap-iens.

ⲓⲱⲧ = آتا *Turkish;* atta, *Gothic,* 'father.'

ⲥⲁϫⲓ = sag-en.

ⲟⲩⲟⲛ = van, 'is,' 'are,' *Magyar.*

ⲟⲩⲟⲣⲡ = werf-en.

ⲕⲟⲗⲡ = κλεπ-τειν.

ϩⲟϥ = ὄφις.

ϣⲟⲛⲧⲓ = sentis.

ⲙⲟϣⲓ = مشي, 'walked,' *Arab.*

ϣⲉⲙϣⲓ = שִׁמֵּשׁ.

ⲫⲱⲧ = fut-ni, 'to flee,' *Magyar.*

ⲟⲩϫⲁⲓ = ὑγιης.

ϣⲃⲱⲧ = שבט

ⲥⲏϥⲓ = سيف, 'sword,' *Arab.*

ϫⲱϫ = coq-uere.

ⲓ = ι-εναι = i-re.

ϣⲉⲙⲏⲣ = חמר, 'leaven.'

ⲓⲏⲥ = חש, 'hasty.'

The use of pronominal affixes is not confined to Hebrew and Coptic, but is found also in Welsh and Magyar; of which the former is an Áryan language, and the latter Turanian. Of the sixteen affixes used in Hebrew, the Coptic coincides exactly in only *two*, the Welsh in *one;* while in the use of *n* for נו, the Welsh agrees with the Coptic, and the Magyar differs only by the addition of *k*, which is in that language the regular affix to mark the plural in all cases. The Magyar agrees also with the Hebrew in the insertion of י $=i$, when the pronominal affix is added to a plural noun. The Welsh uses *t*, and the Magyar *d* as the characteristic of the second person.

On this latter question of pronominal affixes, as pointing to some close analogy between the Coptic and the Hebrew, M. Renan, *Histoire des Langues Sémitiques*, I. 83 sq. (Paris, 1858), has made the following observations:

'Il est, je le sais, des analogies plus profondes et beaucoup plus considérables aux yeux des linguistes, qui semblent rattacher la langue copte aux idiomes sémitiques. L'identité des pronoms, et surtout de la manière de les traiter dans les deux langues, est assurément un fait étrange. Cette identité s'observe jusque dans les détails qui semblent les plus accessoires: plusieurs irrégularités apparentes du pronom sémitique (le changement du ת en ך à l'affixe, par exemple) trouvent même dans la théorie du pronom copte une satisfaisante explication.'

PRONOMS ISOLÉS.

	Copte.	Hébreu.
1re p. sing.	ⲁⲛⲟⲕ	אָנֹכִי
2e p. sing.	ⲛ̄ⲧⲟⲕ et en baschmourique ⲛ̄ⲧⲁⲕ	אַתָּה pour אַנְתָּה
1re p. pl.	ⲁⲛⲟⲛ et en baschmourique ⲁⲛⲁⲛ	אֲנַחְנוּ
2e p. pl.	ⲛ̄ⲧⲱⲧⲛ̄	אַתֶּם pour אַנְתֶּם

PRONOMS SUFFIXES.

	Copte.	Hébreu.
1re p. sing.	ⲓ	י
2e p. sing.	ⲕ	ךָ
3e p. sing.	ϥ	וֹ
1re p. pl.	ⲛ	נוּ
2e p. pl.	ⲧⲉⲛ	כֶם

Les analogies des noms de nombre, signalées par M. Lepsius, ne sont pas moins frappantes. Exemples: ⲥⲛⲁⲩ = שנים; ϣⲟⲙⲧ = שלש; ⲥⲟ = שש; ⲥⲁϣϥ = שבע; ϣⲙⲟⲩⲛ = שמנה, etc. L'agglutination des mots accessoires, l'assimilation des consonnes, le rôle secondaire de la voyelle, son instabilité, qui la fait souvent omettre dans l'écriture, sont autant de traits qui rapprochent singulièrement la grammaire égyptienne de la grammaire hébraïque.—La conjugaison elle-même n'est pas sans quelques analogies dans les deux langues : le présent copte, comme le second temps des langues sémitiques, se forme par l'agglutination du pronom en tête de la racine verbale; les autres temps se forment au moyen d'une composition semblable à celle qu'emploient les langues araméennes. On trouve, en copte, l'emploi d'une forme causative analogue à l'*hiphil*, et la voix passive y est marquée, comme dans les langues sémitiques, par une modification de la voyelle du radical.—La théorie des particules offre aussi, de part et d'autre, quelques ressemblances; la conjonction copte, comme la conjonction arabe, est susceptible de régime; ϩⲱϥ = *etiam ipse;* ⲁϩⲣⲟⲕ = *cur tu.* Enfin, une entente analogue de la phrase et une conception presque identique des rapports grammaticaux établissent entre les deux systèmes de langues d'incontestables affinités.

Mais ces affinités suffisent-elles pour ranger dans une même famille les langues entre lesquelles on les observe? Sont-ce de simples ressemblances comme on en remarque entre toutes les langues, ou des analogies tenant à une commune origine? C'est ici que le problème devient délicat et, à vrai dire, presque insoluble. Il implique une question de méthode sur laquelle, dans l'état actuel de la linguistique, on ne peut rien dire de bien précis. L'histoire naturelle a des signes parfaitement déterminés pour établir les embranchements, les classes, les genres et les espèces; la linguistique n'en a pas : c'est une question de degré, sur laquelle l'appréciation individuelle de chaque linguiste pourra varier. Si l'on veut attribuer à la classification des langues en familles un sens positif, on doit faire correspondre cette division à un fait réel et historique. Elle doit vouloir dire qu'à l'origine de l'humanité le langage apparut sous un ou plusieurs types qui ont produit, par leur développement, toutes les diversités actuelles. Or nous n'avons pas assez de lumières sur les temps primitifs pour aborder ce difficile problème. Le naturaliste n'est pas obligé de décider si chaque genre représente une forme de création primordiale: il se contente de dire que les genres, dans l'état actuel de notre planète, sont irréductibles. Le linguiste, dont les hypothèses impliquent, quoi qu'il fasse, une assertion historique, serait tenu à quelque chose de plus: et pourtant il ne possède qu'un seul critérium pour établir la distinction des familles, c'est l'impossibilité d'expliquer comment le système de l'une a pu sortir du système de l'autre par des transformations régulières. De là au fait primitif, qui seul pourrait offrir aux classifications linguistiques une base solide et clairement intelligible, il y a un abîme qu'aucun esprit sage ne se décidera jamais à franchir.

Du moins, à la question ainsi posée: peut-on expliquer par un développement organique comment le système des langues sémitiques a pu engendrer le système de la langue copte, ou réciproquement? il faut répondre sans hésiter d'une manière négative. Des rapprochements comme ceux que l'on signale sont tout à fait insuffisants pour établir une parenté primitive. Un système grammatical va tout d'une pièce, et il est absurde de supposer que deux groupes de langues possèdent en commun une moitié de leur système grammatical sans se ressembler par l'autre. Certes il nous est difficile d'expliquer l'identité d'éléments en apparence aussi accidentels que les pronoms et les noms de nombre. Quelle raison a pu déterminer les races diverses à prendre le *t* pour caractéristique de la seconde personne du singulier, l'*n* pour caractéristique de la première personne du pluriel? Il serait puéril de le rechercher. Avouons pourtant que les premiers hommes ont pu se laisser guider en cela par des analogies qui nous échappent. La théorie du pronom tient d'une manière si intime à la constitution même de l'esprit humain, qu'elle appartient presque aux catégories de la logique, et doit, comme ses catégories, se retrouver partout la même. Les noms de nombre se rattacheraient de très-près aux pronoms, s'il fallait ajouter foi aux vues ingénieuses que M. Lepsius lui-même, dans la seconde des dissertations précitées, a émises sur ce sujet. Enfin, quelque étrange que puisse paraître un *emprunt* portant sur des éléments linguistiques aussi essentiels, on n'ose regarder un tel emprunt comme impossible, quand on voit le pehlvi (dont la réalité comme langue parlée n'est pas, il est vrai, bien certaine) offrir des pronoms, des noms de nombre, des prépositions, des conjonctions sémitiques, à côté d'éléments non moins fondamentaux appartenant aux idiomes iraniens.'

APPENDIX II.

Religions of the barbarous tribes of Africa.

(See above, p. 433.)

The special interest attaching at the present day to explorations in that mighty tract of unknown country, which is vaguely termed the highlands and lowlands of Central Africa, induces me to add a few brief notes on some remarkable analogies which may be traced between the aspects of religion there and in the other parts of heathendom. I do so from a further wish to illustrate, as far as may be, the religious condition of Egypt anterior to the coming of that second race of immigrants who stamped a widely different character on many of her sacred institutions.

The great work of Dr. Livingstone has pointed here and there to some remote connexion in primeval ages between Egypt and South-Central Africa[1]. Thus, the animal-worship of the Old Egyptians, which had ever formed their strongest and most startling peculiarity in the eyes of Greece and Rome (see above, pp. 456 sq.) is traceable as far southward as the Bechuana tribes. These tribes are also named after certain animals. 'The term *Bakatla* means, "they of the monkey;" *Bakuena*, "they of the alligator;" *Batlápi*, "they of the fish," each tribe having a superstitious dread of the animal after which it is called...*A tribe never eats the animal which is its namesake*, using the term *ila*, "hate" or "dread," in reference to killing it' (*Missionary Travels*, p. 13: cf. above pp. 456, 466). Prichard, in like manner, has collected observations bearing upon this point from earlier travellers in South Africa: 'If a person has been killed by an elephant, they offer a sacrifice, apparently to appease the demon supposed to have actuated the animal. One who kills by accident a *makem*, or Balearic crane, or a *brom-vogel*, a species of tucan, must offer a calf in atonement. Sometimes they imagine that a *shulúga*, or spirit, resides in a particular ox [cf. the *Apis* of Egypt, above, p. 457, and n. 2], and propitiate it by prayers when going on hunting expeditions:' *Researches*, II. 289. From the Rev. J. Shooter's *Kafirs of Natal and the Zulu country*, Lond. 1857, we have learned, again, not only that serpents and some other reptiles are there regarded as 'incarnations of spirits departed' (p. 162), but also that Zulus are very scrupulous in abstaining from the flesh of a particular group of animals (p. 215), some of which, however, as in different nomes of ancient Egypt, are eaten freely by their neighbours.

[1] See also Brosses (Ch. de), *Du Culte des Dieux Fétiches, ou Parallèle de l'ancienne Religion de l'Egypte avec la Religion actuelle de Nigritie*, Paris, 1760.

Dr. Livingstone has further drawn attention to the fact that striking coincidences exist between the customs of Egypt and Central Africa, *e.g.* in pounding maize (p. 196), in dressing the hair (pp. 304, 443), in spinning and weaving (pp. 399, 400), and other matters: but one of the most important links supplied by him for drawing together the first populations of the two districts will be found in his comparison of the African dialects with the language of the Old Egyptians. He thinks it nearly certain (1) that all the tongues now spoken to the South of the Equator, with the exception of the Bush or Hottentot, are strictly *homogeneous*, and (2) that the Sichuana tongue, as now elevated by the powerful Bechuana chieftains, bears, in structure, very close resemblance to the language of Egyptian monuments. He has handled this subject in a small unpublished work, for some knowledge of which I am indebted to the valuable edition of *Dr. Livingstone's Cambridge Lectures*, by the Rev. William Monk (Camb. 1858), pp. 106—121.

But, to my own mind, the most conclusive testimony flowing from late researches of Dr. Livingstone may readily be brought to bear upon a somewhat larger question, *viz.* the affinity in thought and feeling and traditions between the natives of Central Africa and the primitive layer of human population, not in Egypt only, but in other and far-distant countries. As Dr. Livingstone was himself, apparently, unconscious of any such relationship, his observations will of course possess the greater value. I shall cite a few examples; at the same time illustrating Dr. Livingstone's account by references to the Third Part of this work, and by adducing, here and there, the testimony of other writers.

The African idea of God. According to the verdict of early travellers in Southern Africa, the natives of that region were esteemed 'the most brutal and barbarous in the world, neither worshipping God nor any idol;' and the general absence of all forms of public worship, both among the Kafirs and the Bechuanas of the present day, has caused the charge of atheism to be continually repeated (Livingstone, pp. 158, 159). Such also, we have seen already (p. 392), was precisely the condition of the Papuan Family, exposing them to similar charges. Yet in neither case are we at liberty to argue that the thought of a superior race of beings, superhuman and invisible, had been quite obliterated from the native mind. With reference to South Africa, Dr. Livingstone appears to be at variance on this point with Mr. Moffat, his friend and predecessor (*Missionary Labours*, p. 245): for, writing of the people towards the mouths of the Zambesi (pp. 641, 642), he affirms that they have a clear idea of a Supreme Being. That being 'is named *Morimo*, *Molungo*, *Reza*, *Mpámbe*, in the different dialects spoken. The Barotse name him *Nyámpi*, and the Balonda *Zámbi*. All promptly acknowledge him as the ruler over all.' Dr Livingstone, however, confesses plainly in another passage (pp. 158, 159), while speaking of the Kafirs and Bechuanas, that this notion of the deity, though present, seems to be inoperative at the best; and since the form *Morimo* is probably identical with *Barimo*, and both the nouns are also used in the *plural* number as equivalent to 'spirits,' we are fully entitled to infer that there, as in the wild tribes of America, *the* Morimo is only a Great Spirit, acting as the highest member of a group,—in other words, 'the brightest inmate of a crowded pantheon' (above, p. 357). I may observe that *Morimo*, as the nearest possible approximation, has been hitherto adopted by missionaries in rendering the name of the Supreme Being. We further ascertain that in the Kafir tribes some memories are still lingering of a 'Great-Great' and a 'First Appearer;' and in one single district of Natal the Great-Great is actually worshipped, 'though the recollection of him is very dim' (Shooter, p. 160).

Offerings to and for the dead. Hegel seems to fancy (*Phil. of Hist.* p. 99, Lond. 1857) that this kind of worship was the special characteristic of the African negroes, their idea being that departed 'ancestors exercise vengeance and inflict upon man various injuries.' We have seen, however, that the practice was all but universal in China (pp. 290 sq.), among the wild tribes of America (p. 355, n. 1), among the Papuans p. 391), and the Maori (pp. 405 sq.); and was further recognised as one chief part of the religion of the Old Egyptians (p. 471). The soul of the deceased was commonly believed, in Asia, Africa, America, and Oceanica, to linger for a certain period near the place of sepulture, and also to derive while there a sort of gratification from the offerings which were made in her behalf. Thus, to take one striking specimen from Dr. Livingstone's work (p. 434; cf. pp. 319, 641, 642): 'The same superstitious ideas being prevalent through the whole of the country north of the Zambesi, seems to indicate that the people must originally have been one. All believe that the souls of the departed still mingle among the living, and partake in some way of the food they consume. In sickness, sacrifices of fowls and goats are made to appease the spirits. It is imagined that they wish to take the living away from earth and all its enjoyments. When one man has killed another, a sacrifice is made, as if to lay the spirit of the victim. A sect is reported to exist who kill men in order to take their hearts and offer them to the *Barimo*.' Mr. Shooter also, speaking of the Kafirs of Natal, has made a similar observation (p. 161): and when he adds that the attention of departed spirits is thought to be restricted to their own relatives,—a father caring for the family and a chief for the tribe, which they respectively left behind them,—we need only turn to China or New Zealand to discover a most vivid and exact resemblance (above, pp. 291, 405).

Slaughter of servants in honour of their chiefs. The horrible practice of burning widows which had long prevailed in Hindústán, and which was also found by early missionaries in the Wendic tribes of northern Europe (see the letter of Boniface, *Opp.* ed. Giles, I. 132 sq.), had extended southward to the Vítí islands (above, p. 395, n. 1), where slaves and even children of the deceased were put to death at his funeral (cf. Herod. IV. 71, 72). Dr. Livingstone, while speaking of the negroes of South-Central Africa (p. 318), produces the same gloomy picture: 'When a chief dies, a number of servants are slaughtered with him to form his company in the other world.' He then adds: 'As we go north, the people become more bloodily superstitious.'

Transmigration. We have seen that both in civilised and barbarous countries the idea of immortality was always prone to clothe itself in more or less elaborate theories on the transmigration of the human soul. Such theories, we have further seen, prevailed in all the polished circles of Hindústán and Egypt, but the traces of them were observable as well among the wild tribes of America (above, p. 361). It is probable that in almost every case the spirit was supposed to linger for a time in the vicinity of her old dwelling, and then to start upon her wanderings through the different animal forms which she was destined to inhabit. And substantially the same account is brought us by the missionary who has studied the religion of the southern tribes of Africa: 'They believe in the transmigration of souls; and also that while persons are still living they may enter into lions and alligators, and then return again to their own bodies' (Livingstone, p. 642). Mr. Shooter (*Kafirs of Natal*, p. 162) corroborates this statement also, adding that 'departed spirits are believed to revisit the earth and appear to their descendants in the form of certain serpents.'

Bondage to fear. The gloomy terror everywhere inspired alike by the religions of the wild American and by those of Oceanica (above, pp. 359, sq.; 397), has found its counterpart again among the various tribes of Central Africa: 'Their religion, if such it may be called, is one of dread. Numbers of charms are employed to avert the evils with which they feel themselves to be encompassed. Occasionally you meet a man, more cautious or more timid than the rest, with twenty or thirty charms hung round his neck' (Livingstone, p. 435). Again: 'There is nothing more heart-rending than their death-wails. When the natives turn their eyes to the future world, they have a view cheerless enough of their own utter helplessness and hopelessness. They fancy themselves completely in the power of the disembodied spirits, and look upon the prospect of following them, as the greatest of misfortunes. Hence they are constantly deprecating the wrath of departed souls, believing that, if they are appeased, there is no other cause of death but witchcraft, which may be averted by charms' (p. 440).

Circumcision. I have already had occasion to notice the prevalence of this rite in Southern Africa, and also pointed out some traces of it in the Egypt of the Pharaohs, as well as in far distant parts of heathendom: see above, pp. 490, 491, and the references there given.

Black and white men. The following declaration of a 'rain-doctor,' as recorded by Dr. Livingstone (p. 24), is identical with a tradition already noted (above, p. 398) in speaking of the Viti islands: 'He made black men first, and did not love us, as he did the white men. He made you beautiful, and gave you clothing and guns, &c.; but towards us he had no heart. He gave us nothing, except the assegai and cattle and rain-making: and he did not give us hearts like yours. We never love each other.' A legend of precisely the same import (above, p. 403, n. 2) is still preserved among the Tongans (and not improbably among some other of the Polynesian islanders). There too it is the elder son who is depraved and idle, and his children who are destined to change colour, and to pass from white to black, by reason of some moral delinquency of their progenitor,—'because the heart is bad.'

Veneration of the Ficus Indica. Attention has been drawn already to the marvellous frequency with which the nations of South-Eastern Asia and the wilder tribes of Oceanica have betrayed their reverence for the banyan-tree or Indian fig (above, p. 393): but, strange as this may seem, the regions of Central Africa explored of late years by Dr. Livingstone have yielded further testimonies of precisely the same kind. In speaking of the Balonda, he says (p. 290): 'They regard this tree with some sort of veneration as a medicine or charm.' And again, referring to a village in the Barotse valley, he writes (p. 495): 'At this village there is a real Indian banyan-tree, which has spread itself over a considerable space by means of roots from its branches...It is curious that trees of this family are looked upon with veneration, and all the way from the Barotse to Loanda are thought to be preservatives from evil.'

The examples here adduced of some original tie connecting the barbaric tribes of Southern and Central Africa, not only with the earliest masters of the land of Egypt, but with primitive layers of population in Asia, in America, in Oceanica, will serve a highly moral purpose, if they tend to silence the suspicions now again in circulation with regard to the admissibility of Africans into the family of man. I deem it a most cruel falsehood to maintain that any even of the lowest negro tribes are unsusceptible of mental and moral culture; but instead of urging my own opinion, I transcribe the words of one who, by his long and patient study of the question, earned a fairer claim to speak about it than a multitude of philo-slavers: 'The civilisation,' writes Prichard, 'of many African nations is much superior to that of the aborigines of Europe during the ages which preceded the conquests of the Goths and Swedes in the north, and the Romans in the Southern parts. The old Finnish inhabitants of Scandinavia had long, as it has been proved by the learned investigations of Rühs, the religion of fetishes, and a vocabulary as scanty as that of the most barbarous Africans. They had lived from immemorial ages without laws, or government, or social union; every individual the supreme arbiter, in every thing, of his own actions; and they displayed as little capability of emerging from the squalid sloth of their rude and merely animal existence. When conquered by people of Indo-German race, who brought with them from the East the rudiments of mental culture, they emerged more slowly from their pristine barbarism than many of the native African nations have done. Even at the present day there are hordes in various parts of Northern Asia, whose heads have the form belonging to the Tatars, and to Slavonians and other Europeans, but are below many of the African tribes in civilisation.'

INDEX.

CAMBRIDGE: PRINTED BY C. J. CLAY, M.A. AT THE UNIVERSITY PRESS.